Debtor–Creditor Law and Procedure

FOURTH EDITION

Laurence M. Olivo and DeeAnn Gonsalves

 2012
Emond Montgomery Publications
Toronto, Canada

Emond Montgomery Publications Limited
60 Shaftesbury Avenue
Toronto ON M4T 1A3
http://www.emp.ca/college

Printed in Canada.
17 16 15 14 13 12 11   1 2 3 4 5

We acknowledge the financial support of the Government of Canada through the Canada Book Fund for our publishing activities.

The events and characters depicted in this book are fictitious. Any similarity to actual persons, living or dead, is purely coincidental.

Acquisitions editor: Bernard Sandler

Developmental editor: Sarah Gleadow

Marketing manager: Christine Davidson

Director, sales and marketing, higher education: Kevin Smulan

Production and copy editor: Cindy Fujimoto

Proofreader and indexer: Paula Pike

Cover designer: Tara Wells

Cover image: stuartbur, iStockphoto.com

Library and Archives Canada Cataloguing in Publication

Olivo, Laurence M., 1946-
    Debtor-creditor law and procedure / Laurence M. Olivo and DeeAnn Gonsalves. — 4th ed.

Includes bibliographical references and index.
ISBN 978-1-55239-393-2

    1. Debtor and creditor — Ontario — Textbooks.   I. Gonsalves, DeeAnn, 1965-
II. Title.

KEO417.O44 2011   346.71307'7   C2011-906808-7
KF1536.ZB3O44 2011

To Brian, Kevin, and Lauren for their love and support,
and to my co-author for his ongoing patience and support.

To Joyce, as always, and with thanks to my co-author
for chasing the devils that were in the details.

Contents

PART II
DEBT COLLECTION: SELECTED TOPICS

List of Figures

Preface to the Fourth Edition

Since the third edition was published in early 2008, there have been legislative changes that affect the courts and court procedures, including an increase in the monetary limit for Small Claims Court claims from $10,000 to $25,000. Along with the increase in monetary jurisdiction, many of the Small Claims Court forms and procedures were updated and revised, and in some cases, particularly in the area of judgment enforcement, new forms and procedures were added. In all, 11 Small Claims Court rules and 42 forms were revised, which necessitated major overhauls of chapters 8 and 9 (which are now chapters 10 and 11). There have also been some changes to the rules and procedures in the Superior Court following the implementation of many recommendations from the Osborne Report. This required us to update the chapters on debtor–creditor practices and procedures in the Superior Court. In particular, there have been significant changes to the procedures for summary judgment (rule 20) and simplified procedure (rule 76). There have also been modifications in the areas of discovery and case management, plus a variety of more minor changes to pretrial procedure.

Paralegal licensing is now firmly in place and there has been a large increase in the number of students taking paralegal programs and going into practice. We wanted to update the book to continue to make it useful for both law clerks and paralegals, and in particular to include greater reference to the rules and Law Society by-laws that govern paralegals. There have also been updates in the area of construction liens and changes in bankruptcy and consumer proposals since the third edition was published.

In response to reader feedback and in order to permit us to provide detailed and concentrated information on certain topics, two of the larger chapters from past editions — one on file organization and searches and the other on lawsuits and calculations — have now been broken down into four smaller chapters, each on a single topic, making the subject matter less overwhelming and more manageable for students.

While the focus of this text has been on remedies for creditors, a chapter on debtor's rights and remedies has been added to this edition. As a result of economic changes over the past few years, the number of personal and business debtors in Canada has greatly increased, and while remedies for debtors have always been noted throughout the book, including sections on bankruptcy, consumer proposals, Small Claims Court consolidation orders and some information on collection agency regulations that affect debtors, we decided to add a further chapter that sets out that information in one place, and also to go into more detail in these areas, adding other information on how to respond to debt collectors as well as other options such as credit counselling.

As always, we encourage students, instructors, and other readers using the book to forward comments and suggestions to us to help us keep the text current and accurate.

Laurence M. Olivo
DeeAnn Gonsalves
November 2011

Acknowledgments

Nature abhors a vacuum, and whatever we as authors think of vacuums, we know that we did not write this edition in one. First, we are grateful to our families for allowing us the time to focus on writing this new edition. And second, the editorial support we received from our publisher, Emond Montgomery, was, as always, of high quality; we are especially grateful to Cindy Fujimoto for keeping an eagle eye on the work as it took shape, and progressed through to publication. Our colleagues from the School of Legal and Public Administration, the Faculty of Continuing Education, and the students of Seneca College were, as they have been in the past, supportive and helpful — free with their comments and advice, whether we asked them or not.

Laurence M. Olivo
DeeAnn Gonsalves

PART I

The Debt Collection Process

In this part we examine the process of collecting debts, first by attempting to obtain voluntary payment and, if that fails, by commencing proceedings in the Ontario Superior Court of Justice or in the Small Claims Court, depending on the amount of the claim. We then examine the steps and procedures that may be taken to enforce a judgment after one has been obtained.

CHAPTER 1
Introduction

THE NATURE OF A DEBT COLLECTION PRACTICE

Debt collection litigation has some features that allow much of the work to be done by law clerks in law firms or by independent paralegals. This book focuses on doing this work.

Most debt collection cases arise from the failure to pay what is owing on a contract for goods or services or for the loan of money, where the debt is based on a promise to pay and is **unsecured**. Cases fall into three categories:

1. *The debtor cannot pay.* This happens most often in consumer debt situations, where an individual's income is not enough to cover debts as they fall due. Many individuals do not know what to do in this situation. Although they may be entitled to make an **assignment in bankruptcy** or negotiate a **consumer proposal**, often out of ignorance they do nothing when sued, so that a creditor obtains a judgment by default and then proceeds to enforce it.

    A debtor who receives proper advice might make an assignment in bankruptcy or negotiate a consumer proposal, in which case an ordinary creditor's lawsuit will be stayed, and the debt will usually be wiped out in the bankruptcy process or reduced in the consumer proposal.

2. *The debtor will not pay.* In this instance, the debtor could perhaps pay but chooses not to and resorts to various delaying tactics to make it difficult for the creditor to obtain a judgment and to enforce that judgment. This requires some skill and knowledge, which a clever debtor can use to render himself "judgment proof" or to make it so difficult for the creditor to collect that the creditor agrees to take less than what is owed. In this situation, a creditor may obtain a judgment and then find that the debtor has arranged his financial affairs so that there are no assets or income in the debtor's name to seize and sell to pay the amount due to the creditor on the judgment.

    For example, the car the debtor drives and the house he lives in may be in a spouse's name or in a child's name. If so, it is no longer the debtor's legal property and therefore cannot be seized to pay the debtor's debt. Although some consumer debtors engage in these practices, commercial or business debtors are more likely to do so, particularly those who are in a business where cash flow is uneven. Here the business may be sound but, because its income fluctuates, it sometimes cannot pay bills when they fall due. The debtor will try to stave off payment until funds become available. A

unsecured credit
a loan or extension of credit to a debtor where the debtor has not given the creditor a right to seize property belonging to the debtor to satisfy the debt when the debt remains unpaid

assignment in bankruptcy
some debtors find that there is insufficient income to pay debts as they come due and they can retain a trustee in bankruptcy and assign most of their assets to the trustee for distribution to creditors, after which debtors may emerge from bankruptcy with most of their debts wiped out; an assignment in bankruptcy, sometimes called voluntary bankruptcy, is distinguished from a petition in bankruptcy, which is involuntary and where a creditor forces the debtor into bankruptcy by filing a petition in bankruptcy

consumer proposal
a plan put forth by a debtor to her creditors, through a trustee in bankruptcy, wherein a reduction of debt, interest, and/or a longer period to pay debts is suggested

commercial debtor may also delay matters, knowing that the creditor may be prepared to settle for less than the full amount owing rather than spend money on legal fees trying to obtain or enforce a judgment where the expense of doing so may be high when compared with the debt owing. For example, a creditor would probably think twice about paying a lawyer $5,000 in fees and expenses to collect an $8,000 debt. It may be much more rational to accept payment of the principal amount and forgo the interest the creditor is entitled to than to spend thousands of dollars on a case where the creditor collects little or nothing.

3. *The debtor has a defence for nonpayment.* In this situation, the debtor is really a dissatisfied customer for goods or services who has refused to pay because she alleges that the creditor has sold a defective product to the debtor, or the creditor has been negligent in providing a service. If the debtor is aggressive, she may sue the creditor for breach of contract or for furnishing a defective product or service, in which case the lawsuit is framed as an action for breach of contract or for negligence and not framed as an action in debt. However, often the debtor will just refuse to pay and when the creditor sues for payment of the price, the debtor responds with a vigorous defence claiming that the money is not owing because the creditor is in breach of his duty or has breached a contract. In addition, the debtor may **counterclaim** for damages caused by the defective product or service or other wrong done by the creditor.

counterclaim
arises when A sues B and B defends A's claim and makes her own claim against A

Where there is no substantive defence to nonpayment, and the debtor is simply refusing or is unable to pay, cases need not be treated as if they require highly specialized legal services. Rather, these cases can be efficiently processed as routine matters by paralegals. Trained support personnel, such as law clerks, working under the supervision of a lawyer can process undefended cases.

PARALEGALS AND THE DEBT COLLECTION PROCESS

Paralegals are individuals, licensed by the Law Society of Upper Canada, who are authorized to provide some legal services directly to the public.[1] To qualify as a paralegal, an individual must complete an accredited paralegal education program and pass a licensing examination.[2] He must also demonstrate that he is of good character. In order to provide legal services to the public, a paralegal must carry errors and omissions insurance. Paralegals are not lawyers and are restricted in their practice to those areas authorized by the Law Society of Upper Canada. Included in these services are representation in courts and before tribunals where a statute permits agents or non-lawyers to appear. These courts and tribunals are as follows:

- the Ontario Court of Justice, Provincial Offences Court;

- the Ontario Court of Justice, Criminal Court on summary conviction offences where the maximum prison sentence does not exceed six months;

- the Small Claims Court, where actions for damages or the return of property valued at $25,000 or less can be heard;[3] and

- the Ontario Superior Court of Justice, in limited circumstances, where permitted by statute; for example, under the *Construction Lien Act*, a paralegal may appear before the Superior Court of Justice on a construction lien matter where the amount of the lien is less than or equal to the maximum amount permitted in the Small Claims Court;

- tribunals where representation by an agent or non-lawyer is permitted.

NON-PARALEGALS AND THE DEBT COLLECTION PROCESS

In addition to lawyers and paralegals, the Law Society of Upper Canada, under By-Law 4,[4] sets out a number of categories of non-licensed persons who, based on their occupation or relationship to their employer or a family member, may appear before some courts and tribunals such as the Small Claims Court, without a licence.[5] By-Law 4 exempts certain representatives from requiring a licence by deeming their work to not constitute practising law or providing legal services. Such workers include Aboriginal service court workers, among others. The second category of persons not requiring a licence to provide certain legal services includes legal aid clinic workers, parliamentary constituency assistants, in-house legal service providers, and those who occasionally represent friends or family. Also included are persons who provide legal services occasionally as an ancillary part of their job. These persons include some human resources professionals, appraisers, and those working for trade unions.

PARALEGALS AND THE COLLECTION AGENCIES ACT

Debt collectors are regulated under the *Collection Agencies Act* and Regulation 74, which was made under the Act. If you wish to act as a paralegal for creditors on a regular basis in debt collection cases, you should register your business as a collection agency. Employees of a paralegal practising in this area must also be registered.[6] Lawyers in a regular practice and their employees do not have to register.[7] It is not unreasonable to assume that, in the future, licensed and regulated paralegals will be treated the way lawyers are currently treated under the Act. The reason for this assumption is that with regulation, paralegals are required to maintain trust accounts and submit to financial audits of their books and records, as lawyers currently do. The Law Society of Upper Canada's control over paralegals should prevent a paralegal from defrauding creditor-clients, making the bonding and oversight controls in the Act unnecessary. The establishment of enforced codes of conduct would prevent the kinds of abuses the Act focuses on, which are outlined below.

The *Collection Agencies Act* prevents abuse of debtors by those who engage in collection work and ensures that creditors who use a collection agency are paid what they are entitled to out of the collection proceeds. A collection agency is prohibited[8] from

- attempting to collect payment without having sent a notice to the debtor that sets out the name of the creditor to whom the debt is owed, the balance owing on the debt. and advising the debtor that the agency is acting on behalf of the creditor to collect the debt;

- phoning the debtor before the sixth day after mailing the above-mentioned notice;

- commencing proceedings without first giving notice to the debtor of its intention to sue on behalf of the creditor;

- threatening proceedings or other collection activity without authorization in writing by the creditor;

- continuing to contact a debtor when the debtor or his *lawyer* (not a paralegal) has sent a registered letter suggesting that the collector go to court and/or continuing to contact a debtor directly when the debtor has asked that contact be with their lawyer;

- communicating in such a manner or with such frequency as to constitute harassment;

- phoning the debtor on Sunday, before 1 p.m. or after 5 p.m. (local time), on a statutory holiday, or on any other day other than between the hours of 7 a.m. and 9 p.m. local time in the place being called;

- giving false information about a debtor to anyone;

- failing to give full particulars of the debt when contacting a debtor;

- contacting the debtor more than three times in a seven-day period;

- contacting the debtor's spouse, family, relatives, friends, or acquaintances, unless they are a guarantor or consent has been granted to speak to them by the debtor or if the purpose of the contact is to find out the debtor's home address or home telephone number;

- contacting the debtor's employer, unless they are a guarantor or consent has been granted to speak to them by the debtor or to find out the debtor's employment, business title, and business address;

- publishing or threatening to publish the debtor's failure to pay;

- using threatening, profane, intimidating, or coercive language;

- using undue, excessive, or unreasonable pressure;

- collecting or attempting to collect a debt from a person who the collection agency or collector knows or reasonably ought to know is not liable for the debt;

- continuing to contact a person who has stated that he or she is not one and the same person as the debtor the agency is seeking, unless the agency takes all reasonable precautions to ensure that the person is, in fact, who the collection agency intends to contact;

- giving any person any false or misleading information;

- misrepresenting to any person contacted in respect of the debt the purpose of the contact or the identity of the creditor or of the collection agency or collector;

- using, without lawful authority, any summons, notice, demand, or other document that states, suggests, or implies that it is authorized or approved by a court in Canada or another jurisdiction;

- commencing proceedings in its own name, unless it has paid the creditor for the right to collect and keep the amount owing to the creditor; and

- commencing proceedings without written authorization from the creditor.

In order to register as a collection agency, a person must meet certain conditions. These include

- paying the required fees;

- writing an examination;

- operating the agency out of a place of business in Ontario that is open to the public and is not in a private residence;

- posting of a bond, the amount of which is based on the amount of money collected by the agency;[9]

- mandatory filing of copies of all forms and form letters sent to debtors, and all contracts used with creditor-clients, for review by the registrar;[10] and

- the collection agent must be an Ontario resident and have at least two years' experience in the collections business or, in the opinion of the registrar, related equivalent experience.

All moneys collected by the agency are deemed to be held in trust for the creditor in accordance with the collection contract.[11] The required bonding of agencies is designed to provide some assurance that money collected for a creditor is turned over to the creditor. If an agency fails to do this, the bond may be forfeited and its proceeds used to pay creditors.

Catch 22: Complying with the Collection Agencies Act

The Act's requirement of two years' experience as a prerequisite for registration as a collection agency is a bit of a "Catch 22" for paralegals: a paralegal cannot have a collections practice unless he or she has had two years' experience in a collections practice. The actual wording of the *Collection Agency Act's* Regulation 74, ss. 12(1) and (2), is as follows:

> 12(1) No person shall be registered as a collection agency unless the person,
>   (a) has had at least two years of actual experience in all phases of the collection agency business, or has related experience that, in the opinion of the Registrar, is equivalent to that actual experience; and

(b) is 18 years of age or over, if the applicant for registration is an individual.

(2) No person shall be registered as a collector unless the person,

(a) is an individual who is a Canadian citizen or has been lawfully admitted to Canada for permanent residence and who is ordinarily resident in Canada, and

(b) is 18 years of age or over.

A person who makes an isolated collection and whose regular business is not collecting debts for others is exempt from the Act and its registration requirements,[12] but any paralegal who acts on behalf of creditors, on a regular basis, as part of a paralegal practice must register as a collection agency under the Act and have two years' experience in order to do this.

An alternative route would be to persuade the registrar that because a paralegal is a member of a profession that is licensed and regulated by the Law Society, subject to rules of professional conduct, audit controls over moneys handled for others, and a prescribed educational program, additional control by the registrar under the Act is not required. In effect, the argument is that paralegals should be treated like lawyers under the Act.

Another route is to work for an existing collection agency as a collector for a period of two years, and then apply for registration under the Act in the ordinary way.

It is clear, at present, that a paralegal cannot ignore the Act if he or she wishes to establish a Small Claims Court practice that includes collections. But note that a paralegal can act on behalf of debtors without having to register or do anything else under the Act.

LAW CLERKS AND THE DEBT COLLECTION PROCESS

default judgment
a plaintiff obtains a default judgment when the defendant takes no action and files no defence when he is sued—in that case, the defendant is deemed to have admitted the debt and the plaintiff may then present necessary documents to the court clerk, who will then, on behalf of the court, sign a judgment for the amount owing; no hearing is required, no oral submissions are made, and no judge is required to sign a default judgment

If the debt is for more than $25,000, then the matter must be heard in the Ontario Superior Court of Justice. If the debtor contests payment and wishes to have representation in court, a lawyer will be required to appear in court to handle the case, because although a debtor who is not incorporated may appear on their own behalf in any court — including the Supreme Court of Canada — *non-lawyers may not appear in the Superior Court on behalf of paying clients.* However, if the debtor has no defence and the plaintiff can obtain a **default judgment**, the matter does not require a court appearance and it can be handled by a non-lawyer. Note that if the matter is heard in the Superior Court, while a non-lawyer can do the work in default judgment situations, a lawyer should be supervising the work, because non-lawyers have no independent standing in the Superior Court. For this reason, debt collection for amounts of $25,000 and under can be an important part of a paralegal's practice, but a claim in excess of $25,000 should be handled by a lawyer or a law clerk or paralegal working under a lawyer's supervision.

Debt collection work is or can be a large part of a legal practice. It includes the collection of consumer debt, credit card debt, defaults on personal loans, and retail and wholesale customer accounts involving commercial debtors. Often this work can be done economically on a high-volume basis, where the routine nature of most collection cases lends itself to standardized processing. Many law firms still treat debt collection matters in the same way as more complex matters, which results in higher costs to the client and greater inefficiencies. This creates opportunities for collection agencies, paralegal firms, and law firms that are organized efficiently and effectively to do debt collection work.

Such law firms will use law clerks who have some legal training and can participate in the kinds of work done by lawyers, provided that they are supervised by lawyers and that they do not undertake work in a law office that only lawyers are allowed to do. An example of prohibited work is giving a legal opinion or legal advice to a client. This cannot be done by a law clerk. The prohibitions on legal work by a non-licensee are set out in the Law Society of Upper Canada's By-Law 7.1 (see the box below).

Summary of By-Law 7.1 of the Law Society

In general, By-Law 7.1 requires that lawyers closely supervise the work of their non-lawyer staff. Specifically, law clerks and other unlicensed persons are prohibited from

- taking instructions from clients or giving undertakings on behalf of a lawyer, unless the lawyer provides express instructions and authorization to do so and closely supervises the work;

- giving legal advice to clients;

- negotiating with third parties without the client's specific approval and without the lawyer supervising the process;

- signing or sending correspondence, other than on routine or administrative matters, unless it is reviewed by a lawyer;

- using the lawyer's personalized diskette to access the online real property registration system;

- appearing as advocates — the Law Society now requires non-lawyers employed by lawyers who appear before tribunals and lower courts to be licensed paralegals, unless the appearance is limited to routine or administrative matters, such as setting dates for trial in criminal courts; and

- sending collection letters on behalf of a client, unless the letter is prepared under the direct supervision of the lawyer and reviewed, approved, and signed by the lawyer prior to being sent out.

There are other features of collection work that are of interest here. Obtaining a judgment against a debtor is often easy, because many debtors cannot pay what they owe. Because that is not a defence in an action for debt, debtors often do not bother to defend and, with relative ease, the creditor obtains a default judgment as an administrative act. The more difficult job is to enforce the judgment. A judgment is no more than a piece of paper containing an order to pay. It is not self-enforcing; if the debtor pays voluntarily when the order is made, that is the end of the matter. However, if the debtor does not pay, then the creditor must take steps to enforce the judgment, using a variety of legal procedures of which the more common ones are:

judgment debtor
a debtor against whom a judgment has been obtained

judgment creditor
a creditor who has obtained a judgment for debt against a debtor

execution debtor
a debtor who is the subject of enforcement proceedings at the hands of an execution creditor

execution creditor
a creditor who has obtained a judgment and is in the process of executing or enforcing a judgment for debt

- *A writ of seizure and sale* (also called a writ of execution) allows the sheriff to seize and sell goods or land belonging to the **judgment debtor** and apply the proceeds to the **judgment creditor**'s claim.

- *Garnishment* allows the judgment creditor to have someone who owes money to the debtor pay some or all of that money to the creditor to satisfy the creditor's claim against the debtor.

- *Examination in aid of execution* allows the judgment creditor to summon the debtor and require her to answer questions about what income or assets she has that can be seized to satisfy the debt.

The most difficult part of the collection work is enforcement. The tools available are cumbersome, expensive to use, and slow. A skillful **execution debtor** can delay matters, drive up costs, and, in general, make it difficult to seize assets to satisfy the debt. In many cases, the **execution creditor** will decide that the cost of collection is exceeding the benefit to be obtained. At that point, the creditor may decide to "write off" the debt. This is not a dead loss for the creditor because she may deduct the loss from other income for tax purposes, thereby reducing her taxable income and the amount of overall income tax she would otherwise pay. Institutional lenders or creditors with large numbers of customer accounts usually track collection costs and, using formulas, will determine in a rational and dispassionate way when to cease unsuccessful enforcement proceedings or when a compromise should be made with the debtor. Where a creditor is deciding to cut his losses, he will often accept some of what is owing, rather than the total amount, on the assumption that getting partial payment now is better than the risk of recovering less later.

HOW CREDITORS ADMINISTER CREDIT TRANSACTIONS

When a person provides goods or services on contract where some or all of the payment is due in the future, there has been an extension of credit. While the parties may arrange special terms for payment, the customary business arrangement on the sale of goods and services is to offer payment terms of "net 30 days." This means that the debtor has 30 days, including the date of the invoice, to pay the invoiced amount without having to pay interest, and often with a discount of 5 to 10 percent on the invoiced amount to encourage prompt payment.[13] The invoice will usually provide that starting on the 31st day, interest accrues at some percentage per month, usually in the range of 1 to 2 percent. Although that may not sound like much, it works out to between 12 and 24 percent per year, which adds substantially to the debt and makes it more difficult to pay off. As a matter of practice, a knowledgeable debtor may negotiate a late payment by trying to reduce or eliminate the interest component. A creditor may well accept this, knowing that the older a debt is, the harder it is to collect, and take what is offered rather than run the risk of collecting nothing.

Many creditors and some lawyers assume that if there is provision for interest in the invoice, the creditor is legally entitled to payment. This is usually not the case. Unless the debtor specifically agreed to the interest provision at the time of sale or extension of credit, simply including it in an invoice does not make interest an enforceable part of

An Overview of the Debt Collection Process

1. Your client is unable to collect the money owing to him and refers the matter to you.

2. Send a demand letter giving the debtor 10 days to pay.

3. Conduct asset and identification searches of the debtor.

4. Determine the amount owing prior to commencing action.

5. At the expiry of the 10-day period, prepare, issue, and serve pleadings in the appropriate court.

6. If the debtor does not defend within the time provided for filing a defence, have a default judgment signed against the debtor.

7. When a judgment has been obtained, commence proceedings to enforce the judgment.

8. File a writ of execution, issue a garnishment notice, and/or conduct an examination of the judgment debtor to determine the debtor's ability to pay.

the contract. Terms cannot be inserted into a contract in an invoice *after* the contract has been formed. Note that if interest is payable on terms of less than a year (for example, if daily, weekly, bi-weekly, or monthly interest is payable), the contract must set out the yearly rate of interest. If the equivalent annual interest rate is not set out, s. 4 of the *Interest Act* sets out that interest is limited to 5 percent or less per year.

Ideally, creditors should have debtors sign a contract setting out terms of repayment, including interest. Such a contract should also include a consent from the debtor permitting the creditor to conduct a credit bureau search on the debtor. Except among sophisticated institutional lenders, this practice is rare and you should consider recommending to clients who have collection issues to obtain this consent when a debtor–creditor relationship is established. It is easier to get such a consent up front instead of later on when an account goes into default. Privacy legislation requires that consent be obtained. In general, creditors should obtain as much information as possible about the debtor at the outset when the parties are on good terms. The use of a customer information form should be considered to collect data that includes the debtor's full legal name and driver's licence number, as well as asset, debt, and banking information. The form should also secure the debtor's consent to a credit bureau search and release of information in accordance with the *Privacy Act*. In the event of non-payment, a driver's licence search may confirm the debtor's whereabouts. A credit bureau report on the debtor can provide information concerning the debtor's employment, other debts, and repayment history. Driver's and credit bureau searches are discussed in more detail in Chapter 3.

Most commercial extenders of credit will not immediately demand payment on the 31st day after the debt was incurred. Often there is a business relationship that has gone on for some time and is expected to go on in the future. In the interest of continuing the relationship, most creditors will allow the 31st day to pass without taking action. Instead, the overdue debt, called a **receivable**, begins to earn interest. Most businesses will review the receivable at the end of 60 days, and again at 90 days. Depending on the

receivable
refers to money that is owing to a creditor (also called an account receivable); because it describes a right to future payment or income, a creditor can sell or assign its receivables as a way of paying others—a creditor who has done this gives the purchaser or assignee of the receivable the right to be paid the amount of the receivable by the debtor

nature of the relationship, the extender of credit may automatically send a letter in the form of a gentle reminder that payment is due when 60 days have elapsed. When 90 days have elapsed, most lawyers and most businesses consider that there is a problem with the account and there may be difficulties with collecting. Now is the time for the creditor to make personal contact with the debtor and find out why payment has not been made. Sometimes the reason is quite innocent — for example, the person responsible for payment has been ill or is on vacation, or the matter has simply been overlooked. At other times, the creditor may learn that the debtor has a cash flow problem — perhaps business has fallen off, other creditors are demanding payment, or the debtor's own customers have been slow to pay. In times of recession, this can have a ripple effect as one debtor fails to pay his creditor who, in turn, does not have the cash to pay his creditor, and so on. Whatever the reason, the creditor needs to make a decision to alter the terms of payment; extend further time to pay; or turn the matter over to a lawyer, paralegal, or collection agency. This decision requires a balancing of the desire to continue a commercial relationship with the desire to be paid. In the interests of preserving the relationship and profits from it over time, a creditor may choose to forgo all of the interest that he is entitled to and relax the payment terms.

To avoid debts that are difficult to collect, at the commencement of a commercial relationship a creditor will usually require cash on delivery (COD). Once the relationship is ongoing, credit may be extended by allowing payment on terms of net 30 days, as described above, or as the parties otherwise decide.

Another common way to advance credit, particularly in consumer transactions of "big ticket" items such as automobiles, is for the creditor (the seller) to lend the money to the purchaser to buy the seller's product. This is done with a **conditional sale contract** (also called an executory contract, an installment contract, or a purchase money security agreement (see further below for more on conditional sale contracts)). For example, if a consumer buys a car and does not have all of the cash to pay the purchase price, the creditor will give the buyer credit, allowing the buyer to put a down payment on the purchase price and pay the balance of the purchase price plus interest in monthly installments over a period of time. Because this loan may be quite large, the seller may require the purchaser to pledge the car as security for repayment of the loan. This means that, if the purchaser misses an installment payment on the debt, the lender has the right to seize and sell the car and apply the sale proceeds to pay down the loan.[14] Usually, if the debtor still owes money after that happens, the seller has the right to then sue the debtor to collect the balance that is still outstanding. A transaction where the debtor gives the creditor an interest in property of the debtor as a guarantee of payment to the creditor is referred to as a **secured credit transaction** or a secured debt.

SECURED TRANSACTIONS UNDER THE PERSONAL PROPERTY SECURITY ACT

The Ontario *Personal Property Security Act* (PPSA) applies whenever a debtor grants a creditor a secured interest using some or all of his **personal property** as collateral and registers notice of their interest under the Act.[15] The PPSA contains rules to determine and govern the priorities and rights of secured creditors and debtors.

conditional sale contract
with this kind of contract, the vendor finances the debtor's purchase, taking security in the item sold; also called a purchase money security agreement or a hire-purchase agreement; a slang term for this kind of contract is "buying on the never-never," meaning that you never seem to stop paying in order to get title to (own) the chattel

secured credit transaction
a transaction where the debtor has put up some asset of value as collateral that the creditor may use as security for the unpaid debt—if the debtor defaults, the creditor can recover what is owing by seizing the collateral; the debt is said to be secured by the creditor's rights in the collateral

personal property
consists of tangibles such as consumer goods, other goods, inventory and equipment, and intangibles including investments and securities

THE PERSONAL PROPERTY SECURITY REGISTRATION SYSTEM

The Personal Property Security Registration System (PPSR) handles registrations and searches done under the provisions of the PPSA. The PPSR also accepts registration of liens under the *Repair and Storage Liens Act* (RSLA). The RSLA is most commonly used by motor vehicle repair shops to register a non-possessory lien against a motor vehicle to secure unpaid repair work. When a motor vehicle is repaired and a customer does not make full payment for properly authorized repairs, the repairer can either keep the vehicle until payment is made or release the vehicle to the customer upon receipt of an acknowledgment signed by the customer stating that the bill has not been paid in full. The repairer can then use the acknowledgment to register a non-possessory lien against the vehicle. The owner cannot legally sell the vehicle with the lien in place. Liens under the RSLA are effective for three years.

Registration Under the PPSA

In order to obtain priority under the PPSA, a creditor must achieve attachment of the collateral and perfect their secured interest.

ATTACHMENT OF THE SECURED COLLATERAL

For a secured interest to be enforceable under the PPSA against a third party, the interest must attach to the collateral. The most basic form of attachment is for the creditor to keep possession of the property. However, in most cases, a debtor requires possession of the property. When the secured property is to stay in the debtor's possession, the parties will need to execute a security agreement to set out the terms of their agreement. In this case, attachment occurs when the agreement is signed.

SECURITY AGREEMENTS

The parties may enter into either a specific security agreement or a general security agreement. The specific security agreement covers only a single asset. A general security agreement usually covers all present and future assets with the exception of real property, for which a mortgage is required.

Security agreements generally cover matters such as a description of the parties and the collateral, restrictions on the use of the collateral, the obligations of the debtor to maintain and insure the collateral, and remedies for breach of the agreement. An example of a general security agreement is appended to this chapter as figure 1.1.

PERFECTION OF THE SECURITY INTEREST UNDER THE PPSA

Following attachment, in order to obtain priority under the PPSA, the creditor must perfect his interest. Perfection usually occurs upon registration of a financing statement.

Advantages of Registering Under the PPSA

- Registration provides notice of the creditor's secured interest to the public, allowing potential creditors to conduct searches against the debtor to determine whether the debtor has already granted security to another creditor.

- Registration, in most cases, provides the creditor with priority over unregistered interests and over interests registered subsequent to their interest.

- Future advances to a debtor can be secured under the initial registration; however, in the case of consumer goods, a financing statement must be registered each time after execution of a security agreement.

- The Act sets out rules for realization of the security that may result in a faster and less expensive seizure of property.

REGISTERING A FINANCING STATEMENT UNDER THE PPSR

The PPSR is a notice-based system. Security agreements themselves are not registered. Notice of the agreement, in the form of an electronically filed financing statement, is registered in the PPSR system. The financing statement contains the borrower's name, address, and date of birth. It also contains the lender's name and address, along with the registration period, the initial amount of the loan, its maturity date, and a description of the collateral.

A financing statement should be filled out very carefully and proofread thoroughly before registration. Neglecting to include the debtor's middle initial (if they have one), spelling their name incorrectly, or marking off the wrong box on the form may result in a loss of priority under the PPSA. A guide to PPSA registrations is available online at http://www.ontario.ca/en/services_for_business/access_now/STEL02_115702.html. There is a PPSA Assurance Fund to provide compensation for errors made by PPSR staff.

A financing statement must be registered online. Registration can be done online at http://www.ontario.ca/en/services_for_business/access_now/STEL01_086166.html on your own or through a third party for hire. A creditor can register a financing statement for a period of anywhere between 1 to 25 years up to a perpetual registration period.[16] The registration fee is $8 per year for 1 to 25 years or $500 for a registration in perpetuity. Note that for consumer goods the registration period is a maximum of five years.

Within 30 days of registration the creditor must deliver a copy of the registered financing statement to the debtor.[17]

Priority Under the PPSA

If you are the only registered secured creditor against a particular piece of property or inventory, then you have priority over unregistered creditors and trustees in bankruptcy. If, however, there is more than one registered security interest against the property, the PPSA sets out who has priority. A perfected security interest takes priority over an unperfected one. If, for example, the debtor has signed two security agreements and only one of the creditors has registered a financing statement under the PPSA, the registered security interest is the only perfected one and has priority over the unregistered, unperfected interest. If both creditors registered under the Act, the rule of "first in time, first in right" applies, so that the party who first registered a financing statement has priority. There is one category of registration, called the purchase money security interest (PMSI), that takes priority over other perfected interests, even those registered prior to the PMSI. A PMSI occurs, in some cases, when someone lends the debtor funds to purchase a specific item. The creditor then takes a secured interest, in the form of a PMSI, in that item. Under the PPSA, PMSIs must be perfected within 10 days after the debtor obtains possession of the purchased item. PMSIs allow for multiple security on a debtor's property. For example, the debtor may have executed a general security agreement over all of their inventory with a creditor, but then they contract with another lender to borrow money to buy a new item to add inventory covered by the general security agreement. The new creditor will want to register a PMSI in order to take priority on that item against the other creditor, who has security under the general security agreement.

In some cases, with multiple registrations under the PPSA, priorities may be difficult to determine. The PPSA provides that the Superior Court of Justice can be called upon to establish priorities and also to make orders to protect the collateral in the interim. In some cases, a court-ordered injunction to refrain from selling or damaging the property may be of assistance to the creditor.

Enforcement of PPSA Secured Interests

Part V of the PPSA sets out the rights and responsibilities of the parties when realizing upon security under the PPSA. The overriding general rule is that the parties must act in a commercially reasonable manner. Therefore, the creditor must give the debtor time to remedy the default. The Act permits the creditor to seize the secured item and even to render it unusable if it cannot be easily seized. If the collateral consists of consumer goods, under s. 65(1) of the Ontario PPSA, if the debtor has paid at least 60 percent of the indebtedness secured, the secured party must dispose of or contract to dispose of the collateral within 90 days of taking possession. Once 66.66 percent or more of the amount outstanding on consumer goods has been paid, in accordance with schedule A of the *Consumer Protection Act, 2002*, the goods cannot be seized. The PPSA also provides for the granting of injunctions by the court, and for the appointment of a receiver where appropriate. In all cases, a creditor should avoid using violence when realizing upon the security, because charges of assault and trespass against the creditor could result. Once the creditor gains possession of the collateral, she must use reasonable care to preserve it. The creditor can charge the debtor reasonable repair, storage, and insurance costs. The creditor must notify the debtor and other creditors with an interest in the collateral of the seizure and must provide 15 days' notice of any sale of the property. All sales must be at fair market value as determined by two appraisers. The creditor must account to the debtor and the other creditors and must pay any surplus after the sale to the debtor. If there is a shortfall, the creditor may sue for recovery against the debtor.

Example of Priority Ranking Among Secured and Unsecured Creditors of a Debtor

A debtor owes $4,000 to Sedate Motors Ltd. on a conditional sale contract. The debtor's car is collateral for payment to Sedate. The contract was made in 2005 and registered under the PPSA. In 2004, the debtor bought an exercise machine for $1,000 from Bulko Wholesale Ltd. (Bulko). He didn't pay for it and was sued in 2006; the seller obtained judgment and filed a writ of execution against the debtor in 2007. In 2008, the debtor pledged his car to Fly-By-Night Enterprises for a $2,000 loan. Fly-By-Night registered its interest in the car under the PPSA in 2008.

Priority Ranking

1. Sedate, having registered its interest in the collateral in 2005 under the PPSA, has first priority with respect to a claim by the other creditors against this asset.

2. Fly-By-Night, having registered its interest in the same collateral as Sedate, but after Sedate, is in the second priority position with respect to the car. This means that Sedate is entitled to seize and sell the car and take $4,000 from the proceeds to satisfy the debt. If there are any proceeds of sale left over, Fly-By-Night is entitled to take its share from those proceeds.

3. Bulko, as an unsecured creditor, can levy execution on any sale proceeds left over from the sale of the car and against any other assets that are not held as collateral for a secured debt. Although Fly-By-Night's interest arises after Bulko's, Bulko has a lower priority because a registered interest in specific collateral takes priority over any unsecured interest.

CREDITOR APPROACHES TO EXTENDING RETAIL CREDIT

Consumer credit is remarkably easy to obtain. Many retail sellers offer credit to finance purchases, or allow payments on easy terms. Although many of these credit transactions may go into default and require collection, retail sellers rely on the high volume of such sales to generate profits. In the absence of a downturn in the economy with rapidly rising unemployment, this approach usually worked. However, even in the best of times, many consumers take on a debt load that they cannot discharge and find themselves being sued or having their secured property seized. A retail seller who does not want to be in the debt collection business will often sell his right to be repaid, at a discount, to a finance company or other financial institution. This means that the seller will sell the right to collect the debt at a price that is less than the full amount owing to him. Although the seller has not gotten the full purchase price, he has gotten rid of the cost of collecting the debt as well as the risk that the debtor will default. And, of course, the cost of discounting a receivable will often have been factored into the price charged to the retail consumer to begin with.

CHAPTER SUMMARY

In this chapter you were introduced to the nature of a debt collection practice, beginning with the reasons debtors do not pay debts when they are due. The reason for nonpayment often drives the strategies and approaches to collection taken by both parties to the debt. Jurisdictional controls over paralegals and law clerks were then discussed. Under the *Collection Agencies Act*, paralegals running a collection practice may have to register as a collection agency. Paralegals are also limited to certain types of debt collections, particularly those within the limit of the Small Claims Court's monetary jurisdiction. Law clerks, provided that they are working under a lawyer's supervision, may have more varied work, but they do not operate independently. The chapter continued with a discussion of how creditors administer credit transactions, including how interest is determined and charged; how creditors decide when they need to take action to collect a debt; and how creditors decide when a debt is not worth pursuing. Secured transactions under the *Personal Property Security Act* and the Personal Property Security Registration System were then discussed. The chapter concluded with a brief discussion of consumer credit and in what situations retail sellers will sell to a finance company or other financial institution their right to collect on a debt.

KEY TERMS

assignment in bankruptcy

conditional sale contract

consumer proposal

counterclaim

default judgment

execution creditor

execution debtor

judgment creditor

judgment debtor

personal property

receivable

secured credit transaction

unsecured credit

NOTES

1. The jurisdiction of paralegals to appear in court is governed by the *Law Society Act*, RSO 1990, c. L.8 and By-Law 4 of the Law Society of Upper Canada made under the authority of the *Law Society Act.*

2. A list of accredited paralegal education programs can be found at http://rc.lsuc.on.ca/jsp/paralegal/accreditation.jsp. Prior to 2007, some experienced paralegals were grandfathered out of the paralegal education requirement.

3. *Courts of Justice Act*, RSO 1990, c. C.43, s. 23(1) and O. Reg. 626/00, s. 1(1).

4. By-Law 4 is made under the authority of the *Law Society Act*, RSO 1990, c. L.8. The by-law can be found in its entirety at http://rc.lsuc.on.ca/jsp/ home/paralegalindex.jsp.

5. The Law Society of Upper Canada offered a time-limited, integrated licensing program for some persons listed in By-Law 4 as exempt from licensing and for experienced collection agents. In order to be admitted into the program, collection agents must have been registered and in good standing under the *Collection Agencies Act*, RSO 1990, c. C.14 for three out of the previous five years. Candidates took an online course offered by the Law Society. Candidates had until September 30, 2011 to apply for the program and it must have been completed by December 31, 2014. For more information on the integrated licensing program, see http://rc.lsuc.on.ca/jsp/licensingprocessexemptedgroup/index.jsp.

6. *Collection Agencies Act*, RSO 1990, c. C.14, s. 4(1).

7. Ibid., s. 2(a).

8. Ibid., Reg. 74, RRO 1990, ss. 21-24.

9. Ibid., s. 2.

10. Ibid., s. 21(1).

11. Ibid., s. 17.

12. Supra note 6, s. 2(f).

13. Some business owners start the net 30-day period on the day after the purchase has been invoiced; we, however, have followed the more common business practice of using the date of purchase (invoice date) as day 1 of the net 30-day period as the vendor creditor generally wants the net 30-day period to end as soon as possible to ensure a regular cash flow and timely payment of invoices.

14. Section 25 of the *Consumer Protection Act, 2002*, SO 2002, c. 30, sch. A provides that where a consumer under a conditional sale contract has paid two-thirds or more of his or her payment, the repossession/resale provisions of the Act are unenforceable except with leave of the Superior Court of Justice.

15. Some provinces and territories have their own personal property security acts, while others are in the process of enacting such legislation.

16. *Personal Property Security Act*, RSO 1990, c. P.10, s. 51(1).

17. Ibid., s. 46(6).

REFERENCES

Access to Justice Act, SO 2006, c. 21 (Bill 14).

Collection Agencies Act, RSO 1990, c. C.14 and RRO 1990, Reg. 74.

Consumer Protection Act, 2002, SO 2002, C. 30, sch. A.

Construction Lien Act, RSO 1990, c. C.30.

Interest Act, RSC 1985, c. I-15.

Insurance Act, RSO 1990, c. I.8.

Law Society Act, RSO 1990, c. L.8.

Law Society of Upper Canada, *Rules of Professional Conduct* (Toronto: LSUC, 2011) (also available at http://www.lsuc.on.ca).

Personal Property Security Act, RSO 1990, c. P.10 (PPSA).

Privacy Act, RSC 1985, c. P-21.

Repair and Storage Liens Act, RSO 1990, c. R.25 (RSLA).

REVIEW QUESTIONS

1. Bulko Wholesale Ltd. (Bulko) sells exercise machines to fitness clubs and to individual consumers. The machines range in price from $600 to $10,000.

   a. What kind of sale arrangement might Bulko make with a first-time wholesale (commercial) customer?

   b. What kind of sale arrangement might Bulko make with an established wholesale customer?

   c. Suppose that an individual consumer wishes to buy a $6,000 machine, but cannot pay the sale price immediately. What kind of arrangement might Bulko make to sell the machine to the consumer?

   d. If Bulko isn't paid after 30 days, should it sue immediately? After 60 days? After 90 days? Explain your answer.

2. Identify the usual reasons for which a debt remains unpaid.

3. Describe two limitations on the right of paralegals to conduct a debt collection practice.

4. What are the limitations on a law clerk's involvement in the debt collection process?

5. Name two persons, other than a lawyer or a paralegal, who can represent someone in Small Claims Court on a debt collection matter.

6. Define

   a. secured and unsecured transactions

   b. judgment creditor

   c. execution creditor

d. judgment debtor

e. execution debtor

f. conditional sale contract

g. assignment in bankruptcy

7. Give two reasons why a creditor would register a financing statement under the PPSA.

8. Explain two ways in which attachment under the PPSA can take place.

9. How is a security interest perfected under the PPSA?

10. Explain which secured creditor has priority in each of these circumstances:

a. one creditor who has perfected his interest and one who has not perfected his interest

b. two perfected interests

c. a creditor with a perfected interest and one with a PMSI

Figure 1.1 Example of a General Security Agreement

SECURITY AGREEMENT

Crazy Car Parts Manufacturing (the "Company"), the secured party, and Auto Parts Dealer (the "Dealer"), as debtor, agree to the following terms:

1. INDEBTEDNESS SECURED

The Dealer contracts to pay the Company, when due, all debt now owed to the Company and all additional debt later incurred by the Dealer to the Company.

2. COLLATERAL

The collateral that is to be subject to the security interests created under this agreement consists of the Dealer's entire stock of goods, including, but not limited to, all cars, parts, and accessories supplied to the Dealer by the Company and that form part of the Dealer's inventory.

3. GRANTING OF SECURITY INTEREST

As security for payment of the indebtedness and in consideration of this agreement, the Dealer grants to the company a security interest in all paid and unpaid for items of collateral, both of which are referred to in this agreement as the "security interest." Such collateral shall remain as security for the Dealer's entire indebtedness until payment in full is made. The security interest extends to collateral presently in the Dealer's possession and collateral subsequently acquired along with proceeds from the sale or lease of such collateral and any returned or repossessed collateral.

4. ATTACHMENT

The security interest attaches upon execution of this agreement in regard to all collateral that the Dealer has at that time and shall attach to future collateral upon acquisition of same.

5. PROTECTION OF COLLATERAL

The Dealer shall properly store collateral and protect it from injury or damage. The Dealer shall keep the collateral insured with all risk coverage satisfactory to the Company. The Dealer shall provide details of such coverage to the Company. If coverage is not in place, the Company may purchase its own and charge it to the Dealer.

The Dealer shall pay all taxes associated with the collateral.

The Dealer shall keep the collateral free from liens and encumbrances unless they have the written authorization of the Company to lien the property.

6. DEFAULT

The following shall be considered defaults by the Dealer:

a) the Dealer's authority to sell the Company's goods is cancelled,
b) the Dealer defaults in the payment or performance of any obligation owed to the Company,
c) the Dealer fails, upon request, to hand over proceeds or provide further information,
d) the Dealer disposes of the collateral without first obtaining the written consent of the Company,
e) the Dealer enters into bankruptcy.

Figure 1.1   Concluded

7. RIGHTS ON DEFAULT

If default occurs, the Company may:

a) accelerate all debt owed by the Dealer to the Company along with reasonable legal expenses,
b) take possession of any or all collateral,
c) stop delivery of any collateral.

8. REPOSSESSION

For repossession purposes, the Company, to the extent permitted by law, may enter the Dealer's premises to repossess the collateral.

9. SALE OF THE COLLATERAL

The Company may sell the repossessed collateral privately or by public auction. The proceeds of any sale are to be applied to the Company's expenses, then to the Dealer's indebtedness, and, third, to any subordinate security interest where notice has been received by the Company. Any surplus shall be paid to the Dealer, and if there is a shortfall, the Dealer is liable to pay it forthwith.

10. SUCCESSORS AND ASSIGNS

This agreement enures to the benefit of the heirs, executors, successors, and assigns of the Company.

11. AGREEMENT

This agreement becomes effective immediately upon execution by the parties and will continue in effect until replaced by a new agreement.

DATED at _____ this _____ day of _____ , 20 ____.

_____   _____
Dealer   Witness

_____   _____
Company   Witness

CHAPTER 2

Steps to Take Before Commencing Proceedings

This chapter is concerned with setting up and organizing collection litigation files and with client identification and verification procedures.

OBTAINING INFORMATION FROM THE CLIENT

Most debt collection cases rely on documents rather than on oral evidence. It is important to obtain all of the documents that the client relies on to support the claim. These are likely to include documents that create indebtedness, such as sale contracts, promissory notes, invoices, account records, and correspondence. When possible, it is important to obtain and retain in your file the *original* documents — if it is necessary to prove a fact in court with the use of a document, rules of evidence generally require that the original document, rather than a copy of it, be produced. If documents have been produced electronically, then the source, whether it be a computer disk, CD, flash drive, or hard drive, should be available, if required, to authenticate the document sent or produced from it. If only copies, rather than originals, are available, the copies may be used in evidence. Courts generally follow the "best evidence" rule: you should submit the best evidence you have — use originals if you have them.

Clients may provide you with useful background information about the debtor, including address, email address, phone number, assets owned, banks where the debtor does business, and whether the debtor is in financial difficulty. This information allows you to locate the debtor when it is time to sue; it will also tell you what assets may be available to satisfy the debt owed to your client and help you to decide what strategy to take in pursuing the claim. When interviewing the client, use a checklist (figure 2.1) to be sure that you have obtained all the relevant information and documents. A checklist can be used to help the lawyer or paralegal meet their obligations concerning client identification and verification under By-Law 7.1 of the Law Society of Upper Canada. In most cases, a client must be identified, and if a transfer of money is involved (which

Client Identification and Verification

Summary of By-Law 7.1 of the Law Society of Upper Canada

- When a lawyer or paralegal is retained by an individual he must identify the client by obtaining the client's full name, address, telephone number, and occupation(s).

- If a lawyer or paralegal is retained by a business, he must obtain the client's legal business name, address, telephone number, incorporation number or business identification number and place of issue of the number, information on the nature of the business, the name(s), position(s), and contact information for the individual(s) who give instructions on behalf of the business, and in the case of a corporation, the legal service provider must also make reasonable efforts to obtain the name(s) and occupation(s), of each director and the name(s), address(es), and occupation(s) of any person who owns 25 percent or more of the shares of the corporation.

- in receiving, paying, or transferring funds, reasonable steps must be taken to verify a client's identity using a reliable, independent source document such as a driver's licence, passport, or birth certificate for an individual, and in the case of a corporation, a corporate status certificate.

- The legal service provider must keep client identification and verification information for a minimum of six years.

- By-Law 7.1 identification and verification procedures do not apply if the client is the legal service provider's employer or a financial institution.[1]

is the case in most debtor–creditor situations), the client's identity must also be verified. The client identification and verification process was implemented to try to reduce the possibility that a legal service provider[2] might be duped by an unknown client into carrying out fraudulent activities. For more information on By-Law 7.1, refer to the box above.

In addition to recording information received from the client and identifying and verifying the client's identity, a checklist can also be used to track steps taken and progress made on a collection file. The checklist found in figure 2.1 can be used for these purposes.

After obtaining the information required to open and set up your new client file, you will need to determine the amount owed to your client. Work with the client to determine the amount owing. The client can provide you with the necessary information, because the client will have kept track of the accounts, know how the calculations were done, what the balance is, what payments have been missed, what interest has accrued, and so on. The client may have a computerized accounting or bookkeeping system that does calculations, and there is no reason not to use this information; however, it is important that you check the calculations and understand how they were done, in case the debtor argues that the calculations or the creditor's data are in error.

After the client has determined what is owing to a given date, be sure there is enough information to calculate how much the balance will increase from that date because of accruing interest or further installment payments due.[3] After the client has turned the matter over to you, you must calculate the balance actually owing at the time of judgment or payment. In order to do this you will have to know what the interest rate is and how it is being calculated. Calculation of the balance owing is discussed in more detail in chapter 4.

Once you have met with the client and it has been agreed that you will do the work, formalize the contractual relationship by having the client sign a **retainer** (see the example on the next page). Usually, the retainer records that the legal service provider has been hired to do the work specifically described in it, and that a cash deposit has been paid. The retainer may also set out when the client may next expect to be billed and when the client may expect to receive a progress report from you, among other things.

Send a letter to the client as a follow up to the meeting. The letter should acknowledge receipt of the account, set out the basic facts of the account (amount owing, interest rates, and due dates), as well as the billing and reporting structures, and should reiterate the client's instructions. Enclose a copy of the retainer agreement in the letter if you did not give the client a copy when you met. Although this letter is not mandatory, it promotes a more positive and constructive relationship with the client.[4]

FILE ORGANIZATION

Once the client has retained your services, it is important to organize the file in a rational way so that documents can be easily accessed, filed, and stored. Although filing practices vary from office to office, most use a format similar to the one described here.

- *Case file folder.* For each case or matter, you should have a separate retainer and a separate case file, even if you have multiple case files for the same client. Once a case file is set up, all subfiles go inside the case file. The case file folder contains the name of the client — for example, "SMITH v. Slippout"[5] — and should contain on the inside file cover a form with the client's name, address, email address, phone and fax numbers, and other essential information. It should also contain a checklist (see figure 2.1) where steps in the proceeding are checked off, so that anyone picking up the file for the first time will know what stage the proceedings have reached. The file name will also have a file number assigned by the file clerk or accounting clerk — the file number can include codes for the type of file, the lawyer, paralegal or staff person responsible for the file, the date it was opened, and so on. Some offices use different colours of file folders for different types of legal work.

- *Correspondence subfile.* All correspondence related to the file should be here, with the most recent on top. A quick glance at this file should tell you what the matter is about, how it has progressed, the stage the proceeding has reached, and what problems need to be dealt with. At one time this file consisted of letters sent and received, but it is now more likely to be composed of printouts of emails sent and received. While emails can and should be stored electronically on the office computer system, keeping hardcopies is a useful way of ensuring that there are copies if there is a system failure.

- *Notes subfile.* Notes that you or others in your office take should be filed here. If the client later hires someone else to finish the matter for which you were originally retained, you may remove your notes from any materials you return to the client.

retainer
a document that records the contractual relationship between legal service provider and client, usually stating that the legal service provider acts for the client and stipulating generally what the legal service provider has been retained to do; also used to describe an amount of money that the client pays the legal service provider as a down payment for services to be rendered—in this case, the legal service provider is required to account for how this money is used on the client's behalf; also used to describe a situation where a client does not hire a legal service provider for anything specific, but simply wants the legal service provider to be available to her to perform legal work for a specified period—in this case, the legal service provider does not have to account for the money and may use it for his own purposes; he is deemed to be entitled to the money for making himself available to the client, although he may charge for any services actually performed during the period of the retainer

Sample Retainer

Date: May 23, year 0

To: Blodgett, Swine and Cattle, Barristers and Solicitors

From: I.M.A. Client

Re: Debt Collection from U.R. Scapegrace Ltd.

I retain Blodgett, Swine and Cattle, Barristers and Solicitors, to act as my lawyers and to take all necessary steps to collect a debt owing to me in the approximate amount of $45,000 from U.R. Scapegrace Ltd.

This retainer is your authority to proceed to take all necessary steps to collect this debt, including authorization to take legal proceedings and obtain and enforce a judgment. I also authorize you to engage on my behalf any expert you believe is required in this matter and I acknowledge that I am responsible for payment of the expert's fees.

I agree to pay a deposit of $_____ now, and I understand that you will deduct legal fees and expenses incurred on my behalf from this deposit. I also agree to pay further deposits in anticipation of further legal fees and expenses not covered by the initial deposit. I understand that no work will be done until a deposit demanded by you has been paid.

I understand that the following members of the firm may work on the file and that their hourly rates are as follows:

- John Blodgett—$250

- Carl Cattle—$200

- Dan Lawclerk—$100

I understand that these rates may increase annually and I agree to pay them upon receiving written notice of the increase from you.

I understand that I must pay HST on fees and expenses.

I agree that I will pay interest at the rate permitted by the *Solicitors Act* on accounts that are paid later than 30 days after the date they were sent by you.

I acknowledge receipt of this contract.

By my signature below I authorize Blodgett, Swine and Cattle, Barristers and Solicitors or their delegate to search my credit bureau record now or in the future for the purposes of collecting information for any lawsuits brought on my behalf or against me and for the enforcement of any judgments or debts against me. I understand that Blodgett, Swine and Cattle, Barristers and Solicitors will protect my personal information and use it only for the purposes referred to in this retainer. If I require any further information about the use of my personal information, I agree to contact John Blodgett.

Date: _____

_____   per _____
I.M.A. Client   Blodgett, Swine and Cattle

- *Client documents subfile.* Client documents, including copies, should be kept separate from other documents because they may be required to be filed as evidence in a proceeding. These documents are the property of the client and must be returned to the client when the matter is concluded.

- *Client identification and verification.* In order to meet the requirements of By-Law 7.1 and to be organized for a possible Law Society audit, it can be useful to maintain copies of client identity verification documents in a subfile.

- *Pleadings subfile.* All court documents, including copies, should be kept in this file.

- *Miscellaneous subfile.* Documents that do not fit into the preceding categories should be placed here. When this file gets crowded, consider whether additional specific subfiles should be created.

Care should be taken with the storage of files. File storage can become a big issue in an office with a large volume of cases. In large firms, files, like library books, may be checked in and out by staff from a central filing area. In this way, a file can be located easily, and centrally stored when not in use. When a matter has been completed, original documents belonging to the client should be returned to the client along with the final reporting letter and account. The file should be purged of any unnecessary documents such as file copies of routine letters sent to clients. The material remaining should then be stored among the inactive files. Because further work may need to be done, or in case a client becomes dissatisfied and sues for negligence, the file should not be destroyed. Many lawyers used to keep closed files indefinitely, but the Law Society currently suggests that there is no fixed rule regarding file retention. However, By-Law 7.1 requires that client identification verification documents be kept for a minimum of six years.[6] There are a number of factors to consider. Certainly you should keep closed files until after the limitation period for negligence has expired. Other factors include the nature of the actual legal work performed, the working life of the legal document(s), the outcome of the case, and the attitude and capacity, or lack thereof, of the client.[7] Note that storage may not require vast physical space, because files may be scanned onto a disk or put on microfilm. Many law firms get advice from technical experts in deciding on the type of e-storage system they will use.

"TICKLER" SYSTEMS, LIMITATION PERIODS, NOTICE PERIODS, AND "BRING FORWARD DATES"

In any litigation, deadlines must be carefully noted in the file and in a "tickler" system. A tickler system is a date-recording system that alerts you to upcoming deadlines. It can be a datebook, calendar, computer system, hand-held device, or phone app that alerts you to approaching deadlines. In order for these systems to work, the relevant deadlines need to be diarized or entered in the tickler system. The careful and methodical use of a tickler system is absolutely essential, because a missed deadline can be damaging to a client's case. A missed limitation period can cause a client to sue your office for professional negligence.[8]

There are a number of deadlines that can be very important in debt collection proceedings. The first deadline involves limitation periods. Limitation periods are found in federal and provincial legislation, including the Ontario *Limitations Act, 2002*. A limitation period is the time period in which a legal procedure must be commenced. If the procedure is not begun during the specified time period, it cannot be done at all. If the plaintiff does not start proceedings, by issuing a claim, within the time period, he is "statute barred" and may not proceed with the lawsuit at all. The limitation period begins when the right to sue (sometimes called a "cause of action") arises.

Under the *Limitations Act, 2002*, the basic limitation period for almost all causes of action, including actions in debt, is two years from the time the debt was past due (s. 4) or could reasonably be determined to be past due (s. 5). There are some exceptions to this general rule that may affect a debt action:

- *Minors and persons under disability:* The limitation period begins to run only when a litigation guardian is appointed (ss. 6 to 9).

- *Debt actions not subject to any limitation period:* Proceedings to enforce a family law domestic agreement for support; and proceedings by the Crown to collect taxes, reclaim welfare benefits, or recover on defaulted student loans (s. 1).

If a limitation period is set out in another act, it does not apply unless it is set out as an exception to the general provisions of the *Limitations Act, 2002* in the schedule at the back of the Act (s. 19).

There are a number of reasons given for having limitation periods. By requiring an action to be commenced within a specific time period, the defendant does not have the threat of litigation constantly hanging over him. In an action brought soon after the events giving rise to it, witnesses' memories are fresher and evidence is probably more reliable than it would be if recalled long after the event.

In addition to limitation periods, there are also notice periods that should be diarized or noted in the tickler system. For example, when a statement of claim is issued by the Superior Court of Justice, it must be served within six months of the issuing date.[9] Unlike a limitation period, where failure to observe the timelines will be fatal to the action, missing a notice period may be merely a procedural irregularity that can be cured. Overcoming an irregularity will, however, result in a delay and increased costs for the client.

In addition to limitation periods and notice periods, there are other important deadlines or dates that need to be "brought forward" so that you will be able to accomplish the tasks before the time for doing so has passed. Many of these dates are based on common sense rather than on rules. Of particular importance is the timing of the demand letter and the commencement of proceedings. The older a debt is, the harder it is to collect. If the client did not send a letter demanding payment as part of its initial collection efforts, one should be sent as soon as possible. A demand letter should indicate the date on which payment is required. If payment is not made by that date, diarize commencement of proceedings for the next day, and issue the claim on that date. If the action is not defended, diarize the date for signing the default judgment, and submit the default judgment for signing by the court on that date. It is important to diarize and to adhere to a litigation schedule. Delay does not favour a creditor, because the debtor's assets may be shrinking rapidly. Also, sticking firmly to dates sends a psychological message to the debtor that the creditor is determined to pursue the matter diligently and that the matter is not going to fade away.

CHAPTER SUMMARY

Once you have determined that a debt is overdue, there are a number of things that must be done before commencing proceedings, the first of which are being retained and opening a client file. This chapter discusses the various ways in which a file can be organized. In particular, attention is drawn to the use of tickler systems and to the need to keep track of limitation and notice periods. The requirements of client identification and verification under By-Law 7.1 are explained in the chapter.

KEY TERM

retainer

NOTES

1. Sections 22 and 23 of By-Law 7.1 made under the *Law Society Act*.

2. The term "legal service provider" is used because both paralegals and lawyers are now licensed to provide legal services in Ontario.

3. This may happen on a "running account," where the debtor runs up debt with continuous transactions, paying down the debt at stated intervals. In some cases, purchases have been made with payment not yet due, when the creditor decides to take action against the debtor for previous defaults. As recent debts become due after default, those debts will be added to the claim. In many cases this problem is avoided if the creditor, in the contract extending credit, inserts an "acceleration clause." An acceleration clause provides that when there is one act of default by the debtor, all amounts outstanding are deemed to be due and owing immediately rather than on the date they were originally due.

4. One of the most frequent causes of complaints to the Law Society about lawyers is that lawyers fail to communicate with clients. With the licensing of paralegals, it is not unreasonable to expect that this will be a frequent cause of complaint for paralegal licensees as well.

5. Where your client is the debtor (or defendant) rather than the creditor, for filing purposes the client's name should still be first. In this case, the file name would be written: "SMITH ats Snoggle"; "ats" means "at the suit of" and indicates that your client, Smith, is being sued by Snoggle. Uppercase letters are used so that you can quickly see which party is the client. This format allows your client's name to be first whether the client is plaintiff or defendant.

6. Section 23(14) of By-Law 7.1.

7. *Guide to Retention and Destruction of Closed Files*, March 2011, The Law Society of Upper Canada. Online: http://rc.lsuc.on.ca/pdf/practiceGuides/retentionDestructionGuide.pdf.

8. The Ontario Lawyers' Professional Indemnity Company (LawPro) reports that a leading cause of insurance claims against lawyers for professional negligence arises from missed limitation periods — an insurance loss that is almost wholly preventable if a law office is operating efficiently. See http://www.lawpro.ca/LawPRO/Casebook_July2002.pdf.

9. *Rules of Civil Procedure*, rule 14.08.

REFERENCES

Limitations Act, 2002, SO 2002, c. 24, sch. B.

REVIEW QUESTIONS

1. Why are client documents important in collection cases?

2. What information about the debt collection matter would you expect the client to provide?

3. What is a retainer? Why is it advisable to have one signed by the client?

4. Explain the steps to be taken in the process of opening a collection file.

5. What is a "tickler system" and how is it useful?

6. What is a limitation period?

7. Why is it important not to delay work on a collection file?

8. Explain what information a legal service provider must collect when being retained (a) by an individual client and (b) by a corporate client.

Figure 2.1   Client Information Checklist

Client information:

1. Client's full name and any other names client is known by:

   _____

2. Address (home and business): _____

   _____

3. Telephone number(s): _____

4. Fax number: _____

5. Email address: _____

6. Occupation and employer's address (list all that apply):

   _____

   _____

7. Bank and address: _____

8. Credit card — type, number, and expiry date: _____

9. Date of birth and place of birth: _____

List and copy driver's licence information and one other piece of identification to verify client information:

(Note: In all cases, obtain the client's driver's licence number (if they have one) along with one of the following documents (documents should be reviewed and copied): an original government-issued identification that is valid and has not expired, such as a birth certificate, provincial or territorial health card (if volunteered, as no demand for a health card can be made due to privacy legislation), or passport. If non–face-to-face instruction is provided from a client in Canada, then the review and verification of the identification documents can be provided by attestation from a person listed under By-Law 7.1, including a commissioner of oaths or a guarantor (doctor, pharmacist, lawyer, etc.). If the client is outside Canada, an agent who can provide an attestation must be retained — see the by-law for details and/or call the Law Society at 416-947-3315, ext. 3315 for confidential assistance.)

   _____

Date identity verified and by whom: _____

For clients that are a business or organization:

10. Incorporation or business identification number: _____

11. Place of issuance of incorporation/business identification number:

    _____

12. Type of business: _____

13. Name, position and contact information for those individuals authorized to give instructions with respect to the matter for which the licensee is retained (in the case of an organization, reasonable efforts must be made to record the names, addresses, and occupations of all directors and of those persons who own 25 percent or more of the shares of a corporation):

    _____

    _____

    _____

14. Give details of identification reviewed and copied to verify client information:

(Note: The following documents, where applicable, should be reviewed and copied: a certificate of corporate status issued by a public body for corporations, articles of incorporation, or a trust or partnership agreement, or any other similar record that confirms the unincorporated organization's existence. For directors' information, consult corporate minute books or online corporate registry services.)

_____

_____

Where the client is acting for or representing a third-party beneficiary or a principal:

15. Information about the beneficiary or principal as set out in paragraphs 1 to 14, as applicable:

_____

_____

Information about the debtor/defendant:

16. Full name/business name: _____

17. Business type (sole prop., corp., partnership), if applicable: _____

18. Defendant's address: _____

_____

19. Defendant's phone number: _____

20. Fax/email of defendant _____

21. Defendant's representative (if any) and their contact information:

_____

_____

22. Marital status of defendant and name of spouse, if applicable: _____

_____

23. Defendant's employer: _____

Defendant's assets:

24. Real estate (address, lot, plan number, if known): _____

_____

25. Vehicle(s) (licence, VIN, description): _____

_____

26. Bank account numbers and bank addresses: _____

_____

27. Investments (type, number, company, address of company): _____

_____

_____

Details of claim:

28. Type of case (tort, collections, etc.): _____

If collection matter:

29. Original amount: _____

30. Terms, including interest: _____

31. Evidence of debt (contract, invoice, note, security agreement): _____

_____

32. Payment history/default history: _____

33. Co-signors or guarantor information (name, address, phone number):

_____

34. Collateral given as security (if any, and type, location): _____

_____

Documents delivered by client (obtain and secure originals and make copies)**:**

35. Invoices: _____

36. Account records: _____

37. Promissory notes: _____

38. Guarantees: _____

39. Security agreements: _____

40. Demand letters sent by client: _____

41. Other documents (list): _____

42. Searches carried out by client: _____

Client retainer, instructions and action taken:

43. Name of lawyer/paralegal assigned to case: _____

44. Retainer agreement reviewed and signed (write date and copy for file, put retainer funds into trust account): _____

45. Reporting frequency (monthly or details of other): _____

_____

46. Billing frequency (monthly or details of other): _____

_____

47. Conflicts check carried out: _____

48. Tickler date system established: _____

49. Client account opened: _____

50. File number assigned: _____

51. Details of searches carried out (credit bureau, driver's licence, business name, etc.):

_____

52. Demand letter sent and date of letter: _____

53. Time given for payment in demand letter: _____

54. Authority given to discuss settlement and details as to what client will accept:

_____

_____

55. Authority to commence litigation: _____

56. Authority to retain outside counsel: _____

57. Authority to retain experts:_____

58. Date statement of claim issued: _____

59. Date statement of claim served: _____

60. Date default judgment may be requested: _____

61. Pretrial deadline: _____

62. Case management deadlines: _____

63. Judgment date: _____

64. Examination in aid of execution date: _____

65. Date writ of seizure and sale obtained: _____

66. Date for renewal of writ of seizure and sale: _____

67. Date garnishment obtained: _____

68. Date for renewal of garnishment: _____

69. Final reporting and letter to client: _____

70. Client documents and any property on hand returned to client: _____

_____

71. Date file closed: _____

NOTE: This form and copies of any identification verification documents must be kept on file for six years following completion of the matter.

CHAPTER 3

Searches to Carry Out Before Commencing Proceedings

This chapter is concerned with how to carry out the necessary background investigation and information gathering required before commencing collection proceedings.

OBTAINING INFORMATION FROM THE CLIENT

Ask your client to provide you with all the information that they have on the debtor. They may already have information on the client's legal name, address, and credit status. In some cases, a client will have the debtor's driver's licence number in their file. You will usually need to verify and update this information and can do so by carrying out public record searches.

OBTAINING BACKGROUND INFORMATION: PUBLIC RECORD SEARCHES

When creditors come to you, it is because they have tried and failed to collect a debt and expect you to do it for them, usually by suing the debtor. However, that may not be the best strategy if the debtor

- has fled the jurisdiction;

- has recently transferred or encumbered assets that might otherwise be available to satisfy the debt;

- was sued by other creditors who have been unsuccessful in collecting on their judgments;

- had assets seized by other creditors;

- tried to hide assets;

- suffered personal or business financial losses recently; or

- had assets seized by secured creditors who have a collateral interest in those assets and a right to seize them to satisfy the debt when there is default.[1]

In these circumstances, there may be little or no purpose in suing the debtor because there may be no assets available to satisfy the debt or no hope of payment. To obtain the necessary information about the debtor or to confirm information supplied by the client, there are a number of public searches and databases that can yield useful information to help you decide whether to sue or to pursue another strategy. Many of these public searches can be done online, as well as by phone, fax, mail, or in person.

IDENTIFYING AND LOCATING THE DEBTOR

Name Search: Consumer Debtors

If you are suing an individual consumer rather than a business, you should verify the legal name of the debtor. Suing in the wrong name can result in an unenforceable judgment. For example, if you are suing Murray Benek and obtain a judgment in that name, the judgment will be useless if it turns out that Murray's legal first name is really Miroslav, but that he informally changed it to Murray years ago. Most people use their formal legal name for title deeds, banking documents and other "official" documents such as driver's licences. Legally, and certainly for formal purposes, Miroslav Benek exists, but Murray Benek does not, at least for the purposes of obtaining and enforcing a judgment. Getting the debtor's name right at the outset is important both to obtaining a judgment against the debtor in the right name, and to conducting searches to determine whether the debtor is worth suing.

There are several ways in which you can verify a debtor's correct name.

STATEMENT OF DRIVING RECORD

If you have the debtor's driver's licence number, you can request a Statement of Driving Record, which provides a three-year history of the driver, including the name of the driver, licence status information (including a physical description and date of birth), and a record of driving offence convictions. The person's driving record can help you verify the name of the debtor, and verify that you have the right person. In this connection, the information about height, gender, and date of birth might be useful in performing other searches. For example, having the date of birth makes it easier to verify who a debtor is on a *Personal Property Security Act* (PPSA) search. A driving record search may be especially useful with someone who has a common last name, like Singh, Smith, or Wong. Note, however, that this search will not provide an address for the licence holder — privacy restrictions keep addresses out of the public record. However, an authorized user may obtain the driver's address. You may become an "authorized" user if

1. you apply for authorization and enter into an agreement with the Ministry of Transportation, and

2. your search is conducted for one of the purposes for which authorization will be granted, such as debt collection, litigation, claims, and accidents.

Authorized investigators may include private investigators, security guards, lawyers, paralegals, and others acting for these purposes.

For further information about becoming an authorized MTO user, contact:

Supervisor,
Driver and Vehicle Licensing Call Centre
Licensing Administration Office
Ministry of Transportation
2680 Keele Street
Downsview, ON M3M 3E6

Tel.: 416-235-2999
Toll free: 1-800-387-3445

You may conduct your search online, paying by credit card, and receive a driving record abstract. The search site for this record and other driver and automobile related searches is the Service Ontario site on the Ontario Government website, which can be found at: http://www.ontario.ca/en/services_for_residents/053274.html#Important Notes for Abstract.[2]

To see what a Statement of Driving Record abstract looks like, see figure 3.1.

PLATE HISTORY AND VEHICLE HISTORY ABSTRACTS

If you have the Vehicle Identification Number (VIN) or the licence plate number for a vehicle you think is owned by the debtor, you can use either number to do a plate or VIN search, either of which will provide the name of the owner, his or her driver's licence, the date the vehicle was registered, and whether it has changed owners recently.

Again, the address of the owner will not be provided unless you have obtained the authorization described in the previous section. You may also do these searches online using the web address provided in the previous section.

You can see what a Certified Plate Search—Recent Owner looks like in figure 3.2. The VIN search record is similar.

ONLINE SEARCHES

In the last several years various search engines and other online sources have been expanded and refined to allow you to submit the name of a debtor to obtain addresses, telephone numbers, and other information about an individual that can help you verify a name, obtain other identifying information, and locate the person. These searches can be used to find both individual consumer debtors and business debtors operating under a business name. You may also do a **reverse search** on many of these sites by submitting a telephone number, address, email address, or other information that will help you to obtain the correct name and address of a debtor, as well as other information. Reverse searches of phone numbers will often identify the subscriber of unlisted landlines and cell phones. Many sites are free, but some charge for information, in which case you can pay by credit card. The following websites were useful at the time of publication.

reverse search
a reverse search allows you to submit an address, telephone number, or email address to obtain the name of a resident or subscriber

- *Canada411:* http://www.canada411.ca Submitting a name to this site can turn up a telephone number. Reverse searching is also available.

- *WhitePages.ca:* http://www.whitepages.ca This site allows you to look up names to obtain addresses and phone numbers and also allows you to do reverse directory searches of addresses and phone numbers to identify and locate individuals.

- *CanPages:* http://www.canpages.ca Can be used to find the telephone number of an individual or a business along with their address. Reverse searches are possible.

- *Yellow Pages:* http://www.yellowpages.ca Can be used to find the telephone number of a business along with their address. Reverse searches are possible.

- *Yahoo People Canada:* http://ca.people.yahoo.com You may search by name, with or without the city or province. This may turn up addresses and other miscellaneous information, some of which could be useful. Also includes an email address search feature. While the site seems to require American addresses, it does provide data on Canadian residents.

- *Pipl:* http://www.pipl.ca This site searches the "deep web," including online databases, to find references to any name you submit. It accesses databases in many countries.

- *NetTrace:* http://www.nettrace.com.au/resource/search/people.html This Australian site is a gateway to a variety of search sites that allow you to search in various countries, including Canada, by inputting phone numbers, addresses, email addresses, names, and other data. Many of the sites will search various public and private databases, including many in Canada. Some charge fees.

- *Telus:* http://www.mytelus.com/phonebook This site allows you to submit names to obtain addresses and phone numbers, including unlisted cell phone numbers. You may also do reverse searches on phone numbers and addresses to identify and locate individuals.

- *Search Detective:* http://www.searchdetective.net This site allows you to search by phone number and will turn up account holder names and addresses, including those for unlisted landlines and cell phones. Searches may also be done by name, but it is useful only when your subject has a US address.

- *Lycos Search:* http://www.whowhere.com This site can find individuals with a name search for locations in the United States. You can also do reverse searches. The results will yield information about who has the phone or email account, or who owns premises or lives at an address. It may also provide other personal information.

Name Search: Business Debtors

If the debtor is a business debtor, it is important to know the form of business organization used by the debtor. The debtor may be an individual (referred to in law as a natural person) carrying on business in her own name. In that case, the consumer name search techniques discussed in the previous section can be used to verify the name of the debtor. However, if the individual carries on business using a trade name (Mary Ann Chen carrying on business as Mary's Golf Driving Range) or as a partnership or a corporation, it may initially be difficult to determine what the debtor should legally be called in the lawsuit.

- If the business is incorporated, you must sue the corporation in its legal corporate name.

- If you are dealing with a sole proprietorship, you may sue the individual, or you may wish to sue the sole proprietorship in the name in which it carries on business. The *Rules of Civil Procedure* make it easy to sue in the business name, and then expand enforcement rights against the individual who is the sole proprietor, allowing you to seize assets in both the business name, and in the name of the individual.[3]

- If the debtor is a partnership, you may sue in the partnership's name or sue the partners individually in their own names. Again, the *Rules of Civil Procedure* make it easy to sue the partnership in the partnership name and then identify the partners, and expand enforcement rights to include partnership assets, and the personal assets of the partners.

For example, if the creditor's business has been with Mary Ann Chen's golf driving range and the business is incorporated as Chengolf Ltd., the creditor must sue in the correct corporate name. If you sue Mary Ann Chen personally or sue in the name of Mary's Golf Driving Range, you are likely to meet a defence that those persons had no liability because it was the corporation that was legally liable, not Mary Ann Chen as an individual or as an individual carrying on business as Mary's Golf Driving Range. So you must sue Chengolf Ltd.

Similarly, if Mary's Golf Driving Range is operated as a business partnership between Mary Ann Chen and John Parten, you will need to know the name the partnership uses to carry on business, as well as who the partners are. While you can sue in the partnership name, that judgment will only bind partnership assets, such as the golf balls and clubs used in the business. If you also want to have access to the assets of each individual partner, such as their land, cars, and personal bank accounts, you need to know the correct name of each partner, so that they can be given notice that you intend to go after their assets as well as those of the business in order to satisfy the judgment. Some legal service providers sue both the partnership under its name and the partners individually named because some sheriff's officers and bailiffs are reluctant to enforce judgments against persons not individually named in the original proceedings. Rule 8 of the *Rules of Civil Procedure* of the Superior Court provides a complete code for the procedure in suing partners. This includes provisions to obtain disclosure of the names of those who were partners at the relevant time, in order that they can be given notice of the lawsuit as a prerequisite to enforcing a judgment against their personal assets, as well as against any assets in the partnership name.

Any business being carried on in Ontario in a name other than the owner's name must register its business name with the Companies and Personal Property Security Branch, Ministry of Government Services (Companies Branch).[4] To identify individuals who may be liable as business debtors, submission of a business name search will result in the identification of the individual person if the business is a sole proprietorship. You may sue the business by suing the individual sole proprietor or you may sue the business using the business name. If the business is a partnership, submission of the business name will result in identification of the partners. You may sue a partnership by suing in the partnership's name, suing the individuals who are partners, or suing both. This broadens the range of assets available to satisfy the judgment against the partnership. Because some members of a partnership may leave after its initial registration, and some may join, you are entitled to inquire as to who the partners were at the relevant time when the debt was incurred. *Both* the *Rules of the Small Claims Court* and the *Rules of Civil Procedure* explicitly allow for this, and the information is available through pretrial procedures.

Submission for search of the name under which a corporation carries on business will result in the correct corporate name. Unlike with sole proprietorships and partnerships, remember that when suing a corporation, its legal name must be used. For example, if Mary Ann Chen had incorporated her golf driving range business, the corporation must be sued, not Mary Ann Chen (even though she may be the sole officer and shareholder) of Mary's Golf Driving Range. Do not be surprised if the corporate name that turns up has nothing to do with the golf driving range business. The name may well be an assigned registration number given by the Companies Branch, and it may appear, for example, as something like 192356 Ontario Limited. This is sometimes referred to as a "numbered company." There is nothing particularly sinister about a numbered company. For example, if Henry Gold decides to buy and operate a McDonald's franchise, he may run his franchise business as a corporation. If so, there is no point in getting a business name for the company, because it will be carrying on business under the well-known and highly marketable name of the franchiser. In this case, Gold may simply use the number that the Companies Branch assigns to the company when it is incorporated without a name.

A business name search can be done in two ways. You can attend in person at the public search office of the Companies and Personal Property Security Branch, Ministry of Government Services (MGS), 375 University Avenue, 2nd floor, Toronto, Ontario M5G 2M2 where there are computer terminals at which you can conduct a search, or you can conduct an online search from your home or office. You can access the Ministry of Government Services search site at Service Ontario at https://www.services.gov.on .ca/services/searchServices.do?action=service_details&id=11287&locale=EN.

A business names report will identify persons using a business name and will show their address. If the business name is not registered, you can obtain a certificate of non-registration showing that a business name that may be in use has not been registered. (There are penalties for failing to register a business under the *Business Names Act*, although this will not directly affect a creditor's lawsuit against the debtor; however, if the creditor is suing in a name that is not registered, her lawsuit will be **stayed** until the name is registered.)

If a business name search shows that the business is actually a corporation, or you know that you are dealing with a corporation, you can carry out a search of the Initial Return/Notice of Change filing of the corporation to verify that you have the correct corporate name, and to obtain the corporation's address for service, and the names and addresses of the officers and directors of the corporation. An Initial Return/Notice of Change form must be filed by every corporation incorporated in Ontario. A sample of a completed Initial Return/Notice of Change is set out in figure 3.3.

An online search can be inexpensively done, provided that the name you are searching has been registered with the Companies and Personal Property Securities Branch. At the Service Ontario website, http://www.serviceontario.ca, follow the links to the online for business search application, and select Search a Business Name to order an Enhanced Business Name Search. You can see a sample Enhanced Business Name Search online form in figure 3.4. You can search the exact business name, words within the

stayed
a legal proceeding may be stopped from proceeding further, or stayed by a judge, until one of the parties does something they are obliged to do; for example, a plaintiff who is suing using an unregistered business name will have the proceeding stayed until he proves that he has registered the name as he is legally required to do

name, or use the business identification number (if you have it) that all businesses are given when their names are registered. You can pay for the search online by credit card. Searching can also be done, for a fee, online or by telephone through private search companies such as Cyberbahn and Corporate Searchers or through Oncorp, which are all recognized service providers to the Ontario government. You can access Oncorp's search services and also view samples of documents such as a Corporation Profile Report (which contains a corporation's address and the names of its directors) at http:// www.oncorp.com/home/services_onbis_corp.asp. Note that not all business registration documents are available from the government website. Documents such as a Corporation Profile Report are available only through private search sites such as Cyberbahn or Oncorp. You can see a sample Corporation Profile Report in figure 3.5. This report is useful because it sets out the corporation's legal name and the names of the directors. If your business client does not have the information required for you to meet your legal service provider client identification and verification requirements under By-Law 7.1 (as discussed in chapter 2), the Corporation Profile Report can be obtained, at the client's expense, to verify information concerning the business such as the legal business name, address, incorporation number or business identification number, and place of issue of the number.

If you require a document that is not available through the government website or you do not have the time or expertise to search on your own, there are companies that will conduct searches for you for a fee. You may also do your own online searches by using private search and registration services such as the previously mentioned Oncorp (http://www.oncorp.com) or Cyberbahn (http://www.cyberbahngroup.com/ CyberbahnCMS). To use these sites, start at the homepage and follow the directions and links. These search sites will also allow you to conduct a variety of other searches of public business records maintained by the federal and provincial governments. The cost of the search can be passed on as a disbursement to the client that requires the search on their matter. Note that if a corporation is carrying on business in Ontario but is incorporated in another province or is a federally incorporated company, an Ontario corporate search will not be useful. However, either of these search sites can be used to obtain information about companies incorporated federally or in other provinces.

INFORMATION ABOUT THE DEBTOR'S ASSETS AND DEBTS

You have now identified the debtor by its proper name for the purposes of naming the debtor in a lawsuit, and obtained information to locate the debtor for service. You can now also submit an accurate name for a second set of searches that you need to conduct to answer some important questions:

- Is this debtor worth suing?

- Does the debtor have any assets worth seizing to satisfy a judgment?

- Are there secured creditors that will get all the valuable assets before you ever get near them with your judgment?

- Are you the only creditor suing, or are there 15 others all hounding the debtor?

- Has this debtor a long history of defaulting on debts where creditors have had little success in recovering anything on their judgments?

The answers to these questions may indicate that you should advise the creditor that the best advice may be to obtain a judgment, hopefully by default, but to not waste too much time or money trying to enforce it. Or you might advise the client to not waste money by suing, but to simply write the debt off as a business loss for tax purposes. If the debt is written off for tax purposes, the taxpayer must be able to document the reasons for doing so, especially if he or she decided not to sue.

In order to get to the point where you can properly advise a client, you need to conduct some or all of the following searches that can tell you whether there are likely to be assets to seize and whether collection efforts are likely to be successful.

Execution Search

writ of seizure and sale
also called a writ of execution; allows the sheriff to seize and sell goods or land belonging to the judgment debtor and apply the proceeds to the judgment creditor's claim

When a plaintiff obtains a judgment in a lawsuit, the judgment orders the defendant to pay money, but the judgment is not self-enforcing. If the defendant does not pay, it is necessary for the plaintiff to file a **writ of seizure and sale** (also referred to as a "writ of execution") with the sheriff of the county or district where the defendant has assets. Unfortunately, the province has no centralized file of all writs of seizure and sale. This means that you might have to file duplicate writs of execution in sheriff's offices in more than one county or district if you believe the defendant has assets in more than one county or district. Once filed, a writ of execution can be used in one of two ways: (1) if the judgment creditor knows of an asset that can be seized and sold, so that the proceeds of sale can be used to satisfy the judgment, she can direct the sheriff to seize and sell the goods; or (2) the judgment creditor can simply leave the execution sitting on file. Others who do business with the debtor, or who may be lending the debtor money, often search executions to assure themselves that the person they are dealing with is a good credit risk. They may be reluctant to lend or extend credit to a business once they learn of an outstanding writ of execution. In these circumstances, the debtor may be pressured to pay off the execution creditor. Another advantage of filing an execution is that if another judgment creditor enforces their writ you will be entitled to share, on a pro rata basis, in the amount collected. The writ, once filed, is enforceable for six years and can be renewed. Sheriff's offices used to send renewal notices, but now they do not. You will need to diarize the renewal date.

judgment proof
term used to describe a debtor against whom a judgment may be obtained, where the judgment will be unenforceable because the debtor has no assets to pay the judgment or the debtor has hidden or encumbered assets so that they cannot be easily seized; a judgment in these circumstances is sometimes described as a "paper judgment"—that is, it is worth no more than the paper it is printed on because it cannot be enforced in any practical way

It is a good idea to do an execution search against the name of the debtor, because a lot of useful information will be revealed. For example:

- It can be used to verify the debtor's name or the spelling of the name.

- A number of outstanding writs of execution may indicate that the debtor has been sued before and that the judgment creditors have not been able to collect on the judgment.

- Several writs of execution filed recently may indicate that all of the creditors are closing in and that the debtor is likely to be "**judgment proof**," with little likelihood that assets will be available to satisfy the judgment. This pattern may also indicate that the debtor has just gone, or is about to go, bankrupt. Suing may be a waste of time and the creditor may obtain more through bankruptcy.

- Many outstanding writs that are several years old may indicate that the debtor has successfully avoided paying creditors for some time and either has no assets or is adept at hiding them.

- No executions may indicate that there are no prior unsatisfied judgments and that there will be assets available to seize; it may also indicate that the debtor's assets are not located in the county or district where you searched executions.

Even where you find a number of writs on file, it may still be useful to try to obtain a judgment and add your own writ of execution to those on file. The reason for this is that the *Creditors' Relief Act, 2010* requires that execution creditors (all those who have filed writs of execution in that county) share on a pro rata basis if any execution creditor succeeds in seizing and selling assets.[5] When assets are seized and sold, the sheriff is obliged to distribute a share of the money to each of the execution creditors in proportion to what they are owed. This means that execution creditors with large judgments receive a larger share of the money than those who have judgments for smaller amounts (as the box below shows). There are some exceptions to the rule about pro rata distributions. Support creditors and the Crown in respect of unpaid taxes take priority over other judgment creditors.

To conduct a search of executions against the name of a debtor, you can attend at the Sheriff's Office and request a certificate indicating whether there are writs of seizure and sale on file in that office. The Sheriff's Office is usually located in the local Superior Court of Justice courthouse. The local court office and the Sheriff's Office are listed in the blue government pages of the local telephone directory.

In Toronto, execution searches at the Sheriff's Office are done online after payment of the prescribed fee. You key in the same kind of information you would provide for the certificate and the system produces an on-screen response, and, if desired, a printout of that response. In time, this system will extend to other parts of Ontario, and may one day be available online from your office computer.

Give the full name of the debtor; if the debtor is an individual, give middle names as well as the first name, if possible. If the debtor is a business, be sure to give the busi-

Illustration of a Pro Rata Distribution of the Proceeds of Execution

Amount owing to execution creditor A	$500
Amount owing to execution creditor B	$200
Amount owing to execution creditor C	$100
Total	$800

Execution creditor C levies execution and recovers $300 as a net amount after the costs of execution have been deducted from the gross amount.

Formula:

$$\text{amount recovered on levy} \times \frac{\text{amount owing to creditor}}{\text{amount owing to all creditors}} = \text{share paid to creditor}$$

A will receive $300 × $500/800$ = $ 187.50 (62.5%)

B will receive $300 × $200/800$ = $ 75.00 (25.0%)

C will receive $300 × $100/800$ = $ 37.50 (12.5%)

ness's proper legal name. With sole proprietorships and partnerships, it may be wise in most cases to list the name of the individual who is the sole proprietor or the names of the partners. File the certificate in the Sheriff's Office for the county or district where the debtor is likely to have assets, lives, or carries on business. In Toronto, it is possible to use a computer to do your own search, which will give you immediate information on writs on file. Once you have results you can ask for copies of the writs to find out the particulars, such as the name of the judgment creditor, the amount owing, and the length of time the debt has been unsatisfied. You can also call the judgment creditor's lawyer whose name appears on the writ to find out about any attempts to collect that have been made.

You can pay to have an online writ of execution search carried out by using a writs search service provided by Teranet. An Ontario-wide search (OWL—Ontario Writs Locator) can be ordered through Teranet. To access this service you need to register as a member at https://www.teranetexpress.ca/csp. Membership is free. You can also perform execution searches at Cyberbahn at http://www.cyberbahngroup.com/CyberbahnCMS.

Personal Property Security Act Search

Once you have the proper name of the debtor, you can conduct a search under the *Personal Property Security Act* (PPSA). The PPSA allows creditors who have taken an interest in property of the debtor to secure repayment to register notice of their interest in the property so that anyone conducting a search will learn about the creditor's interest in the property. When the property is pledged as security for a loan, it is sometimes referred to as "collateral." Registration of a Financing Statement that makes reference to a security agreement between the creditor and the debtor is notice to the world that the creditor has an interest in the debtor's property, which the creditor may seize if the debt is not repaid. The PPSA also determines priority among secured creditors. Generally, the first to perfect a security interest in the debtor's property has the right to seize property ahead of other creditors whose interest was perfected later.

At this stage, a PPSA search will reveal what assets the debtor owns that are pledged as collateral to other creditors. The nature and range of assets will tell you something about the debtor's business or, if the debtor is a consumer, his spending habits. It will also identify assets that may not be available for you to seize once you obtain a judgment, because the secured creditor has priority over later judgment creditors. If the amount of secured debt is very high, so that none of the assets appear to be available for seizure, it may not be advisable for your client to sue at all because there may be no assets available to be seized and sold to satisfy a judgment. Because the secured creditor is likely to have priority over a later judgment creditor, proceeds of sale after seizure by an unsecured judgment creditor would be used first to pay the secured creditor before proceeds would be available for an ordinary judgment creditor.

After judgment has been obtained, you have a right under the PPSA to ask the secured creditor questions about the security agreement with the debtor, including how much the debtor owes the creditor. You may also write to the secured creditor and ask questions before a judgment has been obtained, but the secured creditor does not have to answer your questions. However, asking questions at this stage sometimes causes the secured creditor to contact the debtor, which may cause the debtor to pay your client.

In order to conduct a PPSA search, you must know the full name of the debtor, including, if possible, the person's middle name. Supplying the debtor's birth date will narrow the search. A search under the name "John Smith" without an accompanying birth date will result in a report with all the registrations against every John Smith in the system. Having the right birth date will help eliminate the John Smiths you are not interested in. You may also search for automobiles owned by the debtor by supplying the VIN.

Filing a PPSA inquiry request results in a report that will identify the category of asset secured along with the secured creditor's name and address. To obtain details about the asset and the debt, it is necessary to contact the secured creditor identified in the report. The report will state whether or not there are registrations against the named debtor. PPSA searches may be done by telephone by calling 1-800-267-8847 (Toronto 416-325-8847). There is a charge for the information given, which may be paid by credit card. Searches may also be conducted online for a fee through Cyberbahn and Oncorp at the URLs set out previously in this chapter. You can also conduct searches online at the Service Ontario site at http://www.ontario.ca/en/services_for_business/access_now/STEL01_086165.html. There is a fee for the search and you can order a report that is certified (one that can be filed as evidence in court) or uncertified. Payment is by credit card, but if you do many PPSA searches, you can open an account.

You may do several types of searches:

- *Individual non-specific:* Submit the last name and the first name. You may search for all possible registrations, or registrations within a specific time period.

- *Individual specific:* Submit the last name, first name, and middle initial along with the birth date.

- *Business debtor inquiry:* Submit the business name.

- *Motor vehicle inquiry:* Submit the VIN. This allows you to track a vehicle given as collateral no matter who owned the car, or what licence plate was on it.

See figures 3.6 to 3.9 for completed samples of these forms.

Bank Act Search

In s. 427 of the federal *Bank Act*, there are provisions under which a business can borrow from a chartered bank and pledge its property as security by giving the bank a s. 427 security interest in the property. This results in a transfer of **title** of the debtor's property to the bank until the loan is repaid. During this time, the debtor remains in possession of the collateral and may use it in the ordinary course of business. For example, a manufacturer may pledge its fleet of delivery trucks as collateral under s. 427. The bank has title and is the legal owner; the manufacturer continues to use the trucks to deliver goods without interference by the bank unless the loan goes into default. When the loan is repaid, title in the trucks passes back to the debtor.

Bank Act searches are not used for most consumer debtors or small businesses. They are likely to be used in a case where there is a large business that has borrowed large sums over a long period of time to finance its operations and is in the business of agriculture, aquaculture, or forestry. These are the circumstances that give rise to a

title
the legal ownership of something; often refers to a document that indicates ownership or an ownership interest—to say someone has title to a car usually means that the car is registered with the province in the name of that person

s. 427 security. A *Bank Act* search is done by examining the registers under the name of the business debtor at the offices of the Bank of Canada. In Ontario, such a search is done through the Canadian Securities Registration Systems office (CSRS). To conduct a search through CSRS, you must first register with their office. You can register by sending a fax to 604-637-4015 that sets out your name, address, and the type of account that you want. For information on the types of accounts, call 416-204-3000. The easiest way to carry out a s. 427 search is to order one online from a private search house such as Cyberbahn or Corporate Searchers. There is a fee for the search report, which may be paid by credit card. An entry in the register will give a file number that can be used to obtain further particulars of the loan. If most or all of the business's assets are pledged as security under s. 427, there may be very few assets available to satisfy the claims of an ordinary judgment debtor, so that suing the business may not be worthwhile.

Section 427 provides for a secured credit registration system similar to that of the PPSA. In fact, assets may be pledged as collateral under both systems. If it is advisable to conduct a *Bank Act* search, it is probably a good idea to do a PPSA search as well; the reverse, however, is not necessarily true, because a PPSA search may be used with consumer debtors and small businesses, where a *Bank Act* search would usually be unnecessary for those classes of debtors.

Because creditors may register against the same debtor in both systems, there can be problems in sorting out which creditor has priority over the other. Where two creditors use the PPSA, for example, the PPSA's internal priority ranking rules will determine which of two PPSA creditors of the same debtor has priority. There is, however, no national statutory solution to resolve a priority conflict between a PPSA registration and a *Bank Act* registration, which has its own separate rules for determining priorities among competing s. 427 registrants.[6]

Bankruptcy and Insolvency Act Searches

A bankruptcy search is useful to determine whether the debtor has gone bankrupt or is about to go bankrupt. If a debtor is bankrupt, there is no point in suing the debtor because any action would be automatically stayed. Instead, the creditor will file a proof of debt claim with the debtor's trustee in bankruptcy. The trustee will review the claim and, if it is in order, the creditor may recover some of the money owing but is unlikely to ever see all of it. Secured creditors are entitled to seize their secured property to satisfy the debt owing to them and to do so ahead of the claims and rights of unsecured creditors claiming through the trustee. Unsecured creditors, which include ordinary judgment creditors, get what is left over. After all of the bankrupt's creditors, both secured and unsecured, have had their interests attended to, the debtor is usually discharged from bankruptcy, free and clear of the debts incurred before bankruptcy, with some exceptions.[7]

As a result of the bankruptcy rules, there is often little of value left for unsecured creditors of the bankrupt. For this reason, unsecured creditors may recover no more than 10 or 20 cents on each dollar owed, because the secured creditors have already taken all the major assets.

There are two ways to go bankrupt: (1) in certain circumstances, an unpaid creditor who is owed $1,000 or more can put a debtor into bankruptcy using a petition for bankruptcy, or (2) the debtor can make an assignment in bankruptcy. As an alternative to bankruptcy, a debtor who owes up to $250,000 (excluding a mortgage) may make a consumer proposal to his creditors through a trustee in bankruptcy. All bankruptcy searches are done through the Office of the Superintendent of Bankruptcy. All bankruptcies and proposals filed in Canada since 1978 are on file. The Office of the Superintendent of Bankruptcy is represented in each province by its Offices of the Official Receiver. Official Receivers are individuals authorized to handle various functions under the *Bankruptcy and Insolvency Act*.[8] There are four offices of the Official Receiver in Ontario. Their locations are set out below. The toll free phone number for all locations is 1-877-376-9902.

- 55 Bay Street North, 9th Floor, Hamilton, Ontario L8R 3P7; fax: 905-572-4066.

- 451 Talbot Street, Suite 303, London, Ontario N6A 5C9; fax: 519-645-5139.

- 160 Elgin Street, 11th Floor, Suite B-100, Ottawa, Ontario K2P 2P7; fax: 613-996-0949.

- 25 St. Clair Avenue East, 6th Floor, Toronto, Ontario M4T 1M2; fax: 416-973-7440.

The bankruptcy and insolvency records database, which includes information on bankruptcies, proposals, and receiverships, may be searched online through the Office of the Superintendent of Bankruptcy at http://www.ic.gc.ca/app/scr/bsf-osb/ins/login.html or by calling 1-877-376-9902 (toll free) instead. In order to conduct searches you must establish a Name Search Account with the Office of the Superintendent of Bankruptcy. You may now register online at https://www.ic.gc.ca/cgi-bin/allsites/registration-inscription/mainScreen.cgi.

A bankruptcy search will also reveal whether the debtor is in receivership. This may happen when a business debtor has defaulted on a loan, which, in some circumstances, gives the creditor the right, on default, to appoint a receiver to run the debtor's business or take it over to liquidate assets. Unless your client has some priority right over the secured lender in this situation, she is unlikely to recover any money, because the secured lender will dispose of virtually all of the assets free of any claim by your client. The Office of the Superintendent of Bankruptcy maintains online records of receiverships nationwide since 1993. Bankruptcy is discussed in more detail in chapter 14.

Credit Bureau Searches

Licensed credit bureaus, which can be found in the Yellow Pages, can provide their members with information on the debtor, including his or her address, past and present employers, outstanding loans, credit cards, and repayment history. Credit reports will also tell you if the debtor has applied for further credit or been given further loans, and may set out judgments against the debtor as well as information on past bankruptcies and consumer proposals. Existing creditors make reports on the debtor's payment record. With this information, you can contact other lenders to obtain more detailed information. Credit bureaus depend on their members to report information about loans, defaults, and payments made by a debtor to get an accurate sense of what kind of credit risk the borrower is. Some credit bureaus have inexpensive online services available to members that allow you to search online for a fee. Both Equifax and TransUnion have websites. Equifax is at http://www.consumer.equifax.ca/home/en_ca and TransUnion is at http://www.transunion.ca.

Credit bureaus can provide commercial or consumer credit reports. You may order a report online using the business name or individual's name. The more identifying information you can supply about the debtor, the more likely you are to obtain an accurate credit report. A credit report provides broader and more detailed information than the other searches we have examined so far. However, the information in the report comes from a variety of sources, some of which may be less than accurate, so caution should be observed with respect to the contents of the report. You can order a report only if you are a member of the Credit Bureau and the debtor has consented to the search. As a legal service provider, you can join the Credit Bureau as a business member. Your client may have obtained the debtor's consent to a credit bureau search if they had the debtor complete a credit application.

Commercial Credit Reports

The following are among the types of information that such reports will likely provide (details on what an Equifax commercial credit report provides are described here). A sample Equifax commercial credit report, using the elements discussed here, is set out in figure 3.10.

- *Identification:* The debtor is identified by name, address, phone number, the date the file was established, and the reporting agency's file number.

- *Summary:* This provides an overview of the degree of risk and the contents of the report. It may include how creditors have been treated and describe negative information, if any. This part can be quite subjective and should be used with caution. Debtors have the right to have errors corrected by the reporting agency. Information on how to correct your credit record is available on the agency's website.[9]

- *Creditor information:* This section identifies the industry or reporting creditors for this debtor. It should include when the information was posted. It often provides information about the "aging" of receivables, which describes how long it takes a debtor to pay creditors. The most recently posted information comes first.

- *Payment trends:* The speed with which payments are received is reported over a two-year period. This allows creditors to view trends and cyclical fluctuations in payment delays that can result from cash flow fluctuations as a result of the nature of the business.

- *Returned cheques:* This provides details on NSF cheques.

- *Collections claims:* This reports creditors' collection claims for a five-year period.

- *Legal information:* This sets out legal information about lawsuits and judgments over a five-year period. Note that not every lawsuit has to do with debts.

- *Information on bankruptcy:* Information from the Superintendent of Bankruptcy about the creditor for a five-year period is noted here.

- *Banking information:* When available, information about bank accounts, loans, and lines of credit is reported here.

- *Company information:* The date of incorporation and information about officers and directors are reported here, if available.

- *Other files:* If the business has had name changes, or is linked to other business entities, any previous credit files about predecessor business entities will be included here, providing a longer historical payment trail. However, assumptions about current behaviour based on the behaviour of predecessors is risky, because past behaviour may be only remotely linked to present behaviour due to changes in the nature of the business and its management.

- *Recent inquiries:* There will be a record here of recent inquiries by other creditors about this debtor.

- *Scoring:* From all the details in the report, a credit reporting agency will provide a credit information score indicating overall risk in dealing with the debtor, and a payment index score indicating the percentage of the total amount owing that is past due. These scores are important to creditors in determining the steps they take with respect to a debtor and how quickly they take them. Discussed below is how these two scores are used by Equifax. Other credit reporting agencies use similar scoring techniques.

  - *Credit information score:* The higher the score, the greater the risk factor. The lowest possible risk score is zero. A zero score is characteristic of less than 1 percent of all businesses, and would describe a business that pays all debts when accounts are presented. A company with a score of more than 40 is considered to be a high risk. Only about 1.06 percent of all businesses score over 40.

    New companies automatically default to a factor of 20, indicating they are neither very safe, nor very risky. As time goes by, and there are few or no negative reports, the risk factor will drop. If there is a bad payment history, the risk factor will rise.

    If a company is reported by the Superintendent of Bankruptcy, it automatically gets a score of 70, indicating the presence of insolvency proceedings.

    A company that scores between 1 and 10 is considered a very good risk. Only about 15 percent of all businesses fall into this low-risk group. A score of 20 represents a "neutral" risk assessment, but a score of over 20 represents increased risk.

    The score is calculated using the seven factors shown in the matrix at the end of the report (see the last page of figure 3.10).

  - *Payment index score:* This index takes the amounts owed in the current, first, second, third, and fourth payment periods past due and calculates them as percentages of the total amount owed. It then uses a formula to work out the average number of days that payment is past due. In Canada, the average score is 22. Accounts are often sent to collection when they reach a score of 60. The highest score would be 100, which would mean that everything owing would have to be in the third period past due. This would mean that all the amounts owing have been unpaid for months, which would be evidence of insolvency. The lowest score would be zero, which indicates that all bills are paid before the due date. Note that the long-term trend of the scores is more important than the score at the moment. Of interest is whether the risk is increasing, which indicates financial problems, or decreasing, which indicates that the business is doing well. Equifax provides nine quarters, or just over two years' worth of scores.

Consumer Credit Reports

Among the types of information that such reports will likely provide are the following (details on what an Equifax consumer credit report provides are described here). A sample Equifax consumer credit report that presents the elements discussed here is set out in figure 3.11.

- *Identification:* The consumer's name, address, and employer are usually provided. This information is provided by member creditors and may be out of date.

- *Credit inquiry information:* The names of bureau members who have recently received a copy of this credit report are listed. Inquiries are automatically purged from the report after three years from the date of inquiry.

- *Banking information:* Information on the consumer's bank accounts is provided, including the name of the bank and the type of account. Banking information is automatically purged from the report six years from the date it was entered into the report.

- *Credit history:* Each creditor sets out when they last reported, the balance outstanding on their debt, the date their debt commenced, and the highest amount that has ever been outstanding. A credit transaction will automatically be purged from the report six years after the date of the last activity. The credit rating assigned by the creditor is also reported. These ratings are called "R" ratings and are known as North American Standard Account Ratings. The "R" represents accounts with revolving credit (such as credit cards, which may have varying balances from month to month). The best possible rating is R1, which indicates that the consumer has always paid this creditor on time. The lowest rating is R9, which indicates a bad debt, such as one that has gone into collection. The spectrum of available "R" designations is as follows:

R0   There is no information to report. For example, a new account may have been approved but not yet used.

R1   The debtor pays within 30 days of the due date or has had only one payment past due.

R2   The debtor pays between 31 and 60 days from the due date or has had two payments past due.

R3   The debtor pays between 61 and 90 days from the due date or has had three payments past due.

R4   The debtor pays between 91 and 120 days from the due date or has had four payments past due.

R5   The debtor is at least 120 days overdue.

R7   The debtor is making regular payments under a special arrangement to settle debts.

R8   Indicates repossession.

R9   Indicates a bad debt, often one placed for collection or in bankruptcy, and may indicate that the debtor moved without giving a new address.

- *Other information:* A consumer credit report may also indicate court judgments and executions, consumer proposals, bankruptcies, and discharges from bankruptcy. Consumer proposals are purged from the report three years from the date creditors have been paid under the proposal. Bankruptcies are purged from the report six years after the date of discharge.

Credit Score

Each file is assigned a credit score. Lenders rely on this score to assess credit risks. The score is based on payment history, number of debts, balances outstanding, how long accounts have been open and used, and any bankruptcies, consumer proposals, or debt management plans. The amount of credit that you have or have applied for is factored in as well. The best possible score is 900, 800 is very good, and 600 is good. The lowest score is 300. You can read more about credit scores at the Financial Consumer Agency of Canada's website at http://www.fcac-acfc.gc.ca. You can obtain a copy of your credit bureau report for free by mail; however, there is a fee of approximately $20 to obtain your credit score.

Bulk Sales Act Search

This is a search that you may be advised to do when the debtor is a business and there is some risk that the business has just sold all of its assets or is about to sell all of its assets, resulting in the business's ceasing to operate or to have **exigible assets**.

While there is nothing wrong with selling the assets of a business, a debtor could sell all of her assets to a **purchaser in good faith**, take the sale proceeds, and leave the jurisdiction, making it difficult or impossible for creditors to obtain payment of what the debtor owes them. The *Bulk Sales Act* requires that a purchaser complete documentation that gives details of the sale in order to protect himself against claims by the vendor's creditors that the purchaser knew the vendor was disposing of assets to defraud his creditors. This documentation is filed in the bulk sales register, which is kept in the court offices of the Superior Court of Justice in the county or district where the purchase occurred. Unfortunately, there is no centralized province-wide registry.[10] The search must therefore be carried out in the appropriate court office, or through a private search provider such as Cyberbahn, Oncorp, or Corporate Searchers. A purchaser who has complied with the Act is protected from claims by the vendor's creditors against the assets sold by the debtor to the purchaser. A search of the register will determine whether the Act has been complied with. If it has not, the purchaser's interest in the assets of the debtor can be attacked by the creditor.

exigible assets
assets that are available to be legally seized under a writ of seizure and sale; non-exigible assets are those that are exempt from seizure under the *Execution Act* or under the provisions of another statute

purchaser in good faith
sometimes given in Latin as *bona fide* purchaser, this phrase describes an individual who has bought something in circumstances where there is nothing to tell her that the seller is trying to unload the asset quickly, get cash, and get away with the cash before creditors manage to seize the asset or its proceeds; where a bad-faith sale has occurred, there are usually signs that tip off a reasonable and prudent buyer—for example, a price below fair market value, secrecy in the transaction, undue haste, insistence on payment in cash, among other things—so that a purchaser would be presumed to be on notice that the seller's title is flawed or questionable and the purchaser is deemed to acquire ownership subject to the claims of creditors

POST-SEARCH STRATEGIES

After completing the searches, evaluate with your client the information you have obtained and get their instructions about how to proceed. Usually, legal proceedings to recover the debt will be commenced, but sometimes other remedies are called for.

If it appears that the debtor has recently been transferring assets to others because creditors are closing in, it is advisable to consider some quick steps to prevent further transfer of these assets before suing to collect the debt. It is possible to apply to the courts to "tag" the property so that others will know ownership rights are in dispute, and that the current "owner" may not have good title to the asset and would be unable to transfer it successfully. There is a common law rule that says that you cannot give a better title or greater ownership interest to a purchaser than you yourself have. For example, if a debtor is being sued and transfers his car to his mother for $10, which is well below market price, his mother may not acquire good title. If so, no one will knowingly buy it from his mother because they know her title is likely to be challenged by someone who has a superior interest, such as the creditor. There are a number of things a creditor in this example can do to "tag" the asset with its superior title interest so that no innocent but careful purchaser would buy the car.

In this situation, the creditor could obtain an interim preservation order without notice to the debtor under the *Courts of Justice Act*, s. 104 and rule 44 of the *Rules of Civil Procedure*, in a fairly streamlined and simple procedure. The creditor would have to show lawful entitlement to the asset or a right to possess it with which the debtor or others have interfered.

If the property is real property (land) in which the creditor claims an interest, the creditor could obtain a certificate of pending litigation. When the certificate is registered on title in the land registration system, it is notice to the world of the creditor's interest, and the debtor would be unable to transfer any interest to a stranger. In the registration system, a potential purchaser is deemed to have notice of the creditor's interest when the certificate of pending litigation is registered, even if the potential purchaser does not search the register. In this situation, a purchaser cannot be a good-faith purchaser because he is deemed to know about the creditor's interest and cannot acquire any title to the land that could eliminate the creditor's interest.

If a debtor is about to leave Ontario with his assets to hinder or defeat creditors, it is possible to obtain an injunction to prevent the removal of assets from Ontario.

If the creditor has a security interest in assets of the debtor, it may not be necessary to sue at all. In most secured transactions, the creditor retains the right to seize and sell an asset if there is a default by the debtor, without going to court. Examples include:

- repossession of an automobile using a licensed, private bailiff;

- starting private power of sale proceedings under a land mortgage where the mortgagor (debtor) has defaulted on payments; or

- seizing a commercial tenant's goods using the landlord's remedy of distress on premises where the tenant is in arrears of rent, or evicting the tenant from the premises.

Although these private law remedies are attractive because they are fast and inexpensive, those using them must comply with both the letter and spirit of the law.

Because the courts do not supervise the process and allow the creditor to run it, if it is not done properly, the debtor can apply to the court for **relief from forfeiture**. If the court finds unfair or inequitable treatment, oppressive behaviour, or failure to comply exactly with required procedure, the court may order return of the asset to the debtor and stay further proceedings.

In conclusion, if the searches show that the debtor's affairs are hopeless, and there is no chance of recovery of the debt by suing, the creditor may be able to petition the debtor into bankruptcy. This prevents further dissipation of assets. However, if most assets are subject to the interests of secured creditors because they have been given as collateral, there may be very little left to liquidate and use to pay unsecured creditors — but it still may be more than an unsecured creditor would otherwise get if he or she did nothing. As well, if there is evidence that the debtor is paying some creditors but not others or transferring assets to relatives or friends, then bankruptcy may be advisable because there are provisions available under the Act that can provide remedies for *bona fide* creditors of the bankrupt that would be otherwise unavailable.

relief from forfeiture
a remedy granted to a debtor whose property has been seized by a creditor who has acted in an oppressive or capricious manner

CHAPTER SUMMARY

Once you have determined that a debt is overdue and have opened a client file, there are a number of things that must be done before commencing proceedings. In this chapter we look at the various searches that should be carried out prior to commencing litigation. Such searches can provide you with the debtor's legal name and address and provide information concerning their assets and liabilities to help you determine whether or not they are worth suing. Driver's licence and vehicle searches can be used to verify a name and an address, as can online searches. Execution, bankruptcy, and *Personal Property Security Act* searches can be used to tell you whether the debtor has assets that can be seized to pay the judgment. These searches may also tell you whether other creditors are trying to collect from the debtor and, if so, whether they have had much success. You may also use a credit bureau service to obtain information about the debtor's credit history. Once you have gathered information about the debtor's identity, assets, and credit history, talk to your client to determine whether to sue or take other measures.

KEY TERMS

exigible assets	reverse search
judgment proof	stayed
purchaser in good faith	title
relief from forfeiture	writ of seizure and sale

NOTES

1. Secured creditors are those who, in exchange for giving credit, ask for an interest in an asset of the debtor (called collateral) to secure payment of the debt. If the debtor defaults, instead of just suing the debtor, the creditor may seize or repossess the collateral without suing or getting a judgment, sell it, and use the proceeds of sale to satisfy the debt. Usually the secured creditor has a prior right to collateral as against an unsecured creditor, who has no right to seize the assets of the debtor until after a judgment is obtained.

2. Because online sites are relatively easy and inexpensive to change compared with paper systems, we have found that websites are often altered, usually for the better, to facilitate searches, and that among commercial and private search sites there is much competition, so sites are frequently transformed with the result that URLs come and go with some frequency. You may have to search and play with links or use Google or another search engine to find a site that seems to have disappeared or is not where you saw it last. This may be frustrating, but that is the way the Internet is these days.

3. Rule 8 of the *Rules of Civil Procedure*, RRO 1990, Reg. 94 made under the *Courts of Justice Act*.

4. See the *Business Names Act*, RSO 1990, c. B.17.

5. See the *Creditors' Relief Act, 2010*, SO 2010, c. 16, sch. 4.

6. In the case of *Bank of Montreal Innovative Credit Union*, 2010 SCC 47, the Supreme Court of Canada held that although a province cannot legislate to oust a bank's rights, they can alter a law as it relates to property and civil rights. A province can, therefore, as Saskatchewan has done, add priority provisions to its provincial PPSA legislation.

7. Although most debts are extinguished on the discharge of the bankrupt, some, such as child support debts and unpaid student loans, are not.

8. This Act and other federal legislation are available online at http://laws .justice.gc.ca.

9. Information on correcting your credit bureau report can be found at http://www.consumer.equifax.ca.

10. Many of the older registration and search systems, such as the system for bulk sales and writs of execution, were developed at a time when most business was done locally and on a small scale. The systems were certainly not designed to be used effectively with large, multinational enterprises or with electronic transfers of assets in a global economy.

REFERENCES

Bank Act, SC 1991, c. 46.

Bankruptcy and Insolvency Act, RSC 1985, c. B-3, as amended.

Bulk Sales Act, RSO 1990, c. B.14.

Business Names Act, RSO 1990, c. B.17.

Courts of Justice Act, RSO 1990, c. C.43.

Creditors' Relief Act, 2010, SO 2010, c. 16, sch. 4.

Execution Act, RSO 1990, c. E.24.

Personal Property Security Act, RSO 1990, c. P.10.

Rules of Civil Procedure, RRO 1990, Reg. 194.

Rules of the Small Claims Court, O. Reg. 258/98.

REVIEW QUESTIONS

1. Describe searches that can be used to identify the debtor.

2. Why is it important to identify the debtor accurately as a legal entity before suing?

3. Explain who can be sued if the debtor is a sole proprietorship, a partnership, or a corporation.

4. What does it mean to "expand enforcement rights" when suing a sole proprietorship or partnership?

5. Describe the searches that can be used to find out information about the debtor that is relevant to the conduct of collection litigation.

6. Describe the searches that can be used to verify the debtor's identity.

7. How does an unsecured credit transaction differ from a secured credit transaction?

8. What problem arises if an asset is pledged as security to two different creditors and one creditor registers its interest under the *Bank Act* while the other creditor registers its interest under the PPSA?

9. What can be done if a creditor finds that the debtor is transferring assets to relatives?

10. In what circumstances is a credit bureau search useful?

11. What is the significance of a credit information score of 35 in a commercial credit report?

12. If a consumer credit report gives the consumer an "R" rating of R1, is this a high or low credit risk?

DISCUSSION QUESTIONS

1. Carol Creditor has come to you with a collection matter. She makes stained glass ornaments and was hired by the Tea for Two Restaurant to create a stained glass canopy depicting lettuce heads to go over the salad bar in a restaurant. She has been dealing with Don Dafoe, the restaurant's manager, who ordered the work done and signed the order form. Carol has heard rumblings that the restaurant may have been sold and that there are other creditors lurking in the wings.

   In this situation, what searches would you perform and why would you perform them? What searches would you not perform?

2. On behalf of a creditor you have done some searches that reveal the following:

   The debtor carries on the business of a lumber yard. It has given a s. 427 security to the Caring Bank for a $100,000 loan, with the security being all of its lumber inventory and all of its vehicles. In addition, it has borrowed from Monopoly Trust and pledged all of its vehicles as collateral for a second loan in the amount of $75,000. A check with the credit bureau indicates that it has not defaulted on any debts, but that payments are often late. There are three executions against the business that were filed five years ago. They total $43,000 and have yet to be paid. Your client has sold supplies to this business on a running account. The account is now at $72,000 and no payments have been made for 65 days. Usually, a payment is received after 40 days.

   a. What options does the client have in this case?

b. What advice would you give to the client on which option to take and why she should pursue that option?

c. In pursuing the option you and your client have chosen, what steps do you have to take to achieve your goal?

Figure 3.1 Statement of Driving Record

Ontario

Location: <u>Ministry Home</u> > <u>Drivers & Vehicles</u> > <u>Ministry Online Service</u> > Order

<u>Back</u>

Ministry	Ministère	Road User	Division de la
of	des	Safety Division	sécurité des usagers
Transportation	Transports		de la route

Ontario

Ministry No./No. Du Ministère Search Date/Date de recherche (Y/A M D/J)
0000-0000-0 1994/08/19

STATEMENT OF DRIVING RECORD/RELEVÉ DU DOSSIER DE CONDUITE PAGE 01

DRIVER INFORMATION/DONNÉE DE CONDUCTEUR

Name/Nom **PUBLIC, JOHN, Q.**
Address/Adresse *

Reference No. or Driver's Licence No./
No de référence ou du permis de conduire **P0000-00000-00000**
Date of Birth/Date de naissance (Y/A M D/J) **1962/12/10**
Sex/Sexe **MALE/HOMME**
Height/Taille **175**
Class/Catégorie **G***
Condition/Restriction ***
Expiry Date/Date d'expirition (Y/A M D/J) **1985/08/31**
STATUS/STATUT **UNLICENCED/PERMIS DE CONDUIRE EXPIRÉ
UNRENEWABLE/NON RENOUVELABLE
SUSPENDED/SUSPENDU**

DATE CONVICTIONS, DISCHARGES AND OTHER ACTIONS
Y/A M D/J CONDAMNATIONS, LIBÉRATIONS ET AUTRES ACTIONS

93/10/12 REINST - SUSP. EXPIRED OR RESCINDED 1128705
REMIS EN VIGUEUR - SUSP. EXPIRÉE OU ANNULÉE

93/10/26 UNSAFE MOVE
MANOEUVRE DANGEREUSE

93/11/10 SUSPENDED RE UNPAID FINE
SUSPENDU, AMENDE IMPAYÉE
SUSPENSION NO./NO DE SUSPENSION 3050140 EXPIRY DATE: 1994/02/01
DATE D'EXPIRATION: 1994/02/01

94/02/01 REINST - SUSP. EXPIRED OR RESCINDED 3050140
REMIS EN VIGUEUR - SUSP. EXPIRÉE OU ANNULÉE

Figure 3.2   Certified Plate Search — Recent Owner

Ontario

**Ministry of
Transportation**

| central site | feedback | search | site map | français |

Location: <u>Ministry Home</u> > <u>Drivers & Vehicles</u> > <u>Ministry Online Service</u> > Order

<u>Back</u>

Ministry   Ministère   Road User   Division de la
of   des   Safety Division   sécurité des usagers
Transportation   Transports   de la route

Ontario

MINISTRY CONTROL NO./NO. DE CONTRÔLE DU MINISTÈRE SEARCH DATE/DATE DE RECHERCHE
000000 94/10/24

SEARCH TYPE/TYPE DE RECHERCHE INQUIRY KEY/ CRITÈRE DE RECHERCHE

PLATE/PLAQUE PLATE/PLAQUE - **AAAAAA**
===
REGISTRANT/CONDUCTEUR
NAME/NOM - **PUBLIC, JOHN, Q.**
ADDRESS/ADRESSE - * STAGGER/ÉCHELONNER - **0509**

-VEHICLE/VÉHICULE
VEHICLE IDENTIFICATION NO./NO D'IDENTIFICATION DU VÉHICULE - **OAOAAOOAOAAOOOOOO**
CLASS/CATÉGORIE - **PASSENGER/VOITURE PARTICULIÈRE** MAKE/MARQUE - **PONT**
MODEL/MODÈLE - **FRS**
BODY TYPE/TYPE DE CARROSSERIE - **2 DOOR SEDAN/COUPÉ**
NO. OF CYLINDERS/NO DE CYLINDRÉE-**04**
MOTIVE POWER/FORCE MOTRICE - **GASOLINE/ESSENCE**
COLOUR/COULEUR - **WHITE/BLANC** YEAR/ANNÉE - **84**
STATUS/STATUT - **FIT/EN ÉTAT DE MARCHE** WEIGHT EMPTY/POIDS À VIDE -
NO. OF AXLES/NO D'ESSIEUX -

-PLATE/PLAQUE
PLATE/PLAQUE - **000YYY** YEAR/ANNÉE -
SERIES/SÉRIE - **OWN CHOICE PASSENGER/PERSONNALISÉE VOITURE PARTICULIÈRE**
STATUS/STATUT - **ATTACHED/FIXÉE**
FORMAT -
PLATE REGISTRATION DATE/DATE D'ENREGISTREMENT DES PLAQUES - **910122**
---VALTAG
NO./NO DE VIGNETTE - **0000000** REGISTERED WEIGHT/POIDS ENREGISTRÉ -
DECLARATION/DÉCLARATION -
STAGGER/ÉCHELONNER - **93/05/10** EXPIRY/EXPIRATION - **94/05/09**
PERMIT NO./NO DE CERTIFICAT - **49815715** DATE ISSUED/DATE DE DÉLIVRANCE - **91/05/09**

Figure 3.3   Initial Return/Notice of Change

Ontario

Ministry of
Government Services

Central Production and
Verification Services Branch
393 University Ave, Suite 200
Toronto ON M5G 2M2

Ministère des
Services gouvernementaux

Direction des services
centraux de production et de vérification
393, av University, bureau 200
Toronto ON M5G 2M2

For Ministry Use Only
À l'usage du ministère seulement
Page/Page 1   of/de _____

Form 1 - Ontario Corporation Initial Return / Notice of Change
Formule 1 - Personnes morales de l'Ontario Rapport initial / Avis de modification
Corporations Information Act / Loi sur les renseignements exigés des personnes morales

Please type or print all information in block capital letters using black ink.
Prière de dactylographier les renseignements ou de les écrire en caractères d'imprimerie à l'encre noire.

1.
Business Corporation/
Société par actions
Not-For-Profit Corporation/
Personne morale sans but
lucratif

Initial Return
Rapport initial

Notice of Change
Avis de modification

2.
Ontario Corporation Number
Numéro matricule de la personne
morale en Ontario

114836

3.
Date of Incorporation or
Amalgamation/
Date de constitution ou fusion
Year/Année Month/Mois Day/Jour

2006   12   11

For Ministry Use Only
À l'usage du ministère seulement

4.   Corporation Name Including Punctuation/Raison sociale de la personne morale, y compris la ponctuation

CHENGOLF LTD.

5.   Address of Registered or Head Office/Adresse du siège social

c/o / a/s

MARY CHEN

Street No./N° civique   Street Name/Nom de la rue

60   CENTRE ST.

Suite/Bureau

#3

Street Name (cont'd)/Nom de la rue (suite)

City/Town/Ville

TORONTO   ONTARIO, CANADA

Postal Code/Code postal

M6Z 3A5

For Ministry Use Only/
À l'usage du ministère seulement

6.   Mailing Address/Adresse postale

✓ Same as Registered or Head Office/
Même que siège social

☐ Not Applicable/
Ne s'applique pas

Street No./N° civique

Street Name/Nom de la rue   Suite/Bureau

Street Name (cont'd)/Nom de la rue (suite)

City/Town/Ville

Province, State/Province, État   Country/Pays   Postal Code/Code postal

7.   Language of Preference/Langue préférée   English - Anglais ✓   French - Français ☐

8.   **Information on Directors/Officers must be completed on Schedule A as requested.** If additional space is required, photocopy Schedule A./**Les renseignements sur les administrateurs ou les dirigeants doivent être fournis dans l'Annexe A, tel que demandé.** Si vous avez besoin de plus d'espace, vous pouvez photocopier l'Annexe A.

Number of Schedule A(s) submitted/Nombre d'Annexes A présentées   1   (At least one Schedule A must be submitted/Au moins une
Annexe A doit être présentée)

9.
I/Je

(Print or type name in full of the person authorizing filing / Dactylographier ou inscrire le
prénom et le nom en caractères d'imprimerie de la personne qui autorise l'enregistrement)

MARY CHEN

certify that the information set out herein, is true and correct.
atteste que les renseignements précités sont véridiques et exacts.

Check appropriate box
Cocher la case pertinente

D) ✓ Director/Administrateur

O) ☐ Officer /Dirigeant

P) ☐ Other individual having knowledge of the
affairs of the Corporation/Autre personne
ayant connaissance des activités de la
personne morale

Note/Remarque : Sections 13 and 14 of the *Corporations Information Act* provide penalties for making false or misleading statements or omissions. Les articles 13 et
14 de la *Loi sur les renseignements exigés des personnes morales* prévoient des peines en cas de déclaration fausse ou trompeuse, ou d'omission.

07200 (2011/06)   © Queen's Printer for Ontario, 2011 / © Imprimeur de la Reine pour l'Ontario, 2011   Page 1 of/de 3

Figure 3.3   Concluded

Form 1 - Ontario Corporation/Formule 1 - Personnes morales de l'Ontario
Schedule A/Annexe A

For Ministry Use Only
À l'usage du ministère seulement
Page/Page _____ of/de _____

Please type or print all information in block capital letters using black ink. Prière de dactylographier les renseignements ou de les écrire en caractères d'imprimerie à l'encre noire.	Ontario Corporation Number Numéro matricule de la personne morale en Ontario 114836	Date of Incorporation or Amalgamation Date de constitution ou fusion Year/Année Month/Mois Day/Jour 2006 | 12 | 11

DIRECTOR / OFFICER INFORMATION - RENSEIGNEMENTS RELATIFS AUX ADMINISTRATEURS/DIRIGEANTS

Full Name and Address for Service/Nom et domicile élu

Last Name/Nom de famille	First Name/Prénom	Middle Names/Autres prénoms
CHEN	MARY	A

Street Number/Numéro civique: 60   Suite/Bureau: #3

Street Name/Nom de la rue: CENTRE ST.

Street Name (cont'd)/Nom de la rue (suite):

City/Town/Ville: TORONTO

Province, State/Province, État: ON   Country/Pays: CANADA   Postal Code/Code postal: M6Z 3A5

*OTHER TITLES (Please Specify)
*AUTRES TITRES (Veuillez préciser)
Chair / Président du conseil
Chair Person / Président du conseil
Chairman / Président du conseil
Chairwoman / Présidente du conseil
Vice-Chair / Vice-président du conseil
Vice-President / Vice-président
Assistant Secretary / Secrétaire adjoint
Assistant Treasurer / Trésorier adjoint
Chief Manager / Directeur exécutif
Executive Director / Directeur administratif
Managing Director / Administrateur délégué
Chief Executive Officer / Directeur général
Chief Financial Officer /
Agent en chef des finances
Chief Information Officer /
Directeur général de l'information
Chief Operating Officer /
Administrateur en chef des opérations
Chief Administrative Officer /
Directeur général de l'administration
Comptroller / Contrôleur
Authorized Signing Officer /
Signataire autorisé
Other (Untitled) / Autre (sans titre)

Director Information/Renseignements relatifs aux administrateurs

Resident Canadian/ ✓ YES/OUI   [ ] NO/NON   (Resident Canadian applies to directors of business corporations only.)/
Résident canadien   (Résident canadien ne s'applique qu'aux administrateurs de sociétés par actions)

Date Elected/Date d'élection: Year/Année ___ Month/Mois ___ Day/Jour ___

Date Ceased/Date de cessation: Year/Année ___ Month/Mois ___ Day/Jour ___

Officer Information/Renseignements relatifs aux dirigeants

	PRESIDENT/PRÉSIDENT			SECRETARY/SECRÉTAIRE			TREASURER/TRÉSORIER			GENERAL MANAGER/ DIRECTEUR GÉNÉRAL			*OTHER/AUTRE		
	Year/Année	Month/Mois	Day/Jour	Year/Année	Month/Mois	Day/Jour	Year/Année	Month/Mois	Day/Jour	Year/Année	Month/Mois	Day/Jour	Year/Année	Month/Mois	Day/Jour
Date Appointed/Date de nomination	2006	12	11												
Date Ceased/Date de cessation															

DIRECTOR / OFFICER INFORMATION - RENSEIGNEMENTS RELATIFS AUX ADMINISTRATEURS/DIRIGEANTS

Full Name and Address for Service/Nom et domicile élu

Last Name/Nom de famille	First Name/Prénom	Middle Names/Autres prénoms
PARTEN	JOHN	E

Street Number/Numéro civique: 25   Suite/Bureau:

Street Name/Nom de la rue: STIPPARD RD.

Street Name (cont'd)/Nom de la rue (suite):

City/Town/Ville: TORONTO

Province, State/Province, État: ON   Country/Pays: CANADA   Postal Code/Code postal: M4R 1M6

*OTHER TITLES (Please Specify)
*AUTRES TITRES (Veuillez préciser)
Chair / Président du conseil
Chair Person / Président du conseil
Chairman / Président du conseil
Chairwoman / Présidente du conseil
Vice-Chair / Vice-président du conseil
Vice-President / Vice-président
Assistant Secretary / Secrétaire adjoint
Assistant Treasurer / Trésorier adjoint
Chief Manager / Directeur exécutif
Executive Director / Directeur administratif
Managing Director / Administrateur délégué
Chief Executive Officer / Directeur général
Chief Financial Officer /
Agent en chef des finances
Chief Information Officer /
Directeur général de l'information
Chief Operating Officer /
Administrateur en chef des opérations
Chief Administrative Officer /
Directeur général de l'administration
Comptroller / Contrôleur
Authorized Signing Officer /
Signataire autorisé
Other (Untitled) / Autre (sans titre)

Director Information/Renseignements relatifs aux administrateurs

Resident Canadian/ ✓ YES/OUI   [ ] NO/NON   (Resident Canadian applies to directors of business corporations only.)/
Résident canadien   (Résident canadien ne s'applique qu'aux administrateurs de sociétés par actions)

Date Elected/Date d'élection: Year/Année 2006 Month/Mois 12 Day/Jour 11

Date Ceased/Date de cessation: Year/Année ___ Month/Mois ___ Day/Jour ___

Officer Information/Renseignements relatifs aux dirigeants

	PRESIDENT/PRÉSIDENT			SECRETARY/SECRÉTAIRE			TREASURER/TRÉSORIER			GENERAL MANAGER/ DIRECTEUR GÉNÉRAL			*OTHER/AUTRE		
	Year/Année	Month/Mois	Day/Jour	Year/Année	Month/Mois	Day/Jour	Year/Année	Month/Mois	Day/Jour	Year/Année	Month/Mois	Day/Jour	Year/Année	Month/Mois	Day/Jour
Date Appointed/Date de nomination				2006	12	11									
Date Ceased/Date de cessation															

07200 (2011/06)

Figure 3.4 Enhanced Business Name Search — Search Criteria

Ontario

HOME | NEWSROOM | SERVICES | YOUR GOVERNMENT | ABOUT ONTARIO

ServiceOntario

Integrated Business Services Application

making it easier

ACCESSIBILITY

Enhanced Business Name Search - Search Criteria

Caution: The Integrated Business Services Application does not support the Browser's Back button. Changes to information can be done at the Summary Screens.

Help With This Page

You must enter either a Business Name or the Ontario Business Identification Number.

Note: It will take approximately 45 seconds to process your search.

Business Name	Fly-By-Night Enterprises
City	BARRIE
Ontario Business Identification Number	
Type of Search *(Required)*	◉ Enhanced Search ○ Exact Search
Type of Report	Detailed Business Names Report

Help With This Page | Next

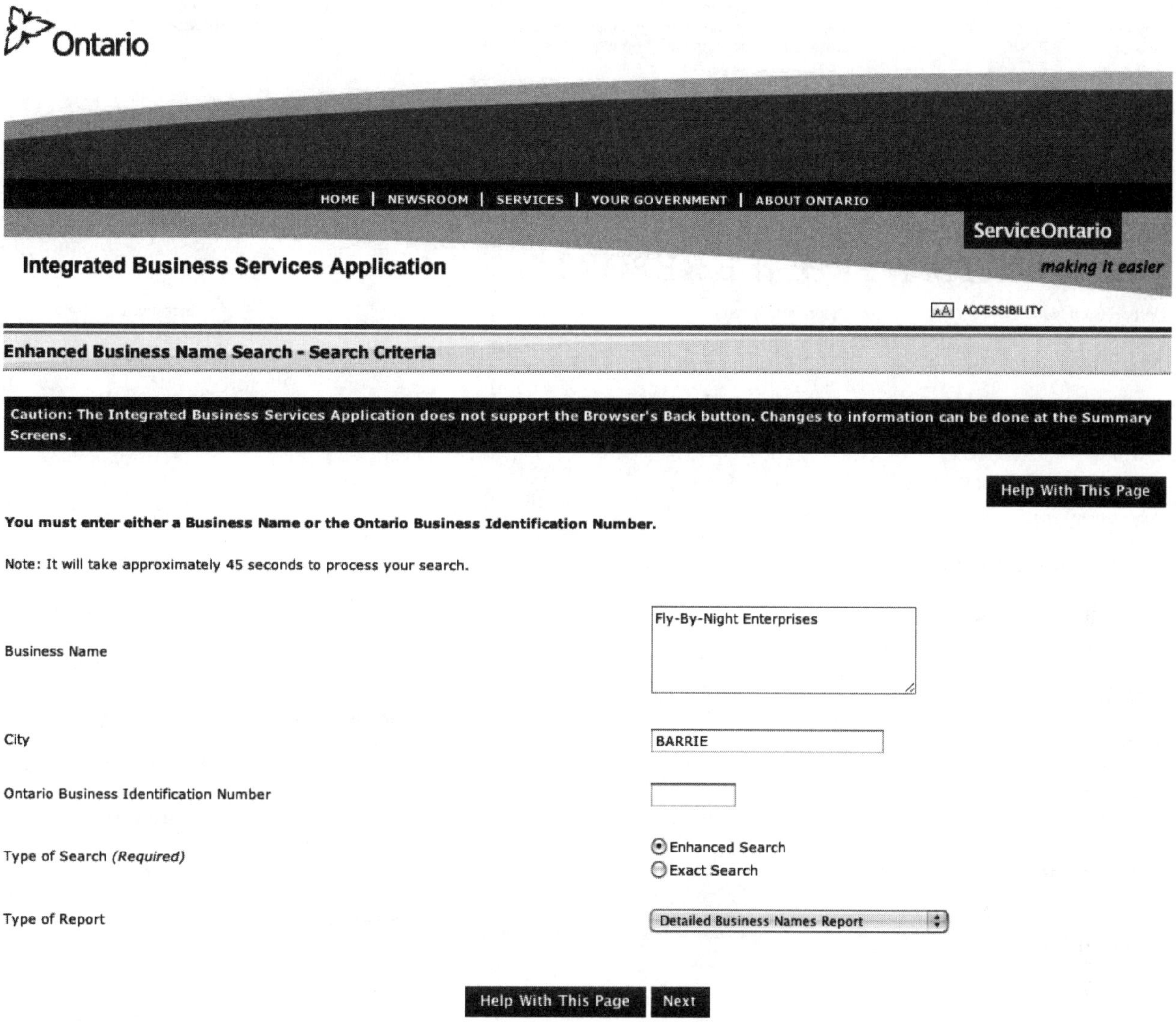

Figure 3.5   Corporation Profile Report

Request ID: 000177620	Province of Ontario	Date Report Produced: 2005/10/21
Transaction ID: 12871109	Ministry of Consumer and Business Services	Time Report Produced: 14:38:07
Category ID: UN/E	Companies and Personal Property Security Branch	Page: 1

CORPORATION PROFILE REPORT

Ontario Corp Number	Corporation Name		Incorporation Date
1990004	TEST		1993/02/25

Jurisdiction

ONTARIO

Corporation Type	Corporation Status		Former Jurisdiction
ONTARIO BUSINESS CORP.	ACTIVE		NOT APPLICABLE

Registered Office Address		Date Amalgamated	Amalgamation Ind.
		NOT APPLICABLE	NOT APPLICABLE

2 QUEEN STREET

	New Amal. Number	Notice Date

Suite # 222
TORONTO
ONTARIO
CANADA   M6M 6M6

NOT APPLICABLE   NOT APPLICABLE

Letter Date

Mailing Address

NOT APPLICABLE

	Revival Date	Continuation Date

2 QUEEN STREET

NOT APPLICABLE   NOT APPLICABLE

Suite # 222
TORONTO
ONTARIO
CANADA   M6M 6M6

Transferred Out Date	Cancel/Inactive Date
NOT APPLICABLE	NOT APPLICABLE

EP Licence Eff.Date	EP Licence Term.Date
NOT APPLICABLE	NOT APPLICABLE

Number of Directors		Date Commenced	Date Ceased
Minimum	Maximum	in Ontario	in Ontario
UNKNOWN	UNKNOWN	NOT APPLICABLE	NOT APPLICABLE

Activity Classification

NOT AVAILABLE

Figure 3.5　Continued

Request ID:　　000177620
Transaction ID:　12871109
Category ID:　　UN/E

Province of Ontario
Ministry of Consumer and Business Services
Companies and Personal Property Security Branch

Date Report Produced:　2005/10/21
Time Report Produced:　14:38:07
Page:　　　　　　　　2

CORPORATION PROFILE REPORT

Ontario Corp Number

1990004

Corporation Name

TEST

Corporate Name History

TEST

Effective Date

1993/02/25

Current Business Name(s) Exist:

Expired Business Name(s) Exist:

YES

YES - SEARCH REQUIRED FOR DETAILS

Administrator:
Name (Individual / Corporation)

ADAM

EVE

Address

77 5TH STREET

KINGSTON
ONTARIO
CANADA　N5N 5N5

Date Began

2004/07/01

Designation

DIRECTOR

First Director

NOT APPLICABLE

Officer Type

Resident Canadian

Y

Figure 3.5 Continued

Request ID: 000177620
Transaction ID: 12871109
Category ID: UN/E

Province of Ontario
Ministry of Consumer and Business Services
Companies and Personal Property Security Branch

Date Report Produced: 2005/10/21
Time Report Produced: 14:38:07
Page: 3

CORPORATION PROFILE REPORT

Ontario Corp Number

Corporation Name

1990004

TEST

Administrator:
Name (Individual / Corporation)

Address

ADAM

EVE

77 5TH STREET

KINGSTON
ONTARIO
CANADA   N5N 5N5

Date Began	First Director
2004/07/01	NOT APPLICABLE

Designation	Officer Type	Resident Canadian
OFFICER	GENERAL MANAGER	Y

Administrator:
Name (Individual / Corporation)

Address

JANE

JANENE

99 15TH AVENUE

OTTAWA
ONTARIO
CANADA   L7L 6K5

Date Began	First Director
2003/02/28	NOT APPLICABLE

Designation	Officer Type	Resident Canadian
DIRECTOR		Y

Figure 3.5   Continued

Request ID: 000177620
Transaction ID: 12871109
Category ID: UN/E

Province of Ontario
Ministry of Consumer and Business Services
Companies and Personal Property Security Branch

Date Report Produced: 2005/10/21
Time Report Produced: 14:38:07
Page: 4

CORPORATION PROFILE REPORT

Ontario Corp Number

1990004

Corporation Name

TEST

Administrator:
Name (Individual / Corporation)

JANE

JANENE

Address

99 15TH AVENUE

OTTAWA
ONTARIO
CANADA   L7L 6K5

Date Began

2003/02/28

First Director

NOT APPLICABLE

Designation

OFFICER

Officer Type

PRESIDENT

Resident Canadian

Y

Administrator:
Name (Individual / Corporation)

JAMES

JONES

Address

2 KING STREET WEST

TORONTO
ONTARIO
CANADA   M7M 7M7

Date Began

1999/05/05

First Director

NOT APPLICABLE

Designation

DIRECTOR

Officer Type

Resident Canadian

Y

Figure 3.5   Continued

Request ID: 000177620
Transaction ID: 12871109
Category ID: UN/E

Province of Ontario
Ministry of Consumer and Business Services
Companies and Personal Property Security Branch

Date Report Produced: 2005/10/21
Time Report Produced: 14:38:07
Page: 5

CORPORATION PROFILE REPORT

Ontario Corp Number

1990004

Corporation Name

TEST

Administrator:
Name (Individual / Corporation)

JOHN
P.
SMITHEX

Address

88 QUEEN STREET NORTH

TORONTO
ONTARIO
CANADA   L7L 5M5

Date Began   First Director

2004/07/01   NOT APPLICABLE

Designation   Officer Type   Resident Canadian

DIRECTOR   Y

Administrator:
Name (Individual / Corporation)

JOHN
P.
SMITHEX

Address

88 QUEEN STREET NORTH

TORONTO
ONTARIO
CANADA   L7L 5M5

Date Began   First Director

2004/07/01   NOT APPLICABLE

Designation   Officer Type   Resident Canadian

OFFICER   SECRETARY   Y

Figure 3.5   Concluded

Request ID: 000177620	Province of Ontario	Date Report Produced: 2005/10/21
Transaction ID: 12871109	Ministry of Consumer and Business Services	Time Report Produced: 14:38:07
Category ID: UN/E	Companies and Personal Property Security Branch	Page: 6

CORPORATION PROFILE REPORT

Ontario Corp Number   Corporation Name

1990004   TEST

Last Document Recorded

Act/Code Description   Form   Date

CIA   CHANGE NOTICE   1   2005/08/30 (ELECTRONIC FILING)

THIS CORPORATION HAS RECEIVED A NOTICE OF INTENTION TO DISSOLVE ON THE DATE INDICATED IN THE "NOTICE DATE" FIELD AND IS SUBJECT TO CANCELLATION.

THIS REPORT SETS OUT THE MOST RECENT INFORMATION FILED BY THE CORPORATION ON OR AFTER JUNE 27, 1992, AND RECORDED IN THE ONTARIO BUSINESS INFORMATION SYSTEM AS AT THE DATE AND TIME OF PRINTING. ALL PERSONS WHO ARE RECORDED AS CURRENT DIRECTORS OR OFFICERS ARE INCLUDED IN THE LIST OF ADMINISTRATORS.

ADDITIONAL HISTORICAL INFORMATION MAY EXIST ON THE COMPANIES AND PERSONAL PROPERTY SECURITY BRANCH MICROFICHE.

The issuance of this report in electronic form is authorized by the Director of Companies and Personal Property Security Branch

Figure 3.6   PPSA Search — Individual Non-Specific

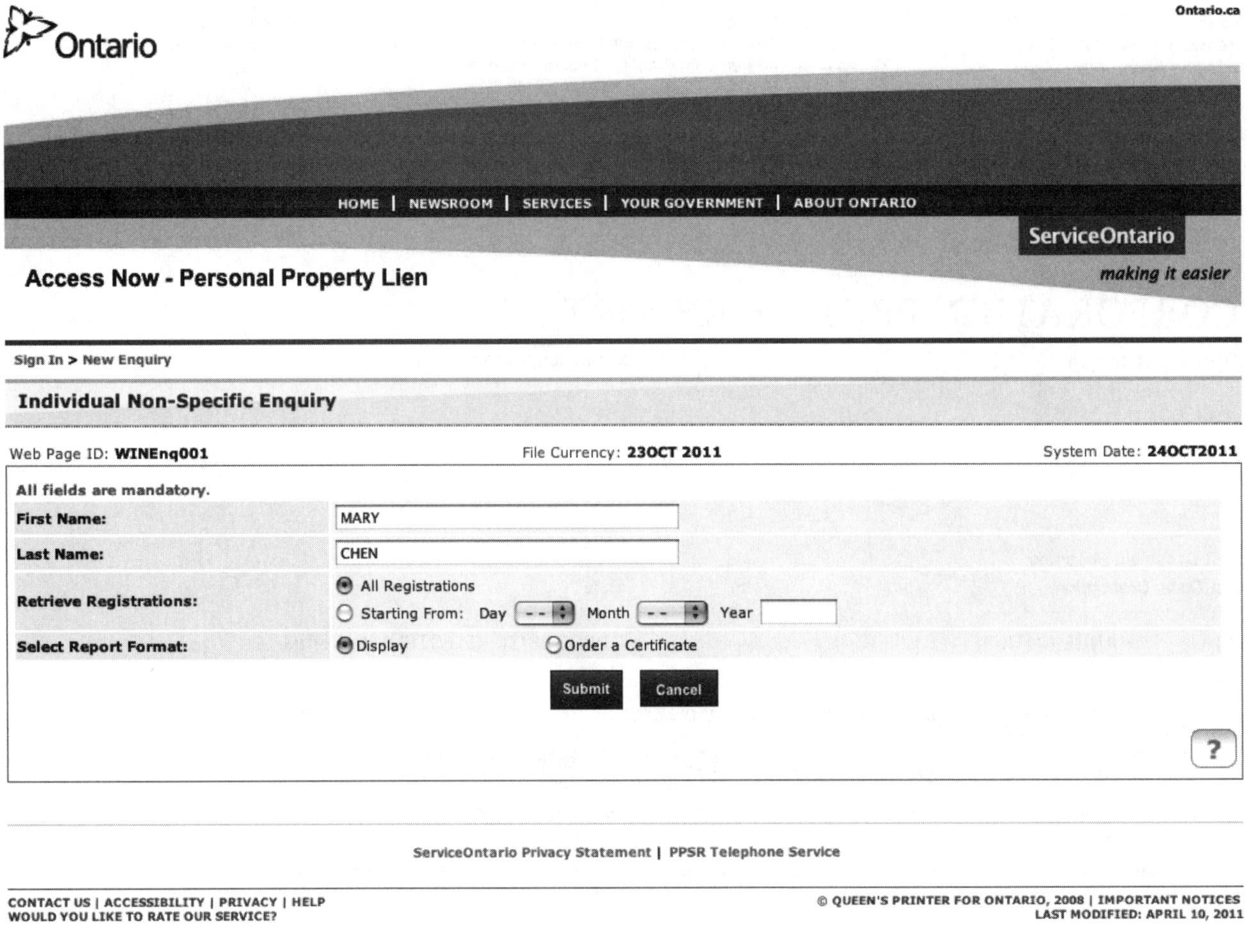

Figure 3.6   PPSA Search — Individual Non-Specific

Figure 3.7   PPSA Search — Individual Specific

Ontario.ca

Ontario

HOME | NEWSROOM | SERVICES | YOUR GOVERNMENT | ABOUT ONTARIO

ServiceOntario

Access Now - Personal Property Lien

making it easier

Sign In > New Enquiry

Individual Specific Enquiry

Web Page ID: **WISEnq001**   File Currency: **23OCT 2011**   System Date: **24OCT2011**

All fields except Middle Initial are mandatory.

First Name:	MARY
Middle Initial:	A
Last Name:	CHEN
Date of Birth:	Day 17 Month OCT Year 1958
Retrieve Registrations:	⦿ All Registrations ○ Starting From: Day -- Month -- Year
Select Report Format:	⦿ Display ○ Order a Certificate

Submit   Cancel

?

ServiceOntario Privacy Statement | PPSR Telephone Service

Figure 3.8   PPSA Search — Business Debtor Enquiry

Ontario.ca

HOME | NEWSROOM | SERVICES | YOUR GOVERNMENT | ABOUT ONTARIO

ServiceOntario

making it easier

Access Now - Personal Property Lien

Sign In > New Enquiry

Business Debtor Enquiry

Web Page ID: **WBDEnq001**   File Currency: **23OCT 2011**   System Date: **24OCT2011**

All fields are mandatory.

Business Name:	MARY'S GOLF DRIVING RANGE
Retrieve Registrations:	● All Registrations ○ Starting From: Day [--] Month [--] Year [ ]
Select Report Format:	● Display ○ Order a Certificate

Submit   Cancel

?

ServiceOntario Privacy Statement | PPSR Telephone Service

Figure 3.9   PPSA Search — Motor Vehicle Enquiry

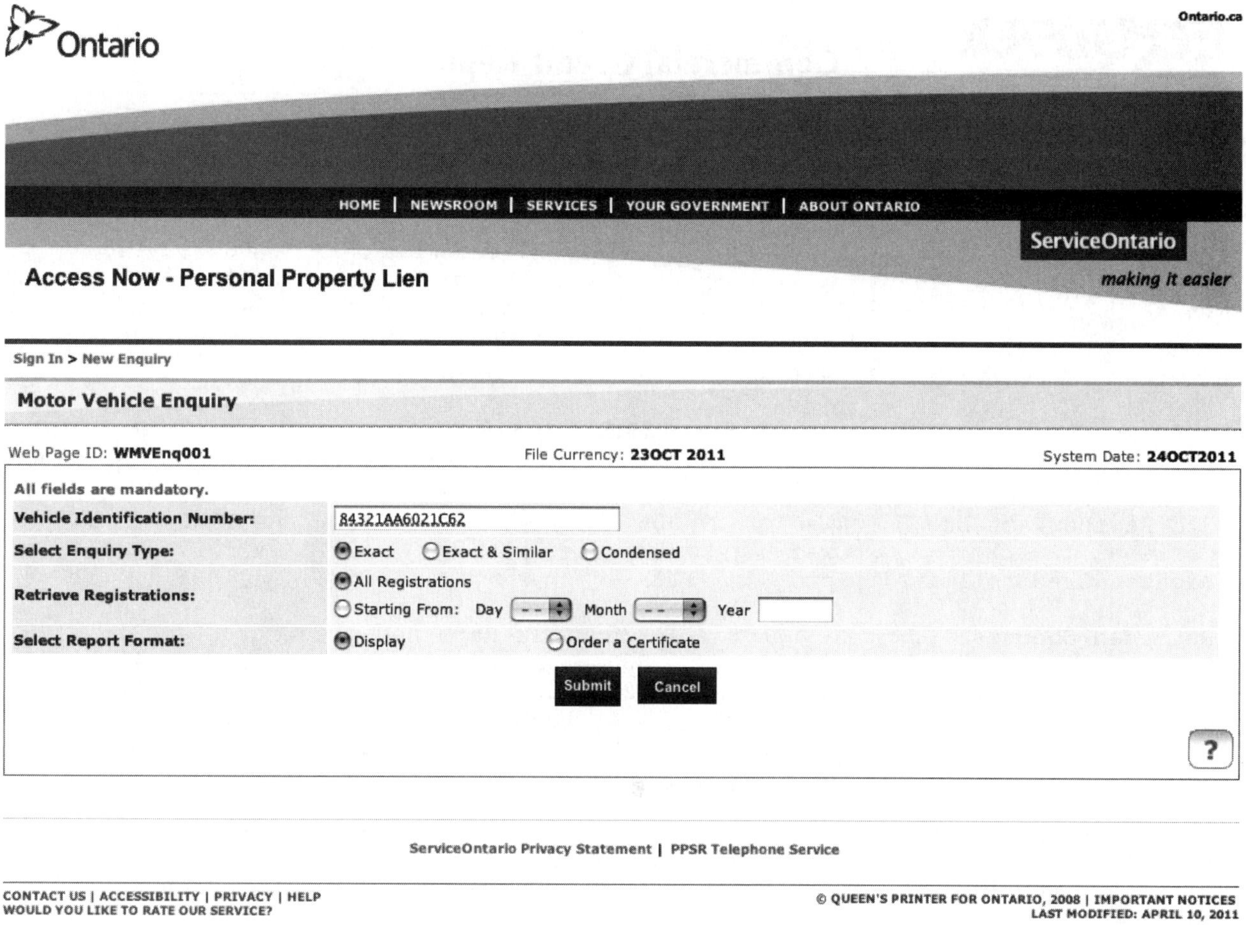

Figure 3.10   Sample Commercial Credit Report

EQUIFAX   Commercial Credit Report

ABC HOMES LTD
12345 FORGE RD SE
CALGARY, AB
T2H 0S9

Report date	: Feb 05, 1999
File opened	: Dec 31, 1979

File Number	: 0000199943
Subject Number	: A13999
Reference Number	: New Business
Requestor ID	: John Test

Telephone : 403-555-0581
Fax   : 403-555-1284

Primary SIC number - 1521 - (Gen Con, Home Improvement)

* * * SUMMARY * * *

					Credit Info	Scores	Payment	
9 Trade Suppliers	Owed	220K		*	23	Current	12	*
3rd Period Past Due	Owed	9,006	or	4%	*	12	4Q1998	14	*
Current	Owed	160K	or	72%	*	5	4Q1997	16	*
Highest Credit Limit	Rptd	116K		*	15	4Q1996	11	*

Returned Cheques	1 for	275	Last Returned Cheque ..	Dec 01, 1998
Collection Claims	1 for	500	Last Claim	Jan 12, 1998
Legal Suits	2 for	492K	Last Legal Suit	Feb 26, 1998
Judgments	1 for	0	Last Judgment	Jun 12, 1998
Other Items	1 for	0	Last Other Item	Jul 31, 1998

* * * TRADE ITEMS * * *

Supplier's Name/Industry	Terms Amount/Comments/Habits					
Rptd Open	High	Total	Current	Past Due/Pay Period		
Date Date	Credit	Owing	$	1st	2nd	3rd

Mfr-Auto & Parts:	DLA-1998/10/01, 839					
Jan* Jun/1997	30,211	20,520	20,520	0	0	0
REVELSTOKE HOME CTRE:	604-899-5555					
Nov*	36,150	36,150	19,521	16,629	0	0
Retail-Bldg/Hardware:						
Nov*	57,347	6,144	553	5,591	0	0
	-------	-------	-------	-------	-------	-------
P.I. = 12 90 Days	123K	62,814	40,594	22,220	0	0
Reported	-------	-------	-------	-------	-------	-------
Mfr-Fabricated Mtl:						
Nov*	116K	116K	90,495	21,488	1,681	3,106
Contr,Masonry,Stone:						
Oct*	33,955	33,955	23,769	3,396	1,019	5,771
SHELL CANADA (WEST):	403-691-2622					
Oct*	2,724	2,724	2,724	0	0	0
Mfr-Paint, Varnishes:						
Oct*	2,000	919	680	110	0	129
Services-Employment:						
Aug*	707	707	707	0	0	0
CANADIAN TURBO INC:	403-294-6431					
Mar*	5,154	3,007	1,594	1,413	0	0
	-------	-------	-------	-------	-------	-------
P.I. = 12 Total	285K	220K	160K	48,627	2,700	9,006
Reported	-------	-------	-------	-------	-------	-------

Note: * Indicates the data was supplied by an accounts receivable submission.

Figure 3.10 Continued

Note: # indicates Long Term Secured Debt which is NOT included in the PI and
      CI calculation.

* * * PAYMENT TRENDS * * *

	Payment	C.I.	Number Of	Total		- $ Overdue -		
Quarters	Index	Score	Suppliers	Owing	Current	1st	2nd	3rd
4 Qtr/1998	14	12	7	483,240	326,251	130,191	8,737	18,061
3 Qtr/1998	12	15	8	483,583	352,171	100,601	19,906	10,905
2 Qtr/1998	15	20	4	305,839	171,552	130,204	1,468	2,615
1 Qtr/1998	17	17	6	173,488	120,544	33,907	4,055	14,982
4 Qtr/1997	16	5	5	495,333	321,001	134,057	13,521	26,754
3 Qtr/1997	15	15	4	237,619	178,573	34,266	3,802	20,978
2 Qtr/1997	17	23	8	311,722	172,597	128,078	0	11,047
1 Qtr/1997	58	25	4	5,134	1,849	513	0	2,772
4 Qtr/1996	11	15	5	25,566	22,498	256	0	2,812

* * * RETURNED CHEQUES * * *

Sys. Date	Bank date	Amount	Reason Returned	Status
Feb 05, 1999	Dec 01, 1998	275.00	NSF	Not Replaced

* * * COLLECTION CLAIMS RECEIVED * * *

Debtor	ABC HOMES LTD	Date Placed	Jan 12, 1998
Creditor	ABC Publishing	Amount Placed	500
Agency	Equifax Accounts Receivable	Amount Paid	0
Comment	In Collection		

* * * LEGAL INFORMATION SECTION * * *

Statement of Claim:

Defendant	ABC HOMES LTD	Date	Feb 26, 1998
Plaintiff	SMART, WARREN	Court	Queen's Bench
Amount	16,364	Location	Calgary
Reason	Damages	File Number	960324546

Statement of Claim:

Defendant	ABC HOMES 1997 LTD	Date	Oct 05, 1995
Plaintiff	VAN SMITH HOMES	Court	Queen's Bench
Amount	476,000	Location	Calgary
Reason	Damages	File Number	970312904

Judgment, Order:

Defendant	ABC HOMES LTD	Date	Jun 12, 1998
Plaintiff	JONES, MARK	Court	Queen's Bench
Amount	0	Location	Calgary
Reason	Damages	File Number	970345568

* * * OTHER LEGAL INFORMATION * * *

Notice of Discontinuance:

Defendant	ABC HOMES 1997 LTD	Date	Jul 31, 1998
Plaintiff	123658 ALBERTA INC	Court	Queen's Bench
		Location	Calgary

Figure 3.10   Continued

```
                                              File Number 960355797
                    * * * BANKING INFORMATION * * *


Reported on: ABC HOMES LTD
Date: 1999/02/05                           File Number: 0000199943
                                           Subject Number: A13999

CANADIAN IMPERIAL BANK OF COMMERCE
628-8TH AVE S.W.
CALGARY, ALBERTA, T2P1G4
Branch: 010, Transit: 00019
Ref. Phone: (403) 544-1234              Ref. Fax: (403) 544-0988


     Account Information:
          Number of Accounts: 2, Current account, US account,
          Opened: For more than 3 years
          Total Balance: Low 6 figures

     *** Returned Cheque Details:
          Quantity: None, Frequency: In the last 3 months

     Line of Credit Details:
          Opened: 1980/12/03
          Authorized Amount: Low 7 figures
          Utilized: 80%
          Rating: Paid as agreed
          Secured: yes, Equipment, Mortgage

     Loan Details:
          Term loan, Opened: 1980/12/04
          Authorized Amount: $ 180,000
          Balance Owing: $ 25,000
          Terms: Monthly, $ 1,280
          Rating: Paid as agreed
          Secured: yes, Mortgage, Inventory

     Signing officer(s):
          WILSON JOHN, WILSON WILMA, WILSON SAMANTHA
          2 signatures required

                    * * * COMPANY INFORMATION * * *

Incorporation  Number: 12345667, Effective Date: 1978/05/01
Provincial Charter / Alberta

 1999/02/05, ALBERTA CORPORATE REGISTRY:REGISTERED OFFICE AND RECORDS
          ADDRESS:12345 FORGE RD SE,CALGARY,AB,T2H0S9.LAST ANNUAL REPORT
          1998-12-01.

 Premises: Owned, Land Only (Reported: 1999/02/26)
          12345 FORGE RD SE CALGARY AB T2H0S9
          Valuation Srce: Municipal Evaluation, Value: $ 500,000

 Number Employees: Full Time: 25, (Reported: 1999/02/05)
                   Part Time: 25, (Reported: 1999/02/05)

 Finances: Sales: $ 1,500,000, (Reported: 1999/02/05)
          Net Worth: $ 2,500,000, (Reported: 1999/02/05)
          A/R Amount: $ 75,000, (Reported: 1999/02/05)
          A/P Amount: $ 50,000, (Reported: 1999/02/05)
```

Figure 3.10   Concluded

```
Officers/Owners: (Reported: 1999/02/05)
     - WILSON, JOHN, President/Shareholder/Administrator
     - WILSON, SAMANTHA, Secretary Treasurer/Administrator
     - WILSON, WILMA, Vice President/Administrator
```

* * * ADDITIONAL COMMENTS * * *

```
1996/03/26, ABC HOMES LTD
          PREVIOUS ADD: 11 GREENBRIER CRES, SHERWOOD PARK, AB, T8A1A2
```

* * * OTHER FILES INCLUDED IN THIS REPORT * * *

```
A B C HOMES LTD.                           File Number    : 0032589944
11 GREENBRIER CRES                         Subject Number : ZZ9980
SHERWOOD PARK, AB   T8A1A2


ABC HOMES LTD                              File Number    : 0085299943
206, 2 ATHABASCA AVENUE                    Subject Number : ZX1668
SHERWOOD PARK, AB   T8A4E3
```

* * * RECENT INQUIRIES * * *

```
Jan 27, 1999  Publisher-Magazine
Dec 04, 1998  Jacks Lumber
Aug 21, 1998  The Great Hardware Store
Nov  3, 1997  Lending Institution
Mar 10, 1996  Pipe Depot                              (416)555-1234
```

* * * CREDIT INFORMATION SCORE * * *

The current CREDIT INFORMATION SCORE is the TOTAL of the following factors:

```
Years on File                              0-1  1.1-2  2.1-4  4.1-9   9.1+
     Score ...............................  10     8      6      4      0  =  0
Current Payment Index                      51+  41-50  31-40  21-30   0-20
     Score ...............................  10     7      5      4      0  =  0
Number of Trade Payment References         0-1   2-3    4-6   7-10    11+
     Score ...............................  10     8      5      3      0  =  3
Last Qtr, PI vs same Qtr, Last Year        41+  21-40  11-20   6-10    0-5
     Score ...............................  10     8      6      4      0  =  0
Number of Negative Occurrences             10+   8-9    5-7    2-4    0-1
     Score ...............................  10     8      5      3      0  =  5
Last Negative Occurrence (months)          1-2   3-4    5-6   7-12    12+
     Score ...............................  10     7      4      3      0  = 10
Amt. Neg. Occ, as % of current owed        100% 51-99% 11-50%  1-10%    0%
     Score ...............................  10     8      5      2      0  =  5

                                   CREDIT INFORMATION SCORE = 23
```

END OF REPORT

Figure 3.11 Sample Consumer Credit Report

EQUIFAX

CONSUMER RELATIONS P.O. BOX 190 STATION JEAN TALON
MONTREAL QUEBEC H1S 2Z2

JANE DOE
10 PLEASANT ST.
TORONTO ONTARIO
M2N 1A2

CONFIDENTIAL INFORMATION
NOT TO BE USED FOR CREDIT PURPOSES
RE: EQUIFAX UNIQUE NUMBER: 3140123054

Dear JANE DOE,

Further to your request, a disclosure of your personal credit file as of **03/27/01** follows:

PERSONAL IDENTIFICATION INFORMATION:

The following personal identification information is currently showing on your credit file. Your date of birth and social insurance number have been partially masked to protect your personal information (ie: Birth Date/Age: 01/xx/60, Social Insurance Number: 123-xxx-789).

DATE FILE OPENED:	07/04/92

NAME:	Doe, Jane
CURRENT ADDRESS:	10 PLEASANT ST. TORONTO,ON
DATE REPORTED: 12/96	
PREVIOUS ADDRESS:	2 AVENUE ST,TORONTO,ON
DATE REPORTED: 12/93	
PRIOR ADDRESS:	3 DU BOULEVARD,MONTREAL,PQ
DATE REPORTED: 07/92	

BIRTH DATE/AGE:	10/XX/1968
SOCIAL INSURANCE NUMBER:	123-XXX-789

OTHER REFERENCE NAMES:	
CURRENT EMPLOYMENT:	EDITOR
PREVIOUS EMPLOYMENT:	TRANSLATOR
PRIOR EMPLOYMENT:	CHEF
OTHER INCOME:	

Figure 3.11   Continued

CREDIT INQUIRIES ON YOUR FILE:

Following is a list of Equifax members who have received a copy of your credit file for credit granting or other permissible purposes. Addresses are available by calling Equifax at 1-800-465-7166.

DATE	REQUESTOR NAME	TELEPHONE
03/02/00	CANADA TRUST MTG	(416) 361-8518
02/22/00	TD BANK	(800) 787-7065
01/16/00	BQE NATIONALE	(450) 677-9122

The following inquiries are for your information only and are not displayed to others. They include requests from authorized parties to update their records regarding your existing account with them.

DATE	REQUESTOR NAME	TELEPHONE
03/23/00	SOC ALCOOLS (not displayed)	(514) 873-6281
03/22/00	CANADA TRUST MTG (not displayed)	(416) 361-8518
02/16/00	CMHC SCHL (not displayed)	(888) 463-6454
01/16/00	AMERICAN EXPRESS (not displayed)	(416) 123-4567

CONSUMER INTERVIEWS AND OTHER SERVICES:
You contacted our office in 12/98 to request a review of your credit file.

CREDIT HISTORY AND/OR BANKING INFORMATION:

The following information was reported to us by organizations listed below.
Information is received every 30 days from most credit grantors. All account numbers with your creditors have been masked to protect your personal account information and only the last three digits will be displayed (i.e.: xxx...123).

GMAC last reported to us in 01/01 rating your installment account as I1, meaning paid as agreed and up to date. The reported balance of your account was $1000. Your account number: xxx...345. The account is in the subject's name only. Date account opened: 04/99. Credit limit or highest amount of credit advanced: $4400. **DATE OF LAST ACTIVITY meaning the last payment or transaction made on this account was in 12/00.** Additional comments: auto loan. Monthly payments.

CANADA TRUST MC last reported to us in 01/01 rating your revolving account as R1, meaning paid as agreed and up to date. At the time the reported balance of your account was $285. Your account number: xxx...234. Date account opened: 06/99. Credit limit or highest amount of credit advanced $2000. **DATE OF LAST ACTIVITY meaning the last payment or transaction made on this account was in 12/00. PREVIOUS PAYMENT STATUS:**
30 DAYS: 1 time (s) account previously R2 meaning one payment past due

PUBLIC RECORDS AND OTHER INFORMATION:

The following information was reported to your file on the date indicated.

A COLLECTION was **assigned** in 10/96 to Commercial Credit by Transamerica Financial in the amount of:$2675. Date reported paid: 07/97. Collection status: PAID. **DATE OF LAST ACTIVITY was in 04/96.** Collection agency reference number: 222222.

Figure 3.11   Continued

A JUDGEMENT was **FILED IN 01/96** in Min Govt Serv. Plaintiff and/or case number: Chrysler Canada 4444. Defendant/other info: joint with Dossier. Amount reported: $7525. Status reported: Satisfied. Date satisfied: 09/97.

A BANKRUPTCY was **FILED IN 08/97** in SC Newmarket. Case number and/or trustee: 5555555 SYNDIC & ASS. Liabilities: $250000.Assets: $8900000.Item classification: individual. Information reported on: The subject only. The item is reported as: DISCHARGED. **DATE SETTLED: 05/98.** Additional comments: absolute discharge from bankruptcy.

THE CONSUMER PROVIDED A PERSONAL STATEMENT to us in 12/98. The statement has been recorded as follows:

RE: BANKRUPTCY, CONSUMER DECLARED BANKRUPTCY DUE TO DIVORCE
This statement is to be removed from the file in: 12/04.

RETENTION PERIOD OF DATA:

CREDIT INQUIRIES TO THE FILE
   • An Inquiry made by a Creditor will automatically purge three (3) years from the date of the inquiry. The system will keep a minimum of five (5) inquiries.

CREDIT HISTORY AND BANKING INFORMATION
   • A credit transaction will automatically purge from the sytem six (6) years from the date of last activity.
   • All banking information (checking or saving account) will automatically purge from the system six (6) years from the date of registration.

VOLUNTARY DEPOSIT - ORDERLY PAYMENT OF DEBTS, CREDIT COUNSELING
   • When voluntary deposit – OPD – credit counseling is paid, it will automatically purge from the sytem three (3) years from the date paid.

REGISTERED CONSUMER PROPOSAL
   • When a registered consumer proposal is paid, it will automatically purge three (3) years from the date paid.

BANKRUPTCY
   • A bankruptcy automatically purges six (6) years from the date of discharge in the case of a single bankruptcy. If the consumer declares several bankruptcies, the system will keep each bankruptcy for fourteen (14) years from the date of each discharge. All accounts included in a bankruptcy remain on file indicating "included in bankruptcy" and will purge six (6) years from the date of last activity.

JUDGMENTS, SEIZURE OF MOVABLE/IMMOVABLE, GARNISHMENT OF WAGES
   • The above will automatically purge from the system six (6) years from the date filed.

COLLECTION ACCOUNTS
   • A collection account under public records will automatically purge from the sytem six (6) years from the date of last activity.

SECURED LOANS
   • A secured loan will automatically purge from the system six (6) years from the date filed.

(Exception: P.E.I. Public Records: seven (7) to ten (10) years.)

The attached Reference Update Form is included for your convenience. If you wish to update your file with more current information or to request a change in the information provided above, please complete this form and return it to Equifax. We will ensure that appropriate measures will be applied if corrections are required.

Figure 3.11   Concluded

Please be advised that the file you have received is for your information only and may not be used for credit purposes.

INFORMATION ABOUT YOUR CREDIT FILE

Every day Canadians purchase goods and services using credit. The decision to extend credit to you, the buyer, is made by the seller – commonly referred to as the "credit grantor". Most often, this decision involves reviewing your personal credit file, which is obtained from a credit reporting agency such as Equifax. The agency is a clearinghouse for credit information. Credit grantors provide the agency with factual information about your credit history.

The reporting agency then assembles this information into your personal file. In return, credit grantors can access your files before granting credit to you or identifying you for security purposes. Only you and the credit grantor can have you personal file modified.

WHAT IS AN INQUIRY?

When you apply for credit a credit grantor carries out an account inquiry. Account inquiries are also done routinely by organizations based on their client lists. If you have dealt with certain organizations, your name would likely be on their client list. At times, they may monitor client accounts or update their client information prior to making promotional offerings. This second type of inquiry is confidential and is not shown to other organizations that may offer you credit.

WHY WAS I DENIED CREDIT?

Equifax neither grants nor denies any application for credit. We simply provide a factual account of your credit history to credit grantors. Each credit granting organization reviews this information and makes an independent decision based on its own individual criteria. If an account/business transaction is joint or you have co-signed, both parties are held equally responsible.

WHY HAS SOMETHING I PAID OFF STILL SHOWS ON MY CREDIT FILE?

The fact that you have paid an account on time or did not pay as agreed is of interest to any potential credit grantor because it reflects your ability to pay your bills. A credit file shows past and present transactions.

WHAT CAN BE DONE IF I SUSPECT I AM A VICTIM OF IDENTIFY FRAUD?

If you have lost or had your personal identification stolen or an institution has contacted you regarding suspected fraud activity, please call Equifax toll free at 1 800 465-7166 or (514) 493-2314. A statement will be added to your file to alert credit grantors that you may be a victim of fraud activity.

CREDIT CLINICS: SHOULD I USE THE SERVICE OF COMPANIES WHO INDICATE THEY CAN HELP FIX MY CREDIT?

That is your choice. Remember, however, that these companies cannot have accurate information removed from your credit file. If there is inaccurate information on you file; Equifax will amend it, at no charge to you.

Consumer Department

CHAPTER 4

Determining the Amount Owing on a Claim

This chapter explains how to calculate simple interest, compound interest, and interest on running accounts for the purposes of sending a demand letter and making a court claim.

DETERMINING THE AMOUNT OWING

Before preparing a demand letter or drafting a claim, you must determine the amount that will be owing as of the date of the letter or claim. You must also show in the claim the basis for determining how that amount grows as interest accrues, so that when judgment is obtained or a payment is made, you will easily be able to tell how much is owing. Note that as the matter proceeds, legal costs may be added to the amount of the debt and interest will accrue on the costs on a judgment as well.

We begin with a discussion of how interest is dealt with in a claim by explaining how prejudgment and postjudgment interest are calculated and then, if the contract requires it, how compound interest is calculated on a debt. This discussion is not exhaustive and you may wish to consult a business math text. Also note that the calculation of compound interest can be tedious and there are computer software programs, such as Excel or Lotus, and scientific calculators that you can use to do the calculations quickly and accurately.

Calculation of Prejudgment and Postjudgment Interest

The *Courts of Justice Act*, ss. 127 to 129, sets out the rules for calculating prejudgment and postjudgment interest. Section 127 sets out the formula for determining prejudgment and postjudgment interest rates. The rate is calculated for each quarter of the year by a person designated by the deputy attorney general. The rate for each quarter is posted on the Attorney General's website at http://www.attorneygeneral.jus.gov.on.ca/english/courts/2nd_Quarter_2011_CJA_Pre_Postjudgment_Interest_EN.pdf.

Below are step-by-step instructions for calculating prejudgment and postjudgment interest on a debt. A sample calculation follows on pages 91 and 92. If you have to do frequent prejudgment and postjudgment interest calculations, there is an online service that, for a monthly fee, will do the calculations for you. The service's website is at http://www.judgmentcalculator.com/on.

1. Decide whether there is a right to interest in the contract itself rather than under the *Courts of Justice Act*.

If the contract provides for interest on unpaid amounts, then you must claim interest in accordance with the terms of the contract. If the contract is silent on interest, then you are entitled to claim interest under ss. 127 to 129.

2. If your claim for interest is based on a rate in the contract, claim interest under the *Courts of Justice Act* in the alternative.

Your claim for relief in your statement of claim should then read:

> *The plaintiff claims prejudgment and postjudgment interest under the terms of the contract and under the provisions of the* Courts of Justice Act, *in the alternative.*

If contractual interest is disallowed for some reason, for example, if the interest rate clause in a contract is deemed to be unenforceable, then you may still get interest under the *Courts of Justice Act* in the alternative, provided you made the claim. If you claim only contract-based interest and fail to get it, you may end up getting no interest at all.

3. If the contract provides for an interest rate, use that rate; otherwise, establish the prejudgment interest rate: ss. 127(1) and (2) and 128(1) and (4).

The rule under the *Courts of Justice Act* is that the *rate of interest to be used is the rate for the quarter in which the action was commenced.*

Do not confuse this with the quarter in which the cause of action (or right to sue) arose. The right to sue arises earlier than the day you act on that right by commencing an action. Often the rate on the day the cause of action arose will be different from the rate on the day when the action was commenced, because the two dates are in different quarters.

The Relationship Between the Date the Cause of Action Arose and the Date the Action Commenced

debt past due: June 12	action commenced: Nov. 4
> date cause of action arose 2nd quarter, rate 3%	> date action commenced 4th quarter, rate 4%

The rate of interest that applies is 4 percent, and it applies to the principal amount of the debt as of June 12. Interest commences June 12 and runs up to and including the day of judgment.

4. Having established the rate, calculate the prejudgment interest: ss. 127(1) and 128.

Determine the date on which interest began to run. On a debt, interest is calculated from the day after the debt was due and not paid. For example, if there were 10 days for payment, and the 10th day was today, then interest runs from tomorrow, which is the first day the debt is past due.

Date from Which Interest Runs

debt incurred	debt due	interest runs
day 1	day 10	from and after day 11 when debt is past due

Having determined the date on which interest began to run (the day after the principal amount of the debt was due), count the days up to and including the day the judgment or order is made. If the number of days covers several months, it is much easier to count days using a "Number of Each Day of the Year" chart (see figure 4.1). If you use the chart, start your count from the day the principal amount of the debt is due, not from the date interest starts. Stop your count on the day of judgment or payment. Whether you use the chart or not, the result is the same. Now calculate the prejudgment interest by using the following formula:

the prejudgment interest calculation formula (simple interest) is

$I = P \times R \times T$

where

I = interest

P = amount of the claim

R = rate of interest from the rate for the quarter when the action was commenced (if no contract rate is given)

T = number of days of interest commencing your count from the day after the principal amount of the debt is due up to and including the day of the judgment. This is expressed as a fraction of a year — 32 days is expressed as $^{32}/_{365}$.

If the debt is expressed as being overdue by a number of months rather than days, then a debt two months overdue would be expressed as $^2/_{12}$.

5. Determine the amount of the judgment including prejudgment interest.

The judgment amount will include:

the amount of the principal debt + prejudgment interest + court costs = amount due under the judgment

6. Determine the postjudgment interest rate: ss. 127 and 129, if no contract rate is used.

Once judgment has been signed, you must calculate postjudgment interest on the amount of the judgment that includes the principal amount on the debt, prejudgment interest to the date of judgment, and costs. The interest rate that applies, for post judgment interest, is the rate for the quarter in which the order or judgment was made. Note that, unless the order specifically disallows postjudgment interest, the court clerk will automatically insert the rate into the following standard wording, which should be added to the bottom of a judgment:

This order is subject to postjudgment interest at the rate of _____% per year.

7. Calculate postjudgment interest.

Calculate postjudgment interest using the following formula:

the postjudgment interest calculation (simple interest) is

$I = P \times R \times T$

where

I = postjudgment interest owing on amount of judgment

P = total amount of judgment (amount of principal debt + prejudgment interest + costs) + postjudgment enforcement costs

R = rate of interest from the rate for the quarter in which judgment was made

T = number of days of postjudgment interest commencing the day after judgment up to and including the day of payment (if using the Number of Each Day of the Year chart (figure 4.1), start the count with the date the judgment was made)

	Summary of How to Use $I = P \times R \times T$	
	Prejudgment Interest	Postjudgment Interest
Principal	Principal Debt Owing	Judgment Amount (principal debt plus prejudgment interest plus costs awarded) plus postjudgment enforcement costs
Rate	Use contract rate, if applicable. • If not, use quarter in which action was commenced.	Use contract rate, if applicable. • If not, use quarter in which judgment was made.
Time	From date cause of action arose up to and including date of judgment	From the day after judgment up to and including date of next step (e.g., date of payment, date of enforcement document)

8. Calculate the total amount due and owing to the plaintiff.

The total amount due equals the amount of the judgment (claim for principal debt, prejudgment interest, and costs) plus postjudgment interest up to and including the date of payment.

Now work through the following example for calculating prejudgment interest and postjudgment interest on the judgment and on any costs incurred in enforcing the judgment.

Sample Calculation of Prejudgment and Postjudgment Interest
Facts

Arnold enters into a contract with Bartolo to deliver goods by July 11, year 0; the price was $10,000 and payment was due on August 10, year 0. No payment was received and an action was commenced on August 21. Judgment was obtained by default on September 11, year 0 and satisfied (paid) on September 30.

Prejudgment interest rates have been set as follows under the Courts of Justice Act:

1st quarter	Jan. 1 to Mar. 31	2%
2nd quarter	Apr. 1 to June 30	3%
3rd quarter	July 1 to Sept. 30	3%
4th quarter	Oct. 1 to Dec. 31	4%

Postjudgment interest rates have been set as follows under the Courts of Justice Act:

1st quarter	Jan. 1 to Mar. 31	4%
2nd quarter	Apr. 1 to June 30	5%
3rd quarter	July 1 to Sept. 30	5%
4th quarter	Oct. 1 to Dec. 31	6%

1. *Determine the basis for claiming prejudgment interest.* There is no indication that the parties agreed to an interest rate for overdue payments in the contract. Therefore you must use the prejudgment and postjudgment interest rates prescribed by ss. 127 to 129.

   Because the action commenced on August 21, in the 3rd quarter, the applicable interest rate is the rate for the 3rd quarter — 3 percent.

2. *Calculate prejudgment interest:*
   a. *Determine the date on which interest begins to run.* This is the date on which the cause of action arose. The cause of action arose on the day after the debt was due — August 11 (or on August 10 if you use the Number of Each Day of the Year chart (figure 4.1)).
   b. *Determine the date on which judgment is given and count the days between the two dates.* Because the debt was due on August 10, prejudgment interest runs from August 11 until and including September 11, the day judgment was given — 32 days.
   c. *Calculate prejudgment interest:*

      $I = P \times R \times T$

      $10,000.00 \times .03 \times {}^{32}/_{365} = \$26.30$

3. *Determine the amount of the judgment* — assume you are awarded $180.00 in costs on the judgment:

   $\$10,000.00 + \$26.30 + \$180.00 = \$10,206.30$

   If you did not receive payment on the day of judgment, go on to calculate postjudgment interest.

4. *Determine the postjudgment interest rate.* Because there is no rate set by the contract, the rate that applies is the rate for the quarter in which the order or judgment was made. The judgment was given on September 11, which is in the 3rd quarter, for which the interest rate is 5 percent.

5. *Calculate the postjudgment interest:*
   a. *Determine the day on which postjudgment interest begins to run.* Interest begins the day after the judgment or order was made. The order was made on September 11. (If you use the Number of Each Day of the Year chart (figure 4.1), start your count with September 11.) Use September 12 as your start date if you are not using the Number of Each Day of the Year chart.
   b. *Count the days from the day after the order is made until and including the date of payment.* The day after the order is made was September 12, and payment was made on September 30, which is 19 days.
   c. *Calculate the postjudgment interest:*

   $I = P \times R \times T$
   $\$10,206.30 \times .05 \times {}^{19}/_{365} = \$26.56$ postjudgment interest

6. *Calculate the amount due on the date of payment, including postjudgment interest:*
   a. $10,206.30 (judgment) + $26.56 (postjudgment interest)
      = $10,232.86

CALCULATION OF SIMPLE AND COMPOUND INTEREST

In the Sample Calculation of Prejudgment and Postjudgment Interest beginning on page 91, we used simple interest — interest that is calculated on the principal amount of the debt only. Simple interest is calculated during the interest period on the principal amount and added to the accumulated interest. Compound interest is calculated on the principal amount as well as on previous interest. The following examples, using the same principal amount and interest rate, show how the calculations are done with simple and compound interest. The effect of using compound interest is that the amount of earned interest is greater than it would be from using simple interest. With large amounts of principal, compound interest results in significantly higher total amounts. You can determine whether compound interest is due by examining the payment and interest provisions in the contract. When the contract or loan agreement describes interest as being "compounded monthly" (or annually, or quarterly, or daily) or states that "interest is calculated on previous arrears of principal and interest" there is cause to compound interest.

Sample Simple Interest Calculation

Calculate the total amount owing on a debt of $10,000 that is 1 month, 2 months, 3 months, and 15 months overdue. The interest rate is 21 percent **per annum**.

per annum
Latin for "per year"

Solution

Use the formula $I = P \times R \times T$

Because we are given the number of months the debt is overdue, rather than the number of days, we will use $^1/_{12}$, $^2/_{12}$, $^3/_{12}$, and $^{15}/_{12}$ as our measurement of time for the formula. This represents time as months as a fraction of the year.

Interest for 1 month   = $10,000 × .21 × $1/12$ = $175

Interest for 2 months = $10,000 × .21 × $2/12$ = $350

Interest for 3 months = $10,000 × .21 × $3/12$ = $525

Interest for 15 months = $10,000 × .21 × $15/12$ = $2,625

Therefore, the total amount of principal and interest would be:

1 month $10,175

2 months $10,350

3 months $10,525

15 months $12,625

Sample Compound Interest Calculation

Calculate the total amount owing on a debt of $10,000 that is 1 month, 2 months, 3 months, and 15 months overdue. The interest rate is 21 percent per annum and the debt is compounded monthly.

Solution

Note: Amounts have been rounded off.

Use the following formula for compound interest:

$$S = P(1 + i)^n$$

where

S = amount owing (principal and interest)

P = principal (amount of the claim)

i = interest rate for each compounding period

n = number of compounding periods

Note: Because the compounding period is one month, we need to calculate the monthly rate of interest. It is $21/12 = .0175$.

The amount owing (S) at the end of month 1 is:

$10,000(1 + .0175)^1 = $10,175.00$

The amount owing at the end of month 2 is:

$10,000(1 + .0175)^2 = $10,353.06$

The amount owing at the end of month 3 is:

$10,000(1 + .0175)^3 = $10,534.24$

The amount owing at the end of month 15 is:

$10,000(1 + .0175)^{15} = $12,972.28$

DETERMINING THE AMOUNT OWING FROM THE CONTRACT

The terms of the contract and the creditor's accounting records usually form the basis for determining the amount due and owing. Often the creditor will do the calculations for you up to a certain date. If so, you need only update the interest from that date to the date you demand payment in your demand letter, or to the date on which you obtain judgment. If the creditor is claiming interest under the contract, remember to check that there is a basis for it in the contract; mere reference to interest in the invoice or bill is not enough by itself. It has to have been agreed to by the parties in the contract itself.

Special care should be taken with a running account. A running account is one where the debtor is a regular customer and has a fluctuating balance from time to time. This happens where the debtor charges purchases to his account and makes payments from time to time. A debtor may not pay off the full amount due at the end of a payment period; the creditor will carry that amount forward into the next payment period, when the debtor will pay some or all of it off. It is possible for a creditor's customer to always have a balance due greater than zero, in which case the creditor is "carrying" the debtor by carrying an unpaid amount that is due and owing. Of course if interest is charged on overdue amounts, then the debtor is being "carried" at some cost to himself.

When determining what is owing on a running account, go back through the debits and credits until you come to a nil balance and start your calculations from there. Calculate the interest on the balance from the time it is due until there is a change in the principal balance because of a further debit or credit. When a payment is received, it is first allocated to outstanding interest, and then to outstanding principal.

An example of a running account and how to determine the amount of a claim is set out below.[1]

Sample Calculation of Amounts Owing on a Running Account

Facts

We act for Artemis Plumbing Supply Ltd. One of its customers, Personable Plumbers Ltd., has a running account for orders that the office manager from Personable phones in to Artemis. There was some activity in July, year 0, but there has been no activity since. The transactions are as follows:

DATE	INVOICE	DEBIT	CREDIT	BALANCE
June 3	0113	20,000		$20,000.00
June 4			20,000	0.00
June 15	0893	32,000		32,000.00
June 21	0896	20,000		52,000.00
July 28			20,000	32,199.89*

* This is the result of applying the July 28 payment first to the interest owing on overdue amounts and then to the principal owing — see solution below.

No further orders have been placed or payments received. The original agreement stated that payments were due within 30 days of billing, after which interest would be charged at the rate of 12 percent per annum.

Assume that it is September 15, year 0. Calculate the amount owing for inclusion in a demand letter that requires the debt to be paid by September 25, year 0.

Solution

Note: Amounts have been rounded off.

1. Determine the rate of interest and type of interest to use. The agreement indicates that there is a contractual interest rate of 12 percent; there is no clear indication that compound interest is required, so assume that it is simple interest and use the simple interest formula, $I = P \times R \times T$.

2. Because there is a nil balance on June 4, start with the debit of $32,000 on June 15. Interest runs from July 15 (30-day interest-free

period ended on July 14) to date when payment is made on July 28, which results in 14 days' interest:

$32,000 × .12 × $^{14}/_{365}$ = $147.29 interest

3. Calculate interest on the next debit of $20,000 on June 21. Interest runs from July 21 (30-day interest-free period ended on July 20) to date when the payment is made on July 28, which results in 8 days' interest:

$20,000 × .12 × $^{8}/_{365}$ = $52.60 interest

4. From the payment of $20,000, subtract the outstanding interest:

$147.29 + $52.60 = $199.89;

$20,000 − $199.89 = $19,800.11

5. Allocate the remainder of the $20,000 payment to outstanding principal:

$52,000 − $19,800.11 = $32,199.89,

which is the outstanding balance as of July 28.

6. Calculate the interest on the outstanding principal from July 29 to September 25 and add it to the outstanding principal to determine the amount owing as of September 25. This amount, plus a reasonable amount for costs, is the amount to claim in the demand letter.

Interest . . . . $32,199.89 × .12 × $^{59}/_{365}$ = $ 624.59

Add principal $32,199.89

Total due on September 25 . . . . $32,824.48

CHAPTER SUMMARY

Chapter 4 takes you through the various steps required to determine the actual amount of a claim, including methods for calculating prejudgment and postjudgment interest, determining the balance owing on a running account, and determining compound interest, where compound interest can be claimed.

KEY TERM

per annum

NOTE

1. In chapter 5, the statement of claim on a running account in figure 5.1 is based on the facts in this example. From this you will see how you would progress from drafting a demand letter to drafting a statement of claim.

REFERENCE

Courts of Justice Act, RSO 1990, c. C.43.

REVIEW QUESTIONS

1. How do you determine the amount to be claimed in a demand letter? What components should be included in determining the total?

2. What determines the rate of interest to be claimed in an action against a debtor?

3. If you are relying on the *Courts of Justice Act* interest rates for prejudgment and postjudgment interest:

   a. how do you determine the rate of interest to be used?

   b. how do you determine the date on which interest begins to run at that rate?

4. What is the difference between simple and compound interest?

Figure 4.1   The Number of Each Day of the Year

Day of Month	Jan.	Feb.	Mar.	Apr.	May	June	July	Aug.	Sept.	Oct.	Nov.	Dec.	Day of Month
1	1	32	60	91	121	152	182	213	244	274	305	335	1
2	2	33	61	92	122	153	183	214	245	275	306	336	2
3	3	34	62	93	123	154	184	215	246	276	307	337	3
4	4	35	63	94	124	155	185	216	247	277	308	338	4
5	5	36	64	95	125	156	186	217	248	278	309	339	5
6	6	37	65	96	126	157	187	218	249	279	310	340	6
7	7	38	66	97	127	158	188	219	250	280	311	341	7
8	8	39	67	98	128	159	189	220	251	281	312	342	8
9	9	40	68	99	129	160	190	221	252	282	313	343	9
10	10	41	69	100	130	161	191	222	253	283	314	344	10
11	11	42	70	101	131	162	192	223	254	284	315	345	11
12	12	43	71	102	132	163	193	224	255	285	316	346	12
13	13	44	72	103	133	164	194	225	256	286	317	347	13
14	14	45	73	104	134	165	195	226	257	287	318	348	14
15	15	46	74	105	135	166	196	227	258	288	319	349	15
16	16	47	75	106	136	167	197	228	259	289	320	350	16
17	17	48	76	107	137	168	198	229	260	290	321	351	17
18	18	49	77	108	138	169	199	230	261	291	322	352	18
19	19	50	78	109	139	170	200	231	262	292	323	353	19
20	20	51	79	110	140	171	201	232	263	293	324	354	20
21	21	52	80	111	141	172	202	233	264	294	325	355	21
22	22	53	81	112	142	173	203	234	265	295	326	356	22
23	23	54	82	113	143	174	204	235	266	296	327	357	23
24	24	55	83	114	144	175	205	236	267	297	328	358	24
25	25	56	84	115	145	176	206	237	268	298	329	359	25
26	26	57	85	116	146	177	207	238	269	299	330	360	26
27	27	58	86	117	147	178	208	239	270	300	331	361	27
28	28	59	87	118	148	179	209	240	271	301	332	362	28
29	29		88	119	149	180	210	241	272	302	333	363	29
30	30		89	120	150	181	211	242	273	303	334	364	30
31	31		90		151		212	243		304		365	31

Notes: (1) For leap years, February 29 becomes day 60 and the numbers in the table must be increased by 1 for all following days. (2) For debts, start your count on the day the debt is due, not on the day after it is due.

CHAPTER 5

Commencement of Proceedings

Chapter 5 explains how to start legal proceedings to collect a debt arising from a simple promise to pay. You should first write a demand letter. If the debtor does not respond, you must then decide which court to sue in and draft, issue, and serve the claim. If the debtor is evading personal service of the court documents, you must then consider approaches to substitutional service. This chapter focuses on proceedings in the Superior Court of Justice. Chapter 10 outlines proceedings in the Small Claims Court.

SENDING A DEMAND LETTER

Typically, the creditor will have made a demand on the debtor for payment, threatening to turn the matter over to legal representatives if the demand has not been met. The client often wishes no further demand letters to be sent and, after discussion with the client, you may agree that this is a prudent course to take, particularly if the debtor's situation is rapidly getting worse. Where the debtor's situation is going from bad to worse, it may be advisable to move quickly and start proceedings or take other action, rather than give further opportunities to the debtor to delay matters. However, if the client has not sent a demand letter in circumstances where one should have been sent, a legal representative's demand letter should be sent (see page 100). Some debtors will ignore a creditor's demand letter, but will respond to the threat of legal action by the creditor's legal representative. There may also be some credit contracts that require the creditor to make a written demand for payment to the debtor before starting proceedings. In that case, a demand letter must be sent and will serve as the required notice. Paralegals who carry out collections work on a regular basis are required, under the *Collection Agencies Act*, to send the debtor a written notice, such as a letter, prior to commencing any litigation.

A legal representative's demand letter should

- be brief and business-like;

- state that you are the agent or are employed by the law firm or paralegal for the creditor and that you are instructed to collect money that is owing to the creditor;

- identify the debt owing and the fact of default in payment;

Example of a Demand Letter

Blodgett, Swine and Cattle
Barristers and Solicitors
39 Chancery Lane
Oriface, ON L6P 2U3
961-368-4220

May 28, year 0

Keepon Trucking Ltd.
231 Circular Road
Oriface, ON L6P 4F4

Attention: Henry Paylate, General Manager

Dear Sir:

Re: Tenacious Tires Ltd.

We are the lawyers for Tenacious Tires Ltd. We have been instructed to collect from Keepon the price of tires sold by our client but not paid for. The amount due and owing is $45,000 inclusive of interest and costs to June 15, year 0.

In order to avoid legal proceedings, please forward a certified cheque in the amount of $45,000 payable to Blodgett, Swine and Cattle, in trust, by June 15, year 0. If we have not received this amount by that date, we will commence legal proceedings without further notice to you. Please note that, in addition to the amount of the debt, you will also be liable for further accrued interest and for court costs.

Kindly govern yourself accordingly.

Yours very truly,

BLODGETT, SWINE AND CATTLE
Carl Cattle

CC/od

- indicate how much is owing, including principal, interest, and costs, as of a date specified for payment, usually 10 days to two weeks after the date of the letter;

- demand payment of that amount as of that date; and

- indicate that failure to pay what is due by the date given will result in civil proceedings being taken to collect what is owing to the creditor.

It is not necessary in this letter to set out the detailed basis for the calculation of the amount owing, but the total amount required should be set out clearly. It is permissible to include in the total an amount that reasonably reflects the cost to your client of collecting the debt, including things like legal fees and expenses paid to conduct various searches. It is recommended that payment be made to the law firm or paralegal firm in trust. This allows you to verify that the cheque will be honoured and that the money has actually been received.

You should require that the cheque be certified to ensure that it is honoured when it is presented for payment. When a cheque is certified, the bank guarantees that the money to honour it will be held in the account until the cheque is presented for payment.[1] Alternatively, the creditor can ask for payment by a bank or postal money order or by electronic transfer if that option is available. It is permissible to state that if payment is not made, proceedings to collect the debt will be taken. However, do not threaten the debtor by writing to tell him that if he does not pay, the creditor will bring criminal proceedings. To threaten criminal proceedings to collect a civil debt is extortion, which is a criminal offence. Although it is possible for your client to lay an **information** that leads to criminal charges against a debtor, this is not the usual course of action because the creditor is much more interested in getting paid than in getting involved in the criminal justice system. There may be times, however, as in debts involving serious fraud, where criminal charges may be appropriate. There is nothing to prevent a creditor from initiating criminal proceedings in respect of acts that are public wrongs, as well as civil proceedings to collect the debt.

information
a sworn written statement made before a justice of the peace that can initiate criminal proceedings against a person

A demand letter (see the example on the facing page) should be sent to each debtor, if there is more than one, and to the **guarantor** of the debt, if there is one. The letter should be sent by registered mail, as the letter can be tracked online at Canada Post: http://www.canadapost.ca, and Canada Post will verify that it has been delivered and signed for. The letter should also be sent by ordinary mail, in case the debtor refuses to accept the registered mail version. A registered letter that cannot be delivered will be returned to the sender.

guarantor
one who is obliged to pay a creditor when the principal debtor defaults

JURISDICTION

If the debtor ignores the demand letter, or your instructions are to start proceedings immediately once the date for payment in the letter has passed, you have to decide which court to sue in.

In Ontario there are three possibilities:

1. *Small Claims Court jurisdiction is for matters of $25,000 or less*, exclusive of costs and interest. The plaintiff can reduce the amount claimed to $25,000 to proceed in this court if they wish, but the court will not award $25,001. Small Claims Court proceedings are discussed in chapter 10.

affidavit

a sworn statement of facts that can be used as evidence in court proceedings in lieu of oral evidence

examination for discovery

a pretrial process where lawyers get to ask the opposite party (plaintiff or defendant) questions about the allegations in the statement of claim or statement of defence

motion

an application to the court within the main proceeding to settle a legal issue that has arisen in the main proceeding—for example, a plaintiff might bring a motion to court asking that the defendant provide more detail in the statement of defence; a motion is brought by a notice of motion, which states what remedy is sought and the reasons for it; the facts in support of the motion are usually presented in an affidavit

affidavit of documents

an affidavit in which a party identifies those documents that are relevant to the issues in the proceeding and that he has in his possession, power, and control and can produce; he must also identify those documents that he once had in his possession, power, and control but no longer has and those that he objects to producing; privileged documents, such as solicitor–client correspondence, will fall in the latter category; the documents being produced and relied on are contained in a document brief that is filed as evidence in the proceeding and may be referred to in court

2. *If the amount is between $25,001 and $100,000*, exclusive of costs and interest, you must sue in the Superior Court of Justice, using the simplified procedure available under rule 76 of the *Rules of Civil Procedure*. The discussion of the simplified procedure that follows is an overview; a detailed discussion is beyond the scope of this text.[2] The procedure is designed to reduce cost and delay by using a streamlined version of the standard civil process. To invoke the rule, you must state in the statement of claim that "the action is brought under the simplified procedure pursuant to rule 76."

If the plaintiff sues for more than $100,000 but recovers less than that amount, the plaintiff may be subject to severe cost penalties for not using the simplified procedure. However, a plaintiff suing for more than $100,000 can use the simplified procedure, unless the defendant objects. An objecting defendant should set out the objection in the statement of defence and ask that the proceeding continue under the ordinary procedural rules. The plaintiff must then either comply or abandon that part of the claim that exceeds $100,000.

The advantage of the simplified procedure is that it speeds up the pretrial process by shortening or eliminating some of the steps in the pretrial stage, and speeds up the trial process by simplifying the presentation of evidence, notably by relying on the option of using **affidavits** rather than oral evidence.

In the pretrial stage, **examinations for discovery** are limited to a total of two hours for each party, however many parties there are to be examined. Cross-examinations on affidavits used in support of court **motions** are not permitted. The parties must deliver an **affidavit of documents**, which lists the documents they are relying on, and provide copies of the documents along with the names and addresses of potential witnesses.

The pretrial stage is further shortened by requiring settlement discussions to be held within 60 days after the first defence has been filed. Of course, if the debtor does not file a statement of defence, the plaintiff may obtain a default judgment in the usual way.

The parties can have a summary trial or proceed with a regular trial. If the parties agree to a summary trial, it proceeds more quickly than does a trial under the standard rules:

a. evidence is given by affidavit rather than orally, although a party may examine the witness for no more than 10 minutes on the affidavit;

b. the opposing party may cross-examine orally on notice, but total cross-examination of all witnesses by a party is limited to 50 minutes;

c. re-examination of the witness following cross-examination is limited to 10 minutes;

d. oral argument at the conclusion of the trial is limited to 45 minutes for each party.

3. *If the amount of the claim exceeds $100,000*, the claim is brought under the ordinary rules for civil trials in the Superior Court. The filing of a claim under these rules is discussed in the balance of this chapter.

With the increase in monetary jurisdiction in 2010, more debts, particularly consumer debts, are likely to be subject to procedures that reduce cost and delay, and make debt recovery quicker and less expensive than it was formerly. Further, rule 1.04(1.1) now requires parties to an action to interpret the rules using the doctrine of proportionality. This means that the complexity of a proceeding must be proportional to the amount claimed in the lawsuit. Where a simpler, more expeditious and less expensive way of proceeding is available and suitable, the parties are expected to use it.

CLAIMS IN FOREIGN CURRENCY

The *Courts of Justice Act*, s. 121, permits a creditor to sue for an amount expressed in a foreign currency. If the debt is expressed in a foreign currency, it must be converted to Canadian dollars, usually as of the date the creditor is paid on the judgment, following the directions in s. 121(1). However, the court has discretion to specify a specific date and method for conversion, if the situation warrants. An exchange rate can be obtained by doing a search of exchange rates reported in the financial pages of a newspaper such as the *Globe and Mail*. Exchange rates can be searched on a currency trading site such as http://www.oanda.com/currency/converter or by calling a currency trader.

NAMING THE PROPER PARTIES TO THE PROCEEDING

Once you have determined what is owing, you must then decide who is liable for payment. The person (or persons) liable for payment is the proper party defendant to the claim. You must first determine who the debtor is and what its status is. For example, when an employee of a company is the person placing an order, it is not the employee who is liable for payment, because she did not order on her own account but was acting for her employer. It is the employer in this example who is liable for payment and who is a proper party defendant.

Once you have determined who is liable, you must next determine what the status of the party is for the purpose of suing and then name the party appropriately. In chapter 3 you learned about the importance of using public searches to determine or verify the type of business organization the debtor used (sole proprietorship, partnership, or limited liability company). You also learned that it is important, once you know the type of business organization the debtor is using, to name the business entity correctly in the lawsuit so that you obtain a judgment against an entity that legally exists.

- If you are suing an individual person carrying on business as a sole proprietor, it is best to sue the individual in his own name and in the business name: sue "Michael DeFalco" and "Michael DeFalco carrying on business as Swiftsure Accounting" or "Swiftsure Accounting." In this way, the sheriff will not hesitate to seize the assets of both the individual and the business.

- If you are suing a partnership, sue the partners and the partnership: sue "Michael DeFalco, John Gertstein, and Swiftsure Accounting." If you sue the partners alone, you can recover judgment only against the personal assets of the individual partners — for example, by seizing and selling Mr. DeFalco's yacht

— but if you name the partnership as well, you can also recover against partnership assets — for example, by seizing and selling the office computer system. Alternatively, under rule 8 of the *Rules of Civil Procedure*, you can sue the partnership in the firm name alone, and give notice to the individual partners that you seek to enforce the judgment against their personal assets.

- If you are suing a corporation, sue in the name of the corporation exactly as it appears in the public search records. If the search record identifies a company as a numbered company, then use the numbered company name, rather than any trade name under which it carries on business.

PREPARING THE STATEMENT OF CLAIM

Once you have determined who the appropriate defendants are, you are ready to draft the statement of claim. An action for debt in the Superior Court commences with a statement of claim. A sample statement of claim for payment of a debt is set out on pages 110 through 113. If the action is brought under the simplified procedure in the *Rules of Civil Procedure*, insert the following just before paragraph 1 of the statement of claim:

> This action is brought against you under the simplified procedure pursuant to rule 76 of the *Rules of Civil Procedure.*

ISSUING AND SERVING THE STATEMENT OF CLAIM

Once you have completed the statement of claim, it is necessary to start the action by having the statement of claim issued by the court office. A court clerk, acting on behalf of the registrar of the court, will, on payment of the prescribed fee, date, sign, and seal the document and assign it a file number.[3] The clerk will hand you back the original document, signed and sealed. You will then write on a copy of the document the file number, date, and signature with quotation marks around it. This copy is called a "true copy" or "trued-up copy." Give it back to the clerk, who will put it in the court file. Along with the statement of claim you now also have to file Form 14F, Information for Court Use, found on pages 106 and 107, which indicates whether the action is brought as a "regular" proceeding, or brought as a simplified procedure under rule 76. You will take the original claim back to the office with you. Make several photocopies for the file and to serve on defendants. The original should be kept in your office file. You will need to produce it at various times — for example, when signing a default judgment.[4]

In Toronto, there are often lengthy line-ups to issue claims. If you are working in the Toronto area, allocate sufficient time for the physical task of attending at the court office to issue claims. The suburban court offices surrounding Toronto are also often quite busy.

The Superior Court has run pilot projects to see whether some court documents can be filed electronically online. A plaintiff, in some circumstances under the rules, now has the option of electronically filing a requisition for noting a defendant in default.[5]

Once a statement of claim has been issued, it must be served within six months of the date of issue.[6] Failure to serve the claim within the six-month time limit is an irregularity. However, the court may allow extra time to serve the claim. A claim must be issued, but not necessarily served, by the time a statutory limitation period expires.

Serving the Proper Parties and Methods of Service

Once you have issued the statement of claim, you will need to consider who is to be served with the statement of claim.

If you are suing an individual, then that is the person to be served by leaving a copy of the statement of claim with that individual. However, if you are suing a corporation, service is effected by leaving a copy of the claim with an officer of the company (for example, the president or the treasurer), a member of the board of directors, an agent of the company, or an individual who appears to be in control or management of the company's place of business. In addition to a head office, it is acceptable to serve persons in charge of branch offices.[7]

If you are suing the partnership only, and not naming the individual partners, you may serve anyone who appears to be in control of the partnership's main place of business.[8] If you wish to name the partners as well as the partnership (because you wish to be able to enforce a judgment against the partners' personal assets as well as the partnership assets), then you must personally serve each partner against whose assets you wish to enforce a judgment.[9]

Rule 16 sets out a comprehensive code for service of documents. Generally, the first document, sometimes referred to as the "originating process" in a lawsuit, must be served on the defendant by personal service or an alternative to personal service. After the first document is served, the rules become more relaxed, permitting copies of subsequent documents to be mailed, emailed (with an acknowledgment of service by email), or faxed to the party or her solicitor.[10] Once a document has been served, you should prepare an affidavit of service. This will be used later in the proceeding to prove service of the document. A sample affidavit of personal service is set out on pages 108 and 109.

Service of a statement of claim by an alternative to personal service makes it easier to serve a defendant. However, you are advised to use personal service, if possible, to avoid having a defendant emerge after he has apparently failed to defend, and ask that a default judgment be set aside because he had no notice of the lawsuit. Motions to set aside default judgments in these circumstances are often successful and a lot of time and money is wasted if you have to begin all over again.

You should use the alternatives to personal service in situations where the defendant and his lawyer know that you will be suing and are prepared to be cooperative about moving the lawsuit along. You may also use it where speed is required and you are not able to personally serve the defendant.

The alternatives to personal service[11] are:

- Service of a document on a lawyer for the party, where it is known she has one, and the lawyer is prepared to accept service on behalf of the client. In this case, proof of service is shown by the lawyer accepting a copy of the document and writing on your copy that he accepts service of the statement of claim on behalf of his client; he writes in the date and signs his name.

Sample Information for Court Use (Form 14F)

Court File no.

ONTARIO

SUPERIOR COURT OF JUSTICE

B E T W E E N:

PRETENTIOUS AUTOMOBILES LTD.

Plaintiff

and

EDWARD GOODWHEEL

Defendant

INFORMATION FOR COURT USE

1. This proceeding is an: [x] action   [ ] application

2. Has it been commenced under the *Class Proceedings Act, 1992*?   [ ] yes   [x] no

3. If the proceeding is an action, does Rule 76 (Simplified Procedure) apply? Note: *Subject to the exceptions found in subrule 76.01(1), it is MANDATORY to proceed under Rule 76 for all cases in which the money amount claimed or the value of real or personal property claimed is $100,000 or less.*	[x] yes [ ] no

4. The claim in this proceeding (action or application) is in respect of:

*(Select the **one** item that **best** describes the nature of the main claim in the proceeding.)*

Bankruptcy or insolvency law	[ ]	Motor vehicle accident	[ ]
Collection of liquidated debt	[x]	Municipal law	[ ]
Constitutional law	[ ]	Partnership law	[ ]
Construction law (other than construction lien)	[ ]	Personal property security	[ ]
Construction lien	[ ]	Product liability	[ ]
Contract law	[ ]	Professional malpractice (other than medical)	[ ]
Corporate law	[ ]	Real property (including leases; excluding mortgage or charge)	[ ]
Defamation	[ ]	Tort: economic injury (other than from medical or professional malpractice)	[ ]
Employment or labour law	[ ]		
Intellectual property law	[ ]	Tort: personal injury (other than from motor vehicle accident)	[ ]
Judicial review	[ ]	Trusts, fiduciary duty	[ ]
Medical malpractice	[ ]	Wills, estates	[ ]
Mortgage or charge	[ ]		

CERTIFICATION

I certify that the above information is correct, to the best of my knowledge.

Date: July 20, year 1 _____

_____
Signature of lawyer

I.M. Just   LSUC #12345A
JUST AND COPING
Barristers and Solicitors
8701 - 365 Bay Street
Toronto, ON M3J 4A9

416-762-1342
FAX 416-762-1343

Lawyers for the Plaintiff

Sample Affidavit of Personal Service (Form 16B)

Court file no. 1234

ONTARIO
SUPERIOR COURT OF JUSTICE

B E T W E E N:

PRETENTIOUS AUTOMOBILES LTD.

Plaintiff

and

EDWARD GOODWHEEL

Defendant

AFFIDAVIT OF PERSONAL SERVICE

I, Henry James, of the City of Toronto, MAKE OATH AND SAY:

1. On Friday, July 25, year 1, at 2:00 pm, at 84 Spokes Boulevard in the City of Toronto, I served the defendant in this proceeding, Edward Goodwheel, with a true copy of the statement of claim in this proceeding by leaving a copy with him.

2. I was able to identify the defendant by his acknowledgment to me that he was Edward Goodwheel.

SWORN before me at the City of	)	
	)	
Toronto, this 2nd day of	)	
	)	
August, year 1	)	*Henry James*
	)	
I.M. Just	)	
	)	
A Commissioner, etc.	)	

RCP-E 16B (January 1, 2008)

Court file no. 1234

PRETENTIOUS
Plaintiff

and

GOODWHEEL
Defendant

ONTARIO
SUPERIOR COURT OF JUSTICE
PROCEEDING COMMENCED at
TORONTO

AFFIDAVIT OF SERVICE
OF HENRY JAMES
Sworn August 2, year 1

I.M. Just   LSUC #12345A
JUST AND COPING
Barristers and Solicitors
8701 - 365 Bay Street
Toronto, ON M3J 4A9

416-762-1342
FAX 416-762-1343

Lawyers for the Plaintiff

RCP-E 4C (July 1, 2007)

Sample Statement of Claim for Debt: Price of Goods Sold and Delivered (From 14A)

Court file no.

ONTARIO

SUPERIOR COURT OF JUSTICE

B E T W E E N:

PRETENTIOUS AUTOMOBILES LTD.

Plaintiff

and

EDWARD GOODWHEEL

Defendant

STATEMENT OF CLAIM

TO THE DEFENDANT

A LEGAL PROCEEDING HAS BEEN COMMENCED AGAINST YOU by the plaintiff. The claim made against you is set out in the following pages.

IF YOU WISH TO DEFEND THIS PROCEEDING, you or an Ontario lawyer acting for you must prepare a statement of defence in Form 18A prescribed by the Rules of Civil Procedure, serve it on the plaintiff's lawyer or, where the plaintiff does not have a lawyer, serve it on the plaintiff, and file it, with proof of service, in this court office, WITHIN TWENTY DAYS after this statement of claim is served on you, if you are served in Ontario.

If you are served in another province or territory of Canada or in the United States of America, the period for serving and filing your statement of defence is forty days. If you are served outside Canada and the United States of America, the period is sixty days.

Instead of serving and filing a statement of defence, you may serve and file a notice of intent to defend in Form 18B prescribed by the Rules of Civil Procedure. This will entitle you to ten more days within which to serve and file your statement of defence.

IF YOU FAIL TO DEFEND THIS PROCEEDING, JUDGMENT MAY BE GIVEN AGAINST YOU IN YOUR ABSENCE AND WITHOUT FURTHER NOTICE TO YOU. IF YOU WISH TO DEFEND THIS PROCEEDING BUT ARE UNABLE TO PAY LEGAL FEES, LEGAL AID MAY BE AVAILABLE TO YOU BY CONTACTING A LOCAL LEGAL AID OFFICE.

IF YOU PAY THE PLAINTIFF'S CLAIM, and $500.00 for costs, within the time for serving and filing your statement of defence, you may move to have this proceeding dismissed by the court. If you believe the amount claimed for costs is excessive, you may pay the plaintiff's claim and $400 for costs and have the costs assessed by the court.

Date July 20, year 1   Issued by ....
                                                      Local registrar

Address of court office: 393 University Ave.
                                          Toronto, ON M5G 1T4

TO: Edward Goodwheel
          84 Spokes Blvd.
          Toronto, ON M6Y 3T4

THIS ACTION IS BROUGHT AGAINST YOU UNDER THE SIMPLIFIED
PROCEDURE PROVIDED IN RULE 76 OF THE RULES OF CIVIL PROCEDURE.

CLAIM

1. The plaintiff claims:

    a. the balance of the purchase price of a year 0 Whizzbang automobile in the liquidated amount of $31,000;

    b. prejudgment and postjudgment interest, as provided for by the *Courts of Justice Act*, at the rate of 21 percent per annum in accordance with the terms of the purchase contract from June 3, year 1 until payment;

    c. in the alternative, prejudgment and postjudgment interest at the rate of interest prescribed by the *Courts of Justice Act* from June 3, year 1 until payment;

    d. the plaintiff's costs of the proceeding including applicable HST; and

    e. such further relief as the Honourable Court deems appropriate.

2. The plaintiff is a corporation, with offices in Toronto, Ontario, and carries on business as a broker and seller of automobiles.

3. The defendant is an individual who resides in the city of Toronto, and is the purchaser from the plaintiff of a year 0 Whizzbang automobile.

4. The plaintiff's claim is for the balance of money owing from the defendant to the plaintiff on a contract for the purchase by the defendant of a year 0 Whizzbang automobile, VIN 398654321, which automobile was delivered to the defendant on June 1, year 1. The purchase price, inclusive of costs and taxes, was $41,000. The defendant paid a cash deposit of $10,000 against the purchase price. The balance of the purchase price, $31,000, was due and payable on June 2, year 1.

5. The defendant failed to pay the balance of the purchase price on June 2, year 1 and, despite demands for payment, has refused or neglected to pay the balance due to the plaintiff.

6. The balance due and owing as of June 3, year 1 is $31,000. The plaintiff also claims interest at the rate of 21 percent per annum pursuant to the terms of the contract governing interest on overdue payments, in accordance with the *Courts of Justice Act.*

7. Attached to this claim and marked as schedule A is a statement of account showing how the balance claimed is calculated.

The Plaintiff proposes that this action be tried at: Toronto

DATED at Toronto   I.M. Just   LSUC #12345A
July 14, year 1   JUST AND COPING, Barristers and Solicitors
                           8701 - 365 Bay Street, Toronto, ON M3J 4A9
                           416-762-1342 FAX 416-762-1343
                           Lawyers for the Plaintiff

SCHEDULE "A" TO THE STATEMENT OF CLAIM

DATE	DEBIT	CREDIT	BALANCE
May 15, year 1	$41,000		$41,000
May 15, year 1		$10,000	$31,000
June 2, year 1		nil[*]	$31,000

Balance due and owing as of June 3, year 1:

$31,000 with interest at 21 percent per annum until payment.

---

[*] A "nil" entry is made to show that the balance was due and unpaid, with interest running from the next day, June 3, on the balance due on June 2. With a simple unpaid account, as in this example, it is not necessary to include the account schedule, and you may omit it. It is provided here for illustrative purposes. It should certainly be included if the claim is on a running account, or is otherwise detailed or complex.

PRETENTIOUS
Plaintiff

and

GOODWHEEL
Defendant

Court file no.

ONTARIO
SUPERIOR COURT OF JUSTICE
PROCEEDING COMMENCED at
TORONTO

STATEMENT OF CLAIM

I.M. Just   LSUC #12345A
JUST AND COPING
Barristers and Solicitors
8701 - 365 Bay Street
Toronto, ON M3J 4A9

416-762-1342
FAX 416-762-1343

Lawyers for the Plaintiff

RCP-E 4C (July 1, 2007)

- Service by mail to the last-known address of the defendant, provided the document is mailed by registered mail; however, to be effective, a signed post office receipt must be received by you. Service is effected as of the date the plaintiff receives the receipt.

- Service by leaving a copy of the claim at the residence of the defendant is permitted provided an attempt is made to effect personal service at the residence; in this case, a copy must be left with an apparently adult member of the same household in a sealed envelope addressed to the defendant and, on the same or following day, another copy must be mailed to the defendant at that address. In this case, service is effected on the fifth day after mailing.

- If the defendant is a corporation, and its head office or business office in Ontario cannot be found, it may be served by mail at the last head office address or address of its agent in Ontario, registered with the Ministry of Government Services.[12]

Substitutional Service

notice of motion
a document that states
what remedy is sought
and the reasons for it

If the defendant appears to have left town or disappeared, or is attempting to evade service, you may apply by **notice of motion** to the court for an order for substitutional service on the defendant. You must demonstrate that any other method is impractical and that the mode of substitutional service you are suggesting would likely bring the matter to the attention of the defendant. You do not have to assure the court that this will happen. In some rare cases, the court may order that service be dispensed with — usually where it is unlikely that any mode of service will reach the defendant.

Substitutional service is often carried out by registered mail on the defendant's last-known address or on someone, such as a close relative, who likely knows where the defendant can be located. It can also be accomplished by newspaper advertisement. This method can be quite expensive and should be avoided if possible. For service to be effected, it is necessary that you carry out the court's order precisely, serving the document in exactly the way the court ordered.

SAMPLE STATEMENTS OF CLAIM

All statements of claim include a standard first page and a backsheet, which are reproduced on pages 110 and 113, respectively. In the sample statements of claim reproduced in figures 5.1 through 5.4, we include only those pages that illustrate the specific claim that you must draft.

STATEMENT OF DEFENCE

In chapter 1, we noted that often there is no defence in a debt action because the reason for nonpayment is often inability to pay, which is not a defence. However, the defendant, depending on where he is served, has:

- 20 days to file a statement of defence if he is served in Ontario;

- 40 days to file a statement of defence if he is served in other parts of Canada or in the United States; and

- 60 days to file a statement of defence if he is served elsewhere.

A defendant may also file a notice of intent to defend (see figure 5.5)[13] which extends the time for filing a statement of defence. The times for filing the statement of defence should be diarized. If none has been received, or you have heard nothing from the defendant, you should begin preparing documents to obtain a default judgment. Chapter 6 discusses how to do this. A sample statement of defence is shown in figure 5.6.

CHAPTER SUMMARY

Chapter 5 takes you through the various steps required to commence proceedings after the decision to sue has been made. We learned that if a demand letter has not been sent, one should be prepared, and there is a discussion of what goes into such a letter. There is a discussion of which court to sue in, and in the case of the Superior Court, whether or not to use the simplified procedure. We then turned to the subject of naming the proper parties to the action. There is a description of how to prepare a statement of claim, issue it, and serve it on the debtor, followed by what the debtor might do to defend the action.

KEY TERMS

affidavit	information
affidavit of documents	motion
examination for discovery	notice of motion
guarantor	

NOTES

1. LAWPRO, which is the errors and omissions insurance company for Ontario lawyers, has reported an increase in fraudulent activity involving phony certified cheques presented by clients for payment into lawyers' trust accounts. For more information, please read the articles at http://www.practicepro.ca/Practice/fraud.asp. You should also be aware that although a certified cheque will normally be honoured, it is possible for

the drawer of the cheque to ask its bank to put a "stop payment" on the certified cheque after it is issued, but before it is presented for payment. In this case, payment will not be made when the cheque is presented even though the cheque is certified. The debtor may do the same thing with a money order prior to the creditor presenting it for payment.

2. Watson and McGowan, *Ontario Civil Practice* (Toronto: Carswell, annual) contains a detailed narrative description with useful commentary on rule 76, as well as the text of the rule. Because *Ontario Civil Practice* is published annually, be sure to use an up-to-date version.

3. Rule 14.07.

4. Rule 19.01.

5. Rule 19.01(1.1).

6. Rule 14.08.

7. Rule 16.02(1)(c).

8. Rule 16.02(1)(m).

9. Rule 8.03.

10. Rules 16.01 to 16.05.

11. Rule 16.03.

12. Rule 16.03(6).

13. Rule 18.02.01.

REFERENCES

Courts of Justice Act, RSO 1990, c. C.43.

Law Society of Upper Canada, *Rules of Professional Conduct* (Toronto: LSUC, 2011) (also available at http://www.lsuc.on.ca).

Ministry of the Attorney General, http://www.attorneygeneral.jus.gov.on.ca.

Rules of Civil Procedure, RRO 1990, Reg. 194.

REVIEW QUESTIONS

1. In what circumstances is it necessary for you to send a lawyer's demand letter to the debtor?

2. What points should be included in a lawyer's demand letter?

3. In what form should payment be demanded?

4. In the demand letter, can you threaten to bring criminal proceedings if the debt is not paid?

5. What courts can you use to sue a debtor? What factors determine the choice of court?

6. What are two advantages that come from using the simplified procedure?

7. Joe Smith, the office manager of Nokando Ltd., has always ordered materials from your client over the phone. The order is shipped to Joe at Nokando's factory, but is addressed to Joe Smith. Who is the proper party for your client to sue if the bills are not paid? Explain your reasons.

8. If Joe Smith was running an unincorporated business that he owned called "Smith Productions," whom would you sue?

9. If Smith Productions was jointly owned and operated by Joe Smith and his wife, Jill Montoya, whom would you sue? Explain your reasons.

10. What are the steps involved in issuing a statement of claim?

11. Suppose you have tried to serve a debtor personally with a statement of claim but he doesn't ever seem to be home when your process server attempts service. A woman who answered the door on the two occasions that the process server attempted service admitted that she was the debtor's spouse and said that he had just stepped out but that she didn't know when he would be back. What options for service do you have in this situation? Among these options, which would you choose in these circumstances?

DISCUSSION QUESTIONS

1. Your client has received a demand letter that says among other things: "If you fail to make the payment required by the due date, we will take all available legal proceedings against you." Is it permissible for the creditor to take this position?

2. You are suing for Penumbuco SA, a Mexican company that is owed 3,000,000 pesetas by a defendant in Ontario. You are told to sue in the Superior Court for the amount of pesetas owing. How do you do this?

CASE STUDIES
Case Study 1

M E M O

DATE: December 3, year 0

TO: U.R. Clerk

FROM: I.M. Principal

RE: Foucault Collection

Our client, Umberto Ecco, the sole shareholder and president of Pendulum Artistics Ltd., has instructed us to collect an overdue debt from a customer, Henri Foucault. Foucault bought a silver pendulum to hang from his living room ceiling for the sum of $44,000 plus taxes and shipping for a total bill of $49,820. Foucault paid a deposit of $4,000 at the time of purchase on September 19, year 0. The pendulum was delivered to Foucault on September 23, year 0. The bill of sale is attached.

Bill of Sale

PENDULUM ARTISTICS LTD.
2223 Yonge Street, Toronto, Ontario M4R 1V6   Tel. 416-234-5678

September 19, year 0

SOLD TO:
Henri Foucault
230 Rosedale Rd.
Toronto, Ontario M6O 3B0

Item	one silver pendulum 43" diameter w. silver $1/2$ inch chain @ 6 ft. to be delivered.
Price	$44,000 + HST + shipping = $49,820
Deposit	$ 4,000
Total due	$45,820

Terms: net 30 days from the date of billing. Overdue balances are subject to interest at the rate of 1.5 percent per month until payment.

Signed: *Umberto Ecco*   Purchaser: *Henri Foucault*

As of November 15, year 0, no payments had been made; Ecco has heard Foucault is in financial difficulty; there has been no response to Ecco's calls.
   Ecco has asked us to collect the amount owing.

1. Draft and send a demand letter requiring payment in full as of December 20, year 0.

2. Assuming that no money is received, draft a statement of claim to be issued on December 21, year 0.

Case Study 2

M E M O

DATE: April 30, year 0
TO: Law Clerk
FROM: I.M. Just
RE: Cookie Caldwell

Cookie Caldwell, the owner of Cookie's Cookies, a sole proprietorship, called and told us that she has a problem. It seems she has been supplying Tina's Tearoom, a division of T. Tuna Corp. Ltd., with chocolate chip cookies for several months. The manager of Tina's has signed a purchase order every month totalling $19,000 per month, with interest at the rate of 10 percent per annum on all overdue accounts. Payments are due 10 days after billing. Tina's has always been a slow payer but the last two invoices, dated February 10 and March 10 and totalling $38,000, have not been paid at all as of this date.

1. Send a demand letter with payment to be made by May 20, year 0.

2. Assume that the demand letter produces no results and draft a statement of claim.

Case Study 3

Assume the same facts as in case study 2 with the exception that Tina has come to you. She's been threatened with legal action by Cookie. She owes for two months but was reluctant to tell Cookie what has been happening. She is having some cash problems, but the primary cause of them is that the last three shipments of cookies from Cookie's have caused customers who eat the cookies to become violently ill — so ill that they "woof their cookies" all over the shop. It is getting to the point where Tina is thinking of handing out airline motion sickness bags to the customers that she has left. Her business has fallen off considerably in the last two months — business losses are estimated to be about 20 percent, or $32,000 so far. The situation would be worse but she has other things on the menu that sell and she isn't ordering any more cookies.

Draft a letter responding to Cookie's demand letter.

Figure 5.1 Sample Statement of Claim on a Running Account (Form 14A)

THIS ACTION IS BROUGHT AGAINST YOU UNDER THE SIMPLIFIED
PROCEDURE PROVIDED IN RULE 76 OF THE RULES OF CIVIL PROCEDURE.

CLAIM

1. The plaintiff claims:

   a. the balance of the purchase price for plumbing supplies sold and delivered in the liquidated amount of $32,199.89;

   b. prejudgment and postjudgment interest, as provided for by the *Courts of Justice Act*, at the rate of 12 percent per annum in accordance with the credit agreement entered into by the parties from July 29, year 0 until payment;

   c. in the alternative, prejudgment and postjudgment interest at the rate of interest prescribed by the *Courts of Justice Act* from July 29, year 0, until payment;

   d. the plaintiff's costs of the proceeding including applicable HST; and

   e. such further relief as the honourable court deems appropriate.

2. The plaintiff is a corporation with offices in the city of Toronto and carries on business as a wholesale plumbing supply company.

3. The defendant is a corporation with offices in the city of Toronto and carries on a plumbing business in the city of Toronto.

4. The plaintiff's claim is for the balance of money owing from the defendant to the plaintiff on a running account. The defendant executed under seal a revolving credit agreement on April 4, year 0, under which the defendant could make purchases on credit from time to time; the terms agreed to by the parties were that the defendant would pay each invoice within 30 days from the date of the invoice, after which interest would accrue at the rate of 12 percent per annum.

5. The defendant made payments from time to time, as set out in schedule A to this statement of claim. The defendant, however, has failed or neglected to make any payments on the balance due on the account from July 28, year 0 to the date of pleading.

Figure 5.1   Continued

6. The balance due and owing as of July 28, year 0 is $32,199.89. The plaintiff also claims interest on this amount at the rate of 12 percent per annum pursuant to the terms of the contract governing interest on overdue payments, in accordance with the *Courts of Justice Act.*

7. Attached to this claim and marked as schedule A is a statement of account showing how the balance claimed is calculated.

The Plaintiff proposes that this action be tried at: Toronto

DATED at Toronto   I.M. Just   LSUC #12345A

September 30, year 0   JUST AND COPING, Barristers and Solicitors

8701 - 365 Bay Street, Toronto, ON M3J 4A9

416-762-1342 FAX 416-762-1343

Lawyers for the Plaintiff

RCP-E 14A (July 1, 2007)

Figure 5.1   Concluded

SCHEDULE A TO THE STATEMENT OF CLAIM

DATE	INVOICE	DEBIT	CREDIT	BALANCE
June 3	0113	$20,000		$20,000.00
June 4			$20,000	0
June 15	0893	$32,000		$32,000.00
June 22	0896	$20,000		$52,000.00
July 28			$20,000	$32,199.89

Figure 5.2   Sample Statement of Claim on a Credit Card Balance (Form 14A)

THIS ACTION IS BROUGHT AGAINST YOU UNDER THE SIMPLIFIED PROCEDURE PROVIDED IN RULE 76 OF THE RULES OF CIVIL PROCEDURE.

CLAIM

1. The plaintiff claims:

    a. money owing to the plaintiff by the defendant under a "Rapacious Credit" cardholder agreement, in the liquidated amount of $29,123.45;

    b. prejudgment and postjudgment interest at the rate of 25 percent per annum as provided for by the cardholder agreement between the parties, pursuant to the *Courts of Justice Act*;

    c. prejudgment and postjudgment interest in accordance with the *Courts of Justice Act*;

    d. the costs of this action, including applicable HST; and

    e. such further relief as this honourable court deems appropriate.

2. The plaintiff is a financial services company, incorporated under the laws of Canada, with offices in Toronto, Ontario. The plaintiff is in the business of extending credit to persons such as the defendant through the use of credit cards.

3. The defendant is an individual who resides in the city of Toronto and who at all relevant times was a credit customer of the plaintiff.

4. On the defendant's application, the plaintiff opened a credit account for the defendant and issued the defendant a "Rapacious Credit" credit card. The card was issued subject to the terms and conditions set out in a cardholder agreement. The defendant was asked to read and sign the cardholder agreement by an agent of the plaintiff. The defendant signed the agreement on May 3, year 0. At that time, the defendant was issued with a credit card and given an account number — 1904 569 3452.

5. By signing the cardholder agreement, the defendant promised to be bound by the terms of the agreement, which allowed him to purchase goods and services on credit and to obtain cash advances on credit by using the credit card provided by the plaintiff. The defendant agreed to pay all debts arising from the use of the credit card to the plaintiff.

Figure 5.2   Concluded

6. The defendant, from and after May 3, year 0, used the credit card to purchase goods and services and make cash advances that were charged to his account with the plaintiff.

7. As a result of late payments or non-payment on the account, interest accrued on the outstanding balance from time to time, payable at the rate in effect from time to time as provided for in the cardholder agreement. At all relevant times, the defendant was given notice of the interest rate from time to time, as required by the cardholder agreement. At present, the rate of interest charged is 25 percent per annum.

8. The defendant has received full particulars of all transactions on his account in monthly statements sent by the plaintiff and from sales and transaction drafts delivered to him at the time of the transactions.

9. The balance of the account outstanding and due and owing by the defendant to the plaintiff is $29,123.45 as of June 15, year 1. The defendant is in default because he has failed to pay any amount since December 3, year 0, despite repeated demands that he pay the balance outstanding in accordance with the provisions of the cardholder agreement.

The Plaintiff proposes that this action be tried at: Toronto

DATED at Toronto
July 3, year 0

I.M. Weasel   LSUC #88512B
Barrister and Solicitor
123 Finch Road, Toronto, ON M2J 2X5
416-223-6789 FAX 416-223-6788
Lawyer for the Plaintiff

RCP-E 14A (July 1, 2007)

Figure 5.3 Sample Statement of Claim: Arrears of Rent in a Commercial Tenancy (Form 14A)

THIS ACTION IS BROUGHT AGAINST YOU UNDER THE SIMPLIFIED PROCEDURE PROVIDED IN RULE 76 OF THE RULES OF CIVIL PROCEDURE.

CLAIM

1. The plaintiff claims:

   a. the liquidated sum of $45,000 due and owing to the plaintiff pursuant to a lease executed by the defendant, dated February 26, year 0;

   b. prejudgment and postjudgment interest in accordance with the provisions of the *Courts of Justice Act** from October 2, year 5 until payment;

   c. the plaintiff's costs of this action including applicable HST; and

   d. such further relief as this honourable court deems appropriate.

2. The plaintiff is an individual who carries on business in the city of Toronto as a landlord of premises leased for commercial purposes.

3. The defendant Verdi and Wagner Music Store, carrying on business in the city of Toronto, is a partnership, of which the defendants Joe Verdi, who resides in the Town of Richmond Hill, and Richard Wagner, who resides in the city of Mississauga, are partners.**

4. The plaintiff's claim is based on rents owed by the defendant Verdi and Wagner Music Store on property it leases at 678 Main Street, Toronto, Ontario, M3Y 2T4. The property was leased by the plaintiff to the defendant Verdi and Wagner Music Store for a period of 5 years under a written lease executed by the defendant Verdi and Wagner Music Store by its principals, Joe Verdi and Richard Wagner, on October 14, year 0, which lease took effect on January 1, year 1.

5. Under the provisions of the lease, the premises were rented to the defendant Verdi and Wagner Music Store for the sum of $180,000 per year; the defendant Verdi and Wagner Music Store was required to pay the annual rent in equal, monthly installments of $15,000 per month in advance, on the first day of each month. The

---

*   It is assumed here that most simple commercial leases do not have interest provisions for when they are in default, so prejudgment and postjudgment interest can be claimed only under the *Courts of Justice Act*.

**   If the partners as well as the partnership are named as defendants, there is a claim by the plaintiff against both the partnership assets and assets of the individual partners. Alternatively, if the individuals are not named, they can be served with notices under rule 8.

Figure 5.3 Concluded

lease further provides that if there is a default in payment of rent, the obligation to pay the balance of the rent due over the term of the lease is accelerated and becomes immediately due and payable.

6. The defendant Verdi and Wagner Music Store defaulted in payment of the rent due on October 1, year 5 and has refused or neglected to pay the balance due and owing to the plaintiff.

7. The balance due and owing to the plaintiff as of October 1, year 5 is $45,000.

8. The plaintiff states that the defendants Joe Verdi and Richard Wagner, as partners and owners of the defendant Verdi and Wagner Music Store, are personally, jointly, and severally liable for the debt to the plaintiff of the defendant Verdi and Wagner Music Store.

9. The plaintiff claims interest on this amount in accordance with the provisions of the *Courts of Justice Act* from October 2, year 5 to the date of payment.

The Plaintiff proposes that this action be tried at: Toronto

DATED at Toronto
July 3, year 0

I.M. Greedy   LSUC #22333C
GREEDY & RAPACIOUS, Barristers and Solicitors
580 - 1234 Yonge Street, Toronto, ON M3F 4T0
416-485-8690 FAX 416-486-8691
Lawyers for the Plaintiff

RCP-E 14A (July 1, 2007)

Figure 5.4   Sample Statement of Claim Against a Principal Debtor and Guarantor (Form 14A)

THIS ACTION IS BROUGHT AGAINST YOU UNDER THE SIMPLIFIED PROCEDURE PROVIDED IN RULE 76 OF THE RULES OF CIVIL PROCEDURE.

CLAIM

1. The plaintiff claims:

    a. money owing to the plaintiff by the defendants under a "Rapacious Credit" cardholder agreement in the liquidated amount of $29,123.45;

    b. prejudgment and postjudgment interest at the rate of 25 percent per annum as provided for by the cardholder agreement between the parties, pursuant to the *Courts of Justice Act*;

    c. prejudgment and postjudgment interest in accordance with the provisions of the *Courts of Justice Act*, in the alternative;

    d. the costs of this action, including applicable HST; and

    e. such further relief as this honourable court deems appropriate.

2. The plaintiff is a financial services company, incorporated under the laws of Canada, with offices in Toronto, Ontario. The plaintiff is in the business of extending credit to persons such as the defendant Alvin Profligate through the use of credit cards.

3. The defendant Alvin Profligate is an individual who resides in the city of Toronto and who at all relevant times was a credit customer of the plaintiff.

4. The defendant Petra Profligate is an individual who resides in the city of Toronto and who is the spouse of Alvin Profligate and guarantor of the payment obligations of Alvin Profligate to the plaintiff.

5. On the defendant Alvin Profligate's application, the plaintiff opened a credit account for him and issued him a "Rapacious Credit" credit card. The card was issued subject to the terms and conditions set out in a cardholder agreement. The defendant Alvin Profligate was asked to read and sign the cardholder agreement by an agent of the plaintiff. The defendant signed the agreement on May 3, year 0. At that time, the defendant was issued with a credit card and given an account number, 1904 569 3452.

6. The defendant Petra Profligate executed a guarantor agreement on May 3, year 0 whereby she agreed to guarantee the debt of the defendant Alvin Profligate in the event that he defaulted on his payment obligations under the cardholder agreement.

Figure 5.4   Concluded

7. By signing the cardholder agreement, the defendant Alvin Profligate promised to be bound by the terms of the agreement, which allowed him to purchase goods and services on credit, and to obtain cash advances on credit by using the credit card provided by the plaintiff. He agreed to pay all debts to the plaintiff arising from the use of the credit card.

8. The defendant Alvin Profligate, from and after May 3, year 0, used the credit card to purchase goods and services and make cash advances, which were charged to his account with the plaintiff.

9. As a result of late payments or non-payment on the account, interest accrued on the outstanding balance from time to time, payable at the rate in effect from time to time as provided for in the cardholder agreement. At all relevant times, the defendant Alvin Profligate was given notice of the interest rate from time to time, as required by the cardholder agreement. At present, the rate of interest charged is 25 percent per annum.

10. The defendant Alvin Profligate has received full particulars of all transactions on his account in monthly statements sent by the plaintiff and from sales and transaction drafts delivered to him at the time of the transactions.

11. The defendant Petra Profligate was given written notice of the default in payment of Alvin Profligate on January 16, year 1, and by this written notice demand was made on her as guarantor to honour the obligations of Alvin Profligate.

12. The balance of the account outstanding and due and owing by the defendants to the plaintiff is $29,123.45 as of June 15, year 1. The defendants are in default because they have failed to pay any amount since December 3, year 0, despite repeated demands that they pay the balance outstanding in accordance with the provisions of the cardholder agreement and the guarantor agreement.

The Plaintiff proposes that this action be tried at: Toronto

DATED at Toronto
July 3, year 1

I.M. Weasel   LSUC #88512B
Barrister and Solicitor
123 Finch Road, Toronto, ON M2J 2X5
416-223-6789 FAX 416-223-6788

Figure 5.5   Sample Notice of Intent to Defend (Form 18B)

Court file no. 6789

ONTARIO

SUPERIOR COURT OF JUSTICE

B E T W E E N:

THE PLUMBER'S DELIGHT LTD.

Plaintiff

and

SEWERS R' US LTD.

Defendant

NOTICE OF INTENT TO DEFEND

The defendant (*or* defendant added by counterclaim *or* third party) intends to defend this action.

May 25, year 0

Susan Snogg   LSUC #98714D
BLODGETT AND SNOGG
Barristers and Solicitors
307 - 301 Cartway Road
Toronto, ON M3R 1P3

416-987-6543
FAX 416-987-6544

Lawyers for the Defendant

TO: I.M. Just   LSUC #12345A
       JUST AND COPING
       Barristers and Solicitors
       8701 - 365 Bay Street
       Toronto, ON M3J 4A9

       416-762-1342
       FAX 416-762-1343

       Lawyers for the Plaintiff

RCP-E 18B (July 1, 2007)

Figure 5.6   Sample Statement of Defence (Form 18A)

Court file no. 6789

ONTARIO

SUPERIOR COURT OF JUSTICE

B E T W E E N:

THE PLUMBER'S DELIGHT LTD.

Plaintiff

and

SEWERS R' US LTD.

Defendant

STATEMENT OF DEFENCE*

1. The defendant admits the allegations contained in paragraphs 2 and 3 of the statement of claim.

2. The defendant denies the allegations contained in paragraphs 1, 4, 5, 6, and 7 of the statement of claim.

3. The defendant did not execute a revolving credit agreement as alleged in paragraph 4 of the statement of claim. The defendant and the plaintiff orally agreed that credit would be extended to the defendant, and that accounts would be rendered from time to time and that the balance would be paid down from time to time. No rate of interest was agreed to in respect of overdue payments.

4. The defendant is obliged to make payments from time to time if the outstanding balance becomes excessively high. At no time has the balance due been excessively high.

---

*   Based on the sample statement of claim on a running account in figure 5.1.

Figure 5.6   Concluded

5. The defendant is not in breach of its obligations to pay the balance due, and is not in breach of its contractual obligations to the plaintiff.

6. The defendant asks that the action be dismissed, with costs.

May 30, year 0

Susan Snogg   LSUC #98714D
BLODGETT AND SNOGG
Barristers and Solicitors
307 - 301 Cartway Road
Toronto, ON M3R 1P3

416-987-6543
FAX 416-987-6544

Lawyers for the Defendant

TO: I.M. Just   LSUC #12345A
JUST AND COPING
Barristers and Solicitors
8701 - 365 Bay Street
Toronto, ON M3J 4A9

416-762-1342
FAX 416-762-1343

Lawyers for the Plaintiff

RCP-E 18A (July 1, 2007)

CHAPTER 6

Default Judgment

Once you have served the statement of claim, the defendant must in turn serve you with a statement of defence within the time provided for in the *Rules of Civil Procedure*. If you receive no statement of defence, the defendant is deemed to have admitted the truth of the facts in the statement of claim and admitted liability and you may obtain a judgment against the defendant in default of a defence. If the claim is a **liquidated amount**, there is a simple, quick, and straightforward administrative process for obtaining a judgment for the amount due. Most debt collection cases are liquidated claims — for example, claims for payment for goods or services sold or supplied, credit card debts, unpaid loans, and unpaid running accounts.

If the claim is not liquidated, even though the defendant is deemed to have admitted the truth of the facts in the statement of claim and to have admitted liability, the plaintiff is obliged to prove the monetary value of damages in court. For example, a claim for general damages for loss of business arising from a breach of contract cannot be simply calculated using a formula. In this case, the plaintiff must lead evidence showing the extent of the business losses to allow a judge to exercise discretion in subjectively deciding how much money to award the plaintiff.

To obtain or sign default judgment on behalf of a plaintiff, you must prepare the following documents and file them with the registrar of the Superior Court. If the documents are properly prepared and in order, the clerk, acting on behalf of the registrar, will sign judgment for the full amount of the claim, prejudgment interest, and costs. The clerk will also award postjudgment interest in accordance with the terms of a contract, or, if there is no contractual rate that applies post judgment, in accordance with the terms of s. 129 of the *Courts of Justice Act*. Be sure that your claim is accurately stated and that the calculations are accurate, because it is embarrassing and time consuming to have to change or amend a judgment later to correct an error.

liquidated amount
a specific sum of money that can be easily and objectively calculated; if a debtor borrows $1,000 for a one-year period at 10 percent interest per year, the amount owing —$1,100—would be a liquidated amount because it is precise and specific and the total is easily calculated using an objective standard or formula

FORMS REQUIRED TO SIGN JUDGMENT

The following forms are required to sign judgment:

1. Affidavit of service proving service of the statement of claim together with the original statement of claim.

2. Requisition for default judgment, noting the defendant in default,[1] stating that the claim is a liquidated claim, coming within the class of claims for

which you may sign default judgment, and showing how much is owing, less payments made by the debtor, if any.

3. Draft bill of costs (original and two copies) to provide a basis for fixing the amount of costs to be included in the judgment.

4. Draft judgment (original and two copies).

5. Requisition for writ of seizure and sale.

6. Writ of seizure and sale (original and two copies).

7. Cheque payable to the Minister of Finance to file the requisition for default judgment and to issue the writ of seizure and sale.[2]

PROCEDURE FOR SIGNING JUDGMENT

Set out below is a step-by-step guide to signing default judgment. There is a default judgment fact situation at the end of this chapter that shows the necessary forms, filled out as required by the court. The requisition for default judgment, the requisition for the writ of seizure and sale, and the writ of seizure and sale are court forms that are prescribed by the *Rules of Civil Procedure*. The bill of costs and the judgment are documents that you draft from precedents or word processing templates. The statement of claim and affidavit of service, or other proof of service, are already in your office file.

Prepare a Requisition for Default Judgment

You will need the original statement of claim attached to the process server's affidavit of service, so that the clerk can see when the claim was served, where it was served, and satisfy herself that the time for filing a statement of defence has indeed elapsed. As you read through the following steps, you will find that they are easier to understand if you have the Requisition for Default Judgment (Form 19D) in front of you (see figure 6.1).

1. On the requisition itself, after the words "TO THE LOCAL REGISTRAR AT … ," type in "I REQUIRE you to note the defendant [*insert defendant's name*] in default in this action and that **pleadings be noted closed** against the defendant on the ground that the defendant has failed to deliver a statement of defence within the time provided for in the rules." Next, insert the defendant's name below "I REQUIRE default judgment to be signed against the defendant."

2. Check off the basis for signing default judgment.

3. Indicate whether any payments have been made on account with respect to the claim. If some payments have been made, complete Part A; if none have been made, complete Part B.

4. If some payments have been made, indicate the principal sum claimed, without interest; then show the payment on account and show how much of that payment is allocated to interest and to principal; then indicate the

pleadings noted closed
the act of noting pleadings closed means that no party may file any further claims, defences, motions, or other court documents; this act brings the pretrial stage to a close—in a defended proceeding, the matter is then listed for trial; in a default proceeding, the defendant is barred from filing a statement of defence and the plaintiff is free to sign judgment

principal amount outstanding, after the allocations have been made. This is "Total A" on the form. Remember that any payment received after the claim issues has to be allocated first to accrued interest, and then to the principal amount claimed.

5. With respect to the calculation of prejudgment interest, indicate the date on which the claim was issued and the date on which the cause of action arose; this allows the clerk (and you) to determine how many days of interest you are entitled to and what the appropriate rate is if interest is calculated under the *Courts of Justice Act* interest provisions.

6. Show how prejudgment interest is calculated. Calculate simple interest unless you have a contractual right to compound interest based on an agreement relied on and set out in the statement of claim. Calculate interest on the principal sum owing from the date of the last payment that you previously identified in the form. To calculate interest from the last payment, count the number of days from the last payment to the date on which judgment is to be signed (the last "End Date" in the form), multiply that number by the annual rate of interest, and multiply that result by the principal sum owing and divide by 365. This is "Total B" on the form.

7. From the calculations in 6, enter Total B and from the calculations in 4, enter Total A in order to fill in the total amount for which to sign judgment.

8. If no payment was received, then complete Part B, indicating amount A, the total amount of the claim less interest, and then provide the interest data including the date on which the claim arose and was issued. Then show your interest calculations, using simple interest, unless you have a contractual right to compound interest and have claimed this in your statement of claim. Count the number of days from the time the cause of action arose to the date of judgment, and do the calculations as described previously for Part A (part payments received). Add the sum claimed — Total A — to the interest claimed — Total B — to determine the amount for which judgment is to be signed.

9. Complete Part C — "Postjudgment Interest and Costs." Insert the rate of postjudgment interest that applies (this is either a contractually agreed-upon rate between the parties or the statutory rate, which is the rate for the quarter in which the judgment is signed) and indicate the basis for claiming interest. Then check off whether you wish the registrar to fix the costs or have them assessed later. The usual practice is to have the registrar fix the costs based on your bill of costs, prepared in accordance with the *Rules of Civil Procedure*. This is much quicker and less expensive than coming back at a later date to have the costs assessed. One might ask to have a bill of costs assessed if, for some reason, the costs to the plaintiff had been much higher than is usually the case for default judgment.

Prepare a Bill of Costs

partial indemnity
usual order for costs, based on a cost grid that establishes hourly rates for tariff items listed in the grid; provides less than full recovery of legal fees for the client

See figure 6.2, Proposed Bill of Costs (Form 57A), at the end of this chapter. In a default judgment situation, as in most civil cases, the loser pays some of the winner's legal costs on a **partial indemnity** scale. The basis for assessing a lawyer's fees on a bill of costs is rule 57.01(1), which creates a broad discretion in determining the fee component of a costs award. However, costs were subject to a Notice from the Costs Subcommittee of the Civil Rules Committee, which established a costs grid. This grid was revoked in 2005. However, in the absence of any other guidelines, the grid figures continue to be used by judges, lawyers, and law clerks, and are included here. The costs grid sets out the following *maximum* rates to be used:

- law clerks: $80.00 per hour

- student-at-law: $60.00 per hour

- lawyer with less than 10 years' experience: $225.00 per hour

- lawyer with more than 10 but less than 20 years' experience: $300.00 per hour

- lawyer with 20 or more years of experience: $350.00 per hour.

However, for simpler matters, including obtaining a default judgment, the rates should be well below the maximums, although there is no prescription or formula to tell you with precision what they should be.

disbursements
amounts paid out by the law office on its own account to third parties on behalf of a client

The lawyer's out-of-pocket expenses, or **disbursements**, are another story. These are covered in tariff A, part II, Disbursements. Here, cost recovery is usually on a dollar-for-dollar basis. For example, if $40.00 is paid to a process server to serve a statement of claim, then that is the amount that will be recovered in costs, although there are limits on some part II disbursements. Court fees and sheriff costs[3] can be recovered in full. The items usually included in the bill of costs on default judgment are as follows:

1. *Pleadings:* Hours spent × appropriate hourly rate from the cost grid.

2. *Court fees paid to issue statement of claim:* Obtain fees from the Schedule of Fees that follows tariffs A and B in commercial editions of the Rules of Practice, such as *Ontario Annual Practice* — note that these fees change regularly, and always in an upward direction.

3. *Fees paid to serve statement of claim:* See tariff A, part II — reasonable cost backed by receipt for payment to process server (this includes HST).

4. *Determination of costs and signing order (default judgment):* Hours spent × appropriate hourly rate on the grid.

5. *Court fees paid to file requisition for default judgment:* as in item 2 above, see the Schedule of Fees.[4]

substantial indemnity
costs scale usually used as a punitive costs award that results in near indemnity for the winner on a dollar-for-dollar basis

In the bill of costs, fees and disbursements are recorded in separate columns and totalled. Disbursements include tariff A, part II items, as well as court fees and sheriff fees. If for any reason you wish to recover costs on a **substantial indemnity** scale, this is a claim for a full recovery of costs and is best dealt with by being set down for hearing before an assessment officer. Recovery on this scale is unusual in default situations, as this scale is usually applied where a party has misconducted himself or herself in the course of the proceedings.

Draft a Judgment

Draft a judgment (see figure 6.3) and make two copies of it. The judgment is a one-paragraph document in which you must insert the sum claimed, composed of the principal amount and interest, taken from the requisition for default judgment, and the costs, taken from the total on the bill of costs. Remember to include a sentence stating that "This judgment bears interest at the rate of _____ percent per year from its date." If this statement is not present in the draft judgment, even though interest is claimed in the statement of claim and identified in the requisition for default judgment, the clerk may not insert the phrase for you and you will not obtain postjudgment interest.

Prepare a Requisition for a Writ of Seizure and Sale

While a requisition for a writ of seizure and sale and a writ of seizure and sale are not required to obtain default judgment, the documents are often prepared when obtaining default judgment because you may wish to file the writ of execution as quickly as possible to catch the debtor's assets before they are dissipated. The requisition (see figure 6.4) should be directed to the sheriff of each county or area where you think the debtor has assets. If the debtor has assets in more than one area, you will, therefore, need to refer in the requisition to each sheriff's office in which you intend to file a writ of seizure and sale. Be sure to accurately set out the name of the debtor. Include the amount to be seized, the amount of costs claimed, and the applicable postjudgment interest rate, all of which can be copied from the judgment.

Prepare a Writ of Seizure and Sale

You should prepare an original and one copy of the writ (see figure 6.5) for each sheriff's office in which you plan to file the writ. When you obtain the default judgment and pay the fee to issue the writ, file the original and one copy with the Sheriff's Office, along with a cover letter instructing the sheriff to file the writ in the land registry and land titles system. If the writ is not filed in the land titles system, the writ will not attach to the execution debtor's land registered in the land titles system. For the land registry system, filing the writ with the sheriff is sufficient to attach an interest in land registered there. Check with the Sheriff's Office to ascertain the fee for filing with the land registry system. Complete each writ, filling in the blanks, using the judgment and the requisition for a writ of seizure and sale as the source of the necessary information. Keep one copy of each writ for your office file. Remember to complete the backsheet by adding in the fee paid to issue the writ, and the lawyer's fee for issuing the writ. Rule 60.19(2)(a) sets the lawyer's fee for preparation of the writ at $50.00. The sheriff is entitled to add these costs to the amounts on the face of the writ that may be collected from the debtor in the future.

Prepare a Cheque Payable to the Minister of Finance

To cover the cost of requisitioning the default judgment and issuing each original writ of seizure and sale, check the current tariffs for court and sheriff's fees for the cost of obtaining default judgment and issuing a writ of seizure and sale, and prepare a cheque payable to the Minister of Finance.

Sample Illustration of a Default Judgment

Having described how to prepare documentation to sign a default judgment, this section sets out the completed documents that you must prepare as models to use, based on the facts in chapter 4 on pages 94 and 95, Sample Calculation of Amounts Owing on a Running Account. The facts are set out below. The statement of claim based on those facts is found in the sample statements of claim at the end of chapter 5 in figure 5.1, Sample Statement of Claim on a Running Account. When preparing court documents, remember that all of them must have a backsheet. See rule 4 of the *Rules of Civil Procedure* for the general rules governing the format and content of court documents.

Facts

We act for Artemis Plumbing Supply Ltd.; one of its customers, Personable Plumbers Ltd. ("Personable"), has a running account for orders that the office manager from Personable phones in to Artemis. There was some activity in June, year 0, but there has been no activity since. The transactions are as follows:

DATE	INVOICE	DEBIT	CREDIT	BALANCE
June 3	0113	$20,000		$20,000.00
June 4			$20,000	0.00
June 15	0893	$32,000		$32,000.00
June 21	0896	$20,000		$52,000.00
July 28			$20,000	$32,199.89*

* This is the result of applying the July 28 payment first to interest on overdue amounts and then to principal.

No further orders have been placed, or payments received. The original agreement stated that payments were due within 30 days of billing, after which interest would be charged at the rate of 12 percent per annum.

On September 15, year 0, a demand letter was sent but there was no response by the deadline in the demand letter, September 25. A statement of claim was issued and served on September 26. It is now October 16, year 0 and no statement of defence has been received.

Prepare documents on the assumption that you will sign default judgment on October 17, year 0. The cost of issuing a claim is $181 (2011). Assume that you paid a process server $40 (inclusive of HST) to serve the statement of claim and provide you with an affidavit of service as proof of service of the claim. Assume that you have receipts to attach to the bill of costs for all disbursements and dockets to support the claim for fees in the bill of costs.

CHAPTER SUMMARY

In this chapter the debt collection process moved on from the commencement of proceedings to what needs to be done if the debtor does not defend. At this point it is necessary for the plaintiff to move for default judgment if the debt is a liquidated claim or demand. For this the following forms must be prepared: requisition for default judgment noting the defendant in default, a draft bill of costs, and a draft judgment. A requisition for a writ of seizure and sale and the writ itself should also be prepared. These documents are then filed with the court. If they are in order, the clerk will verify that the facts and calculations in the requisition for default judgment fit the claim in the statement of claim. The clerk will then assess the plaintiff's costs, and sign judgment. The writ of seizure and sale may then be issued and filed with the Sheriff's Office(s) where the debtor has, or is likely to have, assets.

KEY TERMS

disbursements

liquidated amount

partial indemnity

pleadings noted closed

substantial indemnity

NOTES

1. The defendant may be noted in default by filing a requisition in Form 4E to note the defendant in default. In the blank space on the form where you indicate what administrative act you are requiring the court to perform, state: "I require that you note the defendant in default in this action, on the ground that the defendant has failed to deliver a statement of defence within the time provided for in the rules" (or on other grounds, such as the defence being struck out without leave to amend). It is more usual however to include the default in defence as part of the requisition for default judgment in Form 19D. The effect of noting the defendant in default is to note pleadings closed, which bars the late filing of a statement of defence.

2. Items 5, 6, and 7 are not required to sign default judgment, but are often prepared when signing judgment so that the writ of seizure and sale can be filed as quickly as possible to catch assets before they are dissipated.

3. *Superior Court of Justice and Court of Appeal — Fees*, O. Reg. 293/92, as amended. The tariffs and court fees are set out in the Ontario *Rules of Civil Procedure*. These rules are regulations under the *Courts of Justice Act* and can be found online at http://www.e-laws.gov.on.ca. To find these regulations at the e-laws website, click on Current Consolidated Law and choose "A," then click on the plus sign to the left of the *Administration of Justice Act* entry in the list. This will open up the regulations, which will be listed below the Act.

4. Always check the tariff before preparing a bill of costs because the tariffs and court fees are amended from time to time.

REFERENCES

Administration of Justice Act, RSO 1990, c. A.6.

Courts of Justice Act, RSO 1990, c. C.43.

Ontario Annual Practice (Aurora, ON: Canada Law Book, annual).

Rules of Civil Procedure, RRO 1990, Reg. 194.

Superior Court of Justice and Court of Appeal — Fees, O. Reg. 293/92.

REVIEW QUESTIONS

1. Under what circumstances can you apply to sign default judgment?

2. Explain the difference between a liquidated claim and an unliquidated claim.

3. What documents must you prepare to sign default judgment?

4. What documents must you file with the court in order to sign default judgment?

5. What is the function of providing the registrar with a requisition for default judgment?

6. Suppose the defendant defaults on her defence, but pays some money on account of the amount set out in the statement of claim. How does this affect the process of signing default judgment?

7. What determines the interest rate used for prejudgment and postjudgment interest?

8. How do you determine the amounts that go into the bill of costs?

9. What is the difference between fees and disbursements?

10. What is the difference between partial indemnity costs and substantial indemnity costs?

11. Which scale of costs would you use in signing default judgment? Explain your answer.

12. What are the significant differences between assessing costs and fixing costs?

13. In what circumstances would you have to requisition more than one writ of seizure and sale on signing default judgment?

14. What do you need to tell the sheriff to do when you obtain a writ of seizure and sale to file with the Sheriff's Office?

15. Once the sheriff has the writ, can she collect more from the debtor than the face amount on the judgment, including accrued interest?

CASE STUDY

Prepare documents to sign default judgment in the following case:

B. Hard
8701 – 365 Bay Street
Toronto, ON M5A 1J3

tel.: 416-782-1234

MEMO

DATE: April 26, year 1

TO: U.R. Clerk

FROM: Bodley Head

RE: Default Judgment — Rapacious Lenders v. Ophelia Foot

We issued a claim against Ophelia Foot on March 23, year 1. Foot had signed a promissory note to our client Rapacious Lenders Ltd. for $30,000 on August 1, year 0. The note was due on December 1, year 0. It provided for interest at 12 percent per year from the time it was past due until payment. Interest has been claimed on this basis. The claim was thus for $30,000 plus interest on the overdue amount. On March 1, year 1, Foot paid $2,000 on account, but nothing has been paid since. Foot was served with the statement of claim on March 24, year 1; nothing has happened since.

Because Foot has not defended, and the time for filing a defence has passed, please prepare the necessary documents to sign default judgment on April 28, year 1. The original statement of claim and affidavit of service are in the file, together with a receipt for $40.00 (inclusive of HST) for service of the claim and a receipt for $181.00 from the court for the fee paid to issue the statement of claim. It is rumoured that Foot owns property in Toronto and Oshawa, so be sure to take that into account when requisitioning the writ of seizure and sale.

Figure 6.1   Requisition for Default Judgment (Form 19D)

Court file no. 1234

ONTARIO

SUPERIOR COURT OF JUSTICE

B E T W E E N

ARTEMIS PLUMBING SUPPLY LTD.

Plaintiff

and

PERSONABLE PLUMBERS LTD.

Defendant

REQUISITION FOR DEFAULT JUDGMENT

TO THE LOCAL REGISTRAR AT TORONTO

I REQUIRE you to note the defendant Personable Plumbers Ltd. in default in this action and that pleadings be noted closed against the defendant on the ground that the defendant has failed to deliver a statement of defence within the time provided for in the rules.

I REQUIRE default judgment to be signed against the defendant

Personable Plumbers Ltd.

Default judgment may properly be signed in this action because the claim is for:

[x] a debt or liquidated demand in money

[ ] recovery of possession of land

[ ] recovery of possession of personal property

[ ] foreclosure, sale or redemption of a mortgage

(Debt or liquidated demand)

[x] There has been no payment on account of the claim since the statement of claim was issued. *(Complete Parts B and C.)*

OR

[ ] The following payments have been made on account of the claim since the statement of claim was issued.

(Complete Parts B and C.)

Figure 6.1   Continued

PART A — PAYMENT(S) RECEIVED BY PLAINTIFF

(Complete this part only where part payment of the claim has been received. Where no payment has been received on account of the claim, omit this part and complete Part B.)

1. Principal

Principal sum claimed in statement of claim (without interest) $ ....

Date of Payment	Amount of Payment	Payment Amount Principal	Applied to Interest	Principal Sum Owing
TOTAL	$	$	$	A $ ....

2. Prejudgment interest

(Under section 128 of the Courts of Justice Act, *judgment may be obtained for prejudgment interest from the date the cause of action arose, if claimed in the statement of claim.)*

Date on which statement of claim was issued ....

Date from which prejudgment interest is claimed ....

The plaintiff is entitled to prejudgment interest on the claim, calculated as follows:

(Calculate simple interest only unless an agreement relied on in the statement of claim specifies otherwise. Calculate interest on the principal sum owing from the date of the last payment. To calculate the interest amount, count the number of days since the last payment, multiply that number by the annual rate of interest, multiply the result by the principal sum owing and divide by 365.)

Principal Sum Owing	Start Date	End Date (Date of Payment)	Number of Days	Rate	Interest Amount

TOTAL B $ ....

Principal Sum Owing (Total A above) $ ....

Total Interest Amount (Total B above) $ ....

SIGN JUDGMENT FOR $ ....

Figure 6.1 Continued

PART B — NO PAYMENT RECEIVED BY PLAINTIFF

(Complete this part only where no payment has been received on account of the claim.)

1. Principal

   Principal sum claimed in statement of claim (without interest)   A $ 32,199.89

2. Prejudgment interest

(Under section 128 of the Courts of Justice Act, *judgment may be obtained for prejudgment interest from the date the cause of action arose, if claimed in the statement of claim.)*

   Date on which statement of claim was issued: September 26, year 0

   Date from which prejudgment interest is claimed: July 29, year 0

   The plaintiff is entitled to prejudgment interest on the claim, calculated as follows:

(Calculate simple interest only unless an agreement relied on in the statement of claim specifies otherwise. To calculate the interest amount, count the number of days and multiply that number by the annual rate of interest, multiply the result by the principal sum owing and divide by 365.)

Principal Sum Owing	Start Date	End Date (Date of Payment)	Number of Days	Rate	Interest Amount
32,199.89	July 29, year 0	Oct. 17, year 0	81*	12%	857.42

TOTAL B	$ 857.42
Principal Sum Owing (Total A above)	$ 32,199.89
Total Interest Amount (Total B above)	$ 857.42
SIGN JUDGMENT FOR	$ 33,057.31

---

* When calculating the time (T) factor in interest calculations, the figure is rounded to four decimal places in all text examples. So, here, T = $^{81}/_{365}$ = .2219178, and .2219178 rounded off to four decimal places is .2219:

I = P × R × T = $32,199.89 × .12 × .2219 = $857.42 prejudgment interest.

Figure 6.1 Continued

PART C — POSTJUDGMENT INTEREST AND COSTS

1. Postjudgment interest

   The plaintiff is entitled to postjudgment interest at the rate of   per cent per year,

   [ ] under the *Courts of Justice Act*, as claimed in the statement of claim.

OR

   [x] in accordance with the claim made in the statement of claim.

2. Costs

   The plaintiff wishes costs to be,

   [x] fixed by the local registrar.

OR

   [ ] assessed by an assessment officer.

Date: October 17, year 0

I.M. Just
_____

I.M. Just   LSUC #12345A

JUST AND COPING

Barristers and Solicitors

8701 - 365 Bay Street

Toronto, ON M3J 4A9

416-762-1342

FAX 416-762-1343

Lawyers for the Plaintiff

RCP-E 19D (July 1, 2007)

Figure 6.1　Concluded

ARTEMIS
Plaintiff

and

PERSONABLE
Defendant

Court file no. 1234

ONTARIO
SUPERIOR COURT OF JUSTICE

PROCEEDING COMMENCED at
TORONTO

REQUISITION FOR
DEFAULT JUDGMENT

I.M. Just　LSUC #12345A
JUST AND COPING
Barristers and Solicitors
8701 - 365 Bay Street
Toronto, ON　M3J 4A9

416-762-1342
FAX 416-762-1343

Lawyers for the Plaintiff

RCP-E 4C (July 1, 2007)

Figure 6.2   Proposed Bill of Costs (Form 57A)

Court file no. 1234

ONTARIO
SUPERIOR COURT OF JUSTICE

B E T W E E N

ARTEMIS PLUMBING SUPPLY LTD.

Plaintiff

and

PERSONABLE PLUMBERS LTD.

Defendant

BILL OF COSTS

AMOUNTS CLAIMED FOR FEES AND DISBURSEMENTS

FEES OTHER THAN COUNSEL FEES

1. Preparing and drafting statement of claim,

   I.M. Just, September 25, year 0   1.0 hour

2. Signing default judgment and assessing costs,

   I.M. Just, October 17, year 0   0.6 hour

1.6 hours × $200 = $320.00

TOTAL FEES $320.00

HST ON FEES $41.60

Figure 6.2 Concluded

DISBURSEMENTS*

1. paid to issue statement of claim	$181.00	
2. paid to serve claim (includes HST)	40.00	
3. paid to file requisition for default judgment	127.00	
TOTAL DISBURSEMENTS		$348.00

HST (R0145892)**

TOTAL FEES AND DISBURSEMENTS $709.60

STATEMENT OF EXPERIENCE

A claim for fees is being made with respect to the following lawyers:

Name of lawyer	Years of experience
I.M. Just	12
LSUC #12345A	

THIS BILL assessed and allowed at $_____ this _____ day of _____, _____

_____
Registrar, Ontario Superior Court of Justice

TO: H.E.S. Evasive   LSUC #56785E
     Barrister and Solicitor
     1256 Orfue Rd.
     Toronto, ON M4R 1Y6

     416-645-1267
     FAX 416-645-1268

     Lawyer for the Defendant

RCP-E 57A (November 1, 2005)

---

* The court fees under disbursements here are based on the fees in O. Reg. 293/92, Superior Court of Justice and Court of Appeal — Fees Under the *Administration of Justice Act*. Note that these fees change from time to time — a reminder to always check tariffs and the schedule of fees.

** HST is paid on fees and disbursements paid out to third parties, other than court and government fixed fees, which includes HST to serve the claim in this case. Not all lawyers charge HST on bills of costs, although the better practice is to do so.

Figure 6.3   Proposed Default Judgment (Debt or Liquidated Demand (Form 19A)

Court file no. 1234

ONTARIO

SUPERIOR COURT OF JUSTICE

B E T W E E N

ARTEMIS PLUMBING SUPPLY LTD.

Plaintiff

and

PERSONABLE PLUMBERS LTD.

Defendant

JUDGMENT

On reading the statement of claim in this action and the proof of service of the statement of claim on the defendant, filed, and the defendant having been noted in default,

1. IT IS ORDERED AND ADJUDGED that the defendant pay to the plaintiff the sum of $33,057.31 and the sum of $_____ for the costs of this action.

    This judgment bears interest at the rate of _____ per cent per year from its date.

Date: _____   Signed by: _____

Local Registrar

Address of the court office:

393 University Avenue
Toronto, ON M5G 1T4

RCP-E 19A (November 1, 2005)

Figure 6.4 Requisition for Writ of Seizure and Sale

Court file no. 1234

ONTARIO

SUPERIOR COURT OF JUSTICE

B E T W E E N

ARTEMIS PLUMBING SUPPLY LTD.

Plaintiff

and

PERSONABLE PLUMBERS LTD.

Defendant

REQUISITION FOR WRIT OF SEIZURE AND SALE

TO THE LOCAL REGISTRAR at TORONTO

I REQUIRE a writ of seizure and sale pursuant to an order of this court made on

October 17, year 0 in favour of ARTEMIS PLUMBING SUPPLY LTD. *(name of creditor)*

directed to the Sheriff of the City of Toronto

to seize and sell the real and personal property of

Surname of individual or name of corporation/firm, etc.
PERSONABLE PLUMBERS LTD. *(name of debtor)*

First given name (individual only)	*Second given name (individual only) (if applicable)*	*Third given name (individual only) (if applicable)*

and to realize from the seizure and sale the following sums:

(a) $33,057.31 *(single payment)* and interest at 12 per cent per year commencing on October 17, year 0;

(b) $709.60 for costs together with interest at 12 per cent per year commencing on October 17, year 0; and

(c) your fees and expenses in enforcing this writ.

October 17, year 0

I.M. Just   LSUC #12345A

JUST AND COPING, Barristers and Solicitors

8701 - 365 Bay Street, Toronto, ON M3J 4A9

416-762-1342   FAX 416-762-1343

Lawyers for the Plaintiff

Figure 6.5   Writ of Seizure and Sale (Form 60A)

Court file no. 1234

ONTARIO

SUPERIOR COURT OF JUSTICE

B E T W E E N

ARTEMIS PLUMBING SUPPLY LTD.

Plaintiff

and

PERSONABLE PLUMBERS LTD.

Defendant

WRIT OF SEIZURE AND SALE

TO: the Sheriff of the City of Toronto

Under an order of this court made on October 17, year 0, in favour of ARTEMIS PLUMBING SUPPLY LTD., YOU ARE DIRECTED to seize and sell the real and personal property within your county or district of

Surname of individual or name of corporation/firm, etc. PERSONABLE PLUMBERS LTD.

First given name (individual only)	*Second given name (individual only) (if applicable)*	*Third given name (individual only) (if applicable)*

and to realize from the seizure and sale the following sums:

(a) $33,057.31 *(single payment)* and interest at 12 per cent per year commencing on October 17, year 0;

(b) $709.60 for costs together with interest at 12 per cent per year commencing on October 17, year 0; and

(c)   your fees and expenses in enforcing this writ.

YOU ARE DIRECTED to pay out the proceeds according to law and to report on the execution of this writ if required by the party or lawyer who filed it.

Dated at _____

on October 17, year 0

Issued by: _____

Registrar

Address of court office: 393 University Avenue
                                            Toronto, ON M5G 1T4

RCP-E 60A (July 1, 2007)

Figure 6.5 Concluded

ARTEMIS
Plaintiff(s)

and

PERSONABLE
Defendant(s)

Court file no. 1234

ONTARIO

SUPERIOR COURT OF JUSTICE

PROCEEDING COMMENCED at
TORONTO

WRIT OF SEIZURE AND SALE

CREDITOR'S NAME
ARTEMIS PLUMBING SUPPLY LTD.

Address
c/o JUST AND COPING
Barristers and Solicitors

LAWYER'S NAME
I.M. Just   LSUC #12345A

Address
JUST AND COPING, 8701 - 365 Bay Street
Toronto, ON M3J 4A9

Tel. No.: 416-762-1342
Fax No.: 416-762-1343

RCP-E 4C (July 1, 2007)

FEES		
Fee	Item	Officer
$55.00	Paid for this writ	
$50.00*	Solicitor's fee for issuing writ	
	First renewal	
	Second renewal	
	Third renewal	

RENEWAL	
Date	Officer

---

*   As allowed by rule 60.19(2)(a).

CHAPTER 7

Summary Judgment

SUMMARY JUDGMENT

Where either the plaintiff or defendant believes that the pleadings and the case of the opposite party do not disclose a genuine issue requiring a trial, the party may bring a motion for summary judgment.[1]

As a result of the January 2010 rule amendments, this rule has become much more important than it was, making it easier for a party bringing a summary judgment motion to succeed in obtaining judgment.

The key change is in the test for deciding a summary judgment motion. Formerly, the moving party had to show that there was *no genuine issue for trial*. The moving party now has to show that there is *no genuine issue requiring a trial*. This test effectively lowers the bar for the moving party. Under the amended rule, a respondent may not rest solely on the pleadings, but must set out facts that show that there is a genuine issue that does require a trial. A motion judge (but not a master) now has the authority to go beyond the pleadings, and, with the ability to order a mini trial, the judge may weigh and assess evidence, make findings on credibility, and draw inferences from the evidence.

To assist moving parties, the former assumption that a moving party who failed to obtain judgment must pay substantial indemnity costs has been eliminated. Substantial indemnity costs are now restricted to the role they play elsewhere: to punish unreasonable behaviour by either party. The regular costs provisions now apply to summary judgment motions.

The clear intent of the amendment to rule 20 is to reduce the number of cases that proceed to trial unless a trial is really required, by allowing mini trials and extensive overview by a judge of the pretrial paper record. Clearly, many debt collection cases where defendants have mounted spurious defences can be cleared away under the amended rule 20. Under the old rules, a judge's power to assess evidence was limited, the bar to success was set higher, and the cost consequences to the unsuccessful moving party were punitive. Not surprisingly, counsel were reluctant to move for summary judgment, regarding it as something of a gamble. It remains to be seen whether lawyers make more use of rule 20, and it will require some Court of Appeal decisions to see whether the amended rule will operate as the Rules Committee intended. Under the former version of rule 20, the Court of Appeal made it very difficult for a moving party to succeed.

taking of accounts
a court may order that there be a taking of accounts where an issue involving complex financial transactions needs to be examined in some detail in a less formal process than a trial; accounts may be taken before a judge or other judicial officers, usually masters of the Superior Court; the process is similar to that used in a reference

reference
a judicial proceeding used where it is necessary to inquire into an issue in an action in great detail; rather than tie up the court's time in a formal proceeding, a judge may order a reference to be held before a judge or other judicial official, such as a master, with expertise or time or both to delve into the matter using a less formal process than the process used in a formal trial

motion
an application to the court within the main proceeding to settle a legal issue that has arisen in the main proceeding—for example, a plaintiff might bring a motion to court asking that the defendant provide more detail in the statement of defence; a motion is brought by a notice of motion, which states what remedy is sought and the reasons for it; the facts in support of the motion are usually presented in an affidavit

master
a judicial officer of the Superior Court who decides procedural issues on pretrial matters and performs some other judicial functions

affiant
a person who swears to the truth of statements set out in her affidavit

Note that simplified proceedings under rule 76 are now subject to rule 20 for summary judgment. There is no longer a separate summary judgment procedure under rule 76.

Aside from an order for dismissal of the action, there are a variety of orders a court can make on a motion for summary judgment:

1. If the issue is a question of law alone, arising clearly from the pleadings, affidavits may not be necessary, and the court may dismiss the action or dismiss the motion, in which case the action continues.

2. If the issue is the amount of damages owing, where liability is clear, the court may grant judgment with a reference for the **taking of accounts** or for a **reference**.

3. If the court, having examined the issues, refuses to grant a summary judgment, it may make various orders to expedite or speed up the trial. For example, it may find that certain witnesses need not give oral evidence, or that certain facts are deemed admitted and need not be proved.

4. The court may adjourn a motion for judgment, but payment of part of the disputed sum into court may be the cost of an adjournment, particularly for a defendant.

Summary Judgments in Actions for Debt

Strategically, a motion for summary judgment can be a useful tool in debt actions, because it allows a plaintiff to obtain judgment for all or part of a claim at an early stage in the pretrial proceedings without the cost and delay of discovery and a formal trial. This is particularly useful if the dispute boils down to an argument over the amount of a debt that is actually owing, because a judgment can be given for a reference or to take accounts.

Procedure

In order to obtain summary judgment, the party seeking it must bring a **motion** before a judge or, in limited circumstances, a **master**.[2] In support of the motion, an affidavit (figure 7.3) setting out the evidence on which you rely for the relief requested in the notice of motion (figure 7.2) must also be served with the notice of motion. In response to the moving party's material, the responding party may serve an affidavit in reply. The moving party is then responsible for preparing and filing with the court a motion record (figure 7.1), which contains all of the documents of both parties relevant to the issues arising on the motion. Before the hearing of the motion, both sides must file factums setting out concise statements of the facts and law that they are relying on. If either party wishes to cross-examine an **affiant** on his or her affidavit, it will probably be necessary to adjourn the hearing of the motion to conduct the cross-examination out of court, and then, by a supplementary notice of motion returnable on the date to which the original motion was adjourned, add the transcripts of cross-examination to the material to be used on the motion for summary judgment. Once all this has been done, counsel may appear before the judge or master and make oral submissions, after which the judge may give a judgment dismissing the motion, or granting judgment in the ways described earlier. However, judges now also have the power to hold mini trials and hear oral evidence either from the maker of the affidavit or from other witnesses. This may have the effect of reducing the need to cross-examine on affidavits.

In a motion for summary judgment, the plaintiff, in his affidavit, should focus on refuting with hard evidence the facts relied on by the defendant in the statement of defence. If there is reference to a contract, agreement, or other documents, those should be attached to the affidavit as exhibits, or relevant wording from them should be quoted directly in the affidavit. If there are complex or voluminous documents that are relevant to the issues, consider filing an **affidavit of documents** with a document brief as part of the evidence on which to rely. You would do this, for example, if there was no dispute that some debt was owing, but where there are complex financial records and there is some question about the accuracy of the records and about the amount owing. If necessary, file affidavits of other witnesses who have direct knowledge of evidence relevant to the issues, particularly where the plaintiff does not have direct knowledge. For example, if there is an issue about what payments were made on an account, the plaintiff's accounts receivable manager may be in a better position to give evidence than the plaintiff because the accounts receivable manager is likely to have direct knowledge of the relevant transactions. What is said here generally about organizing a case applies equally to a defendant who is moving for judgment to dismiss the action.

It is not possible here to do more than sketch the procedure for bringing a motion for summary judgment, because it can be complex and is more properly covered in a civil procedure text. Reference should be made to the *Rules of Civil Procedure*, in particular to rule 20 (summary judgment), rule 37 (motions and motion procedure), and rule 39 (evidence on motions and applications).

affidavit of documents
an affidavit in which a party identifies those documents that are relevant to the issues in the proceeding and that he has in his possession, power, and control and can produce; he must also identify those documents that he once had in his possession, power, and control but no longer has and those that he objects to producing; privileged documents, such as solicitor–client correspondence, will fall in the latter category; the documents being produced and relied on are contained in a document brief that is filed as evidence in the proceeding and may be referred to in court

CHAPTER SUMMARY

Chapter 7 identifies the general situations in which you would move for summary judgment and describes the standard you have to meet to obtain summary judgment. Situations in which it is likely you would move for summary judgment in an action for debt are described. The procedure for obtaining summary judgment is set out together with suggestions of the contents required for affidavits and the kinds of documents you should consider relying on. At the back of the chapter the documentation for a typical motion for summary judgment is set out.

KEY TERMS

affiant

affidavit of documents

master

motion

reference

taking of accounts

NOTES

1. *Rules of Civil Procedure*, rule 20.

2. Masters are not available in all judicial regions, but sit in Toronto, Ottawa, and London. The power of a master is more limited than that of a judge.

The power of a master to grant summary judgment under rule 20 is severely limited. A master cannot determine issues of law and does not have the authority to weigh and assess evidence and credibility, and to draw inferences from the evidence. A master could, perhaps, determine a summary judgment motion where the claim is based on an error concerning the quantum of damages where the quantum claimed is in fact based upon a typographical error. Where there is a choice, proceeding before a master may be quicker.

REFERENCES

Rules of Civil Procedure, RRO 1990, Reg. 194.

REVIEW QUESTIONS

1. In what circumstances would a party to a debt action bring a motion for summary judgment?

2. What does a party have to show to obtain a summary judgment?

3. What sort of material should be used as evidence to support a motion?

4. What kinds of orders can a judge make on a matter for summary judgment?

5. In what circumstances would judgment with a reference be given?

6. In what kinds of situations is it advisable to serve, and require from the other party, an affidavit of documents?

7. Describe the procedure and procedural steps to be taken to apply for a summary judgment.

8. How is a motion for summary judgment under the simplified procedure different from the process in an ordinary action?

CASE STUDY

M E M O

DATE: March 16, year 1

TO: U.R. Clerk

FROM: I.M. Principal

RE: Tallis ats Monteverdi

Joe Monteverdi sued our client Thomas Tallis for default on a written guarantee for a loan for his wife, Teodora Tallis. The loan for $100,000 was made on January 6, year 0. It was payable, together with interest at 10 percent per year, on January 6, year 1, the total then due being $110,000. Teodora didn't pay up. Monteverdi sued Teodora and our client based on his failure to honour the guarantee. We defended Thomas, and in the statement of defence said that Teodora and Monteverdi renegotiated the interest rate, raising it to 12 percent. No one told Thomas at the time, but Teodora mentioned it to him on December 15, year 0, when she told our client that she would have problems paying the note on January 6, year 1. Thomas was never given notice or asked to agree to continue his guarantee on the new terms, even though it is well known that when the terms of a contract are altered, where there is a guarantor, the right to claim against the guarantor after the contract is altered is void, unless the guarantor is given notice of the change and consents to it.

Draft a notice of motion and affidavit in support of our client's motion for summary judgment dismissing the plaintiff's action against him.

Figure 7.1   Motion Record

Court file no. 1234

ONTARIO

SUPERIOR COURT OF JUSTICE

B E T W E E N

ARTEMIS PLUMBING SUPPLY LTD.

Plaintiff

and

PERSONABLE PLUMBERS LTD.

Defendant

MOTION RECORD

Lawyers for the plaintiff: I.M. Just

Lawyers for the defendant: H.E.S. Evasive

1. Notice of Motion, dated November 3, year 0   Tab 1

2. Affidavit of Henry Freer, sworn October 28, year 0   Tab 2

    a. Exhibit A — accounts payable records of
        Personable Plumbers Ltd.   Tab A

    b. Exhibit B — cancelled cheque dated July 31, year 0
        in the amount of $32,000   Tab B

3. Statement of claim filed September 30, year 0   Tab 3

4. Statement of defence filed October 10, year 0   Tab 4

Figure 7.2 Notice of Motion for Summary Judgment (Form 37A)

Court file no. 1234

ONTARIO

SUPERIOR COURT OF JUSTICE

B E T W E E N

ARTEMIS PLUMBING SUPPLY LTD.

Plaintiff

and

PERSONABLE PLUMBERS LTD.

Defendant

NOTICE OF MOTION

THE DEFENDANT will make a motion to a judge on Wednesday, November 15, year 0 at 11:00 a.m. or, or as soon after that time as the motion can be heard, at 393 University Avenue, Toronto, ON M5G 1E6.

PROPOSED METHOD OF HEARING: The motion is to be heard

[   ]   in writing under subrule 37.12.1 (1) because it is on consent;

[   ]   in writing as an opposed motion under subrule 37.12.1 (4);

[x]   orally.

THE MOTION IS FOR summary judgment dismissing the action against the defendant pursuant to rule 20 of the *Rules of Civil Procedure*, or for such other order as this court deems appropriate.

THE GROUNDS FOR THE MOTION ARE rule 20 of the *Rules of Civil Procedure*.

Figure 7.2   Concluded

THE FOLLOWING DOCUMENTARY EVIDENCE will be used at the hearing of the motion:

1. The statements of claim and defence.

2. The affidavit of Henry Freer, dated October 28, year 0.

Date: November 11, year 0

H.E.S. Evasive   LSUC #56785E
Barrister and Solicitor
1256 Orfue Rd.
Toronto, ON M4R 1Y6
416-645-1267
FAX 416-645-1268
Lawyer for the Defendant

TO: I.M. Just   LSUC #12345A
JUST AND COPING
Barristers and Solicitors
8701 - 365 Bay Street
Toronto, ON M3J 4A9
416-762-1342
FAX 416-762-1343
Lawyers for the Plaintiff

RCP-E 37A (July 1, 2007)

Figure 7.3   Affidavit in Support of Motion for Summary Judgment

Court file no. 1234

ONTARIO

SUPERIOR COURT OF JUSTICE

B E T W E E N:

ARTEMIS PLUMBING SUPPLY LTD.

Plaintiff

and

PERSONABLE PLUMBERS LTD.

Defendant

AFFIDAVIT

I, Henry Freer, of the City of Toronto, MAKE OATH AND SAY:

1. I am the accounts payable manager of the defendant and, as such, have knowledge of the matters deposed to.

2. I have read the statement of claim and the statement of defence in this action.

3. I monitor all accounts payable, including those payable to the plaintiff. It is the defendant's policy to pay all debts as they become due and to pay down running accounts at regular intervals. Attached to my affidavit and marked Exhibit "A"* is a true copy of the accounts payable record, recording all payments made to the plaintiff for the last year, including the last payment made on July 31, year 0.

4. On July 31, year 0, I mailed a cheque, cheque no. 2345, dated July 31, year 0, payable to the plaintiff, in the amount of $32,000. This cheque was apparently cashed by the plaintiff's bank, and the cancelled cheque was returned to me in the ordinary course of business. Now attached to this affidavit and marked exhibit "B"** is a true copy of the cancelled cheque,

---

*   Exhibit A has been omitted from the affidavit to save space. Typically, copies are attached at the end of the document.

**   Exhibit B has been omitted from the affidavit to save space. Typically, copies are attached at the end of the document.

Figure 7.3 Concluded

payable to the plaintiff, and dated July 31, year 0, showing both the front of the cheque and the back.

5. As of the date of the making of this affidavit, our account records show a credit balance in favour of the defendant and not an unpaid balance as the plaintiff maintains.

SWORN before me at the	)	
	)	
City of Toronto,	)	
	)	*Henry Freer*
this 28th day of October, year 0	)	Henry Freer
	)	
I.M. Just	)	
	)	
A Commissioner, etc.	)	

RCP-E 16B (January 1, 2008)

CHAPTER 8

Defended Proceedings and Settlement

Up to this point we have examined debt proceedings where judgments have been obtained at an early stage of the proceeding either by default or by summary judgment. At this stage, much of the work that has to be done can be done by law clerks or paralegals;[1] a lawyer's involvement is often minimal.

However, if the action is defended with a serious and substantive defence, you will find yourself in a proceeding that may take a year or more to resolve itself through settlement or trial, and where carriage and control is likely to be in the hands of lawyers. The handling of this type of litigation, in detail, is beyond the scope of this book, but set out below is a checklist of the steps to be taken for contested litigation in the Superior Court.

In all cases, both parties should consider the concept of proportionality, as courts are directed to apply the rules of procedure by making orders and giving directions that are proportionate to the issues, the complexity of the case, and the amount involved. Competent lawyers have long applied this concept, even before it was required under the rules.[2]

STEPS IN A DEFENDED PROCEEDING

The following are steps taken in a defended proceeding:

- the plaintiff issues and serves the statement of claim and files Form 14F, Information for Court Use;[3]

- the defendant serves and files a notice of intent to defend[4] (optional) and/or a statement of defence;[5]

- the plaintiff may serve and file a reply with respect to any issue raised in the statement of defence that the plaintiff did not deal with in the statement of claim;

- the pleadings are noted closed — that is, no further pleadings may be filed without the court's permission;

discovery

a process where each party is asked questions under oath about the fact allegations in their pleadings and where the strength of the evidence with respect to the facts alleged can be tested; as well, credibility of the parties can be assessed and settlement options explored

trial record

a record that consists of the pleadings, pretrial orders, a solicitor's certificate that the record is complete, and, depending on the nature of the case, other documents as well; once a record has been served and filed, the registrar will put the matter on the trial list 60 days later

practice direction

a procedural directive issued by the chief justice of Ontario for the Superior Court or by a regional chief judge for a particular judicial region; a practice direction may clarify or supplement the procedural requirements of the *Rules of Civil Procedure*—at one time, there was some question about the authoritativeness of practice directions, but they are now clearly authorized by the *Rules of Civil Procedure*

- the plaintiff and defendant are required to work together to develop a discovery plan for discovery of documents and examination for discovery. The requirement for discovery plans includes specific directions for applying proportionality principles to discovery by requiring the parties to plan and stick to a discovery schedule and to focus on controlling the breadth and scope of discovery so that the time and expense of discovery is commensurate with what is at stake for the parties.[6] This last point is a particular problem when it comes to dealing with e-discovery and the increasing volume of documents due to the use of electronic data sources. Each party then prepares and serves the affidavits of documents and provides a document brief that contains all documents relevant to the action, or makes their documents available for inspection;

- **discovery** of the plaintiff and defendant, where each answers questions under oath on the facts and issues identified in the claim and defence takes place;

- either party may set the case down for trial by preparing, serving, and filing a **trial record**, after which the party filing the record may take no further pretrial proceedings; other parties may continue pretrial proceedings right up until trial;

- 60 days after the record has been filed, the registrar places the matter on the trial list. Note that in Toronto there is a commercial trial list for commercial litigation that includes debt actions; there are special rules that apply here. Some regional court offices have issued **practice directions** that apply to the judicial region whose chief judge issued the direction. Generally, practice directions are found printed along with the particular rule of civil procedure to which they relate. They are also published as notices in *Ontario Reports*, *Ontario Annual Practice*, and other commercially published compilations of the *Rules of Civil Procedure*;

- the registrar schedules a pretrial conference before a judge, where the parties will explore settlement and narrow the issues for trial if no settlement is achieved. Pretrial conferences are mandatory unless the court orders otherwise. A pretrial conference brief must be served and filed by each party;

- both parties can serve requests to admit, in which they ask each other to admit facts or allegations, so that these do not have to be formally proved at trial; and

- a party who intends to call an expert witness at trial must, 90 or more days before trial, serve the other parties with the expert's report that sets out the expert's name, address, and qualifications, as well as the substance of their proposed testimony. If the other party plans to call another expert to challenge the first expert they must serve that expert's report on the other side 60 or more days before trial.

- trial.

SETTLEMENT

Only a small fraction, probably less than 5 percent, of all civil actions commenced in the Superior Court actually go to trial. Most settle along the way. In order to encourage settlement in debt collection proceedings there are some things that should be done, particularly by plaintiffs:

- Stick closely to timelines in demand letters and where the *Rules of Civil Procedure* set out time limits. Adherence to deadlines sends a message that you are serious about collecting the debt and are determined to do so, and that there is no profit in the debtor delaying matters with the hope that you will go away.

- Once you have determined with your client what the bottom line is, consider making a formal offer to settle under rule 49 of the *Rules of Civil Procedure*. A plaintiff who makes an offer that is as good as or more favourable than the judgment obtained at trial will be rewarded with a higher costs award than is usual; a defendant who makes an offer that is as good as or more favourable than the judgment will be insulated from some of the costs that a defendant normally bears if he loses. It is the potentially punitive nature of a costs award that encourages parties to settle where they otherwise might not. The procedure involved in making an offer is discussed in more detail in the next section.

Formal Offers to Settle: Rule 49

Until seven days before the trial or hearing, an offer to settle may be made under rule 49, in writing, to the other side.

- If the plaintiff makes an offer and obtains a judgment that is as good as or more favourable than the offer, the plaintiff is entitled to partial indemnity costs to the date of the offer and substantial indemnity costs after the date of the offer.

- If the defendant makes an offer and the plaintiff obtains a judgment, but the judgment is only as favourable as the offer, or less favourable than the offer, then the plaintiff is entitled to partial indemnity costs to the date of the offer, and the defendant is entitled to partial indemnity costs thereafter.

- This treatment of the plaintiff also applies where the plaintiff's action is dismissed in its entirety at the end of the trial[7] (if no offer was made and the action was dismissed, the defendant would likely have received costs on a partial indemnity basis throughout).

- If both parties make offers to settle, and the judgment is more than the plaintiff's offer, but less than the defendant's offer, the plaintiff will usually receive partial indemnity costs throughout the action.

Offers that fall under the rule 49 costs provisions must be made at least seven days before the trial begins. An offer should be considered and made as early as possible, and certainly as soon as you are able to assess the strengths and weaknesses of your case and that of your opponent. This forces the other side to look at settlement, and can result in a reasonable settlement with greatly reduced litigation costs for both parties. You may be able to assess your case with respect to settlement at the close of pleadings, and should be able to do so on completing discovery — certainly by completion of the pre-trial conference.

A Settlement Timeline

An offer to settle, whether formal or informal, may be made at any time: before proceedings commence, during proceedings, or after judgment. Offers may be made informally, formally under rule 49, "**with prejudice**," or "**without prejudice**." Depending on when an offer to settle is made, there are certain procedural steps that should be taken to safeguard the rights of both parties. The box on the facing page gives an overview of the documentation that you must consider when settling under various circumstances.

When negotiating a settlement, if a debtor misrepresents his affairs so that a creditor accepts less than what she is legally entitled to, she may move to set aside the settlement and sue for false or fraudulent misrepresentation. Therefore, in all settlements for less than the full amount due, including interest and costs, whether before or after judgment, the plaintiff should require the debtor to furnish a statutory declaration (figure 8.6) of the debtor's financial situation covering the last five years. This document should identify assets that have been conveyed and list all the assets of the debtor in that period.

Settlement Before Proceedings Commence

If the debtor agrees to settle for the amount in the demand letter or a negotiated amount less than demanded, the creditor will require a lump-sum payment by certified cheque, or payment with a series of post-dated cheques. The debtor will want to have a release of liability and acknowledgment of payment of the obligation, particularly if the debtor has settled for less than the full amount owing. The creditor should be prepared to provide a release (figure 8.1) once the payment is made. If payment involves post-dated cheques, the creditor should be prepared to acknowledge in writing that a release is held and will be provided to the debtor when the last payment has been made. The creditor should also hold a consent to judgment (figure 8.2) in the event of default allowing the creditor to sue for the debt free of any defence by the debtor.

Settlement After Proceedings Commence

As above, the debtor should provide a certified cheque or post-dated cheques for the agreed amount. Because there is a lawsuit in existence, steps must be taken to conclude it. This can be achieved by both parties signing minutes of settlement (figure 8.3) to dismiss the action, with or without costs; a consent judgment (figure 8.4) dismissing the action must also be prepared and filed after the last payment is made. A release may also be required by the debtor.

The action, however, is not dismissed until the amount due is paid. In the event that the amounts due are not paid, the plaintiff holds a consent to judgment (figure 8.2), agreed to in the minutes of settlement or set out in a separate consent to judgment and signed by both parties. On default of payment, the plaintiff files the consent to judgment, or the minutes containing the consent, and a judgment for the amount agreed to

with prejudice
a phrase used in connection with attempts to settle; when it is used (usually at the start of a letter), it signifies that the writer intends to make an offer that he is prepared to disclose to the court during the trial; such disclosure indicates that the party does not fear that disclosure will prejudice his case; rather the idea is that it will enhance his case by showing him to be reasonable, and otherwise presenting him in a favourable light

without prejudice
a phrase used in connection with attempts to settle; unlike "with prejudice" letters, this phrase means that statements will be made in the letter that are made solely in the context of an offer and the letter may not be disclosed to the court, even if it contains damaging statements or admissions; the making of an offer on a without-prejudice basis allows for a free and frank discussion of settlement, without the loss of the ability to present a case to the court, where the court is not prejudiced by admissions made in the course of settlement

Settlement Timeline

Before Proceedings Commence	After Proceedings Commence	After Judgment
• letter confirming terms of settlement	• minutes of settlement	• letter confirming terms of settlement
• certified cheque or post-dated cheques	• consent to judgment (may be included in minutes of settlement)	• satisfaction piece (accord and satisfaction)
• release for debtor	• certified cheque or post-dated cheques	• file execution
• consent to judgment	• consent to dismiss action (may be included in minutes of settlement)	• certified cheque or post-dated cheques
• statutory declaration	• release for debtor	• lift execution when paid
	• statutory declaration	• statutory declaration

or the original amount claimed and not paid, with the court. This should result in a default judgment because the debtor has no defence to the action. The plaintiff may then proceed to enforce the judgment in the usual ways.

Settlement After Judgment

When the plaintiff has obtained a judgment and then settles with the judgment debtor, the debtor must provide a certified cheque or a series of post-dated cheques to the plaintiff. When this has happened and the payments have been made, the creditor provides the debtor with a satisfaction piece (figure 8.5) (sometimes called an accord and satisfaction), which acknowledges payment of the agreed amount, even if it is less than the judgment. The satisfaction piece indicates that the judgment has been paid and is no longer enforceable. Although the debtor is making the payments, any writs of execution should be left in place and, if they have not been filed, they should be filed in any region or county where the debtor has assets. This will serve to give notice to the plaintiff if other creditors seek to enforce writs against the debtor, and will ensure that the plaintiff has a grip on some share of the assets of the debtor if enforcement by other creditors occurs.[8] Once the final payment has been made, the plaintiff should write to the sheriff to ask for withdrawal of the writ of seizure and sale.

For further assurance that there are assets belonging to the debtor that are available to support the settlement and that no other creditors are waiting in the wings to claim assets, the debtor may be required to provide a statutory declaration setting out the debtor's asset and liability situation. A sample statutory declaration by a debtor is set out in figure 8.6.

CHAPTER SUMMARY

This chapter provides an overview of a contested action from commencement of proceedings to trial. The advantages of settlement are discussed, and formal offers to settle under rule 49 are described, as are other less formal settlement procedures. Settlement is then discussed in terms of the stage of the action reached when settlement occurs. There are different legal requirements and safeguards reflected in the settlement documentation depending on whether settlement occurs before a proceeding is commenced, after a proceeding is commenced, or after judgment has been obtained.

KEY TERMS

discovery

practice direction

trial record

with prejudice

without prejudice

NOTES

1. A paralegal working on a Superior Court of Justice case must do so under a lawyer's supervision, unless the case is in the Small Claims Court where those matters can be done by a paralegal on their own.

2. Rule 1.04(1.1) of the *Rules of Civil Procedure* requires parties to now consider proportionality in every case.

3. A sample of Form 14F can be found at page 106 in chapter 5.

4. A sample notice of intent to defend can be found in chapter 5 in figure 5.5.

5. A sample statement of defence can be found in chapter 5 in figure 5.6.

6. Rules 29.1 and 29.2 set out the requirements for discovery plans.

7. Rule 49 is not explicit about this approach where a plaintiff's action is dismissed, but it is an approach sanctioned by the Ontario Court of Appeal: *Strasser Ltd. v. Richmond Hill* (1990), 1 OR (3d) 243 (CA).

8. You will recall that under the *Creditors' Relief Act*, RSO 1990, c. C.45, all execution creditors share ratably with respect to the proceeds where one creditor has successfully levied execution.

REFERENCES

Ontario Reports, The Law Society of Upper Canada (Toronto: LSUC).

Rules of Civil Procedure, RRO 1990, reg. 194.

REVIEW QUESTIONS

1. What are the steps taken in a defended proceeding?

2. What is the significance of the concept of proportionality?

3. What is the purpose of oral discovery and discovery of documents (affidavit of documents)?

4. What is the Commercial List?

5. Why should a plaintiff make a formal offer to settle? Why should a defendant make one?

6. What are the consequences if the defendant makes an offer to settle and the plaintiff refuses the offer, goes to trial and wins, but obtains judgment for an amount that is less than the offer?

7. What documents do you need to prepare if a debt is settled after a demand letter is sent but before litigation starts?

8. What does "without prejudice" at the top of a letter mean?

9. If the debtor proposes to pay by a series of post-dated cheques and no action is commenced, what should the creditor do to safeguard his interests? What should the debtor require of the creditor once all payments have been made?

10. If the debtor pays the debt after proceedings have been commenced, what must be done to terminate the proceedings?

11. Suppose the debtor agrees to settle the debt after judgment has been obtained. What documents will the creditor require? What documents will the debtor require?

CASE STUDY

MEMO

DATE:　　September 15, year 0

FROM:　　L.A. Principal

TO:　　U.R. Clerk

RE:　　Artesian Wells Ltd. v. Grumble

We sued Samuel Grumble on behalf of our client in June year 0 for $40,000 for drilling a water well on Grumble's lot. The action no. is 3423/year 0. The amount outstanding now with interest is $40,600. I have reviewed our costs to date and they amount to about $500 in recoverable costs. The parties have agreed to a settlement where the defendant will pay $40,200 in total, on September 25, year 0, for all of our client's claim, interest, costs, and expenses.

1. Draft all of the documents except those that the defendant will draft because the defendant has knowledge of the information to be included. Use September 16, year 0, as the date for the minutes. Assume that if payment is not received, then judgment will be signed on November 6, year 0, by the Honourable Mr. Justice Smith.

2. Suppose you are acting for the defendant. He has no debts and owns only the property on which the well was drilled — Part Lot 8, Concession 678, Township of Lutterworth, Haliburton County — which is worth $105,000. He has not sold any property, real or personal, since year −6. Draft the documents that the defendant is required to furnish in the proceeding.

Figure 8.1   Sample Release

BETWEEN

ARTEMIS PLUMBING SUPPLY LTD.

Creditor

and

PERSONABLE PLUMBERS LTD.

Debtor

RELEASE

ARTEMIS PLUMBING SUPPLY LTD. (ARTEMIS), on payment of $32,000 now made to Artemis, releases PERSONABLE PLUMBERS LTD. from all liability arising from a debt on a running account #12345, comprising debits up to and including July 31, year 0. The parties agree that this account has, as of the date of this release, a nil balance.

Dated at Toronto this 6th day of November, year 0

ARTEMIS PLUMBING SUPPLY LTD.

By: _____   *(corporate seal)*
    President*

---

*   A corporation signs documents by the signature of those authorized by its articles or by-laws to sign on its behalf. The corporate seal should also be affixed.

Figure 8.2   Sample Consent to Judgment*

Court file no. 1234

ONTARIO

SUPERIOR COURT OF JUSTICE

B E T W E E N

ARTEMIS PLUMBING SUPPLY LTD.

Plaintiff

and

PERSONABLE PLUMBERS LTD.

Defendant

CONSENT TO JUDGMENT

The parties consent to judgment in this action on the following terms:

1. The defendant acknowledges that it is indebted to the plaintiff in the amount of $32,000 including interest and costs in respect of a running account the defendant maintained with the plaintiff.

2. The defendant undertakes to pay this indebtedness by giving to the plaintiff four post-dated cheques, payable to the plaintiff in the amount of $8,000 each, on the first day of the following months: December year 0, January year 1, February year 1, and March year 1.

3. If the defendant defaults on any of the four payments referred to in paragraph 2 of this consent, the defendant shall be liable to pay the balance then outstanding, which becomes immediately due and owing, and the defendant hereby consents to the plaintiff obtaining a judgment for the balance then outstanding, and for a further $300 in costs.

Dated at Toronto this 6th day of November, year 0

PERSONABLE PLUMBERS LTD.

By: _____   *(corporate seal)*

---

*   If this consent to judgment is used where no action has been commenced, then it should not have the title of proceedings used for court documents, but should have a heading similar to the one in figure 8.1, Sample Release.

Figure 8.3   Sample Minutes of Settlement

Court file no. 1234

ONTARIO

SUPERIOR COURT OF JUSTICE

BETWEEN

ARTEMIS PLUMBING SUPPLY LTD.

Plaintiff

and

PERSONABLE PLUMBERS LTD.

Defendant

MINUTES OF SETTLEMENT

THE PARTIES TO THIS ACTION consent to the dismissal of this action without costs on the following terms:

1. The defendant shall pay to the plaintiff by certified cheque or money order the sum of $32,000 on or before August 10, year 0.

2. Upon receipt of payment from the defendant, the plaintiff shall, by these minutes, consent to dismiss the action without costs and obtain a judgment dismissing the action without costs. The parties consent to a judgment in the form attached hereto as schedule "A."*

3. The parties, by their lawyers, hereby certify that the judgment being consented to does not affect the rights of any person under disability.

4. In the event that the defendant fails to make the payment referred to in paragraph 1 of these minutes, they shall, by these minutes, consent to the plaintiff obtaining a judgment for the sum of $32,000 and a further $500 for costs.

Dated at Toronto this 6th day of November, year 0

ARTEMIS PLUMBING SUPPLY LTD.

By its lawyers: _____

PERSONABLE PLUMBERS LTD.

By its lawyers: _____

---

*   Schedule A is not attached to these minutes; however, figure 8.2 is the draft judgment that would be attached here.

Figure 8.4   Sample Consent Judgment

Court file no. 1234

ONTARIO

SUPERIOR COURT OF JUSTICE

JUSTICE _____   _____day, the ___ day
                                                        of _____, year 0

(court seal)

B E T W E E N

ARTEMIS PLUMBING SUPPLY LTD.

Plaintiff

and

PERSONABLE PLUMBERS LTD.

Defendant

JUDGMENT

On reading the pleadings in this action and the minutes of settlement filed consenting to the dismissal of this action without costs,

1. IT IS ORDERED AND ADJUDGED that this action be dismissed without costs.

This judgment bears interest at the rate of ____ per cent per year from its date.

_____

Figure 8.5   Satisfaction Piece (Acknowledgment of Satisfaction of Judgment)

Court file no. 1234

ONTARIO

SUPERIOR COURT OF JUSTICE

B E T W E E N

ARTEMIS PLUMBING SUPPLY LTD.

Plaintiff

and

PERSONABLE PLUMBERS LTD.

Defendant

ACKNOWLEDGMENT OF SATISFACTION OF JUDGMENT

Satisfaction is acknowledged of the judgment dated Wednesday, November 6, year 0, in

an action in the Ontario Superior Court of Justice, in which Artemis Plumbing Supply

Ltd. was the plaintiff, Personable Plumbers Ltd. was the defendant, and it was adjudged

that the plaintiff should recover from the defendant the sum of $32,000 for debt together

with a further sum of $385 for costs.

Figure 8.5 Concluded

The plaintiff, Artemis Plumbing Supply Ltd., nominates its lawyer, Peter Pugnacious, to witness and attest the plaintiff's acknowledgment of satisfaction of this judgment.

H. Dorkin
_____
Artemis Plumbing Supply Ltd.
by its President, Henry Dorkin

(Signed by Henry Dorkin on
(behalf of the plaintiff on
(February 19, year 1 in
(the presence of Peter
(Pugnacious, a lawyer of
(the Ontario Superior Court
(of Justice.
(AND I, Peter Pugnacious,
(declare myself to be the
(lawyer for the
(plaintiff, expressly named
(by it, and attending at the
(plaintiff's request to
(inform the plaintiff and
(its designated
(representative of the
(nature and effect of this
(acknowledgment of
(satisfaction.
(I so informed the
(plaintiff's designated
(representative before he
(executed the accord and
(satisfaction on behalf of
(the plaintiff.
(In testimony whereof, I
(subscribe my name as
(solicitor for the
(plaintiff.
(
(
(_____
(*Peter Pugnacious*
(Peter Pugnacious
(

Figure 8.6   Statutory Declaration

STATUTORY DECLARATION

CANADA

PROVINCE OF ONTARIO

IN THE MATTER OF A JUDGMENT AGAINST PERSONABLE PLUMBERS LTD. ON WEDNESDAY, THE 6TH DAY OF NOVEMBER, YEAR 0 IN FAVOUR OF ARTEMIS PLUMBING SUPPLY LTD., COURT FILE NO. 1234

TO WIT:

I, I.M. Fitter

of the City **of** Toronto

DO SOLEMNLY DECLARE THAT:

1.   I am a representative of the defendant in the action by Artemis Plumbing Supply Ltd. against Personable Plumbers Ltd. The defendant is indebted to the plaintiff pursuant to a judgment dated November 6, year 0 for the sum of $32,000 and $385 for costs.

2.   The defendant has a 5-year commercial lease, which expires on February 1, year 4 for 15,000 sq. metres of warehouse space at 321 Daynor Dr., North York, ON, unit 25-27. The defendant has and has had no other interest in any real estate in Ontario or elsewhere since October, year –5.

3.   Attached is a list of the assets of the defendant that are worth more than $1,000.

4.   The defendant has not sold, transferred, conveyed, or otherwise disposed of any property, real or personal, other than inventory in the ordinary course of business since October, year –5.

5.   Attached are corporate income tax returns of the defendant, with attached schedules and notices of assessment for the past 5 years.

6.   Attached are audited financial statements of the defendant for the past 5 years.

7.   Attached are a list of all the liabilities of the defendant.

AND I make this solemn Declaration conscientiously believing it to be true, and knowing that it is of the same force and effect as if made under oath.

DECLARED before me at the City

of Toronto

in the Province

of Ontario

this 18th **day of** November, year 0

_____

A Commissioner, etc.

_____

I.M. Fitter

Figure 8.6   Concluded

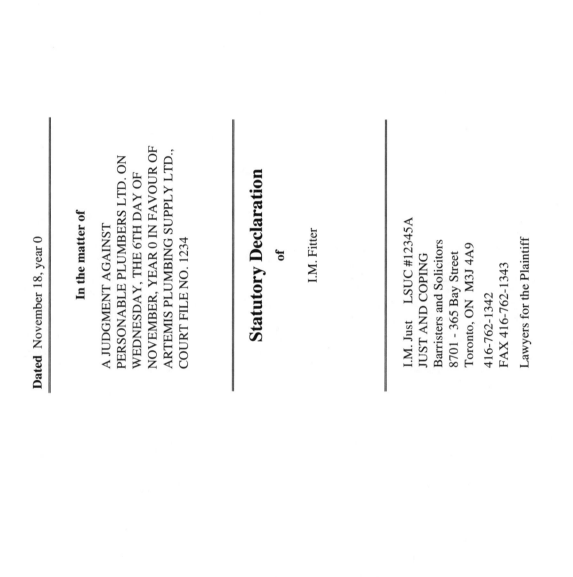

Dated November 18, year 0

In the matter of

A JUDGMENT AGAINST PERSONABLE PLUMBERS LTD. ON WEDNESDAY, THE 6TH DAY OF NOVEMBER, YEAR 0 IN FAVOUR OF ARTEMIS PLUMBING SUPPLY LTD., COURT FILE NO. 1234

Statutory Declaration

of

I.M. Fitter

I.M. Just   LSUC #12345A
JUST AND COPING
Barristers and Solicitors
8701 - 365 Bay Street
Toronto, ON M3J 4A9

416-762-1342
FAX 416-762-1343

Lawyers for the Plaintiff

CHAPTER 9

Enforcement of Superior Court Judgments

In collection matters where the debt is not secured, so that the creditor does not have the right to seize a particular asset to satisfy the debt, Superior Court judgments are usually enforced using some or all of the following enforcement techniques:

- examination in aid of execution, rule 60.18;

- writ of seizure and sale, rule 60.07;

- garnishment, rule 60.18;

- writ of sequestration, rule 60.09;

- injunctions;[1] and

- court appointment of a receiver, rule 60.02.

The most commonly used of these methods in routine collection matters are discussed in some detail in this chapter: examinations in aid of execution (also called judgment debtor examinations), writs of seizure and sale, and garnishment. Rule 60 of the *Rules of Civil Procedure* governs the enforcement process. Rule 60 is set out in Appendix A in Part IV of this book.

EXAMINATION IN AID OF EXECUTION

The examination in aid of execution, or judgment debtor examination (the JD exam), is not usually considered an enforcement technique; rather, it is an investigative tool that allows you to find out what assets of the debtor are available to satisfy a judgment so that you can use enforcement tools such as writs of seizure and sale and garnishment to tap those assets to satisfy the judgment. However, the JD exam also presents an informal opportunity for the debtor to be persuaded to make arrangements with you to pay off the judgment on mutually acceptable terms.

A judgment creditor may examine a judgment debtor under oath, once a year, asking the debtor questions about assets, liabilities, current obligations, expected future income, current income, and so on. The goal is for the creditor to find out all he can about the nature, extent, and location of the debtor's assets. The creditor may ask the debtor why he has not paid the judgment, what his assets consist of, what his income sources are, what other debts he has, whether he has disposed of major assets in the last few years, whether he has transferred assets recently to relatives, and any other relevant questions. Cases indicate that the scope of questions is broad and the court is permissive in allowing creditors a great deal of leeway in framing questions. You should take extensive notes on the debtor's answers about what assets he has. This may enable you to avoid ordering transcripts of the examination, which can be quite expensive.

If the defendant is a corporation, an officer or director of the company may be summoned for examination. The choice of whom to summon is initially that of the creditor and she should choose an officer or director who she knows is knowledgeable about the issues and the company's assets and liabilities. If the creditor simply summons "an officer or director," the defendant may very well send someone who is not knowledgeable and who ends up giving unhelpful answers, requiring motions for re-attendance or for requests for undertakings to find out information. This delays the recovery of assets and raises costs.

Similarly, a partner may be summoned to answer questions on behalf of a partnership debtor, and an owner may be summoned to answer questions on behalf of a sole proprietorship.

If the judgment creditor has had difficulty in enforcing the judgment, has exhausted alternative enforcement options, and can show that some other person has relevant knowledge that will aid in enforcement, Rule 60.18 of the *Rules of Civil Procedure* permits the creditor to ask the court for permission to summons a non-party to be examined. For example, if it appears that the debtor has recently transferred a substantial asset to a relative, you may wish to obtain an order to examine this relative about the circumstances surrounding the transfer to see if it is or appears to be a fraudulent conveyance. Remember, however, that you are asking for an unusual remedy and that the court, in the case of a non-party, is reluctant to draw in non-parties to a proceeding without compelling reasons.

Where the judgment creditor has found that new circumstances have arisen since the last examination, the judgment creditor may also ask the court for permission to examine the judgment debtor more frequently than once a year. Consider the previous example where it appears that the debtor has transferred property to a relative. In addition to examining the relative, you may also have grounds to re-examine the debtor on this transaction — in fact, you may be able to examine both the debtor and the relative in these circumstances.

It is also worth noting that if, during the course of examining a debtor, you discover that a debtor has concealed or moved property to defeat or defraud creditors, you may wish to bring a motion that the debtor be held in contempt. You may bring the motion at the conclusion of the examination, or you may adjourn the examination in order to bring the motion for contempt, and resume the examination after the contempt order is made.

If a judgment debtor does not attend when summoned, refuses to answer questions, or is otherwise uncooperative or obstructive, you may bring a motion to hold the judgment debtor in contempt of court and, in the alternative, ask the court to require the judgment debtor to attend the JD exam again at his own expense. A court will rarely jail someone for contempt on such a motion. Rather, the usual order is for the judgment debtor to re-attend at his own expense to answer your questions. You may and should ask the court to make an order of costs against the judgment debtor if you are successful on the motion, and ask that the costs be fixed and paid immediately as a precondition to being ordered to re-attend to answer questions. Because the court will likely give the debtor a further chance to re-attend to answer questions before using the contempt power to imprison, asking for costs to be fixed and paid helps to drive home to the debtor that you are serious about exercising the creditor's rights. Ultimately, if the judgment debtor is still uncooperative, he can be jailed for contempt.

In situations where a judgment debtor is being uncooperative on the examination, you will want to avoid having to personally serve a second contempt motion if the judgment debtor fails to re-attend or answer questions or otherwise fails to purge himself of his contempt. After all, an uncooperative judgment debtor already cited for contempt once on a motion is hardly likely to make it easy for you to serve him personally on a second contempt motion. In order to avoid having to bring and serve a further contempt motion if the judgment debtor continues to be uncooperative after the first contempt motion has been heard ask the court at the first motion to adjourn your request to commit the debtor to jail for contempt, which will allow you to bring the adjourned part of the motion back to court on short notice if the court orders re-attendance and the debtor continues to be uncooperative. If the judgment debtor is still uncooperative, you may bring the adjourned part of the motion back before the court with minimal paperwork and in a relatively short time, and without having to re-serve the debtor personally.

In order to summons a judgment debtor for examination, it is advisable to serve the judgment debtor personally with a notice of examination (figure 9.1), although you may serve him or her using an alternative to personal service.

The reason for using personal service is that personal service is required to be proved as a prerequisite to finding the judgment debtor in contempt for non-attendance. Some commentators[2] suggest that when serving the notice, you may wish to attach a note to the notice of examination requesting that the person being examined produce detailed information and documents about certain assets or liabilities of which you have some knowledge through earlier investigations at the start of proceedings, or through things you have learned during the proceedings. You may also wish to attach a standard checklist (see the box on page 186) to focus the judgment debtor's mind on assets or interests that are relevant. (Following figure 9.1 are two sets of questions: one to be used when examining an individual debtor, and another to be used when examining an officer or representative of a corporate judgment debtor.)

The particular circumstances of the case should determine the questions you ask, although most people working in this field follow the checklist developed by Frank Bennett for the Law Society Bar Admission Course for individuals and corporations. For adapted versions of these checklists, see pages 205 to 216.

Standard Checklist To Be Attached to Notice of Examination of Judgment Debtor*

To the judgment debtor: In preparing to attend a judgment-debtor examination touching upon your means and ability to pay what you owe to the judgment creditor you are required to provide all documentation in your power, possession, or control, and to provide detailed information with respect to the following:

1. shares and stocks
2. bonds
3. accounts receivable
4. real estate
5. mortgages
6. leases
7. insurance policies
8. debts
9. furniture
10. motor vehicle licence plate and serial numbers
11. bank accounts — account numbers and balances
12. mutual funds — account numbers and current value
13. RRSPs
14. pensions
15. term deposits, GICs
16. jewellery
17. art collections
18. other collections of value
19. watercraft and aircraft
20. assets located outside of Ontario
21. assets located outside of Canada

---

*   Adapted from a checklist suggested by F. Bennett, *Bennett on Collections*, 5th ed. (Toronto: Carswell, 2003), 308-28.

WRIT OF SEIZURE AND SALE

Under the authority of the writ of seizure and sale (also called a writ of execution), the sheriff may seize and sell the real and personal property of the execution debtor, subject to certain exceptions, and sell the seized assets and then distribute the net proceeds of sale ratably among all of the judgment creditors who have filed writs of seizure and sale with the sheriff who has levied execution. Remember that sheriffs operate each within their own county. If a sheriff seizes property in Ottawa, execution creditors with writs filed in Toronto will not share in the proceeds, unless they have also filed duplicate writs with the sheriff in Ottawa.

In chapter 6 in the discussion about obtaining a default judgment, you saw that when you obtained a default judgment you requisitioned the local registrar to issue a writ of seizure and sale. You then filed the writ with the sheriff in each county where you had reason to believe the debtor had property. The writ, when filed, could passively assist the creditor who might share in the proceeds of sale brought about by another execution creditor seizing assets of the debtor. The writ also served as notice to other persons having dealings with the debtor of the creditor's judgment against that creditor. For example, a bank lending the debtor money on a mortgage will not advance funds if it discovers an **execution** filed against the debtor. It will require the execution to be paid off by the debtor before advancing mortgage funds.

The Rules now provide, where available, for the electronic issue of a writ of seizure and sale. Special software is required to do this: see rules 4.05.1 and 60.07(1.1)-(1.4).

Although it is a common and recommended practice to automatically file a writ of seizure and sale on obtaining a judgment, you do not normally instruct the sheriff to seize a particular asset, unless you have

- identified the asset with sufficient particularity that the sheriff is able to locate it and verify its identity;

- obtained a quote from the sheriff as to the cost of seizure and sale and the deposit required to start the process, and obtained the client's consent to incur the expense;

- determined that the debtor has an interest in the asset that can be seized; and

- determined where the asset is located so that the sheriff can be told where to go to seize it.

It is important to note that the sheriff will not do your homework for you or carry out investigations to locate an asset. You have to provide as much information as possible about the asset that you wish to have seized.

Once you have this information, you should complete and send to the sheriff a direction to enforce (figure 9.2). In a direction to enforce you provide

- the date of the judgment and the amount, including costs;

- the postjudgment interest rate;

- the cost of enforcement for issuing the writ of seizure and sale and for the sheriff's fees in filing and enforcing the writ (from the tariff for court and sheriff fees, under the *Administration of Justice Act*, O. Reg. 293/92, as

execution
an act of the sheriff in enforcing a writ of seizure and sale (commonly referred to as a writ of execution), writ of delivery, or writ of sequestration; the word "execution" is also used to describe individual writs of execution on file; when a lawyer "searches executions" she is examining the sheriff's records to see if any writs of seizure and sale are filed with the sheriff

amended). Note that rule 60.19(2)(a) limits the lawyer's preparation fee for a writ to $50;

- the dates and amounts of payments received since the date of judgment, if any; and

- the total amount owing including postjudgment interest to date.

This form does not give the sheriff any useful information to enforce the writ, so you should attach a letter giving explicit directions about what should be seized. Also, you must determine from the Sheriff's Office the amount of the deposit required before the sheriff will seize a **chattel**. If you are seizing bank accounts, try to obtain the location of the branch and the account number. If you are seizing an automobile or any other chattel, provide information about where it can be found. It is useful to provide an up-to-date *Personal Property Security Act* (PPSA) search report to show that assets being seized are either free of the claims of secured creditors or subject to the claims of secured creditors. For example, if you wish to seize the debtor's automobile, you should provide a Statement of Driving Record (figure 3.1, at page 63) and a Certified Plate Search—Recent Owner (figure 3.2, at page 64) from the Ministry of Transportation, along with a PPSA Motor Vehicle Enquiry (figure 3.9, at page 77) in the name of the debtor, and information about where the car is likely to be found and when, so that the sheriff can have it towed away. If your information is correct, the sheriff will attend at the place where the asset is located and seize the asset. If the sheriff meets with resistance, he is entitled to call upon the police to assist his officers in the execution of their duty. If the debtor raises legal objections to a seizure and sues or threatens to sue the sheriff, the sheriff will bring an interpleader motion. This motion asks for direction from the court as to what he is to do with the seized asset. The usual order is to dispose of it by sale, declare the sheriff to be without liability, but hold the proceeds until the court determines the rights of the disputants to the proceeds. Note that the sheriff is not immune from being sued. For example, if the sheriff disposes of assets at an abnormally low price, he can be held to have been negligent in the performance of his duty.

Once you have a judgment, you have an absolute right to enforce it and requisition a writ of seizure and sale. If you don't immediately issue a writ, you may do so at any time within six years of the judgment. If you wish to issue a writ after six years have passed, or if there is a **condition precedent** to be fulfilled before a writ is issued (for example, where payment is specified for a future date), then you must bring a motion, for leave to issue the writ, to the court that gave the judgment. If you obtain an order giving leave to issue the writ, you may issue it at any time within a year of the date on which the order was made (rules 60.07(2) and (3)). Note that the sheriff can decline to enforce a writ. It is important to give the sheriff as much information as possible to enforce a writ. If the sheriff is uncertain as to whether a writ is properly issued or filed, he or she may refuse to enforce it, at which point the creditor may bring a motion for directions. In the past, the sheriff's right of refusal to enforce was implicit (in that you could always bring a motion to get the judicial process to do something), but it is now explicit in rule 60.07(13.1).

The process for filing and executing writs of seizure and sale is changing with the advent of limited use of electronic filings.

- Under rule 60.07(1.1), a creditor is entitled to the electronic issue of one or more writs by electronically filing a requisition under rule 4.05.1(2). The order

chattel
an item of tangible personal property (tangible means it is a thing, like a car); intangible personal property refers to a right to something of value—for example, a cheque, which is a right to payment

condition precedent
a situation where one must do A before one is allowed to do B—A is the condition precedent to the performance of the condition B

on which the writ is based is deemed to have been entered as an order of the Superior Court. This should speed up and simplify the process of issuing a writ, saving both time and money.

- Under rules 60.07(10) and (11.1), where a debtor uses an alias or a variation of the name on the writ, the writ may, on motion, be amended electronically.

- There is now a special rule for electronic filing of writs by the Workplace Safety and Insurance Board.

- If the address of a creditor or a creditor's lawyer changes, the change may be filed electronically under rules 60.07(12.1) and (12.2).

Note that special software is required for electronic filing.

Because a judgment may be unsatisfied for years, and because a writ of seizure and sale expires six years after it is issued, it is necessary to apply to renew the writ. The rules no longer require the sheriff to give notice of expiry of the writ to the creditor's lawyer, so you have to diarize the renewal date. If the creditor wishes to renew the writ, she may do so by filing a request to renew (figure 9.3), in which case the writ is automatically renewed. If a writ has been obtained but not filed with the sheriff, you can renew the writ at the end of six years by requisitioning renewal from the registrar. (Following figure 9.3 is a sample letter to a client with regard to renewal of a writ of seizure and sale.). Under rule 60.07(8.1), you can now electronically file a request to renew a writ.

After suing and obtaining judgment you may discover that the judgment debtor has changed his name legally, goes by another name or alias, or uses a variation of the spelling of his name. If you find this to be the case, you may bring a motion without notice to the debtor, to the court that gave the original judgment, asking that the writ be amended, using the phrase "now known as" or "also known as" followed by the alias, new name, or spelling variation, as the case may be (rule 60.07(10)). The same process may be followed if the address of the creditor or her lawyer changes from the time the writ was first issued (rule 60.07(12)). Under rule 60.07(11.1) the court may grant the creditor leave to file an amendment to the writ electronically under subrule 4.05.1(2) to show the new name, the alias, or the spelling variation.

Procedure Governing Sale

Once the sheriff has seized an asset — for example, the debtor's automobile — the sheriff must follow the procedure set out in rules 60.07(16) to (24). Where personal property is seized, the sheriff must, if requested by the debtor, furnish a list of what has been seized within a reasonable time after the seizure. Before arranging a sale, the sheriff must give public notice of the time and place of the sale and give notice to the creditor and the debtor.

More stringent rules govern the sale of land by the sheriff. First, no step to sell land under a writ may be taken until the writ has been filed for at least four months, and no sale may take place until six months have passed since the writ was filed (rules 60.07(17) and (18)). Notice of sale must be given in the *Ontario Gazette* 30 days before the sale, and in a general circulation newspaper at least once each week in two successive weeks. The successive notices must start no earlier than three weeks before the sale and finish no later than one week before the sale. Notice must also be given by mail to the creditor's lawyer and to the debtor. Notice must also be posted in the Sheriff's Office (rule 60.07(19)). The contents of the notice are prescribed by rule 60.07(20) and include:

- a short description of the land (lot and plan, and municipal address, if any);

- the short title of the proceedings (for example, *Smith v. Jones*);

- the time and place of the intended sale; and

- the name of the debtor whose interest is being sold.

Although the sheriff is not obliged to get the top market price for land or personal property, he must get the best prices he can in the circumstances of a sheriff's sale. Buyers know that sheriff sales are distress sales and that the seller's bargaining power is somewhat less than it would be on the open commercial market. If the sheriff considers it necessary to adjourn a sale to a later date to get the best price possible, he may do so, giving such further notice of the later sale as he deems appropriate. If property remains unsold because there are no buyers, the sheriff must inform the creditor of this fact. On receipt of this notice, the creditor can instruct the sheriff to proceed to sell in a way that will attract buyers and get the best price possible.

Normally, the sheriff will conduct sales by public auction, because that process permits anyone interested to see what prices are offered and that the best price was accepted. If the sheriff obtains an inordinately low price and accepts it rather than trying other sale times or methods, any party affected may be able to sue the sheriff successfully for negligence.

GARNISHMENT

If the judgment debtor does not have assets on which a creditor can levy execution, he may have income from various sources that can be attached. These income sources can be tapped by a creditor using a procedure known as garnishment. Here the creditor (garnishor) obtains an order requiring a third party (garnishee) to pay money the garnishee owes to the debtor to the creditor-garnishor instead. Funds attached in this way reduce the sum the debtor owes to the creditor. The garnishee is deemed to have paid what she owes to the debtor, even though the sum was diverted to the creditor.

Garnishment can be used to attach such things as:

- wages paid by an employer to the debtor;

- commissions earned and paid to the debtor — tips may also be garnisheed;

- cash surrender value of a life insurance policy owned by the debtor;

- pay out of moneys from an RRSP;

- joint bank accounts, up to one-half of the money in the account;

- accounts owned by the debtor;

- mortgage payments to the debtor;

- rental payments to the debtor;

- payments from a mutual fund;

- accounts receivable of the debtor; and

- payments to the debtor from an estate.

The garnishment process is primarily administrative. If neither the garnishee nor the debtor raises a defence to garnishment, there is no court appearance required, and the work can be done by a law clerk.

In order to garnish a debt, you must do the following in the court where the judgment was obtained.

Prepare and File a Requisition for Garnishment

The requisition for garnishment (figure 9.4) will be used by the registrar to prepare the notice of garnishment (figure 9.5) that will be sent to the debtor and the garnishee. It is important that the requisition be accurate. You must provide the following information: the total amount of the garnishment (judgment, costs (including all costs of collection to date as allowed by tariff A and the court and sheriff's fees), and postjudgment interest to date). Note that rule 60.19(2)(a) limits the lawyer's fee for preparation of the requisition to $50.

Prepare an Affidavit in Support of Requisition for Garnishment

An affidavit in support of requisition for garnishment (figure 9.6) may be sworn by the lawyer for the creditor or by the creditor. The affidavit provides the evidence for the facts set out in the requisition. It should give the particulars of the judgment; a copy of the judgment, as **issued and entered**, should be attached to the affidavit. The affidavit should set out the payment history of the debtor since the judgment, as well as calculations showing how the present amount was calculated: principal amount, costs to which you are entitled, postjudgment interest to the date of the affidavit, and requisition. Last, it should set out the basis for the belief that the proposed garnishee is indebted to the debtor; the amount of the indebtedness, if known; and the last known addresses of the debtor, the garnishee, and anyone else to whom the notice will be sent. If the garnishee is outside Ontario, as a prerequisite to the garnishment, you must set out that you would have a right to sue the garnishee for the debt in Ontario. If the garnishee is not yet indebted to the debtor, but will be indebted in the future, set out the circumstances of the debt and the date when it is payable. On receipt of the requisition for garnishment and the supporting affidavit, the registrar will issue a notice of garnishment, describing the persons identified as owing money to the debtor as garnishees. The registrar will send a copy of the notice of garnishment to the sheriff in the county or region where the debtor resides or, if the debtor resides outside Ontario, to the sheriff in the county or region in which the proceedings started.

issued and entered
a judgment or order is issued when it is signed by a judge or registrar and the court's seal is affixed to it; it is then entered—that is, recorded—by the registrar, using a system for referencing and recording an issued judgment; an entered judgment or order will usually have a stamp on it, indicating the microfilm or disk it was recorded on, or will be otherwise referenced so that it can be found in court files

Garnishment of Joint Debts and Dealing with Co-owners

In the past, where income was owed partly to the debtor named in the garnishment notice and partly to a co-owner, matters could be delayed while the share actually owing to the debtor was determined to be available for garnishment. Rule 60.08(1.1) now clearly specifies that one-half of the debt is presumed available for garnishment, or a greater or lesser amount if there has been an order under rule 60.08(16) on a motion to determine the amount owing and available for garnishment. It is now clear under rules 60.08(15.1) and (15.2) that when a creditor is served with a garnishee's notice that a debt is owed to the debtor and a co-owner, a creditor must serve the co-owner with a notice to co-owners of a debt, which sets out the co-owner's rights and liabilities in the proceedings, and also serve a copy of the garnishee's statement. Service must be personal, or by an alternative to personal service. If any party or co-owner asks for a garnishment hearing under rule 60.08(16), the notice of motion must be served on the sheriff. A co-owner wishing to dispute a proposed distribution to the creditor must bring a motion for garnishment hearing within 30 days of service, failing which he or she will be presumed to not dispute payment of the full amount to the creditor.

Issuing and Renewing of Notices of Garnishment

Under rules 60.08(6.1) to (6.5), a notice of garnishment is in effect for six years from the date of issue, and is renewable for an indefinite number of six-year terms. It shall name one debtor and one garnishee. One notice can no longer be used to name several debtors. The notice may be renewed prior to its expiry by filing a requisition for renewal of garnishment where the garnishment was issued, together with a supporting affidavit. The registrar shall renew the garnishment notice, and notice of renewal shall also be served on the sheriff where the debtor resides or on the sheriff of the county or region where the proceeding commenced, if the debtor resides outside Ontario.

Service of Notice of Garnishment

Once the garnishment notice has been issued, the creditor should serve it along with a blank garnishee's statement (figure 9.7), which the garnishee uses to report on payments to be made, or to report that nothing is due and owing to the debtor so that nothing will be paid. Service may be by mail, although service on the debtor should be by personal service, if possible, so that the debtor cannot complain later that he was not served and obstruct the garnishment process once it has begun. If serving a garnishee that is a financial institution or a business with more than one office or location, serve the branch or location where the account is located or where the payment is normally paid from. Remember that you cannot serve a garnishee at a location outside Ontario unless it is a debt for which the garnishee could be sued in Ontario.

    If the garnishee is the **Crown in right of Ontario**, in respect of a debtor who is a provincial civil servant or a contractor with the government, you serve a notice of garnishment to the garnishee and attach a statement of particulars (figure 9.8), setting out the details that will allow Crown officials to identify the debtor and the payment due to

Crown in right of Ontario
the legal title used to refer to the government of Ontario and how the government is usually named when it is a party to a legal proceeding

Illustration of Calculation of Garnishment of Wages

Gross wages:	$1,000	per week
Deductions from gross:	300	income tax deductions
	10	Canada Pension
	20	Employment Insurance
	50	pension plan
	20	health insurance
	30	group life insurance
	$ 430	TOTAL DEDUCTIONS

NET PAY: $1,000 – $430 = $570

AMOUNT AVAILABLE FOR GARNISHMENT: $570 × 0.20 = $114

him, so that they can comply with the notice to garnishee. Include a blank garnishee's statement with your documents for service. If you wish to make the federal Crown a garnishee with respect to a debtor who is a federal civil servant, federally appointed judge, member of Parliament, employee of a Crown corporation (most of them), and others who are paid out of the Consolidated Revenue Fund, you may do so under the *Garnishment, Attachment and Pension Diversion Act* (GAPDA). You should read the statute and the regulations carefully to determine whether the debtor falls under GAPDA, especially if your garnishment target is a federal Crown corporation. Generally, the regulations list the Crown corporations that come under GAPDA. (If the debtor is in receipt of money from Crown corporations that are not on the list, he is governed by the usual provincial garnishment rules.) Once you have determined that the federal Crown is an appropriate garnishee for your debtor, you must serve a notice of intention to garnishee Her Majesty, together with a copy of the judgment and a federal notice to garnishee, with garnishee's statement. The federal Crown may dispute the garnishment and generally has all the rights to respond that an ordinary garnishee would have.

Payments to the Sheriff

When the garnishee has been served, she is obliged to pay to the sheriff the sum set out in the notice, or the sum owed to the debtor if it is less than the sum claimed. The garnishee is also obliged to turn over any of the debtor's property that she has that the debtor has a right to. Payment must be made within 10 days after service of the notice of garnishment or 10 days after payment is due, whichever is later.

Effect of Garnishee Notice

The notice binds debts owed by the garnishee to the debtor at the time the notice is served, up to and including any debt due within six years after the notice is served. If there was a condition precedent to payment by the garnishee and if the condition is performed within six years of service of the notice, payment is deemed to have been made and is deemed to be attached and payable to the sheriff. The garnishee, on responding with payment, should send back the garnishee's statement indicating that payments that are being made and/or will be made in future unless the garnishee is paying the full amount owed to the creditor. The notice should be served on the creditor and debtor and filed with the court within 10 days of service of the notice of garnishment on the garnishee. Note that if you are serving the Crown as garnishee, the Crown, under the *Proceedings Against the Crown Act*, has 30 days from the actual or effective date[3] of service on the Crown to respond. If the garnishee fails to pay, or fails to respond with a garnishee's statement disputing the garnishment, within the time allowed for responding, the creditor is entitled to serve a notice of motion on the garnishee, requesting an order that the garnishee pay the full amount owed by the debtor to the creditor, as if the garnishee were liable directly to the creditor for the debt.

Garnishment Hearing

If any party, including the garnishee, disputes the process, she may, by notice of motion, apply for a garnishment hearing. For example, if you garnish a bank account that appears to be jointly owned with a spouse, a garnishment hearing may be held to determine what the spouse's share of the account is. Note that all interested parties must be served with notice of a hearing and have a right to be heard and make submissions on the motion.

Payment Out by the Sheriff

The sheriff will make payments to the creditor, subject to the terms of the *Creditors' Relief Act*. You will recall that execution creditors shared ratably on any distribution by the sheriff. This is also the case in garnishment proceedings. The sheriff sends a distribution proposal to all execution creditors who have filed writs of execution or garnishment notices with the sheriff. In the distribution proposal, the sheriff records the details of all funds he has seized or otherwise received, and lists the execution creditors who are entitled to share in the proceeds, along with the amounts they are owed, and their pro rata shares.

Garnishing Wages

When garnishing wages,[4] you are allowed by the *Wages Act* to seize 20 percent of the debtor's *net* wages for a pay period. The box on page 193 shows how the amount is calculated.

Assets Exempt from Seizure

exigible
a word used to describe assets that the sheriff may seize when executing a writ of seizure and sale; if an asset is exempt from seizure it is referred to as a non-exigible asset

Some assets of the debtor are non-**exigible** — that is, they may not be seized by the sheriff under a writ nor may they be garnished. At common law, the clothes worn by the debtor cannot be seized, nor can damages paid to the debtor for pain and suffering. However, to these have been added a number of exemptions that are based on statute. Some of these exemptions reflect the concerns of an earlier age — for example, the detailed exemptions allowed to farmers in the *Execution Act*. Another problem with some of the legislation is that certain classes of assets are exempt up to a stated monetary limit. The monetary limits in the *Execution Act* were raised in 2000 for the first time since the 1960s.[5] At the time of writing (October 2011), pursuant to O. Reg. 657/05, the current exemptions and limits for personal property are regulated. The Regulation can be accessed by looking up the statute at http://www.e-laws.gov.on.ca. Click on "Search or Browse Current Consolidated Law," choose "E," and click on the plus sign next to *Execution Act*.

In October 2010, the *Open for Business Act*[6] amended the *Execution Act*, which resulted in a new regime governing personal exemptions. At the time of writing, the new exemption regime had not yet been proclaimed in force.[7] The current exemption rules in O. Reg. 657/05 remain in force until the new exemptions are proclaimed. The new regime works like this:

- The upper limit on necessary clothing for the debtor and dependants is removed. Presumably, if the clothing can be described as "necessaries," it is exempt. The existing law governing "necessaries" for minor's contracts may be useful here to determine what is or is not a "necessary," and is therefore exempt or not from seizure.

- The upper limit on household furnishings is removed and will be set by regulation — presumably some sort of amendment to O. Reg. 657/05.

- The upper limit on tools and property used to earn a living is removed, and there is no longer any distinction between farmer's property and the property of other income earners. The old farming exemptions will be history.

- The upper limit for automobiles, currently $5,650, will be removed and set by regulation.

- There will be provisions to define other personal property as exempt from seizure, and provisions to prescribe upper limits on the value of such property.

- What is really new is a rule that will prescribe an upper limit on the total of all exempt personal property. So while upper limits no longer exist for some categories of property, such as property used to earn a living, there will be a cap on the totals.

To sum up, the use of regulations to set upper limits on most exemptions will continue. There are changes to how the classes of exempt property are described and some classes will have new upper limits, and there will be an upper limit on the total property exemptions for a debtor.

The box on the following page presents an overview of the current exemptions at common law and under provincial and federal legislation. Although most of the exemptions you will run into arise with enforcement of writs of seizure and sale, remember that the exemptions also apply to garnishment proceedings.

Assets Exempt from Seizure

Provincial

PENSIONS, BENEFITS

Compensation for Victims of Crime Act — victim's compensation;

Welfare legislation — section 143 of the *Courts of Justice Act* prohibits garnishment of any benefit, allowance, or assistance payment;

Ontario Municipal Employees Retirement System Act — pensions are exempt except to satisfy a support order; and

Pension Benefits Act — pension benefits are exempt except to satisfy a support order.

INSURANCE BENEFITS

Workplace Safety and Insurance Act — injury insurance benefits and pensions; and

Insurance Act — rights of an insured in an insurance contract and insurance benefits are exempt if a beneficiary is designated who is a close family member.

WAGES

Wages Act — 80 percent of a worker's net wages are exempt from seizure, reduced to 50 percent if enforcement is in respect of a support order. These percentages may be varied upward or downward on application of either the debtor or the creditor.

OTHER ASSETS

Execution Act — exempt from seizure are tools of a trade or calling, up to $11,300 to permit a debtor to gain a livelihood; livestock, equipment up to $28,300, and other farming assets to permit a farmer to earn an income; necessary clothing up to $5,650; household furnishings up to $11,300; vehicles up to $5,650. As noted earlier, the exemptions described here will soon change. **Watch for proclamation of the amendments to the *Execution Act* and to O. Reg. 657/05.**

If a debtor buys a chattel, fails to pay for it, and is sued by the creditor, the creditor may seize the chattel even though it might otherwise be exempt.

The exemptions are not available to corporations, but are available to partnerships and sole proprietorships.

Federal

PENSIONS, BENEFITS

Canada Pension Plan Act — pension benefits are exempt;

Canadian Forces Superannuation Act — pensions are exempt;

Government Annuities Act — annuities and income paid out are exempt under insolvency legislation;

Members of Parliament — pensions are exempt;

Old Age Security Act — benefits are exempt;

Pension Fund Securities Act — the interest of a member in the body of the fund is exempt, and may not be assigned to the creditor or others;

RCMP Superannuation Act — benefits are exempt;

Employment Insurance Act — benefits are exempt; and

War Veterans Allowance Act — allowances are exempt.

Note that most federal pensions are not exempt from garnishment with respect to enforcement of family support judgments under the *Garnishment, Attachment and Pension Diversion Act*.

OTHER ASSETS

Indian Act — real and personal property of status natives on a reserve cannot be seized by a non-native creditor.

OTHER ENFORCEMENT REMEDIES: WRITS OF SEQUESTRATION, INJUNCTIONS, AND RECEIVERSHIPS

Writs of sequestration can be obtained from the court if the creditor is able to show that other enforcement remedies are likely to be ineffective. This is difficult to do, and because the remedy is somewhat out of the ordinary, judges exercise discretion in making such orders. If you do obtain such an order, the effect is that the sheriff may seize and hold personal property and real estate of the debtor, pending further direction by the court. For example, if a debtor is disposing of property to hinder or defeat creditors, you may be allowed to sequester property that you otherwise might not be able to seize, and hold it as a form of security for the property that the debtor is trying to dispose of to prevent you from seizing it.

Injunctions may be obtained on an interim or temporary basis to prevent the debtor from disposing of property before judgment. This goes against the general rule that the creditor may not enforce an unsecured right to payment against the property of a debtor until *after* obtaining a judgment. Because injunctions in these circumstances are extraordinary, they are used sparingly. They are resorted to primarily in cases where the *Fraudulent Conveyances Act* cannot or will not be able to reach assets of the debtor.

Where a creditor can show that there are some assets in Canada belonging to a debtor and that there is a strong risk that they will be removed so as to frustrate enforcement of a judgment, the creditor may be able to persuade the court to issue a **Mareva injunction**, which permits an asset to be seized and held to satisfy the judgment. For example, in the case that gave the Mareva injunction its name, the *Mareva* was the debtor's ship that had happened to dock at a port in the jurisdiction where an action against it had been brought and where there were no other assets. The creditor obtained an injunction to detain the ship and make it available to satisfy the debt, which would otherwise have been unenforceable if the ship had been allowed to leave port. In effect, a debtor who has no exigible assets in Ontario puts at risk any asset he brings within the jurisdiction of Ontario courts.

Receiverships are orders of the court that allow for the appointment of a person to run a business enterprise owned by the debtor, with a view to managing it or selling it. They are often available to deal with property that is security for a debt, and some secured loan agreements will permit the creditor to appoint a receiver without a court order if the debtor is in breach of the loan agreement. Under the *Bankruptcy and Insolvency Act*, it is possible to obtain an order for an interim receivership where there is a danger that an asset, otherwise available to creditors in bankruptcy proceedings, might be dissipated. If an order is made and an interim receiver appointed, the receiver can monitor the use of the asset and safeguard the value in it, but cannot exclude the debtor from using the asset.

As noted earlier, these remedies are exceptional in nature and rarely used, especially in a routine collection practice.

Mareva injunction permits a creditor to obtain an injunction to secure the debtor's assets in a case where it is likely that the debtor will dispose of or remove all assets from the jurisdiction, before judgment, leaving no assets to satisfy the judgment debt

CHAPTER SUMMARY

Chapter 9 examines the enforcement tools used in the Superior Court: examination in aid of execution, writs of seizure and sale, garnishment, writs of sequestration, injunctions, and court-appointed receivers. An examination in aid of execution is an investigative tool that provides information for more effective use of the other enforcement tools. It permits the creditor to question the debtor on her debts, assets, and means. The writ of seizure and sale can be filed with the sheriff. On instructions, the sheriff will then seize and sell the debtor's property, and use the proceeds to pay all creditors who have filed writs in that court. If others owe the debtor money, the creditor may garnish payments owing to the debtor from third parties. If enforcement is proving difficult, in exceptional cases you may get a sequestration order permitting the sheriff to seize property pending further direction from the court. Injunctions can be used to prevent a debtor from disposing of or wasting property prior to judgment. If the debtor is an ongoing business, instead of seizing assets, the court may permit a receiver to be appointed to run the business and arrange to sell it. The remedies of injunction, receivership, and sequestration of assets are exceptional remedies that are not usually used in routine collections.

KEY TERMS

chattel

condition precedent

Crown in right of Ontario

execution

exigible

issued and entered

Mareva injunction

NOTES

1. An injunction is an equitable remedy that is not covered directly by rule 60.

2. F. Bennett, *Bennett on Collections*, 5th ed. (Toronto: Carswell, 2003), 308-9.

3. "Effective date of service" is a reference to service by mail, where the document is deemed served five days after it is mailed. See rule 16.06(2).

4. The *Canadian Oxford Dictionary*, 2nd ed. (Don Mills, ON: Oxford University Press, 2004) notes that both "garnish" and "garnishee" are used to describe the act of a judgment creditor obtaining payment from someone who owes money to the judgment debtor. "He has garnisheed my wages" and "He has garnished my wages" are both acceptable use, although the latter form appears to be the more common usage in Canada.

5. The *Red Tape Reduction Act, 2000*, SO 2000, c. 26, sch. A, s. 8.

6. Bill 68, *Open for Business Act, 2010*.

7. You can check the status of amendments on the e-laws website at http://www.e-laws.gov.on.ca. For the status of amendments to this act, click on "Search or Browse Current Consolidated Law," choose "E," and click on the *Execution Act.*

REFERENCES

Bankruptcy and Insolvency Act, RSC 1985, c. B-3, as amended.

Creditors' Relief Act, RSO 1990, c. C.45.

Execution Act, RSO 1990, c. E.24.

Fraudulent Conveyances Act, RSO 1990, c. F.29.

Garnishment, Attachment and Pension Diversion Act, RSC 1985, c. G-2.

Ontario Gazette (Toronto: Queen's Printer) (also available at http://www.ontariogazette.gov.on.ca).

Personal Property Security Act, RSO 1990, c. P.10.

Proceedings Against the Crown Act, RSO 1990, c. P.27.

Rules of Civil Procedure, RRO 1990, reg. 194.

Wages Act, RSO 1990, c. W.1.

REVIEW QUESTIONS

1. What are the principal methods of enforcing judgments?

2. In what circumstances would you use a Mareva injunction; a writ of seizure and sale; a writ of sequestration; an injunction; and garnishment proceedings?

3. How often can you examine a judgment debtor?

4. Is the judgment debtor the only person you can examine in a JD exam?

5. What should you do before conducting a JD exam with a corporation?

6. What can you do if, on a JD exam, the debtor goes on talking endlessly without answering your questions?

7. Why should you personally serve the notice of examination of a judgment debtor?

8. Suppose you bring a contempt motion against a debtor who is obstructing your judgment debtor examination. On the motion, if the court orders the judgment debtor to re-attend at his own expense, and the debtor does, but continues to be obstructive, how can you avoid having to serve a second contempt motion? And why is this important?

9. Should you file a direction to enforce a writ of seizure with the sheriff every time you file a writ of seizure and sale? Why or why not?

10. What is likely to happen if you direct the sheriff to seize a car and the debtor claims the car seized is not his?

11. How long do you have to file a writ of seizure and sale after it is issued?

12. What do you have to do to prevent a writ of seizure and sale from expiring?

13. Suppose you discover that the judgment debtor is also known by an alias. Will this affect your attempts to enforce the judgment? What steps should you take to deal with this matter?

14. Can you seize the judgment debtor's (a) car; (b) car, if she is a salesperson and uses the car in getting to her customers; (c) Canada Pension benefits; (d) clothing; and (e) set of wrenches if she is a mechanic and the judgment against her is for the unpaid price of the wrenches?

15. If the judgment debtor is a wage earner, can wages be seized to pay a judgment debt?

16. Suppose the creditor has just filed a writ of seizure and sale. Can he direct the sheriff to immediately take steps to sell the debtor's house?

17. Suppose the sheriff on a sale of the asset is offered a small fraction of what a seized asset is worth. Does he have to simply accept it? Should he?

18. Suppose you discover that the judgment debtor has a joint bank account, a car, a house, income from employment, and income from a mortgage that a trustee owns and holds on her behalf. What enforcement remedies would you use?

19. Suppose a garnishee is served with a notice of garnishment for $40,000. He owes the debtor, a building contractor, $10,000 for renovation work. What should the garnishee do in these circumstances? What would happen if the garnishee sat back and did nothing?

20. What happens if you discover that the debtor is an Ontario civil servant and his only asset is his salary? Would it make a difference if the debtor is employed by the federal government?

21. How long is the garnishee liable to make payments to the sheriff?

22. What can the creditor do if the garnishee serves a garnishee statement in which he says that he has no debts owing to the debtor and the creditor thinks this is untrue?

23. When the sheriff receives funds from a garnishee, can he simply turn that amount over to the creditor?

24. In what circumstances would you apply to use a writ of sequestration?

CASE STUDY

M E M O

DATE: January 28, year 0

TO: U.R. Clerk

FROM: Fiona Anoif

RE: Judgment Against Snogglepus Apartments Ltd.

Last week, on January 20, we obtained a judgment against Snogglepus Apartments Ltd. for $36,000, plus prejudgment interest of $430 and costs fixed at $350, on behalf of our client Jerry's Janitorial Services Ltd. Postjudgment interest is at the rate of 10 percent. The plaintiff's address is 123 Main St., Toronto, ON M4Y 2P4.

Our investigations show that Snogglepus Apartments Ltd., not surprisingly, owns Snogglepus Apartments Ltd. at 341 Victory Blvd., Toronto, ON M3R 1V6 and that its head office is in apt. 1 in that building. There are four tenants — G.F. Handel in apt. 2, J.S. Bach in apt. 3, L. Boccherini in apt. 4, and A. Corelli in apt. 5. All pay rent on the first of the month.

1. Complete the necessary documentation to file a writ of seizure and sale so that we can seize the ownership of the apartment building.

2. Complete the necessary forms to garnish rent paid by the tenants of the debtor.

Figure 9.1   Notice of Examination of Judgment Debtor (Form 34A)

Court file no. 1234

ONTARIO

SUPERIOR COURT OF JUSTICE

B E T W E E N

ARTEMIS PLUMBING SUPPLY LTD.

Plaintiff

and

PERSONABLE PLUMBERS LTD.

Defendant

NOTICE OF EXAMINATION

TO: Dagmar Johnson

YOU ARE REQUIRED TO ATTEND, on Friday, December 15, year 0 at 10:30 a.m. at the office of Suleman Kahn, CSR, 721 Bay Street, Suite 300, Toronto, ON M9R 3T4, tel. 416-762-1234 for:

[ ]   Cross-examination on your affidavit dated (*date*)

[ ]   Examination for discovery

[ ]   Examination for discovery on behalf of or in place of (*identify party*)

[ ]   Examination in aid of execution

[x]   Examination in aid of execution on behalf of or in place of Personable Plumbers Ltd.

YOU ARE REQUIRED TO BRING WITH YOU and produce at the examination the documents the following documents and things:

> all books, accounts, invoices, contracts, letters, emails, statements, records, bills, notes, securities, vouchers, plans, photographs, and copies of any of these things in your possession or under your control in any way relating to the matters that are within the scope of these proceedings or that have any reference to these proceedings.

Date: December 2, year 0

I.M. Just LSUC #12345A
JUST AND COPING
Barristers and Solicitors
8701 - 365 Bay Street
Toronto, ON M3J 4A9
416-762-1342
FAX 416-762-1343
Lawyers for the Plaintiff

TO: Dagmar Johannson
87 Pleasant Blvd.
Toronto, ON M3T 1A4

RCP-E 34A (July 1, 2007)

QUESTIONS TO BE USED IN EXAMINING AN INDIVIDUAL DEBTOR

Date of Judgment: _____

Date Writ of Seizure and Sale filed with Sheriff: _____

Date Writ of Seizure and Sale filed with Land Titles Office: _____

Date of Debt: _____

I. PERSONAL DETAILS

A. Personal History

Full name: _____   Birth date:_____

Telephone: _____   Email: _____

Residence address: _____

Are you the Mr./Ms. _____ who owes money to _____

according to this judgment dated _____?

Do you ever use any other name? _____

If so, what name(s)? _____

Spousal Status

Married: _____   Single: _____   Divorced: _____   Common Law: _____

Living Apart: _____

Family Information

Children: _____   No.: _____   Other Dependants: _____

Total family group equals _____ persons.

B. Employment Status

Unemployed: _____   Employed: _____   Self-Employed: _____

Part-Time: _____

What is your occupation? _____   Who is your superior? _____

Name and address of employer: _____

Position: _____   Present Wages: _____

How long have you held this position? _____

When are you paid (obtain day of week)? _____

Bonus schemes (when paid etc.): _____

Commissions: _____

Are you in any way related to your employer? _____

Previous Employers:

Name: _____   Address: _____

How Long? _____

How you ever been in business on your own? _____

When? _____

Where? _____

Inventory? _____   What? _____

Where kept? _____

Have you ever had any employees? _____

Have you been involved in any partnership? _____

When? _____

Where? _____

Have you ever carried on business under any trade or business name? _____

If so, what name? _____

Inventory? _____ What? _____

    Where kept? _____

Are you an Officer or Director of any corporation? _____

If so, which corporation(s)? _____

Have you any part-time jobs? _____

If so, where? (*name and address*) _____

If unemployed, are you subject to recall? _____ When? _____

II. DETAILS OF PLACE OF RESIDENCE

A. Type of Accommodation

Description of Property (e.g., 2-storey, garage, number of bedrooms):

_____

Municipal address: _____

Do you own it?

    (absolute, beneficial, joint tenant, or tenant in common): _____

Legal description: _____

If yes, date of purchase: _____

    – reporting letter _____

Amount paid: _____

    – present value _____

    – air conditioning _____

    – type of heating: oil, gas, or coal _____

    – number of square feet per floor _____

    – number of bathrooms _____

    – unfinished areas _____

Who lives there? _____

Particulars of mortgage including

    – amount: _____

    – balance owing: _____

    – terms: _____

B. If Residence Is Not Owned

Name of building's owner: _____

Address: _____

Do you pay rent? _____ How much? $ _____

When is rent due? _____

Is landlord related to you? _____

Is rent paid up to date? _____

To whom do you give the rent? _____

Do you pay rent by cash or cheque? _____

Who signs the cheque? _____

Is there a lease? _____

Who signed the lease? _____

III. DETAILS ABOUT DEBTOR'S SPOUSE

Full Name: _____

   Maiden Name (if wife): _____

Address: _____

   Age: _____ Telephone: _____

Employment Status

Unemployed: _____   Self-Employed: _____

   Part-Time: _____

Name of Employer: _____

Address: _____

Position: _____   Salary: $ _____

   When paid: _____

How long has he/she worked there? _____

Where did he/she last work? _____

Name: _____

Address: _____

Moneys due: $ _____

How much: $ _____

Any support to other people: _____

IV. PARTICULARS OF CHILDREN

	Name	Age	Address		Employed
1.					Yes/No
2.					Yes/No
3.					Yes/No
4.					Yes/No
5.					Yes/No

V. DETAILS OF PERSONAL BUDGET

Sources of Income and Expenses

Income (Per Month)		*Expenses* (Per Month)	
1. Weekly Salary	$	1. Food	$
2. Part-Time Income	$	2. Clothing	$
3. Room and Board		3. Housing:	
from Others	$	– Rent or Mortgage	$
4. Pensions	$	– Taxes	$
5. Employment Insurance	$	– Fuel	$
6. Workers' Compensation	$	– Phone/Cellphone/Internet	$
7. Family Allowances	$	4. Transportation	$
8. Annuities	$	5. Insurance	$
9. Inheritances	$	6. Education and Recreation	$
10. Other	$	7. Medical and Dental	$
		8. Bank Loans	$
		9. Other	$
Total	$		$

VI. ASSETS OTHER THAN INCOME

A. Real Estate

Do you own any real estate?

Street Address	*City*	*Tenants*
1.		
2.		
3.		

[Obtain municipal address and legal description.]

Do you own other real estate? _____

If not, when did you last own real estate? _____

How did you transfer it? _____

   When? _____

To whom? _____ How much? $_____

Who was the solicitor acting on your behalf? _____

Do you own the furniture in your residence? _____

B. Vehicles

1. Do you own (and/or lease) a car or truck? _____ (Yes/No)

   Make _____ Year _____ Model _____

   Licence No. _____ Chassis No. _____ Engine No. _____

   Where is it kept? _____ What use is made of it? _____

   Value: $ _____

   How much do you still owe on it? $ _____

   To whom? _____ (Name)

   Address: _____

Equity in owned auto? _____

What type of security is there for this debt? _____

Do you own any other automobiles? _____

2. If you do not own an automobile, do you drive an automobile? _____ (Yes/No)

   [If yes, ask who owns the car and particulars under (1), above.]

   When did you last own an automobile? _____

   To whom did you sell it? _____

   For what amount? $_____

   Were there any liens on the car? _____ By whom? _____

3. Do you own, lease, or have the use of a tractor; a snowmobile; an airplane; a motorcycle; or a motor boat? _____ (Yes/No)

   [If yes to one or more, ask particulars under (1), above.]

C. Bank Accounts

1. Do you have any bank accounts or trust company accounts? _____ (Yes/No)

   If yes, give the following information:

	Bank	Address	Type and account number	Balance
a.				
b.				
c.				
d.				

   [Obtain statements and entry books if possible.]

If no, when did you last have a bank account?

Where? _____

When did you close it? _____

When did you last have any claim to or interest in any bank account in any name? _____

When did you last draw a cheque? _____

To whom was that cheque payable? _____

Amount: $ _____ What was it given for? _____

Have you ever had the right of access to any safe deposit box? _____

Box No.: _____ Bank: _____

Address: _____

When was the last time you had a safe deposit box? _____

Do you have any term deposits? _____ When was the last? _____

D. Specific Assets

	Yes	No	Describe

1. Mortgages
2. IOUs
3. Promissory notes
4. Loan agreements
5. Other security for payment of money
6. Government bonds
7. Other bonds
8. Common stock in public and private corporations
9. Preferred stock in public and private corporations
10. RRSP
11. RHOSP
12. RDSP
13. RESP
14. TFSA (Tax Free Savings Account and other tax savings and deferred financial instruments)
15. Television set
16. Refrigerator
17. Stove
18. Washer and dryer
19. Furniture
20. Fur coats
21. Jewellery
22. Gold or silverware
23. Works of art
24. Horses and/or boats
25. Any interest in any patent copyright, process, formula, invention, or royalties
26. Pensions
27. Lottery tickets
28. Coins and stamps
29. Liquor

E. Life Insurance

Do you carry life insurance on yourself? _____ (Yes/No)

    [Check whether term, group, or whole life.]

If yes, please give following information:

Name of Insurance Company	Policy No.	Amount of Policy	Beneficiary	Premium	Who Pays Premium	Cash Surrender Value
1.						
2.						
3.						
4.						

Do you carry life insurance on your wife or any person in which you have an interest? _____

If yes, please give following information:

Name of Insurance Company	Policy No.	Amount of Policy	Beneficiary	Premium	Who Pays Premium	Cash Surrender Value
1.						
2.						
3.						
4.						

F. Moneys Owing to Defendant

Is there money owing to you? _____ (Yes/No)

If yes, give the following information:

	Name of Debtor	Address	Amount	Security Held
1.				
2.				

G. Miscellaneous

1. How much money are you carrying right now? $ _____

2. Have you any income from any other source whatever? _____

3. Have you made a will? _____

4. Have you any interest as beneficiary, remainderman, right of reversion, executor, administrator, trustee, guardian, or otherwise under any will or *inter vivos* of trust or in any estate? _____

5. Have you ever been a party to a trust agreement or other trust instrument? Did you at any time put any money or property of any kind in trust for yourself or anyone else? _____

6. Have you received any money or property of any kind under any will or by inheritance or from any estate? _____

7. Do you have any business deals pending which will likely give you money? _____

VII. ASSETS OF SPOUSE AND CHILDREN

A. Real Estate

Does your spouse own any real estate? _____ (Yes/No)

Do your children own any real estate? _____ (Yes/No)

Locations

	Street Address	City	Tenants
1.			
2.			
3.			

Where did they last own real estate? (give details above)

B. Automobiles

1. Does your wife own an automobile? _____ (Yes/No)

   Make _____ Year _____ Model _____

   Licence No. _____ Serial No. _____

   Where is it kept? _____

What use is made of it? _____

How much does she still owe on it? $ _____

To whom? _____ (Name)

Address: _____

Equity in owned auto? _____

What type of security is there for this debt? _____

Does she own any other cars? _____

2. If she does not own an automobile, does she drive an automobile? _____ (Yes/No)

    [If yes, ask who owns the car and above particulars.]

3. When did she last own an automobile? _____ (Date)

To whom did she sell it? _____ (Name)

Address: _____

Telephone: _____

Amount: $ _____   Security taken: _____

C. Bank Accounts

1. Do your wife or children have any bank accounts? _____ (Yes/No)

If yes, give the following information:

	Bank	Address	Type and account number	Balance
a.				
b.				
c.				
d.				

Do you give them any money to put in the account(s)? _____

If yes, how much? _____

If no, where did they get it? _____

VIII. LIST OF CREDITORS

Present debts (approximate) $ _____

Please list your debts for me, giving the following information:

	Name of Creditor	Address	Amount	Security Held	Judgment
1.					
2.					
3.					
4.					
5.					
6.					
7.					
8.					
9.					
10.					

Give details of payments to other creditors:

Who? _____

How much? _____

When? _____

Why? _____

What is the cause of your financial difficulty?

Explain briefly: _____

    Do you have any identification — for example, a driver's licence? _____

1. Do you hold property in trust for anyone else? (particulars)

_____

2. During the past year did you guarantee any indebtedness for anyone?

_____

3. During the past year did you make or endorse any paper for anyone?

_____

4. When did you last apply for or obtain a loan at any bank, finance company, or other lending institution or from any non-lender, corporation, or person whatsoever?

_____

5. Are you holding in your name or possession for the benefit of anyone else any property of any kind whether real property, personal property, or otherwise?

_____

6. Is anyone holding your property in trust for you?

_____

IX. MISCELLANEOUS MATTERS

1. Have you any judgment or interest in any judgment? _____

2. Have you any claim of any kind against anyone? _____

3. Have you any interest of any kind in any mortgage or any lease or interest in any leasehold on any real or personal property?

_____

4. Are you a party to any agreement of any kind with anyone?

_____

5. Are you a party to any action now pending in the courts?

_____

6. Have you filed your income tax return for the last two years? _____ [Obtain a copy.]

    Any tax refunds? _____

7. Have you ever been bankrupt or made a proposal under the *Bankruptcy Act*? [If so, obtain particulars.]

_____

8. When did you take your last vacation? _____

    [If recently, obtain particulars. If some other person or corporation is in possession of the judgment debtor's property, examine that person or corporation. Ask questions that seek such information.]

X. DISPOSAL OF ASSETS

1. Have you sold any of the assets in the above questions from the debt date
   to present? _____

2. Have you transferred any of the assets in the above questions from the debt date
   to present? _____

   [A debtor should be able to account for every asset that he had at the debt date and every
   asset he acquired from that date to the present.]

3. Did you give your spouse presents for Christmas? Were the presents
   valuable? _____

4. Have you allowed anyone to use your land or property free of charge? Nominal
   charge? _____

5. Have you assigned or transferred any of your property to anyone by way of
   security? _____

XI. PROPOSED SETTLEMENT

The amount owing to our client is $_____ . Is there any possibility that you may be able to get
the money together to pay this debt? _____ (Yes/No)

If yes:

    When? _____

    What terms? _____

Suggested payment: $ _____ per week, month; payments to be made
starting _____.

What arrangements have you made for paying this judgment? _____

Why has the judgment not been paid? _____

QUESTIONS TO BE USED IN EXAMINING AN OFFICER/REPRESENTATIVE OF A CORPORATE JUDGMENT DEBTOR

I. Introduction

1. Name of the officer.
2. Officer's address, telephone/cellphone numbers, and email addresses.
3. Is this the notice of appointment that was served upon you?
4. Are you aware of the amount owing to this creditor as a result of judgment?
5. What is your position with the company?
6. How long have you been with the company?

II. Minute Book

1. Location of minute book.
2. Would you please make minute books available to me if I want to examine them.

III. Financial Statements

1. For present period: books of accounting, general ledger, etc.
2. For five years prior.
3. Particulars of revenues.
4. Particulars of expenses.
5. Particulars of loans, advances, or dividends to shareholders.
6. Salaries paid to officers and directors.
7. Any extraordinary expenses or revenues during period.
8. Has the company during the past five years returned any goods to creditors or paid creditors out of the normal course of business?
9. Copy of bank statements.
10. Who are the company's auditors/accountants/solicitors?

IV. Particulars of Corporation

1. Date of incorporation.
2. What kinds of shares were originally issued by the company? What was their original value? How many shares were originally issued?
3. Who were the original shareholders?
4. Who are the present shareholders?
5. Could you please give me the particulars of the transfer of shares?
6. Were the shares paid for in full?
7. Who were the original directors?
8. Who are the present directors?
9. Who were the original officers?
10. Who are the present officers?
11. Where is the company's head office?
12. Are the premises owned or leased?
13. Were premises ever owned by the company?
14. Could you please describe the type of business?
15. What was the cause for financial difficulties?

V. Creditors of Company

1. Are there any other creditors?

2. What is the status of their claims — that is, do they have secured claims or judgments?

3. Do any creditors have any form of security on the company's assets?

4. If so, what type, when given, and circumstances at time when given?

5. Please provide a list of all the creditors.

6. Does the company owe the bank any money either on a loan or overdraft?

7. How does the bank secure its indebtedness, i.e., assignment of accounts receivable, section 178 security, personal guarantees, or security agreement?

8. Are there any mortgages or liens against automobiles, equipment, furniture, trade fixtures, or general equipment or inventory of the company?

9. Are any of the company's goods taken on consignment or sold on consignment?

VI. Assets of Company

1. Furniture.

2. Office and plant equipment.

3. Vehicles — type, when acquired, how used.

4. Trade fixtures.

5. Inventory.

6. Accounts receivable — obtain list.

7. Lease for office or other leases owned by company.

8. Any holdings outside Canada.

9. If so, with whom did the company deal?

10. Did the company own any bonds?

11. Are any mortgages payable to the company?

12. Are any loan agreements payable to the company?

13. Are any securities payable to the company?

14. Did the company own any common stock in other corporations?

15. Does the company own any other personal property — that is, TV or refrigerator?

16. Does the company own any real property?

17. Does the company own any other property?

Figure 9.2 Direction to Sheriff to Enforce Writ of Seizure and Sale (Form 60F)

Sheriff's file no. 12894

ONTARIO

SUPERIOR COURT OF JUSTICE

B E T W E E N

ARTEMIS PLUMBING SUPPLY LTD.

Creditor(s)

and

PERSONABLE PLUMBERS LTD.

Debtor(s)

DIRECTION TO ENFORCE WRIT OF SEIZURE AND SALE

TO: the Sheriff of the City of Toronto

Under an order of this court in favour of Artemis Plumbing Supply Ltd.

made on October 17, year 0,

Personable Plumbers Ltd. was ordered to pay the sum of $33,057.31

with interest at the rate of 12 per cent per year commencing on October 17, year 0. Since the order was made, the creditor has received the following payments:

Date of payment	*Amount of payment*
nil	

There remains owing today under the order:

Amount of Principal	*Due date*	*Accrued interest*
$33,766.91	due immediately	$144.25*
(prejudgment interest and costs)		to October 30, year 0

---

*   Postjudgment interest is calculated on the judgment plus costs being awarded:
33,057.31 + 709.60 = 33,766.91 × .12 × .0356 (which was $13/365$) = 144.25.

Figure 9.2   Continued

Under rule 60.19 of the *Rules of Civil Procedure*, the creditor is entitled to costs in the amount of,

(a) $50.00 for the preparation of documents in connection with issuing, renewing and filing with the sheriff the writ of execution or notice of garnishment;

(b) $255.00* for disbursements paid to a sheriff, registrar, official examiner, court reporter or other public officer and to which the creditor is entitled under subrule 60.19 (1); *(Attach copy of all receipts.)*

(c) $ .... for an amount determined in accordance with Tariff A for conducting an examination in aid of execution; *(Attach affidavit confirming that examination was conducted.)*

(d) $ .... for any other costs to which the creditor is entitled under subrule 60.19 (1). *(Attach certificate of assessment.)*

YOU ARE DIRECTED to enforce the writ of seizure and sale issued on October 17, year 0 and filed in your office for a sum sufficient to satisfy the total of the amounts set out above, together with subsequent interest, and your fees and expenses.

Date   October 17, year 0
                                                                            I.M. Just
                                                          _____

                                                           (Signature of party or lawyer)

                                            (Name, address and telephone number of party or lawyer)

                                                    I.M. Just   LSUC #12345A
                                                    JUST AND COPING
                                                    Barristers and Solicitors
                                                    8701 - 365 Bay Street
                                                    Toronto, ON M3J 4A9

                                                    416-762-1342
                                                    FAX 416-762-1343

                                                    Lawyers for the Plaintiff

                                                    RCP-E 60F (November 1, 2005)

---

* $55.00 to issue writ

   $100.00 to file with sheriff

   $100.00 to direct enforcement

Figure 9.2   Concluded

Sheriff's file no. 12894

ARTEMIS
Creditor(s)

and

PERSONABLE
Debtor(s)

ONTARIO
SUPERIOR COURT OF JUSTICE
PROCEEDING COMMENCED at
TORONTO

DIRECTION TO
ENFORCE WRIT
(OF SEIZURE AND SALE)

I.M. Just   LSUC #12345A
JUST AND COPING
Barristers and Solicitors
8701 - 365 Bay Street
Toronto, ON M3J 4A9

416-762-1342
FAX 416-762-1343

Lawyers for the Plaintiff

RCP-E 4C (July 1, 2007)

Figure 9.3   Sample Request to Renew Writ of Seizure and Sale (Form 60E)

Court file no. 1234

ONTARIO

SUPERIOR COURT OF JUSTICE

B E T W E E N

ARTEMIS PLUMBING SUPPLY LTD.

Plaintiff

and

PERSONABLE PLUMBERS LTD.

Defendant

REQUEST TO RENEW WRIT OF SEIZURE AND SALE

TO the Sheriff of the City of Toronto

YOU ARE REQUESTED TO RENEW the writ of seizure and sale issued on October 17, year 0 in this proceeding and filed in your office for a period of six years from the date of renewal.

DATE October 4, year 6   Signature   *I.M. Just*

                                          (Signature of party or lawyer)

I.M. Just   LSUC #12345A
JUST AND COPING
Barristers and Solicitors
8701 - 365 Bay Street
Toronto, ON M3J 4A9

416-762-1342
FAX 416-762-1343

Lawyers for the Plaintiff

RCP-E 60E (July 1, 2007)

Sample Letter to Client Re Renewal of Writ of Seizure and Sale

Just and Coping
Barristers and Solicitors
365 Bay Street – 8701
Toronto, ON
M3J 4A9

September 6, year 6

Henry Dorkin, President
Artemis Plumbing Ltd.
100 Laird Avenue
Toronto, ON M6Y 3A4

Dear Sir:

RE: Artemis Plumbing Ltd. v. Personable Plumbers Ltd.

A writ of seizure and sale was filed against Personable Plumbers Ltd. on your behalf on October 17, year 0 for the amount of $33,057.31 together with assessed costs of $709.60. A writ of seizure and sale liens the property for a period of six (6) years, and must be renewed every six (6) years. The cost for the renewal of your writ will be $100 and this renewal must be filed before October 17, year 6.

We look forward to receiving your instructions regarding the renewal of the writ and if you do wish the execution to be renewed against the lands and goods of the defendant, please forward the sum of $100 to our offices, payable to Just and Coping, in Trust.

Yours very truly,

JUST AND COPING
Per:

I.M. Clerk

I.M. Clerk
Law Clerk

Figure 9.4   Requisition for Garnishment (Form 60G)

Court file no. 1234

ONTARIO
SUPERIOR COURT OF JUSTICE

BETWEEN

ARTEMIS PLUMBING SUPPLY LTD.

Creditor(s)

and

PERSONABLE PLUMBERS LTD.

Debtor(s)

and

MURRAY HILL CONTRACTING LTD.

Garnishee

REQUISITION FOR GARNISHMENT

TO: the local registrar at TORONTO

I REQUIRE a notice of garnishment to be issued in this proceeding, in accordance with the attached draft Form 60H. The total amount to be shown in the notice of garnishment is $34,331.16, made up as follows:

1. $33,057.31 for principal owing under the judgment or order, including prejudgment interest.

2. $709.60 for the costs of the action.

3. $50.00 for the preparation of documents in connection with issuing, renewing and filing with the sheriff a writ of execution or notice of garnishment.

4. $370.00* for disbursements paid to a sheriff, registrar, official examiner, court reporter or other public officer and to which the creditor is entitled under subrule 60.19 (1). *(Attach copies of all receipts.)*

5. $ .... for an amount determined in accordance with Tariff A for conducting an examination in aid of execution. *(Attach affidavit confirming that examination was conducted, and a bill of costs.)*

6. $ .... for any other costs to which the creditor is entitled under subrule 60.19 (1). *(Attach certificate of assessment.)*

7. $144.25 for postjudgment interest to today's date.

Date   October 30, year 0

I.M. Just

(Signature of creditor or creditor's lawyer)

I.M. Just   LSUC #12345A
JUST AND COPING, Barristers and Solicitors
8701 - 365 Bay Street
Toronto, ON M3J 4A9

416-762-1342   FAX 416-762-1343

Lawyers for the Plaintiff

* $55.00 to issue writ

    $100.00 to file with sheriff

    $100.00 to direct enforcement

    $115.00 to issue garnishment

RCP-E 60G (November 1, 2005)

Figure 9.5   Notice of Garnishment (Form 60H)

Court file no. 1234

ONTARIO

SUPERIOR COURT OF JUSTICE

B E T W E E N

ARTEMIS PLUMBING SUPPLY LTD.

CREDITOR

and

(Court seal)

PERSONABLE PLUMBERS LTD.

DEBTOR

and

MURRAY HILL CONTRACTING LTD.

GARNISHEE

NOTICE OF GARNISHMENT

TO   MURRAY HILL CONTRACTING LTD.
        123 Dover St., Toronto, ON M1K 5E4

A LEGAL PROCEEDING in this court between the creditor and the debtor has resulted in an order that the debtor pay a sum of money to the creditor. The creditor claims that you owe a debt to the debtor. A debt to the debtor includes both a debt payable to the debtor and a debt payable to the debtor and one or more co-owners. The creditor has had this notice of garnishment directed to you as garnishee in order to seize any debt that you owe or will owe to the debtor. Where the debt is payable to the debtor and to one or more co-owners, you must pay one-half of the indebtedness or the greater or lesser amount specified in an order made under subrule 60.08(16).

YOU ARE REQUIRED TO PAY to the Sheriff of the City of Toronto,

   (a)   within 10 days after this notice is served on you, all debts now payable by you to the debtor; and

   (b)   within 10 days after they become payable, all debts that become payable by you to the debtor within 6 years after this notice is served on you,

subject to the exemptions provided by section 7 of the *Wages Act*. The total amount of all your payments to the sheriff is not to exceed $34,331.16 less $10 for your costs of making each payment.

EACH PAYMENT MUST BE SENT with a copy of the attached garnishee's payment notice to the sheriff at the address shown below.

IF YOU DO NOT PAY THE TOTAL AMOUNT OF $34,331.16 LESS $10 FOR YOUR COSTS OF MAKING EACH PAYMENT WITHIN 10 DAYS after this notice is served on you, because the debt is owed to the debtor and to one or more co-owners or for any other reason, you must within that time serve on the creditor and the debtor and file with the court a garnishee's statement in Form 60I attached to this notice.

IF YOU FAIL TO OBEY THIS NOTICE, THE COURT MAY MAKE AND ENFORCE AN ORDER AGAINST YOU for payment of the amount set out above and the costs of the creditor.

IF YOU MAKE PAYMENT TO ANYONE OTHER THAN THE SHERIFF, YOU MAY BE LIABLE TO PAY AGAIN.

Figure 9.5 Continued

TO THE CREDITOR, THE DEBTOR AND THE GARNISHEE.

Any party may make a motion to the court to determine any matter in relation to this notice of garnishment.

Date   _____October 30, year 0_____   Issued by   _____

Local registrar

Address of
court office   393 University Avenue
Toronto, ON M5G 1T4

Creditor's address	Debtor's address	Sheriff's address
c/o JUST AND COPING Barristers and Solicitors 8701 - 365 Bay Street Toronto, ON M3J4A9 telephone no. 416-762-1342	#25-27 321 Daynor Dr., Toronto, ON M5X 3A1	393 University Avenue 19th Floor Toronto, ON M5G 1E6

....

(The top portion of the garnishee's payment notice is to be completed by the creditor before the notice of garnishment is issued. Where it is anticipated that more than one payment will be made by the garnishee, the creditor should provide extra copies of the payment notice.)

GARNISHEE'S PAYMENT NOTICE

Make payment by cheque or money order payable to the Sheriff of the City of Toronto

and send it, along with a copy of this payment notice, to the   Sheriff at
393 University Avenue
19th Floor
Toronto, ON M5G 1E6

Court   Ontario Superior Court   File no. 1234

Office at   393 University Avenue, Toronto, ON M5G 1E6

Creditor   Artemis Plumbing Supply Ltd.

Debtor   Personable Plumbers Ltd.

Garnishee   Murray Hill Contracting Ltd.

TO BE COMPLETED BY GARNISHEE FOR EACH PAYMENT

Date of payment   _____

Amount enclosed $_____

RCP-E 60H (November 1, 2005)

Figure 9.5   Concluded

Sheriff's file no. 1234

ARTEMIS
CREDITOR

and

PERSONABLE
DEBTOR

and

MURRAY HILL
GARNISHEE

ONTARIO
SUPERIOR COURT OF JUSTICE
PROCEEDING COMMENCED at
TORONTO

NOTICE OF
GARNISHMENT

I.M. Just   LSUC #12345A
JUST AND COPING
Barristers and Solicitors
8701 - 365 Bay Street
Toronto, ON M3J 4A9

416-762-1342
FAX 416-762-1343

Lawyers for the Plaintiff

RCP-E 4C (July 1, 2007)

Figure 9.6   Sample Affidavit in Support of Requisition for Garnishment

Court file no. 1234

ONTARIO

SUPERIOR COURT OF JUSTICE

B E T W E E N

ARTEMIS PLUMBING SUPPLY LTD.

CREDITOR

and

PERSONABLE PLUMBERS LTD.

DEBTOR

and

MURRAY HILL CONTRACTING LTD.

GARNISHEE

AFFIDAVIT

I, Indigo M. Just, of the City of Toronto, MAKE OATH AND SAY:

1. I am a lawyer in the firm of Just and Coping, lawyers for the plaintiff, and as such have knowledge of the matters set forth in this affidavit.

2. Judgment was recovered in this action against the defendant on the 17th day of October, year 0, for the sum of $33,057.31 and the sum of $709.60 for costs. Attached to my affidavit and marked as exhibit "A" is a true copy of this judgment.

3. I have spoken with the accounts receivable manager of the Plaintiff, who advises me and I believe that no payments have been made with respect to this judgment.

Figure 9.6   Concluded

4. I believe that the amount owing at the present time is calculated as follows:

Judgment	$33,057.31
Costs	709.60
Writ of Seizure and Sale	
Fees	50.00
Disbursements	255.00
Notice of Garnishment	
Fees	50.00
Disbursements	370.00
Subtotal	34,491.91
Postjudgment interest at 12% from	
October 17 to October 30 (13 days)	144.25
Balance	$34,636.16

5. Based on the addresses to which the plaintiff shipped plumbing supplies to the defendant, I believe that Murray Hill Contracting Ltd., 123 Dover St., Toronto, ON M1K 5E4 is a customer of the defendant, and is indebted to the defendant in an amount that I am, at present, unable to name.

6. I have conducted a corporate search on the defendant that indicates that its head office is 1131 Fonthill Road, Toronto, ON.

SWORN before me at the   )

)

City of Toronto,   )

)   *I.M. Just*

this 30th day of October, year 0   )   I.M. Just

)

A. Coping   )

A Commissioner, etc.   )

Figure 9.7   Garnishee's Statement

Court file no. 1234

ONTARIO

SUPERIOR COURT OF JUSTICE

B E T W E E N

ARTEMIS PLUMBING SUPPLY LTD.

CREDITOR

and

PERSONABLE PLUMBERS LTD.

DEBTOR

and

MURRAY HILL CONTRACTING LTD.

GARNISHEE

GARNISHEE'S STATEMENT

1.   I/We acknowledge that I/we owe or will owe the debtor or the debtor and one or more co-owners the sum of $, payable on   , because

(Give reasons why you owe the debtor or the debtor and one or more co-owners money. If you are making payment of less than the amount stated in line 2 of this paragraph because the debt is owed to the debtor and to one or more co-owners or for any other reason, give a full explanation of the reason. If you owe the debtor wages, state how often the debtor is paid. State the gross amount of the debtor's wages before any deductions and the net amount after all deductions and attach a copy of a pay slip.)

1.1   *(If debt owed to debtor and one or more co-owners, check here* ☐ *and complete the following*:)

Co-owner(s) of the Debt *(name, address)*

Figure 9.7   Continued

2.   *(If you do not owe the debtor money, explain why. Give any other information that will explain your financial relationship with the debtor.)*

3.   *(If you have been served with any other notice of garnishment or a writ of execution against the debtor, give particulars.)*

Name of creditor	*Location of Sheriff*	*Date of notice or writ*	*Date of service on you*

4.   *(If you have been served outside Ontario and you wish to object on the ground that service outside Ontario was improper, give particulars of your objection.)*

Date ....   Signature of or for garnishee   ....

Name of garnishee   MURRAY HILL CONTRACTING LTD.

Address   ....

....

....

Telephone number   ....

RCP-E 60I (November 1, 2005)

Figure 9.7 Concluded

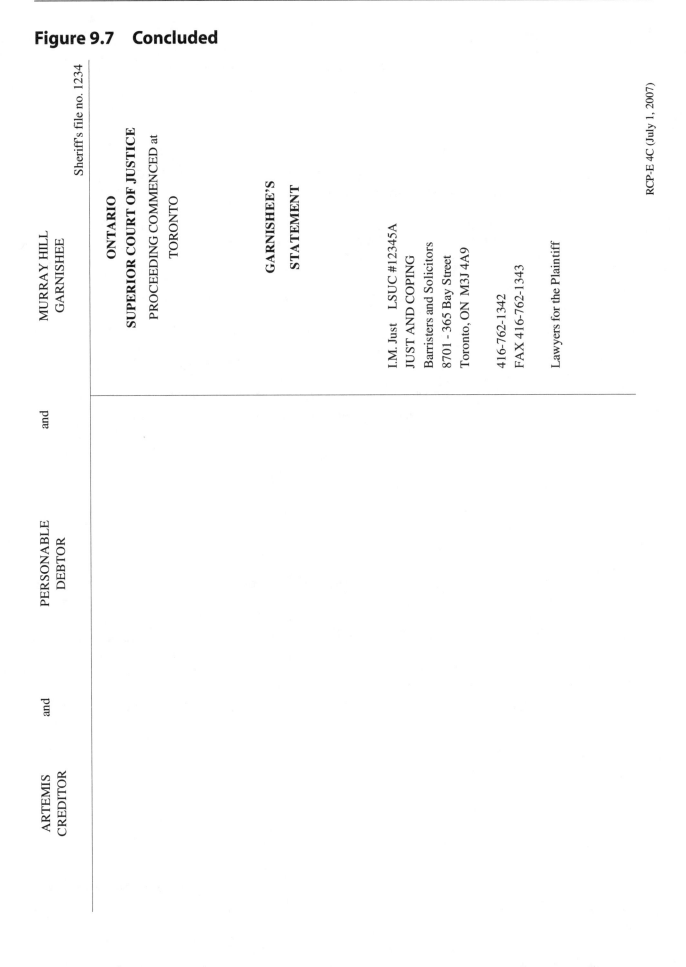

ARTEMIS CREDITOR

and

PERSONABLE DEBTOR

and

MURRAY HILL GARNISHEE

Sheriff's file no. 1234

ONTARIO
SUPERIOR COURT OF JUSTICE
PROCEEDING COMMENCED at
TORONTO

GARNISHEE'S
STATEMENT

I.M. Just   LSUC #12345A
JUST AND COPING
Barristers and Solicitors
8701 - 365 Bay Street
Toronto, ON M3J 4A9

416-762-1342
FAX 416-762-1343

Lawyers for the Plaintiff

RCP-E 4C (July 1, 2007)

Figure 9.8   Sample Statement of Particulars: Garnishment of Civil Servants and Those Receiving Funds from the Province of Ontario

IN THE MATTER OF A GARNISHMENT AGAINST A PROVINCIAL
CIVIL SERVANT AND IN THE MATTER OF THE
PROCEEDINGS AGAINST THE CROWN ACT

STATEMENT OF PARTICULARS

DEBTOR: Darius Milhaud

SIN:

THIS STATEMENT OF PARTICULARS MUST BE SERVED WITH THE NOTICE OF

GARNISHMENT IN ACCORDANCE WITH THE REGULATIONS MADE UNDER THE ACT.

_____

Chief Financial Officer

_____

Administrative Unit

1.   Where the money payable to the debtor is salary, state:

    a.   occupation: assistant deputy minister

    b.   name of employer: Ministry of Education

    c.   section of employer: Community Colleges

    d.   street address: 900 Bay Street, Toronto, ON M5G 1X7

2.   Where the money payable to the debtor is remuneration for goods or services (other than wages), state:

    a.   general description of the goods or services

    b.   approximate date of delivery or performance

    c.   location of delivery or performance

3.   Is the attached notice of garnishment to enforce an order for support or maintenance?

    Yes _____   No _____

_____

Signature of creditor

date: October 18, year 0

[**NOTE:** The regulation under the *Proceedings Against the Crown Act* provides that a notice of garnishment issued against the Crown shall be deemed to be served on the 30th day after the actual date of service or on the 30th day after the effective date of service under the rules of the relevant court.]

Small Claims Court Proceedings

INTRODUCTION

Chapter 10 concerns actions for debt in Small Claims Court. Generally, the techniques and procedures you read about in earlier chapters are applicable to Small Claims Court. In fact, the litigation and enforcement procedures are similar to, and are modelled on, the *Rules of Civil Procedure* of the Superior Court of Justice, except that they are usually simpler and quicker to use than those of the Superior Court. The Small Claims Court has its own rules, namely the *Rules of the Small Claims Court*, which are reproduced in Appendix B of this text.

There is opportunity for paralegals to carry on litigation practice in Small Claims Court. Because of the cost of lawyers' services relative to the amount in issue, and the limits on costs recovery in this court, lawyers are not seen as often as paralegals are in Small Claims Court. There has been a long tradition of having clients represented by court agents who regularly work in these courts, usually for creditors, and often on behalf of collection agencies. A paralegal with a high-volume caseload, where the cases are fairly routine, and often not defended, can operate economically and profitably in the Small Claims Court. Similarly, a law clerk working under a lawyer's supervision can produce and manage the paperwork for the law office's routine small claims collections process, making this part of a practice profitable for a law firm.

Lawyers and paralegals, licensed by the Law Society of Upper Canada, are permitted to appear in Small Claims Court. The Law Society has also authorized certain other groups of persons to appear as representatives in Small Claims Court, including Aboriginal case workers, articling students, and union representatives, among others. For information on these categories of permitted representatives, consult chapter 1. Law clerks are no longer permitted to appear in the court; however, under a lawyer's supervision, a clerk can complete and file Small Claims Court forms.

SMALL CLAIMS COURT CULTURE

Small Claims Court in one form or another has occupied a niche in the justice system of Ontario since the province's colonial beginnings. It was recognized early on that the lawyer-driven civil litigation process in the Superior Court was too expensive, too formal, and too slow to be of practical use where pursuit of a minor claim might cost more than the claim itself. If a small business person or consumer could litigate in a court that was quick, inexpensive, and relatively informal, then justice might be done.

Because of this court's perspective and unique position in the court system, it operates somewhat differently from other courts in Ontario.

- Small Claims Court clerks have a role in assisting litigants by advising them on the use of court procedures and forms; although the clerks do not give legal advice, some may give quasi-legal advice such as on how to determine which defendant to sue.[1] However, you are expected to resolve your own procedural issues. To help you do this, the court makes user-friendly self-help guides and an online forms assistant software program available to the public. These guides and software are designed for litigants who have no experience in conducting cases in this court. There are separate guides for the principal steps in a proceeding. Each guide explains the process and its purpose in plain language, identifies the relevant rules and forms, and gives detailed instructions on how to complete the forms and on how to carry out the court procedure in question. The guides are available at court offices and also online, along with the court forms and forms assistant software program, at http://www .ontariocourtforms.on.ca. Law Help Ontario, a pro bono law organization, operates pro bono legal clinics in the Toronto and Ottawa small claims courts. The Law Help Ontario website at http://www.lawhelpontario.org provides information to assist unrepresented litigants.

- Small Claims Court judges tend to be more interventionist than judges in other courts, particularly if a party is representing himself; the judges will assist litigants in sticking to the real issues, and will sometimes guide the presentation of evidence to eliminate time-consuming efforts spent on legally irrelevant matters. They will also suggest compromises and settlements, where these appear to be feasible, and will screen cases for settlement before they get on the trial list.[2]

JURISDICTION

The court's authority and jurisdiction is found in the *Courts of Justice Act*, ss. 22 to 33.1, and the *Small Claims Court Rules*, which were revised, as were the court forms (in 2011), and can be found in O. Reg. 258/98, as amended. The Small Claims Court is part of the Superior Court of Justice, although it maintains a separate identity, and operates under its own rules.

The court has jurisdiction in most actions for the payment of money where the amount claimed is $25,000 or less, exclusive of costs and interest, or where the plaintiff seeks recovery of personal property where the value of the property is worth $25,000 or less. No cause of action is specifically excluded, but may be implicitly excluded where the remedy claimed is one that is beyond the court's powers. You should note that if you seek more than money damages or recovery of property, you will have to bring your action in the Superior Court. Small Claims Court has no power to give a **declaratory judgment** or grant an injunction or an order for **specific performance**. At any time before trial, on consent of the parties, the registrar of the Superior Court can transfer a case to the Small Claims Court if it is in the latter court's jurisdiction.[3] Although the

---

declaratory judgment
a judgment where the court declares the rights of the parties on some issue before it; also referred to as a declaration

specific performance
in an action for specific performance, the plaintiff claims that she cannot be properly compensated for breach of contract by payment of money damages; instead, she argues that the only just remedy is one where the defendant is compelled by the court to do what he was required to do under the contract—for example, if she has contracted to buy a house with a spectacular view, mere money cannot compensate for the loss of the view; the vendor will be compelled to perform the contract by completing the sale

Superior Court has jurisdiction over all civil cases, whatever the amount of the claim, it is wise to use the Small Claims Court when within its monetary jurisdiction, because there is clear authority for denying a successful plaintiff his costs in the Superior Court, when the claim is for $25,000 or less.[4]

TERRITORIAL JURISDICTION

A plaintiff, under rule 6.01(1), may bring proceedings in the "territorial division" in which the cause of action arose, or where the defendant resides or carries on business. If there is more than one defendant, the plaintiff can bring his claim in the territorial division in which any one of the defendants resides or carries on business. The action may also be brought in the court nearest to a defendant's residence or business. This rule recognizes that a defendant may be closer to a court in an adjacent territorial division than he is to the court in the territorial division in which he resides.

Many credit card companies and institutional lenders specify in their loan contracts that any legal dispute be heard in Toronto, by declaring that the contract is entered into in the city of Toronto in the agreement itself. This means that a defendant who lives in Thunder Bay, who wishes to dispute the amount owing on his credit card, might be compelled to litigate the issue in Toronto and not where he resides. The courts, however, have interpreted these cases narrowly against the plaintiffs. In addition to the fact that the contract sets Toronto as the site of litigation, the court is entitled to look at all the factors, including where the parties entered into the agreement, where the defendant resides, and other factors, before permitting the plaintiff to have its way on the jurisdictional issues. Unless the plaintiff can show that the entire cause of action arose in Toronto, the court is entitled to determine jurisdiction on the basis of a defendant's residence.[5]

While the plaintiff chooses the territorial jurisdiction, the choice can be reviewed at any time by a defendant's motion, by the court on reviewing a request for default judgment, or where several defendants are served outside the court's jurisdiction, and at a settlement conference or trial.

Rule 6.01(2) provides that, on a motion, the court can order that the trial be held at a location other than those described in rule 6.01(1) if "the balance of convenience" substantially favours holding the trial in another place. This is a common law test that looks at where the parties reside, where the witnesses reside, where the costs might be inordinately higher for one side rather than for the other because of location, and so on.

"Territorial division" is defined in rule 1.02(1) as "a county, district or a regional municipality," and also includes various geographical areas, including the City of Toronto. Some territorial divisions have more than one court. A small claims court **gazetteer** can be helpful in determining which court an action should be commenced in.[6]

Proper territorial jurisdiction is something the plaintiff has to prove; this may be done by setting out the facts that relate to the cause of action or the defendant's residence, as the case may be, in the claim. In the alternative, and more usually, the plaintiff can prove territorial jurisdiction by filing an affidavit for jurisdiction (figure 10.1) setting out the facts relevant to jurisdiction. An affidavit will be required if:

- at the time the claim is filed, the address of the defendant is outside the court's territorial division;

gazetteer
a directory in which the entries are arranged by geographical location— various geographical places in the province are listed with corresponding small claims courts to use listed across from the geographical entry

- the defendant is served outside the court's territorial division and does not file a defence before the court grants default judgment; or

- the plaintiff has physically served all defendants outside the court's territorial division, whatever their address appears to be in the claim. The defendant may dispute territorial jurisdiction in her defence, may bring a motion contesting jurisdiction before filing a defence, or may raise the issue later.

Under rule 6.01(3), at a settlement conference or a trial, a judge can change the place of trial if he or she finds that the trial was commenced in the wrong jurisdiction.

COMMENCING PROCEEDINGS

Before commencing proceedings, carry out the usual investigations, giving thought to the costs of doing this balanced against the size of the claim, and ensure that a demand letter has been sent. If there is no response to the demand letter, you should obtain a Plaintiff's Claim form. All Small Claims Court forms can be downloaded from the list of forms for the Small Claims Court at http://www.ontariocourtforms.on.ca.

DETERMINING AND SUING THE PROPER PARTIES

The proper parties to a lawsuit are those who have legal rights and obligations in issue. The issues canvassed in chapter 3 cover these matters — refer to that discussion to refresh your memory.

When suing unincorporated businesses, the *Small Claims Court Rules*, particularly rule 5, are similar to those for the Superior Court. Although it is always wise to cast your net as broadly as possible so that you can enforce a judgment against those who own the business as well as the business itself, rule 5 anticipates that you may not know the identities of the individuals who own a particular business. While you can usually find this information using business name searches, under rule 5.04 you can avoid the cost of searches by requiring the business entity to divulge the name of the individual or individuals who comprise it.

With respect to suing an unincorporated business:

1. You may sue a partnership by naming the partners: "Smith and Jones carrying on business as SJ Enterprises."

2. If you sue the partnership alone, you may do so by suing SJ Enterprises. It is improper to also name the partners if you follow this route. However, some lawyers do sue the partnership and the partners together. The reason for this is that if sheriffs' officers see the names of the partners and the partnership named as parties, they are likely not to hesitate to seize assets of either the partners or the partnership. If they see only the names of the partners, the officers may not be prepared to seize partnership property.

3. If you follow the first example, you may enforce the judgment against the assets of Smith and Jones, as well as against the assets of SJ Enterprises.

4. If you follow the second example, you may enforce the judgment against SJ Enterprises alone. However, in the second example, you may expand your enforcement rights by serving the alleged partners under rule 5.03 with the claim made against the partnership and a notice to the alleged partner (figure 10.2), stating that the plaintiff alleges that the individual served is a partner at the relevant time under rule 5.03. A person who is served in this manner is deemed to be a partner, unless he disputes that fact.

5. If you choose to enforce against individual partners under rule 5.03 *after* obtaining a judgment against the partnership in the partnership name only, not having served notice on any alleged partners, you must bring a motion in the court asking for permission to now name individual partners so that you can enforce the judgment against them.

There may be some situations where you are not sure who the alleged partners were at the relevant time (usually when the cause of action arose) and you want to name them in your lawsuit. For example, if you sue a partnership where some partners have left and others have joined since the cause of action arose, you may wish to narrow down your choice of partners to those who were members, and therefore personally liable, when the cause of action arose. Under rule 5.04(1), you can discover this information by preparing and serving a notice requiring the partnership to disclose in writing the names and addresses of all partners who were members of the partnership on a particular date (figure 10.3).

SOLE PROPRIETORSHIPS

Rule 5 applies with necessary adaptations to sole proprietorships. You may sue the individual who carries on the business in her own name — "Gina McLeod carrying on business as GM Financial Services" — or in the name of the sole proprietorship: "GM Financial Services." It is almost always advisable to sue the individual in her own name. If you are in a situation where you do not know who that is, but know the name of the business when you file your claim, you can use rule 5.04 to find out who the individual sole proprietor is or do a business name search of the sole proprietorship. You may also sue in the business name and serve the sole proprietor in a manner analogous to the way you would serve a partnership. If a sole proprietor or a partnership uses a business name without registering it, the business is not entitled to sue or defend a claim until the business name has been registered.[7]

CORPORATIONS

The rules for suing a corporation are the same as they are in the Superior Court. If the party is a corporation, then the claim must, in most cases, be brought against the corporation in its legal corporate name.

LITIGANTS WHO ARE UNDER A DISABILITY

full legal age and capacity
to sue or be sued, an individual usually has to have reached the age of majority and be mentally capable of taking part in a lawsuit; a person who is capable of participating and who is over 18 years of age is referred to as being of full age and capacity

litigation guardian
an individual who conducts a lawsuit and instructs counsel on behalf of a party who is under a disability or who is not of full age and capacity

Children's Lawyer
a public official whose legal staff looks after the financial and other interests of children who are involved in or have an interest in civil proceedings

Public Guardian and Trustee
a government office whose staff are responsible for looking after the interests of mentally incapable persons (formerly called mentally incompetent) where no attorney under a power of attorney, guardian of the person, or guardian of property has been appointed

If a party, whether plaintiff or defendant, is not of **full legal age and capacity** (a minor or someone who is mentally incapable of looking after his or her own affairs), he or she is deemed to be a party under a disability and must have a **litigation guardian** in order to sue or be sued. However, a minor, under rule 4.01(2), may sue for an amount up to $500 without having a litigation guardian. Rule 4.01(3) requires that a plaintiff under a disability have a litigation guardian file a consent to act as a litigation guardian (figure 10.4) with the claim, or as soon as possible after the claim is filed. The defendant, if under a disability, must do the same, with someone filing a consent to act as litigation guardian for the defendant (figure 10.5) on filing a defence or when ordered to do so by the court. In the consents, you will

- give the minor's date of birth;

- state the nature of the disability;

- set out the relationship of the guardian to the party under a disability, if any;

- state that the guardian has no interest in the proceeding that is adverse to the party under disability; and

- *if appointed on behalf of a plaintiff*, acknowledge personal liability to pay costs awarded against him or her, or against the party under a disability.

When a litigation guardian is used, the title of proceedings should take the form:

Gustave Flaubert, a person under disability, by his litigation guardian, Emma Bovary.

Rule 4.03 sets out who may be a litigation guardian. The person must not be under a disability. For a minor child, a parent or person with custody of the child shall be the guardian; if there is no person who can act as guardian, then the **Children's Lawyer** shall be the guardian.

If the person is mentally incapable but has a guardian or is a person with a power of attorney appointed under the *Substitute Decisions Act*, the guardian or the attorney may act as a litigation guardian if his or her appointment grants the power to act as litigation guardian.

If a mentally incapable person has neither a person acting under a power of attorney nor a guardian appointed in accordance with the *Substitute Decisions Act*, then a "suitable person," with no interest adverse to the mentally incapable person, may be appointed or, in the last resort, the **Public Guardian and Trustee** may be appointed.

In accordance with rule 4.07, no person under a disability may enter into a settlement without court approval. For example, you should never settle a minor's claim without court approval. A release from parents or others in control of the minor will not prevent the minor, once she comes of age, from suing the defendant — and in tort or contract she may have up to two years from the time she reaches the age of majority to commence proceedings.

If you sue a person under a disability, the action must be defended by a litigation guardian. If one does not voluntarily appear when a defence is filed or after the time for filing a defence has passed, then you should serve a demand (figure 10.6) on the defendant; if that brings no response, you must apply to the court by motion for an order appointing a litigation guardian for the defendant who is found to be under a disability. It is advisable to serve the motion on the Children's Lawyer in the case of a minor, or on the Public Guardian and Trustee in the case of a person who is mentally incapable and does not have a guardian appointed to look after his personal needs or his property. The parent or the person having custody of a minor may file a defence and consent to act as litigation guardian, as may the guardian of a person who is mentally incapable.

The duty of a litigation guardian, set out in rule 4.04, is to diligently attend to the interests of the person under a disability and take all steps reasonably necessary for the protection of those interests, including the commencement and conduct of claims against others. A litigation guardian who fails in her duty may be removed by the court, whether or not a motion to do so has been brought. If a litigation guardian for a defendant has not been appointed where one is required, the court will set aside a default judgment.

FILING A CLAIM

A proceeding is commenced by filing a plaintiff's claim (figure 10.7) with the clerk, together with a copy of the claim for each defendant.[8] The clerk, on payment of the prescribed fee, will issue the claim by dating and signing it and putting a seal on it. She will also assign the claim a court file number. Copies of the claim for service should show the clerk's signature. In addition, the clerk will also stamp true copies of the claim to show that it has been issued by the court. The setup of the claim form provides space to set out the reasons for the claim and has blank spaces to fill in the details of the amount claimed and the particulars of the interest claimed. The language used to draft the claim should be concise and non-technical. If the description of the claim requires it, additional pages can be attached.

If there is a document relevant to the claim — such as a promissory note, invoice, or contract — rather than describe it, you must refer to it and attach a copy of it to the claim. You should keep the original document to file in court as documentary evidence as part of your case. You should attach a copy of any relevant documents to your claim. If, for example, you were relying on a promissory note signed by the defendant, you would state in your reasons for claim that a copy of the promissory note was attached to the claim as Document "A." You would then mark a copy of the promissory note as Document "A" and attach it to your claim. You should refer to documents attached to the claim as "document" or "schedule." For a claim you should not use the term "exhibit" because a claim is not a sworn document and the term "exhibit" refers to evidence such as sworn documents or other evidence given to the court on a motion or at trial. (See figure 10.7 for an example of a plaintiff's claim.)

SERVICE OF THE CLAIM

Service is governed by rule 8. As in the Superior Court, the first document in the lawsuit, usually the plaintiff's claim, should be served personally using a process server.[9] Court bailiffs no longer serve claims, summons to witness, or notices of motion unless the court orders them to do so. Some clerks may tell you that the plaintiff may serve the claim herself. This is permissible but inadvisable because there may be a dispute over whether the defendant was properly served. Where there is an issue of credibility, it is better to have a neutral, professional process server giving evidence about the mode of service, rather than someone who has a personal interest in the matter.

You may also use an alternative to personal service to serve individuals, but the alternative service rule cannot be used to serve corporations.

Methods for alternatives to personal service are set out in rule 8.03.

- Alternative service on an individual under rule 8.03(2) may be carried out by leaving a copy of the document in a sealed envelope that is addressed to the defendant with an apparently adult member of the defendant's household *and* you also must, on the same or next day, mail or send by courier a copy to the defendant at that address. Service is deemed to be effective on the fifth day after mailing or on verification of delivery by courier.

- In accordance with rule 8.03(3), a corporation may be served by mail or courier at the last corporate address recorded with the Ministry of Government Services. You must also serve each listed director at his address on file with the ministry by sending him a copy by mail or courier. Service is deemed to be effective on the fifth day after mailing or on verification of delivery by courier. A Corporation Profile Report will reveal the last-known addresses of a corporation. You can search for corporate documents online at http://www .oncorp.com/home/services_onbis_corp.asp. Oncorp is recognized as a filing and search agency. Samples of documents, including a Corporation Profile Report, are readily available on the website.

- You may serve the party's lawyer or an employee in the lawyer's office if the lawyer or employee endorses a copy of the document, accepting service. A lawyer will not do this unless he or she has instructions from the client to accept service. At this time there are no provisions in the rule for service upon a paralegal's office.

- In accordance with rule 8.03(7), you can serve a party by sending a copy of the document by registered mail or courier to the individual's residence. Such service is effective on the date the individual being served, or any person who appears to be a member of the same household, verifies by signature, on a Canada Post or courier delivery confirmation form, their receipt of a copy of the claim.

All documents that come after the claim may be served by mail, courier, or fax on a party, his paralegal, or his lawyer, unless the clerk of the court orders otherwise. If served by mail or courier, the document should be sent to the party at the address given by that party on a previous court document. Once mailed, a document is deemed served on the fifth day after mailing. This should be taken into account when calculating the time for signing a default judgment or if serving motion documents.

The rules set out the requirements for service by fax. If a fax under 16 pages long is served before 5 p.m., the document is deemed to be received on the day it is transmitted, if that day is not a holiday. If the fax is sent after 5 p.m., it is deemed to be received on the next day that is not a holiday. Rule 8.08(2) provides that faxes that are 16 pages or longer must be served between 5 p.m. and 8 a.m. unless consent from the other party to serve the document before 5 p.m. has been granted.

Rule 8 sets out the modes of personal service on a variety of entities. You should refer to the rule whenever you are suing an entity other than an individual of full age and capacity to see what is required to successfully serve the entity personally.

A claim should be served within six months of being issued. If it is not, you need to bring a motion to extend the time for service.

Service is proved by an affidavit of service (figure 10.8), attested to by the process server, and filed with the claim after it has been served.

If you are unable to serve the claim personally or by an alternative to personal service, it is possible to serve the claim by substitutional service. As in the Superior Court, this requires a motion to obtain a court order that must be complied with strictly. If you must serve a party outside Ontario, it is wise to bring a motion to obtain court approval of the costs of service; otherwise, costs of service cannot be recovered by the successful party as part of court costs. Rule 19.01(3) limits the cost of service that can be recovered, without a court order, to $60 for each person served. If you need to find a process server in your area, check the *Yellow Pages* or an online phone directory. If you need to find a process server for service outside Ontario, check the International Process Servers Search Engine Directory at http://www.ipsdirectory.com. Note that claim and defence forms require that plaintiffs and defendants notify the court and all other parties of changes of address within seven days of the change.

When calculating time periods for service, or anything else in the rules, you should take note of rule 1, which defines "holiday," and rule 3, which governs time computation.

In defining "holiday," which includes the expected statutory holidays, rule 1 states the following:

- holiday means any Saturday or Sunday;

- if New Year's Day, Canada Day, or Remembrance Day falls on a Saturday or Sunday, the following Monday is a holiday;

- if Christmas Day falls on a Saturday or Sunday, the following Monday and Tuesday are holidays; and

- if Christmas Day falls on a Friday, the following Monday is a holiday.

Rule 3 states that when the rules prescribe a time period, count the days required by *excluding the first day of the period, and including the last day of the period.* Where the last day of the period falls on a holiday, the time period is deemed to end on the next day after the holiday that is not itself a holiday. For example, if the last day was Labour Day (which is always the first Monday in September), the time would be extended to the next day, Tuesday. If the period ended on Christmas Day, when Christmas day fell on a Friday, then the application of the definition of "holiday" in rule 1 requires that the time period be extended to the following Tuesday.

FILING FEES FOR FREQUENT PLAINTIFFS

A plaintiff who files more than 10 claims in a particular Small Claims Court in a calendar year is termed a "frequent claimant." To issue claims, obtain default judgment, or set matters down for trial or assessment hearings, frequent claimants must pay a higher filing fee as set out in the Small Claims Court Fees and Allowances regulation made under the *Administration of Justice Act*, O. Reg. 432/93. These clients will be given, in advance, pre-assigned court file numbers that they must use. This means that you must keep track of your large-volume clients who are required to pay higher fees and use pre-assigned court file numbers. Ask clients who have a lot of collection work whether they have been classed as large-volume clients. You can also obtain this information from the court.

FILING A DEFENCE

To file a defence under rule 9, the defendant must simply set out, on a defence form, in numbered paragraphs, in non-technical language, the reasons why he disputes the claim, along with the name, address, and phone number of the defendant's lawyer or agent. A defendant, like a plaintiff, is required to attach to the defence a copy of any document on which he relies. If the defendant is unrepresented, he should include his own address and phone number in the defence. The prescribed form for a defence (figure 10.9) is available online at http://www.ontariocourtforms.on.ca.

The defence must be filed within 20 days of service of the claim, unless service was by mail or courier, in which case service is effective on the fifth day after the document is mailed or verified by courier as delivered. The defendant then has 20 days from the date of service to serve and file a defence. A copy of the defence for the court along with a copy for each party must be filed with the court. The court clerk serves the defence by fax or mail on the parties. There is no provision for the clerk to accept a defence, when the time for filing it has passed, without consent in writing from the plaintiff or an order of the court. When acting for a defendant, it is wise to ask the plaintiff to extend the time for filing the defence, if you need the time, and to obtain and file the plaintiff's consent with the defence.

PROPOSALS

Rule 9.03 permits a defendant to admit liability for all or part of the plaintiff's claim, including the monetary amount claimed, and to file a defence that proposes terms of payment. If the plaintiff does not dispute the proposal within 20 days of service of the defence, the defendant should make payment in accordance with the proposal, as if a court order had been made; if the defendant defaults, the plaintiff shall serve a notice of default of payment (figure 10.10)[10] on the defendant and file an affidavit of default of payment (figure 10.11) with the court 15 days after serving the defendant with notice of default if nothing has been paid. The court clerk will then sign judgment for the unpaid balance of the proposal.

If the defendant submits a proposal that the plaintiff wishes to dispute, the plaintiff serves on the defendant and files, with the court, a request to clerk form requesting a terms of payment hearing (figure 10.12). The plaintiff must do this within 20 days of being served with the defendant's defence/proposal. If the defendant is an individual, the clerk will serve a Financial Information Form on the defendant, who must complete it and serve it on the plaintiff prior to the terms of payment hearing. This hopefully will provide some hard evidence of the defendant's ability to pay. If the plaintiff fails to dispute the proposal within the time provided for in the rules, then he or she is deemed to have accepted the proposal.

Once a proposal has been made, the defendant should make payments directly to the plaintiff as proposed, whether the plaintiff objects and whether the proposal has been approved by the court and confirmed in an order. A court is more likely to look favourably on a "cooperative" defendant than on one who is holding off making payment.

In the event that the proposal only admitted partial liability for the claim, the court will schedule the matter for a settlement conference to deal with the part in dispute.

DEFENDANT'S CLAIM

Rule 10 permits a defendant to make a claim against the plaintiff (counterclaim) and anyone else connected with the same event or transaction that gave rise to the plaintiff's claim (third-party claims, cross-claims).

To make a defendant's claim, you must file a defendant's claim (figure 10.13). It must be issued within 20 days of the defence being filed, unless the court permits a later filing. This reduces the opportunity to stall and delay an action by making a "late" defendant's claim. The content of the defendant's claim is set out in rule 10.01(4) and is similar to the required contents of a plaintiff's claim. The clerk will issue the defendant's claim; the defendant will file the original and serve a copy on every other person against whom the claim is made in accordance with the requirements in rule 8 for serving a claim. A party defending a defendant's claim shall file a defence to it within 20 days of service of the defendant's claim. The clerk shall serve any defence to the defendant's claim on the other parties.

The defendant's claim will be decided at the trial of the main action unless the court decides that it would be unduly complicated or would unduly prolong the trial, in which case the court can order that the defendant's claim be tried separately, usually after the main action. A "third party" may defend not only the defendant's claim against him or her, but may defend the main claim as well.

DEFAULT PROCEEDINGS

Rule 11 provides for default proceedings. If the defendant fails to file a defence within the applicable time period, on request the clerk will note the defendant in default (figure 10.14). If the claim was for liquidated damages, the clerk may sign default judgment on proof by the plaintiff that the defendant has been served properly within the territorial division of the court that issued the claim.

1. If the affidavit of service shows that at least one defendant was served within the territorial division of the issuing court, the clerk will sign judgment on any liquidated claim and shall set any general, unliquidated claim down for an assessment of damages in writing or for a hearing.

2. If proof of service shows that no defendant was served in the territorial division, then the plaintiff must prove jurisdiction by filing an affidavit for jurisdiction (figure 10.1) showing that one or more defendants resides or

carries on business within the territorial division of the issuing court (although served somewhere else), or that the cause of action arose within the territorial division of the issuing court, or that it is the court nearest to the place where a defendant resides or carries on business, before the clerk can sign default judgment or set the matter down for a written assessment or for a hearing to prove damages. Oral evidence can be given to prove territorial jurisdiction at an assessment of damages hearing, but it is more efficient to do it by affidavit.

The bottom line is that default judgment can be signed provided that the plaintiff can satisfy the clerk of the court or the judge that at least one defendant resides or carries on business within the territorial division of the issuing court, that the court is the nearest court to the place where a defendant resides or carries on business, or that the cause of action arose within that court's territorial division.

When default judgment is signed, it is for the claim, costs, a claim preparation and filing fee (if applicable), and prejudgment interest, provided the claim is for a liquidated amount. Note that you must specifically claim prejudgment interest in your claim if you are to get it included in the default judgment. Unlike the Superior Court, this court does not require the litigant to prepare all of the documentation. The clerk will prepare the default judgment (figure 10.15) and mail it to the defendant.

If part of the claim was for a liquidated amount and part was not, the clerk may sign default judgment for the part that was for a liquidated amount and set the balance of the claim down for the plaintiff to prove damages on a motion made in writing or at an assessment hearing. An assessment may be obtained by filing a notice of motion and supporting affidavit with attached documentation containing enough evidence to allow a judge to assess unliquidated damages and give judgment. If the documentation on a written motion is insufficient, a judge may schedule a hearing. Once the clerk has noted the defendant in default, the defendant is barred from filing a defence, although, as in the Superior Court, it is possible for the defendant to move to set aside default judgment using rule 11.06 on the grounds that

- he or she has a defence,

- he or she has a reasonable explanation for the default, and

- the motion is made as soon as is reasonably possible in all the circumstances.[11]

If a plaintiff defaults on a defendant's claim, the defendant cannot obtain default judgment. Judgment on the defendant's claim will be given at trial of the main action.

AMENDMENT OF CLAIMS

Rule 12 permits parties to amend claims or defences without the court's permission at any time up to 30 days before trial. In accordance with rule 12, additions to the document should be underlined and any other changes identified. Because there is no formal pretrial discovery, new facts or information that might have surfaced at discovery are now likely to surface later in the process at settlement conferences. This may result in amendments to claims and defences at a relatively late stage in the proceedings. But, to prevent surprise, amendments must be served at least 30 days before the originally scheduled trial date.

SETTLEMENT CONFERENCES

Rule 13 provides for settlement conferences. The purposes of a settlement conference are to

- resolve or narrow the issues in an action;

- speed up the disposition of the action;

- encourage settlement of the action;

- assist the parties in effectively preparing and presenting their case at trial; and

- provide full disclosure between the parties with respect to relevant facts and evidence, including documentary and oral evidence.

There is an expectation, explicitly set out in the rule, that the parties will openly and frankly discuss the issues, that the contents of the discussion will remain confidential, and that statements made in the conference will be treated as having been made on a without-prejudice basis. A judge who presides at a settlement conference cannot preside at the trial.

Under rule 13, a settlement conference is mandatory and must be held in every defended action within 90 days of the filing of the first defence (unless the defence admits liability and sets out a proposal for payment). The clerk will set a time for the settlement conference and send a notice of settlement conference and a blank form 13A, list of proposed witnesses to every party filing a claim or defence. The clerk usually mails the parties a notice of settlement conference when she serves the defence by mail on the plaintiff. The rules require that parties file all documents that were not attached to the claim and defence, and that a party seeks to rely on at trial, including an expert report, along with any other documents or evidence they intend to rely on and that a list of proposed witnesses (figure 10.16) be served and filed at least 14 days prior to the settlement conference. Generally, the court encourages and appreciates full disclosure at this stage. If a person who attends the settlement conference fails to adequately prepare for the settlement conference or does not file the required list of proposed witnesses or documents to be relied upon, the court may award costs against that person.

Judges have been quite creative with this rule and have used it to settle and expedite matters. Judges may use the settlement conference to set a schedule for unrepresented litigants to produce necessary documents or to advise the party of procedural barriers they may face and how they may overcome them, among other things. At the conclusion of the settlement conference, the judge completes a settlement conference memorandum to inform the trial judge of the matters upon which the parties agree, the outstanding issues, the evidentiary issues, the number of witnesses and whether or not any interpreters are required. Any orders made on consent or under the authority of rule 13.05 must be recorded by the judge on an endorsement record.

Where settlement conferences are used to facilitate settlement, the practice is to have the parties sign court form 14D, terms of settlement (figure 10.17). If the defendant defaults, the terms provide that judgment may be obtained, based upon the terms, if the plaintiff brings a motion attesting to the default, or the plaintiff can chose to continue the action as if there had not been a settlement. Theoretically, a party could agree to a settlement for an amount less than the amount claimed and have no intention of making any payments. When default occurs, the plaintiff is then limited to judgment for the lower agreed-upon amount, or has to continue on to trial as if there was not a settlement. Continuing on to trial will require a trial set-down fee plus associated trial costs to be paid, with no guarantee of success. Represented parties will often draft their own minutes of settlement (figure 10.18), which usually contain a provision that states that if the defendant defaults on the terms of the minutes he consents to judgment against him for the amount of the original claim.

These conferences may take place before a court referee. In some divisions, the referee reports back to a judge, who confirms the minutes in a consent order. In Toronto, the practice has not been to confirm the minutes with an order formally, but to include in the minutes a provision for consenting to an order on default of payment.

Once a settlement conference has been scheduled, attendance is mandatory for parties and their representatives unless the court orders otherwise. If you know that a party or a representative will be unable to attend the conference in person, a motion under rule 1.07(1) for permission to attend by phone or video conference should be brought in advance of the conference. If a person who attends a settlement conference does not have the authority to agree to a settlement, she must arrange for the person who has the authority to be available by phone.

Failure to attend a settlement conference will result in costs penalties and the scheduling of an additional settlement conference. Failure to attend a second settlement conference may result in the striking out of the defence and any defendant's claim, and a judgment on a liquidated claim or an assessment of damages on an unliquidated one. If a plaintiff fails to appear, the claim *may* be dismissed, but that is not mandatory. Up to $100 in costs can be levied against an uncooperative party, along with an order to pay related disbursements. If there are special circumstances, more than $100 may be awarded in costs.

If a claim is for less than $2,500, the parties can consent to the judge giving judgment at the end of the settlement conference, saving the cost of a trial. However, a settlement conference judge cannot be the trial judge even if the parties consent.

The old practice of a plaintiff withdrawing a claim after a settlement conference, thereby sticking a defendant with the defendant's own costs, is now prohibited — an order is required and a defendant can ask for and receive costs when a plaintiff withdraws a claim, especially at a late stage in the proceedings.

FORMAL OFFERS TO SETTLE

As is the case with rule 49 of the *Rules of Civil Procedure*, rule 14.07 of the *Small Claims Court Rules* sets up a code for offers to settle that contains cost penalties where a party rejects an offer that turns out to be as good as or better than the judgment. Offers that qualify for costs bonuses and penalties under rule 14 can be made at any stage until seven days before trial; in the absence of a discovery process, offers are likely to be made at the close of a settlement conference. An offer made under rule 14 must be made, accepted, and withdrawn in writing. An offer may take the form of a letter from a lawyer or agent, or it may take the form of an optional court document, form 14A, that lists the provisions of the offer in consecutively numbered paragraphs. (See the offer to settle at figure 10.19.) The offer must remain open for acceptance until the trial commences. It is wise to consider making a counteroffer to an offer that you find unacceptable, rather than reject it outright. Where an offer is made that includes the payment of money, either side can insist on the money being paid into court as a condition of the offer. If the other side accepts, and the money is not paid into court, then the party who was to receive the payment may ask the clerk to sign judgment in accordance with the terms of the offer. This rule also applies when a party fails to comply with an accepted offer, even where there is no order for payment into court.

Under rule 14.07, where the plaintiff makes an offer in writing seven or more days before trial that is not withdrawn and does not expire before trial, and the defendant refuses to accept it, and the plaintiff obtains a judgment *as good as or better* than the offer, then the court may award the plaintiff an award of costs that is up to twice the costs of the action that she otherwise would be entitled to.

Where the defendant makes an offer in writing seven or more days before trial that is not withdrawn and does not expire before trial, and the plaintiff refuses to accept it, and the plaintiff obtains a judgment *as favourable as or less favourable* than the offer, the court may award the defendant an amount for costs that is up to twice the costs awarded to a successful party *from the date the offer was made.*

Note that offers to settle may be made within the seven-day period prior to trial or during the trial, but they will not have the costs benefits/penalties available under rule 14.

MOTIONS

Motions can be brought to deal with pretrial procedural matters. Generally, because of the need to keep court costs down, motions should be used sparingly. In addition to motions, there are two motion-like procedures:

- a request to the clerk to sign a consent order (these are usually minor administrative orders that do not require judicial discretion), and

- a motion to assess damages based on written filings.

If you do decide to bring a motion, you do so using the notice of motion and supporting affidavit form (figure 10.20), unless the court orders otherwise; for example, the court may permit a motion made at trial to be made orally. The form may be served personally, by regular or registered mail, by courier, or by fax on all parties not in default. Service must allow for at least seven full days before the motion is heard if it is served personally, and 12 days if it is served by mail. It must be filed at least three days before the hearing. You must obtain a date for the motion from the clerk *before* you draft and serve the documents. Costs of up to $100 and disbursements of the motion are recoverable by either party. There is now a procedure for motions without notice, where appropriate. There is also a procedure to prohibit a party from bringing further motions where the purpose of that is to delay or hinder proceedings.[12] Motions may be heard by phone or video if an order is obtained in advance under rule 1.07.

THE TRIAL PROCESS

Once the defence has been filed and the settlement conference completed, the clerk shall give the parties a notice to request a trial date if the action is not disposed of in the next 30 days. The plaintiff usually requests a trial and pays the trial set-down fee. The

> ## Sample Illustration of the Formation of the Theory of a Case
>
> In a debt collection case, your client's claim is that the debtor did not pay on a running account. The defence is that payments were made in cash. Your theory may be that the defendant is trying to evade payment of the debt with a story that is not credible. Your strategy will be to discredit his evidence. You will need to give evidence of the accuracy of your accounting records and the debtor's lack of responsiveness to your demands for payment. Documentary supportive evidence would include all of the demand letters and overdue notices, as well as the accounting and banking records for the relevant period.

Settlement Conference Endorsement Record sets out the notice to pay the fee to set the matter down for trial. Once the fee is paid, the clerk fixes the date and sends out the notice of trial to all parties who have filed a claim or defence. If the claim is undefended, but is not a liquidated amount, you may prove your claim by affidavit evidence with affidavits from the witnesses you otherwise would have called at trial. If the judge is not satisfied by the affidavits she can order a hearing.

PREPARING FOR TRIAL

At the time the defence and claims are exchanged, you should have a fairly good idea of what your case is about; you should have developed the theory of your case — based on the facts of the case and applicable law — on which you will base your strategy. The theory of a case cannot be developed until you have interviewed your client, interviewed witnesses, and examined relevant documents. Once you have sifted through the evidence from which you have identified the facts that you are to prove, you can develop your theory (see the box above). If the facts change, you will need to change your theory to fit the facts, not the other way round.

SUMMONS TO WITNESS

When you decide which witnesses you will need to call, you should summons them to attend at trial, unless you are certain that the witnesses will show up. You should know which witnesses you need at the time the claim and defence are filed, and certainly by the close of the settlement conference. If you fail to summons a witness and the witness does not appear, you may be compelled by the court to proceed without that witness. If a summonsed witness fails to appear, you are entitled to an adjournment if you need it; the witness may be apprehended, brought before the court, and held until her presence is no longer required. If the witness is truly unfriendly and refuses to show up for that reason, consider whether it is worth compelling the witness to testify at all, because she may seek to damage your case. If a witness is so hostile that he is not responding in good faith to questions asked on examination-in-chief, you may ask the judge to declare the witness hostile on the grounds of non-responsiveness, in which case you are allowed to cross-examine your own witness and can frame questions to elicit yes/no answers that tie the witness down to precise, responsive answers, rather than rambling, unhelpful discourses.

You may summons a witness by serving her with a summons to witness (figure 10.21). The summons should be for the date of the trial, set out in the notice of trial mailed by the clerk. You should also identify in the summons any documents in the witness's power, possession, or control that you want the witness to bring so that you can introduce them as evidence. You must draft the summons and a request to clerk form asking the court to issue the summons and attend at the court with the appropriate fee for the summons. The summons must be served personally and must be accompanied by a cheque for the witness fee and mileage allowance, referred to in the rules as "attendance money." Experts such as doctors and lawyers are entitled to higher witness fees. The actual amounts required are set out in schedule 3 of the Small Claims Court — Fees and Allowances under the *Administration of Justice Act*. Because these change from time to time, they are not reproduced here. Consult your local court office or obtain them online from http://www.attorneygeneral.jus.gov.on.ca. Click on Court Services, scroll down to Court Fees, and then click on the link for Small Claims Court Fees and Allowances. Although the summons will give the first day of trial as the attendance date, the witness is required to attend on all days of trial until the matter is concluded or the witness is no longer required. You should ask the judge to bind the witnesses over to the next court date if the matter continues past the first day of trial. Proof of service of the summons and attendance money is by affidavit. You should have the affidavit with you in court to show to the judge, in the event that the witness fails to appear. The judge may then issue a warrant for the apprehension of the defaulting witness, requiring that the witness be apprehended and held in custody until the witness's presence is no longer required. If a witness is summonsed needlessly, the court may order that the party summoning the witness pay the witness an amount of money to compensate for inconvenience and expense, above and beyond attendance money already paid.[13]

To prevent surprises, copies of your summons to a witness must be served on all parties so that they can prepare for cross-examination and summons their own reply witnesses.

DOCUMENTARY EVIDENCE AT TRIAL

Most debt collection cases are determined on the basis of documentary evidence rather than on oral evidence. The most important thing for a plaintiff to do in a debt action is to have all the original documents required to prove the case organized and ready for use in court. Rule 18.02 allows you to serve on your opponent, at least 30 days before the trial, a copy of every document you rely on and intend to use at trial to prove your case. Unless the trial judge orders otherwise, these documents may be received in evidence without first having to be identified and commented on by a witness (the usual rule is that documents do not "walk" into court on their own — they have to come in as part of a witness's evidence, where the witness can testify as to what they are, identify them, and otherwise prove their reliability and admissibility). It is advisable to prepare a brief of the documents that you are going to introduce under this rule, with an index identifying each document, listing them in the order that you will be referring to them as part of your case. You should have one copy for the court reporter. The judge and clerk and opposite party should already have copies that were served and filed earlier.

Having extra copies is a good idea, in case served copies have gone missing. These documents may include witness statements and expert reports that include facts and opinions on which the witness could give oral testimony. The use of this class of documents shortens the trial by eliminating the need to call witnesses. If the other side wishes to cross-examine a witness on his statement, he may, under rule 18.02(4), summon him or her as a witness. Also, be aware that judges are reluctant to admit the statements of witnesses that are controversial or that lack credibility. A settlement conference is a good place to settle on which documents and statements would be accepted as evidence if presented in this way. All other documents that would normally be admitted at trial can also be presented in advance in this way. These include accounting records, cheques, promissory notes, contracts, and medical reports.

All documents (including videos and sound discs) that a party intends to rely on at trial must be served on other parties 30 days before the trial date, so that the other parties can prepare to serve reply evidence. The parties should have all relevant documents attached to their pleadings, or should have served and filed them 14 or more days before the settlement conference. From these documents, a party can select the ones to be used at trial and serve them on the other side 30 or more days before trial.

COSTS

As in other civil courts, costs follow the event. This means that if you win, you are reimbursed for some of your legal costs. If you lose, you pay your own costs in full and some of your opponent's costs as well. Remember that the costs rules in rule 19 of the *Small Claims Court Rules* are subject to the costs consequences under rule 14 of refusing or accepting offers to settle made at least seven days before trial, which can double the usual costs award.

The successful party is entitled to have reasonable disbursements paid by the unsuccessful party unless the court orders otherwise. Disbursements include court fees required to issue various documents as well as actual, provable out-of-pocket expenses such as costs of serving documents personally (by a process server) or by mail, the costs of attendance money for witnesses, travel expenses, photocopying, and expert reports. You must be able to provide receipts to prove out-of-pocket expenses.

The court has power to award costs over and above disbursements as follows:

- The court may allow a successful party up to $100 for the preparation and filing of pleadings upon their providing proof that payment of at least $100 was made to a legal representative for claim preparation and filing.

- A representation fee is used to compensate a party who uses a lawyer, articling student, or paralegal. The amount awarded must be reasonable, subject to the limit set out in s. 29 of the *Courts of Justice Act*, which is 15 percent of the amount claimed.

- If the successful party is self-represented, the court may award the successful party up to $500 as compensation for inconvenience.

While a party may expect to recover some of the costs of the action if successful, they still need to have the funds to get the case under way. Where the amount of the claim is relatively small, and where a party has a modest income, court filing fees may present a real barrier to using the court. A poor litigant might be discouraged from proceeding with a meritorious case because of filing fees. It was long thought that the Small Claims Court had no authority to waive fees for those pleading poverty. However, in July 2003, in *Polewsky v. Home Hardware,* the Ontario Divisional Court ruled that the *Courts of Justice Act* should be read as amended to allow Small Claims Court judges to waive fees for parties who have meritorious cases but are unable to pay the fees. The court gave the government a grace period to rewrite the legislation. The fee waiver program is now in place under O. Reg. 2/05 under the *Administration of Justice Act.* An application form to apply for a fee waiver can be obtained from the Small Claims Court office. With a fee waiver, the party does not have to pay any fees and can have an interpreter, in any language, paid for by the court, if required.

VARYING AND SETTING ASIDE JUDGMENTS

Because parties, particularly defendants, may be unrepresented and not realize the necessity of showing up for trial, rule 17 spells out consequences for non-attendance. If neither party shows up, the judge may strike the matter off the trial list, in which case one party or the other will have to reschedule the trial. The judge will not, at this point, dismiss the action or grant default judgment. If one party shows up and the other does not, the judge may proceed in the missing party's absence. If the defendant shows up and the plaintiff does not, the judge may dismiss the action. If the defendant does not show up and the plaintiff does, the judge may grant judgment to the plaintiff or allow the plaintiff to prove his damages. However, if the defendant in his defence had raised the issue of territorial jurisdiction, arguing that the plaintiff had sued in the wrong territorial division, the judge shall make a determination on this issue, and if he or she finds that the action should be tried in another territorial division in accordance with the provisions of rule 6, he or she will make an order directing where the trial should take place. This allows a defendant to have the matter of territorial jurisdiction determined without having to travel a great distance to simply argue that one issue.

Once judgment has been given against a party who has failed to attend trial, it is open to a court to set aside or vary such a judgment. Rule 17 permits motions to set aside default judgments that resulted from inadvertent non-attendance, or because a defendant had no notice of the action because she had not been successfully served. The court in setting aside judgment may do so on terms, often granting to a plaintiff the costs wasted or "thrown away" on the first action. Such a motion must be brought within 30 days of becoming aware of the judgment or the party can ask the court to extend the 30 day period.

If a judgment has been sent from one court to another for enforcement, a motion may be brought in the first court to set the judgment aside. The first court will then notify the second, which will stay enforcement until the matter has been completed in the first court. The key here is that the first court — that is, the one that gave judgment in the first place — determines the outcome of a motion to set aside the judgment and the clerk of the second court will take directions from the clerk of the first court.

A court may also, under rule 17.01(4), on a motion brought within 30 days of the judgment, vary a default judgment after it has been given. Rule 17.04(1) may be used to bring a motion for a new trial if there is relevant evidence that was not available to the party at the time of the original trial and that could not reasonably have been expected to be available at that time. This does provide an alternative to a more costly and formal appeal. Normally a variation of a judgment occurs when the court discovers that, through an inadvertent error, the judgment is incorrect in terms of some detail. For example, a judgment for an amount of money that has been determined on accounting record evidence might be varied if, subsequent to the judgment being made, it was discovered that there had been a calculation error or a misreading of the account records.

ADJOURNMENTS

When a case comes to trial, the judge has the power to postpone or adjourn the trial, but may do so on conditions or terms, and may order one side to compensate the other for inconvenience and costs incurred as a result of the adjournment.

CASE MANAGEMENT

Case management to control delay in the progress of a case is in place in the Small Claims Court.

If a case is undefended and 180 days have passed since the claim was issued, without the defendant being noted in default or the matter placed on a trial list, the clerk shall send the plaintiff a notice of approaching dismissal giving the plaintiff 45 days' notice that the case will be dismissed as abandoned. The plaintiff then has that 45-day period to proceed to default judgment or an assessment of damages. If the delay is due to the fact that the plaintiff is having trouble serving the claim, then he should bring a motion for an extension of time to serve the claim and, if appropriate, for an order for substituted service.

If the case is defended and 150 days have passed without completion of a settlement conference or without the case being put on the trial list or otherwise disposed of, the clerk shall send the plaintiff a notice of approaching dismissal, giving the plaintiff 45 days' notice that the case will be dismissed unless the parties move on to the next step, which is usually to set the matter down for trial.

MOTION FOR A NEW TRIAL AND APPEALS

Within 30 days of the end of a trial, either party may bring a notice of motion asking for a new trial. You must obtain a date from the court clerk and issue the notice of motion within the time provided for in rule 17. You must file proof that you have requested transcripts of the reasons for judgment. On the motion, the court has jurisdiction to grant a new trial, grant the judgment that should have been granted at trial, or vary the judgment only if:

1. There was a purely arithmetical error in the determination of the amount of damages awarded.

2. There is relevant evidence that was not available to the party at the time of trial and could not reasonably be expected to be available at that time.

Where the amount claimed exceeds $2,500, an appeal goes to the Divisional Court. An appeal is appropriate where the judge has made an error in law. The rules for appeals are set out in rule 61 of the *Rules of Civil Procedure*, not in the *Small Claims Court Rules*. To appeal, you must, within 30 days of the judgment being handed down, serve and file a notice of appeal and a certificate that lays out the evidence. There are provisions to extend the time for filing a notice of appeal. The cost of an appeal can easily be more than the amount of the judgment. Transcripts alone cost approximately $400 per day of the trial. Appeal preparation fees and counsel fees on the appeal can easily top $10,000. Appeals can only be brought by lawyers. An appeal is simply not economically feasible in most cases, and is beyond the scope of this text.[14]

CHAPTER SUMMARY

Chapter 10 introduces you to the Small Claims Court and its culture, noting how it differs in its operations from the Superior Court. Court jurisdiction is based on monetary amount and the place where parties reside or the cause of action arose. Determining the proper parties to sue is discussed, with particular attention paid to suing various business entities and parties under a disability. The claim is then prepared, filed, and served, and the various modes of service are examined. Once served, the defendant then has the option of filing a defence or a proposal, and may also file a defendant's claim if he or she has a counterclaim (a claim against the plaintiff), a cross-claim (against another defendant), or a third-party claim (a claim against a person not already a party). How pleadings may be amended is also discussed. Special attention is paid to the mechanics of default proceedings. We then move on to settlement conferences, formal offers to settle, and motions, which usually come into play as the case gets closer to trial. After this, we turn to the trial itself, paying particular attention to trial preparation: summoning witnesses and organizing documentary evidence. We then consider how costs are awarded, how judgments may be varied or set aside, and how appeals are made after the trial has concluded.

KEY TERMS

Children's Lawyer

declaratory judgment

full legal age and capacity

gazetteer

litigation guardian

Public Guardian and Trustee

specific performance

NOTES

1. Marvin Zuker, *Ontario Small Claims Court Practice* (Toronto: Carswell, 2010), 15-16.

2. Reuben Bromstein, "Speedier Justice in Civil Disputes" (Spring 1995), *The Advocates Society Journal* 6.

3. See s. 23(2) of the *Courts of Justice Act*, RSO 1990, c. C.43.

4. See rule 57.05(1) of the *Rules of Civil Procedure*, RRO 1990, reg. 194, as amended.

5. *Ingersoll Press Automation & Machinery v. Tom Saab Industries* (1994), 46 ACWS (3d) 153 (Ont. Sm. Cl. Ct.); *Canada Trust MasterCard v. Nowick* (1982), 27 CPC 183 (Ont. Sm. Cl. Ct.).

6. The *Ontario Legal Directory*, published annually by the University of Toronto Press, contains a Small Claims Court gazetteer.

7. *Business Names Act*, RSO 1990, c. B.17, s. 7(1).

8. The term "plaintiff's claim" is used to distinguish it from a "defendant's claim," which can be used by the defendant in the plaintiff's action for a counterclaim against the plaintiff or a claim against another person whom the defendant thinks is liable (for example, a cross-claim against another defendant or a third-party claim bringing in another party).

9. A summons to a witness and a notice of a contempt hearing must also be served personally.

10. Note that in order to reduce the number of cases used in the example documents in the figures, the *Capricious v. Feckless* case has been shown with a variety of different outcomes: first, as if it was defended, then as if there was a proposal and the proposal had not been met, then as if a proposal was not accepted, and finally as if the claim was undefended and there was default judgment granted.

11. See rule 11.06 of the *Small Claims Court Rules.*

12. See rule 15.04 of the *Small Claims Court Rules.*

13. See rule 18.03(9) of the *Small Claims Court Rules.*

14. For a detailed discussion of an appeal from a judgment of the Small Claims Court, see Zuker, supra note 1, 47.

REFERENCES

Administration of Justice Act, RSO 1990, c. A.6.

Canadian Charter of Rights and Freedoms, part I of the *Constitution Act, 1982*, RSC 1985, app. II, no. 44.

Courts of Justice Act, RSO 1990, c. C.43.

Law Society Act, RSO 1990, c. L.8.

Polewsky v. Home Hardware Stores Ltd., 2003 ONSCDC 10693.

Rules of Civil Procedure, RRO 1990, reg. 194, as amended.

Rules of the Small Claims Court, O. Reg. 258/98, as amended.*

---

* Small Claims Court fees, rules, forms, and procedural guides can be found online at http://www.attorneygeneral.jus.gov.on.ca. Click on Court Services and follow the links.

Small Claims Court — Fees and Allowances, Administration of Justice Act, O. Reg. 432/93, as amended.

Substitute Decisions Act, 1992, SO 1992, c. 30.

REVIEW QUESTIONS

1. In what way does the operation of the Small Claims Court assist litigants who are not represented?

2. What advantages does the Small Claims Court offer to litigants that the Superior Court does not offer?

3. What are the Small Claims Court's jurisdictional limits?

4. If you operate in Kenora and have as part of your standard contract a section that says "the parties consent to all disputes being tried in the Small Claims Court at Kenora," does this allow you to sue for breach of contract in the Kenora Small Claims Court no matter where the defendant resides or carries on business?

5. How do you prove to the court that your claim has been brought in the correct territorial division?

6. What choices do you have if you wish to sue a sole proprietorship; a partnership; a corporation?

7. In what circumstances would a party require a litigation guardian?

8. Suppose you serve a defendant who you know is mentally incapable and no defence has been filed within 20 days of personal service on the defendant. Can you simply ask the clerk to sign default judgment?

9. May the plaintiff personally serve the defendant?

10. Suppose you served a claim and the 20th day after service was effected was Christmas day, which was a Friday. On what day would the defendant be deemed to be in default?

11. If the defendant admits he owes the money claimed by the plaintiff, should he file a defence anyway? What are the advantages in filing a defence? What are the advantages in not filing?

12. Suppose the defendant owes money to the plaintiff, but the plaintiff also owes the defendant a refund on certain purchases, which the plaintiff has not paid yet. How might this situation affect what the defendant includes in his written defence?

13. What are the conditions precedent to having the clerk sign default judgment?

14. If Superior Court discovery is not part of the Small Claims Court procedure, how will you obtain disclosure in order to prepare your case?

15. What are the purposes of the settlement conference?

16. What happens if a settlement conference is called and you fail to attend or have not prepared your case before attending?

17. Suppose the defendant makes an offer to settle. Explain to your client the consequences of not accepting the offer.

18. If the defendant accepts the plaintiff's offer to settle and later reneges on the payment of money required by the settlement, what may the plaintiff do?

19. How do you present evidence at trial?

20. What do you need to do to be sure that your witnesses show up at trial?

21. Tell your client what she can expect to recover for costs if she is successful on her claim for $1,000.

22. Tell your client what her procedural options are if, after trial, you discover that there is new documentary evidence that would have helped her case.

CASE STUDY

M E M O

DATE: September 10, year 0

TO: Collections Clerk

FROM: I.M. Just

RE: Harbour Master v. Pretentious

Our client Harbour Master Ltd., at 2133 Princess Street, Kingston, ON K1R 3T4, is a vendor of sailing supplies. Harbour Master sold a main sheet rig to Peter Pretentious on August 29, year 0 for $1,500 incl. HST. Interest was set out on the bill of sale at 12 percent per year on overdue accounts, with a $25 charge for NSF cheques. We did some checking: Peter lives at 1 Queen's Quay, Suite 1500, Toronto, ON M2J 1P3. His cheque for $1,500 was dishonoured and returned by the bank marked NSF. Calls and letters have received no response. We have been asked to collect the money. Payment was due on the invoice date, August 29.

1. Prepare a claim. The claim was issued on September 15, year 0.

2. Assume that Peter Pretentious was served at home on September 17, year 0. Draft the affidavit of service.

3. Suppose that Mr. Pretentious finds out he's been sued after judgment is obtained. He says he was ill in September year 0 and forgot about being served, so the matter slipped his mind. Had he remembered, he would have defended. Draft the notice of motion and supporting affidavit to set aside default judgment. Assume that the judgment was obtained on October 29, year 0 from the Kingston Small Claims Court, and that you have obtained from the court a motion date for November 13, year 0.

4. Suppose that Mr. Pretentious is successful at getting the judgment set aside; he wants to defend on the basis that the rig he was sold was defective. He wishes to have a sailing crew member who saw the rig and the difficulties it caused testify. Her name is Sara Silandro; she lives at 83 Caulfield Street, Oshawa, ON K3B 1X8; the trial will be at the Kingston Small Claims Court on January 23, year 1. Prepare the necessary documents to ensure that she appears at trial.

Figure 10.1   Affidavit for Jurisdiction

ONTARIO

Superior Court of Justice	**Affidavit for Jurisdiction**
Cour supérieure de justice	*Affidavit établissant la compétence*

Form / *Formule* 11A Ont. Reg. No. / *Règl. de l'Ont.* : 258/98

Toronto

Small Claims Court / *Cour des petites créances de*

SC-10-00012345-0000

Claim No. / *N° de la demande*

47 Sheppard Ave. E., 3rd Floor

Toronto, ON M2N 3X5

Address / *Adresse*

416-326-3554

Phone number / *Numéro de téléphone*

BETWEEN / *ENTRE*

Capricious Credit Corporation Ltd.

Plaintiff(s) / *Demandeur(s)/demanderesse(s)*

and / *et*

Feckless Enterprises

Defendant(s) / *Défendeur(s)/défenderesse(s)*

My name is Charles Dickens

Je m'appelle   (Full name / *Nom et prénoms*)

I live in Toronto, ON

J'habite à   (Municipality & province / *Municipalité et province*)

and I swear/affirm that the following is true:

et je déclare sous serment/j'affirme solennellement que les renseignements suivants sont véridiques :

1. In this action, I am the
   Dans la présente action, je suis le/la

   ☐ plaintiff
       demandeur/demanderesse

   ☒ representative of the plaintiff(s) Capricious Credit Corporation Ltd.
       représentant(e) du/de la/des   (Name of plaintiff(s) / *Nom du/de la/des demandeur(s)/demanderesse(s)*)
       demandeur(s)/demanderesse(s)

2. I make this affidavit in support of the plaintiff's request to note the defendant(s) in default, where all the defendants have been or will be served outside the court's territorial division [R. 11.01 (3)].
   Je fais le présent affidavit à l'appui de la demande du demandeur de faire constater le ou les défendeurs en défaut étant donné que tous les défendeurs ont reçu ou recevront la signification en dehors de la division territoriale du tribunal [par. 11.01 (3)].

Figure 10.1   Concluded

FORM / *FORMULE* 11A   **PAGE 2**   SC-10-00012345-0000

3. The plaintiff is entitled to proceed with this action in this territorial division because this is:
   Le demandeur a le droit de poursuivre cette action dans cette division territoriale parce que :

   ☒   where the event (cause of action) took place.
       l'événement (cause d'action) a eu lieu dans cette division territoriale.

   ☐   where the defendant lives or carries on business.
       le défendeur réside dans cette division territoriale ou y exploite une entreprise.

   ☐   the court nearest to the place where the defendant lives or carries on business [R. 6.01].
       c'est dans cette division territoriale que se trouve le greffe du tribunal qui est le plus près de l'endroit où le défendeur réside ou exploite une entreprise. [règle 6.01].

Sworn/Affirmed before me at **Toronto**
Déclaré sous serment/Affirmé   (Municipality / *municipalité*)
solennellement devant moi à

in **Ontario**
en/à/au   (Province, state or country / *province, État ou pays*)

on **Oct. 30, year 0**   , 20
le

Commissioner for taking affidavits
Commissaire aux affidavits
(Type or print name below if signature is illegible.)
(Dactylographiez le nom ou écrivez-le en caractères d'imprimerie ci-dessous si la signature est illisible.)

Signature
(This form is to be signed in front of a lawyer, justice of the peace, notary public or commissioner for taking affidavits.)
(La présente formule doit être signée en présence d'un avocat, d'un juge de paix, d'un notaire ou d'un commissaire aux affidavits.)

WARNING:	**IT IS AN OFFENCE UNDER THE *CRIMINAL CODE* TO KNOWINGLY SWEAR OR AFFIRM A FALSE AFFIDAVIT.**
AVERTISSEMENT :	***FAIRE SCIEMMENT UN FAUX AFFIDAVIT CONSTITUE UNE INFRACTION AU CODE CRIMINEL.***

Figure 10.2 Notice to Alleged Partner

ONTARIO
Superior Court of Justice
Cour supérieure de justice

Notice to Alleged Partner
Avis au prétendu associé
Form / *Formule* 5A Ont. Reg. No. / *Règl. de l'Ont.* : 258/98

Toronto

Small Claims Court / *Cour des petites créances de*

SC-10-00012345-0000

Claim No. / *N° de la demande*

47 Sheppard Ave. E., 3rd Floor
Toronto, ON M2N 3X5

Address / *Adresse*

416-326-3554

Phone number / *Numéro de téléphone*

BETWEEN / *ENTRE*

Capricious Credit Corporation Ltd.

Plaintiff(s) / *Demandeur(s)/demanderesse(s)*

and / *et*

Feckless Enterprises

Defendant(s) / *Défendeur(s)/défenderesse(s)*

TO: **DESTINATAIRE :**	Name of alleged partner / *Nom du (de la) prétendu(e) associé(e)* **Edward Steerforth**
	Street and number / *Numéro et rue* **108 Elmtree Drive**
	City, province, postal code / *Ville, province, code postal* **Toronto, ON M5W 3A2**

YOU ARE ALLEGED TO HAVE BEEN A PARTNER on **April 1, year -1**   , 20
IL EST ALLÉGUÉ QUE VOUS ÉTIEZ UN(E) ASSOCIÉ(E) le

(or during the period)   , 20   to   , 20
(ou pendant la période du)   *au*

in the partnership/business of **Feckless Enterprises**   ,
de la société en nom collectif/l'entreprise de   (Firm name / *Raison sociale*)

a party named in this proceeding.
désignée comme partie à l'instance.

IF YOU WISH TO DENY THAT YOU WERE A PARTNER at any material time, you must defend this proceeding separately from the partnership, denying that you were a partner at the material time. If you fail to do so, you will be deemed to have been a partner on the date (or during the period) set out above.
SI VOUS SOUHAITEZ NIER QUE VOUS ÉTIEZ UN(E) ASSOCIÉ(E) à l'époque en cause, vous devez présenter dans l'instance une défense distincte de celle de la société en nom collectif, selon laquelle vous niez avoir été un(e) associé(e) à cette époque. À défaut de ce faire, vous serez réputé(e) avoir été une(e) associé(e) à la date (ou pendant la période) susmentionnée.

CAUTION:	**AN ORDER AGAINST THE PARTNERSHIP MAY BE ENFORCED AGAINST YOU PERSONALLY** if you are deemed to have been a partner, if you admit that you were, or if the court finds that you were at the material time.
AVERTISSEMENT :	*UNE ORDONNANCE CONTRE LA SOCIÉTÉ EN NOM COLLECTIF PEUT ÊTRE EXÉCUTÉE CONTRE VOUS PERSONNELLEMENT si vous êtes réputé(e) avoir été un(e) associé(e), si vous admettez ce fait ou si le tribunal conclut que vous étiez un(e) associé(e) à l'époque en cause.*

October 30, year 0   , 20

(Signature of plaintiff or representative / *Signature du demandeur/de la demanderesse ou du/de la représentant(e)*)

SCR 5.03-5A (June 1, 2009 / *1er juin 2009*) CSD

Figure 10.3 Sample Notice Requiring Disclosure of Individual Partner's Names

Claim no. SC-10-00012345-0000

Toronto Small Claims Court

47 Sheppard Avenue East, 3rd Floor

Toronto, ON M2N 2X5

416-326-3554

Plaintiff

Full name

Capricious Credit Corporation Ltd.

Address for service (street & number, city, postal code)

c/o Charles Dickens

8041 Ryder Street

Mississauga, ON L2R 1Y6

Phone no.

905-381-2620

Plaintiff's lawyer/agent (full name)

Charles Dickens

Lawyer/agent's address for service

8041 Ryder Street

Mississauga, ON L2R 1Y6

Lawyer/agent's phone no.

905-381-2620

Defendant

Full name

Feckless Enterprises

Address for service (street & number, city, postal code)

c/o Edward Loquacious

365 Bay Street

Toronto, ON M2N 3A8

Phone no.

416-595-1308

Defendant's lawyer/agent (full name)

Edward Loquacious

Lawyer/agent's address for service

365 Bay Street

Toronto, ON M2N 3A8

Lawyer/agent's phone no.

416-595-1308

Figure 10.3   Concluded

NOTICE REQUIRING DISCLOSURE OF PARTNERS

Take Notice that you are required to disclose and provide to the plaintiff, in writing, the names and addresses of all partners constituting the partnership Feckless Enterprises in April, year –1, pursuant to Rule 5.04 of the Rules of the Small Claims Court.

Where the present address is unknown the partnership will disclose the last known address of the partner(s).

If you fail to comply with this notice, your claim, if any, may be struck out, proceedings may be stayed, or your defence may be struck out.

Dated at Toronto, November 19, year 0

Charles Dickens, Paralegal, LSUC #P02345
8041 Ryder Street
Mississauga, ON L2R 1Y6
905-381-2620

Figure 10.4   Consent to Act as Litigation Guardian (Plaintiff)

ONTARIO

Superior Court of Justice
Cour supérieure de justice

Consent to Act as Litigation Guardian
Consentement pour agir en qualité de tuteur à l'instance
Form / *Formule* 4A Ont. Reg. No. / *Règl. de l'Ont.* : 258/98

Toronto

Small Claims Court / *Cour des petites créances de*

SC-10-00012346-0000

Claim No. / *N° de la demande*

**47 Sheppard Ave. E., 3rd Floor
Toronto, ON M2N 3X5**

Address / *Adresse*

416-326-3554

Phone number / *Numéro de téléphone*

BETWEEN / *ENTRE*

Soroka Smith

Plaintiff(s) / *Demandeur(s)/demanderesse(s)*

and / *et*

Oliver Twist

Defendant(s) / *Défendeur(s)/défenderesse(s)*

My name is *Je m'appelle*	Name / *Nom* **Aphrodite Smith**
And I live at *et j'habite à*	Street and number / *Numéro et rue* **30 Median Way**
	City, province, postal code / *Ville, province, code postal* **Toronto, ON M3R 1X4**
	Phone number and fax number / *Numéro de téléphone et numéro de télécopieur* **416-762-1242**

1. I consent to act as litigation guardian in this action for the
Je consens à agir à titre de tuteur à l'instance dans la présente action au nom du

(Check one box only. / Cochez une seule case.)

☒ plaintiff, named **Soroka Smith**
demandeur suivant :   (Name of plaintiff / *Nom du demandeur/de la demanderesse*)

and I acknowledge that I may be personally responsible for any costs awarded against me or against this person.
et je reconnais que je peux être tenu(e) personnellement responsable des dépens auxquels moi-même ou cette personne pourrions être condamné(e)s.

☐ defendant, named _____ .
défendeur suivant :   (Name of defendant / *Nom du défendeur/de la défenderesse*)

2. The above-named person is under the following disability:
La personne susmentionnée est incapable parce qu'elle est :

(Check appropriate box(es). / Cochez la ou les cases appropriées.)

☒ a minor whose birth date is **April 4, year -15** .
un mineur dont la date de naissance est le   (State date of birth of minor / *Indiquez la date de naissance du mineur*)

☐ mentally incapable within the meaning of Section 6 or Section 45 of the *Substitute Decisions Act, 1992* in respect of an issue in a proceeding.
mentalement incapable au sens de l'article 6 ou 45 de la Loi de 1992 sur la prise de décisions au nom d'autrui *à l'égard d'une question dans une instance.*

☐ an absentee within the meaning of the *Absentees Act*.
une personne absente au sens de la Loi sur les absents.

Figure 10.4   Concluded

FORM / *FORMULE* **4A**   **PAGE 2**   **SC-10-00012346-0000**

Claim No. / *N° de la demande*

3. My relationship to the person under disability is:
   Mon lien de parenté avec l'incapable est le suivant :
   (State your relationship to the person under disability. / Indiquez votre lien de parenté avec l'incapable.)

   Mother

4. I have no interest in this action contrary to that of the person under disability.
   Je n'ai dans la présente action aucun intérêt opposé à celui de l'incapable.

5. I am
   Je

   (Check one box only. / Cochez une seule case.)

   ☒ represented and have given written authority to   **Emily Dickinson**
   suis représenté(e) et j'ai autorisé par écrit :
   (Name of lawyer/agent with authority to act in this proceeding / *Nom de l'avocat/du mandataire autorisé à agir dans la présente instance)*

   of   **365 Queen St. E., Toronto, ON M3R 2X4**
   de   (Address for service / *Adresse aux fins de signification)*

   416-283-0946
   (Phone number and fax number / *Numéro de téléphone et numéro de télécopieur)*

   to act in this proceeding.
   à agir dans la présente instance.

   ☐ not represented by a lawyer/agent.
   ne suis pas représenté(e) par un avocat/un mandataire.

   July 12, year 0   , 20

   (Signature of litigation guardian consenting / *Signature du tuteur à l'instance qui consent)*

   (Signature of witness / *Signature du témoin)*

   Emily Dickinson
   (Name of witness / *Nom du témoin)*

   NOTE: Within seven (7) calendar days of changing your address for service, notify the court and all other parties in writing.
   REMARQUE : *Dans les sept (7) jours civils qui suivent tout changement de votre adresse aux fins de signification, veuillez en aviser par écrit le tribunal et les autres parties.*

Figure 10.5 Consent to Act as Litigation Guardian (Defendant)

ONTARIO

Superior Court of Justice *Cour supérieure de justice*	**Consent to Act as Litigation Guardian** *Consentement pour agir en qualité de tuteur à l'instance* Form / *Formule* 4A Ont. Reg. No. / *Règl. de l'Ont.* : 258/98

Toronto Small Claims Court / *Cour des petites créances de*	**SC-10-00012346-0000** Claim No. / *N° de la demande*
47 Sheppard Ave. E., 3rd Floor **Toronto, ON M2N 3X5**	
Address / *Adresse*	
416-326-3554	
Phone number / *Numéro de téléphone*	

BETWEEN / *ENTRE*

Soroka Smith

Plaintiff(s) / *Demandeur(s)/demanderesse(s)*

and / *et*

Oliver Twist

Defendant(s) / *Défendeur(s)/défenderesse(s)*

My name is *Je m'appelle* **And I live at** *et j'habite à*	Name / *Nom* **Malcolm Twist**
	Street and number / *Numéro et rue* **4905 Yonge St.**
	City, province, postal code / *Ville, province, code postal* **Toronto, ON M3R 2A6**
	Phone number and fax number / *Numéro de téléphone et numéro de télécopieur* **416-233-4547**

1. I consent to act as litigation guardian in this action for the
   Je consens à agir à titre de tuteur à l'instance dans la présente action au nom du

   ☐ plaintiff, named _____
   demandeur suivant :   (Name of plaintiff / *Nom du demandeur/de la demanderesse*)

   (Check one box only. / Cochez une seule case.*)*

   and I acknowledge that I may be personally responsible for any costs awarded against me or against this person.
   et je reconnais que je peux être tenu(e) personnellement responsable des dépens auxquels moi-même ou cette personne pourrions être condamné(e)s.

   ☒ defendant, named **Oliver Twist** _____ .
   défendeur suivant :   (Name of defendant / *Nom du défendeur/de la défenderesse*)

2. The above-named person is under the following disability:
   La personne susmentionnée est incapable parce qu'elle est :

   ☐ a minor whose birth date is _____ .
   un mineur dont la date de naissance est le   (State date of birth of minor / *Indiquez la date de naissance du mineur*)

   (Check appropriate box(es). / Cochez la ou les cases appropriées.*)*

   ☒ mentally incapable within the meaning of Section 6 or Section 45 of the *Substitute Decisions Act, 1992* in respect of an issue in a proceeding.
   mentalement incapable au sens de l'article 6 ou 45 de la Loi de 1992 sur la prise de décisions au nom d'autrui *à l'égard d'une question dans une instance.*

   ☐ an absentee within the meaning of the *Absentees Act*.
   une personne absente au sens de la Loi sur les absents.

Figure 10.5   Concluded

FORM / *FORMULE* 4A   PAGE 2   SC-10-00012346-0000

Claim No. / *N° de la demande*

3. My relationship to the person under disability is:
    Mon lien de parenté avec l'incapable est le suivant :
    (State your relationship to the person under disability. / Indiquez votre lien de parenté avec l'incapable.)
    Father

4. I have no interest in this action contrary to that of the person under disability.
    Je n'ai dans la présente action aucun intérêt opposé à celui de l'incapable.

5. I am
    Je

    (Check one box only. / Cochez une seule case.)

    ☒ represented and have given written authority to   **I.M. Horrendous**

    suis représenté(e) et j'ai autorisé par écrit :   (Name of lawyer/agent with authority to act in this proceeding / *Nom de l'avocat/du mandataire autorisé à agir dans la présente instance*)

    of   **805 Avenue Rd., Toronto, ON M2R 1J6**

    de   (Address for service / *Adresse aux fins de signification*)

    416-964-3101

    (Phone number and fax number / *Numéro de téléphone et numéro de télécopieur*)

    to act in this proceeding.
    à agir dans la présente instance.

    ☐ not represented by a lawyer/agent.
    ne suis pas représenté(e) par un avocat/un mandataire.

    May 8, year 0 _____, 20 _____

    _____
    (Signature of litigation guardian consenting / *Signature du tuteur à l'instance qui consent*)

    _____
    (Signature of witness / *Signature du témoin*)

    I.M. Horrendous
    (Name of witness / *Nom du témoin*)

| **NOTE:** | Within seven (7) calendar days of changing your address for service, notify the court and all other parties in writing. |
| **REMARQUE :** | *Dans les sept (7) jours civils qui suivent tout changement de votre adresse aux fins de signification, veuillez en aviser par écrit le tribunal et les autres parties.* |

Figure 10.6   Sample Demand Served on Person Under Disability

Claim No. SC-10-00012347-0000

Toronto Small Claims Court

47 Sheppard Ave. E., 3rd Floor

Toronto, ON M2N 2X5

416-326-3554

Plaintiff

Full name

O'Hooligan's Bar Ltd.

Address for service

c/o I.M. Horrendous

39 Bedford Avenue

Toronto, ON M3T 9V5

Plaintiff's Representative

I.M. Horrendous

Representative's address for service

39 Bedford Avenue

Toronto, ON M3T 9V5

Representative's phone no.

416-469-3963

Defendant

Full name

Henry Feckless

Address for service

48 Overreach Boulevard

Toronto, ON M2R 5X3

Defendant's Representative

Representative's address for service

Representative's phone no.

Figure 10.6   Concluded

DEMAND

TAKE NOTICE that because Henry Feckless, the above-named defendant, is a party under disability by reason of being a minor under the age of 18 years, he must defend this action by a litigation guardian appointed for this purpose.

AND FURTHER TAKE NOTICE that unless, within 20 days from the receipt of this notice, action is taken to have the defendant's father, mother, or other suitable adult appointed as litigation guardian for the defendant, an application will be made without further notification to you to have the Children's Lawyer appointed litigation guardian for the purpose of this action.

DATED at Toronto, July 28, Year 0

I.M. Horrendous
Representative for the Plaintiff
LSUC # P03478
39 Bedford Avenue
Toronto, ON M3T 9V5
416-369-3963

TO: HENRY FECKLESS, A person under disability
48 Overreach Boulevard
Toronto, ON M2R 5X3

AND TO: HORTENSE FECKLESS, mother of Henry Feckless
48 Overreach Boulevard
Toronto, ON M2R 5X3

Figure 10.7 Plaintiff's Claim

ONTARIO

Superior Court of Justice
Cour supérieure de justice

Plaintiff's Claim
Demande du demandeur

Form / *Formule* 7A Ont. Reg. No. / *Règl. de l'Ont.* : 258/98

Toronto	**SC-10-00012345-0000**
Small Claims Court / *Cour des petites créances de*	Claim No. / *N° de la demande*

Seal / *Sceau*

47 Sheppard Ave. E., 3rd Floor
Toronto, ON M2N 3X5

Address / *Adresse*

416-326-3554

Phone number / *Numéro de téléphone*

Plaintiff No. 1 / *Demandeur n° 1*   ☐ Additional plaintiff(s) listed on attached Form 1A.   ☐ Under 18 years of age.
Le ou les demandeurs additionnels sont mentionnés   *Moins de 18 ans.*
sur la formule 1A ci-jointe.

Last name, or name of company / *Nom de famille ou nom de la compagnie*		
Capricious Credit Corporation Ltd.		
First name / *Premier prénom*	Second name / *Deuxième prénom*	Also known as / *Également connu(e) sous le nom de*
Address (street number, apt., unit) / *Adresse (numéro et rue, app., unité)*		
c/o Charles Dickens 8041 Ryder Street		
City/Town / *Cité/ville*	Province	Phone no. / *N° de téléphone*
Mississauga	**ON**	**905-381-2620**
Postal code / *Code postal*		Fax no. / *N° de télécopieur*
L2R 1Y6		
Representative / *Représentant(e)*		LSUC # / *N° du BHC*
Charles Dickens		**P02345**
Address (street number, apt., unit) / *Adresse (numéro et rue, app., unité)*		
8041 Ryder Street		
City/Town / *Cité/ville*	Province	Phone no. / *N° de téléphone*
Mississauga	**ON**	**905-381-2620**
Postal code / *Code postal*		Fax no. / *N° de télécopieur*
L2R 1Y6		

Defendant No. 1 / *Défendeur n° 1*   ☐ Additional defendant(s) listed on attached Form 1A.   ☐ Under 18 years of age.
Le ou les défendeurs additionnels sont mentionnés   *Moins de 18 ans.*
sur la formule 1A ci-jointe.

Last name, or name of company / *Nom de famille ou nom de la compagnie*		
Feckless Enterprises		
First name / *Premier prénom*	Second name / *Deuxième prénom*	Also known as / *Également connu(e) sous le nom de*
Address (street number, apt., unit) / *Adresse (numéro et rue, app., unité)*		
48 Overreach Blvd.		
City/Town / *Cité/ville*	Province	Phone no. / *N° de téléphone*
Brampton	**ON**	**416-223-4569**
Postal code / *Code postal*		Fax no. / *N° de télécopieur*
L6X 3L7		
Representative / *Représentant(e)*		LSUC # / *N° du BHC*
Address (street number, apt., unit) / *Adresse (numéro et rue, app., unité)*		
City/Town / *Cité/ville*	Province	Phone no. / *N° de téléphone*
Postal code / *Code postal*		Fax no. / *N° de télécopieur*

Figure 10.7   Continued

FORM / *FORMULE* 7A   **PAGE 2**   SC-10-00012345-0000

Claim No. / *N° de la demande*

REASONS FOR CLAIM AND DETAILS / *MOTIFS DE LA DEMANDE ET PRÉCISIONS*

Explain what happened, including where and when. Then explain how much money you are claiming or what goods you want returned.

Expliquez ce qui s'est passé, en précisant où et quand. Ensuite indiquez la somme d'argent que vous demandez ou les biens dont vous demandez la restitution, explication à l'appui.

If you are relying on any documents, you **MUST** attach copies to the claim. If evidence is lost or unavailable, you **MUST** explain why it is not attached.

*Si vous vous appuyez sur des documents, vous **DEVEZ** en annexer des copies à la demande. Si une preuve est perdue ou n'est pas disponible, vous **DEVEZ** expliquer pourquoi elle n'est pas annexée.*

What happened?
Where?
When?

Que s'est-il passé?
Où?
Quand?

The defendant has failed to pay the amount owing to the plaintiff on a promissory note.
The note was signed at Toronto, Ontario.
The note was signed on April 1, year -1 and was due on April 1, year 0.

1. The plaintiff, Capricious Credit Corporation Ltd. (Capricious), is a corporation with its head office in Toronto, Ontario.

2. The defendant, Feckless Enterprises (Feckless), is a partnership located in Toronto, Ontario.

3. Feckless signed a promissory note (note), in favour of Capricious, on April 1, year -1, at Toronto, Ontario.

4. The note, a true copy of which is attached to this claim as Document "A", was in the amount of $3,000 with interest at 10 percent per year both before and after maturity. The note was due on April 1, year 0.

5. Feckless received the amount of $3,000, in accordance with the note, on April 1, year -1.

6. Feckless has neglected or refused to pay the principal and interest due under the note.

Figure 10.7   Concluded

FORM / *FORMULE* 7A   PAGE 3

How much? $ 3,000.00
Combien?   (Principal amount claimed / *Somme demandée*) $

☐   **ADDITIONAL PAGES ARE ATTACHED BECAUSE MORE ROOM WAS NEEDED.**
    DES FEUILLES SUPPLÉMENTAIRES SONT ANNEXÉES EN RAISON DU MANQUE D'ESPACE.

The plaintiff also claims pre-judgment interest from April 1, year 0   **under:**
Le demandeur demande aussi des intérêts   (Date)   ***conformément à :***
antérieurs au jugement de

(Check only   ☐   **the** *Courts of Justice Act*
one box /   *la* **Loi sur les tribunaux judiciaires**
Cochez une
seule case)   ☒   **an agreement at the rate of** 10   **% per year**
                     un accord au taux de   **% par an**

and post-judgment interest, and court costs.
et des intérêts postérieurs au jugement, ainsi que les dépens.

Prepared on: **October 30, year 0**   , 20 _____   _____
Fait le :   (Signature of plaintiff or representative / *Signature du*
                                                           demandeur/de la demanderesse ou du/de la représentant(e))

Issued on: _____ , 20 _____   _____
Délivré le :   (Signature of clerk / *Signature du greffier*)

| **CAUTION TO DEFENDANT:** | **IF YOU DO NOT FILE A DEFENCE** (Form 9A) with the court within twenty (20) calendar days after you have been served with this Plaintiff's Claim, judgment may be obtained without notice and enforced against you. Forms and self-help materials are available at the Small Claims Court and on the following website: www.ontariocourtforms.on.ca. |
| *AVERTISSEMENT AU DÉFENDEUR :* | *SI VOUS NE DÉPOSEZ PAS DE DÉFENSE (formule 9A) auprès du tribunal au plus tard vingt (20) jours civils après avoir reçu signification de la présente demande du demandeur, un jugement peut être obtenu sans préavis et être exécuté contre vous. Vous pouvez obtenir les formules et la documentation à l'usage du client à la Cour des petites créances et sur le site Web suivant : www.ontariocourtforms.on.ca.* |

Figure 10.8   Affidavit of Service

ONTARIO

Superior Court of Justice   **Affidavit of Service**
Cour supérieure de justice   *Affidavit de signification*

Form / *Formule* 8A Ont. Reg. No. / *Règl. de l'Ont.* : 258/98

Toronto   SC-10-00012348-0000

Small Claims Court / *Cour des petites créances de*   Claim No. / *N° de la demande*

47 Sheppard Ave. E., 3rd Floor
Toronto, ON M2N 2X5

Address / *Adresse*

416-326-3554

Phone number / *Numéro de téléphone*

BETWEEN / *ENTRE*

Morris Minor

Plaintiff(s) / *Demandeur(s)/demanderesse(s)*

and / *et*

Robert Cratchit

Defendant(s) / *Défendeur(s)/défenderesse(s)*

My name is Domenico Scarlatti
Je m'appelle   (Full name / *Nom et prénoms*)

I live in Brampton, Ontario
J'habite à   (Municipality & province / *Municipalité et province*)

and I swear/affirm that the following is true:
et je déclare sous serment/j'affirme solennellement que les renseignements suivants sont véridiques :

1. **I served** Robert Cratchit   , on **May 23, year 0**   , 20   ,
   J'ai signifié à   (Full name of person/corporation served / *Nom et prénoms*   , *le*   (Date)
                       de la personne/nom au complet de la personne morale
                       qui a reçu la signification)

   at 105 Dogsbody Road, Toronto, ON
   au   (Address (street and number, unit, municipality, province) / *Adresse (numéro et rue, unité, municipalité, province)*)

   which is ☒ the address of the person's home
   soit   *l'adresse du domicile de la personne*

   ☐ the address of the corporation's place of business
      l'adresse du lieu de travail de l'établissement de la personne morale

   ☐ the address of the person's or corporation's representative on record with the court
      l'adresse du/de la représentant(e) de la personne ou de la personne morale figurant au dossier du tribunal

   ☐ the address on the document most recently filed in court by the party
      l'adresse figurant sur le document déposé le plus récemment au tribunal par la partie

   ☐ the address of the corporation's attorney for service in Ontario
      l'adresse du fondé de pouvoir de la personne morale aux fins de signification en Ontario

   ☐ other address:
      autre adresse :   (Specify. / *Précisez.*)

   with Plaintiff's Claim issued May 6, year 0
   ce qui suit :   (Name(s) of document(s) served / *Titre(s) du ou des documents signifiés*)

Figure 10.8 Continued

FORM / *FORMULE* **8A**   **PAGE 2**   SC-10-00012348-0000

Claim No. / *N° de la demande*

2. **I served the document(s) referred to in paragraph one by the following method:**
   J'ai signifié le ou les documents mentionnés au numéro un de la façon suivante :

   (Tell how service took place by checking appropriate box(es).)
   (Indiquez la façon dont la signification a été effectuée en cochant la ou les cases appropriées.)

Personal service / *Significa- tion à personne*	☒ leaving a copy with the person. *en laissant une copie à la personne.*	
	☐ leaving a copy with the _____ *en laissant une copie au/à la* (Office or position / *Charge ou poste*)	of the corporation. *de la personne morale.*
	☐ leaving a copy with: _____ *en laissant une copie à :* (Specify person's name and office or position. / *Indiquez le nom de la personne ainsi que sa charge ou son poste.*)	

Service at place of residence / *Significa- tion au domicile*

☐ leaving a copy in a sealed envelope addressed to the person at the person's place of residence with a person who appeared to be an adult member of the same household, and sending another copy of the same document(s) to the person's place of residence on the same day or the following day by:
en laissant une copie au domicile de la personne, dans une enveloppe scellée adressée à celle-ci, auprès d'une personne habitant sous le même toit qui semblait majeure et en envoyant une autre copie du ou des mêmes documents au domicile de la personne le même jour ou le jour suivant :

    ☐ regular lettermail.
      par courrier ordinaire.

    ☐ registered mail.
      par courrier recommandé.

    ☐ courier.
      par messagerie.

Service by registered mail / *Significa- tion par courrier recom- mandé*

☐ registered mail.
par courrier recommandé.

(If a copy of a plaintiff's claim or defendant's claim was served by registered mail, attach a copy of the Canada Post delivery confirmation, showing the signature verifying delivery, to this affidavit.)
(Si une copie de la demande du demandeur ou de la demande du défendeur a été signifiée par courrier recommandé, annexez au présent affidavit une copie de la confirmation de livraison remise par Postes Canada sur laquelle figure une signature qui confirme la livraison.)

Service by courier / *Significa- tion par messa- gerie*

☐ courier.
par messagerie.

(If a copy of a plaintiff's claim or defendant's claim was served by courier, attach a copy of the courier's delivery confirmation, showing the signature verifying delivery, to this affidavit.)
(Si une copie de la demande du demandeur ou de la demande du défendeur a été signifiée par messagerie, annexez au présent affidavit une copie de la confirmation de livraison remise par le service de messagerie sur laquelle figure la signature du destinataire de la signification.)

Service on lawyer / *Significa- tion à l'avocat*

☐ leaving a copy with a lawyer who accepted service on the person's behalf.
en laissant une copie avec l'avocat qui a accepté la signification au nom de la personne.

(Attach a copy of the document endorsed with the lawyer's acceptance of service.)
(Annexez une copie du document, sur lequel l'avocat a inscrit qu'il a accepté la signification.)

Service by regular lettermail / *Significa- tion par courrier ordinaire*

☐ regular lettermail.
par courrier ordinaire.

Figure 10.8   Concluded

FORM / *FORMULE* **8A**   **PAGE 3**   SC-10-00012348-0000
                                                                          Claim No. / *N° de la demande*

Service by fax / *Significa- tion par télécopie*	☐ fax sent at _____ (Time / *heure*)	at the following fax number: _____ *au numéro de télécopieur suivant :* (Fax number / *numéro de télécopieur*)

Service to last known address of corporation or attorney for service, and to the directors / *Significa- tion à la dernière adresse connue de la personne morale ou de son fondé de pouvoir aux fins de signification et aux administra- teurs*

☐ mail/courier to corporation or attorney for service at last known address recorded with the Ministry of Government Services, and
d'une part, par la poste/par messagerie à la personne morale ou à son fondé de pouvoir aux fins de signification, à la dernière adresse connue figurant dans les dossiers du ministère des Services gouvernementaux;

mail/courier to each director, as recorded with the Ministry of Government Services, as set out below:
d'autre part, par la poste/par messagerie à chaque administrateur mentionné dans les dossiers du ministère des Services gouvernementaux et dont le nom et l'adresse sont indiqués ci-dessous :

Name of director / *Nom de l'administrateur*	Director's address as recorded with the Ministry of Government Services (street & number, unit, municipality, province) / *Adresse de l'administrateur figurant dans les dossiers du ministère des Services gouvernementaux (numéro et rue, unité, municipalité, province)*
....	....
....	....
....	....
....	....

(Attach separate sheet for additional names if necessary. /
Joignez au besoin une feuille séparée s'il y a d'autres noms à ajouter.)

Substituted service / *Significa- tion indirecte*	☐ substituted service as ordered by the court on _____ , 20 ____ , *par signification indirecte ordonnée par le tribunal le* (Date)
	as follows: (Give details.) *comme suit :* (*Précisez.*)

Sworn/Affirmed before me at   **Toronto**
Déclaré sous serment/Affirmé ....
solennellement devant moi à   (Municipality / *municipalité*)

in **Ontario** ....
en/à/au   (Province, state, or country / *province, État ou pays*)

on **May 25, year 0** _____ , 20 ____ _____
le   Commissioner for taking affidavits
                                              Commissaire aux affidavits
                                              (Type or print name below if signature
                                              is illegible.)
                                              (*Dactylographiez le nom ou écrivez-le
                                              en caractères d'imprimerie ci-dessous
                                              si la signature est illisible.*)

_____
Signature
(This form is to be signed in front of a
lawyer, justice of the peace, notary public or
commissioner for taking affidavits.)
(*La présente formule doit être signée en
présence d'un avocat, d'un juge de paix,
d'un notaire ou d'un commissaire aux
affidavits.*)

Figure 10.9   Defence (to Plaintiff's Claim)

ONTARIO

Superior Court of Justice
Cour supérieure de justice

Defence / *Défense*
Form / *Formule* 9A Ont. Reg. No. / *Règl. de l'Ont.* : 258/98

Toronto

Small Claims Court / *Cour des petites créances de*

SC-10-00012345-0000

Claim No. / *N° de la demande*

47 Sheppard Ave. E., 3rd Floor
Toronto, ON M2N 2X5

Address / *Adresse*

416-326-3554

Phone number / *Numéro de téléphone*

Plaintiff No. 1 / *Demandeur n° 1*

☐ Additional plaintiff(s) listed on attached Form 1A.
Le ou les demandeurs additionnels sont mentionnés sur la formule 1A ci-jointe.

☐ Under 18 years of age.
Moins de 18 ans.

Last name, or name of company / *Nom de famille ou nom de la compagnie*		
Capricious Credit Corporation Ltd.		
First name / *Premier prénom*	Second name / *Deuxième prénom*	Also known as / *Également connu(e) sous le nom de*
Address (street number, apt., unit) / *Adresse (numéro et rue, app., unité)*		
c/o Charles Dickens 8041 Ryder Street		
City/Town / *Cité/ville*	Province	Phone no. / *N° de téléphone*
Mississauga	**ON**	**905-381-2620**
Postal code / *Code postal*		Fax no. / *N° de télécopieur*
L2R 1Y6		
Representative / *Représentant(e)*		LSUC # / *N° du BHC*
Charles Dickens		**P02345**
Address (street number, apt., unit) / *Adresse (numéro et rue, app., unité)*		
8041 Ryder Street		
City/Town / *Cité/ville*	Province	Phone no. / *N° de téléphone*
Mississauga	**ON**	**905-381-2620**
Postal code / *Code postal*		Fax no. / *N° de télécopieur*
L2R 1Y6		

Defendant No. 1 / *Défendeur n° 1*

☐ Additional defendant(s) listed on attached Form 1A.
Le ou les défendeurs additionnels sont mentionnés sur la formule 1A ci-jointe.

☐ Under 18 years of age.
Moins de 18 ans.

Last name, or name of company / *Nom de famille ou nom de la compagnie*		
Feckless Enterprises		
First name / *Premier prénom*	Second name / *Deuxième prénom*	Also known as / *Également connu(e) sous le nom de*
Address (street number, apt., unit) / *Adresse (numéro et rue, app., unité)*		
c/o Edward Loquacious 365 Bay Street		
City/Town / *Cité/ville*	Province	Phone no. / *N° de téléphone*
Toronto	**ON**	**416-595-1308**
Postal code / *Code postal*		Fax no. / *N° de télécopieur*
M2N 3A8		
Representative / *Représentant(e)*		LSUC # / *N° du BHC*
Edward Loquacious		**P02361**
Address (street number, apt., unit) / *Adresse (numéro et rue, app., unité)*		
365 Bay Street		
City/Town / *Cité/ville*	Province	Phone no. / *N° de téléphone*
Toronto	**ON**	**416-595-1308**
Postal code / *Code postal*		Fax no. / *N° de télécopieur*
M2N 3A8		

Figure 10.9   Continued

FORM / *FORMULE* **9A**   **PAGE 2**   SC-10-00012345-0000
                                                                          Claim No. / *N° de la demande*

THIS DEFENCE IS BEING FILED ON BEHALF OF: (Name(s) of defendant(s))
LA PRÉSENTE DÉFENSE EST DÉPOSÉE AU NOM DE : (Nom du/de la ou des défendeur(s)/défenderesse(s))

Feckless Enterprises

and I/we: (Check as many as apply)
et je/nous : (Cochez la ou les cases qui s'appliquent)

☒   Dispute the claim made against me/us.
     conteste/contestons la demande présentée contre moi/nous.

☐   Admit the full claim and propose the following terms of payment:
     reconnais/reconnaissons être redevable(s) de la totalité de la demande et propose/proposons les
     modalités de paiement suivantes :

     $ _____ per _____ commencing _____ , 20 _____ .
       (Amount / *Montant*)   *$ par*   (Week/month / *semaine/mois*)   *à compter du*

☐   Admit part of the claim in the amount of $ _____ and propose the following terms of payment:
     reconnais/reconnaissons être redevable(s)   (Amount / *Montant*)   *$ et propose/proposons les modalités de*
     d'une partie de la demande, soit   *paiement suivantes :*

     $ _____ per _____ commencing _____ , 20 _____ .
       (Amount / *Montant*)   *$ par*   (Week/month / *semaine/mois*)   *à compter du*

REASONS FOR DISPUTING THE CLAIM AND DETAILS:
MOTIFS DE CONTESTATION DE LA DEMANDE ET PRÉCISIONS :

Explain what happened, including where and when. Explain why you do not agree with the claim made against you.
Expliquez ce qui s'est passé, en précisant où et quand. Expliquez pourquoi vous contestez la demande
présentée contre vous.

If you are relying on any documents, you **MUST** attach copies to the Defence. If evidence is lost or unavailable,
you **MUST** explain why it is not attached.
*Si vous vous appuyez sur des documents, vous **DEVEZ** en annexer des copies à la défense. Si une preuve est*
*perdue ou n'est pas disponible, vous **DEVEZ** expliquer pourquoi elle n'est pas annexée.*

What happened?   The defendant signed a promissory note for $3,000.00 on April 1, year -1, maturing
Where?   on April 1, year 0 with interest at 10%.
When?

Que s'est-il   The note was signed at Toronto, Ontario.
passé?
Où?   The defendant paid the plaintiff the full amount due on the promissory note, in cash,
Quand?   on April 1, year 0.

                       The Plaintiff's Claim should be dismissed with costs to the defendant.

Figure 10.9   Concluded

FORM / *FORMULE* 9A   **PAGE 3**   SC-10-00012345-0000
                                                                        Claim No. / *N° de la demande*

Why I/we disagree   The plaintiff was paid in full on April 1, year 0 as agreed.
with all or part of
the claim: /

Je conteste/Nous
contestons la
totalité ou une
partie de la
demande pour les
motifs suivants :

☐   **ADDITIONAL PAGES ARE ATTACHED BECAUSE MORE ROOM WAS NEEDED.**
     DES FEUILLES SUPPLÉMENTAIRES SONT ANNEXÉES EN RAISON DU MANQUE D'ESPACE.

Prepared on: **November 18, year 0**   , 20 ____   _____
Fait le :   (Signature of defendant or representative /
                                            Signature du défendeur/de la défenderesse ou du/de la représentant(e))

NOTE:	Within seven (7) calendar days of changing your address for service, notify the court and all other parties in writing.
REMARQUE :	*Dans les sept (7) jours civils qui suivent tout changement de votre adresse aux fins de signification, veuillez en aviser par écrit le tribunal et les autres parties.*

CAUTION TO PLAINTIFF(S):	If this Defence contains a proposal of terms of payment, you are deemed to have accepted the terms **unless** you file with the clerk and serve on the defendant(s) a Request to Clerk (Form 9B) for a terms of payment hearing **WITHIN TWENTY (20) CALENDAR DAYS** of service of this Defence [R. 9.03(3)].
AVERTISSEMENT AU(X) DEMANDEUR(S) :	*Si la présente défense comprend une proposition à l'égard des modalités de paiement, vous êtes réputé(e)(s) les avoir acceptées, **sauf** si vous déposez auprès du greffier et signifiez au(x) défendeur(s) une demande au greffier (formule 9B) pour la tenue d'une audience relative aux modalités de paiement **DANS LES VINGT (20) JOURS CIVILS** de la signification de la présente défense [par. 9.03 (3)].*

Figure 10.10   Notice of Default of Payment

ONTARIO

Superior Court of Justice
Cour supérieure de justice

Notice of Default of Payment
Avis de défaut de paiement
Form / *Formule* 20L Ont. Reg. No. / *Règl. de l'Ont.* : 258/98

Toronto

Small Claims Court / *Cour des petites créances de*

**47 Sheppard Ave. E., 3rd Floor
Toronto, ON M2N 2X5**

Address / *Adresse*

416-326-3554

Phone number / *Numéro de téléphone*

SC-10-00012345-0000

Claim No. / *N° de la demande*

BETWEEN / *ENTRE*

Capricious Credit Corporation Ltd.

Plaintiff(s)/Creditor(s) / *Demandeur(s)/demanderesse(s)/Créancier(s)/créancière(s)*

and / *et*

Feckless Enterprises

Defendant(s)/Debtor(s) / *Défendeur(s)/défenderesse(s)/Débiteur(s)/débitrice(s)*

TO: Feckless Enterprises
DESTINATAIRE(S) :   (Name of defendant(s)/debtor(s) / *Nom du/de la/des défendeur(s)/défenderesse(s)/débiteur(s)/débitrice(s)*)

TAKE NOTICE that you defaulted in your payment(s) to
VEUILLEZ PRENDRE NOTE *que vous n'avez pas effectué le ou les paiements que vous deviez verser à*

Capricious Credit Corporation Ltd.

(Name of plaintiff(s)/creditor(s) / *Nom du/de la/des demandeur(s)/demanderesse(s)/créancier(s)/créancière(s)*)

(Check appropriate box. / Cochez la case appropriée.)

☐ under an order for periodic payment, dated _____ , 20 _____ .
en vertu d'une ordonnance prescrivant des versements périodiques datée du

According to Rule 20.02(4) of the *Rules of the Small Claims Court*, the order for periodic payment terminates on the day that is 15 days after the creditor serves the debtor with this notice, unless before that date, a Consent (Form 13B) is filed in which the creditor waives the default.
Conformément au paragraphe 20.02 (4) des Règles de la Cour des petites créances, *l'ordonnance prescrivant des versements périodiques prend fin le 15ᵉ jour qui suit la signification par le créancier au débiteur du présent avis, sauf si, avant cette date, le créancier dépose le consentement (formule 13B) dans lequel il renonce à la constatation du défaut.*

☒ under a proposal of terms of payment in the Defence (Form 9A) dated **November 18, year 0** , 20 _____ .
en vertu d'une proposition à l'égard des modalités de paiement dans la défense (formule 9A) datée du

According to Rule 9.03(2)(c) the clerk may sign judgment for the unpaid balance of the undisputed amount on the day that is 15 days after the plaintiff serves the defendant with this notice.
Conformément à l'alinéa 9.03 (2) c), le greffier peut consigner un jugement relativement au solde impayé de la somme non contestée le 15ᵉ jour qui suit la signification par le demandeur au défendeur du présent avis.

Figure 10.10 Concluded

FORM / *FORMULE* 20L   PAGE 2   SC-10-00012345-0000

....

Claim No. / *N° de la demande*

You can get forms and self-help materials at the Small Claims Court or online at: www.ontariocourtforms.on.ca.
*Vous pouvez obtenir les formules et la documentation à l'usage du client auprès de la Cour des petites créances
ou en ligne à l'adresse : www.ontariocourtforms.on.ca.*

NOTE TO DEFENDANT/DEBTOR: / *REMARQUE AU DÉFENDEUR/DÉBITEUR :*

If you / *Si, selon le cas :*

- failed to make payments but intend to do so; or
  vous n'avez pas effectué de paiements mais vous avez l'intention de le faire;

- made payments but the payments were not received by the creditor;
  vous avez effectué des paiements mais le créancier ne les a pas reçus;

contact the plaintiff/creditor to make payment arrangements or correct the reason for non-receipt of payments.
You may obtain the plaintiff/creditor's written consent (Form 13B may be used) to waive the default and file it with
the court within 15 days of being served with this notice. Failure to do so may result in the following:
*communiquez avec le demandeur/créancier pour prendre les dispositions de paiement ou pour régler le motif de la
non-réception des paiements. Vous pouvez obtenir le consentement écrit du demandeur/créancier (vous pouvez utiliser
la formule 13B) pour renoncer à la constatation du défaut et le déposer au tribunal dans les 15 jours de la signification
du présent avis. Si vous ne le faites pas, vous pourriez subir l'une ou l'autre des conséquences suivantes :*

- in the case of default under a proposal of terms of payment in the Defence (Form 9A), the plaintiff may
  obtain default judgment for the unpaid balance of the undisputed amount; or
  *si vous n'effectuez pas les paiements conformément aux modalités de paiement proposées dans la
  défense (formule 9A), le demandeur pourra obtenir un jugement par défaut relativement au solde impayé
  de la somme non contestée;*

- in the case of default under an order for periodic payment, the order will terminate and the creditor may take
  other steps to enforce the order.
  *si vous n'effectuez pas les paiements conformément à une ordonnance prescrivant des versements
  périodiques, l'ordonnance prendra fin et le créancier pourra prendre d'autres mesures en vue de
  l'exécution forcée de l'ordonnance.*

December 15, year 0   , 20

....

(Signature of plaintiff/creditor or representative / *Signature du demandeur/de
la demanderesse/du créancier/de la créancière ou du/de la représentant(e)*)

**Charles Dickens
8041 Ryder St
Mississauga, ON L2R 1Y6**

(Name, address and phone number of plaintiff/creditor or representative /
*Nom, adresse et numéro de téléphone du demandeur/de la
demanderesse/du créancier/de la créancière ou du/de la représentant(e)*)

Figure 10.11   Affidavit of Default of Payment

ONTARIO
Superior Court of Justice
Cour supérieure de justice

Affidavit of Default of Payment
Affidavit de défaut de paiement
Form / *Formule* 20M Ont. Reg. No. / *Règl. de l'Ont.* : 258/98

Toronto

Small Claims Court / *Cour des petites créances de*

SC-10-00012345-0000

Claim No. / *N° de la demande*

47 Sheppard Ave. E., 3rd Floor
Toronto, ON M2N 2X5

Address / *Adresse*

416-326-3554

Phone number / *Numéro de téléphone*

BETWEEN / *ENTRE*

Capricious Credit Corporation Ltd.

Plaintiff(s)/Creditor(s) / *Demandeur(s)/demanderesse(s)/Créancier(s)/créancière(s)*

and / *et*

Feckless Enterprises

Defendant(s)/Debtor(s) / *Défendeur(s)/défenderesse(s)/Débiteur(s)/débitrice(s)*

My name is Charles Dickens
Je m'appelle
(Full name / *Nom et prénoms*)

I live in Toronto, Ontario
J'habite à
(Municipality & province / *Municipalité et province*)

and I swear/affirm that the following is true:
et je déclare sous serment/j'affirme solennellement que les renseignements suivants sont véridiques :

1. In this action, I am the
    Dans la présente action, je suis le/la

    (Check one box only. / Cochez une seule case.)

    ☐ plaintiff/creditor.
        demandeur/demanderesse/créancier/créancière.

    ☒ representative of the
        plaintiff(s)/creditor(s) **Capricious Credit Corporation Ltd.**
        représentant(e) du/de la/des demandeur(s)/demanderesse(s)   (Name of plaintiff(s)/creditor(s) / *Nom du/de la/des*
        ou du/de la/des créancier(s)/créancière(s)   *demandeur(s)/demanderesse(s) ou du/de la/des*
                                                          créancier(s)/créancière(s)

2. To date, I have received from the defendant(s)/debtor(s) $ _____ **40.00** , the last payment being made
    À ce jour, j'ai reçu du ou des défendeurs/débiteurs   (Amount / *Montant*)   *$, soit le dernier paiement ayant*

    on or about **December 1, year 0** , 20 _____ .
    été effectué le ou vers le

3. I make this affidavit in support of a request that:
    Je fais le présent affidavit à l'appui d'une demande visant à :

    (Check appropriate box and complete paragraph. / Cochez la case appropriée et remplissez le point.)

    ☒ the clerk of the court issue a Default Judgment (Form 11B) [R. 9.03(2)(c)]. The defendant(s)
        enjoindre au greffier du tribunal de rendre un jugement par défaut (formule 11B) [alinéa 9.03 (2) c)].
        Le ou les défendeurs

        Feckless Enterprises

        (Name(s) of defendant(s) / *Nom du/de la/des défendeur(s)/défenderesse(s)*)

        failed to make payment in accordance with the proposed terms of payment in the Defence
        n'ont pas effectué les paiements conformément aux modalités de paiement proposées dans la défense

        (Form 9A) dated **November 18, year 0** , 20 _____ and fifteen (15) days have passed since the
        (formule 9A) datée du   *et quinze (15) jours se sont écoulés depuis*

        defendant was served with a Notice of Default of Payment (Form 20L).
        la signification de l'avis de défaut de paiement au défendeur (formule 20L).

Figure 10.11   Continued

FORM / *FORMULE* **20M**   **PAGE 2**   SC-10-00012345-0000

Claim No. / *N° de la demande*

☐ the clerk of the court issue a Default Judgment (Form 11B) [R. 9.03(7)]. The defendant(s)
enjoindre au greffier du tribunal de rendre un jugement par défaut (formule 11B) [par. 9.03 (7)]. Le ou les défendeurs

_____
(Name of defendant(s) / *Nom du/de la/des défendeur(s)/défenderesse(s)*

failed to make payment in accordance with the terms of payment order
n'ont pas effectué les paiements conformément à l'ordonnance relative aux modalités de paiement

(Check appropriate box and complete paragraph. / Cochez la case appropriée et remplissez le point.)

dated _____ , 20 _____ .
datée du

☐ I may enforce the judgment [R. 20.02(3)]. The debtor(s)
m'autoriser à exécuter le jugement [par. 20.02 (3)]. Le ou les débiteurs

_____
(Name(s) of debtor(s) / *Nom du/de la/des débiteur(s)/débitrice(s)*

failed to make payment in accordance with the order for periodic payment dated
n'ont pas effectué les paiements conformément à l'ordonnance prescrivant des versements périodiques datée du

_____ , 20 _____ , and fifteen (15) days have passed since the debtor(s) has/have
et quinze (15) jours se sont écoulés depuis la signification

been served with a Notice of Default of Payment (Form 20L). A Consent (Form 13B) in which the creditor waives the default has not been filed.
de l'avis de défaut de paiement (formule 20L) au ou aux débiteurs. Un consentement (formule 13B) dans lequel le créancier renonce à la constatation du défaut n'a pas été déposé.

4. The unpaid balance is calculated as follows:
Le solde impayé est calculé de la façon suivante :

(A) **DEBT** $ _____ 3,000.00
   LA CRÉANCE $

(B) **PRE-JUDGMENT INTEREST** calculated
   LES INTÉRÊTS ANTÉRIEURS AU JUGEMENT calculés

on the sum of $ _____ 3,000.00 _____ at the rate of **10** %
sur la somme de $ *au taux de* *pour cent*

per annum from **April 1, year -1** , 20 ___ to **Dec. 1, year 0** , 20 ___ ,
par an du *au*

being **610** days. $ _____ 501.37
soit *jours.* $

NOTE:	Calculation of interest is always on the amount owing from time to time as payments are received. This is true for both pre-judgment and post-judgment interest. Attach a separate sheet setting out how you calculated the total amount of any pre/post-judgment interest.
REMARQUE :	*Les intérêts doivent toujours être calculés sur la somme due. Le calcul doit tenir compte des paiements reçus de temps à autre. Ceci s'applique autant aux intérêts antérieurs au jugement qu'aux intérêts postérieurs au jugement. Annexez une feuille distincte indiquant comment vous avez calculé le montant total des intérêts antérieurs et postérieurs au jugement.*

SUBTOTAL (amount of judgment) $ _____ 3,501.37
TOTAL PARTIEL *(montant du jugement)* $

Figure 10.11   Concluded

FORM / FORMULE 20M   **PAGE 3**   SC-10-00012345-0000

Claim No. / N° de la demande

(C) **COSTS** to date of judgment $ _____ 75.00

LES DÉPENS à la date du jugement $

(D) **TOTAL AMOUNT OF PAYMENTS RECEIVED FROM DEBTOR**

after judgment (if any)   (minus) $ _____ 40.00

LE MONTANT TOTAL DES PAIEMENTS REÇUS DU DÉBITEUR   *(moins)* $

après le jugement (le cas échéant)

(E) **POST-JUDGMENT INTEREST** to date calculated

LES INTÉRÊTS POSTÉRIEURS AU JUGEMENT à ce jour, calculés

on the sum of $ _____ 3,536.37   at the rate of __10__ %

sur la somme de _____ $ *au taux de* _____ *pour cent*

per annum from **Nov. 18, year 0** , 20 _____ to **Dec. 2, year 0** , 20 _____ ,

par an du _____ *Au*

being **15** _____ days. $ _____ 14.53

soit _____ *jours.* $

(F) **SUBSEQUENT COSTS** incurred after judgment (including the cost of serving

the Notice of Default of Payment (Form 20L)) $ _____ 19.00

LES DÉPENS SUBSÉQUENTS engagés après le jugement (y compris le coût de $

signification de l'avis de défaut de paiement (formule 20L))

TOTAL DUE $ _____ 3,569.90

SOLDE DÛ $

Sworn/Affirmed before me at   **Toronto** _____

Déclaré sous serment/Affirmé   (Municipality / municipalité)

solennellement devant moi à

in **Ontario** _____

en/à/au   (Province, state, or county / province, État ou pays)

on **Dec. 2, year 0** ____ , 20 ____   _____

le   Commissioner for taking affidavits

Commissaire aux affidavits

(Type or print name below if signature is

illegible.)

(Dactylographiez le nom ou écrivez-le en

caractères d'imprimerie ci-dessous si la

signature est illisible.)

_____

Signature

(This form is to be signed in front of a

lawyer, justice of the peace, notary public

or commissioner for taking affidavits.)

(La présente formule doit être signée en

présence d'un avocat, d'un juge de paix,

d'un notaire ou d'un commissaire aux

affidavits.)

WARNING:	**IT IS AN OFFENCE UNDER THE *CRIMINAL CODE* TO KNOWINGLY SWEAR OR AFFIRM A FALSE AFFIDAVIT.**
AVERTISSEMENT :	*FAIRE SCIEMMENT UN FAUX AFFIDAVIT CONSTITUE UNE INFRACTION AU CODE CRIMINEL.*

Figure 10.12   Request to Clerk (for a Hearing)

ONTARIO

Superior Court of Justice
Cour supérieure de justice

Request to Clerk
Demande au greffier
Form / *Formule* 9B Ont. Reg. No. / *Règl. de l'Ont.* : 258/98

Toronto

Small Claims Court / *Cour des petites créances de*

47 Sheppard Ave. E., 3rd Floor
Toronto, ON M2N 2X5

Address / *Adresse*

416-326-3554

Phone number / *Numéro de téléphone*

SC-10-00012345-0000

Claim No. / *N° de la demande*

BETWEEN / *ENTRE*

Capricious Credit Corporation Ltd.

Plaintiff(s) / *Demandeur(s)/demanderesse(s)*

and / *et*

Feckless Enterprises

Defendant(s) / *Défendeur(s)/défenderesse(s)*

TO THE CLERK OF THE Toronto   **SMALL CLAIMS COURT:**
AU GREFFIER DE LA COUR   (Name of Small Claims Court location / *Emplacement de la*
DES PETITES CRÉANCES DE   *Cour des petites créances*) :

My name is   Charles Dickens   **and I request that the clerk of the court:**
Je m'appelle   (Name of party/representative / *Nom de la partie ou du/de la*   *et je demande au greffier du tribunal*
                                    représentant(e))   *de faire ce qui suit :*

(Check appropriate box(es). / Cochez la ou les cases appropriées.)

☐   note defendant(s) _____
     constater le ou les défendeurs   (Name of defendant(s) / *Nom du/de la/des défendeur(s)/défenderesse(s)*)

     in default for failing to file a Defence (Form 9A) within the prescribed time period [R. 11.01(1)].
     en défaut pour n'avoir pas déposé de défense (formule 9A) dans le délai prescrit [par. 11.01 (1)].

☐   schedule an assessment hearing (all defendants have been noted in default) [R. 11.03(2)(b)].
     fixer la date d'une audience d'évaluation (tous les défendeurs ont été constatés en défaut) [alinéa
     11.03 (2) b)].

☒   schedule a terms of payment hearing because I dispute the defendant's proposed terms of payment
     contained in the Defence (Form 9A) [R. 9.03(3)].
     fixer la date d'une audience relative aux modalités de paiement parce que je conteste les modalités de
     paiement proposées par le défendeur dans la défense (formule 9A) [par. 9.03 (3)].

☐   schedule a trial [R. 16.01(1)(b)].
     fixer une date de procès [alinéa 16.01 (1) b)].

Figure 10.12   Concluded

FORM / *FORMULE* **9B**   **PAGE 2**   SC-10-00012345-0000

                                                                Claim No. / *N° de la demande*

☐   accept payment in the amount of $ _____ into court
     accepter que le paiement de   (Amount / *montant*)   *$ soit consigné au tribunal,*

   ☐   according to an order of the court, dated _____ , 20 ____ .
       conformément à une ordonnance du tribunal datée du

   ☐   for a person under disability according to an order or settlement dated
       au nom d'un incapable, conformément à une ordonnance ou à une transaction datée du

       _____ , 20 ____   [R. 4.08(1)].
                                   [par. 4.08 (1)].

   ☐   pursuant to the attached written offer to settle, dated _____ , 20 ____   [R. 14.05(2)].
       aux termes de l'offre de transaction écrite ci-jointe datée du   *[par. 14.05 (2)].*

   ☐   according to the following legislation:
       conformément à la disposition législative suivante :

       _____ .
             (Name of statute or regulation and section / *Titre de la loi ou du règlement et mention de l'article*)

☐   Other: (Specify.)
     Autre :   *(Précisez.)*

June 2, year 0 _____ , 20 ____   _____
                                               (Signature of party or representative / *Signature de la partie ou du/de la*
                                                                    représentant(e))

CAUTION:	To obtain an assessment of damages, all defendants must be noted in default. If one or more defendants has filed a defence, the matter must proceed to a settlement conference. To bring a motion in writing for an assessment of damages, file a Notice of Motion and Supporting Affidavit (Form 15A). You can get forms at court offices or online at www.ontariocourtforms.on.ca.
AVERTISSEMENT :	*Pour obtenir une évaluation des dommages-intérêts, tous les défendeurs doivent être constatés en défaut. Si un ou plusieurs défendeurs ont déposé une défense, l'affaire doit passer à l'étape de la conférence en vue d'une transaction. Pour présenter une motion par écrit en vue d'une évaluation des dommages-intérêts, déposez un avis de motion et affidavit à l'appui (formule 15A). Vous pouvez obtenir les formules aux greffes des tribunaux ou en ligne à l'adresse www.ontariocourtforms.on.ca.*

Figure 10.13 Defendant's Claim

ONTARIO
Superior Court of Justice
Cour supérieure de justice

Defendant's Claim
Demande du défendeur
Form / *Formule* 10A Ont. Reg. No. / *Règl. de l'Ont.* : 258/98

Seal / *Sceau*

Toronto
Small Claims Court / *Cour des petites créances de*

SC-10-00012349-0001
Claim No. / *N° de la demande*

47 Sheppard Ave. E., 3rd Floor
Toronto, ON M2N 2X5
Address / *Adresse*

416-326-3554
Phone number / *Numéro de téléphone*

Plaintiff by Defendant's Claim No. 1 /
Demandeur dans la demande du défendeur n° 1

☐ Additional plaintiff(s) listed on attached Form 1A. *Le ou les demandeurs additionnels sont mentionnés sur la formule 1A ci-jointe.*

☐ Under 18 years of age. *Moins de 18 ans.*

Last name, or name of company / *Nom de famille ou nom de la compagnie*		
Feckless Enterprises		
First name / *Premier prénom*	Second name / *Deuxième prénom*	Also known as / *Également connu(e) sous le nom de*
Address (street number, apt., unit) / *Adresse (numéro et rue, app., unité)*		
c/o Edward Loquacious 365 Bay Street		
City/Town / *Cité/ville* **Toronto**	Province **ON**	Phone no. / *N° de téléphone* **416-595-1308**
Postal code / *Code postal* **M2N 3A8**		Fax no. / *N° de télécopieur*
Representative / *Représentant(e)* **Edward Loquacious**		LSUC # / *N° du BHC* **P02361**
Address (street number, apt., unit) / *Adresse (numéro et rue, app., unité)*		
365 Bay Street		
City/Town / *Cité/ville* **Toronto**	Province **ON**	Phone no. / *N° de téléphone* **416-595-1308**
Postal code / *Code postal* **M2N 3A8**		Fax no. / *N° de télécopieur*

Defendant by Defendant's Claim No. 1 /
Défendeur dans la demande du défendeur n° 1

☐ Additional defendant(s) listed on attached Form 1A. *Le ou les défendeurs additionnels sont mentionnés sur la formule 1A ci-jointe.*

☐ Under 18 years of age. *Moins de 18 ans.*

Last name, or name of company / *Nom de famille ou nom de la compagnie*		
Slipaway		
First name / *Premier prénom* **Sharon**	Second name / *Deuxième prénom*	Also known as / *Également connu(e) sous le nom de*
Address (street number, apt., unit) / *Adresse (numéro et rue, app., unité)*		
33 Gardenia Crescent		
City/Town / *Cité/ville* **Toronto**	Province **ON**	Phone no. / *N° de téléphone* **416-223-0641**
Postal code / *Code postal* **M2N 2A8**		Fax no. / *N° de télécopieur*
Representative / *Représentant(e)*		LSUC # / *N° du BHC*
Address (street number, apt., unit) / *Adresse (numéro et rue, app., unité)*		
City/Town / *Cité/ville*	Province	Phone no. / *N° de téléphone*
Postal code / *Code postal*		Fax no. / *N° de télécopieur*

Figure 10.13 Continued

FORM / FORMULE 10A PAGE 2 SC-10-00012349-0001
Claim No. / *N° de la demande*

REASONS FOR CLAIM AND DETAILS / *MOTIFS DE LA DEMANDE ET PRÉCISIONS*

Explain what happened, including where and when. Then explain how much money you are claiming or what goods you want returned.
Expliquez ce qui s'est passé, en précisant où et quand. Ensuite indiquez la somme d'argent que vous demandez ou les biens dont vous demandez la restitution, explication à l'appui.

If you are relying on any documents, you **MUST** attach copies to the claim. If evidence is lost or unavailable, you **MUST** explain why it is not attached.
*Si vous vous appuyez sur des documents, vous **DEVEZ** en annexer des copies à la demande. Si une preuve est perdue ou n'est pas disponible, vous **DEVEZ** expliquer pourquoi elle n'est pas annexée.*

What happened?
Where?
When?

Que s'est-il passé?
Où?
Quand?

The plaintiff by defendant's claim, Feckless Enterprises, (Feckless) signed a promissory note in favour of Capricious Credit Corporation Ltd. (Capricious) in the amount of $3,000 plus interest at 10%. The note was signed on April 1, year -1.
The defendant by defendant's claim, Sharon Slipaway (Slipaway), agreed to pay $1,000 of this promissory note if Feckless was obliged to honour its promissory note to Capricious.
The agreement between Feckless and Slipaway was entered into at Toronto, Ontario.

1. Feckless is a business located in Toronto, Ontario. Slipaway is an individual residing in Toronto, Ontario.

2. On April 1, year -1, Feckless signed a promissory note for $3,000 plus interest of 10%, in favour of Capricious. The note was due one year later, on April 1, year 0.

3. On April 2, year -1, Slipaway applied for an account with Feckless. As a conditon of maintaining an account with Feckless, Slipaway agreed to pay the sum of $1,000 toward the promissory note that Feckless had with Capricious. The $1,000 would bear interest at the rate of 10% per year from the time a demand was made to pay it.

4. Capricious called in its note on April 1, year 0.

5. On April 3, year 0, Feckless demanded the sum of $1,000 toward the note from Slipaway as agreed.

6. As of the date of the preparation of this claim, Slipaway has refused to pay the amount due.

7. The amount of $1,000 plus interest at the rate of 10% per year is due from Slipaway from April 3, year 0 to now.

Figure 10.13   Concluded

FORM / *FORMULE* **10A**   **PAGE 3**   SC-10-00012349-0001
                                                                          Claim No. / *N° de la demande*

How much?	$ .... 1,000 $
Combien?	(Principal amount claimed / *Somme demandée*)

☐   **ADDITIONAL PAGES ARE ATTACHED BECAUSE MORE ROOM WAS NEEDED.**
     DES FEUILLES SUPPLÉMENTAIRES SONT ANNEXÉES EN RAISON DU MANQUE D'ESPACE.

The plaintiff by defendant's claim also claims pre-judgment interest from   April 4, year 0   under:
Le demandeur dans la demande du défendeur demande aussi des   (Date)   *conformément à :*
intérêts antérieurs au jugement à compter du

(Check only   ☐   **the *Courts of Justice Act***
one box /   *la* **Loi sur les tribunaux judiciaires**
Cochez une
seule case)   ☒   **an agreement at the rate of** 10   **% per year**
                           un accord au taux de   **% par an**

and post-judgment interest, and court costs.
et des intérêts postérieurs au jugement, ainsi que les dépens.

Prepared on: **November 18, year 0**   , 20 _____   _____
Fait le :   (Signature of plaintiff or representative / *Signature du*
                                                                          demandeur/de la demanderesse ou du/de la représentant(e))

Issued on: **November 18, year 0**   , 20 _____   _____
Délivré le :   (Signature of clerk / *Signature du greffier*)

CAUTION TO DEFENDANT BY DEFENDANT'S CLAIM: ***AVERTISSEMENT AU DÉFENDEUR DANS LA DEMANDE DU DÉFENDEUR :***	**IF YOU DO NOT FILE A DEFENCE** (Form 9A) with the court within twenty (20) calendar days after you have been served with this Defendant's Claim, judgment may be obtained by Defendant's Claim without notice and enforced against you. Forms and self-help materials are available at the Small Claims Court and on the following website: www.ontariocourtforms.on.ca. ***SI VOUS NE DÉPOSEZ PAS DE DÉFENSE*** *(formule 9A) auprès du tribunal au plus tard vingt (20) jours civils après avoir reçu signification de la présente demande du défendeur, un jugement peut être obtenu par suite de cette demande sans préavis et être exécuté contre vous. Vous pouvez obtenir les formules et la documentation à l'usage du client à la Cour des petites créances et sur le site Web suivant : www.ontariocourtforms.on.ca.*

Figure 10.14 Request to Clerk (to Note Defendant in Default)

ONTARIO

Superior Court of Justice
Cour supérieure de justice

Request to Clerk
Demande au greffier
Form / *Formule* 9B Ont. Reg. No. / *Règl. de l'Ont.* : 258/98

Toronto

Small Claims Court / *Cour des petites créances de*

SC-10-00012345-0000

Claim No. / *N° de la demande*

47 Sheppard Ave. E., 3rd Floor
Toronto, ON M2N 2X5

Address / *Adresse*

416-326-3554

Phone number / *Numéro de téléphone*

BETWEEN / *ENTRE*

Capricious Credit Corporation Ltd.

Plaintiff(s) / *Demandeur(s)/demanderesse(s)*

and / *et*

Feckless Enterprises

Defendant(s) / *Défendeur(s)/défenderesse(s)*

TO THE CLERK OF THE Toronto
AU GREFFIER DE LA COUR
DES PETITES CRÉANCES DE

(Name of Small Claims Court location / *Emplacement de la*
Cour des petites créances) :

SMALL CLAIMS COURT:

My name is Charles Dickens
Je m'appelle

(Name of party/representative / *Nom de la partie ou du/de la*
représentant(e))

and I request that the clerk of the court:
et je demande au greffier du tribunal
de faire ce qui suit :

(Check appropriate box(es). / Cochez la ou les cases appropriées.)

☒ note defendant(s) **Feckless Enterprises**
constater le ou les défendeurs

(Name of defendant(s) / *Nom du/de la/des défendeur(s)/défenderesse(s)*)

in default for failing to file a Defence (Form 9A) within the prescribed time period [R. 11.01(1)].
en défaut pour n'avoir pas déposé de défense (formule 9A) dans le délai prescrit [par. 11.01 (1)].

☐ schedule an assessment hearing (all defendants have been noted in default) [R. 11.03(2)(b)].
fixer la date d'une audience d'évaluation (tous les défendeurs ont été constatés en défaut) [alinéa
11.03 (2) b)].

☐ schedule a terms of payment hearing because I dispute the defendant's proposed terms of payment
contained in the Defence (Form 9A) [R. 9.03(3)].
fixer la date d'une audience relative aux modalités de paiement parce que je conteste les modalités de
paiement proposées par le défendeur dans la défense (formule 9A) [par. 9.03 (3)].

☐ schedule a trial [R. 16.01(1)(b)].
fixer une date de procès [alinéa 16.01 (1) b)].

Figure 10.14   Concluded

FORM / *FORMULE* 9B   PAGE 2   <u>SC-10-00012345-0000</u>
                                                                                   Claim No. / *N° de la demande*

☐ accept payment in the amount of $ _____ into court
     accepter que le paiement de   (Amount / *montant*) *$ soit consigné au tribunal,*

   ☐ according to an order of the court, dated _____ , 20 _____ .
     conformément à une ordonnance du tribunal datée du

   ☐ for a person under disability according to an order or settlement dated
     au nom d'un incapable, conformément à une ordonnance ou à une transaction datée du
     _____ , 20 _____ [R. 4.08(1)].
                         [par. 4.08 (1)].

   ☐ pursuant to the attached written offer to settle, dated _____ , 20 _____ [R. 14.05(2)].
     aux termes de l'offre de transaction écrite ci-jointe datée du   *[par. 14.05 (2)].*

   ☐ according to the following legislation:
     conformément à la disposition législative suivante :

   _____ .
         (Name of statute or regulation and section / *Titre de la loi ou du règlement et mention de l'article*)

☐ Other: (Specify.)
     Autre : (*Précisez.*)

November 20, year 0 _____ , 20 _____   _____
                                                    (Signature of party or representative / *Signature de la partie ou du/de la*
                                                    représentant(e))

CAUTION:	To obtain an assessment of damages, all defendants must be noted in default. If one or more defendants has filed a defence, the matter must proceed to a settlement conference. To bring a motion in writing for an assessment of damages, file a Notice of Motion and Supporting Affidavit (Form 15A). You can get forms at court offices or online at www.ontariocourtforms.on.ca.
AVERTISSEMENT :	*Pour obtenir une évaluation des dommages-intérêts, tous les défendeurs doivent être constatés en défaut. Si un ou plusieurs défendeurs ont déposé une défense, l'affaire doit passer à l'étape de la conférence en vue d'une transaction. Pour présenter une motion par écrit en vue d'une évaluation des dommages-intérêts, déposez un avis de motion et affidavit à l'appui (formule 15A). Vous pouvez obtenir les formules aux greffes des tribunaux ou en ligne à l'adresse www.ontariocourtforms.on.ca.*

Figure 10.15   Default Judgment

ONTARIO

Superior Court of Justice
Cour supérieure de justice

Default Judgment
Jugement par défaut

Form / *Formule* 11B Ont. Reg. No. / *Règl. de l'Ont.* : 258/98

Seal / *Sceau*

Toronto

Small Claims Court / *Cour des petites créances de*

47 Sheppard Ave. E., 3rd Floor
Toronto, ON M2N 2X5

Address / *Adresse*

416-326-3554

Phone number / *Numéro de téléphone*

SC-10-00012345-0000

Claim No. / *N° de la demande*

Plaintiff No. 1 / *Demandeur n° 1*   ☐ Additional plaintiff(s) listed on attached Form 1A.
Le ou les demandeurs additionnels sont mentionnés sur la formule 1A ci-jointe.

Last name, or name of company / *Nom de famille ou nom de la compagnie*		
Capricious Credit Corporation Ltd.		
First name / *Premier prénom*	Second name / *Deuxième prénom*	Also known as / *Également connu(e) sous le nom de*
Address (street number, apt., unit) / *Adresse (numéro et rue, app., unité)*		
c/o Charles Dickens 8041 Ryder Street		
City/Town / *Cité/ville*	Province	Phone no. / *N° de téléphone*
Mississauga	**ON**	**905-381-2620**
Postal code / *Code postal*		Fax no. / *N° de télécopieur*
L2R 1Y6		
Representative / *Représentant(e)*		LSUC # / *N° du BHC*
Charles Dickens		**P02345**
Address (street number, apt., unit) / *Adresse (numéro et rue, app., unité)*		
8041 Ryder Street		
City/Town / *Cité/ville*	Province	Phone no. / *N° de téléphone*
Mississauga	**ON**	**905-381-2620**
Postal code / *Code postal*		Fax no. / *N° de télécopieur*
L2R 1Y6		

Defendant No. 1 / *Défendeur n° 1*   ☐ Additional defendant(s) listed on attached Form 1A.
Le ou les défendeurs additionnels sont mentionnés sur la formule 1A ci-jointe.

Last name, or name of company / *Nom de famille ou nom de la compagnie*		
Feckless Enterprises		
First name / *Premier prénom*	Second name / *Deuxième prénom*	Also known as / *Également connu(e) sous le nom de*
Address (street number, apt., unit) / *Adresse (numéro et rue, app., unité)*		
c/o Edward Loquacious 365 Bay Street		
City/Town / *Cité/ville*	Province	Phone no. / *N° de téléphone*
Toronto	**ON**	**416-595-1308**
Postal code / *Code postal*		Fax no. / *N° de télécopieur*
M2N 3A8		
Representative / *Représentant(e)*		LSUC # / *N° du BHC*
Edward Loquacious		**P02361**
Address (street number, apt., unit) / *Adresse (numéro et rue, app., unité)*		
365 Bay Street		
City/Town / *Cité/ville*	Province	Phone no. / *N° de téléphone*
Toronto	**ON**	**416-595-1308**
Postal code / *Code postal*		Fax no. / *N° de télécopieur*
M2N 3A8		

Figure 10.15 Continued

FORM / *FORMULE* **11B**   **PAGE 2**

NOTICE TO THE DEFENDANT(S):
AVIS AU(X) DÉFENDEUR(S) :

(*Check one box only. /* Cochez une seule case.)

☒ You have been noted in default according to Rule 11.01.
vous avez été constaté(e) en défaut aux termes de la règle 11.01.

☐ You have defaulted in your payment according to Rule 9.03(2)(b), pursuant to
vous n'avez pas effectué vos paiements aux termes de l'alinéa 9.03 (2) b), conformément à/au

_____ dated _____ , 20 _____ ,
(Name of document / *Titre du document*)   *daté(e) du*

and 15 days have passed since you were served with a Notice of Default of Payment (Form 20L).
et 15 jours se sont écoulés depuis qu'un avis de défaut de paiement vous a été signifié (formule 20L).

DEFAULT JUDGMENT IS GIVEN against the following defendant(s):
UN JUGEMENT PAR DÉFAUT EST RENDU contre le ou les défendeurs suivants :

Last name, or name of company / *Nom de famille ou nom de la compagnie*		
Feckless Enterprises		
First name / *Premier prénom*	Second name / *Deuxième prénom*	Also known as / *Également connu(e) sous le nom de*

Last name, or name of company / *Nom de famille ou nom de la compagnie*		
First name / *Premier prénom*	Second name / *Deuxième prénom*	Also known as / *Également connu(e) sous le nom de*

Last name, or name of company / *Nom de famille ou nom de la compagnie*		
First name / *Premier prénom*	Second name / *Deuxième prénom*	Also known as / *Également connu(e) sous le nom de*

☐ Additional defendant(s) listed on attached page (*list in same format*).
Défendeur(s) additionnel(s) mentionné(s) sur une feuille annexée (énumérez-les en suivant le même format).

THE DEFENDANT(S) MUST PAY to the plaintiff(s) the following sums:
LE OU LES DÉFENDEURS DOIVENT VERSER au(x) demandeur(s) les sommes suivantes :

(A) **DEBT** (principal amount claimed minus any payments received since the plaintiff's
claim was issued) $ _____ 3,000.00
LA CRÉANCE (somme demandée moins tout paiement reçu depuis la délivrance $
de la demande du demandeur)

(B) **PRE-JUDGMENT INTEREST** calculated
LES INTÉRÊTS ANTÉRIEURS AU JUGEMENT calculés

on the sum of $ _____ 3,000.00 at the rate of **10** _____ %
sur la somme de   *$ au taux de*   *pour cent*

per annum from **April 1, year -1** , 20 _____ , to **Nov. 20, year 0** , 20 _____ ,
par an du   *au*

being **599** _____ days. $ _____ 492.33
soit   *jours.* $

Figure 10.15 Concluded

FORM / *FORMULE* **11B**   **PAGE 3**   <u>SC-10-00012345-0000</u>

Claim No. / *N° de la demande*

(C) **COSTS** to date (including the cost of issuing this judgment) $ <u>   130.00</u>
   LES DÉPENS à ce jour (dont les frais afférents à la prononciation $
   du présent jugement)

                                                                         TOTAL $ <u>   3,622.33</u>

                                                                                                         $

This judgment bears post-judgment interest at <u>**3**   </u>   % per annum commencing this date.
Le présent jugement porte des intérêts postérieurs   *pour cent à partir de la date du présent jugement.*
au jugement calculés au taux annuel de

<u>**November 20, year 0**   </u> **, 20** <u>   </u>   <u>   </u>

                                                                         (Signature of clerk / *Signature du greffier*)

CAUTION TO DEFENDANT:	**YOU MUST PAY THE AMOUNT OF THIS JUDGMENT DIRECTLY TO THE PLAINTIFF(S) IMMEDIATELY.** Failure to do so may result in additional post-judgment interest and enforcement costs.
AVERTISSEMENT AU DÉFENDEUR :	*VOUS DEVEZ VERSER DIRECTEMENT AU(X) DEMANDEUR(S) LE MONTANT DÛ AUX TERMES DU PRÉSENT JUGEMENT IMMÉDIATEMENT, à défaut de quoi d'autres intérêts postérieurs au jugement et dépens de l'exécution forcée pourront vous être imputés.*

Figure 10.16   List of Proposed Witnesses

ONTARIO

Superior Court of Justice
Cour supérieure de justice

List of Proposed Witnesses
Liste des témoins proposés

Form / *Formule* 13A Ont. Reg. No. / *Règl. de l'Ont.* : 258/98

Toronto	**SC-10-00012345-0000**
Small Claims Court / *Cour des petites créances de*	Claim No. / *N° de la demande*

47 Sheppard Ave. E., 3rd Floor
Toronto, ON M2N 2X5

Address / *Adresse*

416-326-3554

Phone number / *Numéro de téléphone*

BETWEEN / *ENTRE*

Capricious Credit Corporation Ltd.

Plaintiff(s) / *Demandeur(s)/demanderesse(s)*

and / *et*

Feckless Enterprises

Defendant(s) / *Défendeur(s)/défenderesse(s)*

My name is Edward Loquacious
Je m'appelle   (Name of party/representative / *Nom de la partie ou du/de la représentant(e)*)

The following is my list of proposed witnesses in this case:
La liste suivante constitue ma liste des témoins proposés dans la présente cause :

Name of witness / *Nom du témoin*	Address, phone and fax numbers / *Adresse, numéros de téléphone et de télécopieur*
1. Henry Snorglepus	35 Morton Avenue
	Toronto, ON M2K 3J5
	416-222-5549
2.	
3.	

Figure 10.16   Concluded

FORM / *FORMULE* **13A**   **PAGE 2**   SC-10-00012345-0000
                                                                          Claim No. / *N° de la demande*

4.

5.

The following is my list of other persons with knowledge of the matter in dispute in this case:
La liste suivante constitue ma liste des autres personnes qui ont connaissance des questions en litige dans la présente cause :

Name of person / *Nom de la personne*	**Address, phone and fax numbers /** *Adresse, numéros de téléphone et de télécopieur*
1.	
2.	

(Attach a separate sheet in the above format for additional witnesses or other persons.)
(En cas de témoins ou de personnes additionnels, annexez une autre feuille reproduisant le format ci-dessus.)

November 25, year 0   , 20
                                                          (Signature of party or representative / *Signature de la partie ou du/de la représentant(e)*)

                                                          (Name, address and phone number of party or representative / *Nom, adresse et numéro de téléphone de la partie ou du/de la représentant(e)*)

NOTE:	EACH PARTY MUST SERVE THIS LIST on all other parties and file it with the court at least fourteen (14) days before the settlement conference [R. 13.03(2)(b)].
REMARQUE :	*CHAQUE PARTIE DOIT SIGNIFIER LA PRÉSENTE LISTE à toutes les autres parties et la déposer auprès du tribunal au moins quatorze (14) jours avant la tenue de la conférence en vue d'une transaction [alinéa 13.03 (2) b)].*

Figure 10.17   Terms of Settlement

ONTARIO

Superior Court of Justice
Cour supérieure de justice

Terms of Settlement
Conditions de la transaction
Form / *Formule* 14D Ont. Reg. No. / *Règl. de l'Ont.* : 258/98

Toronto
Small Claims Court / *Cour des petites créances de*

SC-10-00012345-0000
Claim No. / *N° de la demande*

**47 Sheppard Ave. E., 3rd Floor
Toronto, ON M2N 2X5**

Address / *Adresse*

416-326-3554
Phone number / *Numéro de téléphone*

BETWEEN / *ENTRE*

Capricious Credit Corporation Ltd.

Plaintiff(s) / *Demandeur(s)/demanderesse(s)*

and / *et*

Feckless Enterprises

Defendant(s) / *Défendeur(s)/défenderesse(s)*

We have agreed to settle this action on the following terms:
Nous avons convenu de régler la présente action selon les conditions suivantes :

1. **Feckless Enterprises**

    (Name of party(ies) / *Nom de la ou des parties*)

    Capricious Credit Corporation Ltd.

    (Name of party(ies) / *Nom de la ou des parties*)

    shall pay to
    verse à

    the sum of
    la somme de

$ **3,000.00**   as follows as full and final settlement of the claim, inclusive of interest and costs:
$ comme suit, à titre de transaction complète et définitive sur la demande, y compris les intérêts et les dépens :

(Provide terms of payment such as start date, frequency, amount and duration / *Indiquez les modalités de paiement telles que la date de début des versements ainsi que leur fréquence, leur montant et leur durée.*)

The sum of $1,000.00 shall be paid to the plaintiff on each of the first days of December year 0, January year 1, and February year 1 for a total of $3,000.00, commencing December 1, year 0.

Put a line through any blank space and initial.
Tracez une ligne en travers de tout espace laissé en blanc et apposez vos initiales.

Figure 10.17   Concluded

FORM / *FORMULE* 14D   **PAGE 2**   SC-10-00012345-0000

Claim No. / *N° de la demande*

2.   This claim (and Defendant's Claim, if any) is withdrawn.
Cette demande (et celle du défendeur, le cas échéant) est retirée (sont retirées).

3.   If a party to these terms of settlement fails to comply, judgment in the terms of settlement may be obtained against that party on motion to the court or this action may continue as if there has been no settlement.
Si une partie aux présentes conditions de la transaction n'en observe pas les conditions, un jugement suivant les conditions de la transaction peut être obtenu contre cette partie sur présentation d'une motion au tribunal ou la présente action peut continuer comme s'il n'y avait jamais eu de transaction.

4.   Provided that the terms of settlement are complied with, the parties above fully and finally release one another from all claims related to the facts and issues raised in this action.
Pourvu que les conditions de la transaction soient observées, les parties susmentionnées se dégagent l'une et l'autre complètement et définitivement de toutes demandes liées aux faits et questions en litige soulevés dans la présente action.

The parties do not need to sign terms of settlement on the same day, but each must sign in the presence of his or her witness who signs a moment later. (For additional parties' signatures, attach a separate sheet in the below format.)
Les parties ne sont pas tenues de signer les conditions de la transaction le même jour, mais chacune doit les signer en présence de son témoin, qui les signe à son tour aussitôt après. (S'il y a lieu, annexez une autre feuille portant la signature des parties additionnelles présentée selon le format indiqué ci-dessous.)

November 26, year 0 _____ , 20 _____

_____
(Signature of party / *Signature de la partie*)

Capricious Credit Corporation Ltd.
(Name of party / *Nom de la partie*)

_____
(Signature of witness / *Signature du témoin*)

_____
(Name of witness / *Nom du témoin*)

_____ , 20 _____

_____
(Signature of party / *Signature de la partie*)

_____
(Name of party / *Nom de la partie*)

_____
(Signature of witness / *Signature du témoin*)

_____
(Name of witness / *Nom du témoin*)

November 26, year 0 _____ , 20 _____

_____
(Signature of party / *Signature de la partie*)

Feckless Enterprises
(Name of party / *Nom de la partie*)

_____
(Signature of witness / *Signature du témoin*)

_____
(Name of witness / *Nom du témoin*)

_____ , 20 _____

_____
(Signature of party / *Signature de la partie*)

_____
(Name of party / *Nom de la partie*)

_____
(Signature of witness / *Signature du témoin*)

_____
(Name of witness / *Nom du témoin*)

Figure 10.18   Sample Minutes of Settlement — Settlement Conference

Claim No. SC-10-00012345-0000

Toronto Small Claims Court

47 Sheppard Ave. E., 3rd Floor

Toronto, ON M2N 2X5

416-326-3554

Capricious Credit Corporation Ltd.
Plaintiff

and

Feckless Enterprises
Defendant

MINUTES OF SETTLEMENT

The above parties have agreed to settle this action on the following terms:

1. The Defendant shall pay to the Plaintiff the sum of $3,000 as follows:

    the sum of $1,000 shall be paid to the plaintiff on each of the first days of December year 0, January year 1, and February year 1, for a total of $3,000, commencing December 1, year 0

    as full settlement of this claim, inclusive of interest and costs.

2. This Claim is dismissed upon payment in full.

3. In the event that the Defendant defaults in payment, the Plaintiff may ask the Clerk of the Court to sign judgment, without notice, for $3,000, plus interest and costs, less any payments made.

4. Once these terms of settlement are complied with, the parties each fully and finally release one another from all claims related to the facts and issues raised in this action.

Dated at Toronto, Ontario, this 26th day of November, year 0

Capricious Credit Corporation Ltd.   Feckless Enterprises

Plaintiff   Defendant

Per: _____   Per: _____

Witness: _____   Witness: _____

Figure 10.19 Offer to Settle

ONTARIO

Superior Court of Justice
Cour supérieure de justice

Offer to Settle
Offre de transaction
Form / *Formule* 14A Ont. Reg. No. / *Règl. de l'Ont.* : 258/98

Toronto
Small Claims Court / *Cour des petites créances de*

SC-10-00012345-0000
Claim No. / *N° de la demande*

Address / *Adresse*

Phone number / *Numéro de téléphone*

BETWEEN / *ENTRE*

Capricious Credit Corporation Ltd.

Plaintiff(s) / *Demandeur(s)/demanderesse(s)*

and / *et*

Feckless Enterprises

Defendant(s) / *Défendeur(s)/défenderesse(s)*

My name is Charles Dickens
Je m'appelle
(Full name / *Nom et prénoms*)

1. In this action, I am the
   Dans la présente action, je suis le/la

   ☐ Plaintiff
      demandeur/demanderesse

   ☐ Defendant
      défendeur/défenderesse

   ☒ representative of **Capricious Credit Corporation Ltd.**
      représentant(e) de (Name of party(ies) / *Nom de la ou des parties*)

2. I offer to settle this action against **Feckless Enterprises**
   Je présente une offre de transaction dans cette action contre (Name of party(ies) / *Nom de la ou des parties*)

   on the following terms: *(Set out terms in numbered paragraphs, or on an attached sheet.)*
   selon les conditions suivantes : (Indiquez les conditions sous forme de paragraphes numérotés ou sur une feuille annexée.)

   The defendant shall pay to the plaintiff the sum of $3,000 with $1,000 to be paid December 1, year 0, January 1, year 1, and February 1, year 1.

Figure 10.19 Concluded

FORM / *FORMULE* 14A   PAGE 2   SC-10-00012345-0000

Claim No. / *N° de la demande*

3. This offer to settle is available for acceptance until **November 26, year 0**   , 20 _____ .
    L'acceptation de la présente offre de transaction peut se faire jusqu'au

This offer to settle may be accepted by serving an acceptance of offer to settle (Form 14B may be used) on the party who made it, at any time before it is withdrawn or before the court disposes of the claim to which the offer applies [R. 14.05(1)]. You can get forms at court offices or online at www.ontariocourtforms.on.ca.
La présente offre de transaction peut être acceptée en signifiant une acceptation de l'offre de transaction (la formule 14B peut être utilisée) à la partie qui l'a faite, avant que l'offre ne soit retirée ou avant que le tribunal ne décide la demande qui en fait l'objet [par. 14.05 (1)]. Vous pouvez obtenir des formules aux greffes des tribunaux ou en ligne à l'adresse www.ontariocourtforms.on.ca.

November 25, year 0   , 20 _____   _____

(Signature of party or representative making offer / *Signature de la partie ou du/de la représentant(e)*)

_____

(Name, address and phone number of party or representative / *Nom, adresse et numéro de téléphone de la partie ou du/de la représentant(e)*)

NOTE:	**IF YOU ACCEPT AN OFFER TO SETTLE, THEN FAIL TO COMPLY WITH ITS TERMS,** judgment in the terms of the accepted offer may be obtained against you on motion to the court, or the action may continue as if there has been no offer to settle [R. 14.06].
REMARQUE :	*SI VOUS ACCEPTEZ UNE OFFRE DE TRANSACTION MAIS QU'ENSUITE VOUS N'EN OBSERVEZ PAS LES CONDITIONS, un jugement suivant les conditions de l'offre acceptée peut être obtenu contre vous sur présentation d'une motion au tribunal ou l'action peut continuer comme s'il n'y avait jamais eu d'offre de transaction [règle 14.06].*

NOTE:	**IF THIS OFFER TO SETTLE IS NOT ACCEPTED, IT SHALL NOT BE FILED WITH THE COURT OR DISCLOSED** to the trial judge until all questions of liability and relief (other than costs) have been determined [R. 14.04].
REMARQUE :	*SI LA PRÉSENTE OFFRE DE TRANSACTION N'EST PAS ACCEPTÉE, ELLE NE DOIT PAS ÊTRE DÉPOSÉE AUPRÈS DU TRIBUNAL NI DIVULGUÉE au juge du procès tant que toutes les questions relatives à la responsabilité et aux mesures de redressement (à l'exclusion des dépens) n'ont pas été décidées [règle 14.04].*

Figure 10.20 Notice of Motion and Supporting Affidavit

ONTARIO

Superior Court of Justice
Cour supérieure de justice

Notice of Motion and Supporting Affidavit
Avis de motion et affidavit à l'appui
Form / *Formule* 15A Ont. Reg. No. / *Règl. de l'Ont.* : 258/98

Toronto	SC-10-00012345-0000
Small Claims Court / *Cour des petites créances de*	Claim No. / *N° de la demande*

47 Sheppard Ave. E., 3rd Floor
Toronto, ON M2N 2X5

Address / *Adresse*

416-326-3554

Phone number / *Numéro de téléphone*

Plaintiff No. 1 / *Demandeur n° 1* ☐ Additional plaintiff(s) listed on attached Form 1A.
Le ou les demandeurs additionnels sont mentionnés sur la formule 1A ci-jointe.

Last name, or name of company / *Nom de famille ou nom de la compagnie*		
Capricious Credit Corporation Ltd.		
First name / *Premier prénom*	Second name / *Deuxième prénom*	Also known as / *Également connu(e) sous le nom de*
Address (street number, apt., unit) / *Adresse (numéro et rue, app., unité)*		
c/o Charles Dickens 8041 Ryder Street		
City/Town / *Cité/ville*	Province	Phone no. / *N° de téléphone*
Mississauga	**ON**	**905-381-2620**
Postal code / *Code postal*		Fax no. / *N° de télécopieur*
M5R 1K3		
Representative / *Représentant(e)*		LSUC # / *N° du BHC*
Charles Dickens		**P02345**
Address (street number, apt., unit) / *Adresse (numéro et rue, app., unité)*		
8041 Ryder Street		
City/Town / *Cité/ville*	Province	Phone no. / *N° de téléphone*
Mississauga	**ON**	**905-381-2620**
Postal code / *Code postal*		Fax no. / *N° de télécopieur*
L2R 1Y6		

Defendant No. 1 / *Défendeur n° 1* ☐ Additional defendant(s) listed on attached Form 1A.
Le ou les défendeurs additionnels sont mentionnés sur la formule 1A ci-jointe.

Last name, or name of company / *Nom de famille ou nom de la compagnie*		
Feckless Enterprises		
First name / *Premier prénom*	Second name / *Deuxième prénom*	Also known as / *Également connu(e) sous le nom de*
Address (street number, apt., unit) / *Adresse (numéro et rue, app., unité)*		
c/o Edward Loquacious 365 Bay Street		
City/Town / *Cité/ville*	Province	Phone no. / *N° de téléphone*
Toronto	**ON**	**416-595-1308**
Postal code / *Code postal*		Fax no. / *N° de télécopieur*
M2N 3A8		
Representative / *Représentant(e)*		LSUC # / *N° du BHC*
Edward Loquacious		**P02361**
Address (street number, apt., unit) / *Adresse (numéro et rue, app., unité)*		
365 Bay Street		
City/Town / *Cité/ville*	Province	Phone no. / *N° de téléphone*
Toronto	**ON**	**416-595-1308**
Postal code / *Code postal*		Fax no. / *N° de télécopieur*
M2N 3A8		

Figure 10.20   Continued

FORM / *FORMULE* 15A   PAGE 2   SC-10-00012345-0000

Claim No. / *N° de la demande*

THIS COURT WILL HEAR A MOTION on November 15, year 0   , 20 ____ , at 10:00 a.m.   ,
LE TRIBUNAL PRÉCITÉ ENTENDRA UNE MOTION le   **, à**   (Time / *heure*)

or as soon as possible after that time, at   47 Sheppard Ave. E., Toronto, ON   Courtroom 4
ou dès que possible par la suite à/au   (Address of court location and courtroom number / *Adresse du tribunal et numéro de la salle d'audience*)

Complete Part A <u>or</u> Part B below, then complete the affidavit in support of motion on page 3. / *Remplissez la partie A <u>ou</u> la partie B ci-dessous. Remplissez ensuite l'affidavit à l'appui de la motion à la page 3.*

A.   This motion will be made in person
       by   Feckless Enterprises   ,
       La motion sera présentée en personne par :   (Name of party / *Nom de la partie*)

       for the following order : / *en vue d'obtenir l'ordonnance suivante :*

☐   the court's permission to extend time to (Specify)
      l'autorisation du tribunal de proroger le délai pour (Précisez)

                                                                                    .

☐   set aside default judgment and noting in default.
      l'annulation du jugement par défaut et la constatation du défaut.

☐   set aside noting in default.
      l'annulation de la constatation du défaut.

☐   permission to file a Defence.
      l'autorisation de déposer une défense.

☐   permission to file a Defendant's Claim.
      l'autorisation de déposer une demande du défendeur.

☐   set aside order dismissing claim as abandoned.
      l'annulation d'une demande pour cause de renonciation

☐   terminate garnishment and/or withdraw writ(s).
      la mainlevée de la saisie-arrêt ou le retrait d'un ou de plusieurs brefs, ou les deux.

☒   Other:
      Autre :
      An order requiring the plaintiff to disclose its accounting records.

☐   **ADDITIONAL PAGES ARE ATTACHED BECAUSE MORE ROOM WAS NEEDED.**
      DES FEUILLES SUPPLÉMENTAIRES SONT ANNEXÉES EN RAISON DU MANQUE D'ESPACE.

☐   **DOCUMENTS ARE ATTACHED.**
      PIÈCES JOINTES.

NOTE:	**IF YOU FAIL TO ATTEND AN IN-PERSON MOTION,** an order may be made against you, with costs, in your absence. If you want to attend the motion by telephone or video conference, complete and file a Request for Telephone or Video Conference (Form 1B). If the court permits it, the clerk will make the necessary arrangements and notify the parties [R. 1.07(5)].
REMARQUE :	*SI VOUS NE VOUS PRÉSENTEZ PAS EN PERSONNE À L'AUDITION DE LA MOTION,* une ordonnance peut être rendue contre vous en votre absence, avec dépens. Si vous voulez assister à l'audition de la motion par conférence téléphonique ou vidéoconférence, remplissez et déposez la Demande de conférence téléphonique ou vidéoconférence (formule 1B). Si le tribunal l'autorise, le greffier prendra les dispositions nécessaires et en avisera les parties [par. 1.07 (5)].

Figure 10.20 Continued

FORM / *FORMULE* **15A**   **PAGE 3**   SC-10-00012345-0000

Claim No. / *N° de la demande*

B. **This motion in writing for an assessment of damages is made by**
La présente motion par écrit en vue d'une évaluation des dommages-intérêts est présentée par

_____ ,

(Name of plaintiff / *Nom du demandeur/de la demanderesse*)

who asks the court for an order assessing damages against
qui demande au tribunal de rendre une ordonnance d'évaluation des dommages-intérêts contre

_____

(Name of defendant(s) / *Nom du/de la/des défendeur(s)/défenderesse(s)*)

who have/has been noted in default.
qui a/ont été constaté(e)(s) en défaut.

AFFIDAVIT IN SUPPORT OF MOTION / *AFFIDAVIT À L'APPUI DE LA MOTION*

My name is Henry Feckless
Je m'appelle   (Full name / *Nom et prénoms*)

I live in Toronto, Ontario
J'habite à   (Municipality & province / *Municipalité et province*)

I swear/affirm that the following is true:
Je déclare sous serment/j'affirme solennellement que les renseignements suivants sont véridiques :

Set out the facts in numbered paragraphs. If you learned a fact from someone else, you must give that person's name and state that you believe that fact to be true.
Indiquez les faits sous forme de dispositions numérotées. Si vous avez pris connaissance d'un fait par l'entremise d'une autre personne, vous devez indiquer le nom de cette personne et déclarer que vous croyez que ce fait est véridique.

1. I am the defendant in this matter.

2. My defence is that I paid the plaintiff the amount claimed to be owing by cash payment.

3. I do not have a record of the cash payment; however, the plaintiff's accounting records should show receipt of the cash payment made by me in satisfaction of the promissory note between us.

4. My paralegal, Edward Loquacious, has requested the plaintiff's accounting records for inspection, but to date has not had a response.

5. I make this affidavit in support of this motion and for no other purpose.

Figure 10.20   Concluded

FORM / *FORMULE* 15A   PAGE 4   SC-10-00012345-0000
                                                                 Claim No. / *N° de la demande*

AFFIDAVIT IN SUPPORT OF MOTION, continued / *AFFIDAVIT À L'APPUI DE LA MOTION, suite*

If more space is required, attach and initial extra pages. / Si vous avez besoin de plus d'espace, annexez une ou des feuilles supplémentaires et paraphez-les.

Sworn/Affirmed before me at **Toronto**
Déclaré sous serment/Affirmé   (Municipality / *municipalité*)
solennellement devant moi à

in **Ontario**
en/à/au   (Province, state or country / *province, État ou pays*)

on **Dec. 3, year 0**   , 20
le   Commissioner for taking affidavits
                             Commissaire aux affidavits
                 (Type or print name below if signature is illegible.)
                 (Dactylographiez le nom ou écrivez-le en
                 caractères d'imprimerie ci-dessous si la
                 signature est illisible.)

———————————————————
Signature
(This form is to be signed in front of a
lawyer, justice of the peace, notary public
or commissioner for taking affidavits.)
(La présente formule doit être signée en
présence d'un avocat, d'un juge de paix,
d'un notaire ou d'un commissaire aux
affidavits.)

WARNING:	IT IS AN OFFENCE UNDER THE *CRIMINAL CODE* TO KNOWINGLY SWEAR OR AFFIRM A FALSE AFFIDAVIT.
AVERTISSEMENT :	*FAIRE SCIEMMENT UN FAUX AFFIDAVIT CONSTITUE UNE INFRACTION AU* CODE CRIMINEL.

Figure 10.21   Summons to Witness

ONTARIO

Superior Court of Justice
Cour supérieure de justice

Summons to Witness
Assignation de témoin

Form / *Formule* 18A Ont. Reg. No. / *Règl. de l'Ont.* : 258/98

Seal / *Sceau*

Toronto	SC-10-00012345-0000
Small Claims Court / *Cour des petites créances de*	Claim No. / *N° de la demande*

47 Sheppard Ave. E., 3rd Floor
Toronto, ON M2N 2X5

Address / *Adresse*

416-326-3554

Phone number / *Numéro de téléphone*

BETWEEN / *ENTRE*

Capricious Credit Corporation Ltd.

Plaintiff(s) / *Demandeur(s)/demanderesse(s)*

and / *et*

Feckless Enterprises

Defendant(s) / *Défendeur(s)/défenderesse(s)*

TO: Henry Snorglepus
DESTINATAIRE :

(Name of witness / *Nom du témoin*)

YOU ARE REQUIRED TO ATTEND AND TO GIVE EVIDENCE IN COURT at the trial of this action on
VOUS ÊTES REQUIS(E) DE VOUS PRÉSENTER DEVANT LE TRIBUNAL POUR TÉMOIGNER *à l'instruction de cette action le*

December 21, year 0   , 20 ____   **at** 10:00 a.m.   **, at**
                                              à   (Time / *heure*)   ***à/au***

47 Sheppard Avenue E., Toronto, ON M2N 2X5

(Address of court location / *Adresse du tribunal*)

and to remain until your attendance is no longer required. You may be required to return to court from time to time.
et d'y demeurer jusqu'à ce que votre présence ne soit plus requise. Vous pourriez être requis(e) de vous présenter à nouveau devant le tribunal à l'occasion.

YOU ARE ALSO REQUIRED TO BRING WITH YOU AND PRODUCE AT THE TRIAL the following documents
or other things in your possession, control or power: (Identify and describe particular documents and other things required)
***VOUS ÊTES EN OUTRE REQUIS(E) D'APPORTER AVEC VOUS ET DE PRODUIRE LORS DE
L'INSTRUCTION*** *les documents ou autres objets suivants dont vous avez la garde, la possession ou le contrôle :*
(Indiquez et décrivez les documents et autres objets particuliers qui sont requis)

**All papers, documents, articles, or things in your possession, power, and control and in particular a
copy of the defendant's promissory note, dated April 1, year -1.**

Figure 10.21   Concluded

FORM / *FORMULE* 18A   PAGE 2   SC-10-00012345-0000
                                                                                          Claim No. / *N° de la demande*

and all other documents or other things in your possession, control or power relating to the action.
ainsi que tous les autres documents ou autres objets dont vous avez la garde, la possession ou le contrôle et qui se rapportent à l'action.

Feckless Enterprises   has requested the clerk to issue this summons.
                         (Name of party / *Nom de la partie*)   *a demandé au greffier de délivrer la présente
                                                                      assignation.*

November 28, year 0   , 20
                                                                      (Signature of clerk / *Signature du greffier*)

NOTE:	THIS SUMMONS MUST BE SERVED personally, at least 10 days before the trial date, on the person to be summoned together with attendance money calculated in accordance with the Small Claims Court Schedule of Fees, which is a regulation under the *Administration of Justice Act*. To obtain a copy of the regulation, attend the nearest Small Claims Court or access the following website: www.e-laws.gov.on.ca.
REMARQUE :	*LA PRÉSENTE ASSIGNATION DOIT ÊTRE SIGNIFIÉE à personne, au moins 10 jours avant la date du procès, à la personne devant être assignée, avec l'indemnité de présence calculée conformément au barème des honoraires et frais de la Cour des petites créances qui constitue un règlement pris en application de la Loi sur l'administration de la justice. Vous pouvez obtenir un exemplaire du règlement auprès de la Cour des petites créances de votre localité ou en consultant le site Web suivant : www.lois-en-ligne.gouv.on.ca.*

CAUTION:	**IF YOU FAIL TO ATTEND OR REMAIN IN ATTENDANCE AS REQUIRED BY THIS SUMMONS, A WARRANT MAY BE ISSUED FOR YOUR ARREST.**
AVERTISSEMENT :	*SI VOUS NE VOUS PRÉSENTEZ PAS OU SI VOUS NE DEMEUREZ PAS PRÉSENT(E) COMME L'EXIGE LA PRÉSENTE ASSIGNATION, UN MANDAT D'ARRÊT PEUT ÊTRE DÉLIVRÉ CONTRE VOUS.*

CHAPTER 11

Small Claims Court Enforcement Proceedings

THE ENFORCEMENT ENVIRONMENT

A high percentage of Small Claims Court cases are undefended. Many of these cases are for small amounts.[1] Many of the defendants are consumer debtors who are in debt for relatively small amounts and who are simply unable — or think they are unable — to pay what they owe. The Small Claims Court enforcement procedures in rule 20 of the *Small Claims Court Rules* reflect the reality of an environment where debtors owe relatively small amounts. The usual enforcement mechanisms found in the Superior Court are also found here:

- judgment debtor examinations;

- writs of seizure and sale of land and personal property;

- writs of delivery (for recovery of personal property); and

- garnishment.

However, the usual mechanisms outlined above are not of much use where a debtor is broke and has few assets. In this environment, the *Small Claims Court Rules* provide other solutions that allow a debtor to consolidate debts, have payments scheduled over time, have periodic payment amounts fixed, and have other enforcement proceedings stayed while payments are being made. This permits debtors to avoid being hounded by creditors, and it permits creditors to get their money through installment payments over time. This is an advantage for creditors, who might otherwise find the debtor going bankrupt. If the debtor goes bankrupt, creditors would likely recover far less than they would using the small claims enforcement provisions. In fact, it may be better financially for a debtor to go bankrupt than pay out all that she owes on installment payments in the Small Claims Court over a long period of time.

Rule 20.02 gives the court the general power to stay enforcement proceedings. This means that if such an order is made, enforcement proceedings stop, including payments by garnishees on garnishment orders. Stays can be ordered, for example, on the filing of an appeal or on the making of a consolidation order where small claims creditors of the same debtor receive a portion of periodic installment payments from the debtor, as ordered by the court. Where the court has made an order for payment of a judgment debt by installments, any party may bring a motion to vary the times and proportions in which money is paid if the debtor's circumstances have changed. A debtor whose situation has become worse may apply to have his or her payments reduced. Where the debtor's situation has improved, a creditor may apply to increase the amounts. Rule 20.02(2) now makes it quite clear that creditors may not take enforcement proceedings while the debtor is subject to an order to pay creditors by installments, except that a creditor may require the clerk to issue a writ of seizure and sale against land and file it with the sheriff.

Rule 20.12 requires a debtor to clear his or her credit record after paying a judgment debt, by bringing a motion to have a judgment noted as satisfied.

ENFORCEMENT IN A DIFFERENT TERRITORIAL DIVISION

If, for example, you obtained judgment in the court in North Bay, and there has been default in payment and you wish the judgment enforced against property in the court in Kingston, you must direct the court in Kingston to enforce the North Bay order or judgment. In this situation you must obtain a certificate of judgment (figure 11.1) from the North Bay court. To do this, the clerk of the North Bay court must prepare the certificate showing the amount still owing (inclusive of postjudgment interest), the date and the original amount of the order, and the rate of postjudgment interest payable. You need to file an affidavit with the clerk, verifying the amount still owing before the clerk issues the certificate. The certificate is then sent to the clerk of the court where you seek enforcement — in this example, the Kingston court.

EXAMINATION OF JUDGMENT DEBTORS

Although it is wise to file a writ of seizure and sale against personal property and one against land immediately after obtaining a judgment, unless you know a lot about the debtor's financial circumstances, it is a good idea to schedule an examination of the judgment debtor before embarking on any serious and expensive enforcement efforts.

The procedure for doing this is as follows:

1. Request, by letter, that the clerk of the court where the debtor resides or carries on business issue a notice of examination (figure 11.2).

2. Enclose an affidavit for enforcement request (figure 11.3) that sets out the date of the order and amount awarded, the territorial division in which the order was made, the rate of postjudgment interest payable, the total amount of any payments received since judgment was given, and the amount owing,

including postjudgment interest. (This affidavit must be filed to support any enforcement remedy requested.)

3. Enclose a certificate of judgment (figure 11.1) if the judgment was from a different territorial division than the one that is issuing the notice of examination.

4. The clerk issues the notice and serves it on the debtor personally, together with a blank Financial Information Form (figure 11.4), which the debtor must complete and serve on the creditor prior to the examination. The debtor must also bring a copy of the completed Financial Information Form to the examination, along with any documents that support the information in the form.

The rules permit service by alternatives to personal service but, if it is necessary to bring contempt proceedings for non-attendance, it will be easier to conclusively prove service if the debtor was personally served.

The examination takes place in most territorial divisions under the supervision of a judge or referee. This approach recognizes that where parties are not represented by lawyers or paralegals, the whole business may degenerate into an unseemly and unproductive performance. The judge or referee may take quite an active part in the process. The examination is also private, unless the court orders it to be held in public. At the end of the examination hearing, the court may make an order for payment in full, by installments, and otherwise use its discretion to construct an orderly system for payment. Following an examination, if payments are being made under an order, no other enforcement remedies may be taken, except for filing a writ of seizure and sale against land with the sheriff.

The questions to be asked on an examination are the same as those set out in chapter 9.

You may also request that witnesses be examined, other than or in addition to the debtor, if they have knowledge concerning the debtor's assets, liabilities, and means of complying with the judgment. The scope of the examination is broad and covers the same grounds as an examination in the Superior Court. If the debtor is a corporation, partnership, or sole proprietorship, you have the same right as in the Superior Court to examine officers, directors, partners, and owners of sole proprietorships.

If the debtor or other person summoned fails to attend the examination, or attends but is obstructive, uncooperative, or refuses to answer questions, you may ask that the court find the person in **contempt**. In the past, Small Claims Court judges could not make a contempt order based on *ex facie* **contempt**. However, rule 20.11(2) now provides that a Small Claims Court judge can order a person who has failed to attend an examination to attend a contempt hearing. The court provides the creditor with a notice of contempt hearing form, which the creditor must personally serve on the debtor and file with the court at least seven days before the hearing. The burden of proof is on the debtor to show that he is not in contempt. Under rule 20.11(7) the court may order the debtor to be apprehended and jailed for up to five days. If the debtor is in the courtroom when the contempt takes place, the contempt is considered to be *in facie* and can also be dealt with by a Small Claims Court judge.

If an order jailing the person is issued, the clerk issues a warrant of committal (figure 11.5). The warrant directs police in Ontario to apprehend the person found in

contempt
a contemptuous act demonstrates disrespect or defiance of the court and the administration of justice

***ex facie* contempt**
is contempt that occurs outside the courtroom

***in facie* contempt**
is contempt that occurs in the courtroom, in the face of the court

to purge contempt
when an order has been made by the court finding someone in contempt, the person may avoid punishment for contempt by doing what was required of him; this is referred to as purging his contempt—for example, a person who refuses to answer questions on an examination may purge his contempt by re-attending and answering the questions

contempt and jail him in the nearest provincial correctional institution. He may be discharged at the end of five days, or earlier if he **purges his contempt** by doing what was originally required of him.

THE WRIT OF DELIVERY

The Small Claims Court has jurisdiction to order the return to the plaintiff of property unlawfully taken or held by the defendant, when the property is worth $25,000 or less. After recovering such a judgment, it is wise to write to the defendant, enclosing a copy of the order, demanding that the property be delivered to a specific place on or before a fixed date. If the defendant fails to deliver the property, you may proceed to enforce the order for the recovery of property. Your client must swear an affidavit that the property has not been delivered to him and the letter demanding return should be attached as an exhibit to the affidavit. You then make a request to the clerk to issue a writ of delivery (figure 11.6) and to send it to the court bailiff for enforcement. If the bailiff is unable to recover the specific property referred to, he or she will report this to the clerk, who will advise you. At this stage you may bring a motion to the court requesting an order directing the bailiff to seize other personal property of the defendant. If you know of specific property that could be seized, your client should refer to it in his supporting affidavit. In effect, you are going to be permitted to take hostage some of the defendant's personal property until he returns the property that he has been wrongfully withholding from your client. The bailiff, however, does not turn this property over to you; instead he holds it "hostage" and awaits other orders of the court regarding the property's disposal.

In seizing personal property, the court bailiff may hire a private, licensed bailiff. Licensed bailiffs are in the business of seizing property where there is a legal right to seize it. Much of their business concerns repossession of consumer durables, like automobiles, that are collateral on secured credit contracts where the debtor has defaulted and the lender wishes to exercise his right to seize collateral. When there is any doubt about the right to seize someone else's property, a secured lender may litigate the issue by suing for a writ of delivery; otherwise the secured lender will resort to hiring a private bailiff to exercise the contract right to seize the collateral without obtaining a court order. Whether the bailiff is private or a court's officer and whether the seizure is an exercise in self-help or an execution of a court order, s. 20 of the *Execution Act* permits a bailiff to use reasonable force to seize property if it is located someplace other than a residence. If it is in a residence, a court order is required for permission to use reasonable force. Bailiffs who act without an order or use unreasonable force can be civilly liable for trespass and assault, and may be criminally liable as well.

THE WRIT OF SEIZURE AND SALE OF PERSONAL PROPERTY

This writ is similar in function to the writ of the same name in the Superior Court, as is the procedure for using it. To obtain a writ, pay the prescribed fee and file an affidavit for enforcement request (see figure 11.3) with the clerk where the writ (figure 11.7) is issued showing the amount outstanding, including costs and postjudgment interest, less any amount received. Once the writ is issued, it is filed with the bailiff. Enforcement of the writ can be requested by filing a direction to enforce a writ of seizure and sale of personal property (figure 11.8). The bailiff will enforce the writ for the amount owing plus bailiff's costs. However, before you send the bailiff out, be sure to give instructions in writing about any property you are aware of that is available for seizure. A judgment debtor examination is a useful way to obtain this information; you may also have information from earlier investigations and searches.

In seizing property, the bailiff is subject to the provisions of the *Creditors' Relief Act, 2010* requiring pro rata distribution among other execution creditors in the territorial division who filed writs of seizure and sale prior to the execution or within one month after the money is received by the bailiff.[2] The bailiff is also subject to the restrictions on and exemptions from seizure, outlined in chapter 9. In selling property, the bailiff is subject to the same general requirements as the sheriff concerning an open and fair selling process, obtaining a reasonable price, and so on. Rule 20 of the *Small Claims Court Rules* specifically requires that, on the debtor's request, the bailiff deliver to the debtor an inventory of goods seized; that he give notice of the time and place of sale to the debtor and creditor, at least 30 days before the sale; and that he advertise the sale "in a manner that is likely to bring it to the public's attention." Unlike the sheriff's requirement, there are no specific requirements for advertising. A writ is in force for six years from the date it is issued. Under rule 20.06(1.1), if more than six years have passed since the judgment was made, a writ may only be issued with leave of the court. You must then issue the writ within one year of the order or seek a further order for more time to issue the writ. Once you have a writ, it may be renewed for a further six years. You should diarize the renewal date and keep track of renewals. There is a new request to renew writ of seizure and sale form (figure 11.9) that can be filed before the writ expires.

THE WRIT OF SEIZURE AND SALE OF LAND

If you wish to enforce against land, use a writ of seizure and sale of land (figure 11.10). First, deliver an affidavit for enforcement request (figure 11.3) to the clerk, setting out the amount still owing, as you did to start the procedure to use a writ for the seizure and sale of personal property. You may use the same affidavit to support the request for both writs. Then request that the clerk issue a writ of seizure and sale of land to the sheriff (not to the bailiff) in the county or region where the debtor's land is located. Thereafter, the writ may be enforced by the sheriff against land only, and you are subject to the same procedure as you would be if the writ had been issued by the Superior Court: rule 60 of the *Rules of Civil Procedure* applies (see chapter 9). Rule 60 is reproduced in Appendix A to this book.

GARNISHMENT

If you know of a third party who owes money to the debtor, you may garnish the third party. To do this, you need an affidavit for enforcement request (see figure 11.3), and if the garnishee is located in a different territory, a certificate of judgment (figure 11.1). The clerk will issue a notice of garnishment (figure 11.11) when these documents have been filed.

The rules now clearly permit the garnishment of joint debts. A joint debt is one where the garnishee owes a sum of money to the debtor together with another person who co-owns the right to that sum. The general rule is that the creditor may require the garnishee to pay half the amount of a garnished joint debt into court. However, the creditor, debtor, co-owner of the debt, or garnishee may apply for an order increasing or decreasing the amount the creditor may seize by garnishment. This may occur, for example, where a creditor argues that the so-called joint debt is a sham arrangement, which may happen where the debtor is owed money by a garnishee that is a family-run business.

Where a garnishee is aware of the existence of a co-owner of the debt, the garnishee should serve a notice to co-owner of debt (figure 11.12) on all parties, including, of course, the co-owner.

The affidavit for enforcement request (figure 11.3) should be sworn by the creditor, and its paragraphs should cover the following by setting out:

- the date of the order and the amount awarded;

- the territorial division in which the order was made;

- the rate of postjudgment interest payable;

- the total amount of any payments received since the order was granted;

- the amount owing, including postjudgment interest to date;

- the name and address of each person to whom a notice of garnishment should be directed;

- a statement to the effect that the creditor believes that those persons are or will become indebted to the debtor and the grounds for that belief; and

- the amount owing by the garnishee to the debtor — if the amount is not known, include a statement to that effect.

The clerk will then issue a notice of garnishment to each person named in the affidavit and serve it by mail, by personal service, or by an alternative to personal service on the debtor, and by *registered* mail, personal service, or an alternative to personal service on the garnishee. Service on a bank or trust company must be to the branch where the debt is payable by the garnishee. The garnishment notice takes effect at the time it is served, and attaches all funds owing to the debtor as of that time. The garnishee must pay to the clerk any amount owing, up to the total amount shown in the notice, within 10 days of service of the notice, or 10 days after the debt became payable, whichever is later. For example, if the notice is served on October 1 and the debt is not payable until October 12, then the garnishee need not pay the clerk until October 22. The garnishment notice will stay in effect and attach debts owing for 24 months after it was served.

The garnishee who admits the debt owing to the debtor will pay the debt to the clerk in accordance with instructions in the notice of garnishment. If the garnishee is an employer, he will pay out 20 percent of the net wages in accordance with the *Wages Act.*

It may be the case that there are several garnishment notices issued by several creditors of the same debtor. When this happens, those who have filed notices in the territorial division where the funds are being paid share the amount seized equally (and not on a pro rata basis, as is the case for execution creditors on writs of seizure and sale). The first payment to garnishors takes place 30 days after funds are received by the clerk, with subsequent payments being made as the clerk receives funds.[3] For example, if one creditor garnishes a bank account and another garnishes wages, the court receiving the money from both garnishees will divide the total among all creditors who have filed notices in that court. This will, arguably, include creditors whose own notices of garnishment have not yet produced any payment.

If a garnishee wishes to dispute the garnishment because no money is owing to the debtor or because the garnishee will be paying less than the amount in the notice, the garnishee must file with the court a garnishee's statement (figure 11.13) setting out the nature of the dispute or underpayment, as the case may be, along with the facts on which the dispute is based. The statement should be sent to the court that issued the notice within 10 days of the notice having been served on the garnishee.

A creditor, debtor, or garnishee may, by notice of motion, request a hearing to determine any matter concerning the garnishment. This may include, but is not limited to, the following situations:

- the creditor, debtor, or co-owner of a debt questions the position taken by a garnishee in refusing to pay into court or in paying into court the amounts requested;

- the creditor questions a situation where the garnishee's debt to the debtor has been assigned by the debtor to someone else. In such a case, the garnishee would owe nothing to the debtor if the debtor has assigned his right to the debt; or

- a party seeks to end or vary periodic payments under a garnishment notice.

As is the case in the Superior Court with garnishment, where the garnishee neither pays nor files a garnishee's statement disputing payment, the creditor may obtain an order requiring the garnishee to pay the clerk the entire amount set out in the notice, as if the garnishee were the principal debtor. Payment of the amount required to another person, other than the clerk, exposes the garnishee to liability to pay the debt again to the clerk. This latter situation can arise in cases where the debtor assigns his right to be paid to someone else and the garnishee then pays the assignee, rather than the clerk, as described above. Garnishments are effective for six years and can be renewed. Once a judgment has been paid in full, a notice of termination of garnishment should be served on the garnishee and the court clerk.

CONSOLIDATION ORDERS

It is not unusual for consumer debtors to have several small claims judgments filed against them. When this happens the debtor may find himself in an unpleasant situation as he is badgered by creditors. To solve this problem, a debtor who has two or more unsatisfied judgments against him can bring a motion in the court for a consolidation order. If the court is satisfied that the debtor is entitled to a consolidation order, it can order the debtor to make installment payments of a specified amount, to be divided equally among participating creditors. The clerk will pay the creditors every six months.

To obtain this order the debtor must file an affidavit in support of a motion for a consolidation order (see figure 11.14) that sets out:

- the names and addresses of judgment creditors and the amounts outstanding on each judgment;

- the debtor's income from all sources, identifying each source; and

- the debtor's current financial obligations and any other relevant facts.

All judgment creditors mentioned in the affidavit should be served by mail, by personal service, or by an alternative to personal service with the affidavit and the notice of motion for a consolidation order. Allow seven days' notice of the date of the hearing. Be sure to obtain a motion date before serving the documents so you will have enough time to serve the creditors seven full days before the date set for the hearing.

At the hearing, the creditors may all be heard and make submissions on the propriety of making the order. If the court makes an order, it will set out in the order:

- a list of unsatisfied orders, including the date, court, amount, and amount unpaid;

- the amounts to be paid into court by the debtor under this order; and

- the dates on which the payments are to be made.

The total amount paid by the debtor on the order is not to exceed the amount of the debtor's income available for seizure under s. 7 of the *Wages Act*. This means that 20 percent of the debtor's net wages are available for payment of the consolidation order. In order not to lose the benefit of a consolidation order, the debtor must not be sued further for debt. If a judgment is obtained against the debtor *after* the consolidation order was made for a debt incurred *after* the consolidation order was made, the consolidation order is terminated. However, if the judgment was obtained *after* the consolidation order was made for a debt incurred *before* the consolidation order was made, if the creditor obtains a certified copy of the judgment, the judgment may be added to the consolidation order and the creditor may share equally in the payments made under the order. If the consolidation order is terminated, the clerk will notify the creditors and no further order may be made for one year from the date the order was terminated. A consolidation order may also terminate if it is in default for 21 days.

CONTROL OF FUNDS HELD BY THE SMALL CLAIMS COURT

The courts receive and disburse money in the following situations when payments have been made into court:

- when garnishees make payments into court;

- when the bailiff is holding funds from a seizure and sale; and

- when funds have been ordered to be paid into court — for example, on a settlement offer.

The sheriff, under the *Creditors' Relief Act, 2010*, has the authority to seize funds paid into the Small Claims Court and distribute them among execution creditors from the Superior Court of Justice.

Section 3(4) of the *Creditors' Relief Act, 2010* states that when money recovered by garnishment is paid to a Small Claims Court clerk, the sheriff may, on the request of an execution creditor, demand and receive the money from the clerk of the court to distribute it to the judgment creditors. The garnishment creditor, however, under s. 3(5), is entitled to share in the distribution of the money in respect of her claim against the debtor.

Under s. 10(1) of the *Creditors' Relief Act, 2010*, if the sheriff does not find property of an execution debtor that is sufficient to satisfy all amounts in respect of executions filed with the sheriff, and the sheriff is advised that the bailiff of the Small Claims Court holds personal property of the debtor or proceeds from personal property of the debtor under an execution or attachment against the debtor, at the request of an execution creditor, the sheriff shall demand the property or proceeds from the bailiff and the bailiff shall promptly deliver to the sheriff:

1. the property or proceeds;

2. a copy of every execution and attachment against the debtor that has been filed with the bailiff; and

3. a memorandum showing the amount to be paid under each execution, including the bailiff's fees, and the date when each execution and attachment was filed with the bailiff.

For the purposes of determining to whom the proceeds may be distributed, the Small Claims Court execution creditors are treated as if their executions had been filed with the sheriff.

CHAPTER SUMMARY

Chapter 11 begins with a discussion of the Small Claims Court enforcement environment, noting how it differs from that in the Superior Court with various procedures for structuring debt repayment. The enforcement methods include judgment debtor examinations to obtain enforcement information followed by writs of seizure and sale for personal property and land, writs of delivery of personal property, and garnishment. Enforcement in a different territorial division requires a certificate of judgment to be filed in the enforcing court and debtors may ask for debt payments to be structured by the use of consolidation orders. Last, note is made of how funds that have been seized are distributed. This includes situations where the Small Claims Court may have to pay out seized funds to the sheriff enforcing Superior Court judgments.

KEY TERMS

contempt	*in facie* contempt
ex facie contempt	to purge contempt

NOTES

1. Ministry of the Attorney General, Ontario, in Marvin Zuker, *Small Claims Court Practice* (Toronto: Carswell, 1997), 419-20.

2. *Creditor's Relief Act, 2010*, SO 2010, c. 16, sch. 4, s. 4(1).

3. See rule 20.08(20.1) of the *Small Claims Court Rules.*

REFERENCES

Administration of Justice Act, Small Claims Court — Fees and Allowances, O. Reg. 432/93, as amended; online at http://www.e-laws.gov.on.ca/html/regs/english/elaws_regs_930432_e.htm.

Courts of Justice Act, RSO 1990, c. C.43.

Creditors' Relief Act, 2010, SO 2010, c. 16, sch. 4.

Execution Act, RSO 1990, c. E.24.

Proceedings Against the Crown Act, RSO 1990, c. P.27.

Rules of Civil Procedure, RRO 1990, reg. 194.

Rules of the Small Claims Court, O. Reg. 258/98, as amended by O. Reg. 78/06, in force July 1, 2006.

Wages Act, RSO 1990, c. W.1.

REVIEW QUESTIONS

1. How does the enforcement environment in the Small Claims Court differ from that in the Superior Court? What accounts for these differences?

2. Does the court have any power to alter or stop an order after it is made?

3. If you sued the debtor in Brampton and obtained a judgment there, but seek to seize the debtor's boat that you found located in Belleville, what do you need to do before you can enforce the order?

4. What do you need to do in order to bring a judgment debtor before the court for a judgment debtor examination?

5. What do you do if the debtor shows up but refuses to answer questions at the examination?

6. Suppose you have requested that the clerk issue a writ of delivery. The bailiff is unable to locate the specific property named in the writ and is getting no cooperation from the debtor. Is there anything else you can do to recover the property?

7. What must you do to issue a writ of seizure and sale against personal property? Is the process different if you wish to issue a writ of execution against land? What are the differences, if any?

8. Tell your client what you will have to do to garnish funds from someone who owes money to the debtor.

9. How will the money paid by garnishees to the court be divided up if there are several creditors who have filed garnishment notices in respect of the same debtor?

10. What do you need to do that you would not otherwise have to do in the garnishment process if a garnishee owes money to a debtor together with another person as a co-owner?

11. If a garnishee asks you if she has to do anything when served with a garnishment notice if she doesn't owe the debtor any money, what do you tell her?

12. Suppose a debtor tells you he has four judgments against him in the Toronto Small Claims Court and he is constantly being bothered by bailiffs looking for things to seize — is there anything he can do to prevent his creditors from badgering him?

13. Explain what might happen to a consolidation order if the debtor incurs another debt for $500 after the consolidation order is made and the creditor later obtains a judgment in respect of the $500 debt.

14. If you have a Superior Court judgment and have filed a writ of execution, is there any useful purpose in having the sheriff attempt to enforce the writ against the debtor by making a demand on the bailiff or clerk of the Small Claims Court?

CASE STUDY

I. Need-Help
Barrister & Solicitor
111 - 392 Bay Street
Toronto, ON M3P 1J8

tel.: 416-383-5679

MEMO

DATE: September 3, year 0

TO: U.R. Clerk

FROM: I. Need-Help

RE: Enforcement of Small Claims Judgment

OUR CLIENT: Eatom Shredlu

JUDGMENT DEBTOR: Doofus Tinamou

Our client obtained a judgment against the debtor on June 28, year 0 in the Toronto Small Claims Court, court file #6875/year 0, for the sum of $3,000, prejudgment interest of $24.42, and costs of $329. The judgment was for failure to honour a promissory note due June 1, year 0. The interest on the note was 11 percent per year. The judgment bears postjudgment interest at 11 percent.

The creditor lives at 123 Anywho St., Toronto, ON M5K 1J6 and the phone number is 416-833-1234.

The debtor lives at 31 Hardcase Road, Toronto, ON M4P 1X3. The house is owned by him alone. He has a car, a 1998 Ford Taurus sedan, lic. BAAL 678 Ont., VIN 123456768. It does not appear to be collateral on any loan. Tinamou works as an engraver for Junk Jewel Ltd., 93 Dorfus Road, Toronto, ON M7S 1Y8 and the phone number is 416-667-3101. He earns about $1,400 a week gross, but we are not exactly sure of the amount he actually makes.

Prepare the necessary documentation to enforce the judgment through the use of writs of seizure and sale and garnishment. Also, prepare the necessary documentation to conduct a judgment debtor examination. All documents are to be filed with the court as of September 15, year 0.

Figure 11.1 Certificate of Judgment

ONTARIO

Superior Court of Justice
Cour supérieure de justice

Certificate of Judgment
Certificat de jugement

Form / *Formule* 20A Ont. Reg. No. / *Règl. de l'Ont.* : 258/98

Seal / *Sceau*

North Bay

Small Claims Court / *Cour des petites créances de*

360 Plouffe Street
North Bay, ON P1B 9L5

Address / *Adresse*

705-495-8309

Phone number / *Numéro de téléphone*

SC-10-00012350-0000

Claim No. / *N° de la demande*

BETWEEN / *ENTRE*

Abdullah Karim

Creditor(s) / *Créancier(s)/créancière(s)*

and / *et*

Antonio Salieri

Debtor(s) / *Débiteur(s)/débitrice(s)*

A judgment was made in this action on May 8, year 0 **, 20** **, in the**
Un jugement a été rendu dans la présente action le **, à la**

North Bay Small Claims Court

(Name of court where judgment was made / *Nom de la cour où le jugement a été rendu*)

against / *contre*

Last name of debtor, or name of company / *Nom de famille du débiteur/de la débitrice ou nom de la compagnie*		
Salieri		
First name / *Premier prénom*	Second name / *Deuxième prénom*	Third name / *Troisième prénom*
Antonio		
Address / *Adresse*		
177 Main Street, Kingston, ON K7L 2T2		

Last name of debtor, or name of company / *Nom de famille du débiteur/de la débitrice ou nom de la compagnie*		
First name / *Premier prénom*	Second name / *Deuxième prénom*	Third name / *Troisième prénom*
Address / *Adresse*		

Last name of debtor, or name of company / *Nom de famille du débiteur/de la débitrice ou nom de la compagnie*		
First name / *Premier prénom*	Second name / *Deuxième prénom*	Third name / *Troisième prénom*
Address / *Adresse*		

☐ Additional debtor(s) and also known as names are listed on attached Form 1A.1.
Le ou les débiteur(s) additionnel(s) et le ou les noms sous lesquels les débiteurs sont également connus sont mentionnés sur la formule 1A.1 ci-jointe.

Figure 11.1 Concluded

FORM / *FORMULE* **20A** **PAGE 2** SC-10-00012350-0000

Claim No. / *N° de la demande*

Judgment was made for the following sums:
Un jugement a été rendu à l'égard des sommes suivantes :

(A) **AMOUNT OF JUDGMENT** (debt and pre-judgment interest) $ 3,000.00
LE MONTANT DU JUGEMENT *(créance et intérêts antérieurs au jugement)* $

(B) **COSTS** to date of judgment $ 195.00
LES DÉPENS *à la date du jugement* $

Post-judgment interest continues to accrue at **4** % per annum.
Les intérêts postérieurs au jugement continuent (Interest rate / % *par an.*
à courir au taux de *Taux d'intérêt)*

May 20, year 0 , 20 _____

(Signature of clerk / *Signature du greffier)*

TO THE CLERK OF THE Toronto **SMALL CLAIMS COURT:**
AU GREFFIER DE LA COUR DES PETITES (Name of court to where the judgment is to be filed
CRÉANCES DE / *Nom du tribunal où le jugement doit être déposé)*

The person requesting this certificate is **Abdullah Karim**
La personne qui demande le présent certificat est (Name of party requesting certificate / *Nom de la partie qui demande le certificat)*

280 Queen Street, North Bay, ON P2P 3A5

(Address of party requesting certificate / *Adresse de la partie qui demande le certificat)*

Figure 11.2   Notice of Examination

ONTARIO

Superior Court of Justice
Cour supérieure de justice

Notice of Examination
Avis d'interrogatoire
Form / *Formule* 20H Ont. Reg. No. / *Règl. de l'Ont.* : 258/98

(Seal / *Sceau*)

Toronto
Small Claims Court / *Cour des petites créances de*

SC-10-00012345-0000
Claim No. / *N° de la demande*

47 Sheppard Ave. E., 3rd Floor
Toronto, ON M2N 2X5

Address / *Adresse*

416-326-3554

Phone number / *Numéro de téléphone*

BETWEEN / *ENTRE*

Capricious Credit Corporation Ltd.

Creditor(s) / *Créancier(s)/créancière(s)*

and / *et*

Feckless Enterprises

Debtor(s) / *Débiteur(s)/débitrice(s)*

TO: Henry Feckless
DESTINATAIRE :

(Name of person to be examined / *Nom de la personne qui doit être interrogée*)

of **48 Overreach Blvd. Toronto, ON M2R 5X3**
de/du

(Address of person to be examined / *Adresse de la personne qui doit être interrogée*)

The creditor has obtained a judgment against **Feckless Enterprises**
Le créancier a obtenu un jugement contre

(Name of debtor / *Nom du débiteur/de la débitrice*)

on **November 20, year 0**   , 20   in the
le   *à la Cour des petites créances de*

Toronto Small Claims Court   Small Claims Court.

(Name of court where judgment was made / *Nom du tribunal où le jugement a été rendu*)

According to the supporting affidavit filed by the creditor, the total due on the judgment is
Selon l'affidavit à l'appui déposé par le créancier, le solde somme due aux termes du jugement s'élève à

$ **3,660.20** .   *(This amount must match the total amount identified in the supporting affidavit.)*
        (Total)   ***$.***   *(Ce montant doit correspondre au montant total énoncé dans l'affidavit à l'appui.)*

This total due takes into account all money received, accrued post-judgment interest and costs to
Ce solde somme due tient compte de toutes les sommes reçues, des intérêts postérieurs au jugement courus et des dépens

this date: **November 30, year 0**   , 20   .   *(This date must match the date of the supporting affidavit.)*
à cette date :   *(Cette date doit correspondre à celle de l'affidavit à l'appui.)*

YOU ARE REQUIRED TO ATTEND AN EXAMINATION HEARING to explain how the debtor will pay this judgment and if there are any reasons for not doing so.
VOUS ÊTES REQUIS(E) DE VOUS PRÉSENTER À UN INTERROGATOIRE *pour expliquer de quelle façon le débiteur acquittera la somme due aux termes de ce jugement et s'il existe quelque motif que ce soit de ne pas le faire.*

Figure 11.2   Concluded

FORM / *FORMULE* 20H   PAGE 2   SC-10-00012345-0000

Claim No. / *N° de la demande*

THIS COURT WILL HOLD AN EXAMINATION HEARING
LE TRIBUNAL PRÉCITÉ TIENDRA UN INTERROGATOIRE

or as soon as possible after that time, at

on December 15, year 0   , 20 _____ , at 10:00 a.m.
le _____ , *à*   (Time / *heure*)   *ou dès que possible par la suite à/au*

47 Sheppard Ave. E., Toronto, ON M2N 2X5
(Address of court location / *Adresse du tribunal*)

4
(Courtroom number / *Numéro de la salle d'audience*)

November 20, year 0 _____ , 20 _____
(Signature of clerk / *Signature du greffier*)

CAUTION TO PERSON BEING EXAMINED:	If you fail to attend the examination hearing or attend and refuse to answer questions or produce documents, you may be ordered to attend a contempt hearing. At the contempt hearing, you may be found in contempt of court and the court may order you to be jailed.
AVERTISSEMENT À LA PERSONNE QUI EST INTERROGÉE :	*Si vous ne vous présentez pas à l'interrogatoire ou si vous vous présentez mais que vous refusez de répondre aux questions ou de produire des documents, le tribunal peut ordonner que vous vous présentiez à une audience pour outrage. Lors de l'audience pour outrage, vous pouvez être reconnu(e) coupable d'outrage au tribunal et le tribunal peut ordonner que vous soyez incarcéré(e).*

NOTE TO DEBTOR:	A debtor who is an individual must serve on the creditor a completed Financial Information Form (Form 20I) prior to the hearing. This form must **not** be filed with the court. The debtor must provide a completed copy of this form to the judge at the examination hearing. The debtor must also bring to the hearing documents that support the information given in this form.
REMARQUE AU DÉBITEUR :	*Le débiteur qui est un particulier doit signifier au créancier une formule de renseignements financiers remplie (formule 20I) avant l'interrogatoire. Cette formule ne doit **pas** être déposée auprès du tribunal. Le débiteur doit remettre la formule dûment remplie au juge chargé de l'audience. Le débiteur doit aussi apporter à l'audience les documents qui appuient l'information donnée sur cette formule.*

Figure 11.3   Affidavit for Enforcement Request

ONTARIO

Superior Court of Justice
Cour supérieure de justice

Affidavit for Enforcement Request
Affidavit relatif à une demande d'exécution forcée
Form / *Formule* 20P Ont. Reg. No. / *Règl. de l'Ont.* : 258/98

Toronto
Small Claims Court / *Cour des petites créances de*

SC-10-00012345-0000
Claim No. / *N° de la demande*

47 Sheppard Ave. E., 3rd Floor
Toronto, ON M2N 2X5

Address / *Adresse*

416-326-3554
Phone number / *Numéro de téléphone*

BETWEEN / *ENTRE*

Capricious Credit Corporation Ltd.
Plaintiff(s)/Creditor(s) / *Demandeur(s)/demanderesse(s)/Créancier(s)/créancière(s)*

and / *et*

Feckless Enterprises
Defendant(s)/Debtor(s) / *Défendeur(s)/défenderesse(s)/Débiteur(s)/débitrice(s)*

My name is Charles Dickens
Je m'appelle
(Full name / *Nom et prénoms*)

I live in Toronto, Ontario
J'habite à
(Municipality & province / *Municipalité et province*)

and I swear/affirm that the following is true:
et je déclare sous serment/j'affirme solennellement que les renseignements suivants sont véridiques :

1. **In this action, I am the**
    Dans la présente action, je suis le/la

(Check one
box only. /
*Cochez une
seule case.*)

☐ plaintiff/creditor.
    demandeur/demanderesse/créancier/créancière.

☒ representative of the plaintiff(s)/creditor(s).
    représentant(e) du/de la/des demandeur(s)/demanderesse(s)/créancier(s)/créancière(s).

I make this affidavit in support of a request that the clerk of the court issue the following enforcement process(es):
Je fais le présent affidavit à l'appui d'une demande visant à enjoindre au greffier du tribunal de délivrer l'acte ou les actes de procédure portant exécution forcée suivants :

☐ Certificate of Judgment (Form 20A) to the clerk of the
    Certificat de jugement (formule 20A), au greffier
    de la Cour des petites créances de

(Name of court where the judgment is to be filed / *Nom du tribunal
où le jugement doit être déposé*)

Small Claims Court.

☐ Writ of Seizure and Sale of Personal Property (Form 20C) directed to the bailiff of
    Bref de saisie-exécution de biens meubles (formule 20C) adressé à l'huissier de la Cour des petites créances de

Small Claims Court.

(Name of court location / *Emplacement du tribunal*)

☐ Writ of Seizure and Sale of Land (Form 20D) directed to the sheriff of
    Bref de saisie-exécution de biens-fonds (formule 20D) adressé
    au shérif du/de la

(Name of county/region in which the
enforcement office is located / *Comté/région où
est situé le bureau de l'exécution*)

Figure 11.3   Continued

FORM / *FORMULE* 20P   PAGE 2   SC-10-00012345-0000
                                                                                  Claim No. / *N° de la demande*

☐ Notice of Garnishment (Form 20E)/Notice of Renewal of Garnishment (Form 20E.1).
   Avis de saisie-arrêt (formule 20E)/Avis de renouvellement de la saisie-arrêt (formule 20E.1).

   I believe that the garnishee _____
   Je crois que le tiers saisi   (Name of garnishee / *Nom du tiers saisi*)

   at _____
   à/au   (Address of garnishee / *Adresse du tiers saisi*)

   is indebted to the debtor or will become indebted to the debtor for the following reasons:
   est ou sera redevable d'une dette au débiteur pour les motifs suivants :

   The Notice will be served on the debtor _____
   L'avis sera signifié au débiteur,   (Name of debtor / *Nom du débiteur/de la débitrice*)

   at _____
   à/au   (Address of debtor for service / *Adresse du débiteur/de la débitrice aux fins de signification*)

   within five days of serving it on the garnishee.
   dans les cinq jours qui suivent sa signification au tiers saisi.

☒ Notice of Examination (Form 20H).
   Avis d'interrogatoire (formule 20H).

☐ Writ of Delivery (Form 20B).
   Bref de délaissement (formule 20B).

☐ Other *(Set out the nature of your request):*
   Autre (Indiquez la nature de votre demande) *:*

Complete this section if you are requesting a Writ of Delivery.
Remplissez la présente section si vous demandez un bref de délaissement.

2. An order for the delivery of the following personal property:
   Une ordonnance de délaissement des biens meubles suivants :
   (According to the court order, set out a description of the property to be delivered. Identify any marks or serial numbers. / Selon l'ordonnance du tribunal, donnez la description des biens qui doivent être restitués. Indiquez toute marque d'identification ou tout numéro de série y figurant.)

Figure 11.3   Continued

FORM / *FORMULE* 20P   PAGE 3   SC-10-00012345-0000

Claim No. / *N° de la demande*

was made in this action against: _____

a été rendue dans l'action contre :   (Name of person against whom the order was made / *Nom de la personne contre qui
l'ordonnance a été rendue*)

on _____ , 20 _____ , in the _____

le _____   *à la Cour des petites*   (Name of court location where order was made / *Emplacement
créances de*   *du tribunal où l'ordonnance a été rendue*)

Small Claims Court. Since the above listed personal property has not been delivered, I make this affidavit in
support of a request that the clerk of the court issue a Writ of Delivery (Form 20B) to the bailiff of the
*Étant donné que les biens meubles susmentionnés n'ont pas été restitués, je fais le présent affidavit à l'appui
d'une demande visant à enjoindre au greffier du tribunal de délivrer un bref de délaissement (formule 20B) à
l'huissier de la Cour des petites créances de*

_____ Small Claims Court.

(Name of court location / *Emplacement du tribunal*)

Complete this section if you are requesting a Certificate of Judgment, Writ of Seizure and Sale of Personal Property, Writ of Seizure and Sale of Land, Notice of Garnishment, Notice of Renewal of Garnishment or Notice of Examination.
Remplissez la présente section si vous demandez un certificat de jugement, un bref de saisie-exécution de biens meubles, un bref de saisie-exécution de biens-fonds, un avis de saisie-arrêt, un avis de renouvellement de la saisie-arrêt ou un avis d'interrogatoire.

3. A judgment was made in this action against   **Feckless Enterprises** _____
Un jugement a été rendu dans l'action contre   (Name of debtor(s) / *Nom du/de la/des débiteur(s)/débitrice(s)*)

on **Nov. 20, year 0** _____ , 20 _____ in the _____
le   *à la Cour des petites créances de*

Toronto _____ Small Claims Court
                (Name of court where judgment was made / *Nom du tribunal où le jugement a été rendu*)

for the following sums:
à l'égard des sommes suivantes :

(A) **DEBT** $ _____ 3,000.00
     LA CRÉANCE $

(B) **PRE-JUDGMENT INTEREST** calculated
     LES INTÉRÊTS ANTÉRIEURS AU JUGEMENT calculés

     on the sum of $ _____ 3,000.00   at the rate of **10** _____ %
     sur la somme de $ *au taux de*   *pour cent*

     per annum from **April 1, year -1** , 20 ____ to **Nov. 20, year 0** , 20 ____ ,
     par an du   *au*

     being **599** _____ days. $ _____ 492.33
     soit   *jours.* $

                          SUBTOTAL (Amount of Judgment) $ 3,492.33
                          TOTAL PARTIEL (montant du jugement) $

(C) **COSTS** to date of judgment $ _____ 130.00
     LES DÉPENS à la date du jugement $

Figure 11.3   Concluded

FORM / *FORMULE* **20P**   **PAGE 4**   SC-10-00012345-0000
                                                          Claim No. / *N° de la demande*

(D) **TOTAL AMOUNT OF PAYMENTS RECEIVED FROM DEBTOR**
    after judgment (if any)   (minus) $ _____ nil
    LE MONTANT TOTAL DES PAIEMENTS REÇUS DU   *(moins)* $
    DÉBITEUR après le jugement (le cas échéant)

(E) **POST-JUDGMENT INTEREST** to date calculated
    LES INTÉRÊTS POSTÉRIEURS AU JUGEMENT à ce jour, calculés

    on the sum of $ _____ 3,492.33 ____ at the rate of **3** ____ %
    sur la somme de $ *au taux de*   *pour cent*

    per annum from **Nov. 21, year 0** , 20 ____ to **July 30, year 0** , 20 ____ ,
    par an du   *au*

    being **10** _____ days. $ _____ 2.87
    soit   *jours.* $

    > **NOTE:** Calculation of interest is always on the amount owing from time to time as payments are
    > received. This is true for both pre-judgment and post-judgment interest. Attach a separate sheet
    > setting out how you calculated the total amount of any pre/post-judgment interest.
    > *REMARQUE : Les intérêts doivent toujours être calculés sur la somme due. Le calcul doit tenir
    > compte des paiements reçus de temps à autre. Ceci s'applique autant aux intérêts antérieurs au
    > jugement qu'aux intérêts postérieurs au jugement. Annexez une feuille distincte indiquant comment
    > vous avez calculé le montant total des intérêts antérieurs et postérieurs au jugement.*

(F) **SUBSEQUENT COSTS** incurred after judgment (including the cost of issuing
    the requested enforcement(s)) $ _____ 35.00
    LES DÉPENS SUBSÉQUENTS engagés après le jugement (y compris le $
    coût de la délivrance de la ou des mesures d'exécution forcée demandées)

                                         TOTAL DUE $ _____ 3,660.20
                                         SOLDE DÛ $

Sworn/Affirmed before me at **Toronto**
Déclaré sous serment/Affirmé   (Municipality / *municipalité*)
solennellement devant moi à

in **Ontario** _____
en/à/au   (Province, state or country / *province, État ou pays*)

on **Nov. 30, year 0** , 20 ____   _____
le   Signature
                            Commissioner for taking affidavits   (This form is to be signed in front of a
                            Commissaire aux affidavits   lawyer, justice of the peace, notary public
                            (Type or print name below if signature is illegible.)   or commissioner for taking affidavits.)
                            (Dactylographiez le nom ou écrivez-le en caractères   *(La présente formule doit être signée en*
                            d'imprimerie ci-dessous si la signature est illisible.)   *présence d'un avocat, d'un juge de paix, d'un*
                                                                   notaire ou d'un commissaire aux affidavits.)

WARNING: **IT IS AN OFFENCE UNDER THE** *CRIMINAL CODE* **TO KNOWINGLY SWEAR OR**
                     AFFIRM A FALSE AFFIDAVIT.
AVERTISSEMENT :   *FAIRE SCIEMMENT UN FAUX AFFIDAVIT CONSTITUE UNE INFRACTION AU CODE*
                     CRIMINEL.

Figure 11.4   Financial Information Form

FINANCIAL INFORMATION FORM
FORMULE DE RENSEIGNEMENTS FINANCIERS
Form / *Formule* 20I Ont. Reg. No. / *Règl. de l'Ont.* : 258/98

This form is to be completed by the debtor and served on the creditor.
La présente formule doit être remplie par le débiteur et signifiée au créancier.

This form is not to be filed at the court office. The debtor must provide a completed copy of this form to the Judge at the examination hearing. The debtor must also bring to the hearing documents that support the information given in this form.
Cette formule ne doit pas être déposée au bureau du tribunal. Le débiteur doit remettre la formule dûment remplie au juge chargé de l'audience. Le débiteur doit aussi apporter à l'audience les documents qui appuient l'information donnée sur cette formule.

MONTHLY INCOME *REVENU MENSUEL*		MONTHLY EXPENSES *DÉPENSES MENSUELLES*	
Employer(s) _____ *Employeur(s)*		Rent/Mortgage *Loyer/Hypothèque*	$ _____ $
Employer(s) _____ *Employeur(s)*		Maintenance/Support Payments *Versements d'aliments*	$ _____ $
Net salary *Salaire net*	$ _____ $	Property taxes *Impôts fonciers*	$ _____ $
Commissions *Commissions*	$ _____ $	Utilities (heat, water & light) *Services d'utilité publique (chauffage, eau et éclairage)*	$ _____ $
Tips and gratuities *Pourboires et gratifications*	$ _____ $	Phone *Téléphone*	$ _____ $
Employment insurance *Prestations d'assurance-emploi*	$ _____ $	Cable *Câblodistribution*	$ _____ $
Pension income *Revenu de pension*	$ _____ $	House/Tenant insurance *Assurance-habitation /assurance de responsabilité locative*	$ _____ $
Investment income *Revenu de placements*	$ _____ $	Life insurance *Assurance-vie*	$ _____ $
Rental income *Revenu de location*	$ _____ $	Food *Nourriture*	$ _____ $
Business income *Revenu tiré d'une entreprise*	$ _____ $	Childcare/Babysitting *Garderie/gardiennage d'enfants*	$ _____ $
Child tax benefit *Prestation fiscale pour enfants*	$ _____ $	Motor vehicle (lease or loan) *Véhicule automobile (location à bail ou prêt)*	$ _____ $
Maintenance *(if any)* *Aliments (le cas échéant)*	$ _____ $	(licence, insurance, fuel & maintenance) *(permis, assurance, essence et entretien)*	$ _____ $
Monthly income of other adult household members *Revenu mensuel des autres membres adultes du ménage*	$ _____ $	Transportation (public) *Transports (en commun)*	$ _____ $
Other *Autre*	$ _____ $		
Income assistance *Aide au revenu*	$ _____ $		
INCOME TOTAL $ _____ *REVENU TOTAL* $		**EXPENSES TOTAL** $ _____ *DÉPENSES TOTALES* $	

Figure 11.4   Concluded

FORM / *FORMULE* **20I**   **PAGE 2**

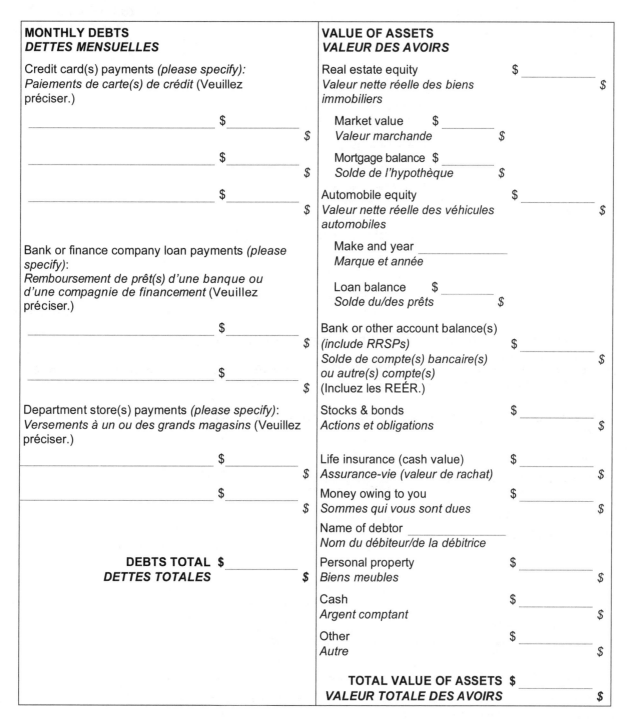

MONTHLY DEBTS / *DETTES MENSUELLES*	VALUE OF ASSETS / *VALEUR DES AVOIRS*
Credit card(s) payments *(please specify):* / *Paiements de carte(s) de crédit* (Veuillez préciser.)	Real estate equity $ / *Valeur nette réelle des biens immobiliers* $
_____ $ _____ $	Market value $ _____ / *Valeur marchande* $
_____ $ _____ $	Mortgage balance $ _____ / *Solde de l'hypothèque* $
_____ $ _____ $	Automobile equity $ _____ / *Valeur nette réelle des véhicules automobiles* $
Bank or finance company loan payments *(please specify):* / *Remboursement de prêt(s) d'une banque ou d'une compagnie de financement* (Veuillez préciser.)	Make and year _____ / *Marque et année*
	Loan balance $ _____ / *Solde du/des prêts* $
_____ $ _____ $	Bank or other account balance(s) *(include RRSPs)* $ _____ / *Solde de compte(s) bancaire(s) ou autre(s) compte(s)* (Incluez les REÉR.) $
_____ $ _____ $	
Department store(s) payments *(please specify):* / *Versements à un ou des grands magasins* (Veuillez préciser.)	Stocks & bonds $ _____ / *Actions et obligations* $
_____ $ _____ $	Life insurance (cash value) $ _____ / *Assurance-vie (valeur de rachat)* $
_____ $ _____ $	Money owing to you $ _____ / *Sommes qui vous sont dues* $
	Name of debtor _____ / *Nom du débiteur/de la débitrice*
DEBTS TOTAL $ _____ / ***DETTES TOTALES*** $	Personal property $ _____ / *Biens meubles* $
	Cash $ _____ / *Argent comptant* $
	Other $ _____ / *Autre* $
	TOTAL VALUE OF ASSETS $ _____ / ***VALEUR TOTALE DES AVOIRS*** $

Figure 11.5   Warrant of Commital

ONTARIO

Superior Court of Justice
Cour supérieure de justice

Warrant of Committal
Mandat de dépôt

Form / *Formule* 20J Ont. Reg. No. / *Règl. de l'Ont.* : 258/98

Seal / *Sceau*

Toronto
Small Claims Court / *Cour des petites créances de*

SC-10-00012345-0000
Claim No. / *N° de la demande*

47 Sheppard Ave. E., 3rd Floor
Toronto, ON M2N 2X5

Address / *Adresse*
416-326-3554

Phone number / *Numéro de téléphone*

BETWEEN / *ENTRE*

Capricious Credit Corporation Ltd.

Plaintiff(s) / *Demandeur(s)/demanderesse(s)*

and / *et*

Feckless Enterprises

Defendant(s) / *Défendeur(s)/défenderesse(s)*

TO ALL POLICE OFFICERS IN ONTARIO AND TO THE OFFICERS OF ALL CORRECTIONAL INSTITUTIONS IN ONTARIO:
À TOUS LES AGENTS DE POLICE DE L'ONTARIO ET AUX AGENTS DE TOUS LES ÉTABLISSEMENTS CORRECTIONNELS DE L'ONTARIO :

THIS WARRANT IS FOR THE COMMITTAL OF / *LE PRÉSENT MANDAT EST DÉCERNÉ POUR L'INCARCÉRATION DE*

Last name / *Nom de famille*		
Feckless		
First name / *Premier prénom*	Second name / *Deuxième prénom*	Also known as / *Également connu(e) sous le nom de*
Henry		
Address (street number, apt., unit) / *Adresse (numéro et rue, app., unité)*		
48 Overreach Blvd.		
City/Town / *Cité/ville*	Province	Phone no. / *N° de téléphone*
Toronto	**ON**	**416-223-4569**
Postal code / *Code postal*		Fax no. / *N° de télécopieur*
M5R 5X3		

A Notice of Contempt Hearing was issued from this court which required
Un avis d'audience pour outrage a été délivré par le tribunal précité ordonnant à

Henry Feckless

(Name of person required to attend contempt hearing / *Nom de la personne tenue de se présenter à l'audience pour outrage*)

to attend the sittings of this court at   **Toronto**   on **November 20, year 0** , 20 _____ .
de se présenter aux séances du   (Time / *Heure*)   *le*   (Date)
tribunal à

At the contempt hearing, it was duly proven that the Notice of Contempt Hearing was properly served, and
Lors de l'audience pour outrage, il a été dûment prouvé que l'avis d'audience pour outrage a été signifié en bonne et due forme et

Figure 11.5 Concluded

FORM / *FORMULE* **20J** **PAGE 2** SC-10-00012345-0000

Claim No. / *N° de la demande*

this court found this person to be in contempt of court because he/she:
d'autre part, le tribunal a reconnu la personne susmentionnée coupable d'outrage au tribunal pour l'un des motifs suivants :

(Check appropriate box. / Cochez la case appropriée.)

☒ wilfully failed to attend an examination hearing as required by a Notice of Examination (Form 20H), which was properly served.
elle a délibérément omis de se présenter à un interrogatoire comme l'exigeait un avis d'interrogatoire (formule 20H), qui a été signifié en bonne et due forme.

☐ attended the examination hearing, refused to answer questions or produce documents or records, and failed to show cause why he/she should not be held in contempt for refusing to answer questions or produce documents or records.
elle s'est présentée à l'interrogatoire mais a refusé de répondre aux questions ou de produire des documents ou des dossiers et a omis de justifier pourquoi elle ne devrait pas être accusée pour outrage pour avoir refusé de répondre aux questions ou de produire des documents ou des dossiers.

At the contempt hearing, a judge of this court ordered this person to be committed.
Lors de l'audience pour outrage, un juge du tribunal a ordonné l'incarcération de la personne susmentionnée.

YOU ARE ORDERED to take the person named above to the nearest correctional institution and admit and
IL VOUS EST ORDONNÉ d'amener la personne susmentionnée à l'établissement correctionnel le plus proche

detain him or her there for **5** days.
et de l'y admettre et l'y détenir pendant *jours.*

This warrant expires twelve (12) months from the date of issue, unless renewed by court order. If renewed, the warrant expires twelve (12) months from the date of the renewal.
Le présent mandat expire douze (12) mois à compter de la date de sa délivrance, sauf si le tribunal le renouvelle par ordonnance. S'il est renouvelé, le mandat expire douze (12) mois à compter de la date du renouvellement.

December 12, year 0 , 20

(Signature of clerk / *Signature du greffier*)

Figure 11.6   Writ of Delivery

ONTARIO

Superior Court of Justice   **Writ of Delivery**
Cour supérieure de justice   *Bref de délaissement*

Form / *Formule* 20B Ont. Reg. No. / *Règl. de l'Ont.* : 258/98

Seal / *Sceau*

North Bay   **SC-10-00012350-0000**

Small Claims Court / *Cour des petites créances de*   Claim No. / *N° de la demande*

360 Plouffe Street
North Bay, ON P1B 9L5

Address / *Adresse*

705-495-8309

Phone number / *Numéro de téléphone*

BETWEEN / *ENTRE*

Abdullah Karim

Plaintiff(s) / *Demandeur(s)/demanderesse(s)*

and / *et*

Antonio Salieri

Defendant(s) / *Défendeur(s)/défenderesse(s)*

TO THE BAILIFF OF North Bay   **SMALL CLAIMS COURT:**
À L'HUISSIER DE LA COUR   (Name of Small Claims Court location / *Emplacement de la Cour*
DES PETITES CRÉANCES DE   *des petites créances*)

Under an order of this court made on **November 30, year 0**   , 20 ____
En vertu d'une ordonnance rendue par le tribunal précité le

YOU ARE DIRECTED to seize from **Antonio Salieri**
NOUS VOUS ENJOIGNONS de saisir auprès de   (Name of person against whom the order was made / *Nom de la personne*
contre qui l'ordonnance a été rendue)

and to deliver without delay to | Name of person in whose favour the order was made / *Nom de la personne en faveur de qui*
et de remettre sans retard à | *l'ordonnance a été rendue*
Abdullah Karim

Street and number / *Numéro et rue*
280 Queen Street

City, province, postal code / *Ville, province, code postal*
North Bay, ON P2P 3A5

Phone number and fax number, if any / *Numéro de téléphone et numéro de télécopieur, le cas échéant*
705-732-4561

possession of the following personal property:
la possession des biens meubles suivants :

(According to the court order, set out a description of the property to be delivered. Identify any marks or serial numbers. If the order refers to
items set out in the issued claim, attach a copy of the issued claim.)
(Conformément à l'ordonnance du tribunal, donnez la description des biens qui doivent être remis. Indiquez toute marque d'identification ou tout
numéro de série y figurant. Si l'ordonnance vise des articles énoncés dans la demande délivrée, annexez une copie de la demande délivrée.)

One Stradivarius violin, red-brown in colour

Figure 11.6   Concluded

FORM / *FORMULE* 20B   PAGE 2   SC-10-00012350-0000
                                                                                  Claim No. / *N° de la demande*

The above personal property is located at: **Faculty of Music, Queen's University, Kingston, ON**
Les biens meubles susmentionnés se trouvent à/au :   (Address / *Adresse*)

If the address provided does not clearly identify where the items are located, please attach a detailed map that
shows the nearest intersection.
Si l'adresse fournie n'indique pas clairement l'emplacement des articles, veuillez annexer un plan détaillé qui
montre l'intersection la plus rapprochée.

(To be completed by the clerk of the court. / Section à remplir par le greffier du tribunal.)	☐ **THE COURT HAS EXPRESSLY ORDERED** that you are authorized to use reasonable force to enter a private dwelling to execute this writ of delivery, if necessary [*Execution Act*, s. 20(2)]. A copy of the court's order on the endorsement record is attached. *EN VERTU D'UNE ORDONNANCE EXPRESSE DU TRIBUNAL, vous êtes autorisé(e) à avoir recours à la force raisonnable pour pénétrer dans un logement privé pour exécuter le présent bref de délaissement, si cela est nécessaire [Loi sur l'exécution forcée, par. 20 (2)]. Une copie de l'ordonnance du tribunal qui figure au dossier des inscriptions est annexée.*

December 15, year 0   , 20   _____

                                                                 (Signature of clerk / *Signature du greffier*)

Figure 11.7   Writ of Seizure and Sale of Personal Property

ONTARIO

Superior Court of Justice
Cour supérieure de justice

Writ of Seizure and Sale of Personal Property
Bref de saisie-exécution de biens meubles
Form / *Formule* 20C Ont. Reg. No. / *Règl. de l'Ont.* : 258/98

Seal / *Sceau*

Toronto

Small Claims Court / *Cour des petites créances de*

SC-10-00012345-0000

Claim No. / *N° de la demande*

47 Sheppard Ave. E., 3rd Floor
Toronto, ON M2N 2X5

Address / *Adresse*

416-326-3554

Phone number / *Numéro de téléphone*

Creditor No. 1 / *Créancier n° 1*

☐ Additional party(ies) listed on attached Form 1A.
La ou les parties additionnelles sont mentionnées sur la formule 1A ci-jointe.

Last name, or name of company / *Nom de famille ou nom de la compagnie*		
Capricious Credit Corporation Ltd.		
First name / *Premier prénom*	Second name / *Deuxième prénom*	Also known as / *Également connu(e) sous le nom de*
Address (street number, apt., unit) / *Adresse (numéro et rue, app., unité)*		
c/o Charles Dickens 8041 Ryder Street		
City/Town / *Cité/ville* **Mississauga**	Province **ON**	Phone no. / *N° de téléphone* **905-381-2620**
Postal code / *Code postal* **L2R 1Y6**		Fax no. / *N° de télécopieur*
Representative / *Représentant(e)* **Charles Dickens**		LSUC # / *N° du BHC* **P02345**
Address (street number, apt., unit) / *Adresse (numéro et rue, app., unité)*		
8041 Ryder Street		
City/Town / *Cité/ville* **Mississauga**	Province **ON**	Phone no. / *N° de téléphone* **905-381-2620**
Postal code / *Code postal* **L2R 1Y6**		Fax no. / *N° de télécopieur*

Debtor No. 1 / *Débiteur n° 1*

☐ Additional party(ies) listed on attached Form 1A.
La ou les parties additionnelles sont mentionnées sur la formule 1A ci-jointe.

Last name, or name of company / *Nom de famille ou nom de la compagnie*		
Feckless Enterprises		
First name / *Premier prénom*	Second name / *Deuxième prénom*	Also known as / *Également connu(e) sous le nom de*
Address (street number, apt., unit) / *Adresse (numéro et rue, app., unité)*		
c/o Edward Loquacious 365 Bay Street		
City/Town / *Cité/ville* **Toronto**	Province **ON**	Phone no. / *N° de téléphone* **416-595-1308**
Postal code / *Code postal* **M2N 3A8**		Fax no. / *N° de télécopieur*
Representative / *Représentant(e)* **Edward Loquacious**		LSUC # / *N° du BHC* **P02361**
Address (street number, apt., unit) / *Adresse (numéro et rue, app., unité)*		
365 Bay Street		
City/Town / *Cité/ville* **Toronto**	Province **ON**	Phone no. / *N° de téléphone* **416-595-1308**
Postal code / *Code postal* **M2N 3A8**		Fax no. / *N° de télécopieur*

Figure 11.7 Continued

FORM / *FORMULE* 20C   **PAGE 2**   SC-10-00012345-0000
                                                                              Claim No. / *N° de la demande*

TO THE BAILIFF OF THE Toronto   **SMALL CLAIMS COURT:**
À L'HUISSIER DE LA COUR   (Small Claims Court location / *Emplacement de la Cour des*
DES PETITES CRÉANCES DE   *petites créances*)

Under an order of this court made on **November 20, year 0**   , 20 _____ , in favour of
En vertu d'une ordonnance rendue par ce tribunal le   *, en faveur de*

Capricious Credit Corporation Ltd.

                        (Name of creditor(s) / *Nom du/de la/des créancier(s)/créancière(s)*)

YOU ARE DIRECTED to seize and sell the personal property of
NOUS VOUS ENJOIGNONS *de saisir les biens meubles de*

Last name, or name of company / *Nom de famille ou nom de la compagnie*		
Feckless Enterprises		
First name / *Premier prénom*	Second name / *Deuxième prénom*	Third name / *Troisième prénom*

☐ Additional debtor(s) and also known as names listed on attached Form 1A.1.
   Le ou les débiteurs additionnels et le ou les noms sous lesquels ils sont également connus sont mentionnés
   sur la formule 1A.1 ci-jointe.

situated within your jurisdiction and to realize from the seizure and sale the following sums:
qui se trouvent dans votre ressort et de procéder à leur vente pour réaliser les sommes suivantes :

(A) **AMOUNT OF JUDGMENT** (debt and pre-judgment interest) $ 3,492.33
    LE MONTANT DU JUGEMENT *(créance et intérêts antérieurs au jugement)* $

(B) **COSTS** to date of judgment $ 130.00
    LES DÉPENS *à la date du jugement* $

(C) **TOTAL AMOUNT OF PAYMENTS RECEIVED FROM DEBTOR** after
    judgment (if any) $ nil
    LE MONTANT TOTAL DES PAIEMENTS REÇUS DU DÉBITEUR *après le* $
    jugement (le cas échéant)

    Post-judgment interest continues to accrue
    Les intérêts postérieurs au jugement continuent à courir

    at the rate of **3** _____ % per annum from **November 21, year 0** , 20 _____ .
    au taux de   % *par an à compter du*

(D) **SUBSEQUENT COSTS** incurred after judgment (including the cost of issuing this writ) $ 35.00
    LES DÉPENS SUBSÉQUENTS *engagés après le jugement (y compris le coût* $
    de délivrance du présent bref)

(E) Your fees and expenses in enforcing this writ.
    Les honoraires et frais qui vous sont dus pour l'exécution forcée du présent bref.

Figure 11.7   Concluded

FORM / *FORMULE* 20C   **PAGE 3**   SC-10-00012345-0000

Claim No. / *N° de la demande*

YOU ARE DIRECTED to calculate the amount owing at the time of enforcement and to pay the proceeds over to the clerk of this court for the creditor.

ET NOUS VOUS ENJOIGNONS de calculer la somme due au moment de l'exécution forcée et de verser le produit de la vente au greffier du tribunal précité pour le compte du créancier.

November 30, year 0   , 20 _____   _____

(Signature of clerk / *Signature du greffier*)

Reasonable disbursements necessarily incurred to enforce this writ $	(filled in and initialled by $
Débours raisonnables qui ont dû être engagés pour exécuter le présent bref	the enforcement office /
(Bailiff (enforcement office) fees and expenses / *Honoraires et frais de l'huissier (bureau de l'exécution)*)	*à remplir et à parapher par le bureau de l'exécution*)

NOTE:	**THIS WRIT REMAINS IN FORCE FOR SIX YEARS** after the date of its issue and for a further six years after each renewal. The writ may be renewed before it expires by filing a Request to Renew a Writ of Seizure and Sale (Form 20N) with the bailiff (enforcement office).
REMARQUE :	*LE PRÉSENT BREF RESTE EN VIGUEUR PENDANT SIX ANS après la date de sa délivrance ou après chaque renouvellement. Le bref peut être renouvelé avant qu'il n'expire en déposant une demande de renouvellement du bref de saisie-exécution (formule 20N) auprès de l'huissier (bureau de l'exécution).*

Figure 11.8 Direction to Enforce Writ of Seizure and Sale of Personal Property

ONTARIO

Superior Court of Justice
Cour supérieure de justice

Direction to Enforce Writ of Seizure and Sale of Personal Property
Ordre d'exécution d'un bref de saisie-exécution de biens meubles

Form / *Formule* 20O Ont. Reg. No. / *Règl. de l'Ont.* : 258/98

Toronto	**SC-10-00012345-0000**
Small Claims Court / *Cour des petites créances de*	Claim No. / *N° de la demande*

47 Sheppard Ave. E., 3rd Floor
Toronto, ON M2N 2X5

Address / *Adresse*

416-326-3554

Phone number / *Numéro de téléphone*

BETWEEN / *ENTRE*

Capricious Credit Corporation Ltd.

Creditor(s) / *Créancier(s)/créancière(s)*

and / *et*

Feckless Enterprises

Debtor(s) / *Débiteur(s)/débitrice(s)*

My name is **Charles Dickens**
Je m'appelle

(Full name / *Nom et prénoms*)

1. In this action, I am the
   Dans la présente action, je suis le/la

   (Check one box only. / *Cochez une seule case.*)

   ☐ creditor.
   créancier/créancière.

   ☒ representative of the creditor(s).
   représentant(e) du/de la/des créancier(s)/créancière(s).

   A Writ of Seizure and Sale of Personal Property (Form 20C) directed to the bailiff of the
   Un bref de saisie-exécution de biens meubles (formule 20C) adressé à l'huissier de la Cour des petites créances de

   Toronto Small Claims Court was issued on:
   (Small Claims Court location / *emplacement de la Cour des petites créances*) *a été délivré le :*

   November 20, year 0 , 20 _____ , in favour of **Capricious Credit Corporation Ltd.**
   , en faveur de (Name of creditor / *Nom du/de la créancier/créancière*)

2. I am filing this direction to enforce the Writ of Seizure and Sale of Personal Property, and direct the bailiff to seize and sell (if required) the personal property belonging to the following debtor(s):
   Je dépose le présent ordre d'exécution du bref de saisie-exécution de biens meubles et ordonne à l'huissier de saisir et de vendre (s'il y a lieu) les biens meubles appartenant au(x) débiteur(s) suivant(s) :

Last name, or name of company / *Nom de famille ou nom de la compagnie*		
Feckless Enterprises		
First name / *Premier prénom*	Second name / *Deuxième prénom*	Third given name (individual only) (if applicable) / *Troisième prénom (particulier seulement) (s'il y a lieu)*

☐ Additional debtor(s) and also known as names are listed on attached Form 1A.1.
Le ou les débiteurs additionnels et le ou les noms sous lesquels les débiteurs sont également connus sont mentionnés sur la formule 1A.1 ci-jointe.

Set out a description of the property to be seized. Identify any marks or serial numbers.
Donnez la description des biens qui doivent être saisis. Indiquez toute marque d'identification ou tout numéro de série y figurant.

Figure 11.8   Concluded

FORM / *FORMULE* 20O   PAGE 2   SC-10-00012345-0000

Claim No. / *N° de la demande*

3. The above personal property is located at: **48 Overreach Blvd., Toronto, ON M2R 5X3**
   Les biens meubles susmentionnés se trouvent à/au :   (Address / *Adresse*)

   If the address provided does not clearly identify where the property is located, please attach a detailed map showing the nearest intersection.
   Si l'adresse fournie n'indique pas clairement l'emplacement des biens, veuillez annexer un plan détaillé qui montre l'intersection la plus rapprochée.

4. From the date that the Writ of Seizure and Sale of Personal Property was issued, the following payments have been received from the debtor and/or subsequent costs incurred by the creditor:
   Depuis la date de délivrance du bref de saisie-exécution de biens meubles, les paiements suivants ont été reçus du débiteur ou les dépens subséquents engagés par le créancier :

   (A) **PAYMENTS RECEIVED FROM DEBTOR**
   PAIEMENTS REÇUS DU DÉBITEUR

Date of Payment *Date du paiement*	Payment Amount *Montant du paiement*	
	$	$
	$	$
	$	$
	$	$

   ☐ List of additional payments attached
       Liste de paiements additionnels ci-jointe

   (B) **SUBSEQUENT COSTS** incurred since issuance of Writ of Seizure and Sale of Personal Property
   ***DÉPENS SUBSÉQUENTS** engagés depuis la délivrance du bref de saisie-exécution de biens meubles*

Reason cost was incurred *Raison pour laquelle les dépens ont été engagés*	Cost Amount *Montant des dépens*	
	$	$
	$	$
	$	$
	$	$

   ☐ List of additional costs attached
       Liste de dépens additionnels ci-jointe

The bailiff will calculate the amount owing based on the information provided within the Writ of Seizure and Sale of Personal Property and the details provided above. This amount will include any reasonable disbursements necessarily incurred to enforce this writ.
L'huissier calculera la somme due en fonction des renseignements donnés dans le bref de saisie-exécution de biens meubles et des précisions données ci-dessus. Cette somme inclura les débours raisonnables qui ont dû être engagés pour exécuter ce bref.

_____ , 20 _____   _____

                                             (Signature of creditor or representative / *Signature du créancier/de la*
                                             créancière ou du/de la représentant(e))

                                             _____

                                             (Name, address and phone number of creditor or representative / *Nom, adresse et*
                                             numéro de téléphone du créancier/de la créancière ou du/de la représentant(e))

Figure 11.9   Request to Renew Writ of Seizure and Sale

ONTARIO

Superior Court of Justice
Cour supérieure de justice

Request to Renew Writ of Seizure and Sale
Demande de renouvellement du bref de saisie-exécution

Form / *Formule* 20N Ont. Reg. No. / *Règl. de l'Ont.* : 258/98

Toronto
Small Claims Court / *Cour des petites créances de*

SC-10-00012345-0000
Claim No. / *N° de la demande*

47 Sheppard Ave. E., 3rd Floor
Toronto, ON M2N 2X5

Address / *Adresse*

416-326-3554
Phone number / *Numéro de téléphone*

BETWEEN / *ENTRE*

Capricious Credit Corporation Ltd.

Creditor(s) / *Créancier(s)/créancière(s)*

and / *et*

Feckless Enterprises

Debtor(s) / *Débiteur(s)/débitrice(s)*

TO THE SHERIFF/BAILIFF OF Toronto   :
AU SHÉRIF/À L'HUISSIER DU/DE LA   (Name of county/region and city/town in which the enforcement office is located / *Nom du comté/de la région et de la cité/ville où est situé le bureau de l'exécution*)

YOU ARE REQUESTED TO RENEW the
VOUS ÊTES PRIÉ(E) DE RENOUVELER le

☒ Writ of Seizure and Sale of Personal Property (Form 20C)
bref de saisie-exécution de biens meubles (formule 20C)

☐ Writ of Seizure and Sale of Land (Form 20D)
bref de saisie-exécution de biens-fonds (formule 20D)

issued on **November 20, year 0**   , 20 _____ , in this proceeding and filed in your office for a period of
délivré le   *dans la présente instance et déposé à votre bureau, pour*

six years from the date of renewal.
une période de six ans à compter de la date du renouvellement.

November 1, year 6   , 20 _____

(Signature of creditor or representative / *Signature du créancier/de la créancière ou du/de la représentant(e)*)

Charles Dickens
8041 Ryder St.
Mississauga, ON L2R 1Y6

(Name, address and phone number of creditor or representative / *Nom, adresse et numéro de téléphone du créancier/de la créancière ou du/de la représentant(e)*)

NOTE: **A WRIT OF SEIZURE AND SALE OF LAND OR OF PERSONAL PROPERTY** remains in force for six years after the date of its issue and for a further six years after each renewal.
REMARQUE : *LE BREF DE SAISIE-EXÉCUTION DE BIENS-FONDS OU DE BIENS MEUBLES reste en vigueur pendant six ans après la date de sa délivrance ou après chaque renouvellement.*

Figure 11.10   Writ of Seizure and Sale of Land

ONTARIO

Superior Court of Justice
Cour supérieure de justice

Writ of Seizure and Sale of Land
Bref de saisie-exécution de biens-fonds

Form / *Formule* 20D Ont. Reg. No. / *Règl. de l'Ont.* : 258/98

Seal / *Sceau*

Toronto	**SC-10-00012345-0000**
Small Claims Court / *Cour des petites créances de*	Claim No. / *N° de la demande*

47 Sheppard Ave. E., 3rd Floor
Toronto, ON M2N 2X5

Address / *Adresse*

416-326-3554

Phone number / *Numéro de téléphone*

☐ Additional party(ies) listed on attached Form 1A.
La ou les parties additionnelles sont mentionnées sur la formule 1A ci-jointe.

Creditor No. 1 / *Créancier n° 1*

Last name, or name of company / *Nom de famille ou nom de la compagnie*		
Capricious Credit Corporation Ltd.		
First name / *Premier prénom*	Second name / *Deuxième prénom*	Also known as / *Également connu(e) sous le nom de*
Address (street number, apt., unit) / *Adresse (numéro et rue, app., unité)*		
c/o Charles Dickens 8041 Ryder St.		
City/Town / *Cité/ville* **Mississauga**	Province **ON**	Phone no. / *N° de téléphone* **905-381-2620**
Postal code / *Code postal* **L2R 1Y6**		Fax no. / *N° de télécopieur*
Representative / *Représentant(e)* **Charles Dickens**		LSUC # / *N° du BHC* **P02345**
Address (street number, apt., unit) / *Adresse (numéro et rue, app., unité)*		
8041 Ryder St.		
City/Town / *Cité/ville* **Mississauga**	Province **ON**	Phone no. / *N° de téléphone* **905-381-2620**
Postal code / *Code postal* **L2R 1Y6**		Fax no. / *N° de télécopieur*

☐ Additional party(ies) listed on attached Form 1A.
La ou les parties additionnelles sont mentionnées sur la formule 1A ci-jointe.

Debtor No. 1 / *Débiteur n° 1*

Last name, or name of company / *Nom de famille ou nom de la compagnie*		
Feckless Enterprises		
First name / *Premier prénom*	Second name / *Deuxième prénom*	Also known as / *Également connu(e) sous le nom de*
Address (street number, apt., unit) / *Adresse (numéro et rue, app., unité)*		
c/o Edward Loquacious 365 Bay Street		
City/Town / *Cité/ville* **Toronto**	Province **ON**	Phone no. / *N° de téléphone* **416-595-1308**
Postal code / *Code postal* **M2N 3A8**		Fax no. / *N° de télécopieur*
Representative / *Représentant(e)* **Edward Loquacious**		LSUC # / *N° du BHC* **P02361**
Address (street number, apt., unit) / *Adresse (numéro et rue, app., unité)*		
365 Bay Street		
City/Town / *Cité/ville* **Toronto**	Province **ON**	Phone no. / *N° de téléphone* **416-595-1308**
Postal code / *Code postal* **M2N 3A8**		Fax no. / *N° de télécopieur*

NOTE:	**THIS WRIT REMAINS IN FORCE FOR SIX YEARS** after the date of its issue and for a further six years after each renewal. The writ may be renewed before it expires by filing a Request to Renew a Writ of Seizure and Sale (Form 20N) with the sheriff (enforcement office.)
REMARQUE :	*LE PRÉSENT BREF RESTE EN VIGUEUR PENDANT SIX ANS après la date de sa délivrance ou après chaque renouvellement. Le bref peut être renouvelé avant qu'il n'expire en déposant une demande de renouvellement du bref de saisie-exécution (formule 20N) auprès du shérif (bureau de l'exécution).*

Figure 11.10   Concluded

FORM / *FORMULE* 20D	PAGE 2	SC-10-00012345-0000

Claim No. / *N° de la demande*

TO THE SHERIFF OF   Toronto   :
AU SHÉRIF DE   (Name of county/region in which the enforcement office is located / *Nom du comté/de la région où est situé le bureau de l'exécution*)

Under an order of this court made on **November 20, year 0** , 20 _____ , in favour of
En vertu d'une ordonnance rendue par ce tribunal le   *, en faveur de*

Capricious Credit Corporation Ltd.

(Name of creditor(s) / *Nom du/de la/des créancier(s)/créancière(s)*)

YOU ARE DIRECTED to seize and sell the real property of
NOUS VOUS ENJOIGNONS *de saisir les biens immeubles de*

Last name, or name of company / *Nom de famille ou nom de la compagnie*		
Feckless Enterprises		
First name / *Premier prénom*	Second name / *Deuxième prénom*	Third name / *Troisième prénom*

☐   Additional debtor(s) and also known as names listed on attached Form 1A.1.
     Le ou les débiteurs additionnels et le ou les noms sous lesquels ils sont également connus sont mentionnés sur la formule 1A.1 ci-jointe.

situated within your jurisdiction and to realize from the seizure and sale the following sums:
qui se trouvent dans votre ressort et de procéder à leur vente pour réaliser les sommes suivantes :

(A)   **AMOUNT OF JUDGMENT** (debt and pre-judgment interest) $ _____ 3.492.33
     MONTANT DU JUGEMENT *(créance et intérêts antérieurs au jugement)* $

(B)   **COSTS** to date of judgment $ _____ 130.00
     LES DÉPENS *à la date du jugement* $

(C)   **TOTAL AMOUNT OF PAYMENTS RECEIVED FROM DEBTOR** after
     judgment (if any) $ _____ nil
     LE MONTANT TOTAL DES PAIEMENTS REÇUS DU DÉBITEUR *après le* $
     jugement (le cas échéant)

     Post-judgment interest continues to accrue
     Les intérêts postérieurs au jugement continuent à courir

     at the rate of **3**   % per annum from **November 21, year 0** , 20 _____ .
     au taux de   *% par an à compter du*

(D)   **SUBSEQUENT COSTS** incurred after judgment (including the cost of issuing this writ) $ _____ 35.00
     LES DÉPENS SUBSÉQUENTS *engagés après le jugement (y compris le coût* $
     de délivrance du présent bref)

(E)   Your fees and expenses in enforcing this writ.
     Les honoraires et frais qui vous sont dus pour l'exécution forcée du présent bref.

YOU ARE DIRECTED to calculate the amount owing at the time of enforcement and pay out the proceeds according to law and to report on the execution of this writ if required by a party who filed this writ.
ET NOUS VOUS ENJOIGNONS *de calculer la somme due au moment de l'exécution forcée et de verser le produit de la vente conformément à la loi et de faire un rapport sur l'exécution forcée du présent bref si la partie qui l'a déposé l'exige.*

November 30, year 0 _____ , 20 _____   _____

                                                     (Signature of clerk / *Signature du greffier*)

Figure 11.11   Notice of Garnishment

ONTARIO
Superior Court of Justice
Cour supérieure de justice

Notice of Garnishment
Avis de saisie-arrêt
Form / *Formule* 20E Ont. Reg. No. / *Règl. de l'Ont.* : 258/98

(Seal / *Sceau*)

North Bay
Small Claims Court / *Cour des petites créances de*

SC-10-00012350-0000
Claim No. / *N° de la demande*

360 Plouffe Street
North Bay, ON   P1B 9L5
Address / *Adresse*

705-495-8309
Phone number / *Numéro de téléphone*

☐ Additional creditor(s) listed on the attached Form 1A.
Le ou les créanciers additionnels sont mentionnés sur la formule 1A ci-jointe.

Creditor / *Créancier*

Last name, or name of company / *Nom de famille ou nom de la compagnie* **Karim**		
First name / *Premier prénom* **Abdullah**	Second name / *Deuxième prénom*	Also known as / *Également connu(e) sous le nom de*
Address (street number, apt., unit) / *Adresse (numéro et rue, app., unité)* **280 Queen Street**		
City/Town / *Cité/ville* **North Bay**	Province **ON**	Phone no. / *N° de téléphone* **705-732-4561**
Postal code / *Code postal* **P2P 3A5**		Fax no. / *N° de télécopieur*
Representative / *Représentant(e)*		LSUC # / *N° du BHC*
Address (street number, apt., unit) / *Adresse (numéro et rue, app., unité)*		
City/Town / *Cité/ville*	Province	Phone no. / *N° de téléphone*
Postal code / *Code postal*		Fax no. / *N° de télécopieur*

Debtor / *Débiteur*

Last name, or name of company / *Nom de famille ou nom de la compagnie* **Salieri**		
First name / *Premier prénom* **Antonio**	Second name / *Deuxième prénom*	Also known as / *Également connu(e) sous le nom de*
Address (street number, apt., unit) / *Adresse (numéro et rue, app., unité)* **177 Main Street**		
City/Town / *Cité/ville* **Kingston**	Province **ON**	Phone no. / *N° de téléphone* **613-223-4564**
Postal code / *Code postal* **K7L 2T2**		Fax no. / *N° de télécopieur*

Garnishee / *Tiers saisi*

Last name, or name of company / *Nom de famille ou nom de la compagnie* **Queen's University**		
First name / *Premier prénom*	Second name / *Deuxième prénom*	Also known as / *Également connu(e) sous le nom de*
Address (street number, apt., unit) / *Adresse (numéro et rue, app., unité)* **99 University Avenue**		
City/Town / *Cité/ville* **Kingston**	Province **ON**	Phone no. / *N° de téléphone* **613-595-2300**
Postal code / *Code postal* **K7L 3N6**		Fax no. / *N° de télécopieur*

NOTE: **THE CREDITOR SHALL SERVE THIS NOTICE** on the debtor with an Affidavit for Enforcement Request (Form 20P) and serve on the garnishee this notice with a blank Garnishee's Statement (Form 20F).

REMARQUE : *LE CRÉANCIER SIGNIFIE LE PRÉSENT AVIS au débiteur conjointement avec un affidavit en vue d'une demande d'exécution (formule 20P) et signifie au tiers saisi le présent avis avec une déclaration du tiers saisi (formule 20F) en blanc.*

Figure 11.11   Continued

FORM / *FORMULE* **20E**   **PAGE 2**   <u>SC-10-00012350-0000</u>
Claim No. / N° de la demande

TO THE GARNISHEE:
AU TIERS SAISI :

The creditor has obtained a court order against the debtor. The creditor claims that you owe or will owe the debtor a debt in the form of wages, salary, pension payments, rent, annuity or other debt that you pay out in a lump-sum, periodically or by instalments. (A debt to the debtor includes both a debt payable to the debtor alone and a joint debt payable to the debtor and one or more co-owners.)
Le créancier a obtenu une ordonnance du tribunal contre le débiteur. Le créancier prétend que vous êtes ou serez redevable au débiteur d'une dette sous forme de salaire, de prestations de retraite, de loyer, de rente ou autre que vous payez par somme forfaitaire, périodiquement ou par versements échelonnés. (Une dette envers le débiteur comprend à la fois une dette payable au débiteur seul et une dette payable conjointement au débiteur et à un ou plusieurs autres cotitulaires de la créance.)

YOU ARE REQUIRED TO PAY to the clerk of the   **North Bay**   Small Claims Court
VOUS ÊTES REQUIS(E) DE PAYER au greffier   (Garnishment issuing court / *Tribunal qui prononce la*
de la Cour des petites créances de   *saisie-arrêt*)

(a)   all debts now payable by you to the debtor, **within 10 days** after this notice is served on you; **and**
d'une part, toutes les dettes dont vous êtes maintenant redevable au débiteur, dans les 10 jours qui suivent la signification du présent avis;

(b)   all debts that become payable by you to the debtor after this notice is served on you and **within 6 years** after this notice is issued, **within 10 days** after they become payable.
d'autre part, toutes les dettes dont vous deviendrez redevable au débiteur après la signification du présent avis et dans les 6 années qui suivent sa délivrance, dans les 10 jours qui suivent la date à laquelle elles deviennent exigibles.

The total amount of all your payments to the clerk is not to exceed $ 3,200.00 .
La totalité des paiements que vous ferez au greffier ne doit pas dépasser   (Amount unsatisfied /   **$.**
                    Montant impayé)

THIS NOTICE IS LEGALLY BINDING ON YOU until it expires or is changed, renewed, terminated or satisfied. If you do not pay the total amount or such lesser amount as you are liable to pay, you must serve a Garnishee's Statement (Form 20F) on the creditor and debtor, and file it with the clerk within 10 days after this notice is served on you.
LE PRÉSENT AVIS VOUS LIE LÉGALEMENT jusqu'à ce qu'il expire ou qu'il soit modifié, renouvelé ou résilié, ou qu'il y soit satisfait. Si vous ne payez pas le montant total ou le montant moindre dont vous êtes redevable, vous devez signifier une déclaration du tiers saisi (formule 20F) au créancier et au débiteur et la déposer auprès du greffier dans les 10 jours qui suivent la signification du présent avis.

EACH PAYMENT, payable to the Minister of Finance, MUST BE SENT with a copy of the attached garnishee's payment notice to the clerk at the above court address.
CHAQUE PAIEMENT, libellé à l'ordre du ministre des Finances, DOIT ÊTRE ENVOYÉ au greffier, à l'adresse du tribunal indiquée ci-dessus, avec une copie de l'avis de paiement du tiers saisi ci-joint.

If your debt is jointly owed to the debtor and to one or more co-owners, you must pay the debtor's appropriate share of the amount now payable, or which becomes payable, or such a percentage as the court may order.
Si votre dette est payable conjointement au débiteur et à un ou plusieurs autres cotitulaires de la créance, vous devez payer la quote-part appropriée du débiteur du montant dont vous êtes maintenant redevable, ou qui devient redevable, ou le pourcentage que le tribunal ordonne.

Figure 11.11   Continued

FORM / *FORMULE* 20E   **PAGE 3**   SC-10-00012350-0000

‾‾‾‾‾‾‾‾‾‾‾‾‾‾‾‾‾‾‾‾‾‾‾‾‾
Claim No. / *N° de la demande*

The amounts paid into court shall not exceed the portion of the debtor's wages that are subject to seizure or garnishment under Section 7 of the *Wages Act* (information available at: www.attorneygeneral.jus.gov.on.ca and www.e-laws.gov.on.ca). The portion of wages that can be garnished may be increased or decreased only by order of the court. If such a court order is attached to this notice or is served on you, you must follow the direction in that court order.

Les montants consignés au tribunal ne doivent pas dépasser la partie du salaire du débiteur qui peut faire l'objet d'une saisie ou d'une saisie-arrêt aux termes de l'article 7 de la Loi sur les salaires (pour de plus amples renseignements, reportez-vous aux adresses : www.attorneygeneral.jus.gov.on.ca et www.lois-en-ligne.gouv.on.ca). La partie saisissable du salaire ne peut être augmentée ou réduite que sur ordonnance du tribunal. Si une telle ordonnance du tribunal est annexée au présent avis ou vous est signifiée, vous devez vous conformer à la directive qui y est énoncée.

July 20, year 0   , 20 _____   ‾‾‾‾‾‾‾‾‾‾‾‾‾‾‾‾‾‾‾‾‾‾‾‾‾‾‾‾‾‾‾

(Signature of clerk / *Signature du greffier*)

CAUTION TO GARNISHEE:	**IF YOU FAIL TO PAY** to the clerk the amount set out in this notice and do not file a Garnishee's Statement (Form 20F) disputing garnishment, **JUDGMENT MAY BE OBTAINED AGAINST YOU BY THE CREDITOR** for payment of the amount set out above, plus costs. If you make a payment to anyone other than the clerk of the court, you may be liable to pay again [R. 20.08(17) and (18)].
AVERTISSEMENT AU TIERS SAISI :	*SI VOUS NE VERSEZ PAS au greffier le montant précisé dans le présent avis et ne déposez pas la déclaration du tiers saisi (formule 20F) contestant la saisie-arrêt, LE CRÉANCIER PEUT OBTENIR CONTRE VOUS UN JUGEMENT ordonnant le paiement du montant précisé ci-dessus et des dépens. Si vous effectuez un paiement à une personne qui n'est pas le greffier du tribunal, vous pouvez être tenu(e) de payer de nouveau [par. 20.08 (17) et (18)].*

NOTE:	Any party or interested person may complete and serve a Notice of Garnishment Hearing (Form 20Q) to determine any matter related to this notice. To obtain forms and self-help materials, attend the nearest Small Claims Court or access the following website: www.ontariocourtforms.on.ca.
REMARQUE :	*Toute partie ou personne intéressée peut remplir et signifier un avis d'audience sur la saisie-arrêt (formule 20Q) en vue de décider une question relative au présent avis. Vous pouvez obtenir les formules et la documentation à l'usage du client auprès de la Cour des petites créances de votre localité ou en consultant le site Web suivant : www.ontariocourtforms.on.ca.*

Figure 11.11 Concluded

FORM / *FORMULE* 20E   **PAGE 4**   SC-10-00012350-0000

The top portion of the garnishee's payment notice, below, is to be completed by the creditor before the Notice of Garnishment is issued. Where it is anticipated that more than one payment will be made by the garnishee, the creditor should supply extra copies of the garnishee's payment notice. Additional copies of the garnishee's payment notice are available at court offices or online at www.ontariocourtforms.on.ca (see Form 20E or 20E.1). *Le créancier doit remplir la partie supérieure de l'avis de paiement du tiers saisi figurant ci-dessous avant la délivrance de l'avis de saisie-arrêt. S'il est prévu que le tiers saisi fera plus d'un paiement, le créancier doit fournir des exemplaires supplémentaires de l'avis de paiement du tiers saisi. Vous pouvez obtenir des exemplaires supplémentaires de l'avis de paiement du tiers saisi aux greffes des tribunaux ou en ligne à l'adresse www.ontariocourtforms.on.ca (consultez la formule 20E ou 20E.1).*

GARNISHEE'S PAYMENT NOTICE / *AVIS DE PAIEMENT DU TIERS SAISI*

Make payment by cheque or money order payable to the Minister of Finance and send it, along with this payment notice to the clerk of the court at the following address:
Effectuez le paiement par chèque ou mandat-poste à l'ordre du ministre des Finances et envoyez-le, avec une copie du présent avis de paiement, au greffier du tribunal à l'adresse suivante :

Court address: **360 Plouffe Street, North Bay, ON P1B 9L5**
Adresse du tribunal :

Claim No.: **1008**
N° de la demande :

Creditor: **Abdullah Karim**
Créancier/créancière :

Debtor: **Antonio Salieri**
Débiteur/débitrice :

Garnishee: **Queen's University**
Tiers saisi :

TO BE COMPLETED BY GARNISHEE FOR EACH PAYMENT
À REMPLIR PAR LE TIERS SAISI LORS DE CHAQUE PAIEMENT

Date of payment: _____ , 20 _____
Date du paiement :

Amount enclosed: $ _____
Montant inclus : $

Figure 11.12   Notice to Co-owner of Debt

ONTARIO

Superior Court of Justice *Cour supérieure de justice*	**Notice to Co-owner of Debt** ***Avis au cotitulaire d'une créance*** Form / *Formule* 20G Ont. Reg. No. / *Règl. de l'Ont.* : 258/98

North Bay Small Claims Court / *Cour des petites créances de*	**SC-10-00012350-0000** Claim No. / *N° de la demande*
360 Plouffe Street **North Bay, ON P1B 9L5** Address / *Adresse*	
705-495-8309 Phone number / *Numéro de téléphone*	

☐ Additional creditor(s) listed on the attached Form 1A.
Le ou les créanciers additionnels sont mentionnés sur la formule 1A ci-jointe.

Creditor / *Créancier*

Last name, or name of company / *Nom de famille ou nom de la compagnie* **Karim**		
First name / *Premier prénom* **Abdullah**	Second name / *Deuxième prénom*	Also known as / *Également connu(e) sous le nom de*
Address (street number, apt., unit) / *Adresse (numéro et rue, app., unité)* **280 Queen Street**		
City/Town / *Cité/ville* **North Bay**	Province **ON**	Phone no. / *N° de téléphone* **705-732-4561**
Postal code / *Code postal* **P2P 3A5**		Fax no. / *N° de télécopieur*
Representative / *Représentant(e)*		LSUC # / *N° du BHC*
Address (street number, apt., unit) / *Adresse (numéro et rue, app., unité)*		
City/Town / *Cité/ville*	Province	Phone no. / *N° de téléphone*
Postal code / *Code postal*		Fax no. / *N° de télécopieur*

Debtor / *Débiteur*

Last name, or name of company / *Nom de famille ou nom de la compagnie* **Salieri**		
First name / *Premier prénom* **Antonio**	Second name / *Deuxième prénom*	Also known as / *Également connu(e) sous le nom de*
Address (street number, apt., unit) / *Adresse (numéro et rue, app., unité)* **177 Main Street**		
City/Town / *Cité/ville* **Kingston**	Province **ON**	Phone no. / *N° de téléphone* **613-223-4564**
Postal code / *Code postal* **K7L 2T2**		Fax no. / *N° de télécopieur*

Garnishee / *Tiers saisi*

Last name, or name of company / *Nom de famille ou nom de la compagnie* **Queen's University**		
First name / *Premier prénom*	Second name / *Deuxième prénom*	Also known as / *Également connu(e) sous le nom de*
Address (street number, apt., unit) / *Adresse (numéro et rue, app., unité)* **99 University Avenue**		
City/Town / *Cité/ville* **Kingston**	Province **ON**	Phone no. / *N° de téléphone* **613-595-2300**
Postal code / *Code postal* **K7L 3N6**		Fax no. / *N° de télécopieur*

NOTE:	**THIS NOTICE SHALL BE SERVED BY THE CREDITOR** on each co-owner of debt together with a copy of the Garnishee's Statement (Form 20F) received from the garnishee.
REMARQUE :	***LE CRÉANCIER SIGNIFIE LE PRÉSENT AVIS*** *à chaque cotitulaire d'une créance conjointement avec une copie de la déclaration du tiers saisi (formule 20F) qu'il reçoit du tiers saisi.*

Figure 11.12   Concluded

FORM / *FORMULE* **20G**   **PAGE 2**   SC-10-00012350-0000

Claim No. / *N° de la demande*

TO: ***DESTINATAIRE :*** *(Attach a separate sheet, in the same format, for additional co-owners of debt. /* Annexez une autre feuille, présentée selon le même format, en cas d'autres cotitulaires de la créance.)	Name of co-owner(s) of debt / *Nom du ou des cotitulaires de la créance* **W.A. Mozart**
	Street and number / *Numéro et rue* **c/o Faculty of Music, Queen's University** **99 University Avenue**
	City, province, postal code / *Ville, province, code postal* **Kingston, ON K7L 3N6**

The creditor has obtained a court order against the debtor. The creditor has served a Notice of Garnishment
Le créancier a obtenu une ordonnance du tribunal contre le débiteur. Le créancier a signifié un avis de saisie-arrêt

(Form 20E), dated **July 20, year 0**   , 20   , on **Queen's University**   ,
(formule 20E), daté du   *à*   (Name of garnishee / *Nom du tiers saisi*)

claiming that the garnishee owes or will owe the debtor a debt in the form of wages, salary, pension payments, rent, annuity, or other debt that the garnishee pays out in a lump-sum, periodically or by instalments. (A debt to the debtor includes both a debt payable to the debtor alone and a joint debt payable to the debtor and one or more co-owners.)
dans lequel il prétend que le tiers saisi est ou sera redevable au débiteur d'une dette sous forme de salaire, de prestations de retraite, de loyer, de rente ou autre que le tiers saisi paie par somme forfaitaire, périodiquement ou par versements échelonnés. (Une dette envers le débiteur comprend à la fois une dette payable au débiteur seul et une dette payable conjointement au débiteur et à un ou plusieurs autres cotitulaires de la créance.)

The garnishee has set out in the attached Garnishee's Statement (Form 20F) that you are a co-owner of debt. Under the Notice of Garnishment, the garnishee has paid or will pay to the clerk of the Small Claims Court the appropriate share of the amount payable or such a percentage as the court may order.
Le tiers saisi a indiqué dans la déclaration du tiers saisi annexée (formule 20F) que vous êtes un cotitulaire de la créance. Aux termes de l'avis de saisie-arrêt, le tiers saisi a payé ou paiera au greffier de la Cour des petites créances la quote-part appropriée du montant redevable ou le pourcentage que le tribunal ordonne.

IF YOU HAVE A CLAIM to the money being paid to the clerk of the Small Claims Court by the garnishee, you have 30 days from service of this notice to request a garnishment hearing by completing and serving a Notice of Garnishment Hearing (Form 20Q) on the creditor, debtor and garnishee, and filing it with the clerk. If you fail to do so, you are not entitled to dispute the enforcement of the creditor's order for the payment or recovery of money and the funds may be paid out to the creditor unless the court orders otherwise.
SI VOUS PRÉTENDEZ AVOIR UN DROIT sur l'argent que le tiers saisi verse au greffier de la Cour des petites créances, vous disposez de 30 jours à compter de la signification du présent avis pour demander une audience sur la saisie-arrêt en remplissant et en signifiant un avis d'audience sur la saisie-arrêt (formule 20Q) au créancier, au débiteur et au tiers saisi, et en le déposant auprès du greffier. Si vous ne le faites pas, vous n'aurez pas le droit par la suite de contester l'exécution forcée de l'ordonnance obtenue par le créancier en vue du paiement ou du recouvrement de sommes d'argent et ces sommes pourront être remises au créancier, sauf ordonnance contraire du tribunal.

To obtain forms and self-help materials, attend the nearest Small Claims Court or access the following website: www.ontariocourtforms.on.ca.
Vous pouvez obtenir les formules et la documentation à l'usage du client auprès de la Cour des petites créances de votre localité ou en consultant le site Web suivant : www.ontariocourtforms.on.ca.

July 30, year 0   , 20   _____

(Signature of creditor or representative / *Signature du créancier/de la créancière ou du/de la représentant(e)*)

NOTE:	Within seven (7) calendar days of changing your address for service, notify the court and all other parties in writing.
REMARQUE :	*Dans les sept (7) jours civils qui suivent tout changement de votre adresse aux fins de signification, veuillez en aviser par écrit le tribunal et les autres parties.*

Figure 11.13 Garnishee's Statement

ONTARIO
Superior Court of Justice
Cour supérieure de justice

Garnishee's Statement
Déclaration du tiers saisi
Form / *Formule* 20F Ont. Reg. No. / *Règl. de l'Ont.* : 258/98

North Bay
Small Claims Court / *Cour des petites créances de*

SC-10-00012350-0000
Claim No. / *N° de la demande*

360 Plouffe Street
North Bay, ON P1B 9L5
Address / *Adresse*

705-495-8309
Phone number / *Numéro de téléphone*

BETWEEN / *ENTRE*

Abdullah Karim

Creditor(s) / *Créancier(s)/créancière(s)*

and / *et*

Antonio Salieri

Debtor(s) / *Débiteur(s)/débitrice(s)*

Name of Garnishee **Queen's University**
Nom du tiers saisi   (Full legal name of garnishee / *Nom et prénoms officiels du tiers saisi*)

A Notice of Garnishment was issued on **July 20, year 0**   , 20 _____ , naming me/us as garnishee.
Un avis de saisie-arrêt a été délivré le _____ , *me/nous désignant comme tiers saisi(s).*

☐ **I/WE DO NOT OWE** and do not expect to owe to the debtor the amount set out in the Notice of Garnishment
for the following reason(s):
JE NE SUIS/NOUS NE SOMMES PAS REDEVABLE(S) et je ne m'attends/nous ne nous attendons pas à
être redevable(s) au débiteur du montant énoncé dans l'avis de saisie-arrêt pour le ou les motifs suivants :

☒ **I/WE OWE OR WILL OWE** the debtor (or the debtor and one or more co-owners), wages or periodic
payments based on the terms explained below:
JE SUIS OU SERAI/NOUS SOMMES OU SERONS REDEVABLE(S) au débiteur (ou au débiteur et à un ou
plusieurs autres cotitulaires de la créance) des montants suivants exigibles à titre de salaire ou de
versements périodiques et selon les modalités suivantes :

(State the amount(s) and how often the debtor is paid. If the debtor is paid wages, state the gross amount of the debtor's wages before
any deductions required by law and the net amount after those deductions, and attach a copy of a pay slip. If you owe or will owe the
debtor a lump sum, state when and how much will be paid.)

(Indiquez le ou les montants et la fréquence des paiements faits au débiteur. Si le débiteur touche un salaire, indiquez son salaire brut
avant les retenues que vous êtes tenu(e)(s) de déduire, selon la loi, ainsi que le montant net après les retenues, et annexez une copie
d'un bordereau de paie. Si vous êtes ou serez redevable(s) d'une somme forfaitaire au débiteur, indiquez-en le montant et à quel
moment le paiement sera effectué.)

a lump sum of $500 payable on September 4, year 0

Figure 11.13　Concluded

FORM / *FORMULE* **20F**　　　　　　　　**PAGE 2**　　　　　　　　SC-10-00012350-0000

Claim No. / *N° de la demande*

☒ **I/We are making payment of less than** the amount stated because the debt is owed to the debtor and to one or more co-owners, or for another reason explained below:
J'effectue/Nous effectuons un paiement inférieur au montant indiqué parce qu'il s'agit d'une dette envers le débiteur et envers un ou plusieurs autres cotitulaires de la créance, ou pour un autre motif indiqué ci-dessous :

50% ($250) owing to each of Antonio Salieri and W.A. Mozart

(Identify the amount(s) and percentage owed to the debtor and each co-owner / *Précisez le ou les montants et le pourcentage redevable au débiteur et à chaque autre cotitulaire de la créance*)

Co-owner(s) of the debt:　**W.A. Mozart**
Cotitulaire(s) de la créance :　　　　　　　　　(Full legal name(s) / *Nom et prénoms officiels*)

c/o Faculty of Music, Queen's University, 99 University Avenue, Kingston, ON K7L 3N6

(Address (street & number, unit, municipality, province) / *Adresse (numéro et rue, unité, municipalité, province)*)

☐ **I/We are not making a payment at this time or are making a payment of less than the amount stated** because I/we have been served with other notice(s) of garnishment against the debtor. (Provide details below.)
Je n'effectue/Nous n'effectuons aucun paiement présentement ou j'effectue/nous effectuons un paiement inférieur au montant indiqué parce que j'ai/nous avons reçu signification d'un ou de plusieurs autres avis de saisie-arrêt contre le débiteur. *(Donnez-en les détails ci-dessous.)*

Name of creditor *Nom du créancier*	Name of issuing court *Nom du tribunal délivreur*	Location of court or Sheriff's Office where payment is currently being made *Emplacement du tribunal ou bureau du shérif où le paiement est actuellement effectué*	Date Notice of Garnishment received *Date de réception de l'avis de saisie-arrêt*

☐ **I/We will dispute the garnishment** by completing and serving a Notice of Garnishment Hearing (Form 20Q) on the creditor, debtor and co-owner(s) of the debt (if any) and any other interested person, and filing it with the clerk of the court.
Je contesterai/Nous contesterons la saisie-arrêt en remplissant et en signifiant un avis d'audience sur la saisie-arrêt (formule 20Q) au créancier, au débiteur et au(x) cotitulaire(s) de la créance (le cas échéant) et à tout autre intéressé et en le déposant auprès du greffier du tribunal.

August 11, year 0　　　　　　　, 20　　　　　

(Signature of garnishee or representative / *Signature du tiers saisi ou du/de la représentant(e)*)

99 University Avenue
Kingston,ON K7L 3N6 613-595-2300

(Address, phone and fax number of garnishee or representative / *Adresse, numéro de téléphone et de télécopieur du tiers saisi ou du/de la représentant(e)*)

NOTE TO GARNISHEE: *REMARQUE AU TIERS SAISI :*	The garnishee must serve a copy of the Garnishee's Statement on the creditor and the debtor and file it with the court. You can get an electronic version of this form online at www.ontariocourtforms.on.ca. *Le tiers saisi doit signifier une copie de la déclaration du tiers saisi au créancier et au débiteur et la déposer auprès du tribunal. Vous pouvez obtenir une version électronique de la présente formule en ligne à l'adresse www.ontariocourtforms.on.ca.*

NOTE TO CREDITOR: *REMARQUE AU CRÉANCIER :*	A creditor who is served with a Garnishee's Statement must send it to the co-owners of the debt, if any, together with a Notice to Co-owner of Debt (Form 20G). You can get forms at court offices or online at www.ontariocourtforms.on.ca. *Le créancier qui reçoit signification de la déclaration du tiers saisi doit la faire parvenir aux cotitulaires de la créance, le cas échéant, avec l'avis au cotitulaire d'une créance (formule 20G). Vous pouvez obtenir des formules aux greffes des tribunaux ou en ligne à l'adresse www.ontariocourtforms.on.ca.*

Figure 11.14   Affidavit in Support of a Motion for a Consolidation Order*

ONTARIO

Superior Court of Justice
Cour supérieure de justice

Affidavit
Affidavit

Form / *Formule* 15B Ont. Reg. No. / *Règl. de l'Ont.* : 258/98

SC-10-00012345-0000,
SC-10-00013789-0000,
SC-10-00012344-0000

Claim No. / *N° de la demande*

Toronto
Small Claims Court / *Cour des petites créances de*

47 Sheppard Ave. E., 3rd Floor
Toronto, ON M2N 2X5

Address / *Adresse*

416-326-3554
Phone number / *Numéro de téléphone*

BETWEEN / *ENTRE*

Capricious Credit Corporation Ltd.

Plaintiff(s)/Creditor(s) / *Demandeur(s)/demanderesse(s)/créancier(s)/créancière(s)*

and / *et*

Feckless Enterprises

Defendant(s)/Debtor(s) / *Défendeur(s)/défenderesse(s)/débiteur(s)/débitrice(s)*

My name is Feckless Enterprises
Je m'appelle

(Full name / *Nom et prénoms*)

I live in Toronto, Ontario
J'habite à

(Municipality & province / *Municipalité et province*)

Claim Numbers SC-10-00012345-0000, SC-10-00013789-0000,
SC-10-00012344-0000

I make this affidavit in relation to:
Je fais le présent affidavit relativement à :   (Specify why the affidavit is being filed with the court. / *Précisez les raisons pour lesquelles l'affidavit est déposé auprès du tribunal.*)

and I swear/affirm that the following is true:
et je déclare sous serment/j'affirme solennellement que les renseignements suivants sont véridiques :

Set out the facts in numbered paragraphs. If you learned a fact from someone else, you must give that person's name and state that you believe that fact to be true.
Indiquez les faits sous forme de dispositions numérotées. Si vous avez pris connaissance d'un fait par l'entremise d'une autre personne, vous devez indiquer le nom de cette personne et déclarer que vous croyez que ce fait est véridique.

---

*   A Financial Information Form (see figure 11.4) can be used to provide income and expense information, and can be attached as an exhibit to the affidavit or be referred to in the affidavit and filed with it.

Figure 11.14 Continued (Additional Parties)

ONTARIO

Superior Court of Justice
Cour supérieure de justice

PAGE 1A

Additional Parties
Parties additionnelles
Form / *Formule* 1A Ont. Reg. No. / *Règl. de l'Ont.* : 258/98

SC-10-00013789-0000,
SC-10-00012344-0000

Claim No. / *N° de la demande*

☒ **Plaintiff No. /** *Demandeur n°* 2   ☐ **Defendant No. /** *Défendeur n°*

Last name, or name of company / *Nom de famille ou nom de la compagnie*		
Forsythe		
First name / *Premier prénom* Wanda	Second name / *Deuxième prénom*	Also known as / *Également connu(e) sous le nom de*
Address (street number, apt., unit) / *Adresse (numéro et rue, app., unité)* 800 Any Street		
City/Town / *Cité/ville* Toronto	Province ON	Phone no. / *N° de téléphone*
Postal code / *Code postal* M3J T8J		Fax no. / *N° de télécopieur*
Representative / *Représentant(e)*		LSUC # / *N° du BHC*
Address (street number, apt., unit) / *Adresse (numéro et rue, app., unité)*		
City/Town / *Cité/ville*	Province	Phone no. / *N° de téléphone*
Postal code / *Code postal*		Fax no. / *N° de télécopieur*

☒ **Plaintiff No. /** *Demandeur n°* 3   ☐ **Defendant No. /** *Défendeur n°*

Last name, or name of company / *Nom de famille ou nom de la compagnie*		
Pasternak		
First name / *Premier prénom* Linda	Second name / *Deuxième prénom*	Also known as / *Également connu(e) sous le nom de*
Address (street number, apt., unit) / *Adresse (numéro et rue, app., unité)* 932 Anyother Street		
City/Town / *Cité/ville* Toronto	Province ON	Phone no. / *N° de téléphone*
Postal code / *Code postal* M4R 1Y6		Fax no. / *N° de télécopieur*
Representative / *Représentant(e)*		LSUC # / *N° du BHC*
Address (street number, apt., unit) / *Adresse (numéro et rue, app., unité)*		
City/Town / *Cité/ville*	Province	Phone no. / *N° de téléphone*
Postal code / *Code postal*		Fax no. / *N° de télécopieur*

☐ **Plaintiff No. /** *Demandeur n°*   ☐ **Defendant No. /** *Défendeur n°*

Last name, or name of company / *Nom de famille ou nom de la compagnie*		
First name / *Premier prénom*	Second name / *Deuxième prénom*	Also known as / *Également connu(e) sous le nom de*
Address (street number, apt., unit) / *Adresse (numéro et rue, app., unité)*		
City/Town / *Cité/ville*	Province	Phone no. / *N° de téléphone*
Postal code / *Code postal*		Fax no. / *N° de télécopieur*
Representative / *Représentant(e)*		LSUC # / *N° du BHC*
Address (street number, apt., unit) / *Adresse (numéro et rue, app., unité)*		
City/Town / *Cité/ville*	Province	Phone no. / *N° de téléphone*
Postal code / *Code postal*		Fax no. / *N° de télécopieur*

Figure 11.14   Concluded

FORM / *FORMULE* **15B**   **PAGE 2**   **SC-10-00012345-0000,**
SC-10-00013789-0000,
SC-10-00012344-0000

Claim No. / *N° de la demande*

1. I am the owner of Feckless Enterprises, a business located in Toronto, Ontario.

2. I am the debtor in the above-noted actions against me and as such have knowledge of the matters sworn to in this affidavit.

3. The following creditors have obtained judgments against me that remain unsatisfied:

a) Capricious Credit Corporation Ltd., 601 - 310 Bay Street, Toronto, ON M5R 1K3, Claim Number SC-10-00012345-0000-0000,
b) Wanda Forsythe, 800 Any Street, Toronto, ON M3J T8J, Claim Number SC-10-00013789-0000, and
c) Linda Pasternak, 932 Anyother Street, Toronto, ON M4R 1Y6, Claim Number SC-10-00012344-0000.

4. I owe $3,000.00 to Capricious Credit Corporation Ltd., $2,000.00 to Wanda Forsythe, and $1,000.00 to Linda Pasternak.

4. My monthly income from all sources is as follows:
Salary (net) $2,000.00
Interest   2.00
Royalties   10.00
Total $2,012.00

5. My current monthly expenses are as follows:
Housing $1,000.00
Food   200.00
Car payment   200.00
Utilities   200.00
Total $1,600.00

6. My current employment situation is uncertain. My main customer, Slippout Sheet Metal, has told its employees that they are likely to close down and our work from them is likely to terminate in March year 1.

If more space is required, attach and initial extra pages. / Si vous avez besoin de plus d'espace, annexez une ou des feuilles supplémentaires et paraphez-les.

Sworn/Affirmed before me at **Toronto** *Déclaré sous serment/Affirmé* *solennellement devant moi à* (Municipality / *municipalité*) in **Ontario** *en/à/au* (Province, state or country / *province, État ou pays*) on **Nov. 7, year 0** , 20 _____ *le* Commissioner for taking affidavits *Commissaire aux affidavits* (Type or print name below if signature is illegible.) *(Dactylographiez le nom ou écrivez-le en caractères d'imprimerie ci-dessous si la signature est illisible.)*	Signature (This form is to be signed in front of a lawyer, justice of the peace, notary public or commissioner for taking affidavits.) *(La présente formule doit être signée en présence d'un avocat, d'un juge de paix, d'un notaire ou d'un commissaire aux affidavits.)*

WARNING:	**IT IS AN OFFENCE UNDER THE *CRIMINAL CODE* TO KNOWINGLY SWEAR OR AFFIRM A FALSE AFFIDAVIT.**
AVERTISSEMENT :	*FAIRE SCIEMMENT UN FAUX AFFIDAVIT CONSTITUE UNE INFRACTION AU CODE CRIMINEL.*

PART II

Debt Collection: Selected Topics

Thus far, we have examined the process of suing and obtaining a judgment for debt, and then enforcing the judgment in both the Superior Court and in the Small Claims Court. In particular, we focused on the parts of that process with which law clerks and paralegals are most likely to be involved. We now turn to an examination of some legal topics about which paralegals and law clerks should have a basic knowledge.

CHAPTER 12

Collections and Deceased Debtors

When a debtor dies, as a matter of law, his estate becomes the entity that participates in any collections matter in which the deceased debtor was involved. Although the death of a debtor does not usually create problems in a collections case, there are some procedural steps that you must take to commence, continue, or conclude an action against a debtor.

WHO REPRESENTS THE ESTATE?

When a debtor dies, the law requires that the estate of the deceased carry on in the deceased's place and that the estate have a representative to act on its behalf. This means that court proceedings against a debtor will stop on her death, and a creditor will be prevented from enforcing a judgment until a legal representative is available to represent the estate. If the deceased had a will, the creditors will have to wait for a legal representative to take control of the estate and its assets; if there is no will, the creditors will have to wait for a representative to apply to the court for authority to administer the estate. In Ontario, the legal name for an estate representative is an estate trustee with a will or an estate trustee without a will, depending on whether or not there is a will. Most financial institutions still refer to the estate trustee as the executor if there is a will.

If a person dies without a will, an individual, usually a relative of the deceased, must apply for a **certificate of appointment of estate trustee without a will**. In Ontario, if a person dies without a will the *Succession Law Reform Act* sets out who has first right to apply to be the estate trustee. The deceased's spouse (including a common law spouse) has first right to be estate trustee, followed by the deceased's children, then grandchildren, followed by other descendants. If there are no descendants, then the deceased's parents, followed by their siblings, have the right to apply to be the estate trustee. Where there are no living relatives, the Public Guardian and Trustee may be appointed as the estate trustee. A creditor may apply to be the estate trustee. If a party with a prior right to be the estate trustee does not want to be appointed, he or she must renounce the position by filing a renunciation with the court. Sometimes no one steps forward and applies, or relatives disagree about who should do it. In this case, it may be necessary for

certificate of appointment of estate trustee without a will when someone dies without a will, it is necessary for someone, usually a relative, to apply to the court for a certificate of appointment of estate trustee without a will; until the appointment is made, no one has authority to do anything with the deceased's assets; once an appointment is made, the estate trustee may deal with the estate, settling its debts and distributing remaining assets to relatives in accordance with a statutory formula that determines the shares family members get some other interested party to make an application, or at least have the court appoint someone to represent the estate for the limited purpose of defending or commencing a legal proceeding.

If the debtor has a will where an **estate trustee** has been named in the will, that person has the authority to deal with the estate's assets from the moment of the deceased's death. However, because the contents of a will may not be known to others, a creditor does not necessarily know who the estate trustee is. In most cases, particularly where the deceased owned property, the estate trustee will apply to the registrar of the Superior Court at the court office in the county or regional municipality where the deceased resided for a **certificate of appointment of estate trustee with a will** (formerly known as a grant of "letters probate"). The certificate does not create the authority for the estate trustee to act; that authority was given by the testator in the will itself — the certificate merely confirms the power granted by the will and certifies that the will is authentic. You may search the records of the court to see if a certificate has been filed. In some cases, a deceased will have made split wills. Split wills consist of two validly co-existing wills executed by the testator. One will deals with assets that require a court certificate in order to have the assets transferred out of the estate. Real estate and publicly traded shares held solely in the deceased's name are examples of such assets. A second will is drafted to deal with assets that do not require a certificate in order to be transferred out of the estate; for example, jewellery and most privately held shares. The advantage of having the second will is that probate fees do not have to be paid on the value of the assets dealt with in the second will.[1] If, as a creditor, you are trying to determine from the will what assets the estate may have, you should make inquiries of the estate trustee to determine whether there is another will. The searches described in chapter 3 can also help the creditor to determine the deceased's assets. These searches should be done soon after the deceased's death because, in some cases, assets may be moved into estate accounts and liquidated fairly quickly.

If the debtor left a will but did not name an estate trustee, or the estate trustee predeceased the **testator**, or the estate trustee refuses to act or is unable to act because of a disability, someone close to the debtor — usually a relative — will have to come forward and apply for a "certificate of appointment" (formerly called "letters of administration with the will annexed"). Note that anyone with a recognizable interest in the administration of the estate could be appointed. This includes creditors of the deceased. However, anyone with a prior right to apply to be the estate trustee would have to renounce his or her right to apply or the court would have to make an order dispensing with a renunciation.

Whether there is a will or not, the person who administers the estate has the task of collecting and valuing the estate assets, determining liabilities, paying creditors, taking proceedings or administrative steps to safeguard assets, and distributing the residue of the estate subject to any **testamentary trusts** that are to be administered into the future. Until the court appoints or, in the case of the will, certifies the appointment of someone to do this job, all proceedings for debt against the deceased are stayed. Once an estate trustee has been appointed or certified, the estate trustee can defend or settle any lawsuit against the deceased. Until an estate trustee is appointed, the estate cannot act or respond, because it does not have an authorized representative in place to do so. A lawsuit against the debtor cannot proceed until an estate trustee has been appointed by the court. This may have dire consequences for a creditor of a deceased debtor who may have to stand by while assets diminish in value.

estate trustee
the deceased's legal representative for estate administration purposes; the estate trustee may be named in the will or approved by the court

certificate of appointment of estate trustee with a will
when someone dies with a will, he has usually named an executor (known as an estate trustee) to administer the estate in accordance with the will; an executor's authority is derived from the will itself; the certificate of appointment granted by the court merely indicates that the will is the last valid will and confirms the executor as estate trustee; an executor will often be named to act not only as estate trustee, but also as a trustee for the administration of any testamentary trusts contained in the will— such trusts are often established for beneficiaries who are under a disability, including minors and mentally incapacitated persons; these trusts may require the executor and trustee to administer them over a long period of time

testator
one who makes a will to dispose of his estate on death

Sample Notice to Creditors

All claims against the Estate of [*name of deceased*], late of the [*City of _____, Province of _____*], who died on [*date of death*], must be filed with the undersigned estate trustee on or before the [*give date, which is usually at least one month from date of first publication of ad*], after which date the estate will be distributed having regard only to the claims of which the estate trustee then shall have notice.

DATED at [*city*], this [____] day of [*month*], [*year*].

[*name of estate trustee*]
Estate trustee of the estate of
[*deceased's name*]
By his lawyers
[*give firm name and address*]

You can check to see whether an estate trustee has been appointed by searching the court records in the court office in the county or regional municipality where the deceased resided at the time of his death for a certificate appointing or, in the case of a will, certifying an estate trustee. Anyone with a financial interest in the estate, including creditors, can file a request with the court in order to receive notice of the commencement of any estate proceedings. If someone applies for a certificate of appointment, anyone who has filed a request for notice will be notified of the application. A request for notice is good for three years, after which time another request may be filed.

Once an estate trustee is appointed, if you act for a creditor, including one who has not commenced any proceedings, you should write to the trustee and send details of the claim to her so that the trustee is on notice as to the claim (see the example on the next page). The tone of this letter should be informative rather than demanding — the estate trustee may know nothing about the deceased's debts and your letter may be the first piece of information she gets. However, do insist on a reply within two weeks and a promise of payment. If you receive no response to this letter within the time you have allotted and diarized, advise your client to continue this as a collection matter and be prepared to sue the estate, either directly or through the summary procedure in the *Estates Act*, which is discussed later in this chapter.

An estate trustee has no statutory duty to advertise for creditors, although it is common to do so where the debtor was engaged in business or other activities where she was likely to have creditors. The reason for this is that the estate trustee may be held personally liable if he failed to give adequate notice to creditors of his intention to distribute assets to estate beneficiaries and then went on and distributed estate assets without paying creditors. Normally, an estate trustee will protect himself from this type of liability by advertising on at least two separate occasions, at least one week apart, in a major daily newspaper. At least one month's notice from the date of the first publication should be given to creditors to come forward with their claims. There is no special form, but the notice should provide the name of the deceased and the date of death, and advise creditors to submit claims to the estate administrator by a given date, after which the estate will be distributed. The executor's address (usually in care of his lawyer) must also be included. A sample notice to creditors is provided in the box at the top of this page.

testamentary trust
a trust set up by the testator in a will to preserve and administer assets for specific purposes after the rest of the estate has been wound up—for example, for a child beneficiary; here, capital is set aside for investment by a trustee (often the estate executor and trustee), with the income to be used for the child's benefit until the child reaches an age set by the trust, at which time the capital may be paid out; if an individual sets up a trust during his or her lifetime, the trust is called an *inter vivos* trust; once a trust is set up, the person who establishes it, called a settlor, no longer owns or controls the trust property; the trustee is then the legal owner; however, the trustee's ownership rights are controlled by the trust terms, which require the trustee to use the property for the benefit of the beneficiary (sometimes called a *cestui que* trust)

Sample Letter from Creditor to Estate Trustee

FOOEY, ARGENT
Barristers and Solicitors
43 Cutpurse Road
Toronto, ON M4R 1D6

January 31, year 0

Ms. Mary Cashedin
100 Moor Hen Way
Toronto, ON M5Q 1W2

Dear Ms. Cashedin:

RE: The Estate of William Cashedin, Deceased

We are lawyers for Triple Q Finance Ltd. According to court records, we understand that you are the estate trustee of the deceased, having been named executor in his will.

Our client loaned the late Mr. Cashedin $27,000 on January 1, year −1 with interest at 12 percent per annum. Mr. Cashedin provided our client with a promissory note in which he promised to pay the sum of $30,240 on January 1, year 0 to discharge this loan. As of this date, that sum remains outstanding and interest continues to accumulate, since the due date, at $8.88 per day.

To avoid further interest charges, we would appreciate it if you would give this matter your urgent attention and now ask that you pay the sum of $30,595.20, including interest, on February 10, year 0, so that this debt can be discharged. Please make your cheque payable to "Fooey, Argent in Trust."

A copy of the promissory note is enclosed.

Yours very truly,

Filbert Fooey

Filbert Fooey

If you are involved in a collections practice, you should get into the habit of reading the legal notices in the business section of your local newspapers to watch for any notice that might be relevant to one of your clients. Once notice has been given, the estate trustee may distribute estate assets if no creditor has made a claim within the time provided for in the notice (usually one month from the time of the first publication of the notice). If the debtor died **intestate**, the estate trustee must advertise for creditors, as described here, or he must wait at least one year from the date of the deceased's death to distribute estate assets. While these steps will protect the estate trustee from personal liability, a creditor who has not notified the estate trustee before distribution may still be able to bring an action and, if he can "trace" assets from the estate to others, may successfully recover judgment and enforce that judgment against traceable assets in the hands of beneficiaries or other creditors who made claims against the estate in a timely manner.[2]

intestate, intestacy
when a person dies without having made a will, he is said to have died intestate; dying without a will is said to create an intestacy—that is, a situation where the estate will have to be administered without a will

APPOINTING AN ESTATE TRUSTEE DURING LITIGATION

If a relative, beneficiary, or other person contests the validity of the will, the certificate of appointment will be held up until the matter is settled and no one will represent the estate, perhaps for years. In this situation, the creditor in an existing action, or on bringing an action, may wish to consider applying to the court where the will validity litigation is being brought, on a motion for advice and directions, to ask that an **estate trustee during litigation** be appointed for the limited purpose of tending to the estate's interests during the litigation. The estate trustee in this situation may well be the named executor, but he or she, in the absence of a court order, has no authority to pay anything out of the estate until the validity of the will has been determined by the court. During litigation, an estate trustee generally maintains an estate, attending to such tasks as income tax return filings and maintaining insurance on estate matters. At any time, such a trustee can seek direction from the court as to how to proceed in a given situation.

estate trustee during litigation
a grant made under a court order appointing someone to act for the estate when there is a dispute about the validity of the will or about who should administer the estate; during litigation the estate trustee has control of estate assets but has no authority to make payouts until the court has dealt with the validity of the will or decided who should administer the estate, as the case may be

The procedure for appointing an estate trustee during litigation is as follows: If an action has been commenced to contest the will, bring a motion to the court where the litigation is occurring; if one has not been commenced, the creditor may bring an application in the court location where the deceased debtor resided. Either the motion or the application should be accompanied by an affidavit setting out why the creditor is applying to be the estate trustee during litigation. An estate trustee will be appointed during litigation when no one is administering, or is likely to administer, the estate in a timely manner. In some cases, the estate trustee suffers from a disability and is unable to carry out his responsibilities. In other cases, there may be issues about the validity of the will that require the appointment of a neutral trustee during litigation. The affidavit should describe the assets in the estate and their value, to the extent the affiant knows them. Lastly, the affiant should request that an estate trustee during litigation be appointed. Along with the affidavit, the creditor should also file the written consent of the proposed trustee to act and, if the creditor can get them, the consents of potential beneficiaries to the estate. The affidavits should be accompanied by affidavits of execution, sworn in your office, in which you confirm that the consents were validly executed. If the court is satisfied with the application or motion on the merits, it will appoint the estate trustee during litigation.

Types of Estate Trustees

Estate trustee with a will	a person appointed by the will to act and administer the estate
Estate trustee without a will	usually a relative, appointed and authorized to administer the estate of an individual who died without a will
Estate trustee during litigation	a person appointed to represent the interest of the estate and to protect the estate if there is a dispute about the validity of a will or a dispute about who should act as personal representative

PROCEDURE FOR MAKING A CLAIM AGAINST THE ESTATE

Under the *Estates Act* there is a procedure that allows a creditor to establish a claim against the deceased's estate or to continue a separate action against the estate that originally was brought against the debtor. To do this, it is necessary to wait for the estate trustee to be appointed.

Continuing an Existing Proceeding

If the creditor sued the debtor and the debtor died before judgment was obtained, the lawsuit is stayed until an estate trustee is in place. Then the creditor may obtain an order to proceed against the estate by transmission of interest to the estate under rule 11 of the *Rules of Civil Procedure*, which is obtained by a requisition (figure 12.1) in the court where the action was started requesting that the action be permitted to continue against the estate. The requisition must be supported by an affidavit (figure 12.2) that sets out the facts on which transmission of liability from the deceased to his estate is based. On the basis of these documents, an order (figure 12.3) will be made permitting the action to continue against "Mary Cashedin, Estate Trustee of William Cashedin." The plaintiff may now continue the action.

Commencing a Claim Against an Estate

Where your client has a claim against a debtor who has died, or a claim against the estate that became due after the debtor died, it is advisable to contact the estate trustee to see about having it paid (see the sample letter on page 360). If the claim is not paid, providing that an estate trustee has been appointed, it is possible to pursue the claim against the estate using a summary procedure under s. 44 of the *Estates Act* in the estates office of the Superior Court.

If you present a claim to an estate trustee and she declines to pay it but also declines to contest it, you must proceed in the ordinary way by suing the estate in the Superior

Payment of Creditors

The estate trustee, once satisfied that a debt is legitimate, must pay the creditor. The creditor will usually be required to sign a release of any further interest in the estate before the funds are released to him. In some cases, the estate may not have enough assets to pay all of its debts. If this is the case, the estate trustee must abate (reduce) inheritances to free up money to pay the creditors. Inheritances are usually abated in the following order:

1. The residue of the estate is abated. Residue is that part of the estate left over after all gifts have been paid.

2. General legacies are then abated. General legacies are non-specific gifts to a beneficiary; for example, "I give my wife $25,000."

3. Demonstrative legacies abate next. Demonstrative legacies are gifts where the source of the gift is set out in the will; for example, if you leave $10,000 from a certain account to your spouse.

4. Specific legacies abate last. A specific legacy is a particular gift to a beneficiary, such as a car.

Court. If the estate trustee declines to pay, she may issue a notice of contestation, which brings the summary procedure in the *Estates Act* into play. The creditor now has 30 days from receipt of the notice of contestation to file a statement of claim, although the creditor can apply for leave to the court for a further three months to file. An affidavit must be filed with the statement of claim, verifying the claim as well as a copy of the notice of contestation. When this is done, the matter is set down for trial without any further pretrial proceedings. At trial, the court may require all those with an interest in the outcome to be given notice of proceedings. This order will usually affect estate beneficiaries. If the beneficiaries are minors, notice may have to be given to the Children's Lawyer who may protect their interest.

If there is no estate trustee, a creditor may file a notice of the claim, verified by affidavit, in the estates office where the deceased resided. This will serve to give public notice to others of a claim against the estate.

An estate trustee has a choice about using the *Estates Act* summary procedure. If the claim is within Small Claims Court jurisdiction, it should proceed in that court in the ordinary way. The estate trustee may object, in which case the claim could proceed under the *Estates Act* procedure. However, any claim for more than $800 may, at the estate trustee's request, be brought in the Superior Court in the ordinary way, which would bring it under the rule 76 simplified procedure. There seems very little use in doing this, because rule 76 also provides for a summary procedure — unless you have a reason to opt out of the simplified procedure too.

If the creditor establishes his claim, he will require leave of the court to enforce the order against the estate. This can be done during or at the conclusion of the hearing so that leave to enforce can be included in the judgment. The judgment can then be filed in the court office in the county or regional municipality where the deceased resided or where he had property, to be enforced in the usual ways.

INSOLVENT ESTATES

If an estate's liabilities exceed its assets, the estate trustee should request leave of the court to file an assignment in bankruptcy. If not, all debtors share on a pro rata basis, regardless of the nature of the debt. Bankruptcy is likely to give the beneficiaries more protection from creditors than they would otherwise have if the estate is insolvent. A creditor may also petition an insolvent estate into bankruptcy. A debtor owing $75,000 or less may make a consumer proposal to deal with his or her debts. Leave of the court to have the proposal approved is required. However, if your client's claim is small and the estate is insolvent, it may be best to write the debt off.

CHAPTER SUMMARY

When a debtor dies, steps must be taken by a creditor to continue to try to collect the debt. The estate of the debtor is responsible for carrying out the obligations of the debtor. Court proceedings against the debtor must stop until an estate trustee takes charge of the estate. When that happens, the litigation can continue, naming the estate and its trustee, because the debtor is no longer personally a party to the proceeding. Who the estate trustee is depends on whether or not the debtor made a will. In some cases no representative comes forward. When this happens, someone with an interest in the estate must apply to represent it. In some cases, a debtor may also apply to have a representative appointed for the sole purpose of completing litigation already under way against the debtor. If a claim is made against an estate, it may be the continuation of an existing proceeding, in which case you need to take steps to replace the name of the debtor with that of the estate trustee. There are other considerations if you are commencing proceedings against an estate. Last, if the estate is insolvent, consider whether litigation against the estate is either worthwhile or possible.

KEY TERMS

certificate of appointment of estate
   trustee with a will

certificate of appointment of estate
   trustee without a will

estate trustee

estate trustee during litigation

intestate, intestacy

testamentary trust

testator

NOTES

1. In the 1990s, the NDP government in Ontario tripled the rate of probate fees for estates valued at over $50,000. The rate for assets above $50,000 went from $5 per $1,000 of value to $15 per $1,000 of value. To reduce probate fees, the practice of preparing split wills for large estates was developed. This practice was challenged in the courts. The Ontario Court

of Appeal ruled that the practice was a valid one and that the government, having tripled fees, could not bar people from using split wills to minimize fees.

2. An estate trustee who is also the sole beneficiary of the estate will usually not advertise for creditors. Although the ad would absolve the estate trustee from liability to unknown creditors, she would still be liable in her capacity as beneficiary.

REFERENCES

Estates Act, RSO 1990, c. E.21.

Rules of Civil Procedure, RRO 1990, reg. 194.

Succession Law Reform Act, RSO 1990, c. S.26.

REVIEW QUESTIONS

1. Your client has come to you with the news that a debtor who owes her money has just died. Your client wonders if this will cause any problems. Explain to your client what the consequences of the debtor's death might be.

2. Explain what needs to be done before an estate trustee can act where

   a. the debtor died without leaving a will;

   b. the debtor died leaving a will; and

   c. the debtor died leaving a will, but there is a dispute about its validity.

3. How do you know if an estate has an estate trustee?

4. What are the duties of an estate trustee?

5. How does an estate trustee protect herself from personal liability on claims from creditors of the estate?

6. In what circumstances is an estate trustee during litigation appointed?

7. Explain how an order for transmission of interest to an estate is obtained.

8. If your client has a claim against an estate but has not commenced proceedings, what options does the client have in pursuing the claim?

9. What options does your client have as creditor of an estate in which the liabilities are greater than the assets?

CASE STUDY

M E M O

DATE: April 15, year 0

TO: Litigation Clerk

FROM: U.R. Ruffled

RE: Snorkelpus Investments Ltd. v. Deer-Lee Departed

Our client Snorkelpus started an action against Deer-Lee Departed for failure to repay a personal loan in the amount of $33,000. The loan was due on August 4, year −1 and has not been paid off. We commenced proceedings in the Superior Court on September 3, year −1. Deer-Lee Departed died on November 3, year −1, having filed a statement of defence. We have determined that the deceased did not have a will and that Deer-Lee's husband, Dogpart Departed, applied for and obtained a certificate of appointment of estate trustee without a will, on December 3, year −1, from the Superior Court offices at Toronto.

Draft the necessary documents to obtain an order of transmission of interest to the estate.

Figure 12.1   Sample Requisition for an Order to Continue Proceeding Against an Estate

Court file no. 4567

ONTARIO
SUPERIOR COURT OF JUSTICE

B E T W E E N

TRIPLE Q FINANCE LTD.

Plaintiff

and

WILLIAM CASHEDIN

Defendant

REQUISITION

TO THE LOCAL REGISTRAR at Toronto

I REQUIRE

An order to continue this proceeding originally commenced in this court, amending the title of proceedings to "Triple Q Finance Ltd." as plaintiff and "Mary Cashedin, estate trustee of the Estate of William Cashedin," as defendant.

THE GROUNDS FOR THIS REQUISITION ARE:

1. The affidavit of Filbert Fooey, sworn February 25, year 0.

2. The certificate of appointment of estate trustee with a will issued by the registrar of this court on December 10, year –1 appointing Mary Cashedin as the estate trustee with a will of the estate of William Cashedin.

3. Rule 11.02 of the *Rules of Civil Procedure*.

February 27, year 0

Filbert Fooey LSUC #66591F
FOOEY, ARGENT
Barristers and Solicitors
43 Cutpurse Road
Toronto, ON M4R 1D6
416-223-4567
fax 416-223-4566
Lawyers for the Plaintiff

Figure 12.2   Sample Affidavit Verifying Transmission of Interest to Estate

Court file no. 4567

ONTARIO

SUPERIOR COURT OF JUSTICE

BETWEEN

TRIPLE Q FINANCE LTD.

Plaintiff

and

WILLIAM CASHEDIN

Defendant

AFFIDAVIT

I, Filbert Fooey, of the City of Toronto, MAKE OATH AND SAY:

1. I am a partner in the law firm of Fooey, Argent, solicitors for the plaintiff in this action, and have knowledge of the matters set out in this affidavit.

2. On November 3, year –1, on the instructions of the plaintiff, our firm commenced proceedings against the defendant, now deceased, for payment on a promissory note.

3. On November 15, year –1 the defendant died.

4. On December 10, year –1, the certificate of appointment of estate trustee with a will was issued by the registrar of this court confirming Mary Cashedin as the estate trustee of the Estate of William Cashedin. Attached to this affidavit and marked exhibit "A" is a true copy of the certificate issued by the court.

5. The lawyers for the plaintiff now request that the local registrar grant an order permitting this proceeding to continue and naming Mary Cashedin, estate trustee of the estate of William Cashedin, as defendant.

SWORN before me in the	)
	)
City of Toronto,	)
	)
this 25th day of February, year 0	) Filbert Fooey
	)
	)
A commissioner, etc.	)

Figure 12.3 Sample Transmission Order Transferring Liability to Estate

Court file no. 4567

ONTARIO
SUPERIOR COURT OF JUSTICE

B E T W E E N

TRIPLE Q FINANCE LTD.

Plaintiff

and

WILLIAM CASHEDIN

Defendant

ORDER

ON THE REQUISITION of the plaintiff and on reading the affidavit of Filbert Fooey, sworn February 25, year 0, filed, and on reading the certificate appointing Mary Cashedin as estate trustee with a will, dated December 10, year –1,

IT IS ORDERED that this proceeding continue with Triple Q Finance as plaintiff and Mary Cashedin, estate trustee of William Cashedin, as defendant, and that the title of proceeding be amended as noted in this order on all documents issued, served, or filed after the date of this order.

Dated: February 27, year 0.

_____

Local Registrar

CHAPTER 13

Construction Liens

RATIONALE AND BASIC PRINCIPLES

The *Construction Lien Act*[1] gives those persons whose work results in an improvement to real property a right to place a **lien** on that property for the value of the work done. If those doing work or furnishing materials are not paid, they can exercise their lien rights by forcing the sale of the property and obtaining their money from the sale proceeds. The Act also provides for a holdback system to ensure that there is a pool of funds from which to pay subcontractors, suppliers, and trade persons. The Act also provides a remedy for a breach of trust action. A breach of trust action does not require a registered lien and may be brought in Small Claims Court if the remedy is for $25,000 or less.

Legislation creating these rights has existed in Ontario since 1875. The rationale behind such legislation is that trades persons, labourers, and material suppliers normally would only have the right to sue the person they contracted with for breach of contract if they were not paid for the work done or the materials supplied. There would be no special right to attach the claim to the increased value of the real property that their efforts had improved. Other creditors who had priority rights — such as mortgagees — would have the right to seize the property to satisfy the debts owing to them, while those who had improved the value of the property would have to wait in line with other ordinary judgment creditors. By giving lien rights to those who improved the property, the legislation ensured that they would be able to secure payment by being able to claim directly on the value of the property they improved.

In addition to lien rights, the Act also provides for a summary construction lien trial process that is designed to be quick and inexpensive, to save workers and small trades persons the cost and delay of more formal legal proceedings.

The Act also contains provisions that allow a labourer — for example, one hired by a building contractor — to make a claim through the lien claim system against the landowner if the labourer is not paid, even though he has no contract with the landowner. Normally, the labourer would be bound by the common law rule about **privity of contract**, where the parties to a contract are the only ones who can sue for breach of that contract. If the privity rule applied, the labourer would only have the right to sue the contractor with whom he had privity of contract. He would have no claim against the owner of the property, even though that person had benefited from the work done by the labourer. The Act gives the labourer a right to directly lien the property that has

lien
a claim to a right to sell or seize property, either real or personal, on the fulfillment of certain conditions

privity of contract
a rule that only parties to a contract can enforce contract rights

been improved, in addition to rights against the contractor. This means that everyone involved in doing work on a large construction project will have lien rights, no matter how far they are contractually from the landowner.

Although the original legislation was designed to benefit small trades persons and labourers, it also applies to large projects where the players include large construction companies and contractors, large landowners, and large banks as lenders. The result is that, when a large project gets into trouble, hundreds of lien claims are filed, and the banks and lien claimants make conflicting claims about which parties' claims have priority. Scores of lawyers become involved, and a construction lien action becomes horrendously complicated and expensive. What was originally designed to be a simple, non-technical, summary process becomes more complicated and difficult to manage than an ordinary civil action in the Superior Court.

THE CONSTRUCTION PYRAMID

The operation of the Act can best be understood by thinking of a construction project as a pyramid, with the owner at the top, the contractor with whom he has a building contract under him (the general contractor), the subcontractors under the general contractor, and subcontractors of subcontractors further down, and so on. Each level of contractual relations represents a class of claimants. As you go further down the contractual chain from the owner you have more and more class members as the classes become larger, which gives the contractual linkages and relationships a pyramid shape, as in the box on the facing page.

You will see some other things in the construction pyramid that require explanation. First you will notice that each class, or layer, shares the same class of payers — in the box on the facing page, the class of subcontractors is paying the class of workers. Subcontractors include persons who supply services or materials to improve the property. Improvement is defined in the Act to mean:

> (a) any alteration, addition or repair to the land,
> (b) any construction, erection or installation on the land, including the installation of industrial, mechanical, electrical or other equipment on the land or on any building, structure, or works on the land that is essential to the normal or intended use of the land, building, structure or works, or
> (c) the complete or partial demolition or removal of any building, structure, or works on the land; …[2]

What defines the class relationship is that there is privity of contract between the classes. You will also notice another relationship illustrated — that is, the general contractor, in paying the subcontractor class, holds back 10 percent of the amount due until all liens that may be claimed have expired, or have been satisfied, discharged, or vacated (see s. 26 of the Act). Lien claimants generally have 45 days from the date that they completed their work or last supplied materials to make a claim for lien. A payer holds back 10 percent for those who are two steps or classes below him on the construction pyramid. This is illustrated in the box on page 373.

The holdback is mandatory; parties to construction contracts are not allowed to waive holdback rights (see s. 22(1) of the Act). Any agreement to waive such rights is illegal and unenforceable in the courts. The box on page 374 provides an example to

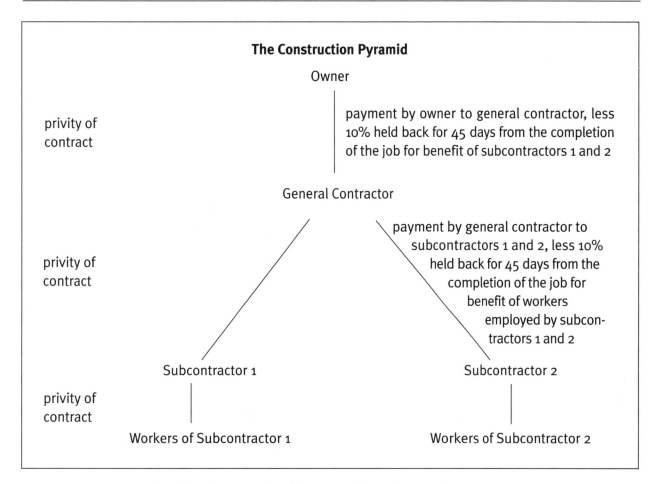

The Construction Pyramid

Owner

privity of
contract

payment by owner to general contractor, less
10% held back for 45 days from the completion
of the job for benefit of subcontractors 1 and 2

General Contractor

privity of
contract

payment by general contractor to
subcontractors 1 and 2, less 10%
held back for 45 days from the
completion of the job for
benefit of workers
employed by subcon-
tractors 1 and 2

Subcontractor 1

Subcontractor 2

privity of
contract

Workers of Subcontractor 1

Workers of Subcontractor 2

show how the holdback works. When the owner pays the $10,000 that is due to the general contractor, he must hold back 10 percent, or $1,000, from the payment. He holds this money in trust for the subcontractors two steps below him. If they are not paid within a short period of time by the general contractor, they must register a claim for lien against the property, and they must do so within 45 days of the last work done or materials furnished. If no claim is made within the 45-day period, then the holdback moneys may be released, in this case by the owner to the general contractor. In a large project, a contract supervisor, usually an engineering firm, is required by the Act to function as a payment certifier and give notice of the payment in construction trade newspapers, in which case those with lien rights have 45 days from publication of the notice to register their liens. When an owner receives a notice of lien, either by searching the property's title or by receiving notice of the lien directly, he will make the holdback available to the lien claimants. If he does this, the lien claimants must take their claim out of the holdback, the owner is discharged from any further obligation, and the liens are vacated and cease to be a claim on the land. If the holdback is insufficient to fully compensate the lien claimant, he may continue with a court action for the shortfall against the person with whom he has a contract.

If the owner failed to retain the holdback, or retained it but did not observe the trust requirements and spent it on something else, then the lien holders may enforce their lien rights against the land and force its sale. On both large and small projects, the failure to retain a holdback or make payments on the principal contract occurs from time to time. Many construction projects, particularly large ones, are financed by banks

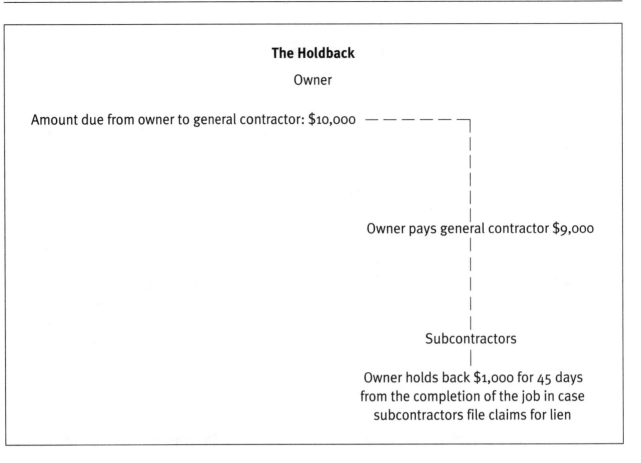

The Holdback

Owner

Amount due from owner to general contractor: $10,000

Owner pays general contractor $9,000

Subcontractors

Owner holds back $1,000 for 45 days from the completion of the job in case subcontractors file claims for lien

and other financial institutions. On a large project, the lender will give a building mortgage where the amount loaned is paid out in installments as stages of the construction are completed rather than in one payment of the total amount. When the owner receives an installment at the completion of a stage of the project (called a progress draw), he pays his general contractor, who in turn uses the money to pay her subcontractors, and so on down the pyramid. In effect, everyone is relying on the bank to provide the cash to keep the project going. If one contractor in the chain of contracts defaults on payments, a flurry of liens may be registered. This, in turn, may cause the bank to suspend further payments, triggering yet more liens from other classes of lien claimants and bringing the project to a halt. Disputes may also arise about who among claimants and the bank has priority for eventual payout if the building is sold in a lien action, further complicating matters. On smaller projects, a payer with a cash flow problem who is late or who defaults on paying his workers may trigger lien claims and bring the project to a halt.

Because of the legislation's intention to create a simple and quick remedy for trades persons and construction workers, the Act allows a person authorized under the *Law Society Act* to represent a lien claimant where the monetary value of the claim is within the monetary jurisdiction of the Small Claims Court (see s. 67(5) of the Act). However, the Act requires that the action must be brought in the Superior Court. This is one of the few times an agent can appear in this court as an advocate.

You should be aware that construction lien litigation is specialized work; involvement in a complex construction lien case is something that most lawyers refer to those firms that are experienced in this kind of work. The fact that a paralegal may act in any claim that comes within the Small Claims Court jurisdiction does not guarantee that such a claim will be simple. For example, if your client is one of thousands in a complex construction lien proceeding, you will need more specialized knowledge than can be conveyed here. It is important for an agent not to take on work that is beyond the agent's knowledge or experience. However, it is not inappropriate for an agent to take on simpler claim proceedings — for example, where a homeowner hires a contractor to carry out home renovations. In such a case, there are likely to be only a few potential classes of lien claimants, and only a few claimants within those classes.[3] The discussion of the lien claim procedure that follows will be based on the following illustration of a relatively simple lien claim case.

A SIMPLE CONSTRUCTION CLAIM

Hi Volt Electrical Ltd. (Hi Volt) is an electrical contractor. Hi Volt was retained by Nicholas Construction Ltd. (Nicholas) to do the electrical work on a small office building owned by Real Land Inc. The building is located at 328 Banburn Drive, Toronto, ON M6R 3Y6. On May 5, year 0, Hi Volt entered into a contract with Nicholas to do the electrical work. The contract price was $7,500 and payments were to be made in installments of $2,500 on September 1, October 1, and November 1, year 0. Hi Volt began work, supplying materials and labour from June 1, year 0 to September 2, year 0. When Hi Volt was not paid on September 1, it decided to stop work on September 2. On September 20, Hi Volt registered a claim for lien; on September 22, Hi Volt made a written demand to Real Land for payment. Having received no reply from either Real Land or Nicholas, Hi Volt wishes to exercise its lien rights and sell the land.

Description of the Lien

Because Hi Volt has supplied materials and labour to improve the property, it is entitled to claim a lien against the property for the value of the work done. It is also entitled to claim all of its contract remedies against Nicholas with whom it has privity. If Real Land had kept a holdback on payments to Nicholas, Hi Volt would share in the holdback on a pro rata basis with other lien claimants who also had Nicholas as a payer and who had privity of contract with Nicholas.

Who May File a Lien?

Anyone who furnishes materials, services, or labour to improve a particular property may file a lien. This includes contractors, subcontractors, employees of contractors and subcontractors, material suppliers, equipment renters, engineers, and design professionals, including architects. Thus, Hi Volt can file a lien as a supplier of materials and services, and Hi Volt's employees, suppliers, and equipment renters on this job could file liens if Hi Volt failed to pay them.

What May Be Liened?

If a supplier of materials or services supplies them for use on an identifiable property and can prove their incorporation or use on that property, then a lien may attach to the owner's interest. Here, Hi Volt has supplied electrical contracting services that improve the value of the building on the property, so the owner's interest in the property can be liened. Note that if the lien arises after a mortgage, the lien claim may be made only against the **owner's equity** that remains after the mortgage loan has been paid off. Also, the lien claim is limited to the value of the improvements, not the price of the contract. Hi Volt, for example, has a $7,500 contract, but had only done $2,500 worth of work before it abandoned the contract because of nonpayment. Its lien claim will be limited to $2,500 against the property because that is probably the value of its improvement (although it may argue it did work valued at more than the first progress payment; on the other hand, Real Land may argue that Hi Volt did far less than $2,500 worth of work). Hi Volt's dispute with Nicholas, however, may well be for more than the $2,500 that was due — there is the loss to Hi Volt of the profit had the contract been completed and other losses associated with the breach of contract that would be available to Hi Volt in its claim against Nicholas.

owner's equity
refers to how much of a property's value is actually that of the owner's—for example, if a house is worth $100,000 and is mortgaged for $50,000, the mortgagee is entitled to $50,000 to cover what is owing by the owner on the mortgage loan; the remaining $50,000 is free and clear of the mortgage claim and is the owner's equity in the house

Holdbacks

As noted, the owner, and any other payer in the pyramid, must hold back 10 percent of any payment made for the benefit of those who have privity of contract with the recipient of the payment. The holdback should only be released if there are no lien claims on title and the time for any other lien claims to be made has passed. The time period for the holdback is generally 45 days after the work has been completed or the materials have been supplied. The person maintaining the holdback is only liable up to the amount of the holdback, and all those claiming against the holdback claim on a pro rata basis from the holdback amount. Here, Real Land was obliged to hold back 10 percent of any payment it made to Nicholas, and Hi Volt has a right to claim against the holdback by making a written demand for payment on the holdback within the 45-day period that it has to register a claim for lien. In effect, the lien claimant who has privity with the owner actually claims against land; the others, who do not have privity with the owner, such as subcontractors, claim against the holdback. Note that if the defaulting party is a subcontractor, the owner is only personally liable to those below the subcontractor for an amount equal to the lesser of their own holdback or the defaulter's holdback amount (see s. 23(3) of the Act).

Breach of Trust

Under s. 13 of the Act, a director, officer, employee, or agent of a corporation who assents to or acquiesces in conduct that he knows or reasonably ought to know amounts to breach of trust by the corporation may be liable for the breach of trust. If, for example, a subcontractor is paid funds by the general contractor for work done and fails to set up the required holdback or pass on payment to a materials supplier, the supplier can argue breach of trust for a misappropriation of funds by the subcontractor while acting in a fiduciary capacity. Breach of trust cases for $25,000 or less can be brought in the Small Claims Court.

As a lien is not required for a breach of trust claim, such a claim is often brought when the time to register a lien has been missed.

Registration of a Claim for Lien

When Hi Volt decides to enforce its lien, you should do the following:

1. *Interview the client:* Interview the client as soon as possible. Remember, you are up against a time limit. Potential lien claimants are often reluctant to register lien claims because they may want to maintain a working business relationship for the future and do not want to jeopardize it by appearing to be adversarial. Consequently, they may not give you instructions until the 45-day period is almost up.

2. *Obtain information for the lien claim:* The following information should be obtained in order to draft the claim:

   - the name, address, and phone number of the client — this information should be verified by the provision of photo identification from the client; if the client is a corporation, the proper corporate name should be obtained and a corporate search carried out to ensure that the corporation has not been dissolved;

   - the name, address, and phone number of the party with whom the client is contracting;

   - the name, address, and phone number of the property owner;

   - the name, address, and phone number of the general contractor;

   - the name, address, and phone number of the architect/payment certifier (if any);

   - the name, address, and phone number of the lender/bank;

   - the name, address, and phone number of subcontractors and others in the client's class;

   - a description of work done and/or materials furnished;

   - the time period in which the work was done and the date of the last work/ materials supplied;

   - the contract and the payment particulars — invoices, statement of accounts (including information on receivables), and calculation of amount due and owing — do not include interest (this is prohibited under s. 14(2) of the Act);

   - the location and the legal description of the property, including lot and plan number, property identification number assigned, municipal address, identification of owners, and type of interest being liened (leasehold, joint tenancy, tenancy in common, or freehold);

   - a title subsearch to verify the legal description and address of the property, owner, mortgagees, and other lien holders; and

   - an execution search against the registered owner to discover any competing claims for the land (for details on how to conduct an execution search, see chapter 3).

Note that the Act itself acknowledges that in some cases information is needed from the defendant in order to complete a claim. The plaintiff may use s. 39 of the Act to request information from the defendant.

3. *Draft the claim for lien:* Prepare a claim for lien (figure 13.1) suitable for registration.[4] (In order to determine where to register the land, you need to know the municipality. As creditors often will not know the lot and plan numbers, you may find this out by inputting the street address into the Teraview electronic search and registration software system.) Lot and plan numbers are required for registration of the lien, although you may use a property identification number if one has been given. If a building does not yet have a street address (as in a new subdivision) you may have to check the **white prints** in the relevant registry office, which will show plans of new subdivisions. It is very important that you have the legal description for registration accurately identified because if you do not register the claim for lien on the right property before the 45-day period is up, the lien rights will be lost and you will have to sue the debtor in the ordinary course.

4. *In the claim for lien you must include:*

   - the name and address of the owner and, if they are different, the person for whom the materials or services were supplied — if the owner or recipient is a corporation, you should carry out a search for the proper corporate name to use (information on conducting corporate searches can be found in chapter 3);

   - the name and address of the lien claimant;

   - a brief description of the work done or materials furnished;

   - the contract price;

   - the amount claimed (be careful not to exaggerate the amount to be claimed because there are cost consequences for exaggerating the size of a claim); and

   - a description of the property that includes the municipal or street address, lot and plan numbers, and/or property identification number, if any.

5. *Preserve the lien:* Once you have completed the claim for lien, it must be preserved. In most cases, the lien is preserved by registering it on title to the property. A lien that does not attach to the land, such as a lien on a municipal road, is preserved by service of the claim for lien on the defendant. For the majority of liens that are registered on title, registration can be done electronically using Teraview. In order to preserve the lien, registration must take place within 45 days after the work was completed or materials were last supplied. In our example, provided that you registered the claim for lien on the right property and did so within the 45-day period, you will have preserved Hi Volt's lien.

6. *Perfect the lien:* Once the lien has been preserved, it must then be perfected. To do this, commence a court action in the Superior Court office for the region or county where the property is located. The lien claimant must draft,

white prints
large maps of subdivisions that are kept in a file of subdivisions and that show all of the lots in the subdivision; the white print will usually show an existing street or other identifiable landmark at the edge of the subdivision that will allow one to identify and locate a particular property, identified as a lot on the plan

issue, and serve an ordinary statement of claim (figure 13.2), together with Form 14F, Information for Court Use (an example of Form 14F can be found in chapter 5 on pages 106 and 107). The defendants will be Real Land, as landowner, and Nicholas Construction, as the party directly liable on the contract for payment. The statement of claim must be issued prior to the end of the 45-day period next following the last day for preservation (see s. 36(2) of the Act). Many lawyers make it a practice to issue the claim within 45 days of the date of preservation even if they preserved the lien on a date less than 45 days after the completion of the work. In some cases a lien can be perfected by sheltering under a certificate of action registered by another lien claimant. Sheltering is a complex matter beyond the scope of this text. A text on construction liens procedure should be consulted for more information. Because a missed deadline can be fatal to the lien claim, it is better to err on the side of caution when preserving and perfecting a lien. After the claim has been issued, you must obtain a certificate of action (figure 13.3) from the Registrar of the court. The certificate is proof that the claim has been issued. The certificate of action must then be registered on title. Again, this can usually be filed electronically using Teraview. This provides notice to the public that the lien claim has been perfected. You have 90 days from the time it is issued to serve the statement of claim. The defendants may serve a statement of defence within 20 days of service of the statement of claim.

7. *Discovery:* There is not an automatic right to an examination for discovery or to the production of documents. A motion must be brought if discoveries are sought. Note that motions are only permitted with the consent of the court. The motion must be for necessary relief or to provide for an order that would expedite the case (see s. 67(2) of the Act). An examination may allow you to obtain information that may allow a lien to be vacated on a reduced amount of security. An examination may reveal an irregularity that might facilitate the discharge of a lien. An examination may also help to establish the actual date that work was completed, and in some cases a defendant could discover that a lien claimant is out of time with respect to the lien.

8. *Set the lien claim down for trial within two years:* A claim for lien matter must be set down for trial within two years from the date upon which the statement of claim was issued. An order fixing a trial date must be obtained within that time period.[5] A notice of trial must then be served on all parties and an affidavit of service filed with the court. If the matter is not set down for trial within this time, the claim for lien expires (see s. 37(1) of the Act). The action will now be tried by a judge in the Superior Court; in Toronto, the plaintiff may bring a motion directing a reference for trial under s. 58 of the Act to have the action heard by a master who will conduct the trial and give judgment in the form of a report to be confirmed by a judge. A sample judgment directing a reference for trial can be found in figure 13.4. In either case, the first day of a complex matter will be devoted to settlement discussions and sorting out and proving claims. In a straightforward case, the matter will simply be tried like any other civil case. As with other types of cases, the parties may agree to mediation or arbitration to resolve their case. There are mediators and arbitrators who specialize in construction lien

litigation. The website of the Canadian College of Construction Lawyers at
http://www.cccl.org maintains a list of experienced mediators and arbitrators.
With a settlement in the plaintiff's favour, the plaintiff will want to ensure
that the settlement moneys are paid. The defendant will want to ensure that
the lien is discharged, the registration of the claim for lien and the certificate
of action are vacated, and the court action is dismissed.

Vacating, Postponing, or Discharging Liens

In response to a lien claim, a defendant can serve and file a statement of defence, leaving
the lien in place until the matter is resolved. However, in some circumstances, a defendant will need to have the lien vacated from title in order to deal with the property. If, for
example, the defendant is trying to sell his home and a claim for lien is registered on
title, the claim must be removed from the title before the property can be transferred.
The Act provides that any lien can be vacated by court order, made without notice to the
plaintiff, if the defendant pays into court a sum equal to the amount of the lien claim
plus the lesser of $50,000 or 25 percent of the amount of the lien claimed in order to
secure costs (see Part VII of the Act). The plaintiff shall provide the court with a motion
record including an affidavit setting out the details as to how the amount of security to
be paid into court has been determined. A draft order should be given to the court along
with a certified copy of the lien. A sample draft order to vacate a lien upon posting security with the court can be found in figure 13.5. In some areas, the local court also
requires a copy of a title subsearch. The practitioner should consult with their local
court office to determine the local practice.[6] Payment can be made by certified cheque
payable to the Accountant of the Superior Court of Justice or by posting security, such
as a letter of credit, with the court. A motion may be brought to reduce the amount of
security to be posted. When a lien is vacated, the lien claim is still preserved and the
matter will continue to be before the courts.

   In some cases, both parties will agree to postpone a lien claim. For example, if a
mortgage advance cannot be made with the lien on title, the parties may agree to postpone the lien claim so that funds can be advanced, with the lien claim being restored
after the funds have been advanced.

   If a lien claim has expired because it was not preserved or perfected in time, a declaration can be sought from the court that the lien has expired. A sample order declaring
that a lien has expired can be found in figure 13.6.

   If the claim for lien is settled on consent, the plaintiff or the defendant may make a
motion to the court for an order to have the lien discharged from title. In addition to
the discharge of the claim for lien from title, the minutes and the court order should
also deal with the discharge of the registration of the certificate of action and dismissal
of the action itself. A sample order discharging a lien on consent can be found in
figure 13.7.

CHAPTER SUMMARY

In chapter 13 we introduce the principles underlying the *Construction Lien Act*: that
those who provide improvements to property are entitled to file a lien claim against an
owner for the value of the improvement if they are not paid for work done or materials

furnished, even when they have no privity of contract with the owner. The chapter goes on to examine the "construction pyramid" and the requirements for holdback on payments. We then present a typical simple lien claim, noting that paralegals may act on a lien claim if it is within the monetary jurisdiction of the Small Claims Court, even though the action is in the Superior Court. We note who may file a lien, what they may file the lien on, how the holdback system works, how a claim for lien is drafted and registered on title, how a statement of claim is prepared and filed, and how a certificate of action is registered on title. The chapter concludes with a discussion of situations where a lien may be vacated, postponed, or discharged.

KEY TERMS

lien

owner's equity

privity of contract

white prints

NOTES

1. *Construction Lien Act*, RSO 1990, c. C.30, as amended.

2. *Ibid.*, s. 1(1).

3. *Conduct of a Lien Action* by Duncan W. Glaholt (Toronto: Thomson Carswell, 2011) is recommended as an excellent source of procedural tips for lien claims, particularly for those made in the Toronto court.

4. If the lien and the certificate of action are being registered in the registry system, these documents have to be attached to a document general. In this example, the claim is being registered in the land titles registry system. For more information on the mechanics of registration, see JoAnn Kurtz, Joan Emmans, and Arlene Blatt, *Residential Real Estate Transactions*, 3rd Edition (Toronto: Emond Montgomery, 2009).

5. See *310 Waste v. Casboro Industries Ltd.* (2006), 83 OR (3d) 314 (CA) for a court decision upholding the dismissal of a claim for lien action where the plaintiff failed to set the claim down for trial within the mandatory two-year period. The court found that the lien claim had expired.

6. For Toronto court procedures on construction liens, Duncan Glaholt's book, *Conduct of a Lien Action*, supra note 3, is an excellent reference.

REFERENCES

Construction Lien Act, RSO 1990, c. C.30, as amended.

Kurtz, JoAnn, Joan Emmans, and Arlene Blatt, *Residential Real Estate Transactions*, 3rd Edition (Toronto: Emond Montgomery, 2009).

Law Society Act, RSO 1990, c. L.8, as amended.

REVIEW QUESTIONS

1. What are the principal features of the *Construction Lien Act* that are beneficial to suppliers of materials and services that improve property?

2. Describe the construction pyramid in terms of the relationships, rights, and remedies among those that make up the pyramid.

3. What defines a class of claimants under the Act?

4. Describe what a holdback is and how it works.

5. When might it be useful to bring a breach of trust claim?

6. Under what circumstances may a paralegal represent a lien claimant?

7. Under what circumstances *should* a paralegal represent a lien claimant?

8. Who may file a lien?

9. On what property can a lien be filed?

10. Will the amount in the claim for a lien against the owner be the same as the amount claimed against the payer with whom the lienor had privity of contract? Explain.

11. When registering a claim for lien, speed is important. Explain why that is the case.

12. What information do you need about the property in order to register a claim for a lien?

13. How do you preserve and perfect a lien?

14. How does the trial process on lien claims in Toronto differ from the lien claim trial process in other parts of the province?

15. What is the time limit for setting a lien claim down for trial?

16. Explain how a defendant in a lien claim can have a lien claim removed from title prior to trial.

CASE STUDY

**Belsize Nappy
Barrister & Solicitor
504 - 365 Bay Street
Toronto, ON M6W 13Y**

tel.: 416-557-1234

MEMO

DATE: January 6, year 0

TO: Morris Clerk

FROM: Belsize Nappy

RE: Construction Lien Claim — Bumble Construction

Our client, Bumble Construction Ltd., had a contract to renovate the kitchen and bathroom of a house owned by Peter Pugnani at 345 Scarlatti Street, Toronto, ON M4R 1D3. The contract was entered into on May 1, year −1 for the amount of $5,500. Our client started work on May 15, year −1. The work was finally completed on December 20, year −1. Pugnani had paid $2,000 when work started but has paid nothing since. Our client's foreman came by on December 22 to pick up the balance and was told to come back after the holidays. Our client doesn't like the smell of this and wants us to lien the property. The results of a title search show that the property is located on part of Lot 68, Plan M-53, city of Toronto, and is registered in the Land Titles Division of Toronto (no. 66).

Prepare the necessary documents to preserve and perfect the lien.

Figure 13.1   Claim for Lien (Form 8)

FORM 8

CLAIM FOR LIEN UNDER SECTION 34 OF THE ACT

Construction Lien Act

Name of lien claimant: ... Hi Volt Electrical Ltd.
c/o James Snorglepus

Address for service: ..... 1234 Bay Street, Toronto, ON M6P 1R2

Name of owner: .... Real Land Inc.

Address: .... c/o Banburn Drive, Toronto, ON M6R 1Y6

Name of person to whom lien claimant supplied services or materials: ....

.... Nicholas Construction Ltd.

Address: .... 2801 Western Road, Brantford ON N7A 3C2

Time within which services or materials were supplied:

from .... June 1, year 0 .... to .... September 2, year 0 ....
(date supply commenced) .... *(date of most recent supply)*

Short description of services or materials that have been supplied:

..... electrical services and materials at 328 Banburn Drive, Toronto, ON M6R 1Y6

Contract price or subcontract price: .... $ .7,500 ...

Amount claimed as owing in respect of services or materials that have been supplied: .... $ .2,500 ...

(Use A where the lien attaches to the premises; use B where the lien does not attach to the premises).

A. The lien claimant *(if claimant is personal representative or assignee this must be stated)* claims a lien against the interest of every person identified above as an owner of the premises described in Schedule A to this claim for lien.

B. ~~The lien claimant *(if claimant is personal representative or assignee this must be stated)* claims a charge against the holdbacks required to be retained under the Act and any additional amount owed by a payer to the contractor or to any subcontractor whose contract or subcontract was in whole or in part performed by the services or materials that have been supplied by the lien claimant in relation to the premises at:~~

....
(address or other identification of the location of the premises)

Date: .. September 20, year 0 .... Hi Volt Electrical Ltd. ......
                                                         (signature of claimant or agent)
                                                         per H. Ampere, President

Figure 13.1   Continued

Construction Lien Act

SCHEDULE A

To the claim for lien of   Hi Volt Electrical Ltd. ....

Description of premises:

(Where the lien attaches to the premises, provide a description of the premises sufficient for registration under the Land Titles Act or the Registry Act, as the case may be).

parts of lot 68, plan M-59 in the Land Titles Division of the City of Toronto, no. 66

Figure 13.1   Concluded

HI VOLT ELECTRICAL LTD.

v.

REAL LAND INC.

and

NICHOLAS CONSTRUCTION LTD.

Construction Lien Act
CLAIM FOR LIEN

JAMES Q. SNORGLEPUS   LSUC #81021S
1234 Bay Street
Toronto, ON M6P 1R2
416-456-7890
FAX 416-456-7891

Lawyer for the lien claimant

Figure 13.2   Statement of Claim

Court file no. 1831

ONTARIO

SUPERIOR COURT OF JUSTICE

B E T W E E N:

HI VOLT ELECTRICAL LTD.

Plaintiff

and

NICHOLAS CONSTRUCTION LTD. and REAL LAND INC.

Defendants

STATEMENT OF CLAIM

TO THE DEFENDANTS

A LEGAL PROCEEDING HAS BEEN COMMENCED AGAINST YOU by the plaintiff. The claim made against you is set out in the following pages.

IF YOU WISH TO DEFEND THIS PROCEEDING, you or an Ontario lawyer acting for you must prepare a statement of defence in Form 18A prescribed by the Rules of Civil Procedure, serve it on the plaintiff's lawyer or, where the plaintiff does not have a lawyer, serve it on the plaintiff, and file it, with proof of service, in this court office, WITHIN TWENTY DAYS after this statement of claim is served on you, if you are served in Ontario.

If you are served in another province or territory of Canada or in the United States of America, the period for serving and filing your statement of defence is forty days. If you are served outside Canada and the United States of America, the period is sixty days.

Instead of serving and filing a statement of defence, you may serve and file a notice of intent to defend in Form 18B prescribed by the Rules of Civil Procedure. This will entitle you to ten more days within which to serve and file your statement of defence.

IF YOU FAIL TO DEFEND THIS PROCEEDING, JUDGMENT MAY BE GIVEN AGAINST YOU IN YOUR ABSENCE AND WITHOUT FURTHER NOTICE TO YOU. IF YOU WISH TO DEFEND THIS PROCEEDING BUT ARE UNABLE TO PAY LEGAL FEES, LEGAL AID MAY BE AVAILABLE TO YOU BY CONTACTING A LOCAL LEGAL AID OFFICE.

IF YOU PAY THE PLAINTIFF'S CLAIM, and $500.00 for costs, within the time for serving and filing your statement of defence, you may move to have this proceeding dismissed by the court. If you believe the amount claimed for costs is excessive, you may pay the plaintiff's claim and $400 for costs and have the costs assessed by the court.

Date October 3, year 0   Issued by ....
                                              Local registrar

                                    Address of court office: 393 University Ave.
                                                              Toronto, ON M5G 1T4

TO: Nicholas Construction
     2801 Western Road
     Brantford, ON N7A 3C2

AND

TO: Real Land Inc.
     328 Banburn Drive
     Toronto, ON M6R 1Y6

Figure 13.2 Continued

~~THIS ACTION IS BROUGHT AGAINST YOU UNDER THE SIMPLIFIED PROCEDURE PROVIDED IN RULE 76 OF THE RULES OF CIVIL PROCEDURE.~~

CLAIM

1. The plaintiff claims:

   a. payment in the amount of $2,500 by the defendants for services and materials supplied under a building construction contract;

   b. payment by the defendant, Nicholas Construction Ltd., for general damages for loss of profit in the amount of $5,000;

   c. in the alternative, payments of the amount owing to the plaintiff in paragraph 1(a) from the holdback required to be maintained by the defendant Real Land Inc. pursuant to the *Construction Lien Act*, RSO 1990, c. C.30 as amended;

   d. in default of payment, that the interest of the defendant Real Land Inc., in the lands and premises located at 328 Banburn Drive in the City of Toronto, be sold pursuant to the provisions of the *Construction Lien Act*, and that amounts owing to the plaintiff be paid out of the proceeds of sale in accordance with the provisions of the *Construction Lien Act*;

   e. prejudgment and postjudgment interest;

   f. cost of the action; and

   g. such further relief as to this honourable court seems appropriate.

2. The plaintiff is a limited company, incorporated pursuant to the laws of Ontario, with its head office located in the City of Toronto. The plaintiff carries on business as an electrical contractor.

3. The defendant Nicholas Construction Ltd. (hereinafter referred to as "Nicholas") is a limited company, incorporated pursuant to the law of Ontario, with its head office located at Brantford, Ontario. Nicholas carries on business as a building contractor.

4. The defendant Real Land Inc. (hereinafter referred to as "Real Land") is a limited company, incorporated pursuant to the law of Quebec, and at all relevant times was the owner of lands and premises located at 328 Banburn Drive in the city of Toronto.

5. At times and places and on terms unknown to the plaintiff at the time of pleading, Real Land entered into an agreement with Nicholas to construct a building at 328 Banburn Drive. Full particulars of this agreement are not within the knowledge of the plaintiff but are within the knowledge of both defendants.

6. In furtherance of its obligations under the contract referred to in paragraph 5, Nicholas, on or about May 5, year 0, entered into a contract with the plaintiff whereby the plaintiff undertook to provide electrician services and materials for the building being constructed at 328 Banburn Rd. The contract price was $7,500 and payments were to be made in installments of $2,500 each on September 1, year 0, October 1, year 0, and November 1, year 0.

Figure 13.2   Continued

7. In accordance with this contract, the plaintiff provided materials and services from June 1, year 0 to September 2, year 0.

8. Nicholas failed to make the $2,500 payment due on September 1, year 0. As a result, the plaintiff ceased work under the contract on September 2, year 0.

9. The plaintiff has not been paid the amount due to it under the provisions of the contract and, as a result of Nicholas's breach, regards the contract as at an end. As a result of its performance of the contract, the plaintiff became entitled to a lien on the interest of Real Land in the lands and premises at 328 Banburn Drive.

10. On September 20, year 0, the plaintiff registered a claim for lien against the interest of Real Land in the lands and premises located at 328 Banburn Drive, as instrument number 60231 CT in the Land Titles Division of Toronto (no. 66). On September 22, year 0, the plaintiff, by notice in writing, demanded of Real Land that it make the contract payments owing to it by Nicholas out of the holdback required to be maintained under the provisions of the *Construction Lien Act*.

11. Real Land has refused or neglected to make such payments as required.

12. The plaintiff pleads and relies on the provisions of the *Construction Lien Act*, RSO 1990, c. C.30, as amended.

13. Because of the refusal or failure of Real Land to make such payments as are required under the Act, the plaintiff requests that Real Land's interest in the premises at 328 Banburn Drive be sold and that the proceeds of sale be used to satisfy the claim of the plaintiff in this action.

The Plaintiff proposes that this action be tried at: Toronto

DATED at Toronto   JAMES Q. SNORGLEPUS   LSUC #81021S
Oct. 2, year 0   1234 Bay Street, Toronto, ON M6P 1R2
                                             416-456-7890 FAX 416-456-7891
                                             Lawyer for the Plaintiff

RCP-E 14A (July 1, 2007)

Figure 13.2 Concluded

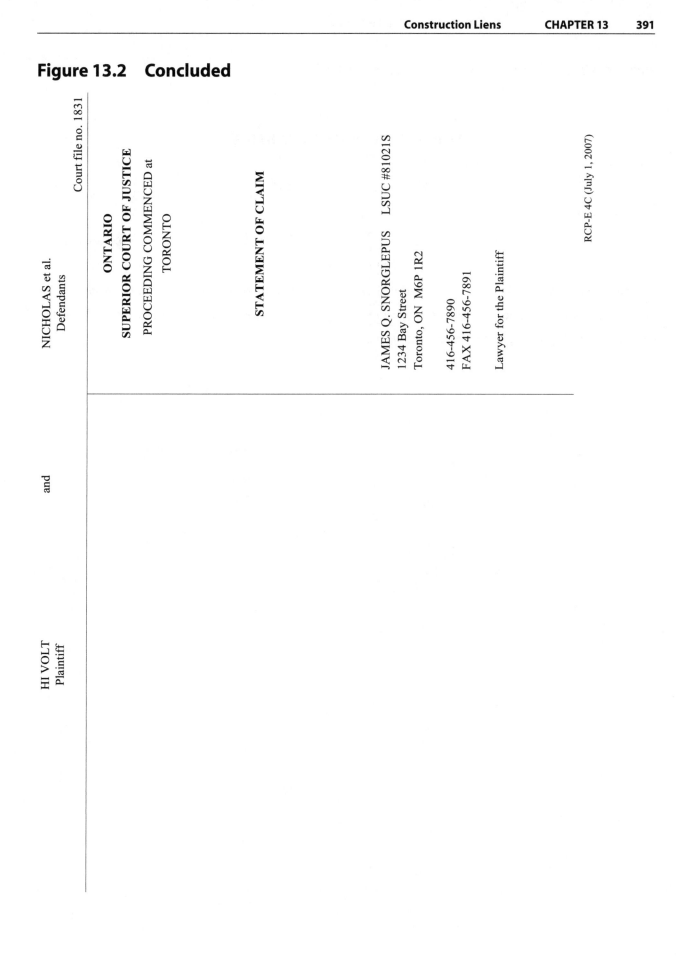

Figure 13.3   Certificate of Action (Form 10)

Court File No.

.... 1831 ....

ONTARIO

SUPERIOR COURT OF JUSTICE

BETWEEN

.... HI VOLT ELECTRICAL LTD. ....,   Plaintiff(s)

(court seal)   and

.... NICHOLAS CONSTRUCTION LTD. and REAL LAND INC. ....,   Defendant(s)

CERTIFICATE OF ACTION

I certify that an action has been commenced in the Ontario Superior Court of Justice under the *Construction Lien Act* between the above parties in respect of the premises described in Schedule A to this certificate, and relating to the the claim(s) for lien bearing the following registration numbers:

....

Date: ...., ...,

                                                        (registrar or local registrar)

Figure 13.3   Concluded

SCHEDULE A

Description of Premises:

(The description of the premises must be the same as in the statement of claim, and must be sufficient for registration under the Land Titles Act or Registry Act, as the case may be.)

Part of lot 68, Plan M-59 in the Land Titles Division of the City of Toronto, no. 66

Figure 13.4   Judgment Directing Reference for Trial Under s. 58 of Act (Form 16)

Court File No.

ONTARIO   1831

SUPERIOR COURT OF JUSTICE

JUSTICE _____   _____ day the ___ day
                                                   of _____, year 0
BETWEEN

(court seal)   HI VOLT ELECTRICAL LTD. .... **Plaintiff(s)**

                                                    and

                        NICHOLAS CONSTRUCTION LTD. and REAL LAND INC. .... **Defendant(s)**

JUDGMENT

On motion of the plaintiff made under subsection 58 (1) of the *Construction Lien Act* in the presence of counsel for the plaintiff(s) and the defendant(s), and on reading the pleadings in this action and on hearing what was alleged by counsel for the parties (*or the parties by their counsel consenting to judgment, or as the case may be*),

1. THIS COURT ORDERS AND ADJUDGES that this action be referred to the master at Toronto (*or other place*) for trial.

2. AND THIS COURT ORDERS AND ADJUDGES that the parties found liable forthwith after confirmation of the report of the master pay to the parties the respective amounts due them.

3. AND THIS COURT ORDERS AND ADJUDGES that the master determine all questions arising in this action and on the reference and all questions arising under the *Construction Lien Act* and that the findings of the master be effective on the confirmation of the report.

4. AND THIS COURT ORDERS AND ADJUDGES that the master determine the question of costs in this action and of the reference, and the costs be taxed and paid as the master shall direct.

Date: ....   Signed by: ....
                                                                        (judge)
                                                              (registrar or local registrar)

R.R.O. 1990, Reg. 175, Form 16

Figure 13.5 Order to Vacate Lien by Posting Security

<table>
<tr><td></td><td align="center">**ONTARIO**</td><td align="right">Court File No.
1831
. . . .</td></tr>
</table>

SUPERIOR COURT OF JUSTICE

JUSTICE _____

BETWEEN

_____day the ___ day
of _____, year 0

HI VOLT ELECTRICAL LTD.
. . . . Plaintiff(s)

(court seal)

and

NICHOLAS CONSTRUCTION LTD. and REAL LAND INC.
. . . . Defendant(s)

JUDGMENT

THIS MOTION made by the general contractor Nicholas Construction Ltd., without notice, pursuant to section 44(1) of the *Construction Lien Act*, RSO 1990, c. C.30, as amended, vacating the registration of the Claim for Lien of Hi Volt Electrical Ltd., registered against the title to the lands and premises described in Schedule "A" attached hereto, was heard this day at the Court House, 393 University Avenue, Toronto, Ontario.

ON READING a copy of the Claim for Lien of Hi Volt Electrical Ltd., the Parcel Register (Abbreviated) for Property Identifier 12345-6789 (LT), filed, and upon hearing submissions of counsel on behalf of the General Contractor, Nicholas Construction Ltd., and upon it appearing that the General Contractor, Nicholas Construction Ltd. having posted cash security in the amount of $3,125.00 with the Accountant of the *Ontario* Superior Court of Justice,

1. THIS COURT ORDERS that the amount of the security to be posted with the Accountant of the Ontario Superior Court of Justice by the General Contractor, Nicholas Construction Ltd., to vacate the registration of the Claim for Lien of Hi Volt Electrical Ltd., described in paragraph 2 herein, be the sum of $2,500.00, together with the sum of $625.00 as security for costs, for a total of $3,125.00.

2. THIS COURT ORDERS that the registration of the Claim for Lien of Hi Volt Electrical Ltd. dated September 20, year 0, in the amount of $2,500.00 and registered on September 20, year 0, as Instrument No. 987654, in the Land Registry Office for the Land Titles Division of the City of Toronto, against the title to the lands and premises described in Schedule "A" attached hereto be vacated.

3. THIS COURT ORDERS that this Order be entered forthwith.

4. THIS COURT ORDERS that a copy of this Order shall be served upon counsel for the Lien Claimant, Hi Volt Electrical Ltd., forthwith after entry.

Date: . . . .   Signed by: . . . .

(judge)
(registrar or local registrar)

Figure 13.5   Concluded

SCHEDULE A

Description of Premises:

Parts of lot 68, Plan M-59 in the Land Titles Division of the City of Toronto Land Registry No. 66.

Figure 13.6   Order Declaring Lien Expired

ONTARIO

SUPERIOR COURT OF JUSTICE

Court File No.
1831

JUSTICE _____

_____day the ___ day

BETWEEN

of _____, year 0

HI VOLT ELECTRICAL LTD. ....   Plaintiff(s)

(court seal)

and

NICHOLAS CONSTRUCTION LTD. and REAL LAND INC. ....   Defendant(s)

ORDER

THIS MOTION made by the Defendant, Nicholas Construction Ltd., without notice, for an Order, declaring expired the Claim for Lien of the Plaintiff, Hi Volt Electrical Ltd. (the Plaintiff), vacating the registration of the Claim for Lien of the Plaintiff, vacating the registration of the Certificate of the Plaintiff, and dismissing the within action, without costs, was heard this day at the Court House, 393 University Avenue, Toronto, Ontario.

ON READING the Notice of Motion, filed, the Affidavit of Brian Nicholas sworn November 30, year 0, and Exhibits thereto, filed, being *inter alia*, certified copies of the Claim for Lien of the Plaintiff, a certified copy of the Certificate for Action of the Plaintiff, a certified copy of the Abstract Index (Abbreviated for Property Identifier 12345-6789), and an Abstract of Title, all filed, and upon hearing submissions of counsel for the Defendant, Nicholas Construction Ltd.,

1. **THIS COURT DECLARES** that the lien of the Plaintiff, Hi Volt Electrical Ltd., dated September 20, year 0, in the amount of $2,500.00 and registered in the Land Registry Office for the Land Titles Division of the City of Toronto, against the title to the lands and premises described in Schedule "A" attached hereto is expired;

2. **THIS COURT ORDERS** that the registration of the Claim for Lien of the Plaintiff, Hi Volt Electrical Ltd., dated September 20, year 0, in the amount of $2,500.00 and registered on September 20, year 0, as Instrument No. 987654, in the Land Registry Office for the Land Titles Division of the City of Toronto, against the title to the lands and premises described in Schedule "A" attached hereto be vacated;

3. **THIS COURT ORDERS** that the registration of the Certificate of Action of the Plaintiff, Hi Volt Electrical Ltd., dated September 20, year 0, and registered on dated September 20, year 0 as Instrument No. 987654, in the Land Registry Office for the Land Titles Division of the City of Toronto, against the title to the lands and premises described in Schedule "A" attached hereto be vacated;

4. **THIS COURT ORDERS** that the within action be dismissed, without costs.

Date: ....

Signed by: ....

(judge)
(registrar or local registrar)

Figure 13.6   Concluded

SCHEDULE A

Description of Premises:

Parts of lot 68, Plan M-59 in the Land Titles Division of the City of Toronto Land Registry No. 66.

Figure 13.7   Order Vacating Claim for Lien and Discharging Construction Lien

ONTARIO

Court File No.
1831
. . . .

SUPERIOR COURT OF JUSTICE

JUSTICE _____

_____day the ___ day
of _____, year 0

BETWEEN

HI VOLT ELECTRICAL LTD.
. . . .   Plaintiff(s)

(court seal)

and

NICHOLAS CONSTRUCTION LTD. and REAL LAND INC.
. . . .   Defendant(s)

ORDER

THIS MOTION, made by the Plaintiff Hi Volt Electrical Ltd., for an Order vacating and discharging its Claim for Lien, vacating the registration of its Certificate of Action and dismissing the within action without costs, was heard this day at the Court House, 393 University Avenue, Toronto, Ontario.

ON READING the Notice of Motion, filed, the Affidavit of Henry Ampere sworn October 30, year 0, and Exhibits attached thereto, filed, and upon hearing the consent of the Plaintiff and the Consent of the Defendants, Nicholas Construction Ltd., filed, and upon being advised that the within action was discontinued as against the defendant, Nicholas Construction Ltd., on October 30, year 0 and upon hearing submissions of counsel for the Plaintiff, Hi Volt Electrical Ltd.,

1. **THIS COURT ORDERS** that the claim for lien of Hi Volt Electrical Ltd. in the amount of $2,500.00, registered on September 20, year 0 as Instrument No. 987654, in the Land Registry Office for the Land Titles Division of the City of Toronto, Ontario, against the title to the lands and premises described in Schedule "A" hereto, be vacated and the lien be discharged.

2. **THIS COURT ORDERS** that the Certificate of Action of Hi Volt Electrical Ltd., registered on September 20, year 0 as Instrument No. 987654, in the Land Registry Office for the Land Titles Division of the City of Toronto, Ontario, against the lands and premises set out in Schedule "A" hereto be vacated.

3. **THIS COURT ORDERS** that the within action be dismissed without costs.

Date: . . . .

Signed by: . . . .

(judge)
(registrar or local registrar)

Figure 13.7   Concluded

SCHEDULE A

Description of Premises:

Parts of lot 68, Plan M-59 in the Land Titles Division of the City of Toronto Land Registry No. 66.

Bankruptcy and Safeguards Against Fraud

Chapter 14 gives an overview of the rights and remedies available under the federal *Bankruptcy and Insolvency Act* (BIA) and under provincial legislation to control fraudulent activity by debtors.[1]

WHAT IS BANKRUPTCY?

Bankruptcy is a legal process carried out under the provisions of the BIA. The process involves disclosure of all assets and liabilities, along with a surrender of property. The debtor must also undergo debt counselling and, in some cases, make a series of monthly payments to a trustee. Bankruptcy relieves the debtor of responsibility for his debts, subject to some exclusions.

WHO SHOULD GO BANKRUPT?

A Canadian resident, or someone who carries on business in Canada, who owes a minimum of $1,000 and has committed an "act of bankruptcy" within the preceding six months is eligible to make an assignment into bankruptcy or be petitioned into bankruptcy by a creditor. There are various "acts of bankruptcy" set out in s. 42 of the BIA. The most common "act of bankruptcy" is insolvency. An insolvent person is someone who is unable to meet his obligations to creditors as they come due or who has ceased paying debts in the ordinary course of business. Note that someone whose liabilities are greater than his assets is not necessarily bankrupt. Many individuals, particularly when they are buying homes, have large mortgages that make their liabilities (debts) greater than their assets. The key is whether they can pay their monthly bills. A temporary shortfall does not mean bankruptcy, nor does a situation where credit counselling or a small claims consolidation order results in a debt restructuring so that the debtor can make payments.

The effect of bankruptcy is that the individual turns over most of her assets (referred to as her estate) to a **trustee in bankruptcy** licensed under the BIA, who will then

trustee in bankruptcy
an individual, usually an accountant, who is licensed to act as a trustee under the *Bankruptcy and Insolvency Act*—such individuals advertise their services in the *Yellow Pages*; an individual or corporation that wishes to make a proposal or an assignment in bankruptcy begins by consulting a trustee; the trustee, once retained, is paid out of the debtor's/bankrupt's estate and becomes trustee over the estate for the benefit of the creditors to whom he is ultimately responsible for the administration and liquidation of the estate

Property Exempt from Seizure

Under Federal Legislation

REGISTERED RETIREMENT SAVINGS PLANS

Registered Retirement Savings Plans (RRSPs) are exempt from seizure in a bankruptcy, provided that the contributions were made at least one year prior to the assignment of bankruptcy.

INDIAN ACT PROPERTY

There are provisions in the *Indian Act* that exempt certain property of status Indians from ordinary seizure in a bankruptcy.

FEDERAL BENEFITS

Benefits paid under the Canada Pension Plan, Old Age Security, Employment Insurance, and Veteran's Allowances are exempt from seizure in a bankruptcy.

Under Provincial Legislation

INSURANCE ACT

Under some provincial insurance acts, including the Ontario *Insurance Act*, the cash value portion of a whole life or universal life insurance policy where a close family member is named as the beneficiary is exempt from seizure. A close family member is defined as being a spouse, child, grandchild, or parent. RRSPs in which there is an insurance component with a close family member named as beneficiary are also exempt from seizure. Segregated funds, an insurance product, held inside or outside of an RRSP, with a close family member listed as beneficiary are eligible for exemption from seizure in a bankruptcy.

EXECUTION ACT

As of the time of publication, under provincial execution acts, including the Ontario *Execution Act* (s. 35), there are exemptions from seizure for the following items:

- household furnishings up to $11,300 in value,

- ordinary and necessary clothing up to $5,650 in value,

- tools of the trade up to $11,300 in value,

- farm equipment up to $28,300 in value, and

- vehicles up to $5,650 in value.

Note that the *Execution Act* has been amended by the *Open for Business Act, 2010*; however, as of the time of publication, the amendments had not yet been proclaimed. The amendments will revise the above-noted exemptions to remove the higher exemption for farm equipment, will add a new exemption for medical aids, and will set an overall exemption limit on personal property. Newly prescribed monetary limits for different types of exempt property are also expected.*

Other Reasons Property Can Be Exempt from Seizure

Property held in trust by the bankrupt for the benefit of another person is exempt from seizure in the bankruptcy as is property that is the subject of a secured interest. Secured creditors have the option under the BIA of seizing their security. Most do so, because they are likely to recover far more that way than they ever would if they abandoned their security rights and chose to participate in the bankruptcy proceedings.

If the bankrupt has property that would be of no financial benefit to the bankrupt's estate it will not be seized. Such property might consist of items that would cost the trustee more to seize and sell than the value of the item itself. In some cases the courts may order certain assets exempt from seizure.

---

* You can examine Ontario statutes and regulations at http://www.e-laws.gov. on.ca under the section on Current Consolidated Law. In this case, to find the statute, click on the "E" and move down to "Execution Act." To see the Act itself, click on the title, or click on the "+" sign to the left of the Act's title to access any regulations made under the Act. Sections that have not yet been proclaimed are generally highlighted in grey.

liquidate the assets and distribute funds to creditors. In bankruptcy, creditors rarely recover the full amount they are owed; however, at the end of the process, with a few exceptions, the bankrupt is stripped of most assets, save those exempt from seizure, and her debts are wiped out, with a few exceptions. If a first-time bankrupt completing the monthly income and expense statement (figure 14.1) has surplus income, then a portion of this surplus, based on her income and family size, must be paid to the trustee for a period of 21 months. The trustee handles the bankrupt's income tax returns for the bankruptcy period and receives any refunds for the benefit of the creditors. Generally, if the bankrupt has not engaged in fraudulent activity, she will be discharged from bankruptcy when the estate is fully administered. Because her debts have been discharged by the bankruptcy process, she will not be sued for those debts, nor can judgments in respect of them be enforced against her. The discharged bankrupt is free to go her own way. Contrary to what is often assumed, a bankrupt can rebuild a credit rating and borrow money. However, someone who repeatedly goes bankrupt will have great difficulty re-establishing a credit rating.

BANKRUPTCY OPTIONS

Under the BIA there are three options available.

Consumer Proposals

A consumer proposal is a plan to repay unsecured debtors put forward by an insolvent natural person (an individual as opposed to an artificial corporation such as a limited company) through an administrator under the *Bankruptcy and Insolvency Act*. A sample consumer proposal form can be found in figure 14.2. The proposal may request that unsecured creditors accept a reduction in interest or extend the overall period for payments of principal and interest, or both. Under the BIA, proposals must be

superintendent of bankruptcy
a government official in Ottawa who supervises and oversees the administration of the *Bankruptcy and Insolvency Act*

Official Receiver
a government official in the Office of the Superintendent of Bankruptcy who receives proposals, examines bankrupts under oath, and chairs meetings of creditors

completed in five years or less.[2] A debtor whose debts are higher in total than $5,000 but do not exceed $250,000 exclusive of a home mortgage, can use the proposal process.[3] Spouses or others who share a debt load under $250,000 may make a joint proposal. A trustee in bankruptcy or proposal administrator approved by the **superintendent of bankruptcy** must review the debtor's financial and property affairs and provide counselling to the debtor. The administrator will help draft a proposal to pay unsecured creditors of the debtor on terms that the debtor can meet. A proposal will not be possible unless the debtor has sufficient monthly income to make payments on the proposal. The proposal is filed with the **Official Receiver**. Within 10 days of filing, the administrator must send the Official Receiver a report of his investigation of the debtor's property and financial affairs; a statement of the debtor's assets, liabilities, income, and expenses; a list of creditors over $250; and an opinion as to whether the proposal is reasonable and fair and whether the debtor will be able to perform it. A copy of the proposal and the report is also sent by the trustee or proposal administrator to all creditors along with a proof of claim form and a statement setting out that a meeting of creditors will not be called unless one is requested, and also that a court review of the proposal will not be made unless requested. A meeting will be held if the Official Receiver directs one to be called or in the event that creditors, having in the aggregate at least 25 percent in value of the proven claims, request one.[4] If no meeting is held, the proposal is deemed to be accepted 45 days after its filing.[5] If a meeting is held, a simple majority of unsecured creditors carries the vote. If the creditors accept the proposal, it is binding on the debtor and on all unsecured creditors. A proposal is deemed to have been approved by the court 15 days after the creditors' acceptance or deemed acceptance. The debtor makes payments to the trustee or administrator, who will distribute payments to unsecured creditors every three months. A consumer proposal stays all court and collection actions against the debtor, subject to any exceptions such as an action concerning fraud against the debtor.

If the proposal is rejected, the debtor may decide to make an assignment into bankruptcy, may be petitioned into bankruptcy by a creditor, or may return to the situation that he was in prior to making the proposal. Without a proposal in place, if the debtor does not enter into bankruptcy, the creditors may initiate or continue all lawsuits and judgment enforcements against him. Note that if a proposal is accepted, the debtor is not bankrupt and does not acquire the legal status of a bankrupt. The major advantage of a consumer proposal is that the debtor keeps her property. The fee paid to a trustee or an administrator for a consumer proposal is less than the fee for a bankruptcy.

Voluntary Assignment into Bankruptcy

Where a debtor cannot or chooses not to make a proposal, or where a proposal is rejected, he can voluntarily seek the status of a bankrupt and go through bankruptcy proceedings. If the debtor has realizable assets worth $10,000 or less, the bankruptcy can proceed in a summary manner.[6] With a summary administration of bankruptcy, the trustee is not required to post security, the bankruptcy is not advertised in a newspaper, inspectors are usually not appointed, and a meeting of creditors is not held unless requested by the creditors. If the debtor has realizable assets valued at over $10,000, the bankruptcy proceeds in the ordinary fashion with a meeting of creditors being held within 21 days of the trustee's appointment. The steps involved in an ordinary bankruptcy are set out below.

Duties of the Bankrupt

Section 158 of the *Bankruptcy and Insolvency Act* provides that the bankrupt must do the following:

1. Provide disclosure of all assets and liabilities to the trustee and deliver all property, subject to exemptions, to the trustee.

2. Advise the trustee of any property disposed of in the past year.

3. Deliver all books, records, and documents concerning property and income tax records to the trustee.

4. Within five days of making an assignment into bankruptcy, provide the trustee with a Statement of Affairs.

5. Advise the trustee of any gifts of property made in the last five years.

6. Surrender all credit cards to the trustee for cancellation.

7. Attend for an oral examination under oath with the Official Receiver if requested to do so.

8. Attend any meetings of creditors.

9. Advise the trustee of any change in address.

10. Assist the trustee in making an inventory of assets.

11. Sign any required documents.

12. Examine the correctness of any Proofs of Claim.

13. Aid in the distribution of the proceeds.

STEPS INVOLVED IN AN ORDINARY BANKRUPTCY

1. *Initial meeting with trustee:* The debtor will meet with a trustee in bankruptcy to review her financial situation and the options available to her. The trustee will obtain information on the debtor's assets, income, liabilities, and details of property disposed of in the last five years. The trustee will use this information to prepare a Form 79 Statement of Affairs for the debtor. Form 79 is set out in figure 14.3. The bankrupt then attends her first counselling session. In order to be discharged from bankruptcy, the bankrupt must attend for at least two counselling sessions. Counselling is provided concerning financial management and prudent use of credit. The trustee may also make referrals for the bankrupt to receive counselling on non-financial matters such as addictions or familial problems. The trustee will review the debtor's household income and expenses and determine whether the bankrupt has surplus income available to be paid to the trustee each month for distribution to the creditors until the discharge.[7] The Superintendent of Bankruptcy has established guidelines, which are revised periodically, to determine the surplus amount for household income. The surplus income guidelines are contained in Directive No. 11R, which can be found online at http://strategis.ic.gc.ca/epic/site/bsf-osb.nsf/en/br01055e.html#appA. The trustee will also have the bankrupt sign a credit bureau authorization and an

authorization letter for the Canada Revenue Agency that permits the trustee to represent her. The trustee will also review the bankrupt's duties under the *Bankruptcy and Insolvency Act.* Failure to abide by these duties can result in a negative discharge report, a fine, or, in some cases, a jail sentence. The bankrupt's duties are set out in the box on the previous page.

2. *Assignment into bankruptcy:* The trustee files the assignment into bankruptcy with the Official Receiver. The bankrupt's property then vests in the trustee, subject to any exemptions under the *Execution Act* or otherwise as set out in the box on page 402. All legal and collection actions (such as garnishments and the execution of writs) against the bankrupt are stayed except for any cases involving fraud that the court may permit to continue.

3. *Notice given to creditors:* The trustee, within five days of the assignment into bankruptcy, will notify the creditors of the bankruptcy by sending them a notice of first meeting, or in the case of a summary administration of bankruptcy, a notice that there will not be a meeting unless one is requested. The trustee will also include a list of creditors, a blank proof of claim form, and a proxy form to be used in the event that the creditor cannot attend the first meeting.

4. *Examination by the Official Receiver:* The bankrupt may be required to present himself, under oath, before an Official Receiver to answer questions concerning his financial situation. A sample of the questions used in an examination of a non-business bankrupt are set out in figure 14.4.

5. *First meeting of creditors:* In an ordinary bankruptcy or in a bankruptcy proceeding by summary administration where a meeting has been requested, a meeting of creditors will be held within 21 days of the assignment into bankruptcy. The bankrupt must attend the meeting. The trustee's appointment will be confirmed and inspectors may be appointed.

6. *Second counselling session:* A second counselling session for the bankrupt is held between the date set for the first meeting of creditors and 90 days after the assignment into bankruptcy.

7. *Trustee's report on the bankruptcy and request for discharge:* The trustee must prepare a report on the bankruptcy for the creditors (those who requested a copy of the report will receive one) and the court. This report must be filed with the court along with a requisition for a discharge from bankruptcy. A sample of Form 82, used for the report, is found in figure 14.5.

8. *Realization of assets:* The trustee will sell the assets and provide an accounting of the proceeds.

9. *Distribution of assets:* The trustee must distribute the assets in accordance with the *Bankruptcy and Insolvency Act.* The costs of administering the estate will be paid first. The trustee is paid a fee equivalent to a percentage of the estate set under the BIA. Preferred creditors will then be paid, followed by ordinary unsecured creditors, on a pro rata basis. Preferred creditors include the Canada Revenue Agency,[8] employees (for unpaid wages), and landlords (for unpaid past and future rent of three months duration).

Debts That Survive a Bankruptcy

A discharge from bankruptcy terminates most of the bankrupt's debts; however, there are some debts that survive a bankruptcy. The most common ones are:

- Spousal and child support debts.

- Damages owed by the bankrupt in respect of an assault or an order of restitution made in a criminal case.

- Court fines.

- Debt arising from fraud. Creditors that have been defrauded by the bankrupt should plead fraud in their statements of claim and request a finding of fraud in their court orders in order to have proof of the fraud for the trustee and the bankruptcy court.

- Student loans survive debt and are non-dischargeable for a period of seven years after a student ceases to be a full- or part-time student. In cases where maintaining liability for all or some of their student debt causes undue hardship and the student acted in good faith in respect of the loan (that is, they used it to pay for their education), the student may apply for a discharge of the loan after five years. Students or former students experiencing financial hardship should consider contacting the Canadian Student Loan Program Debt Management Assistance department to discuss restructuring their loan payments. More information on student loan repayment management can be found at http://www.canlearn.ca/eng/after/repaymentassistance/index.shtml.

- If there is a debt with a co-signor or a guarantor who did not go bankrupt, the creditor may pursue payment from the co-signor/guarantor.

10. *Application for discharge from bankruptcy:* The court will consider the discharge application and usually discharge the bankrupt. The trustee must also apply to be discharged from his duties. When the bankrupt's application for discharge comes before the court, the judge will usually make one of the following decisions:

- *Absolute discharge:* The debtor is relieved of all debts before bankruptcy except those that are not dischargeable, such as family support order obligations. The judge, in considering the application for discharge, will take into account the bankrupt's performance of their duties and their rehabilitation.

- *Conditional discharge:* The debtor will be discharged upon meeting certain conditions, such as providing additional funds to distribute to creditors. The period in which the bankrupt is an undischarged bankrupt is extended to allow payments to be made. This punishes the debtor by extending the period of time before they can be discharged and begin rebuilding their financial situation. A conditional discharge will often call for additional payments to be made over a period of time ranging from 1 to 12 additional months.

- *Suspended discharge:* The debtor's discharge is delayed due to such things as an ongoing criminal investigation or an objection by a creditor, a trustee, or the superintendent of bankruptcy. Common objections include situations where a debtor failed to account for the disposal of an asset, or continued to get credit while unable to pay.

- *Refusal to grant a discharge:* In some cases, a discharge will not be granted. This may occur if the bankrupt has gone through more than two bankruptcies in the past, has committed fraud, or has falsified records.

A Creditor Petitions the Debtor into Bankruptcy

Bankruptcy Court
in Ontario, several judges of the Superior Court with expertise in bankruptcy law have been assigned to sit in what is called Bankruptcy Court, which is not a formal statutory part of the Superior Court; its judges sit in Toronto, Ottawa, and London

Where the debtor is unable to or does not make a proposal or is unwilling to make a voluntary assignment in bankruptcy, a creditor may petition the debtor into bankruptcy. The debt due to the petitioner must be at least $1,000 after deduction of any secured debt, and the petitioner must prove that the debtor has committed an act of bankruptcy within the preceding six months, the most common of which is being unable to meet debts as they fall due. If the petitioner can meet these preconditions, she files a petition for a receiving order with the registrar of the **Bankruptcy Court** (in Ontario, a branch of the Superior Court) in the place of the court's sitting nearest to where the debtor resides or carries on business. If the petition is filed in Toronto, it goes onto the Commercial List, which is regulated by various practice directions available from the Superior Court office at Toronto. The petition must be served on the debtor personally or in accordance with an order for substituted service. On the day fixed for the hearing, if the debtor does not show up, the bankruptcy judge will grant a receiving order. The order appoints a trustee to act as receiver of the assets of the bankrupt to investigate the assets and liabilities and liquidate them for the benefit of creditors.

As this process can take some time, a petition may also request the appointment of an interim receiver; such an order may be granted if assets are subject to rapid waste or there is evidence of fraud. An interim receiver does not have the broad powers of the trustee — she can only conserve assets, oversee the debtor's operations, and ensure compliance with the law until the trustee is appointed. Should the petition for a receiving order fail, the petitioning creditor may find himself liable for any acts of the interim receiver that caused the debtor damage.

If a debtor disputes the petition, he may do so by arguing that he has committed no act of bankruptcy or that he does not owe the debt the petitioner claims he does.

A creditor should be aware that a petition could be both risky and expensive; however, there are some sound reasons for taking this route. If a debtor is truly insolvent, the sooner he goes bankrupt the better for creditors, because assets may rapidly waste or disappear, leaving very little for creditors. A bankruptcy petition, particularly with a request for an interim receiver, can stabilize the assets of the debtor until the trustee can take over.

A second reason is that the BIA gives the creditor some means of investigating and controlling fraudulent preferences and activity by the debtor. Where this is taking place, a petition, with an interim receiver in place, can stop the misconduct. As well, once a trustee is in place, he has broad powers to investigate, as has the Official Receiver, and there are remedies available under the BIA and under provincial insolvency law that the trustee can use. The trustee may sue creditors given a fraudulent preference and attack transfers for less than fair market value or transfers to relatives and business associates if the debtor has:

- paid some creditor within three months of bankruptcy, but not others, while insolvent;

- transferred property for less than fair market value or in suspicious circumstances; or

- transferred property to a blood relation or to someone who shares control of a business within one year of bankruptcy.

In addition to getting the assets back into the estate, the trustee will also be able to hold up the discharge of an individual (companies are usually liquidated as a result of bankruptcy and do not emerge from it because they cease to exist).

CONTROLLING DEBTOR FRAUD, ASSIGNMENTS, AND PREFERENCES UNDER THE BANKRUPTCY AND INSOLVENCY ACT

A debtor may attempt to defraud creditors by transferring property to friends or family members for little or no consideration. There may be an agreement between the parties that the property is actually to be held in trust for the debtor and returned to him after he has been discharged from bankruptcy. In order to return such property to the bankrupt's estate, for the benefit of the creditors, the BIA has certain provisions giving the trustee the power to review and, in some cases, void such transactions.

Section 96 of the BIA provides that any undervalue transfer of property made within the one-year period prior to the bankruptcy to a non-related party or within the five-year period before bankruptcy to a related party may be void as against the trustee. Once it has been established that the undervalue transfer took place within one or five years of the bankruptcy, the onus switches to the transferee to rebut the presumption that the transfer is void. A valid defence might be that the consideration paid was reasonable for the property.

Section 95 of the BIA gives the trustee the power to recover preferential payments made by the bankrupt to a creditor and property that is fraudulently conveyed or mortgaged to a creditor by the bankrupt. To establish a fraudulent preference, the trustee must prove that the transfer, charge, or payment was made within three months of the bankruptcy in the case of unrelated persons, and within the last 12 months if the parties are related. The trustee must also prove that the bankrupt was an insolvent person at the date of the alleged preference and, furthermore, the trustee must show that as a result of the transfer, charge, or payment the creditor received a preference. Once these three factors are proven, the onus is on the creditor to prove to the court that there was no intention to prefer this creditor.

PROVINCIAL LEGISLATION CONTROLLING DEBTOR FRAUD

Although the *Bankruptcy and Insolvency Act* has some powerful remedies against debtor's fraudulent activities in hiding or transferring assets, as a prerequisite for using the remedies, the debtor must be bankrupt. Where the debtor is not bankrupt but is hiding assets and hindering the execution of a judgment, there is provincial legislation that can be of some assistance.

The Fraudulent Conveyances Act

The *Fraudulent Conveyances Act* (FCA) is designed to nullify transfers of assets by the debtor to third parties where the intent of the transfer is to defraud creditors. Where, for example, a debtor who has been sued transfers title to his house to his spouse for little or no payment, the creditor may attack this transaction and obtain an order that sets the transaction aside and vests title with the debtor, so that the creditor can seize the property to satisfy a judgment. It is interesting to note that there is no limitation period affecting this action — it can be brought at any time after the cause of action arose.

To obtain an order, it is necessary to sue the debtor and the transferee in an ordinary lawsuit in the Superior Court. This can be expensive and time consuming. In such an action, the focus is on the intention of the debtor and others involved. The intention is derived from an examination of the facts surrounding a transaction. Although there is rarely a "smoking gun," reasonable inferences may be drawn from the factual circumstances. Over time, the case law has identified "badges of fraud" that, when present, lead to an inference on the balance of probabilities that the transaction is tainted.[9]

The usual badges of fraud to watch for are:

1. the debtor was insolvent when the transfers were made;

2. the debtor was disposing of nearly all assets on the eve of execution of a judgment;

3. the price paid for the asset was clearly inadequate given its value;

4. the transferee was a close relative, business associate, or friend;

5. there was unusual haste in closing the transaction;

6. there was secrecy surrounding the transaction; and

7. there was continued use of the asset by the debtor after transfer.

In addition to the common law badges of fraud, there are some presumptions in the statute from which unlawful intent can be presumed. Where the transferee receives no money, there is a presumption of fraud, as there is if the transferee is a close relative. However, a debtor is free to advance evidence that will rebut the presumption and show that the transaction is innocent. Similarly, a transferee may be able to show that he is a bona fide purchaser for value without notice of any defect in the title. To do this, the purchaser must show that he paid a fair market price and that he had no grounds to suspect fraudulent intent by the debtor. If the transferee cannot mount a defence and has sold the property to someone else, the transferee may be ordered to pay an amount equal to the value of the asset. In this situation, where the transferee has conveyed the property to a stranger, the stranger might very well succeed with the defence of being a bona fide purchaser but his vendor may be obliged to pay an amount equal to the value of the asset.

In addition to the FCA, there are some other ways to curtail the fraudulent debtor. If the creditor has an interest in the land of a debtor, he can register a caution or a notice of pending litigation on title, which will warn potential purchasers that they buy subject to the rights of the creditor. A Mareva injunction or a writ of sequestration, discussed in chapter 9, may also be useful here.

The Assignments and Preferences Act

The *Assignments and Preferences Act* (APA) is provincial legislation that was enacted prior to the BIA. The APA allows insolvent persons to turn over assets to an assignee for distribution to creditors. The APA is especially useful in zeroing in on an unjust preference. This happens when a debtor in financial difficulties pays one creditor but not others, conferring a preference on the creditor who was paid. Other creditors may move to set aside the transaction to obtain the return of money or goods to the debtor where these assets will become available to other creditors to satisfy debts owing to them. For example, if a debtor gives security to one creditor for a past debt, but not to others, that is arguably an unjust preference, as would be a transaction where one creditor is paid in full while others receive nothing. In these circumstances the transactions might be set aside. As with the FCA, intention of the parties, inferred from surrounding circumstances, is important in determining the validity of the transaction.

When seeking remedies under the APA, it is important to note that only unjust preferences can be set aside. In some circumstances, the preference of one creditor over another may be permissible. For example, any payment made by the debtor in the ordinary course of business or on a regular periodic basis is permitted. This includes wages and some monthly bills. Payment to a secured creditor to the value of the security is permitted, because the secured creditor could seize the collateral ahead of other creditors anyway. Giving security to a creditor where there is an advance of funds or something of value at the time security is given is permissible if there is evidence that the advance will assist the debtor to stay in business and become solvent. Last, if there is pressure on a debtor to pay — for example, from a threat of legal action — and there is evidence that the debtor will be able to continue in business and remain solvent if he responds to the pressure to pay, that may be permitted. However, if the transaction resulted from pressure by a creditor, and it is challenged within 60 days of its occurrence, there is a presumption that the intention was to unjustly prefer a payment, and pressure will not provide the debtor or the transferee with a defence. The statutory presumption arising under the "60-day rule" is, however, rebuttable.

CHAPTER SUMMARY

A bankrupt is defined as a person who is unable to meet his or her obligations as they come due. There are three routes that a debtor may pursue through a trustee in bankruptcy. First, a debtor may make a proposal to restructure payment on unsecured debt in certain circumstances. Second, a debtor may make an assignment in bankruptcy by voluntarily filing for bankruptcy. Last, creditors may petition a debtor into bankruptcy. The effect of bankruptcy is that a debtor is stripped of his or her assets, less those exempt from seizure. Once the bankrupt is discharged, he or she cannot be sued for prior debts, with some exceptions. Bankruptcy legislation has a number of safeguards to protect creditors from fraud by the bankrupt. In addition to bankruptcy legislation, there are provincial statutes that can be used to control debtor fraud when a debtor is not bankrupt. The *Fraudulent Conveyances Act* is designed to set aside transactions where the debtor has tried to transfer assets to others to prevent creditors from seizing them. The *Assignments and Preferences Act* permits creditors to trace proceeds of sale of property by debtors to others where an unjust preference may have been given to one creditor over another.

KEY TERMS

Bankruptcy Court

Official Receiver

superintendent of bankruptcy

trustee in bankruptcy

NOTES

1. *Bankruptcy and Insolvency Act*, RSC 1985, c. B-3, as amended.

2. BIA, s. 66.12(5).

3. If the debtor's debt exceeds $250,000 she cannot make a consumer proposal. However, she can make a Division I proposal—there is no limit on the amount of debt; however, the period for creditors to accept the proposal is short—only 21 days. It is also more difficult to get creditor approval. A majority of creditors holding at least two-thirds of the value of the debt must accept the proposal. If the proposal is not accepted, the debtor automatically goes into bankruptcy.

4. BIA, s. 66.15.

5. BIA, s. 66.18.

6. BIA, s. 155.

7. A bankrupt with surplus income is not eligible for an automatic discharge nine months after his or her assignment into bankruptcy. The bankrupt remains in bankruptcy for a further 12 months and continues to make surplus income payments to the trustee. With a second bankruptcy, the bankrupt must remain in bankruptcy for a further three years or longer, and make surplus income payments during that time.

8. Individuals who owe more than $200,000 in personal income taxes representing 75 percent or more of their unsecured debt are not eligible for an automatic discharge. A court order for a discharge must be sought.

9. For a discussion of the *Fraudulent Conveyances Act*, badges of fraud, and the role of debtor's intent, see *Abakhan & Associates Inc. v. Braydon Investments Ltd.*, 2009 BCCA 521.

REFERENCES

Assignments and Preferences Act, RSO 1990, c. A.33.

Bankruptcy and Insolvency Act, RSC 1985, c. B-3, as amended.

Execution Act, RSO 1990, c. E.24, as amended.

Fraudulent Conveyances Act, RSO 1990, c. F.29.

Indian Act, RSC 1985, c. I-5.

Insurance Act, RSO 1990, C. I.8.

REVIEW QUESTIONS

1. Under what circumstances could a debtor be said to be bankrupt?

2. Why are only unsecured creditors involved in bankruptcy proceedings?

3. If your client wants to know what options in respect of bankruptcy are available to him, what would you tell him?

4. What remedies does the *Bankruptcy and Insolvency Act* (BIA) provide to control fraudulent activity by bankrupts?

5. What are the advantages and disadvantages for a creditor in petitioning a debtor into bankruptcy?

6. In what circumstances is it useful to use the *Fraudulent Conveyances Act* (FCA)?

7. For a creditor, what advantages does the FCA have over the bankruptcy legislation?

8. What are the badges of fraud that can assist a creditor under the FCA?

9. What are the statutory presumptions that can assist a creditor under the FCA?

10. How is the *Assignments and Preferences Act* (APA) similar to the FCA? How is it different?

Figure 14.1 Monthly Income and Expense Statement (Form 65)

FORM 65

Monthly Income and Expense Statement of the Bankrupt and the Family Unit
and Information (*or* Amended Information) Concerning
the Financial Situation of the Individual Bankrupt
(Section 68 and Subsection 102(3) of the Act and Rule 105(4))

Title Form 1

The information concerning the monthly income and expense statement of the bankrupt and the family unit, the financial situation of the bankrupt and the bankrupt's obligation to make payments required under section 68 of the Act to the estate of the bankrupt are as follows:

MONTHLY INCOME	Bankrupt	Other members of the family unit	Total
Net employment income	_____		
Net pension/Annuities	_____		
Net child support	_____		
Net spousal support	_____		
Net employment insurance benefits	_____		
Net social assistance	_____		
Self-employment income			
Gross _____ Net	_____		
Other net income	_____		
(Provide details _____)			

TOTAL MONTHLY INCOME . . . . $_____(1) $_____(2)*

TOTAL MONTHLY INCOME OF
THE FAMILY UNIT ((1) + (2))   ➤$_____(3)

MONTHLY NON-DISCRETIONARY
EXPENSES

Child support payments	_____	
Spousal support payments	_____	
Child care	_____	
Medical condition expenses	_____	
Fines/Penalties imposed by the court	_____	
Expenses as a condition of employment . . .	_____	
Debts where stay has been lifted	_____	
Other expenses	_____	
(Provide details_____)		

TOTAL MONTHLY NON-
DISCRETIONARY EXPENSES . . . . $_____(4) $_____ (5)

TOTAL MONTHLY NON-DISCRETIONARY
EXPENSES OF THE FAMILY UNIT ((4) + (5))   ➤$_____(6)

AVAILABLE MONTHLY INCOME
OF THE BANKRUPT ((1) - (4)) . . . . $_____ (7)

AVAILABLE MONTHLY INCOME
OF THE FAMILY UNIT ((3) - (6))   ➤$_____(8)

BANKRUPT'S PORTION OF THE AVAILABLE
MONTHLY FAMILY UNIT INCOME
((7) / (8) X 100))   ➤% _____(9)

---

*Where one or more members of the family unit have refused to divulge this information, please provide details as required by section 10 of Directive 11R.

Figure 14.1   Concluded

FORM 65 -- *Concluded*

MONTHLY DISCRETIONARY EXPENSES: *(Family unit)*

Housing expenses

    Rent/Mortgage . . . . _____

    Property taxes/Condo fees . . . . _____

    Heating/Gas/Oil . . . . _____

    Telephone . . . . _____

    Cable . . . . _____

    Hydro . . . . _____

    Water . . . . _____

    Furniture . . . . _____

    Other . . . . _____

Personal expenses

    Smoking . . . . _____

    Alcohol . . . . _____

    Dining/Lunches/Restaurants . . . . _____

    Entertainment/Sports . . . . _____

    Gifts/Charitable donations . . . . _____

    Allowances . . . . _____

    Other . . . . _____

Non-recoverable medical expenses

    Prescriptions . . . . _____

    Dental . . . . _____

    Other . . . . _____

Living expenses

    Food/Grocery . . . . _____

    Laundry/Dry cleaning . . . . _____

    Grooming/Toiletries . . . . _____

    Clothing . . . . _____

    Other . . . . _____

Transportation expenses

    Car lease/Payments . . . . _____

    Repair/ Maintenance/Gas . . . . _____

    Public transportation . . . . _____

    Other . . . . _____

Insurance expenses

    Vehicle . . . . _____

    House . . . . _____

    Furniture/Contents . . . . _____

    Life insurance . . . . _____

    Other . . . . _____

Payments

    To the estate . . . . _____

    To secured creditor . . . . _____

    (Other than mortgage and vehicle) . . . _____

    Other . . . . _____

TOTAL MONTHLY DISCRETIONARY EXPENSES (FAMILY UNIT) . . . . - \$_____ (10)

MONTHLY SURPLUS OR (DEFICIT) FAMILY UNIT ((8) - (10)) . . . . = \$_____ (11)

Information (*or* Amended Information) Concerning the Financial Situation of the Individual Bankrupt

Payments to the estate as per agreement

Number of persons in household family unit, including bankrupt: _____

Total amount bankrupt has agreed to pay monthly . . . . _____ (12)

Amount bankrupt has agreed to pay monthly to repurchase assets

*(provide details)*_____ . . . . _____ (13)

Residual amount paid into the estate ((12) - (13)) . . . . _____ (14)

Payments required by the Directive on Surplus Income

Monthly amount required by the Directive on Surplus Income based on percentage established on line (9) . . . . _____ (15)

Difference between amounts at lines (14) and (15) . . . . _____ (16)

Other applicable comments: *(If amount at line (14) is less than amount at line (15),*

*explain why the required payments are not being made:*_____*)*

Amendment or material change: *(If the information relates to a material change*

or an amendment, provide details: _____*)*

Dated at _____, this _____ day of _____ _____.

_____   _____

        Trustee   Bankrupt

Note: In a joint assignment, only one form is required and each bankrupt's monthly income and non-discretionary expenses have to be explained in detail.

Figure 14.2   Consumer Proposal (Form 47)

FORM 47

Consumer Proposal
(Paragraph 66.13(2)(c) of the Act)

(Title Form 1)

I, _____, a consumer debtor, hereby make the following consumer proposal under the Act:

1. That payment of the claims of secured creditors be made in the following manner:

(Set out the terms of the proposal in respect of secured claims.)

2. That payment of all claims directed by the Act to be paid in priority to other claims in the distribution of my property be made in the following manner:

(Set out the terms of the proposal in respect of preferred claims.)

3. That payment of the fees and expenses of the administrator of the consumer proposal and payment of the fees and expenses of any person in respect of counselling given by such person pursuant to the Act be made in the following manner:

(Set out the terms of the proposal in respect of these fees and expenses.)

4. That the following payments be made to _____, the administrator of the consumer proposal, for the benefit of the unsecured creditors:

(Set out the schedule of payments and the total amount to be paid in respect of unsecured claims.)

5. That the administrator of the consumer proposal distribute the moneys received to the unsecured creditors in accordance with the following schedule:

(Describe the manner for distributing dividends.)

6. That the proposal may include the following additional terms:

(a) the creditors may appoint up to three inspectors responsible for the consumer proposal of the consumer debtor. The inspectors may have, in addition to any powers of inspectors under the Act, the power to
   (i)   receive any notice of default in the performance of a provision of the consumer proposal and waive any such default, and

Figure 14.2   Concluded

FORM 47 -- *Concluded*

(ii)   approve any amendment to the consumer proposal without calling a meeting of creditors, if the amendment would alter the schedule for and the amount of the payments to be made by the consumer debtor, but would not change the total amount to be paid; and

(b) such other terms as may be proposed.

Dated at _____, this _____ day of _____ _____.

_____
Witness

_____
Consumer Debtor

Figure 14.3 Statement of Affairs (Form 79)

FORM 79

Statement of Affairs (Non-Business Bankruptcy)
(Paragraph 158(d) of the Act)

(*Title Form 1*)

ASSETS						
Type of assets		Description *(Provide details)*	Estimated Dollar Value	Exempt Property		Secured Amount/ Liens	Estimated net realizable dollar value *
				Yes	No		
1. Cash on hand							
2. Furniture							
3. Personal effects							
4. Cash-surrender value of life insurance policies, RRSPs, etc.							
5. Securities							
6. Real Property	House						
	Cottage						
	Land						
7. Motor vehicle	Automobile						
	Motorcycle						
	Snowmobile						
	Other						
8. Recreational equipment							
9. Estimated tax refund							
10. Other assets							
TOTAL							

_____
Date

_____
Bankrupt

* For a summary administration, indicate value net of the direct realization costs referred to in Rule 128 (1) of the BIA.

Figure 14.3   Continued

FORM 79 -- *Continued*

LIABILITIES						
			Liabilities type code (LTP) 1 Real Property Mortgage 2 Bank Loans (except real property mortgage) 3 Finance Company Loans 4 Credit Cards Bank/Trust Companies Issuers 5 Credit Cards Other Issuers 6 Taxes Federal/Provincial/Municipal 7 Student Loans 8 Loans from Individuals 9 Other			
Creditor	Address including postal code	Account No.	Amount of debt			Enter LTP
			Unsecured	Secured	Preferred	
1						
2						
3						
4						
5						
6						
7						
8						
9						
10						
11						
11						
12						
13						
14						
15						
16						
17						
18						
19						
20						
	TOTAL	Unsecured				
	TOTAL	Secured				
	TOTAL	Preferred				
				TOTAL		

_____   _____
Date   Bankrupt

Figure 14.3 Continued

FORM 79 -- *Continued*

INFORMATION RELATING TO THE AFFAIRS OF THE BANKRUPT				
A. PERSONAL DATA				
1. Family name:	Given names:		Date of birth: _____ / ___ / ___ YYYY / MM / DD	
	Gender : F ☐ M ☐			
2. Also known as:				
3. Complete address, including postal code:				
4. Marital status: *(Specify month and year of event if it occurred in the last five years)*	___ ___ Married ___ ___ Widowed ___ ___ Divorced		___ ___ Single ___ ___ Separated ___ ___ Common-law partner	
5. Full name of spouse or common-law partner:				
6. Name of present employer:		Occupation (Bankrupt):		
7A. Number of persons in household family unit, including bankrupt:				
7B. Number of persons 17 years of age or less:				
8. Have you operated a business within the last five years?	Yes	No	(If yes) Name, type and period of operation:	
B. WITHIN THE 12 MONTHS PRIOR TO THE DATE OF THE INITIAL BANKRUPTCY EVENT, HAVE YOU, EITHER IN CANADA OR ELSEWHERE:				
9A. Sold or disposed of any of your property?			Yes	No
9B. Made payments in excess of the regular payments to creditors?			Yes	No
9C. Had any property seized by a creditor?			Yes	No
C. WITHIN FIVE YEARS PRIOR TO THE DATE OF THE INITIAL BANKRUPTCY EVENT, WHILE YOU KNEW YOURSELF TO BE INSOLVENT, HAVE YOU, EITHER IN CANADA OR ELSEWHERE:				
10A. Sold or disposed of any property?			Yes	No
10B. Made any gifts to relatives or others in excess of $500?			Yes	No

Figure 14.3   Concluded

FORM 79 -- *Concluded*

D. BUDGET INFORMATION: *Attach Form 65 to this Form.*

11A. Have you ever made a proposal under the *Bankruptcy and Insolvency Act*?   Yes ___   No ___

11B. Have you been bankrupt before, either in Canada or elsewhere?   Yes ___   No ___

(If you answered Yes, provide the following details for all insolvency proceedings: (a) Filing date and location of the proceedings; (b) Name of trustee or administrator; (c) If applicable, was the proposal successful; (d) Date on which Certificate of Full Performance or Discharge was obtained.)

_____

_____

_____

---

12. Do you expect to receive any sums of money which are not related to your normal income, or any other property within the next 12 months?   Yes ___   No ___

---

13. If you answered Yes to any of questions 9, 10 and 12, provide details:

_____

_____

_____

---

14. Give reasons for your financial difficulties:

_____

_____

_____

I, _____ , of the _____ of _____ in the Province of _____ , do swear (*or* solemnly declare) that this statement is, to the best of my knowledge, a full, true and complete statement of my affairs on the _____ day of _____ ____ and fully discloses all property and transactions of every description that is or was in my possession or that may devolve on me in accordance with section 67 of the *Bankruptcy and Insolvency Act.*

SWORN (*or* SOLEMNLY DECLARED)
before me at the _____ of _____ in the Province of _____ this _____ day of _____ _____ .

_____

Commissioner of Oaths   Bankrupt
for the Province of _____

Figure 14.4 Questions for Examination of Non-Business Bankrupt (Form 27)

FORM 27

Examination of Bankrupt by Official Receiver
(Non-Business)
(Section 161 of the Act)

Instructions to Official Receiver

The following questions, or questions to a like effect, are to be put to the person examined under section 161 by the official receiver. The questions should be expanded or supplemented by the official receiver in an endeavour to extract from the examination the maximum of essential information and to determine as nearly as possible the true cause of the bankruptcy, the disposition of the property and the conduct of the bankrupt.

OFFICIAL RECEIVER'S NOTES (*To be completed by Official Receiver*)

Previous Bankruptcy(ies):

Reviewable Transactions:

Undisclosed Assets:

Undisclosed Debts:

Preferential Payments:

Excessive Credit Use:

Settlements:

Other Matters or Concerns:

_____

Official Receiver

Figure 14.4   Continued

FORM 27 -- *Continued*

1.   Give your full legal name (and aliases) and your birthday.

2.   What is your current address?

3.   Have you ever been the owner, or are the current owner of the residence that you live in, or does a family member own it?

4.   How much is your rent, or your mortgage payments?

5.   Have you been informed of your duties, according to the *Bankruptcy & Insolvency Act*?

6.   Approximately on what date did you become aware that you were unable to meet your debts as they became due and what made you aware of this fact?

7.   Did you use or obtain credit after this date? If yes, from whom did you obtain credit?

8.   Have you ever been bankrupt before, or made a proposal to your creditors? If yes, when?

9.   Do you have any credit cards in your possession at this time?

10. Who is your present employer, and how much is your monthly "Take Home" pay?

11. Do you have any other source of income, other than your job? If yes, what is the source and amount of the income?

12. What bank or banks do you have accounts at, and what is your present balance?

13. Do you have any other debts that you have not disclosed on your Statement of Affairs? If yes, give details.

14. Do you have any other assets that you have not disclosed on your Statement of Affairs? If yes, give details.

15. Explain the following debts, giving the date they were started, and the reason or cause of the debt.

16. Have you sold, given away or disposed of any assets in the 12 months prior to the date of the initial bankruptcy event? If so, give details.

17. From the sale of the above assets, how much money did you receive, and what did you do with the money?

18. Did you sell or give away anything that you bought on credit before it was fully paid for? If so, give details.

Figure 14.4 Continued

FORM 27 -- *Continued*

19. Have you paid back any debts to family members in the 12 months prior to the date of the initial bankruptcy event? If so, give details.

20. Did you pay your trustee at the time of signing your papers? If so, how much?

21. Are you presently making payments to your trustee? If so, how much?

22. Did you consider any other formal insolvency options before you filed your bankruptcy?

23. What creditors did you make payments to in the 3 months prior to filing bankruptcy? Did you pay any of these creditors in full, or give them larger than normal payments?

24. Are you aware of anyone holding any assets in trust? If so, give details.

25. Are you preparing monthly income and expense statements for your trustee?

26. List all monthly income, including that of your spouse (including common-law), and the source of the income.

27. List all monthly expenses, with the dollar amounts beside them.

28. If your expenses are more than your income, please explain what expenses you are not paying, and what you are doing to correct this problem.

29. Who advised you in regard to your financial problems?

30. Do you own or lease a motor vehicle? If yes, give details (are you paying the trustee to keep the vehicle, or who are paying to keep it, and what amount is being paid).

31. Are you presently borrowing a motor vehicle? If yes, give details.

32. Did you obtain any cash advances on any credit cards in the 12 months prior to the date of the initial bankruptcy event? If so, list them giving cash amounts and the last date an advance was taken.

33. Did you pay for any trips with your credit cards in the 12 months prior to the date of the initial bankruptcy event? If yes, what trips did you take, and how much money was charged on the cards?

34. Please explain why and how you ran up a total credit card debt of over $x.xx on your credit cards. I.e., what type of purchases were made and over what period of time?

35. What do you believe are the causes of your bankruptcy? Please give a brief explanation.

Figure 14.4   Concluded

FORM 27 -- *Concluded*

36.   Do you feel you are directly or partially responsible for your bankruptcy? Please explain your answer.

NOTE TO OFFICIAL RECEIVER

Any additional questions put by the official receiver and the answers to them should be entered in the space provided below or on a sheet to be attached to this form.

I, _____, of the _____ of _____, in the Province of_____, do swear (*or* solemnly declare) that to the best of my knowledge the above answers are true in every respect. I understand that this examination is being adjourned *sine die* and may be continued at a later date if necessary.

SWORN (*or* SOLEMNLY DECLARED)
before me at the _____
_____ of _____ in the Province
of _____, this ____ day
of _____ ____.

_____   _____
Official Receiver for Bankruptcy   Bankrupt
Division No_____ of the
Bankruptcy District of

_____

Figure 14.5   Trustee's Report on Bankrupt's Application for Discharge (Form 82)

FORM 82

Report of Trustee on Bankrupt's
Application for Discharge
(Subsection 170(1) of the Act)

(*Title Form 1*)

Date of bankruptcy:		Date of initial bankruptcy event:	
Marital status:			
Type of employment:	Number of persons in household family unit, including bankrupt:		
AMOUNT OF LIABILITIES			
	Secured	Preferred	Unsecured
Declared	$	$	$
Proven	$	$	$
AMOUNT OF ASSETS			
Description	Value as per Statement of Affairs	Amount realized	Estimate of assets to be realized
	$	$	$
TOTAL			
ANTICIPATED RATE OF DIVIDENDS			
Preferred creditors:		Unsecured creditors:	

A: CAUSES OF BANKRUPTCY

1.   Provide details of the causes of bankruptcy:

_____
_____
_____

B: INFORMATION CONCERNING THE FINANCIAL SITUATION *(The same method of calculation must be used to establish the available monthly income of the bankrupt and the family unit at date of bankruptcy and at date of this report. Explain any material changes.)*

2.   (a) Available monthly income of the bankrupt at date of bankruptcy
        (Same amount as line (7) on Form 65): . . . . $_____

        (b) Available monthly income of the bankrupt at date of this report: . . . . $_____

3.   (a) Available monthly income of the family unit at date of bankruptcy
        (Same amount as line (8) on Form 65): . . . . $_____

        (b) Available monthly income of the family unit at date of this report: . . . . $_____

Figure 14.5 Continued

FORM 82 -- *Continued*

C: CONDUCT OF THE BANKRUPT

4.   (a) Was the bankrupt required to pay to the estate an amount established by the Directive on Surplus Income? *(If yes, attach Appendix A)*   ☐ Yes ☐ No

      (b) Could the bankrupt have made a viable proposal rather than proceeding with bankruptcy? *(If yes, attach Appendix A)*   ☐ Yes ☐No

5.   (a) Did the bankrupt fail to perform any of the duties imposed on the bankrupt under the Act? *(If yes, provide details)*   ☐ Yes ☐ No

      (b) Can the bankrupt be justly held responsible for any of the facts referred pursuant to section 173 of the Act? *(If yes, provide details)*   ☐ Yes ☐No

      (c) Did the bankrupt commit any offence in connection with the bankruptcy? *(If yes, provide details)*   ☐ Yes ☐ No

6.   (a) Did the bankrupt ever make a proposal under the *Bankruptcy and Insolvency Act*? *(If yes, provide details)*   ☐ Yes ☐ No

      (b) Has the bankrupt been bankrupt before either in Canada or elsewhere? *(If yes, provide details)* ☐ Yes ☐ No

7.   Were inspectors appointed in this estate?
(Provide details if the trustee has reasonable grounds to believe that the inspectors will not approve this report. Attach a copy of the resolution.)   ☐ Yes ☐ No

D: DISCHARGE OF THE BANKRUPT

8.   (a) Is it the intention of the trustee to oppose the bankrupt's discharge? *(If yes, provide details)*   ☐ Yes ☐ No

      (b) Does the trustee have reasonable grounds to believe that a creditor or the Superintendent will oppose the bankrupt's discharge for a reason other than those set out in section 173(1)(m) or (n) of the Act? *(If yes, provide details)*   ☐ Yes ☐ No

9.   Did the bankrupt refuse or neglect to receive counselling pursuant to the Directive on Counselling in insolvency matters? *(If yes, provide details)*   ☐ Yes ☐ No

10.   Are there other facts, matters or circumstances that would justify the Court in refusing an absolute order of discharge? *(If yes, provide details)*   ☐ Yes ☐ No

11.   Other pertinent information? *(e.g. Exceptional personal circumstances, preferential payments, etc. If yes, provide details.)*   ☐ Yes ☐ No

Additional details as required

Number   **Additional information**

_____

_____

_____

_____

Dated at _____, this _____ day of _____, _____.

_____

                                             Trustee

Figure 14.5   Concluded

FORM 82 -- *Concluded*

APPENDIX A

A: AMOUNT REQUIRED TO BE PAID MONTHLY BY THE BANKRUPT

Monthly amount required by the Directive on Surplus Income
(Same amount as line (15) on Form 65): . . . . $_____(1)
Amount bankrupt has agreed to pay monthly *(Same amount as line (14) on Form 65):* . . . . $_____(2)
Difference between amounts at lines (1) and (2): . . . . $_____
Amount bankrupt has agreed to pay monthly to repurchase assets
(Same amount as line (13) on Form 65, provide details): . . . . $_____(3)
Total anticipated payments, lines (2) + (3): . . . . $_____

B: SURPLUS INCOME

1.   Did bankrupt make all required payments pursuant to section 68 of the Act? *(If no, provide details)* ❑ No ❑Yes

2.   Does amount established to be paid correspond with Directive on Surplus Income?
      (If no, provide details of any extenuating circumstances
      that would affect amount to be paid as per Directive)   ❑ No ❑ Yes

3.   Was the bankrupt made aware of the possibility of requesting mediation?   ❑ No ❑ Yes

4.   Any amendment or material changes during period of bankruptcy? *(If yes, provide details)*   ❑ Yes ❑ No

5.   Was mediation necessary under subsection 68(6) or 68(7)
      of the Act to determine the amount to be paid by the bankrupt?   ❑ Yes ❑ No

C: RECOMMENDATION ON THE BANKRUPT'S DISCHARGE

(Do not complete this part if:
      -the bankrupt has previously been a bankrupt;
      -the discharge of the bankrupt is opposed on grounds other than those mentioned at section 170.1 of the Act; or
      -the bankrupt has refused or neglected to receive counselling pursuant to the Directive on Counselling in insolvency
      matters)

6.   Recommendation of the trustee pursuant to section 170.1 of the Act:

      ❑   bankrupt to be discharged without conditions; *(Provide justification for unconditional discharge)*

      ❑   bankrupt to be discharged subject to conditions (deemed opposition) based on the following grounds under
                 subsection 170.1(2) of the Act; *(Provide details, including amount and period of payments)*

                 ❑ the bankrupt has not complied with a requirement imposed on the bankrupt under section 68 of the Act;

                 ❑ the total amount paid to the estate by the bankrupt is disproportionate in relation to the bankrupt's
                 indebtedness and financial resources;

                 ❑ the bankrupt could have made a viable proposal, but chose to proceed with bankruptcy, rather than make a
                 proposal as the means to resolve the indebtedness;

      ❑   bankrupt to be discharged after fulfilling obligations under mediation agreement. *(Provide details, including*
                 amount and period of payments.)

7.   Does the trustee have reasonable grounds to believe that the debtor
      agrees to the conditions recommended by the trustee?   ❑ Yes ❑ No

8.   Was the bankrupt made aware of the possibility of requesting mediation?   ❑ Yes ❑ No

Dated at _____, this _____ day of _____, _____.

———————————————————
                                                                              Trustee

PART III

Debtors' Remedies

In the previous chapters, debtors have primarily been dealt with in the context of a creditor's collection action. With the exception of the chapter on bankruptcy, the focus has been on the creditor, with some mention, from time to time, of possible actions that the debtor might take.

In this final chapter we bring together the range of strategies that a debtor might be able to exercise proactively or in response to a creditor's action against them. Additional information, not available elsewhere in the text, on debt management, credit counselling, and credit report rectification is included in this part.

CHAPTER 15

Debtors' Remedies

Dealt with in this chapter are various strategies that a debtor might use to

- renegotiate debt,

- defend debt actions,

- bring court motions for installment payments and consolidation orders,

- enter into credit counselling and a debt management plan, and

- file a consumer proposal or bankruptcy.

Information is also included on how to make proposals to pay debts in the Small Claims Court and to effectively participate in a judgment-debtor examination.

PAYING THE DEBT

An agreement between a debtor and a creditor is a contract. The debtor should review the contractual terms of the agreement, whether it is a credit card agreement, loan agreement, or security agreement, to determine what the consequences are for missing a payment or making a late payment. Some agreements contain a clause wherein a debtor may be late on making or miss one payment, but make up the payment later before the contract ends with minimal or no penalty. If a debtor intends to rely on such a clause to get over a short-term cash flow problem, it is a good idea to contact the creditor to make them aware of his intention to rely on that clause for that particular month.

Most agreements contain an **acceleration clause**, whereby if one payment is missed, the entire debt, at the creditor's option, becomes due. In that case, instead of facing a one-month catch-up payment, the debtor would have to come up with the money to pay the entire loan.

As well as facing additional costs from not paying the debt, the following consequences may occur:

- The debtor's credit rating and overall credit score will be negatively affected, such that it may be difficult to secure further credit, rental premises, insurance, or, in some cases, even a job.

- The debtor may have to deal with repeated calls and contact from a collection agency.

acceleration clause
provides that if the debtor misses a payment, the entire debt is accelerated and becomes immediately due and payable

- The debtor may be sued, which will result in a judgment against him and possibly a writ of seizure and sale against him, which can block the sale of his real estate or prevent him from obtaining a mortgage. A judgment against him can also result in a garnishment of his wages, other income, bank accounts, and investments.

- The debtor may be petitioned into bankruptcy by a creditor.

- If the debtor gave collateral to secure the loan, then the collateral may be repossessed. For example, if the loan was used to buy a car and that car was the collateral, the vehicle can be seized if the debtor has not paid at least two-thirds of the loan. The *Consumer Protection Act, 2002*, however, provides that if a consumer has paid more than two-thirds of a consumer loan, then the collateral cannot be repossessed.

In most cases, it is to the debtor's advantage to find the funds to pay the debts owed. In some cases, preparing a debt-focused budget (see the worksheet in figure 15.1) can help identify expenses that can be cut or opportunities to sell assets to obtain funds to pay the debt. In many cases, debt is caused by excess spending on gambling or substance abuse. If this is the case, a debtor can seek support by contacting the Ontario Problem Gambling Helpline at 1-888-230-3505 or at http://www.opgh.on.ca or the Drug and Alcohol Helpline at 1-800-565-8603 or at http://www.drugandalcoholhelpline.ca. If the debtor is able to do so, he may be able to take on a part-time, temporary, or seasonal position to earn funds to pay the debt. There are a variety of good debt-payment and budgeting books on the market that can help a debtor to organize his affairs to pay his debts.[1]

CONSOLIDATION OF DEBT LOANS

It is useful for a debtor to list all of her debts (figure 15.1) and set out the interest rate applied to each debt. In some cases she may be able to shift higher interest debt to a lower interest rate credit card or line of credit. If her credit rating is good, she may be able to apply for a lower interest rate card. A better interest rate can usually be obtained by requesting a credit card or line of credit from the institution where the debtor does most of her banking. If her credit rating is good and she has the monthly income to do so, it is usually advantageous to try to qualify for a bank consolidation-of-debt loan. Monthly credit card payments at various rates of, often high, interest would be replaced by one monthly payment, usually at a lower rate of interest. A better rate of interest can sometimes be obtained if the debtor has real estate or a vehicle that can be offered as collateral. The lender will usually want to see the debtor's monthly budget, list of debts, and proof of income (usually in the form of paystubs) to ensure that the debtor can make the monthly loan payments. In some cases the lender will request that someone co-sign the loan along with the debtor as extra security for repayment of the loan.

RENEGOTIATION OF DEBT

The debtor may be able to approach the creditor to discuss renegotiation of the debt. As mentioned earlier, some credit agreements provide that one payment may be missed and added onto the end of the debt. When asking to change payment terms, loan balances, or interest rates, it is usually helpful if, in his request for new terms on the debt, the debtor is honest with the creditor and explains what hardship has resulted from the debt. The creditor may be able to move the credit card balance over to another lower interest card or unsecured or secured line of credit, which should result in a better rate, or may even provide a loan to replace the debt. Remember that creditors may be receptive to renegotiation of a debt, even if the creditor ends up collecting less than the full value of the debts outstanding. Creditors are not in the morality business; they recognize that "a bird in the hand is worth two in the bush" — that is, they may take less than the full amount due if they think they have little chance of recovering all of the debt, or if they have to spend more to collect the full amount than they would get if they settled with the debtor.

If the debt is a student loan, the debtor should contact the Canada Student Loans Program Repayment Assistance Plan to discuss restructuring his loan payments. While the amount owing cannot be altered, monthly payments can be reduced and spread out over a longer period of time. Information on the Repayment Assistance Plan can be found at http://www.canlearn.ca/eng/after/repaymentassistance/index.shtml. A student loan cannot be included in a bankruptcy until seven years after the student has left school; however, in hardship cases, this waiting period may be reduced to five years.

If the debt is for unpaid income tax, the Canada Revenue Agency has a department that handles requests for individuals to request payment plan arrangements to spread payments out over a longer time period. In some cases, the Agency will consider a reduction on compassionate grounds, such as the occurrence of a natural disaster or serious illness. To discuss alternative income tax payment arrangements, the debtor should call the CRA Debt Management Call Center at 1-888-863-8657.

In the event that the debtor and the creditor agree to a new arrangement for payment of the debt, the details should be confirmed in writing.

RESPONDING TO A COLLECTION AGENT

Once a payment on a debt is late or has been missed, the debtor may be contacted by a collection agent. Before a collection agent can contact a debtor by telephone, the agent must send the debtor a written notice that sets out the debt that she is handling and confirms who she is and who she is acting for. Once the agent has provided the debtor with this notice, she may contact the debtor by phone or email three times over the next seven days, or more often with the debtor's consent. The *Collection Agencies Act*, as detailed in chapter 1, restricts the times during which an agent may call.

Debtors can stop a collection agent from contacting them in two ways:

- by sending a letter to the collection agency disputing the debt and suggesting that they take the matter to court, or

- by having a lawyer send a letter to the agency confirming that they are acting for the debtor and directing that the agency deal with the lawyer.

If a collection agent persists in contacting the debtor after he has done one of the above, or calls the debtor outside of permitted hours or more often than he has allowed, the debtor should request the agent's registration identification number. Complaints about collection agents should be directed to the Ministry of Government Services at 1-800-889-9768.

RESPONDING TO A SUPERIOR COURT ACTION

If the debt is for more than $25,000, the creditor may commence a lawsuit in the Superior Court of Justice to obtain judgment for the debt. The debtor, upon being served with such a claim, may want to ignore it; however, doing so can result in increased costs against the debtor. The debtor should review the claim for accuracy and to identify possible defences concerning any product quality, limitation periods, or other issues. Superior Court documents and procedures are fairly technical and most people use the services of a lawyer to represent them. But in many cases a debtor cannot afford a lawyer. A debtor can obtain a free 30-minute consultation with a lawyer specializing in debtor–creditor law by contacting the Law Society of Upper Canada's Lawyer Referral Service at 1-800-268-8326. Debtors experiencing severe hardship may obtain assistance through the Law Help pro bono legal clinic. For more information on Law Help, go to their website at http://www.lawhelpontario.org.

For those who are not eligible for legal aid and who cannot afford the usual services offered by lawyers and paralegals, there may be another solution. As of September 2011, the Law Society of Upper Canada has approved limited retainers, also known as the "unbundling of legal services." Clients who cannot afford the full range of a lawyer's or paralegal's services may agree to have the lawyer provide some services, with the client doing the rest. A debtor who wants to make this kind of arrangement should discuss the options carefully with the lawyer, and the services to be provided by the lawyer should be clearly spelled out in the retainer. As this is a new procedure in Ontario, practices and procedures will evolve over time.

Lastly, a debtor who cannot afford to defend a lawsuit may apply for a fee waiver with respect to court filing fees. A guide and accompanying forms for fee waivers can be found on the Attorney General's website at http://www.attorneygeneral.jus.gov.on.ca/english/courts/feewaiver/guide-forms.asp.

A debtor served with a statement of claim can find the contact information for the creditor's lawyer on the first and last pages of the claim. If the debtor acknowledges the debt but would like to make payment arrangements, possibly avoiding a judgment against her, she should call the creditor's lawyer and inquire about making an offer to settle the case. The lawyer has a duty to pass on any offers made to the creditor for its consideration. In order to save the time and expense associated with going further with the court claim, a settlement may be possible.

In some cases a debtor may be judgment proof and will at that point in time not have anything to lose by not responding to a lawsuit. If the debtor's income is from welfare, CPP, or Old Age Security pension, these funds cannot be garnished in order to pay a judgment unless it was for child or spousal support. However, if a judgment is made against the debtor and a writ put in place, if the debtor's circumstances change, perhaps as a result of an inheritance, the creditor will then be able to enforce its judgment plus accumulated costs and interest. The debtor will then end up paying more to the creditor than if she had responded to the claim at the time it was served and made arrangements to pay at that time.

RESPONDING TO A SMALL CLAIMS COURT CLAIM

If the debtor is served with a Small Claims Court action he may be able to represent himself with the help of the guides and forms available online at http://www .ontariocourtforms.on.ca. Most consumer debt claims in Ontario are brought in the Small Claims Court because they are claims for $25,000 or less. If served with a Small Claims Court claim, the debtor may consider one of the following responses:

- Contact the plaintiff's lawyer or paralegal to discuss a possible settlement of the claim.

- File a defence form that contains a proposal to pay some or all of the debt in monthly payments. If the creditor does not respond within 20 days, the debtor should begin making the payments proposed to the creditor. If the creditor disagrees with the proposal, she can request a hearing with the court to determine payments. If the proposal is for partial payment, the court will schedule a settlement conference wherein the parties will be encouraged to try to resolve the matter by agreement. The fee to file a defence is $40. If it is a financial hardship for the defendant to pay the filing fee and the defendant has limited assets, he may apply to the court for a Fee Waiver Assistance form that will allow him to file a defence and any other court paperwork for free and to obtain an interpreter paid for by the court, should one be needed. The Law Help pro bono office mentioned above has offices at the Small Claims Court in Toronto and Ottawa that can provide some assistance to qualifying parties.

- File a defence and possibly a defendant's claim for any issues—for example, product quality—that he may have in defence of his failure to pay. See chapter 10 for more information on defences and defendant's claims. Once a defence is filed, the court will schedule a settlement conference for the parties to attend.

- If you do not defend the claim and a judgment is made against the debtor, the debtor can bring a motion in court to request that he be allowed to pay the judgment in installments. Once an installment order is made, the creditor cannot take any steps to enforce the judgment other than to issue and file a writ of seizure and sale of land.

- If the defendant already has one or more Small Claims Court judgments against him, when this latest judgment is made he can bring a motion requesting a consolidation order to bring the orders together and permit one monthly payment to be made to the court. A consolidation order prevents the creditor from taking any steps to enforce, other than to issue and file a writ of seizure and sale of land.

RESPONDING TO ENFORCEMENT PROCEEDINGS

Once a creditor has obtained a judgment, he may try to enforce it through the use of garnishments and writs, and may schedule an examination in aid of execution of the debtor.

Examination in Aid of Execution

A judgment debtor is required to attend an examination in aid of execution up to once a year, or more often if ordered by the court. The debtor should complete the required Financial Information Form and bring it to the examination along with supporting financial documentation. A judge in Small Claims Court presides over the examination and, even at this stage, payment agreements can sometimes be reached. The debtor should be forthright and honest at all times. Failure to attend an examination or to respond to relevant questions asked can result in a contempt of court order and a possible jail sentence.

Garnishments

A debtor may find that 20 percent of her net pay has been garnished to pay an outstanding judgment. In some cases this may cause financial hardship to the debtor. The debtor can bring a motion under the *Wages Act* to increase the exempt portion of her wages from 80 percent to a higher exempt amount, resulting in a reduction in the amount garnished.

Writs of Seizure and Sale

A judgment creditor will usually issue and file a writ of seizure and sale of land, and in some cases of personal property, against the name of the judgment debtor. A writ filed against land prevents the debtor from selling real property or obtaining a mortgage. In order to remove the writ, the creditor will usually want full payment of the judgment and accrued interest and costs. If the property is to be sold, the creditor and the debtor's real estate lawyer can usually make arrangements to have the writ lifted provided that the debtor's lawyer agrees to direct funds from the sale proceeds to pay the debt.

If the debtor chooses to execute the land writ and have the sheriff seize and sell the real estate, the debtor should closely monitor market conditions, listing price, and expenses charged to get the property ready for sale. If it appears that the sheriff is undervaluing the property or spending excessive sums of money to ready the property for sale, the debtor may bring an interpleader motion to the court for direction on these matters from the court.

If the debtor exercises a writ of seizure and sale of personal property, the debtor is entitled to demand from the bailiff an inventory of all of the items sold. The debtor should also familiarize herself with the provisions of the *Execution Act* that stipulate property that is exempt from seizure. More information on the *Execution Act* can be found in chapter 9.

CREDIT COUNSELLING AND DEBT MANAGEMENT PLANS

If a debtor is unable to qualify for a debt consolidation loan from a financial institution, he may wish to consider seeking help from a credit counsellor and possibly entering into a debt management plan. A credit counselling agency can be found in the yellow pages of the phone book or at http://www.yellowpages.ca. Credit counsellors are unregulated and unlicensed and do not require any training. As such, the debtor should be careful to select a reputable agency. Most credit counselling agencies are run on a not-for-profit basis and are in fact funded by commercial creditors.

If a debtor is lacking in budgeting skills, credit counselling is a good place to start. With a careful budget, funds with which to start paying off debts can sometimes be found.

If a debtor is seeking relief from the interest they are paying, a credit counsellor can put forward a debt management plan to the debtor's creditors, which, if accepted, usually gives the debtor a longer time period in which to pay and a reduced interest rate. The principal due is usually not reduced. Unlike a consumer proposal (see below), the debt management plan does not stop creditors from taking other enforcement actions if they wish to do so. A debt management plan is usually made to run over a 4- to 5-year period, with the debtor making one monthly payment to the credit counsellor who then pays the creditors. A debt management plan is voluntary for creditors to join in or not, so the debtor may be faced with making the monthly plan payment and payments to creditors who did not join the plan.

Consumer Proposals and Bankruptcy

Under the federal *Bankruptcy and Insolvency Act*, a debtor may hire a trustee in bankruptcy to either make a consumer proposal to their creditors or file for bankruptcy. As well, a creditor may petition a debtor into bankruptcy. The filing of a consumer proposal or a bankruptcy stops all enforcement action by the creditor.

CONSUMER PROPOSALS

A debtor who owes $250,000 or less, exclusive of a mortgage, may make a consumer proposal to their creditors to pay a reduced amount of the debt. Generally the proposal is to pay 35 to 50 percent of the amount owed. The creditors have 45 days to vote on the proposal, which must be accepted by a 50 percent plus 1 vote from the creditors. If a proposal is not accepted, bankruptcy is not automatic. The debtor can then choose to do nothing or to go bankrupt. Once a consumer proposal is filed, all interest stops accruing on the debts. The debtor surrenders his credit cards to the trustee and makes one monthly payment to the trustee. Consumer proposals may be set up to run over a five-year period of time. All of the creditors are bound by the proposal. The advantage of a consumer proposal is that the debtor gets to keep all of her property and pays a reduced amount over a longer time period.

If the debtor owes more than $250,000, then she may make a Division I proposal, for which there is no set monetary limit. With a Division I proposal, a higher percentage of creditors must accept the proposal in a shorter period of time (21 days). If the Division I proposal is not accepted, then the debtor is automatically put into bankruptcy.

BANKRUPTCY

A Canadian resident who owes at least $1,000 may file for bankruptcy. With a bankruptcy, the debtor surrenders most of his property to a trustee to sell and pay the sale proceeds to his creditors. A bankruptcy clears most of the debtor's debts. A few debts, however, such as child and spousal support, court fines, judgments based on fraud, and court orders to pay damages for personal injuries or assault, survive the bankruptcy and must be paid. Compared with a consumer proposal, there is a higher fee to be paid to a trustee to go bankrupt. If the debtor, based on his net income and family size, is considered to have surplus income (over $1,870 per month for a single person), he then must pay the surplus monthly income to the trustee for the benefit of his creditors for 21 months on a first bankruptcy. Once all of the debtor's obligations under the bankruptcy are met, the trustee applies for a discharge from the bankruptcy.

Bankruptcy and Consumer Proposal Comparison

BANKRUPTCY	CONSUMER PROPOSAL
Must owe at least $1,000	Must owe at least $5,000
No maximum limit	Must be debts of $250,000 or less (though a Division I proposal can be made if debt is higher)
Debtor must surrender most property to the trustee	Debtor keeps all of his property
Property is liquidated and funds used to pay creditors	Payments on a reduced debt amount are made to creditors
If surplus income, monthly payments are made for 21 months on a first bankruptcy	Payments made to creditors over a 5-year time period
Credit rating drops to R9	Credit rating drops to R7
Discharged from first bankruptcy in 9 to 21 months from time of filing depending on where payments being made	Proposal is generally paid in 5 years' time
Bankruptcy remains on credit record for 6 years from discharge date	Proposal remains on credit record for 3 years after final payment has been made
Student loans can be included in bankruptcy for 7 years after debtor ceases to be a student	Student loans cannot form part of the proposal
Higher fee to be paid to trustee	Lower trustee fee

CREDIT REPORTS

Anyone who has ever applied for a bank account or credit card has a credit record. There are two major credit bureaus in Canada: Equifax and TransUnion. A debtor should annually review his credit record with each of the bureaus to ensure accuracy and to flag any suspicious activity that may be a sign of identity theft. Credit reports are available to debtors through the mail at no cost.

Credit bureaus obtain their information from debtors, creditors, collection agencies, and public agencies. Whenever a debtor fills out a credit application or applies for a job, to become a tenant, or to buy insurance, the information on the form is provided, with their consent, to the credit bureaus. Creditors provide information to the bureaus on how much the debtor owes and what payments have been made. Public agencies such as the Superintendent of Bankruptcy and the courts provide information to the bureaus on proposals, bankruptcies, and judgments and executions against the debtor.

A credit report has two sets of payment data in it — the nine-point R rating scale and the overall credit score. The free report that can be obtained has a debtor's R ratings on it. R stands for revolving credit such as credit cards and reflects the debtor's payment trends on his credit cards. If a debtor has an R1 rating, which is the highest, this means that all debts are paid on time. The filing of a consumer proposal drops the debtor's rating to R7, while a bankruptcy drops it to R9. However, on discharge from bankruptcy, the rating status is zero. The debtor can then work to build up a new credit rating. Some banks will give the discharged bankrupt the opportunity to have a secured credit card whereby the debtor gives the bank $1,000 to hold in exchange for a $500 secured credit card. If all payments are made in full and on time, the debtor will start to slowly repair his credit rating.

Credit scores range from 300 to 850 and are based on payment history, how long the debtor has been using credit, his recent history, how many credit cards he has, and how high the outstanding debt on those cards is. A high score is ideal and can result in lower insurance premiums and better credit limits on approved cards. To keep the score favourable, a debtor should not use more than 30 to 50 percent of the available credit on his cards. As well, the debtor should not make several credit card applications at the same time, because this will reduce his score.

Correcting Inaccuracies on Credit Reports

When a debtor checks her credit bureau report, she may find inaccuracies. She should put the inaccuracies in writing and submit them to the credit bureau and to the financial institutions they relate to and request a correction. If the financial institution agrees that an error has been made, the credit bureau has 30 days to correct the report. If the correction cannot be made, the debtor can submit an entry of her own, consisting of 100 words or less to be added to the report. If there is a complaint against the financial institution or credit bureau about the debtor's report, she can call the Financial Consumer Agency of Canada at 1-866-461-3222.

The best ways to build and maintain a good credit report are to:

- review the credit report annually;

- demand in writing that errors be fixed — if they cannot, add a personal statement of explanation to the report;

- accurately complete credit card applications;

- apply for a minimum number of credit cards;

- pay all bills on time;

- pay bills, if possible, in full by the due date — if this is not possible, try to pay more than the minimum payment amounts;

- pay debts off as soon as possible;

- keep card balances well below the credit limit;

- open a bank savings account and make regular deposits after a consumer proposal or a bankruptcy has concluded; and

- obtain a secured credit card after a consumer proposal or bankruptcy to start rebuilding a positive credit report.

CHAPTER SUMMARY

This chapter pulls together in one place the various remedies that debtors can avail themselves of. It compares bankruptcy to consumer proposals, and gives information on credit counselling and debt management and on how to obtain and repair one's credit report.

KEY TERM

acceleration clause

NOTE

1. An excellent Canadian book on debt management is *Debt-Free Forever* by Gail Vaz-Oxlade, published in 2009 and available from HarperCollins.

REFERENCES

Bankruptcy and Insolvency Act, RSC 1985, c. B-3, as amended.

Collection Agencies Act, RSO 1990, c. C.14.

Execution Act, RSO 1990, c. E.24.

Wages Act, RSO 1990, c. W.1.

REVIEW QUESTIONS

1. Outline three possible consequences of failing to pay a debt.

2. Describe two criteria that a lender will look for before approving a debtor for a consolidation loan.

3. List three options that a debtor has to respond to a Small Claims Court debt collection claim against him.

4. List two ways in which a debtor can request that a collection agent stop contacting him.

5. Who should consider using credit counselling?

6. What is the difference between a debt management plan and a consumer proposal?

7. Give two advantages that a consumer proposal has over a bankruptcy.

8. Explain how student loans can be dealt with in a bankruptcy.

9. Explain the difference between a credit rating and a credit score.

10. What should a debtor do if she finds an error in her credit report?

DISCUSSION QUESTION

Andrea owes $35,000 in credit card debt. Her husband left her and took up with another woman outside the country. Before he left, he charged his trip and various purchases to their joint credit cards. Andrea has been late in making some payments and has missed other payments altogether. She now has a poor credit rating. She is a single mother with three children. She works full time earning $40,000 per year. She has a heavily mortgaged house and a six-year-old car that has been paid off. The interest rates on four of her credit cards with outstanding balances run from 8 to 19 percent. Explain what options Andrea has to deal with this situation.

Figure 15.1   Debtor Budget Worksheet

DEBTOR BUDGET WORKSHEET

DEBTS AT A GLANCE

Creditor	Amount Owing	Interest Rate	Minimum Monthly Payment

TOTAL OWED: _____

TOTAL MONTHLY MINIMUM PAYMENTS: _____

MAJOR ASSETS AT A GLANCE

Asset	Value	Debt on the Asset

INCOME FROM EMPLOYMENT

Full time job: _____   Monthly salary: _____

Part time jobs: _____   Monthly salary: _____

Bonuses: _____   Monthly amount: _____

Self-employment: _____   Monthly income: _____

Figure 15.1   Continued

OTHER INCOME

Benefit payments: _____
(EI, WSIB, Disability)

Pension payments: _____

Old Age Security pension: _____

Spousal/Child support: _____

Child Tax Benefit: _____

Universal Child Tax Benefit: _____

HST Rebate Credit: _____

Investment income: _____

Rental Income: _____

Gifts: _____

TOTAL MONTHLY INCOME: _____

EXPENSES

Work-Related Expenses

Expense	Monthly Amount Spent
Income tax	
CPP	
EI	
Pension contribution	
Union dues/Prof. fees	
Health benefits plan	
Workplace life insurance	

TOTAL: _____

Transportation Costs

Expense	Monthly Amount Spent
Gas	
Public transit/Taxis	
Car insurance	
Parking	
Car repairs, maintenance and licensing	
Car loan/lease payments	

TOTAL: _____

Figure 15.1   Continued

Housing Costs

Expense	Monthly Amount Spent
Rent or Mortgage	
Property taxes	
Condo fees	
Property insurance	
Repairs and maintenance	
Water	
Heating	
Hot Water tank rental	
Electricity	
Furniture	
Cable/Satellite TV/Radio	
Internet	
Electricity	

TOTAL: _____

Health Costs

Expense	Monthly Amount Spent
Dental expenses	
Medicines	
Vitamins/Supplements	
Eye care	
Hearing care	
Therapy: physio, chiropractor, massage	
Private insurance: life, disability, critical illness, health	

TOTAL: _____

Personal Expenses

Expense	Monthly Amount Spent
Clothes	
Hair care, nails, beauty treatments	
Other	

TOTAL: _____

Figure 15.1   Continued

Household Expenses

Expense	Monthly Amount Spent
Groceries	
Meals out and takeout	
Pet care	
Dry cleaning	
Other	

TOTAL: _____

Children's Expenses

Expense	Monthly Amount Spent
Daycare/Babysitters/ Summer camp	
Education-related expenses	
Gifts for birthday parties	
Lessons/Sports	
RESP contributions	
Clothing	
Child support paid	
Other	

TOTAL: _____

Investment Expenses

Expense	Monthly Amount Spent
RRSP contributions	
Automatic deposit savings	
RESP contributions	
Banking service fees	
Safety deposit box fee	
Other	

TOTAL: _____

Figure 15.1   Concluded

Recreational Spending

Expense	Monthly Amount Spent
Movies/Theatre	
Video and game rentals	
Lottery tickets	
Sports: golf, swimming, skating, skiing entry fees	
Books and periodicals	
Gambling: casinos and video terminals	
Alcohol	
Tobacco	
Hobbies	
Gifts	
Vacations	
Other	

TOTAL: _____

DEBT PAYMENTS

Expense	Monthly Amount Spent
Total minimum credit card payments	
Total line of credit minimum payments	
Total loan payments	
Payments on court judgments	
Spousal support payments	
Other	

TOTAL: _____

Total Monthly Income _____ – Total Monthly Expenses _____ = Surplus/Deficit _____

PART IV

Supplementary Materials

Appendix A of this part contains rules 4, 8, 11, 19, 20, 37, 39, 44, 49, 57, 60, 61, and 76 of the *Rules of Civil Procedure* of the Superior Court of Justice. These rules deal with court documents, interim preservation orders, offers to settle, costs, default and summary judgments, motions, and judgment enforcement procedures.

Appendix B contains the *Rules of the Small Claims Court*, which set out the procedural rules that govern proceedings in that court.

APPENDIX A

Rules of Civil Procedure

GENERAL MATTERS

RULE 4   COURT DOCUMENTS

FORMAT

Standards — Documents in Writing

4.01(1) A document in writing in a proceeding shall meet the following standards:

1. The text shall be printed, typewritten, written or reproduced legibly, with double spaces between the lines and a margin of approximately 40 millimetres on the left-hand side.

2. The characters used shall be of at least 12 point or 10 pitch size.

3. Good quality white paper or good quality near white recycled paper 216 millimetres by 279 millimetres shall be used.

One Side or Both

(2) The text may appear on one side or on both sides of the paper.

Standards — Electronic Documents

(3) A document mentioned in rule 4.05.1 is sufficient, despite subrule (1), if it meets the standards of the software authorized by the Ministry of the Attorney General.

(4)-(11) Revoked.

4.01.1 Revoked.

CONTENTS

General Heading

4.02(1) Every document in a proceeding shall have a heading in accordance with Form 4A (actions) or 4B (applications) that sets out,

(a) the name of the court and the court file number; and

(b) the title of the proceeding in accordance with rule 14.06 (action or application), but in a document other than an originating process, pleading, record, order or report, where there are more than two parties to the proceeding, a short title showing the names of the first party on each side followed by the words "and others" may be used.

(1.1) Clause (1)(b) does not apply to documents in proceedings under Rules 74 and 75.

Body of Document

(2) Every document in a proceeding shall contain,

(a) the title of the document;

(b) its date;

(c) where the document is filed by a party and not issued by a registrar or is an originating process, the name, address and telephone number of the lawyer filing the document or, where a party acts in person, his or her name, address for service and telephone number; and

(d) where the document is issued by a registrar, the address of the court office in which the proceeding was commenced or, in the case of an application to the Divisional Court, the address of the court office in the place where the application is to be heard.

Backsheet

(3) Every document in a proceeding shall have a backsheet in accordance with Form 4C that sets out,

(a) the short title of the proceeding;

(b) the name of the court and the court file number;

(c) in the case of an affidavit, the deponent's name and the date when he or she swore it;

(d) the location of the court office in which the proceeding was commenced;

(e) the title of the document;

(f) The name, address, telephone number and law society Registration number of the lawyer serving or filing the document or, where a party acts in person, his or her name, address for service and telephone number;

(g) the fax number, if any, of the lawyer serving or filing the document or, where a party acts in person, his or her fax number, if any; and

(h) the fax number, if known, of the person on whom the document is served.

(4) Revoked.

BILINGUAL DOCUMENTS

4.02.1 A pleading or other documents written in French that may be filed under section 126 of the *Courts of Justice Act* may also include a version of all or part of the text written in English.

CERTIFIED COPIES OF COURT DOCUMENTS

4.03 On the requisition of a person entitled to see a document in the court file under section 137 of the *Courts of Justice Act* and on payment of the prescribed fee the registrar shall issue a certified copy of the document.

NOTICE TO BE GIVEN IN WRITING OR ELECTRONICALLY

4.04(1) A notice required to be given by these rules shall be given,

(a) in writing; or

(b) electronically, if the use of electronic means is authorized.

(2) Revoked.

(3) Revoked.

ISSUING AND FILING OF DOCUMENTS

Issuing Documents

4.05(1) A document may be issued on personal attendance in the court office by the party seeking to issue it or by someone on the party's behalf.

Electronic Issuing

(1.1) A document mentioned in rule 4.05.1 may be issued electronically by using the authorized software.

Deemed Issuing

(1.2) A document issued under subrule (1.1) shall be deemed to have been issued by the Superior Court of Justice.

(1.2.1), (1.2.2) Revoked.

Notice — Document Issued

(1.3) After a document is issued electronically, notice that it was issued shall be sent to the party that had it issued.

Place of Filing

(2) The following requirements govern the place of filing of documents in proceedings, unless the documents are filed in the course of a hearing or these rules provide otherwise:

1. All documents required to be filed in a proceeding shall be filed in the court office in which the proceeding was commenced, subject to paragraphs 2, 3 and 4.

2. If the proceeding has been transferred to another county in accordance with rule 13.1.02, the documents shall be filed in the court office in the new county, subject to paragraph 3.

3. An affidavit, transcript, record or factum to be used at a hearing shall be filed in the court office in the county where the hearing is to be held.

4. Documents relating to a motion to transfer a proceeding to another county under rule 13.1.02 shall be filed in the court office of the county to which the transfer is sought, if subrule 13.1.02(3.1) applies.

(3) Revoked.

Filing by Leaving in Court Office or by Mail

(4) Any document, other than one that is to be issued, may be filed by leaving it in the proper court office or mailing it to the proper court office, accompanied by the prescribed fee.

Electronic Filing

(4.1) A document mentioned in rule 4.05.1 may be filed electronically by using the authorized software.

(4.1.1), (4.1.2) Revoked.

Notice — Document Filed

(4.2) After a document is filed electronically, notice that it was filed shall be sent to the party that filed it.

Date of Filing where Filed by Mail

(5) Where a document is filed by mail, the date of the filing stamp of the court office on the document shall be deemed to be the date of its filing, unless the court orders otherwise.

Where Document Filed by Mail Not Received

(6) Where a court office has no record of the receipt of a document alleged to have been filed by mail, the document shall be deemed not to have been filed, unless the court orders otherwise.

ELECTRONIC DOCUMENTS

4.05.1(1) Revoked.

(2) A lawyer, another person who has filed a requisition with the registrar or the Workplace Safety and Insurance Board may use the authorized software to issue or to file

electronically the following documents, to date them and to record the date of issue or filing:

1. A declaration under subrule 60.02(3) to enforce a certificate of assessment.

2. A requisition under subrule 60.07(1.1) or (1.2).

3. A writ of seizure and sale under subrule 60.07(1.1) or (1.2).

4. A request to renew under subrule 60.07(8.1).

5. An amendment to the writ under subrule 60.07(11.1).

6. A change of address under subrule 60.07(12.2).

7. A withdrawal of writ under subrule 60.15(4).

(3) The Minister of Finance may use the authorized software to file electronically the following documents, to date them and to record the date of issue or filing:

1. A warrant described in rule 60.07.1.

2. A request to renew under subrule 60.07(8.1) that relates to a warrant described in rule 60.07.1.

3. An amendment under subrule 60.07(11.1) that relates to a warrant described in rule 60.07.1.

4. A withdrawal under subrule 60.15(4) that relates to a warrant described in rule 60.07.1.

4.05.2 Revoked.

AFFIDAVITS
Format

4.06(1) An affidavit used in a proceeding shall,

(a) be in Form 4D;

(b) be expressed in the first person;

(c) state the full name of the deponent and, if the deponent is a party or a lawyer, officer, director, member or employee of a party, shall state that fact;

(d) be divided into paragraphs, numbered consecutively, with each paragraph being confined as far as possible to a particular statement of fact; and

(e) be signed by the deponent and sworn or affirmed before a person authorized to administer oaths or affirmations.

Contents

(2) An affidavit shall be confined to the statement of facts within the personal knowledge of the deponent or to other evidence that the deponent could give if testifying as a witness in court, except where these rules provide otherwise.

Exhibits

(3) An exhibit that is referred to in an affidavit shall be marked as such by the person taking the affidavit and where the exhibit,

(a) is referred to as being attached to the affidavit, it shall be attached to and filed with the affidavit;

(b) is referred to as being produced and shown to the deponent, it shall not be attached to the affidavit or filed with it, but shall be left with the registrar for the use of the court, and on the disposition of the matter in respect of which the affidavit was filed, the exhibit shall be returned to the lawyer or party who filed the affidavit, unless the court orders otherwise; and

(c) is a document, a copy shall be served with the affidavit, unless it is impractical to do so.

By Two or More Deponents

(4) Where an affidavit is made by two or more deponents, there shall be a separate jurat for each deponent, unless all the deponents make the affidavit before the same person at the same time, in which case one jurat containing the words "Sworn (or affirmed) by the above-named deponents" may be used.

For a Corporation

(5) Where these rules require an affidavit to be made by a party and the party is a corporation, the affidavit may be made for the corporation by an officer, director or employee of the corporation.

For a Partnership

(6) Where these rules require an affidavit to be made by a party and the party is a partnership, the affidavit may be made for the partnership by a member or employee of the partnership.

By an Illiterate or Blind Person

(7) Where it appears to a person taking an affidavit that the deponent is illiterate or blind, the person shall certify in the jurat that the affidavit was read in his or her presence to the deponent, that the deponent appeared to understand it, and that the deponent signed the affidavit or placed his or her mark on it in the presence of the person taking the affidavit.

By a Person Who Does Not Understand the Language

(8) Where it appears to a person taking an affidavit that the deponent does not understand the language used in the affidavit, the person shall certify in the jurat that the affidavit was interpreted to the deponent in the person's presence by a named interpreter who took an oath or made an affirmation before him or her to interpret the affidavit correctly.

Alterations

(9) Any interlineation, erasure or other alteration in an affidavit shall be initialled by the person taking the affidavit and, unless so initialled, the affidavit shall not be used without leave of the presiding judge or officer.

BINDING OF DOCUMENTS
Records

4.07(1) Records for motions, applications, trials and appeals shall have a light blue backsheet.

Transcripts

(2) Transcripts of evidence for use on a motion or application or at trial shall have a light grey backsheet.

Appeal Book and Compendium

(3) An appeal book and compendium shall be bound front and back in buff covers.

Transcripts on Appeal

(4) Transcripts of evidence for use in an appeal shall be bound front and back in red covers, except where the transcript forms part of the appeal book and compendium or record and, where there is more than one volume of transcripts, the volumes shall be clearly numbered.

Factums and Case Books

(5) A factum or case book filed by an applicant, moving party or appellant shall be bound front and back in white covers, and a factum or case book of a respondent or responding party shall be bound front and back in green covers.

(5.1) Revoked.

Cover Stock

(6) Backsheets and covers shall be of 176g/m² cover stock.

REQUISITION

4.08 Where a party is entitled to require the registrar to carry out a duty under these rules, the party may do so by filing a requisition (Form 4E) and paying the prescribed fee, if any.

TRANSCRIPTS

Paper Size

4.09(1) Evidence shall be transcribed on paper 216 millimetres by 279 millimetres in size with a margin 25 millimetres wide on the left side delimited by a vertical line.

Heading

(2) The name of the court or, in the case of an examiner, the examiner's name, title and location shall be stated on a single line no more than 15 millimetres from the top of the first page.

Standards

(3) The text shall be typewritten on thirty-two lines numbered in the margin at every fifth line.

(4) Headings, such as swearing of a witness, direct examination and cross-examination, shall be capitalized and separated from the preceding text by the space of a numbered line, and the number of lines of text on the page may be reduced by one for each heading that appears on the page.

(5) Every question shall commence on a new line and shall begin with the designation "Q.", followed, within 10 millimetres, by the question.

(6) Every answer shall commence on a new line and shall begin with the designation "A.", followed, within 10 millimetres, by the answer.

(7) The first line of a question or answer shall be indented 35 millimetres from the margin and shall be 130 millimetres in length.

(8) In a transcript of evidence taken in court, every line of a question or answer, other than the first line, shall begin at the margin and shall be 165 millimetres in length.

(9) In a transcript of evidence taken out of court, every line of a question or answer, other than the first line, shall begin 15 millimetres from the margin and shall be 150 millimetres in length, and questions shall be numbered consecutively by means of a number placed in the 15 millimetres to the right of the margin.

(10) Lines of text other than questions and answers shall be indented 35 millimetres from the margin and shall be 130 millimetres in length.

(11) Every transcript of evidence taken in court or out of court shall have,

    (a) a cover page setting out,

        (i) the court,

        (ii) the title of the proceeding,

        (iii) the nature of the hearing or examination,

        (iv) the place and date of the hearing or examination,

        (v) the name of the presiding judge or officer, and

        (vi) the names of the lawyers representing the parties; and

    (b) a table of contents setting out,

        (i) the name of each witness with the page number at which the examination, cross-examination and re-examination of the witness commence,

        (ii) the page number at which the charge to the jury, the objections to the charge and the re-charge commence,

        (iii) the page number at which the reasons for judgment commence,

        (iv) a list of the exhibits with the page number at which they were made exhibits, and

(v) at the foot of the page, the date the transcript was ordered, the date it was completed and the date the parties were notified of its completion.

TRANSMISSION OF DOCUMENTS

4.10(1) Where documents filed with the court or exhibits in the custody of an officer are required for use at another location, the registrar shall send them to the registrar at the other location on a party's requisition, on payment of the prescribed fee.

(2) Documents or exhibits that have been filed at or sent to a location other than where the proceeding was commenced for a hearing at that location shall be sent by the registrar, after the completion of the hearing, to the registrar at the court office where the proceeding was commenced.

NOTICE OF CONSTITUTIONAL QUESTION

4.11 The notice of constitutional question referred to in section 109 of the *Courts of Justice Act* shall be in Form 4F.

RULE 4.1   DUTY OF EXPERT

DUTY OF EXPERT

4.1.01(1) It is the duty of every expert engaged by or on behalf of a party to provide evidence in relation to a proceeding under these rules,

(a) to provide opinion evidence that is fair, objective and non-partisan;

(b) to provide opinion evidence that is related only to matters that are within the expert's area of expertise; and

(c) to provide such additional assistance as the court may reasonably require to determine a matter in issue.

Duty Prevails

(2) The duty in subrule (1) prevails over any obligation owed by the expert to the party by whom or on whose behalf he or she is engaged.

PARTIES AND JOINDER

RULE 8   PARTNERSHIPS AND SOLE PROPRIETORSHIPS

PARTNERSHIPS

8.01(1) A proceeding by or against two or more persons as partners may be commenced using the firm name of the partnership.

(2) Subrule (1) extends to a proceeding between partnerships having one or more partners in common.

DEFENCE

8.02 Where a proceeding is commenced against a partnership using the firm name, the partnership's defence shall be delivered in the firm name and no person who admits having been a partner at any material time may defend the proceeding separately, except with leave of the court.

NOTICE TO ALLEGED PARTNER WHERE
ENFORCEMENT SOUGHT AGAINST PARTNER

8.03(1) In a proceeding against a partnership using the firm name, where a plaintiff or applicant seeks an order that will be enforceable personally against a person as a partner, the plaintiff or applicant may serve the person with the originating process, together with a notice to alleged partner (Form 8A) stating that the person was a partner at a material time specified in the notice.

(2) A person served as provided in subrule (1) shall be deemed to have been a partner at the material time, unless the person defends the proceeding separately denying that he or she was a partner at the material time.

PERSON DEFENDING SEPARATELY

8.04 A person becomes a party to a proceeding as a defendant or respondent, and the title of the proceeding shall be amended accordingly, if the person defends a proceeding separately,

(a) denying having been a partner at the material time; or

(b) with leave of the court under rule 8.02.

DISCLOSURE OF PARTNERS

8.05(1) Where a proceeding is commenced by or against a partnership using the firm name, any other party may serve a notice requiring the partnership to disclose forthwith in writing the names and addresses of all the partners constituting the partnership at a time specified in the notice and, where the present address of a partner is unknown, the partnership shall disclose the last known address of that partner.

(2) Where a partnership fails to comply with a notice under subrule (1), its claim may be dismissed or the proceeding stayed or its defence may be struck out.

(3) Where the name of a partner is disclosed pursuant to a notice under subrule (1) and the partner has not been served as provided in rule 8.03, the partner may be so served within fifteen days after the name is disclosed.

ENFORCEMENT OF ORDER

Against Partnership Property

8.06(1) An order against a partnership using the firm name may be enforced against the property of the partnership.

Against Person Served as Alleged Partner

(2) An order against a partnership using the firm name may also be enforced, where the order or a subsequent order so provides, against any person who was served as provided in rule 8.03 and who,

(a) under that rule, is deemed to have been a partner;

(b) has admitted having been a partner; or

(c) has been adjudged to have been a partner,

at the material time.

Against Person not Served as Alleged Partner

(3) Where, after an order has been made against a partnership using the firm name, the party obtaining it claims to be entitled to enforce it against any person alleged to be a partner other than a person who was served as provided in rule 8.03, the party may move before a judge for leave to do so, and the judge may grant leave if the liability of the person as a partner is not disputed or, if disputed, after the liability has been determined in such manner as the judge directs.

SOLE PROPRIETORSHIPS

8.07(1) Where a person carries on business in a business name other than his or her own name, a proceeding may be commenced by or against the person using the business name.

(2) Rules 8.01 to 8.06 apply, with necessary modifications, to a proceeding by or against a sole proprietor using a business name, as though the sole proprietor were a partner and the business name were the firm name of a partnership.

RULE 11   TRANSFER OR TRANSMISSION OF INTEREST

EFFECT OF TRANSFER OR TRANSMISSION

11.01 Where at any stage of a proceeding the interest or liability of a party is transferred or transmitted to another person by assignment, bankruptcy, death or other means, the proceeding shall be stayed with respect to the party whose interest or liability has been transferred or transmitted until an order to continue the proceeding by or against the other person has been obtained.

ORDER TO CONTINUE

11.02(1) Where a transfer or transmission of the interest or liability of a party takes place while a proceeding is pending, any interested person may, on filing an affidavit verifying the transfer or transmission of interest or liability, obtain on requisition from the registrar an order to continue (Form 11A), without notice to any other party.

(2) An order to continue shall be served forthwith on every other party.

FAILURE TO OBTAIN ORDER TO CONTINUE ACTION

11.03 Where a transfer or transmission of the interest of a plaintiff takes place while an action is pending and no order to continue is obtained within a reasonable time, a defendant may move to have the action dismissed for delay, and rules 24.02 to 24.05 apply, with necessary modifications.

DISPOSITION WITHOUT TRIAL

RULE 19   DEFAULT PROCEEDINGS

NOTING DEFAULT

Where No Defence Delivered

19.01(1) Where a defendant fails to deliver a statement of defence within the prescribed time, the plaintiff may, on filing proof of service of the statement of claim, or of deemed service under subrule 16.01(2), require the registrar to note the defendant in default.

Noting Default Electronically

(1.1) Where a plaintiff files electronically a requisition for the noting in default of a defendant and the registrar notes the defendant in default, the registrar shall send the plaintiff confirmation of the noting in default.

Where Defence Struck Out

(2) Where the statement of defence of a defendant has been struck out,

   (a) without leave to deliver another; or

   (b) with leave to deliver another, and the defendant has failed to deliver another within the time allowed,

the plaintiff may, on filing a copy of the order striking out the statement of defence, require the registrar to note the defendant in default.

Noting of Default by Co-defendant

(3) Where a plaintiff has failed to require the registrar to note a defendant in default, the court on motion of any other defendant who has delivered a statement of defence, on notice to the plaintiff, may order the registrar to note the other defendant in default.

Party Under Disability

(4) If a party to an action is under disability, the party may be noted in default only with leave of a judge obtained on motion under rule 7.07.

Late Delivery of Defence

(5) A defendant may deliver a statement of defence at any time before being noted in default under this rule.

CONSEQUENCES OF NOTING DEFAULT

19.02(1) A defendant who has been noted in default,

(a) is deemed to admit the truth of all allegations of fact made in the statement of claim; and

(b) shall not deliver a statement of defence or take any other step in the action, other than a motion to set aside the noting of default or any judgment obtained by reason of the default, except with leave of the court or the consent of the plaintiff.

(2) Despite any other rule, where a defendant has been noted in default, any step in the action that requires the consent of a defendant may be taken without the consent of the defendant in default.

(3) Despite any other rule, a defendant who has been noted in default is not entitled to notice of any step in the action and need not be served with any document in the action, except where the court orders otherwise or where a party requires the personal attendance of the defendant, and except as provided in,

(a) subrule 26.04(3) (amended pleading);

(b) subrule 27.04(3) (counterclaim);

(c) subrule 28.04(2) (crossclaim);

(d) subrule 29.11(2) (fourth or subsequent party claim);

(e) subrule 54.08(1) (motion for confirmation of report on reference);

(f) subrule 54.09(1) (report on reference);

(g) subrule 54.09(3) (motion to oppose confirmation of report on reference);

(h) subrule 55.02(2) (notice of hearing for directions on reference);

(i) clause 64.03(8)(a) (notice of taking of account in foreclosure action);

(j) subrule 64.03(24) (notice of reference in action converted from foreclosure to sale);

(k) subrule 64.04(7) (notice of taking of account in sale action);

(l) subrule 64.06(8) (notice of reference in mortgage action);

(m) subrule 64.06(17) (report on reference in mortgage action); and

(n) subrule 64.06(21) (notice of change of account);

(o) Revoked: O. Reg. 131/04, s. 10(2).

(p) Revoked: O. Reg. 131/04, s. 10(2).

SETTING ASIDE THE NOTING OF DEFAULT

19.03(1) The noting of default may be set aside by the court on such terms as are just.

(2) Where a defendant delivers a statement of defence with the consent of the plaintiff under clause 19.02(1)(b), the noting of default against the defendant shall be deemed to have been set aside.

BY SIGNING DEFAULT JUDGMENT

Where Available

19.04(1) Where a defendant has been noted in default, the plaintiff may require the registrar to sign judgment against the defendant in respect of a claim for,

(a) a debt or liquidated demand in money, including interest if claimed in the statement of claim (Form 19A);

(b) the recovery of possession of land (Form 19B);

(c) the recovery of possession of personal property (Form 19C); or

(d) foreclosure, sale or redemption of a mortgage (Forms 64B to 64D, 64G to 64K and 64M).

(1.1) Revoked.

Requisition for Default Judgment

(2) Before the signing of default judgment, the plaintiff shall file with the registrar a requisition for default judgment (Form 19D),

(a) stating that the claim comes within the class of cases for which default judgment may properly be signed;

(b) stating whether there has been any partial payment of the claim and setting out the date and amount of any partial payment;

(c) where the plaintiff has claimed prejudgment interest in the statement of claim, setting out how the interest is calculated;

(d) where the plaintiff has claimed postjudgment interest in the statement of claim at a rate other than as provided in section 129 of the *Courts of Justice Act*, setting out the rate; and

(e) stating whether the plaintiff wishes costs to be fixed by the registrar or assessed.

Registrar May Decline to Sign Default Judgment

(3) The registrar may decline to sign default judgment if uncertain,

(a) whether the claim comes within the class of cases for which default judgment may properly be signed; or

(b) of the amount or rate that is properly recoverable for prejudgment or postjudgment interest.

(3.1) If the registrar declines to sign default judgment, the plaintiff may,

(a) move before a judge for judgment under rule 19.05; or

(b) in the case of a claim referred to in subrule (1), make a motion to the court for default judgment.

Where Claim Partially Satisfied

(4) Where the claim has been partially satisfied, the default judgment shall be confined to the remainder of the claim.

Postjudgment Interest

(5) Where the registrar signs default judgment and the plaintiff has claimed postjudgment interest in the statement of claim at a rate other than as provided in section 129 of the *Courts of Justice Act*, the default judgment shall provide for postjudgment interest at the rate claimed.

Costs

(6) On signing a default judgment, the registrar shall fix the costs under Tariff A to which the plaintiff is entitled against the defendant in default and shall include the costs in the judgment unless,

(a) the judgment directs a reference; or

(b) the plaintiff states in the requisition that he or she wishes to have the costs assessed,

in which case the judgment shall include costs to be determined on the reference or on assessment.

BY MOTION FOR JUDGMENT

19.05(1) Where a defendant has been noted in default, the plaintiff may move before a judge for judgment against the defendant on the statement of claim in respect of any claim for which default judgment has not been signed.

(2) A motion for judgment under subrule (1) shall be supported by evidence given by affidavit if the claim is for unliquidated damages.

(3) On a motion for judgment under subrule (1), the judge may grant judgment, dismiss the action or order that the action proceed to trial and that oral evidence be presented.

(4) Where an action proceeds to trial, a motion for judgment on the statement of claim against a defendant noted in default may be made at the trial.

FACTS MUST ENTITLE PLAINTIFF TO JUDGMENT

19.06 A plaintiff is not entitled to judgment on a motion for judgment or at trial merely because the facts alleged in the statement of claim are deemed to be admitted, unless the facts entitle the plaintiff to judgment.

EFFECT OF DEFAULT JUDGMENT

19.07 A judgment obtained against a defendant who has been noted in default does not prevent the plaintiff from proceeding against the same defendant for any other relief.

SETTING ASIDE DEFAULT JUDGMENT

19.08(1) A judgment against a defendant who has been noted in default that is signed by the registrar or granted by the court on motion under rule 19.04 may be set aside or varied by the court on such terms as are just.

(2) A judgment against a defendant who has been noted in default that is obtained on a motion for judgment on the statement of claim under rule 19.05 or that is obtained after trial may be set aside or varied by a judge on such terms as are just.

(3) On setting aside a judgment under subrule (1) or (2) the court or judge may also set aside the noting of default under rule 19.03.

APPLICATION TO COUNTERCLAIMS, CROSSCLAIMS AND THIRD PARTY CLAIMS

19.09 Rules 19.01 to 19.08 apply, with necessary modifications, to counterclaims, crossclaims and third party claims, subject to rules 28.07 (default of defence to crossclaim) and 29.07 (default of defence to third party claim).

RULE 20   SUMMARY JUDGMENT

WHERE AVAILABLE
To Plaintiff

20.01(1) A plaintiff may, after the defendant has delivered a statement of defence or served a notice of motion, move with supporting affidavit material or other evidence for summary judgment on all or part of the claim in the statement of claim.

(2) The plaintiff may move, without notice, for leave to serve a notice of motion for summary judgment together with the statement of claim, and leave may be given where special urgency is shown, subject to such directions as are just.

To Defendant

(3) A defendant may, after delivering a statement of defence, move with supporting affidavit material or other evidence for summary judgment dismissing all or part of the claim in the statement of claim.

EVIDENCE ON MOTION

20.02(1) An affidavit for use on a motion for summary judgment may be made on information and belief as provided in subrule 39.01(4), but, on the hearing of the motion, the court may, if appropriate, draw an adverse inference from the failure of a party to provide the evidence of any person having personal knowledge of contested facts.

(2) In response to affidavit material or other evidence supporting a motion for summary judgment, a responding party may not rest solely on the allegations or denials in the party's pleadings, but must set out, in affidavit material or other evidence, specific facts showing that there is a genuine issue requiring a trial.

FACTUMS REQUIRED

20.03(1) On a motion for summary judgment, each party shall serve on every other party to the motion a factum consisting of a concise argument stating the facts and law relied on by the party.

(2) The moving party's factum shall be served and filed with proof of service in the court office where the motion is to be heard at least seven days before the hearing.

(3) The responding party's factum shall be served and filed with proof of service in the court office where the motion is to be heard at least four days before the hearing.

(4) Revoked.

DISPOSITION OF MOTION

General

20.04(1) Revoked.

(2) The court shall grant summary judgment if,

(a) the court is satisfied that there is no genuine issue requiring a trial with respect to a claim or defence; or

(b) the parties agree to have all or part of the claim determined by a summary judgment and the court is satisfied that it is appropriate to grant summary judgment.

Powers

(2.1) In determining under clause (2)(a) whether there is a genuine issue requiring a trial, the court shall consider the evidence submitted by the parties and, if the determination is being made by a judge, the judge may exercise any of the following powers for the purpose, unless it is in the interest of justice for such powers to be exercised only at a trial:

1. Weighing the evidence.
2. Evaluating the credibility of a deponent.
3. Drawing any reasonable inference from the evidence.

Oral Evidence (Mini-Trial)

(2.2) A judge may, for the purposes of exercising any of the powers set out in subrule (2.1), order that oral evidence be presented by one or more parties, with or without time limits on its presentation.

Only Genuine Issue is Amount

(3) Where the court is satisfied that the only genuine issue is the amount to which the moving party is entitled, the court may order a trial of that issue or grant judgment with a reference to determine the amount.

Only Genuine Issue is Question of Law

(4) Where the court is satisfied that the only genuine issue is a question of law, the court may determine the question and grant judgment accordingly, but where the motion is made to a master, it shall be adjourned to be heard by a judge.

Only Claim Is for an Accounting

(5) Where the plaintiff is the moving party and claims an accounting and the defendant fails to satisfy the court that there is a preliminary issue to be tried, the court may grant judgment on the claim with a reference to take the accounts.

WHERE TRIAL IS NECESSARY

Powers of Court

20.05(1) Where summary judgment is refused or is granted only in part, the court may make an order specifying what material facts are not in dispute and defining the issues to be tried, and order that the action proceed to trial expeditiously.

Directions and Terms

(2) If an action is ordered to proceed to trial under subrule (1), the court may give such directions or impose such terms as are just, including an order,

(a) that each party deliver, within a specified time, an affidavit of documents in accordance with the court's directions;

(b) that any motions be brought within a specified time;

(c) that a statement setting out what material facts are not in dispute be filed within a specified time;

(d) that examinations for discovery be conducted in accordance with a discovery plan established by the court, which may set a schedule for examinations and impose such limits on the right of discovery as are just, including a limit on the scope of discovery to matters not covered by the affidavits or any other evidence filed on the motion and any cross-examinations on them;

(e) that a discovery plan agreed to by the parties under Rule 29.1 (discovery plan) be amended;

(f) that the affidavits or any other evidence filed on the motion and any cross-examinations on them may be used at trial in the same manner as an examination for discovery;

(g) that any examination of a person under Rule 36 (taking evidence before trial) be subject to a time limit;

(h) that a party deliver, within a specified time, a written summary of the anticipated evidence of a witness;

(i) that any oral examination of a witness at trial be subject to a time limit;

(j) that the evidence of a witness be given in whole or in part by affidavit;

(k) that any experts engaged by or on behalf of the parties in relation to the action meet on a without prejudice basis in order to identify the issues on which the experts agree and the issues on which they do not agree, to attempt to clarify and resolve any issues that are the subject of disagreement and to prepare a joint statement setting out the areas of agreement and any areas of disagreement and the reasons for it if, in the opinion of the court, the cost or time savings or other benefits that may be achieved from the meeting are proportionate to the amounts at stake or the importance of the issues involved in the case and,

(i) there is a reasonable prospect for agreement on some or all of the issues, or

(ii) the rationale for opposing expert opinions is unknown and clarification on areas of disagreement would assist the parties or the court;

(l) that each of the parties deliver a concise summary of his or her opening statement;

(m) that the parties appear before the court by a specified date, at which appearance the court may make any order that may be made under this subrule;

(n) that the action be set down for trial on a particular date or on a particular trial list, subject to the direction of the regional senior judge;

(o) for payment into court of all or part of the claim; and

(p) for security for costs.

Specified Facts

(3) At the trial, any facts specified under subrule (1) or clause (2)(c) shall be deemed to be established unless the trial judge orders otherwise to prevent injustice.

Order re Affidavit Evidence

(4) In deciding whether to make an order under clause (2)(j), the fact that an adverse party may reasonably require the attendance of the deponent at trial for cross-examination is a relevant consideration.

Order re Experts, Costs

(5) If an order is made under clause (2)(k), each party shall bear his or her own costs.

Failure to Comply with Order

(6) Where a party fails to comply with an order under clause (2)(o) for payment into court or under clause (2)(p) for security for costs, the court on motion of the opposite party may dismiss the action, strike out the statement of defence or make such other order as is just.

(7) Where on a motion under subrule (6) the statement of defence is struck out, the defendant shall be deemed to be noted in default.

COSTS SANCTIONS FOR IMPROPER USE OF RULE

20.06 The court may fix and order payment of the costs of a motion for summary judgment by a party on a substantial indemnity basis if,

(a) the party acted unreasonably by making or responding to the motion; or

(b) the party acted in bad faith for the purpose of delay.

EFFECT OF SUMMARY JUDGMENT

20.07 A plaintiff who obtains summary judgment may proceed against the same defendant for any other relief.

STAY OF EXECUTION

20.08 Where it appears that the enforcement of a summary judgment ought to be stayed pending the determination of any other issue in the action or a counterclaim, crossclaim or third party claim, the court may so order on such terms as are just.

APPLICATION TO COUNTERCLAIMS, CROSSCLAIMS AND THIRD PARTY CLAIMS

20.09 Rules 20.01 to 20.08 apply, with necessary modifications, to counterclaims, crossclaims and third party claims.

MOTIONS AND APPLICATIONS

RULE 37   MOTIONS — JURISDICTION AND PROCEDURE

NOTICE OF MOTION

37.01 A motion shall be made by a notice of motion (Form 37A) unless the nature of the motion or the circumstances make a notice of motion unnecessary.

JURISDICTION TO HEAR A MOTION

Jurisdiction of Judge

37.02(1) A judge has jurisdiction to hear any motion in a proceeding.

Jurisdiction of a Master

(2) A master has jurisdiction to hear any motion in a proceeding, and has all the jurisdiction of a judge in respect of a motion, except a motion,

(a) where the power to grant the relief sought is conferred expressly on a judge by a statute or rule;

(b) to set aside, vary or amend an order of a judge;

(c) to abridge or extend a time prescribed by an order that a master could not have made;

(d) for judgment on consent in favour of or against a party under disability;

(e) relating to the liberty of the subject;

(f) under section 4 or 5 of the *Judicial Review Procedure Act*; or

(g) in an appeal.

Jurisdiction of Registrar

(3) The registrar shall make an order granting the relief sought on a motion for an order on consent, if,

(a) the consent of all parties (including the consent of any party to be added, deleted or substituted) is filed;

(b) the consent states that no party affected by the order is under disability; and

(c) the order sought is for,

(i) amendment of a pleading, notice of application or notice of motion,

(ii) addition, deletion or substitution of a party,

(iii) removal of a lawyer as lawyer of record;

(iv) setting aside the noting of a party in default,

(v) setting aside a default judgment,

(vi) discharge of a certificate of pending litigation,

(vii) security for costs in a specified amount,

(viii) re-attendance of a witness to answer questions on an examination,

(ix) fulfilment of undertakings given on an examination, or

(x) dismissal of a proceeding, with or without costs.

PLACE OF HEARING OF MOTIONS

37.03(1) All motions shall be brought and heard in the county where the proceeding was commenced or to which it has been transferred under rule 13.1.02, unless the court orders otherwise.

(2) Revoked.

(3) Spent.

MOTIONS — TO WHOM TO BE MADE

37.04 A motion shall be made to the court if it is within the jurisdiction of a master or registrar and otherwise shall be made to a judge.

HEARING DATE FOR MOTIONS
Where no practice direction

37.05(1) At any place where no practice direction concerning the scheduling of motions is in effect, a motion may be set down for hearing on any day on which a judge or master is scheduled to hear motions.

Exception, lengthy hearing

(2) If a lawyer estimates that the hearing of the motion will be more than two hours long, a hearing date shall be obtained from the registrar before the notice of motion is served.

Urgent motion

(3) An urgent motion may be set down for hearing on any day on which a judge or master is scheduled to hear motions, even if a lawyer estimates that the hearing is likely to be more than two hours long.

CONTENT OF NOTICE

37.06 Every notice of motion (Form 37A) shall,

(a) state the precise relief sought;

(b) state the grounds to be argued, including a reference to any statutory provision or rule to be relied on; and

(c) list the documentary evidence to be used at the hearing of the motion.

SERVICE OF NOTICE

Required as General Rule

37.07(1) The notice of motion shall be served on any party or other person who will be affected by the order sought, unless these rules provide otherwise.

Where Not Required

(2) Where the nature of the motion or the circumstances render service of the notice of motion impracticable or unnecessary, the court may make an order without notice.

(3) Where the delay necessary to effect service might entail serious consequences, the court may make an interim order without notice.

(4) Unless the court orders or these rules provide otherwise, an order made without notice to a party or other person affected by the order shall be served on the party or other person, together with a copy of the notice of motion and all affidavits and other documents used at the hearing of the motion.

Where Notice Ought to Have Been Served

(5) Where it appears to the court that the notice of motion ought to have been served on a person who has not been served, the court may,

(a) dismiss the motion or dismiss it only against the person who was not served;

(b) adjourn the motion and direct that the notice of motion be served on the person; or

(c) direct that any order made on the motion be served on the person.

Minimum Notice Period

(6) Where a motion is made on notice, the notice of motion shall be served at least seven days before the date on which the motion is to be heard.

FILING OF NOTICE OF MOTION

37.08(1) Where a motion is made on notice, the notice of motion shall be filed with proof of service at least seven days before the hearing date in the court office where the motion is to be heard.

(2) Where service of the notice of motion is not required, it shall be filed at or before the hearing.

ABANDONED MOTIONS

37.09(1) A party who makes a motion may abandon it by delivering a notice of abandonment. R.R.O. 1990, Reg. 194, r. 37.09(1).

(2) A party who serves a notice of motion and does not file it or appear at the hearing shall be deemed to have abandoned the motion unless the court orders otherwise.

(3) Where a motion is abandoned or is deemed to have been abandoned, a responding party on whom the notice of motion was served is entitled to the costs of the motion forthwith, unless the court orders otherwise.

MATERIAL FOR USE ON MOTIONS

Where Motion Record Required

37.10(1) Where a motion is made on notice, the moving party shall, unless the court orders otherwise before or at the hearing of the motion, serve a motion record on every other party to the motion and file it, with proof of service, in the court office where the motion is to be heard, at least seven days before the hearing, and the court file shall not be placed before the judge or master hearing the motion unless he or she requests it or a party requisitions it.

Contents of Motion Record

(2) The motion record shall contain, in consecutively numbered pages arranged in the following order,

(a) a table of contents describing each document, including each exhibit, by its nature and date and, in the case of an exhibit, by exhibit number or letter;

(b) a copy of the notice of motion;

(c) a copy of all affidavits and other material served by any party for use on the motion;

(d) a list of all relevant transcripts of evidence in chronological order, but not necessarily the transcripts themselves; and

(e) a copy of any other material in the court file that is necessary for the hearing of the motion.

Responding Party's Motion Record

(3) Where a motion record is served a responding party who is of the opinion that it is incomplete may serve on every other party, and file, with proof of service, in the court office where the motion is to be heard, at least four days before the hearing, a responding party's motion record containing, in consecutively numbered pages arranged in the following order,

(a) a table of contents describing each document, including each exhibit, by its nature and date and, in the case of an exhibit, by exhibit number or letter; and

(b) a copy of any material to be used by the responding party on the motion and not included in the motion record.

Material May Be Filed as Part of Record

(4) A notice of motion and any other material served by a party for use on a motion may be filed, together with proof of service, as part of the party's motion record and need not be filed separately.

Transcript of Evidence

(5) A party who intends to refer to a transcript of evidence at the hearing of a motion shall file a copy of the transcript as provided by rule 34.18.

Factum

(6) A party may serve on every other party a factum consisting of a concise argument stating the facts and law relied on by the party.

(7) The moving party's factum, if any, shall be served and filed with proof of service in the court office where the motion is to be heard at least seven days before the hearing.

(8) The responding party's factum, if any, shall be served and filed with proof of service in the court office where the motion is to be heard at least four days before the hearing.

(9) Revoked.

Refusals and Undertakings Chart

(10) On a motion to compel answers or to have undertakings given on an examination or cross-examination satisfied,

(a) the moving party shall serve on every other party to the motion and file with proof of service, in the court office where the motion is to be heard, at least seven days before the hearing, a refusals and undertakings chart (Form 37C) that sets out,

(i) the issue that is the subject of the refusal or undertaking and its connection to the pleadings or affidavit,

(ii) the question number and a reference to the page of the transcript where the question appears, and

(iii) the exact words of the question; and

(b) the responding party shall serve on the moving party and every other party to the motion and file with proof of service, in the court office where the motion is to be heard, at least four days before the hearing, a copy of the undertakings and refusals chart that was served by the moving party completed so as to show,

(i) the answer provided, or

(ii) the basis for the refusal to answer the question or satisfy the undertaking.

CONFIRMATION OF MOTION

Confirmation of Motion

37.10.1(1) A party who makes a motion on notice to another party shall,

(a) confer or attempt to confer with the other party;

(b) not later than 2 p.m. three days before the hearing date, give the registrar a confirmation of motion (Form 37B) by,

(i) sending it by fax, or by e-mail if available in the court office, or

(ii) leaving it at the court office; and

(c) send a copy of the confirmation of motion to the other party by fax or e-mail.

Effect of Failure to Confirm

(2) If no confirmation is given, the motion shall not be heard, except by order of the court.

Duty to Update

(3) A party who has given a confirmation of motion and later determines that the confirmation is no longer correct shall immediately,

(a) give the registrar a corrected confirmation of motion (Form 37B) by,

(i) sending it by fax, or by e-mail if available in the court office, or

(ii) leaving it at the court office; and

(b) send a copy of the corrected confirmation of motion to the other party by fax or e-mail.

HEARING IN ABSENCE OF PUBLIC

37.11(1) A motion may be heard in the absence of the public where,

(a) the motion is to be heard and determined without oral argument;

(b) because of urgency, it is impractical to have the motion heard in public;

(c) the motion is to be heard by conference telephone;

(d) the motion is made in the course of a pre-trial conference; or

(e) the motion is before a single judge of an appellate court.

(2) The hearing of all other motions shall be open to the public, except as provided in section 135 of the *Courts of Justice Act*, in which case the presiding judge or officer shall endorse on the notice of motion leave for a hearing in the absence of the public.

37.12 Revoked.

HEARING WITHOUT ORAL ARGUMENT

Consent Motions, Unopposed Motions and Motions Without Notice

37.12.1(1) Where a motion is on consent, unopposed or without notice under subrule 37.07(2), the motion may be heard in writing without the attendance of the parties, unless the court orders otherwise.

(2) Where the motion is on consent, the consent and a draft order shall be filed with the notice of motion.

(3) Where the motion is unopposed, a notice from the responding party stating that the party does not oppose the motion and a draft order shall be filed with the notice of motion.

Opposed Motions in Writing

(4) Where the issues of fact and law are not complex, the moving party may propose in the notice of motion that the motion be heard in writing without the attendance of the parties, in which case,

(a) the motion shall be made on at least fourteen days notice;

(b) the moving party shall serve with the notice of motion and immediately file, with proof of service in the court office where the motion is to be heard, a motion record, a draft order and a factum entitled factum for a motion in writing, setting out the moving party's argument;

(c) the motion may be heard in writing without the attendance of the parties, unless the court orders otherwise.

(5) Within ten days after being served with the moving party's material, the responding party shall serve and file, with proof of service, in the court office where the motion is to be heard,

(a) a consent to the motion;

(b) a notice that the responding party does not oppose the motion;

(c) a motion record, a notice that the responding party agrees to have the motion heard and determined in writing under this rule and a factum entitled factum for a motion in writing, setting out the party's argument; or

(d) a notice that the responding party intends to make oral argument, along with any material intended to be relied upon by the party.

(6) Where the responding party delivers a notice under subrule (5) that the party intends to make oral argument, the moving party may either attend the hearing and make oral argument or not attend and rely on the party's motion record and factum.

DISPOSITION OF MOTION

37.13(1) On the hearing of a motion, the presiding judge or officer may grant the relief sought or dismiss or adjourn the motion, in whole or in part and with or without terms, and may,

(a) where the proceeding is an action, order that it be placed forthwith, or within a specified time, on a list of cases requiring speedy trial; or

(b) where the proceeding is an application, order that it be heard at such time and place as are just.

(2) A judge who hears a motion may,

(a) in proper case, order that the motion be converted into a motion for judgment; or

(b) order the trial of an issue, with such directions as are just, and adjourn the motion to be disposed of by the trial judge.

(3) Where on a motion a judge directs the trial of an issue, subrules 38.10(2) and (3) (issue treated as action) apply with necessary modifications.

Exception, Motions in Estate Matters

(4) Clause (2)(b) and subrule (3) do not apply to motions under Rules 74 and 75.

SETTING ASIDE, VARYING OR AMENDING ORDERS

Motion to Set Aside or Vary

37.14(1) A party or other person who,

(a) is affected by an order obtained on motion without notice;

(b) fails to appear on a motion through accident, mistake or insufficient notice; or

(c) is affected by an order of a registrar,

may move to set aside or vary the order, by a notice of motion that is served forthwith after the order comes to the person's attention and names the first available hearing date that is at least three days after service of the notice of motion.

(2) On a motion under subrule (1), the court may set aside or vary the order on such terms as are just.

Order Made by Registrar

(3) A motion under subrule (1) or any other rule to set aside, vary or amend an order of a registrar may be made to a judge or master, at a place determined in accordance with rule 37.03 (place of hearing of motions).

Order Made by Judge

(4) A motion under subrule (1) or any other rule to set aside, vary or amend an order of a judge may be made,

(a) to the judge who made it, at any place; or

(b) to any other judge, at a place determined in accordance with rule 37.03 (place of hearing of motions).

Order Made by Master

(5) A motion under subrule (1) or any other rule to set aside, vary or amend an order of a master may be made,

(a) to the master who made it, at any place; or

(b) to any other master or to a judge, at a place determined in accordance with rule 37.03 (place of hearing of motions).

Order Made in Court of Appeal or Divisional Court

(6) A motion under subrule (1) or any other rule to set aside, vary or amend an order made by a judge or panel of the Court of Appeal or Divisional Court may be made,

(a) where the order was made by a judge, to the judge who made it or any other judge of the court; or

(b) where the order was made by a panel of the court, to the panel that made it or any other panel of the court.

MOTIONS IN A COMPLICATED PROCEEDING OR SERIES OF PROCEEDINGS

37.15(1) Where a proceeding involves complicated issues or where there are two or more proceedings that involve similar issues, the Chief Justice or Associate Chief Justice of the Superior Court of Justice, a regional senior judge of the Superior Court of Justice or a judge designated by any of them may direct that all motions in the proceeding or proceedings be heard by a particular judge, and rule 37.03 (place of hearing of motions) does not apply to those motions.

(1.1) A judge who is directed to hear all motions under subrule (1) may refer to a master any motion within the jurisdiction of a master under subrule 37.02(2) unless the judge who made the direction under subrule (1) directs otherwise.

(1.2) A judge who is directed to hear all motions under subrule (1) and a master to whom a motion is referred under subrule (1.1) may give such directions and make such procedural orders as are necessary to promote the most expeditious and least expensive determination of the proceeding.

(2) A judge who hears motions pursuant to a direction under subrule (1) shall not preside at the trial of the actions or the hearing of the applications except with the written consent of all parties.

PROHIBITING MOTIONS WITHOUT LEAVE

37.16 On motion by any party, a judge or master may by order prohibit another party from making further motions in the proceeding without leave, where the judge or master on the hearing of the motion is satisfied that the other party is attempting to delay or add to the costs of the proceeding or otherwise abuse the process of the court by a multiplicity of frivolous or vexatious motions.

MOTION BEFORE COMMENCEMENT OF PROCEEDING

37.17 In an urgent case, a motion may be made before the commencement of a proceeding on the moving party's undertaking to commence the proceeding forthwith.

RULE 39   EVIDENCE ON MOTIONS AND APPLICATIONS

EVIDENCE BY AFFIDAVIT
Generally

39.01(1) Evidence on a motion or application may be given by affidavit unless a statute or these rules provide otherwise.

Service and Filing

(2) Where a motion or application is made on notice, the affidavits on which the motion or application is founded shall be served with the notice of motion or notice of application and shall be filed with proof of service in the court office where the motion or application is to be heard at least seven days before the hearing.

(3) All affidavits to be used at the hearing in opposition to a motion or application or in reply shall be served and filed with proof of service in the court office where the motion or application is to be heard at least four days before the hearing.

Contents — Motions

(4) An affidavit for use on a motion may contain statements of the deponent's information and belief, if the source of the information and the fact of the belief are specified in the affidavit.

Contents — Applications

(5) An affidavit for use on an application may contain statements of the deponent's information and belief with respect to facts that are not contentious, if the source of the information and the fact of the belief are specified in the affidavit.

Full and Fair Disclosure on Motion or Application Without Notice

(6) Where a motion or application is made without notice, the moving party or applicant shall make full and fair disclosure of all material facts, and failure to do so is in itself sufficient ground for setting aside any order obtained on the motion or application.

EVIDENCE BY CROSS-EXAMINATION ON AFFIDAVIT
On a Motion or Application

39.02(1) A party to a motion or application who has served every affidavit on which the party intends to rely and has completed all examinations under rule 39.03 may cross-examine the deponent of any affidavit served by a party who is adverse in interest on the motion or application.

(2) A party who has cross-examined on an affidavit delivered by an adverse party shall not subsequently deliver an affidavit for use at the hearing or conduct an examination under rule 39.03 without leave or consent, and the court shall grant leave, on such terms as are just, where it is satisfied that the party ought to be permitted to respond to any matter raised on the cross-examination with evidence in the form of an affidavit or a transcript of an examination conducted under rule 39.03.

To be Exercised with Reasonable Diligence

(3) The right to cross-examine shall be exercised with reasonable diligence, and the court may refuse an adjournment of a motion or application for the purpose of cross-examination where the party seeking the adjournment has failed to act with reasonable diligence.

Additional Provisions Applicable to Motions

(4) On a motion other than a motion for summary judgment or a contempt order, a party who cross-examines on an affidavit,

(a) shall, where the party orders a transcript of the examination, purchase and serve a copy on every adverse party on the motion, free of charge; and

(b) is liable for the partial indemnity costs of every adverse party on the motion in respect of the cross-examination, regardless of the outcome of the proceeding, unless the court orders otherwise.

EVIDENCE BY EXAMINATION OF A WITNESS
Before the Hearing

39.03(1) Subject to subrule 39.02(2), a person may be examined as a witness before the hearing of a pending motion or application for the purpose of having a transcript of his or her evidence available for use at the hearing.

(2) A witness examined under subrule (1) may be cross-examined by the examining party and any other party and may then be re-examined by the examining party on matters raised by other parties, and the re-examination may take the form of cross-examination.

To be Exercised with Reasonable Diligence

(3) The right to examine shall be exercised with reasonable diligence, and the court may refuse an adjournment of a motion or application for the purpose of an examination where the party seeking the adjournment has failed to act with reasonable diligence.

At the Hearing

(4) With leave of the presiding judge or officer, a person may be examined at the hearing of a motion or application in the same manner as at a trial.

Summons to Witness

(5) The attendance of a person to be examined under subrule (4) may be compelled in the same manner as provided in Rule 53 for a witness at a trial.

EVIDENCE BY EXAMINATION FOR DISCOVERY
Adverse Party's Examination

39.04(1) On the hearing of a motion, a party may use in evidence an adverse party's examination for discovery or the examination for discovery of any person examined on behalf or in place of, or in addition to, the adverse party, and rule 31.11 (use of discovery at trial) applies with necessary modifications.

Party's Examination

(2) On the hearing of a motion, a party may not use in evidence the party's own examination for discovery or the examination for discovery of any person examined on behalf or in place of, or in addition to, the party unless the other parties consent.

PRESERVATION OF RIGHTS IN PENDING LITIGATION

RULE 44   INTERIM RECOVERY OF PERSONAL PROPERTY

MOTION FOR INTERIM ORDER

44.01(1) An interim order under section 104 of the *Courts of Justice Act* for recovery of possession of personal property may be obtained on motion by the plaintiff, supported by an affidavit setting out,

    (a) a description of the property sufficient to make it readily identifiable;

    (b) the value of the property;

    (c) that the plaintiff is the owner or lawfully entitled to possession of the property;

    (d) that the property was unlawfully taken from the possession of the plaintiff or is unlawfully detained by the defendant; and

    (e) the facts and circumstances giving rise to the unlawful taking or detention.

(2) The notice of motion shall be served on the defendant unless the court is satisfied that there is reason to believe that the defendant may improperly attempt to prevent recovery of possession of the property or that, for any other sufficient reason, the order should be made without notice.

ORDER TO CONTAIN DESCRIPTION AND VALUE OF PROPERTY

44.02 An interim order for recovery of possession of personal property shall contain a description of the property sufficient to make it readily identifiable and shall state the value of the property.

DISPOSITION OF MOTION

Where Made on Notice

44.03(1) On a motion for an interim order for recovery of possession of personal property made on notice to the defendant, the court may,

    (a) order the plaintiff to pay into court as security twice the value of the property as stated in the order, or such other amount as the court directs, or to give the appropriate sheriff security in such form and amount as the court approves, and direct the sheriff to take the property from the defendant and give it to the plaintiff;

    (b) order the defendant to pay into court as security twice the value of the property as stated in the order, or such other amount as the court directs, or to give the plaintiff security in such form and amount as the court approves, and direct that the property remain in the possession of the defendant; or

    (c) make such other order as is just.

Where Made Without Notice

(2) On a motion for an interim order for the recovery of possession of personal property made without notice to the defendant, the court may,

    (a) order the plaintiff to pay into court as security twice the value of the property as stated in the order, or such other amount as the court directs, or to give the appropriate sheriff security in such form and amount as the court approves, and direct the sheriff to take and detain the property for a period of ten days after service of the interim order on the defendant before giving it to the plaintiff; or

    (b) make such other order as is just.

CONDITION AND FORM OF SECURITY

44.04(1) Where an interim order for the recovery of possession of personal property requires either party to give security, the condition of the security shall be that the party providing the security will return the property to the opposite party without delay when ordered to do so, and pay any damages and costs the opposite party has sustained by reason of the interim order.

(2) Where the security is by bond, the bond shall be in Form 44A and shall remain in force until the security is released under rule 44.06.

(3) Where the bond is to be given by a person other than an insurer licensed under the Insurance Act to write surety and fidelity insurance, the person giving the bond shall first be approved by the court.

SETTING ASIDE ORDER

44.05 The court on motion may set aside or vary an interim order for the recovery of possession of personal property or stay enforcement of the order.

RELEASE OF SECURITY

44.06 Any security furnished pursuant to an order made under rule 44.03 may be released on the filing of the written consent of the parties or by order of the court.

DUTY OF SHERIFF

44.07(1) Before proceeding to enforce an interim order for the recovery of possession of personal property, the sheriff shall ascertain that any security required by the order has been given.

(2) The sheriff shall serve the order on the defendant when the property or any part of it is recovered or as soon thereafter as is possible.

(3) Where the sheriff is unable to comply with the order, or it is dangerous to do so, the sheriff may move for directions from the court.

(4) The sheriff shall, without delay after attempting to enforce the order and in any event within ten days after service of the order, report to the plaintiff on what property has been recovered and, where the sheriff has failed to recover possession of all or part of the property, on what property has not been recovered and the reason for his or her failure to recover it.

WHERE DEFENDANT PREVENTS RECOVERY

44.08 Where the sheriff reports that the defendant has prevented the recovery of all or part of the property, the court may make an order,

(a) directing the sheriff to take any other personal property of the defendant, to the value of the property that the sheriff was prevented from recovering, and give it to the plaintiff; and

(b) directing the plaintiff to hold the substituted property until the defendant surrenders to the plaintiff the property that the sheriff was prevented from recovering.

PRE-TRIAL PROCEDURES

RULE 49   OFFER TO SETTLE

DEFINITIONS

49.01 In rules 49.02 to 49.14,

"defendant" includes a respondent; ("défendeur")

"plaintiff" includes an applicant. ("demandeur")

WHERE AVAILABLE

49.02(1) A party to a proceeding may serve on any other party an offer to settle any one or more of the claims in the proceeding on the terms specified in the offer to settle (Form 49A).

(2) Subrule (1) and rules 49.03 to 49.14 also apply to motions, with necessary modifications.

TIME FOR MAKING OFFER

49.03 An offer to settle may be made at any time, but where the offer to settle is made less than seven days before the hearing commences, the costs consequences referred to in rule 49.10 do not apply.

WITHDRAWAL OR EXPIRY OF OFFER

Withdrawal

49.04(1) An offer to settle may be withdrawn at any time before it is accepted by serving written notice of withdrawal of the offer on the party to whom the offer was made.

(2) The notice of withdrawal of the offer may be in Form 49B.

Offer Expiring after Limited Time

(3) Where an offer to settle specifies a time within which it may be accepted and it is not accepted or withdrawn within that time, it shall be deemed to have been withdrawn when the time expires.

Offer Expires when Court Disposes of Claim

(4) An offer may not be accepted after the court disposes of the claim in respect of which the offer is made.

EFFECT OF OFFER

49.05 An offer to settle shall be deemed to be an offer of compromise made without prejudice.

DISCLOSURE OF OFFER TO COURT

49.06(1) No statement of the fact that an offer to settle has been made shall be contained in any pleading.

(2) Where an offer to settle is not accepted, no communication respecting the offer shall be made to the court at the hearing of the proceeding until all questions of liability and the relief to be granted, other than costs, have been determined.

(3) An offer to settle shall not be filed until all questions of liability and the relief to be granted in the proceeding, other than costs, have been determined.

ACCEPTANCE OF OFFER

Generally

49.07(1) An offer to settle may be accepted by serving an acceptance of offer (Form 49C) on the party who made the offer, at any time before it is withdrawn or the court disposes of the claim in respect of which it is made.

(2) Where a party to whom an offer to settle is made rejects the offer or responds with a counter-offer that is not accepted, the party may thereafter accept the original offer to settle, unless it has been withdrawn or the court has disposed of the claim in respect of which it was made.

Payment into Court or to Trustee as Term of Offer

(3) An offer by a plaintiff to settle a claim in return for the payment of money by a defendant may include a term that the defendant pay the money into court or to a trustee and the defendant may accept the offer only by paying the money in accordance with the offer and notifying the plaintiff of the payment.

Payment into Court or to Trustee as a Condition of Acceptance

(4) Where a defendant offers to pay money to the plaintiff in settlement of a claim, the plaintiff may accept the offer with the condition that the defendant pay the money into court or to a trustee and, where the offer is so accepted and the defendant fails to pay the money in accordance with the acceptance, the plaintiff may proceed as provided in rule 49.09 for failure to comply with the terms of an accepted offer.

Costs

(5) Where an accepted offer to settle does not provide for the disposition of costs, the plaintiff is entitled,

(a) where the offer was made by the defendant, to the plaintiff's costs assessed to the date the plaintiff was served with the offer; or

(b) where the offer was made by the plaintiff, to the plaintiff's costs assessed to the date that the notice of acceptance was served.

Incorporating into Judgment

(6) Where an offer is accepted, the court may incorporate any of its terms into a judgment.

Payment Out of Court

(7) Where money is paid into court under subrule (3) or (4), it may be paid out on consent or by order.

PARTIES UNDER DISABILITY

49.08 A party under disability may make, withdraw and accept an offer to settle, but no acceptance of an offer made by the party and no acceptance by the party of an offer made by another party is binding on the party until the settlement has been approved as provided in rule 7.08.

FAILURE TO COMPLY WITH ACCEPTED OFFER

49.09 Where a party to an accepted offer to settle fails to comply with the terms of the offer, the other party may,

(a) make a motion to a judge for judgment in the terms of the accepted offer, and the judge may grant judgment accordingly; or

(b) continue the proceeding as if there had been no accepted offer to settle.

COSTS CONSEQUENCES OF FAILURE TO ACCEPT
Plaintiff's Offer

49.10(1) Where an offer to settle,

(a) is made by a plaintiff at least seven days before the commencement of the hearing;

(b) is not withdrawn and does not expire before the commencement of the hearing; and

(c) is not accepted by the defendant,

and the plaintiff obtains a judgment as favourable as or more favourable than the terms of the offer to settle, the plaintiff is entitled to partial indemnity costs to the date the offer to settle was served and substantial indemnity costs from that date, unless the court orders otherwise.

Defendant's Offer

(2) Where an offer to settle,

(a) is made by a defendant at least seven days before the commencement of the hearing;

(b) is not withdrawn and does not expire before the commencement of the hearing; and

(c) is not accepted by the plaintiff,

and the plaintiff obtains a judgment as favourable as or less favourable than the terms of the offer to settle, the plaintiff is entitled to partial indemnity costs to the date the offer was served and the defendant is entitled to partial indemnity costs from that date, unless the court orders otherwise.

Burden of Proof

(3) The burden of proving that the judgment is as favourable as the terms of the offer to settle, or more or less favourable, as the case may be, is on the party who claims the benefit of subrule (1) or (2).

MULTIPLE DEFENDANTS

49.11 Where there are two or more defendants, the plaintiff may offer to settle with any defendant and any defendant may offer to settle with the plaintiff, but where the defendants are alleged to be jointly or jointly and severally liable to the plaintiff in respect of a claim and rights of contribution or indemnity may exist between the defendants, the costs consequences prescribed by rule 49.10 do not apply to an offer to settle unless,

(a) in the case of an offer made by the plaintiff, the offer is made to all the defendants, and is an offer to settle the claim against all the defendants; or

(b) in the case of an offer made to the plaintiff,

(i) the offer is an offer to settle the plaintiff's claim against all the defendants and to pay the costs of any defendant who does not join in making the offer, or

(ii) the offer is made by all the defendants and is an offer to settle the claim against all the defendants, and, by the terms of the offer, they are made jointly and severally liable to the plaintiff for the whole amount of the offer.

OFFER TO CONTRIBUTE

49.12(1) Where two or more defendants are alleged to be jointly or jointly and severally liable to the plaintiff in respect of a claim, any defendant may serve on any other defendant an offer to contribute (Form 49D) toward a settlement of the claim.

(2) The court may take an offer to contribute into account in determining whether another defendant should be ordered,

(a) to pay the costs of the defendant who made the offer; or

(b) to indemnify the defendant who made the offer for any costs that defendant is liable to pay to the plaintiff,

or to do both.

(3) Rules 49.04, 49.05, 49.06 and 49.13 apply to an offer to contribute as if it were an offer to settle.

DISCRETION OF COURT

49.13 Despite rules 49.03, 49.10 and 49.11, the court, in exercising its discretion with respect to costs, may take into account any offer to settle made in writing, the date the offer was made and the terms of the offer.

APPLICATION TO COUNTERCLAIMS, CROSSCLAIMS AND THIRD PARTY CLAIMS

49.14 Rules 49.01 to 49.13 apply, with necessary modifications, to counterclaims, crossclaims and third party claims.

COSTS

RULE 57   COSTS OF PROCEEDINGS

GENERAL PRINCIPLES

Factors in Discretion

57.01(1) In exercising its discretion under section 131 of the *Courts of Justice Act* to award costs, the court may consider, in addition to the result in the proceeding and any offer to settle or to contribute made in writing,

(0.a) the principle of indemnity, including, where applicable, the experience of the lawyer for the party entitled to the costs as well as the rates charged and the hours spent by that lawyer;

(0.b) the amount of costs that an unsuccessful party could reasonably expect to pay in relation to the step in the proceeding for which costs are being fixed;

(a) the amount claimed and the amount recovered in the proceeding;

(b) the apportionment of liability;

(c) the complexity of the proceeding;

(d) the importance of the issues;

(e) the conduct of any party that tended to shorten or to lengthen unnecessarily the duration of the proceeding;

(f) whether any step in the proceeding was,

(i) improper, vexatious or unnecessary, or

(ii) taken through negligence, mistake or excessive caution;

(g) a party's denial of or refusal to admit anything that should have been admitted;

(h) whether it is appropriate to award any costs or more than one set of costs where a party,

(i) commenced separate proceedings for claims that should have been made in one proceeding, or

(ii) in defending a proceeding separated unnecessarily from another party in the same interest or defended by a different lawyer; and

(i) any other matter relevant to the question of costs.

Costs Against Successful Party

(2) The fact that a party is successful in a proceeding or a step in a proceeding does not prevent the court from awarding costs against the party in a proper case.

Fixing Costs: Tariffs

(3) When the court awards costs, it shall fix them in accordance with subrule (1) and the Tariffs.

Assessment in Exceptional Cases

(3.1) Despite subrule (3), in an exceptional case the court may refer costs for assessment under Rule 58.

Authority of Court

(4) Nothing in this rule or rules 57.02 to 57.07 affects the authority of the court under section 131 of the *Courts of Justice Act*,

(a) to award or refuse costs in respect of a particular issue or part of a proceeding;

(b) to award a percentage of assessed costs or award assessed costs up to or from a particular stage of a proceeding;

(c) to award all or part of the costs on a substantial indemnity basis;

(d) to award costs in an amount that represents full indemnity; or

(e) to award costs to a party acting in person.

Bill of Costs

(5) After a trial, the hearing of a motion that disposes of a proceeding or the hearing of an application, a party who is awarded costs shall serve a bill of costs (Form 57A) on the other parties and shall file it, with proof of service.

Costs Outline

(6) Unless the parties have agreed on the costs that it would be appropriate to award for a step in a proceeding, every party who intends to seek costs for that step shall give to every other party involved in the same step, and bring to the hearing, a costs outline (Form 57B) not exceeding three pages in length.

Process for Fixing Costs

(7) The court shall devise and adopt the simplest, least expensive and most expeditious process for fixing costs and, without limiting the generality of the foregoing, costs may be fixed after receiving written submissions, without the attendance of the parties.

DIRECTIONS TO ASSESSMENT OFFICER

57.02(1) Where costs are to be assessed, the court may give directions to the assessment officer in respect of any matter referred to in rule 57.01.

(2) The court shall record,

(a) any direction to the assessment officer;

(b) any direction that is requested by a party and refused; and

(c) any direction that is requested by a party and that the court declines to make but leaves to the discretion of the assessment officer.

COSTS OF A MOTION

Contested Motion

57.03(1) On the hearing of a contested motion, unless the court is satisfied that a different order would be more just, the court shall,

(a) fix the costs of the motion and order them to be paid within 30 days; or

(b) in an exceptional case, refer the costs of the motion for assessment under Rule 58 and order them to be paid within 30 days after assessment.

(2) Where a party fails to pay the costs of a motion as required under subrule (1), the court may dismiss or stay the party's proceeding, strike out the party's defence or make such other order as is just.

Motion Without Notice

(3) On a motion made without notice, there shall be no costs to any party, unless the court orders otherwise.

COSTS ON SETTLEMENT

57.04 Where a proceeding is settled on the basis that a party shall pay or recover costs and the amount of costs is not included in or determined by the settlement, the costs may be assessed under Rule 58 on the filing of a copy of the minutes of settlement in the office of the assessment officer.

COSTS WHERE ACTION BROUGHT IN WRONG COURT

Recovery within Monetary Jurisdiction of Small Claims Court

57.05(1) If a plaintiff recovers an amount within the monetary jurisdiction of the Small Claims Court, the court may order that the plaintiff shall not recover any costs.

(2) Subrule (1) does not apply to an action transferred to the Superior Court of Justice under section 107 of the *Courts of Justice Act.*

Default Judgment Within Monetary Jurisdiction of Small Claims Court

(3) If the plaintiff obtains a default judgment that is within the monetary jurisdiction of the Small Claims Court, costs shall be assessed in accordance with that court's tariff.

Proceeding Dismissed for Want of Jurisdiction

(4) Where a proceeding is dismissed for want of jurisdiction, the court may make an order for the costs of the proceeding.

COSTS OF LITIGATION GUARDIAN

57.06(1) The court may order a successful party to pay the costs of the litigation guardian of a party under disability who is a defendant or respondent, but may further order that the successful party pay those costs only to the extent that the successful party is able to recover them from the party liable for the successful party's costs.

(2) A litigation guardian who has been ordered to pay costs is entitled to recover them from the person under disability for whom he or she has acted, unless the court orders otherwise.

LIABILITY OF LAWYER FOR COSTS

57.07(1) Where a lawyer for a party has caused costs to be incurred without reasonable cause or to be wasted by undue delay, negligence or other default, the court may make an order,

(a) disallowing costs between the lawyer and client or directing the lawyer to repay to the client money paid on account of costs;

(b) directing the lawyer to reimburse the client for any costs that the client has been ordered to pay to any other party; and

(c) requiring the lawyer personally to pay the costs of any party.

(2) An order under subrule (1) may be made by the court on its own initiative or on the motion of any party to the proceeding, but no such order shall be made unless the lawyer is given a reasonable opportunity to make representations to the court.

(3) The court may direct that notice of an order against a lawyer under subrule (1) be given to the client in the manner specified in the order.

ORDERS

RULE 60   ENFORCEMENT OF ORDERS

DEFINITIONS

60.01 In rules 60.02 to 60.19,

"creditor" means a person who is entitled to enforce an order for the payment or recovery of money; ("créancier")

"debtor" means a person against whom an order for the payment or recovery of money may be enforced. ("débiteur")

ENFORCEMENT OF ORDER FOR PAYMENT OR RECOVERY OF MONEY

General

60.02(1) In addition to any other method of enforcement provided by law, an order for the payment or recovery of money may be enforced by,

(a) a writ of seizure and sale (Form 60A) under rule 60.07;

(b) garnishment under rule 60.08;

(c) a writ of sequestration (Form 60B) under rule 60.09; and

(d) the appointment of a receiver.

Recovery of Costs Without Order Awarding Costs

(2) Where under these rules a party is entitled to costs on the basis of a certificate of assessment of costs without an order awarding costs, and the costs are not paid within seven days after the certificate of assessment of costs is signed, the party may enforce payment of the costs by the means set out in subrule (1) on filing with the registrar an affidavit setting out the basis of entitlement to costs and attaching a copy of the certificate of assessment.

Electronic Filing of Declaration

(3) Where a party may enforce payment of costs under subrule (2), payment may be enforced under rule 60.07 by a writ of seizure and sale (Form 60A) by filing electronically under subrule 4.05.1(2) a declaration setting out the basis of the entitlement to costs.

ENFORCEMENT OF ORDER FOR POSSESSION OF LAND

60.03 An order for the recovery or delivery of the possession of land may be enforced by a writ of possession (Form 60C) under rule 60.10.

ENFORCEMENT OF ORDER FOR RECOVERY OF PERSONAL PROPERTY

60.04(1) An order for the recovery of possession of personal property other than money may be enforced by a writ of delivery (Form 60D), which may be obtained on filing with the registrar where the proceeding was commenced a requisition together with a copy of the order as entered.

(2) Where the property is not delivered up under a writ of delivery, the order may be enforced by a writ of sequestration (Form 60B) under rule 60.09.

ENFORCEMENT OF ORDER TO DO OR ABSTAIN FROM DOING ANY ACT

60.05 An order requiring a person to do an act, other than the payment of money, or to abstain from doing an act, may be enforced against the person refusing or neglecting to obey the order by a contempt order under rule 60.11.

ENFORCEMENT BY OR AGAINST A PERSON NOT A PARTY

60.06(1) An order that is made for the benefit of a person who is not a party may be enforced by that person in the same manner as if the person were a party.

(2) An order that may be enforced against a person who is not a party may be enforced against that person in the same manner as if the person were a party.

WRIT OF SEIZURE AND SALE
Where Available Without Leave

60.07(1) Where an order may be enforced by a writ of seizure and sale, the creditor is entitled to the issue of one or more writs of seizure and sale (Form 60A), on filing with the registrar where the proceeding was commenced a requisition setting out,

    (a) the date and amount of any payment received since the order was made; and

    (b) the amount owing and the rate of postjudgment interest,

together with a copy of the order as entered and any other evidence necessary to establish the amount awarded and the creditor's entitlement.

Electronic Issue of Writ

(1.1) Where an order may be enforced by a writ of seizure and sale, a creditor is entitled to the electronic issue of one or more writs of seizure and sale on filing electronically under subrule 4.05.1(2) a requisition setting out,

    (a) the date and amount of any payment received since the order was made; and

    (b) the amount owing and the rate of postjudgment interest.

(1.2) Where the Workplace Safety and Insurance Board is entitled to file a certificate under section 139 of the *Workplace Safety and Insurance Act, 1997*, the Board is entitled to the electronic issue of one or more writs of seizure and sale on filing electronically a requisition setting out,

(a) the date and amount of any payment received since the order was made; and

(b) the amount owing and the rate of postjudgment interest.

Order Deemed Entered

(1.3) Where a creditor files a requisition under subrule (1.1), the order to which the requisition relates shall be deemed to have been entered as an order of the Superior Court of Justice.

(1.4) Where the Workplace Safety and Insurance Board files a requisition under subrule (1.2), the certificate referred to in that subrule shall be deemed to have been entered as an order of the Superior Court of Justice.

Where Leave Is Required

(2) If six years or more have elapsed since the date of the order, or if its enforcement is subject to a condition, a writ of seizure and sale shall not be issued unless leave of the court is first obtained.

(3) An order granting leave to issue a writ of seizure and sale ceases to have effect if the writ is not issued within one year after the date of the order granting leave, but the court may grant leave again on a subsequent motion.

Order for Payment into Court

(4) Where an order is for the payment of money into court, the writ of seizure and sale shall contain a notice that all money realized by the sheriff under the writ is to be paid into court.

Order for Payment at Future Time

(5) Where an order is for payment at or after a specified future time, the writ of seizure and sale shall not be issued until after the expiration of that time.

Duration and Renewal

(6) A writ of seizure and sale remains in force for six years from the date of its issue and for a further six years from each renewal.

(7) Revoked.

(8) A writ of seizure and sale that is filed with a sheriff may be renewed before its expiration by filing a request to renew (Form 60E) with the sheriff, who shall record the date of renewal.

(8.1) A creditor may file electronically under subrule 4.05.1(2) a request to renew under subrule (8).

(9) A writ of seizure and sale that is not filed with a sheriff may be renewed before its expiration by filing with the registrar who issued it a requisition to renew the writ, and the registrar shall renew the writ and record the date of renewal.

Change or Variation of Debtor's Name

(10) Where a debtor named in a writ of seizure and sale,

(a) changes his, her or its name after the writ is issued;

(b) uses an alias; or

(c) uses a variation of spelling of the name,

the creditor may on motion made without notice seek a change or variation to the writ.

(11) On a motion referred to in subrule (10), the court may order the sheriff to,

(a) amend the writ by adding the words "now or also known as", followed by the new name of the debtor, the alias or the spelling variation;

(b) amend the index of writs to show the new name, the alias or the spelling variation; and

(c) if a copy of the writ was sent to the land registrar for filing under the *Land Titles Act*, send a copy of the amended writ to the land registrar.

(11.1) On a motion referred to in subrule (10), the court may grant the creditor leave to file an amendment to the writ electronically under subrule 4.05.1(2) to show the new name, the alias or the spelling variation.

Writ to Bear Creditor's Address

(12) Every writ of seizure and sale shall bear the name and address of the creditor and the creditor's lawyer, if any.

Change of Address

(12.1) If the address of the creditor or the creditor's lawyer changes after the writ is issued, the creditor may have the new address noted on the writ by filing a requisition to that effect with the sheriff.

(12.2) If the address of the creditor or the creditor's lawyer changes after the writ is issued, the creditor may have the new address recorded by filing a change of address form electronically under subrule 4.05.1(2).

Direction to Enforce

(13) Where an order may be enforced by a writ of seizure and sale, a creditor who has filed a writ of seizure and sale with a sheriff may file with the sheriff a copy of the order as entered, together with a direction to enforce (Form 60F) setting out,

(a) the date of the order and the amount awarded;

(b) the rate of postjudgment interest payable;

(c) the costs of enforcement to which the creditor is entitled under rule 60.19;

(d) the date and amount of any payment received since the order was made; and

(e) the amount owing, including postjudgment interest,

and directing the sheriff to enforce the writ for the amount owing, subsequent interest and the sheriff's fees and expenses.

Sheriff May Decline to Enforce

(13.1) The sheriff may decline to enforce the writ of seizure and sale, and the creditor may make a motion to the court for directions, where the sheriff is uncertain whether the writ of seizure and sale has been properly issued or filed.

Property in Hands of Receiver

(14) A writ of seizure and sale shall not be enforced against property in the hands of a receiver appointed by a court.

Seizure of Personal Property

(15) Where personal property is seized under a writ of seizure and sale, the sheriff shall, on request, deliver an inventory of the property seized to the debtor or the debtor's agent or employee before or, where this is not practicable, within a reasonable time after the property is removed from the premises on which it was seized.

Sale of Personal Property

(16) Personal property seized under a writ of seizure and sale shall not be sold by the sheriff unless notice of the time and place of the sale has been,

(a) mailed to the creditor at the address shown on the writ or the creditor's lawyer and to the debtor at the debtor's last known address, at least ten days before the sale; and

(b) published in a newspaper of general circulation in the place where the property was seized.

Sale of Land

(17) A creditor may not take any step to sell land under a writ of seizure and sale until four months after the writ was filed with the sheriff or, where the writ has been withdrawn, four months after the writ was re-filed.

(18) No sale of land under a writ of seizure and sale may be held until six months after the writ was filed with the sheriff or, where the writ has been withdrawn, six months after the writ was re-filed.

(19) A sale of land shall not be held under a writ of seizure and sale unless notice of the time and place of sale has been,

(a) mailed to the creditor at the address shown on the writ or to the creditor's lawyer and to the debtor at the debtor's last known address, at least thirty days before the sale;

(b) published in *The Ontario Gazette* once at least thirty days before the sale and in a newspaper of general circulation in the place where the land is situate, once each week for two successive weeks, the last notice to be published not less than one week nor more than three weeks before the date of sale; and

(c) posted in a conspicuous place in the sheriff's office for at least thirty days before the sale.

(20) The notice shall set out,

(a) a short description of the property to be sold;

(b) the short title of the proceeding;

(c) the time and place of the intended sale; and

(d) the name of the debtor whose interest is to be sold.

(21) The sheriff may adjourn a sale to a later date where the sheriff considers it necessary in order to realize the best price that can be obtained in all the circumstances, and where the sale is adjourned, it may be conducted on the later date with such further notice, if any, as the sheriff considers advisable.

(22) Where notice of a sale of land under a writ of seizure and sale is published in *The Ontario Gazette* before the writ expires, the sale may be completed by a sale and transfer of the land after the writ expires.

Abortive Sale

(23) Where personal property or land seized under a writ of seizure and sale remains unsold for want of buyers, the sheriff shall notify the creditor of the date and place of the attempted sale and of any other relevant circumstances.

(24) On receipt of a notice under subrule (23), the creditor may instruct the sheriff in writing to sell the personal property or land in such manner as the sheriff considers will realize the best price that can be obtained.

WARRANT ISSUED BY MINISTER OF FINANCE
Application of Rules

60.07.1(1) These rules apply, with necessary modifications, to a warrant that is issued by the Minister of Finance under an Act and directed to a sheriff, as if the warrant were a writ of seizure and sale.

Electronic Filing

(2) A warrant described in subrule (1) may be filed electronically under subrule 4.05.1(3).

Direction to Enforce

(3) When a warrant described in subrule (1) has been filed with the sheriff, the Minister of Finance may file with the sheriff a direction to enforce setting out,

  (a) the date and amount of the warrant;

  (b) the rate of interest payable;

  (c) the date and amount of any payment received since the warrant was issued; and

  (d) the amount owing under the warrant, including interest,

and directing the sheriff to enforce the warrant for the amount owing, subsequent interest and the sheriff's fees and expenses.

GARNISHMENT
Where Available

60.08(1) A creditor under an order for the payment or recovery of money may enforce it by garnishment of debts payable to the debtor by other persons.

Joint Debts Garnishable

(1.1) Where a debt is payable to the debtor and to one or more co-owners, one-half of the indebtedness or a greater or lesser amount specified in an order made under subrule (16) may be garnished.

Where Leave Required

(2) If six years or more have elapsed since the date of the order, or if its enforcement is subject to a condition, a notice of garnishment shall not be issued unless leave of the court is first obtained.

(3) An order granting leave to issue a notice of garnishment ceases to have effect if the notice is not issued within one year after the date of the order granting leave, but the court may grant leave again on a subsequent motion.

Renewal

(3.1) A notice of renewal of garnishment may be issued under subrule (6.4) without leave of the court before the original notice of garnishment or any subsequent notice of renewal of garnishment expires.

Obtaining Notice of Garnishment

(4) A creditor under an order for the payment or recovery of money who seeks to enforce it by garnishment shall file with the registrar where the proceeding was commenced a requisition for garnishment (Form 60G) together with a copy of the order as entered, any other evidence necessary to establish the amount awarded and the creditor's entitlement, and an affidavit stating,

  (a) the date and amount of any payment received since the order was made;

  (b) the amount owing, including postjudgment interest;

  (c) details of how the amount owing and the postjudgment interest are calculated;

  (c.1) the address of the debtor;

  (d) the name and address of each person to whom a notice of garnishment is to be directed;

  (e) that the creditor believes that those persons are or will become indebted to the debtor and the grounds for the belief;

  (f) such particulars of the debts as are known to the creditor;

  (g) where a person to whom a notice of garnishment is to be directed is not in Ontario, that the debtor is entitled to sue that person in Ontario to recover the debt, and the basis of entitlement to sue in Ontario; and

(h) where a person to whom a notice of garnishment is to be directed is not then indebted but will become indebted to the debtor, such particulars of the date on and the circumstances under which the debt will arise as are known to the creditor.

(5) The affidavit required by subrule (4) may contain statements of the deponent's information and belief, if the source of the information and the fact of the belief are specified in the affidavit.

(6) On the filing of the requisition and affidavit required by subrule (4), the registrar shall issue notices of garnishment (Form 60H) naming as garnishees the persons named in the affidavit and shall send a copy of each notice of garnishment to the sheriff of the county in which the debtor resides or, if the debtor resides outside Ontario, to the sheriff of the county in which the proceeding was commenced.

(6.1) A notice of garnishment issued under subrule (6) shall name one debtor and one garnishee.

Duration and Renewal

(6.2) A notice of garnishment remains in force for six years from the date of its issue and for a further six years from each renewal.

(6.3) A notice of garnishment may be renewed before its expiration by filing with the registrar where the proceeding was commenced a requisition for renewal of garnishment (Form 60G.1) together with the affidavit required by subrule (4).

(6.4) On the filing of the requisition and affidavit required by subrule (6.3), the registrar shall issue notices of renewal of garnishment (Form 60H.1) naming as garnishees the persons named in the affidavit and shall send a copy of each notice of renewal of garnishment to the sheriff of the county in which the debtor resides or, if the debtor resides outside Ontario, to the sheriff of the county in which the proceeding was commenced.

(6.5) The provisions of these rules that apply with respect to notices of garnishment also apply with respect to notices of renewal of garnishment.

Service of Notice of Garnishment

(7) The creditor shall serve the notice of garnishment,

(a) on the debtor, together with a copy of the affidavit required by subrule (4); and

(b) on the garnishee, with a blank garnishee's statement (Form 60I) attached.

(8) The notice of garnishment shall be served by ordinary mail, or by personal service or an alternative to personal service under rule 16.03.

(9) A notice of garnishment may be served outside Ontario if the debtor would be entitled to sue the garnishee in Ontario to recover the debt.

(10) If the garnishee is a financial institution, the notice of garnishment and all further notices required to be served under this rule shall be served at the branch at which the debt is payable.

(10.1) Revoked.

Garnishee Liable from Time of Service

(11) The garnishee is liable to pay to the sheriff any debt of the garnishee to the debtor, up to the amount shown in the notice of garnishment or supplementary notice of garnishment, less $10 for the cost of making each payment, within ten days after service on the garnishee or ten days after the debt becomes payable, whichever is later.

(12) For the purposes of subrule (11), a debt of the garnishee to the debtor includes,

(a) a debt payable at the time the notice of garnishment is served; and

(b) a debt payable (whether absolutely or on the fulfilment of a condition) after the notice is served and within six years after it is issued.

(13) For the purposes of subrule (11), a debt of the garnishee to the debtor does not include,

(a) if the garnishee is a financial institution, money in an account opened after the notice of garnishment is served;

(b) if the garnishee is an employer, a debt arising out of employment that commences after the notice is served; or

(c) if the garnishee is an insurer, a debt payable under an insurance policy that is entered into after the notice is served.

Payment by Garnishee to Sheriff

(14) A garnishee who admits owing a debt to the debtor shall pay it to the sheriff in the manner prescribed by the notice of garnishment, subject to section 7 of the Wages Act.

When Garnishee Must Serve Statement

(15) A garnishee who wishes for any reason to dispute the garnishment or who pays to the sheriff less than the amount set out in the notice of garnishment because the debt is owed to the debtor and to one or more co-owners or for any other reason shall, within 10 days after service of the notice of garnishment, serve on the creditor and the debtor and file with the court a garnishee's statement (Form 60I) setting out the particulars.

Notice to Co-owner of the Debt

(15.1) When a creditor is served with a garnishee's statement that indicates that the debt is owed to the debtor and to one or more co-owners, the creditor shall forthwith serve the co-owners with a notice to co-owner of the debt (Form 60I.1) and a copy of the garnishee's statement.

(15.2) The notice to co-owner of the debt and the copy of the garnishee's statement shall be served by personal service or an alternative to personal service under rule 16.03.

Garnishment Hearing

(16) On motion by a creditor, debtor, garnishee, co-owner of the debt or any other interested person, the court may,

(a) where it is alleged that the debt of the garnishee to the debtor has been assigned or encumbered, order the assignee or encumbrancer to appear and state the nature and particulars of the claim;

(b) determine the rights and liabilities of the garnishee, the debtor, any co-owner of the debt and any assignee or encumbrancer;

(c) vary or suspend periodic payments under a notice of garnishment; or

(d) determine any other matter in relation to a notice of garnishment,

and the court may proceed in a summary manner, but where the motion is made to a master and raises a genuine issue of fact or of law, it shall be adjourned to be heard by a judge.

(16.1) A copy of a notice of motion for a garnishment hearing shall be served on the sheriff by ordinary mail, or by personal service or an alternative to personal service under rule 16.03.

Time for Motion

(16.2) A person who has been served with a notice to co-owner is not entitled to dispute the enforcement of the creditor's order for the payment or recovery of money or a payment made in accordance with the *Creditors' Relief Act* unless the person moves for a garnishment hearing within 30 days after being served with the notice.

Enforcement Against Garnishee

(17) Where the garnishee does not pay to the sheriff the amount set out in the notice of garnishment as owing by the garnishee to the debtor and does not serve and file a garnishee's statement, the creditor is entitled on motion to the court, on notice to the garnishee, to an order against the garnishee for payment of the amount that the court finds is payable to the debtor by the garnishee, or the amount set out in the notice, whichever is less.

Payment by Garnishee to Person Other Than Sheriff

(18) Where, after service of a notice of garnishment, the garnishee pays a debt attached by the notice to a person other than the sheriff, the garnishee remains liable to pay the debt in accordance with the notice.

Effect of Payment to Sheriff

(19) Payment of a debt by a garnishee in accordance with a notice of garnishment is a valid discharge of the debt, as between the garnishee and the debtor, and any co-owner of the debt, to the extent of the payment, including the amount deducted for the cost of making payment under subrule (11).

Creditor to Give Notice When Order Satisfied

(20) When the amount owing under an order that is enforced by garnishment has been paid, the creditor shall forthwith serve a notice of termination of garnishment (Form 60J) on the garnishee and on the sheriff.

Payment When Debt Jointly Owned

(21) Where a payment of a debt owed to the debtor and one or more co-owners has been made to the sheriff, no notice of motion for a garnishment hearing is delivered and the time for doing so has expired, the creditor may file with the sheriff, within 30 days thereafter,

(a) proof of service of the notice to co-owner; and

(b) an affidavit stating that the creditor believes that no co-owner of the debt is a person under disability and the grounds for the belief.

(22) The affidavit required by subrule (21) may contain statements of the deponent's information and belief, if the source of the information and the fact of the belief are specified in the affidavit.

(23) Where the creditor does not file the material referred to in subrule (21), the sheriff shall return the money to the garnishee.

WRIT OF SEQUESTRATION
Leave Required

60.09(1) A writ of sequestration (Form 60B), directing a sheriff to take possession of and hold the property of a person against whom an order has been made and to collect and hold any income from the property until the person complies with the order, may be issued only with leave of the court, obtained on motion.

(2) The court may grant leave to issue a writ of sequestration only where it is satisfied that other enforcement measures are or are likely to be ineffective.

(3) In granting leave to issue a writ of sequestration, the court may order that the writ be enforced against all or part of the person's real and personal property.

Variation or Discharge

(4) The court on motion may discharge or vary a writ of sequestration on such terms as are just.

WRIT OF POSSESSION
Leave Required

60.10(1) A writ of possession (Form 60C) may be issued only with leave of the court, obtained on motion without notice or at the time an order entitling a party to possession is made.

(2) The court may grant leave to issue a writ of possession only where it is satisfied that all persons in actual possession of any part of the land have received sufficient notice of the proceeding in which the order was obtained to have enabled them to apply to the court for relief.

Duration

(3) A writ of possession remains in force for one year from the date of the order authorizing its issue, and may, before its expiry, be renewed by order for a period of one year from each renewal.

CONTEMPT ORDER

Motion for Contempt Order

60.11(1) A contempt order to enforce an order requiring a person to do an act, other than the payment of money, or to abstain from doing an act, may be obtained only on motion to a judge in the proceeding in which the order to be enforced was made.

(2) The notice of motion shall be served personally on the person against whom a contempt order is sought, and not by an alternative to personal service, unless the court orders otherwise.

(3) An affidavit in support of a motion for a contempt order may contain statements of the deponent's information and belief only with respect to facts that are not contentious, and the source of the information and the fact of the belief shall be specified in the affidavit.

Warrant for Arrest

(4) A judge may issue a warrant (Form 60K) for the arrest of the person against whom a contempt order is sought where the judge is of the opinion that the person's attendance at the hearing is necessary in the interest of justice and it appears that the person is not likely to attend voluntarily.

Content of Order

(5) In disposing of a motion under subrule (1), the judge may make such order as is just, and where a finding of contempt is made, the judge may order that the person in contempt,

    (a) be imprisoned for such period and on such terms as are just;

    (b) be imprisoned if the person fails to comply with a term of the order;

    (c) pay a fine;

    (d) do or refrain from doing an act;

    (e) pay such costs as are just; and

    (f) comply with any other order that the judge considers necessary,

and may grant leave to issue a writ of sequestration under rule 60.09 against the person's property.

Where Corporation Is in Contempt

(6) Where a corporation is in contempt, the judge may also make an order under subrule (5) against any officer or director of the corporation and may grant leave to issue a writ of sequestration under rule 60.09 against his or her property.

Warrant of Committal

(7) An order under subrule (5) for imprisonment may be enforced by the issue of a warrant of committal (Form 60L).

Discharging or Setting Aside Contempt Order

(8) On motion, a judge may discharge, set aside, vary or give directions in respect of an order under subrule (5) or (6) and may grant such other relief and make such other order as is just.

Order that Act Be Done by Another Person

(9) Where a person fails to comply with an order requiring the doing of an act, other than the payment of money, a judge on motion may, instead of or in addition to making a contempt order, order the act to be done, at the expense of the disobedient person, by the party enforcing the order or any other person appointed by the judge.

(10) The party enforcing the order and any person appointed by the judge are entitled to the costs of the motion under subrule (9) and the expenses incurred in doing the act ordered to be done, fixed by the judge or assessed by an assessment officer in accordance with Rule 58.

FAILURE TO COMPLY WITH INTERLOCUTORY ORDER

60.12 Where a party fails to comply with an interlocutory order, the court may, in addition to any other sanction provided by these rules,

    (a) stay the party's proceeding;

    (b) dismiss the party's proceeding or strike out the party's defence; or

    (c) make such other order as is just.

DISPUTE OF OWNERSHIP OF PROPERTY SEIZED BY SHERIFF

60.13(1) A person who makes a claim in respect of property or the proceeds of property taken or intended to be taken by a sheriff in the execution of any enforcement process against another person shall give notice to the sheriff of the claim and the address for service of the person making the claim.

(2) On receiving a claim, the sheriff shall forthwith give notice of claim (Form 60M) to every creditor of the debtor who has filed an enforcement process with the sheriff, by mail addressed to the creditor at the address shown on the enforcement process, and the creditor shall within seven days after receiving the notice give the sheriff notice in writing stating whether the creditor admits or disputes the claim.

(3) Where the sheriff,

    (a) receives a notice admitting the claim from every creditor; or

    (b) receives a notice admitting the claim from the creditor at whose direction the sheriff took or intended to take the property and does not receive a notice disputing the claim from any other creditor,

he or she shall release the property in respect of which the claim is admitted.

Interpleader Proceedings

(4) Where the sheriff,

    (a) does not receive a notice disputing the claim; or

    (b) does not receive a notice disputing the claim from the creditor at whose direction the sheriff took or intended to take the property and receives a notice admitting the claim from every other creditor,

the sheriff shall give notice to every creditor who has filed an enforcement process with the sheriff, by mail addressed to the creditor at the address shown on the enforcement process that, unless the creditor seeks an interpleader order under Rule 43 within 60 days of the date of the notice, the sheriff will release the property.

(5) Where the sheriff receives a notice disputing the claim, the sheriff shall give notice to the person making the claim by mail addressed to the person's address for service that, unless the person seeks an interpleader order under Rule 43 within 60 days of the date of the notice, the sheriff shall proceed as if the claim had been abandoned.

SHERIFF'S REPORT ON EXECUTION OF WRIT

60.14(1) A party or lawyer who has filed a writ with a sheriff may in writing require the sheriff to report the manner in which he or she has executed the writ and the sheriff shall do so forthwith by mailing to the party or lawyer a sheriff's report (Form 60N).

(2) Where the sheriff fails to comply with a request made under subrule (1) within a reasonable time, the party serving the request may move before a judge for an order directing the sheriff to comply with the request.

REMOVAL OR WITHDRAWAL OF WRIT FROM SHERIFF'S FILE

Sheriff's Procedure — Executed and Expired Writs

60.15(1) When a writ has been fully executed or has expired, the sheriff shall so indicate in his or her file, and the writ shall be removed from the active file, transferred to a separate file of executed, expired and withdrawn writs and retained there.

Sheriff's Procedure — Withdrawn Writs

(2) When a writ is withdrawn, the sheriff shall record the date and time of the withdrawal, and if the writ is withdrawn as against all the debtors named in it, it shall be removed from the active file, transferred to a separate file of executed, expired and withdrawn writs and retained there.

Withdrawal of Writ by Person Who Filed It

(3) A party or lawyer who has filed a writ with a sheriff may withdraw it as against one or more of the debtors named in it by giving the sheriff written instructions to that effect.

(4) A party who has filed a writ with a sheriff may withdraw it as against one or more of the debtors named in it by filing a withdrawal of writ electronically under subrule 4.05.1(2).

Withdrawal of Writ on Debtor's Request

(5) When a judgment debt has been released by an order of discharge or by a certificate of full performance under the *Bankruptcy and Insolvency Act* (Canada), the debtor may request that the writ be withdrawn by giving the sheriff,

(a) a written request to withdraw the writ (Form 60O); and

(b) a certified copy of the order of discharge or a copy of the certificate of full performance.

(6) On receiving the documents described in subrule (5), the sheriff shall forthwith send the creditor, by mail addressed to the creditor at the address shown on the writ, a copy of the documents and a notice that the writ will be withdrawn unless the creditor,

(a) makes a motion for an order under the *Bankruptcy and Insolvency Act* (Canada) that the judgment debt is not released by the order of discharge or certificate of full performance; and

(b) within 30 days after the date of the sheriff's notice, serves the sheriff with a copy of the notice of motion and a copy of all affidavits and other material served for use on the motion.

(7) The sheriff shall withdraw the writ after the day that is 30 days after the date of the notice to the creditor, unless the creditor has taken the steps described in clause (6)(b).

(8) If the creditor takes the steps described in clause (6)(b), the sheriff shall not withdraw the writ at the debtor's request unless the court orders otherwise.

DUTY OF PERSON FILING WRIT WITH SHERIFF

60.16(1) Where a writ of seizure and sale has been filed with a sheriff and any payment has been received by or on behalf of the creditor, the creditor shall forthwith give the sheriff notice of the payment.

(2) Where an order has been satisfied in full, the creditor shall withdraw all writs of execution relating to the order from the office of any sheriff with whom they have been filed.

(3) Where the creditor fails to withdraw a writ as required by subrule (2), the court on motion by the debtor may order that the writ be withdrawn.

MOTION FOR DIRECTIONS

60.17 Where a question arises in relation to the measures to be taken by a sheriff in carrying out an order, writ of execution or notice of garnishment, the sheriff or any interested person may make a motion for directions,

(a) to the judge or officer who made the original order, at any place;

(b) to a judge or officer who had jurisdiction to make the original order, in the sheriff's county, despite rule 37.03 (place of hearing of motions); or

(c) where an appeal has been taken from the original order, to a judge of the court to which the appeal has been taken, at any place.

EXAMINATION IN AID OF EXECUTION

Definitions

60.18(1) In subrules (2) to (6),

"creditor" includes a person entitled to obtain or enforce a writ of possession, delivery or sequestration; ("créancier")

"debtor" includes a person against whom a writ of possession, delivery or sequestration may be or has been issued. ("débiteur")

Examination of Debtor

(2) A creditor may examine the debtor in relation to,

(a) the reason for nonpayment or nonperformance of the order;

(b) the debtor's income and property;

(c) the debts owed to and by the debtor;

(d) the disposal the debtor has made of any property either before or after the making of the order;

(e) the debtor's present, past and future means to satisfy the order;

(f) whether the debtor intends to obey the order or has any reason for not doing so; and

(g) any other matter pertinent to the enforcement of the order.

(3) An officer or director of a corporate debtor, or, in the case of a debtor that is a partnership or sole proprietorship, a partner or sole proprietor against whom the order may be enforced, may be examined on behalf of the debtor in relation to the matters set out in subrule (2).

(4) Only one examination under subrule (2) or (3) may be held in a twelve month period in respect of a debtor in the same proceeding, unless the court orders otherwise.

(5) Where it appears from an examination under subrules (2) to (4) that a debtor has concealed or made away with property to defeat or defraud creditors, a judge may make a contempt order against the debtor.

Examination of Person Other Than Debtor

(6) Where any difficulty arises concerning the enforcement of an order, the court may,

(a) make an order for the examination of any person who the court is satisfied may have knowledge of the matters set out in subrule (2); and

(b) make such order for the examination of any other person as is just.

Service on Debtor

(7) Despite clause 34.04(1)(a) (service on lawyer), a party who is to be examined in aid of execution shall be served with a notice of examination personally or by an alternative to personal service.

COSTS OF ENFORCEMENT

60.19(1) A party who is entitled to enforce an order is entitled to the costs of the following steps on a partial indemnity scale, unless the court on motion orders otherwise:

1. An examination in aid of execution.

2. The issuing, service, filing, enforcement and renewal of a writ of execution and notice of garnishment.

3. Any other procedure authorized by these rules for enforcing the order.

(2) A party entitled to costs under subrule (1) may include in or collect under a writ of execution or notice of garnishment,

(a) $50 for the preparation of documents in connection with issuing, renewing and filing with the sheriff the writ of execution or notice of garnishment;

(b) disbursements paid to a sheriff, registrar, official examiner, court reporter or other public officer and to which the party is entitled under subrule (1), on filing with the sheriff or registrar a copy of a receipt for each disbursement;

(c) an amount determined in accordance with Tariff A for conducting an examination in aid of execution, on filing with the sheriff or registrar an affidavit stating that the examination was conducted; and

(d) any other costs to which the party is entitled under subrule (1), on filing with the sheriff or registrar a certificate of assessment of the costs.

(3) A sheriff or registrar may fix costs under clause (2)(c),

(a) if all the parties consent; or

(b) if the lawyer's fee does not exceed $2,000, exclusive of goods and services tax.

(4) Under clause (3)(b), the sheriff or registrar shall fix costs of $750 plus disbursements.

(5) When costs are to be fixed by the sheriff or registrar under subrule (3), the party who is entitled to costs shall file a bill of costs with the sheriff or registrar.

APPEALS

RULE 61   APPEALS TO AN APPELLATE COURT

APPLICATION OF THE RULE

61.01 Rules 61.02 to 61.16 apply to all appeals to an appellate court except as provided in clause 62.01(1)(b) or rule 62.02 and, with necessary modifications, to proceedings in an appellate court by way of,

(a) stated case under a statute;

(b) special case under rule 22.03, subject to any directions given under subrule 22.03(2); and

(c) reference under section 8 of the *Courts of Justice Act.*

DEFINITION

61.02 In rules 61.03 to 61.16,

"Registrar" means,

(a) in the Court of Appeal, the Registrar of the Court of Appeal, or

(b) in the Divisional Court, the registrar in the regional centre of the region where the appeal is to be heard in accordance with subsection 20(1) of the *Courts of Justice Act.*

MOTION FOR LEAVE TO APPEAL TO DIVISIONAL COURT

Notice of Motion for Leave

61.03(1) Where an appeal to the Divisional Court requires the leave of that court, the notice of motion for leave shall,

(a) state that the motion will be heard on a date to be fixed by the Registrar;

(b) be served within 15 days after the making of the order or decision from which leave to appeal is sought, unless a statute provides otherwise; and

(c) be filed with proof of service in the office of the Registrar, within five days after service.

Motion Record, Factum and Transcripts

(2) On a motion for leave to appeal to the Divisional Court, the moving party shall serve,

(a) a motion record containing, in consecutively numbered pages arranged in the following order,

(i) a table of contents describing each document, including each exhibit, by its nature and date and, in the case of an exhibit, by exhibit number or letter,

(ii) a copy of the notice of motion,

(iii) a copy of the order or decision from which leave to appeal is sought, as signed and entered,

(iv) a copy of the reasons of the court or tribunal from which leave to appeal is sought with a further typed or printed copy if the reasons are handwritten,

(iv.1) a copy of any order or decision that was the subject of the hearing before the court or tribunal from which leave to appeal is sought,

(iv.2) a copy of any reasons for the order or decision referred to in subclause (iv.1), with a further typed or printed copy if the reasons are handwritten,

(v) a copy of all affidavits and other material used before the court or tribunal from which leave to appeal is sought,

(vi) a list of all relevant transcripts of evidence in chronological order, but not necessarily the transcripts themselves, and

(vii) a copy of any other material in the court file that is necessary for the hearing of the motion;

(b) a factum consisting of a concise argument stating the facts and law relied on by the moving party; and

(c) relevant transcripts of evidence, if they are not included in the motion record,

and shall file three copies of the motion record, factum and transcripts, if any, with proof of service, within thirty days after the filing of the notice of motion for leave to appeal.

(3) On a motion for leave to appeal to the Divisional Court, the responding party may, where he or she is of the opinion that the moving party's motion record is incomplete, serve a motion record containing, in consecutively numbered pages arranged in the following order,

(a) a table of contents describing each document, including each exhibit, by its nature and date and, in the case of an exhibit, by exhibit number or letter; and

(b) a copy of any material to be used by the responding party on the motion and not included in the motion record,

and may serve a factum consisting of a concise argument stating the facts and law relied on by the responding party, and shall file three copies of the responding party's motion record and factum, if any, with proof of service, within fifteen days after service of the moving party's motion record, factum and transcripts, if any.

Notice and Factum to State Questions on Appeal

(4) The moving party's notice of motion and factum shall, where practicable, set out the specific questions that it is proposed the Divisional Court should answer if leave to appeal is granted.

Date for Hearing

(5) The Registrar shall fix a date for the hearing of the motion which shall not, except with the responding party's consent, be earlier than fifteen days after the filing of the moving party's motion record, factum and transcripts, if any.

Time for Delivering Notice of Appeal

(6) Where leave is granted, the notice of appeal shall be delivered within seven days after the granting of leave.

Costs Appeal Joined with Appeal as of Right

(7) Where a party seeks to join an appeal under clause 133(b) of the *Courts of Justice Act* with an appeal as of right,

(a) the request for leave to appeal shall be included in the notice of appeal or in a supplementary notice of appeal as part of the relief sought;

(b) leave to appeal shall be sought from the panel of the Divisional Court hearing the appeal as of right; and

(c) where leave is granted, the panel may then hear the appeal.

Costs Cross-Appeal Joined with Appeal or Cross-Appeal as of Right

(8) Where a party seeks to join a cross-appeal under a statute that requires leave for an appeal with an appeal or cross-appeal as of right,

(a) the request for leave to appeal shall be included in the notice of appeal or cross-appeal or in a supplementary notice of appeal or cross-appeal as part of the relief sought;

(b) leave to appeal shall be sought from the panel of the Divisional Court hearing the appeal or cross-appeal as of right; and

(c) where leave is granted, the panel may then hear the appeal.

Application of Rules

(9) Subrules (1) to (6) do not apply where subrules (7) and (8) apply.

MOTION FOR LEAVE TO APPEAL TO COURT OF APPEAL
Motion in Writing

61.03.1(1) Where an appeal to the Court of Appeal requires the leave of that court, the motion for leave shall be heard in writing, without the attendance of parties or lawyers.

Notice of Motion

(2) The notice of motion for leave to appeal shall state that the court will hear the motion in writing, 36 days after service of the moving party's motion record, factum and transcripts, if any, or on the filing of the moving party's reply factum, if any, whichever is earlier.

(3) The notice of motion,

(a) shall be served within 15 days after the making of the order or decision from which leave to appeal is sought, unless a statute provides otherwise; and

(b) shall be filed with proof of service in the office of the Registrar within five days after service.

Moving Party's Motion Record, Factum and Transcripts

(4) The moving party shall serve a motion record and transcripts of evidence, if any, as provided in subrule 61.03(2), and a factum consisting of the following elements:

1. Part I, containing a statement identifying the moving party and the court from which it is proposed to appeal, and stating the result in that court.

2. Part II, containing a concise summary of the facts relevant to the issues on the proposed appeal, with such reference to the evidence by page and line as is necessary.

3. Part III, containing the specific questions that it is proposed the court should answer if leave to appeal is granted.

4. Part IV, containing a statement of each issue raised, immediately followed by a concise statement of the law and authorities relating to that issue.

5. Schedule A, containing a list of the authorities referred to.

6. Schedule B, containing the text of all relevant provisions of statutes, regulations and by-laws.

(5) Parts I to IV shall be arranged in paragraphs numbered consecutively throughout the factum.

(6) The moving party shall file three copies of the motion record, factum and transcripts, if any, and may file three copies of a book of authorities, if any, with proof of service, within 30 days after the filing of the notice of motion for leave to appeal.

Responding Party's Motion Record and Factum

(7) The responding party may, if of the opinion that the moving party's motion record is incomplete, serve a motion record as provided in subrule 61.03(3).

(8) The responding party shall serve a factum consisting of the following elements:

1. Part I, containing a statement of the facts in the moving party's summary of relevant facts that the responding party accepts as correct and those facts with which the responding party disagrees and a concise summary of any additional facts relied on, with such reference to the evidence by page and line as is necessary.

2. Part II, containing the responding party's position with respect to each issue raised by the moving party, immediately followed by a concise statement of the law and authorities relating to it.

3. Part III, containing a statement of any additional issues raised by the responding party, the statement of each issue to be followed by a concise statement of the law and authorities relating to it.

4. Schedule A, containing a list of the authorities referred to.

5. Schedule B, containing the text of all relevant provisions of statutes, regulations and by-laws.

(9) Parts I to III shall be arranged in paragraphs numbered consecutively throughout the factum.

(10) The responding party shall file three copies of the factum, and of the motion record, if any, and may file three copies of a book of authorities, if any, with proof of service, within 25 days after service of the moving party's motion record and other documents.

Moving Party's Reply Factum

(11) If the responding party's factum raises an issue on which the moving party has not taken a position in the moving party's factum, that party may serve a reply factum.

(12) The reply factum shall contain consecutively numbered paragraphs setting out the moving party's position on the issue, followed by a concise statement of the law and authorities relating to it.

(13) The moving party shall file three copies of the reply factum with proof of service within 10 days after service of the responding party's factum.

Determination of Motion

(14) Thirty-six days after service of the moving party's motion record and factum, and transcripts, if any, or on the filing of the moving party's reply factum, if any, whichever is earlier, the motion shall be submitted to the court for consideration, and,

(a) if it appears from the written material that no oral hearing is warranted, the court shall determine the motion;

(b) otherwise, the court shall order an oral hearing to determine the motion.

Date for Oral Hearing

(15) If the court orders an oral hearing, the Registrar shall fix a date for it.

Time for Delivering Notice of Appeal

(16) Where leave is granted, the notice of appeal shall be delivered within seven days after the granting of leave.

Costs Appeal Joined with Appeal as of Right

(17) Where a party seeks to join an appeal under clause 133(b) of the *Courts of Justice Act* with an appeal as of right,

(a) the request for leave to appeal shall be included in the notice of appeal or in a supplementary notice of appeal as part of the relief sought;

(b) leave to appeal shall be sought from the panel of the Court of Appeal hearing the appeal as of right;

(c) where leave is granted, the panel may then hear the appeal.

Costs Cross-Appeal Joined with Appeal or Cross-Appeal as of Right

(18) Where a party seeks to join a cross-appeal under a statute that requires leave for an appeal with an appeal or cross-appeal as of right,

(a) the request for leave to appeal shall be included in the notice of appeal or cross-appeal or in a supplementary notice of appeal or cross-appeal as part of the relief sought;

(b) leave to appeal shall be sought from the panel of the Court of Appeal hearing the appeal or cross-appeal as of right;

(c) where leave is granted, the panel may then hear the appeal.

Application of Rules

(19) Subrules (1) to (16) do not apply where subrules (17) and (18) apply.

COMMENCEMENT OF APPEALS

Time for Appeal and Service of Notice

61.04(1) An appeal to an appellate court shall be commenced by serving a notice of appeal (Form 61A) together with the certificate required by subrule 61.05(1), within 30 days after the making of the order appealed from, unless a statute or these rules provide otherwise,

(a) on every party whose interest may be affected by the appeal, subject to subrule (1.1); and

(b) on any person entitled by statute to be heard on the appeal.

(1.1) The notice of appeal and certificate need not be served on,

(a) a defendant who was noted in default; or

(b) a respondent who has not delivered a notice of appearance, unless the respondent was heard at the hearing with leave.

Title of Proceeding

(2) The title of the proceeding in an appeal shall be in accordance with Form 61B.

Notice of Appeal

(3) The notice of appeal (Form 61A) shall state,

(a) the relief sought;

(b) the grounds of appeal; and

(c) the basis for the appellate court's jurisdiction, including references to,

(i) any provision of a statute or regulation establishing jurisdiction,

(ii) whether the order appealed from is final or interlocutory,

(iii) whether leave to appeal is necessary and if so whether it has been granted, and

(iv) any other facts relevant to establishing jurisdiction.

(4) The notice of appeal, with proof of service, shall be filed in accordance with sub-rule 4.05(4) (leaving in or mailing to court office) in the Registrar's office within ten days after service.

CERTIFICATE OR AGREEMENT RESPECTING EVIDENCE

Appellant's Certificate Respecting Evidence

61.05(1) In order to minimize the number of documents and the length of the transcript required for an appeal, the appellant shall serve with the notice of appeal an appellant's certificate respecting evidence (Form 61C) setting out only the portions of the evidence that, in the appellant's opinion, are required for the appeal.

Respondent's Certificate Respecting Evidence

(2) Within fifteen days after service of the appellant's certificate, the respondent shall serve on the appellant a respondent's certificate respecting evidence (Form 61D), confirming the appellant's certificate or setting out any additions to or deletions from it.

(3) A respondent who fails to serve a respondent's certificate within the prescribed time shall be deemed to have confirmed the appellant's certificate.

Agreement Respecting Evidence

(4) Instead of complying with subrules (1) to (3), the parties may, within thirty days after service of the notice of appeal, make an agreement respecting the documents to be included in the appeal book and compendium and the transcript required for the appeal.

Ordering Transcripts

(5) The appellant shall within thirty days after filing the notice of appeal file proof that the appellant has ordered a transcript of all oral evidence that the parties have not agreed to omit, subject to any direction under subrule 61.09(4) (relief from compliance).

(6) A party who has previously ordered a transcript of oral evidence shall forthwith modify the order in writing to comply with the certificates or agreement.

(7) When the evidence has been transcribed, the court reporter shall forthwith give written notice to all parties and the Registrar.

Costs Sanctions for Unnecessary Evidence

(8) The court may impose costs sanctions where evidence is transcribed or exhibits are reproduced unnecessarily.

SECURITY FOR COSTS OF APPEAL

61.06(1) In an appeal where it appears that,

(a) there is good reason to believe that the appeal is frivolous and vexatious and that the appellant has insufficient assets in Ontario to pay the costs of the appeal;

(b) an order for security for costs could be made against the appellant under rule 56.01; or

(c) for other good reason, security for costs should be ordered,

a judge of the appellate court, on motion by the respondent, may make such order for security for costs of the proceeding and of the appeal as is just.

(1.1) If an order is made under subrule (1), rules 56.04, 56.05, 56.07 and 56.08 apply, with necessary modifications.

(2) If an appellant fails to comply with an order under subrule (1), a judge of the appellate court on motion may dismiss the appeal.

CROSS-APPEALS

61.07(1) A respondent who,

(a) seeks to set aside or vary the order appealed from; or

(b) will seek, if the appeal is allowed in whole or in part, other relief or a different disposition than the order appealed from,

shall, within fifteen days after service of the notice of appeal, serve a notice of cross-appeal (Form 61E) on all parties whose interests may be affected by the cross-appeal and on any person entitled by statute to be heard on the appeal, stating the relief sought and the grounds of the cross-appeal.

(1.1) A respondent may, subject to subrule (1.2), serve a notice of cross-appeal without obtaining leave to appeal for the cross-appeal if,

(a) there is an appeal as of right; or

(b) leave to appeal has been granted.

(1.2) The respondent shall obtain leave to appeal in the manner provided by subrule 61.03(8) or 61.03.1(18), as the case may be, if the cross-appeal is taken under a statute that requires leave for an appeal.

(2) The notice of cross-appeal, with proof of service, shall be filed in the office of the Registrar within ten days after service.

(3) Where a respondent has not delivered a notice of cross-appeal, no cross-appeal may be heard except with leave of the court hearing the appeal.

AMENDMENT OF NOTICE OF APPEAL OR CROSS-APPEAL

Supplementary Notice to Be Served and Filed

61.08(1) The notice of appeal or cross-appeal may be amended without leave, before the appeal is perfected, by serving on each of the parties on whom the notice was served a supplementary notice of appeal or cross-appeal (Form 61F) and filing it with proof of service.

Argument Limited to Grounds Stated

(2) No grounds other than those stated in the notice of appeal or cross-appeal or supplementary notice may be relied on at the hearing, except with leave of the court hearing the appeal.

Relief Limited

(3) No relief other than that sought in the notice of appeal or cross-appeal or supplementary notice may be sought at the hearing, except with the leave of the court hearing the appeal.

PERFECTING APPEALS

Time for Perfecting

61.09(1) The appellant shall perfect the appeal by complying with subrules (2) and (3),

(a) where no transcript of evidence is required for the appeal, within thirty days after filing the notice of appeal; or

(b) where a transcript of evidence is required for the appeal, within 60 days after receiving notice that the evidence has been transcribed.

Record and Exhibits Only If Required

(2) If the appellant or the respondent believes that a part of the record or the original exhibits from the court or tribunal from which the appeal is taken is required for the proper hearing of the appeal, the appellant or respondent may move before a judge of the appellate court for an order that they be sent to the Registrar.

Material to Be Served and Filed

(3) The appellant shall,

(a) serve on every other party to the appeal and any other person entitled by statute or an order under rule 13.03 (intervention in appeal) to be heard on the appeal,

(i) the appeal book and compendium referred to in rule 61.10,

(ii) the exhibit book referred to in rule 61.10.1,

(iii) a typed or printed copy of the transcript of evidence,

(iv) an electronic version of the transcript of evidence, unless the court reporter did not prepare an electronic version, and

(v) a typed or printed copy of the appellant's factum referred to in rule 61.11;

(b) file with the Registrar, with proof of service,

(i) three copies of the appeal book and compendium, and where the appeal is to be heard by five judges, two additional copies,

(ii) one copy of the exhibit book,

(iii) a typed or printed copy of the transcript of evidence,

(iv) an electronic version of the transcript of evidence, unless the court reporter did not prepare an electronic version,

(v) three typed or printed copies of the appellant's factum, and where the appeal is to be heard by five judges, two additional copies, and

(vi) an electronic version of the appellant's factum; and

(c) file with the Registrar a certificate of perfection,

(i) stating that the appeal book and compendium, exhibit book, transcripts, if any, and appellant's factum have been filed, and

(ii) setting out, with respect to every party to the appeal and any other person entitled by statute or by an order under rule 13.03 (intervention in appeal) to be heard on the appeal,

(A) the name, address and telephone number of the party's or other person's lawyer, or

(B) the name, address for service and telephone number of the party or other person, if acting in person.

Relief from Compliance

(4) If it is necessary to do so in the interest of justice, a judge of the appellate court may give special directions and vary the rules governing the appeal book and compendium, the exhibit book, the transcript of evidence and the appellant's factum.

Notice of Listing for Hearing

(5) When an appeal is perfected, the Registrar shall place it on the list of cases to be heard at the appropriate place of hearing and shall mail a notice of listing for hearing (Form 61G) to every person listed in the certificate of perfection.

APPEAL BOOK AND COMPENDIUM

61.10(1) The appeal book and compendium shall contain, in consecutively numbered pages with numbered tabs arranged in the following order,

(a) a table of contents describing each document by its nature and date;

(b) a copy of the notice of appeal and of any notice of cross-appeal or supplementary notice of appeal or cross-appeal;

(c) a copy of the order or decision appealed from as signed and entered;

(d) a copy of the reasons of the court or tribunal appealed from, with a further typed or printed copy if the reasons are handwritten;

(e) if an earlier order or decision was the subject of the hearing before the court or tribunal appealed from, a copy of the order or decision, as signed and entered, and a copy of any reasons for it, with a further typed or printed copy if the reasons are handwritten;

(f) a copy of the pleadings or notice of application or of any other document that initiated the proceeding or defines the issues in it;

(g) a copy of any excerpts from a transcript of evidence that are referred to in the appellant's factum;

(h) a copy of any exhibits that are referred to in the appellant's factum;

(i) a copy of any other documents relevant to the hearing of the appeal that are referred to in the appellant's factum;

(j) a copy of the certificates or agreement respecting evidence referred to in rule 61.05;

(k) a copy of any order made in respect of the conduct of the appeal; and

(l) a certificate (Form 61H) signed by the appellant's lawyer, or on the lawyer's behalf by someone he or she has specifically authorized, stating that the contents of the appeal book and compendium are complete and legible.

(2) The Registrar may refuse to accept an appeal book and compendium if it does not comply with these rules or is not legible.

EXHIBIT BOOK

61.10.1 The exhibit book shall contain, in consecutively numbered pages with numbered tabs arranged in the following order,

(a) a table of contents describing each exhibit by its nature, date and exhibit number or letter;

(b) any affidavit evidence, including exhibits, that the parties have not agreed to omit;

(c) transcripts of evidence used on a motion or application that the parties have not agreed to omit; and

(d) a copy of each exhibit filed at a hearing or marked on an examination that the parties have not agreed to omit, arranged in order by date (or, if there are documents with common characteristics, grouped accordingly in order by date) and not by exhibit number.

APPELLANT'S FACTUM

61.11(1) The appellant's factum shall be signed by the appellant's lawyer, or on the lawyer's behalf by someone he or she has specifically authorized, and shall consist of,

(a) Part I, containing a statement identifying the appellant and the court or tribunal appealed from and stating the result in that court or tribunal;

(b) Part II, containing a concise overview statement describing the nature of the case and of the issues;

(c) Part III, containing a concise summary of the facts relevant to the issues on the appeal, with such reference to the transcript of evidence and the exhibits as is necessary;

(d) Part IV, containing a statement of each issue raised, immediately followed by a concise argument with reference to the law and authorities relating to that issue;

(d.1) Part V, containing a statement of the order that the appellate court will be asked to make, including any order for costs;

(e) a certificate stating,

(i) that an order under subrule 61.09(2) (original record and exhibits) has been obtained or is not required, and

(ii) how much time (expressed in hours or fractions of an hour) the lawyer estimates will be required for his or her oral argument, not including reply;

(f) Schedule A, containing a list of the authorities referred to; and

(g) Schedule B, containing the text of all relevant provisions of statutes, regulations and by-laws.

(1.1) References to the transcript of evidence shall be by tab, page number and line in the appeal book and compendium, and references to exhibits shall be by page number in the exhibit book and by tab and page number in the appeal book and compendium.

(2) Parts I to V shall be arranged in paragraphs numbered consecutively throughout the factum.

RESPONDENT'S FACTUM AND COMPENDIUM
Filing and Service

61.12(1) Every respondent shall,
    (a) serve on every other party to the appeal,
        (i) a typed or printed copy of the respondent's factum, and
        (ii) the respondent's compendium;
    (b) file with the Registrar, with proof of service,
        (i) three typed or printed copies of the respondent's factum, and where the appeal is to be heard by five judges, two additional copies, and
        (ii) three copies of the respondent's compendium, and where the appeal is to be heard by five judges, two additional copies; and
    (c) file with the Registrar an electronic version of the respondent's factum.

Time for Delivery

(2) The respondent's factum and compendium shall be delivered within 60 days after service of the appeal book and compendium, exhibit book, transcript of evidence, if any, and appellant's factum.

Contents of Respondent's Factum

(3) The respondent's factum shall be signed by the respondent's lawyer, or on the lawyer's behalf by someone he or she has specifically authorized, and shall consist of,
    (a) Part I, containing a concise overview statement describing the nature of the case and of the issues;
    (b) Part II, containing a statement of the facts in the appellant's summary of relevant facts that the respondent accepts as correct and those facts with which the respondent disagrees, and a concise summary of any additional facts relied on, with such reference to the transcript of evidence and the exhibits as is necessary;
    (c) Part III, containing the position of the respondent with respect to each issue raised by the appellant, immediately followed by a concise argument with reference to the law and authorities relating to that issue;
    (d) Part IV, containing a statement of any additional issues raised by the respondent, the statement of each issue to be followed by a concise argument with reference to the law and authorities relating to that issue;
    (e) Part V, containing a statement of the order that the appellate court will be asked to make, including any order for costs;
    (f) a certificate stating,
        (i) that an order under subrule 61.09(2) (original record and exhibits) has been obtained or is not required, and
        (ii) how much time (expressed in hours or fractions of an hour) the lawyer estimates will be required for his or her oral argument, not including reply;
    (g) Schedule A, containing a list of the authorities referred to; and
    (h) Schedule B, containing the text of all relevant provisions of statutes, regulations and by-laws that are not included in Schedule B to the appellant's factum.
(4) References to the transcript of evidence shall be by tab, page number and line in the respondent's compendium, and references to exhibits shall be by page number in the exhibit book and by tab and page number in the respondent's compendium.
(5) Parts I to V shall be arranged in paragraphs numbered consecutively throughout the factum.

Cross-Appeal

(6) Where a respondent has served a notice of cross-appeal under rule 61.07,

(a) the respondent shall prepare a factum as an appellant by cross-appeal and deliver it with or incorporate it in the respondent's factum; and

(b) the appellant shall deliver a factum as a respondent to the cross-appeal within 10 days after service of the respondent's factum.

Contents of Respondent's Compendium

(7) The respondent's compendium shall contain, in consecutively numbered pages with numbered tabs arranged in the following order,

(a) a table of contents describing each document by its nature and date;

(b) a copy of any excerpts from a transcript of evidence that are referred to in the respondent's factum;

(c) a copy of any exhibits that are referred to in the respondent's factum; and

(d) a copy of any other documents relevant to the hearing of the appeal that are referred to in the respondent's factum.

Relief from Compliance

(8) If it is necessary to do so in the interest of justice, a judge of the appellate court may give special directions and vary the rules governing the respondent's factum and the respondent's compendium.

61.12.1 Revoked.

DISMISSAL FOR DELAY

Motion by Respondent

61.13(1) Where an appellant has not,

(a) filed proof that a transcript of evidence that the parties have not agreed to omit was ordered within the time prescribed by subrule 61.05(5); or

(b) perfected the appeal within the time prescribed by subrule 61.09(1) or by an order of the appellate court or a judge of that court,

the respondent may make a motion to the Registrar, on ten days notice to the appellant, to have the appeal dismissed for delay.

Notice by Registrar

(2) Where the appellant has not,

(a) filed a transcript of evidence within 60 days after the Registrar received notice that the evidence has been transcribed; or

(b) perfected the appeal within one year after filing the notice of appeal,

the Registrar may serve notice on the appellant that the appeal will be dismissed for delay unless it is perfected within ten days after service of the notice.

(2.1) Where no transcript of evidence is required for the appeal and the appellant has not perfected it within the time prescribed by subrule 61.09(1) or by an order of the appellate court or a judge of that court, the Registrar may serve notice on the appellant that the appeal will be dismissed for delay unless it is perfected within 10 days after service of the notice.

Registrar to Dismiss Where Default Not Cured

(3) Where the appellant does not cure the default,

(a) in the case of a motion under subrule (1), before the hearing of the motion; or

(b) in the case of a notice under subrule (2) or (2.1), within ten days after service of the notice,

or within such longer period as a judge of the appellate court allows, the Registrar shall make an order in (Form 61I) dismissing the appeal for delay, with costs fixed at $750, despite rule 58.13 and shall serve the order on the respondent.

Cross-Appeals

(4) Where a respondent who has served a notice of cross-appeal has not delivered a factum in the cross-appeal within 60 days after service of the appeal book and compendium, transcript of evidence and appellant's factum, the appellant may make a motion to the Registrar, on five days notice to the respondent, to have the cross-appeal dismissed for delay.

(5) Where the respondent does not deliver a factum in the cross-appeal before the hearing of the motion under subrule (4) or within such longer period as a judge of the appellate court allows, the Registrar shall make an order in (Form 61I) dismissing the cross-appeal for delay, with costs fixed at $750, despite rule 58.13.

Motions for Leave

(6) On a motion for leave to appeal, where the moving party has not served and filed the motion record and other documents in accordance with subrule 61.03(2) or subrules 61.03.1(4) to (6), the responding party may make a motion to the Registrar, on 10 days notice to the moving party, to have the motion for leave to appeal dismissed for delay.

(7) On a motion for leave to appeal, where the moving party has not served and filed the motion record and other documents within 60 days after the filing of the notice of motion for leave to appeal, the Registrar may serve notice on the moving party that the motion will be dismissed for delay unless the documents are served and filed within 10 days after service of the notice.

(8) On a motion for leave to appeal, where the moving party,

(a) in the case of a motion under subrule (6), does not serve and file the documents before the hearing of that motion, or within such longer period as a judge of the appellate court allows;

(b) in the case of a notice under subrule (7), does not serve and file the documents within ten days after service of the notice or within such longer period as a judge of the appellate court allows,

the Registrar shall make an order in (Form 61J) dismissing the motion for delay, with costs fixed at $750, despite rule 58.13.

FAILURE TO OBTAIN ORDER TO CONTINUE APPEAL

61.13.1(1) If a transfer or transmission of an appellant's interest or liability takes place while an appeal is pending and no order to continue is obtained within a reasonable time, a respondent may make a motion to the Registrar, on 10 days notice to the appellant, to have the appeal dismissed for delay.

(2) If the appellant does not obtain an order to continue before the hearing of the motion or within the longer period allowed by a judge of the appellate court, the Registrar shall make an order dismissing the appeal for delay, with costs fixed at $750, despite rule 58.13.

ABANDONED APPEALS

Delivery of Notice of Abandonment

61.14(1) A party may abandon an appeal or cross-appeal by delivering a notice of abandonment (Form 61K).

Deemed Abandonment

(2) A party who serves a notice of appeal or cross-appeal and does not file it within ten days after service shall be deemed to have abandoned the appeal or cross-appeal, unless the court orders otherwise.

Effect of Abandonment

(3) Where an appeal or cross-appeal is abandoned or is deemed to have been abandoned, the appeal or cross-appeal is at an end, and the respondent or appellant is entitled to the costs of the appeal or cross-appeal, unless a judge of the appellate court orders otherwise.

CROSS-APPEAL WHERE APPEAL DISMISSED FOR DELAY OR ABANDONED

61.15(1) Where an appeal is dismissed for delay or is abandoned, a respondent who has cross-appealed may,

(a) within fifteen days thereafter, deliver a notice of election to proceed (Form 61L); and

(b) make a motion to a judge of the appellate court for directions in respect of the cross-appeal.

(2) Where the respondent does not deliver a notice of election to proceed within fifteen days, the cross-appeal shall be deemed to be abandoned without costs unless a judge of the appellate court orders otherwise.

MOTIONS IN APPELLATE COURT

Rule 37 Applies Generally

61.16(1) Rule 37, except rules 37.02 to 37.04 (jurisdiction to hear motions, place of hearing, to whom to be made) and rule 37.17 (motion before commencement of proceeding), applies to motions in an appellate court, with necessary modifications.

Motion to Receive Further Evidence

(2) A motion under clause 134(4)(b) of the *Courts of Justice Act* (motion to receive further evidence) shall be made to the panel hearing the appeal.

Motions Required to Be Heard by One Judge

(2.1) A motion required by subsection 7(2) or 21(3) of the *Courts of Justice Act* to be heard and determined by one judge may be heard and determined by a panel hearing an appeal or another motion in the proceeding properly made to the panel.

Motions Required to Be Heard by Panel

(2.2) A motion in the Court of Appeal for an order that finally determines an appeal, other than an order dismissing the appeal on consent, shall be heard and determined by a panel consisting of not fewer than three judges sitting together, and always of an uneven number of judges.

Motion to Be Heard by More Than One Judge

(3) Where a motion in an appellate court is to be heard by more than one judge, the notice of motion shall state that the motion will be heard on a date to be fixed by the Registrar.

(3.1) Revoked.

Certificate of Estimated Time for Argument

(3.2) The notice of motion shall contain a certificate stating how much time (expressed in hours or fractions of an hour) the lawyer estimates will be required for his or her oral argument, not including reply.

Motion Record and Factum

(4) On a motion referred to in subrule (3),

(a) the moving party,

(i) shall serve a motion record that contains the documents referred to in subrule 37.10(2) and a factum consisting of a concise argument stating the facts and law relied on by the moving party, and

(ii) shall file three copies of the moving party's motion record and factum, with proof of service, within 30 days after filing the notice of motion;

(b) the responding party,

(i) may, if of the opinion that the moving party's motion record is incomplete, serve a motion record that contains the documents referred to in subrule 37.10(3),

(ii) shall serve a factum consisting of a concise argument stating the facts and law relied on by the responding party, and

(iii) shall file three copies of the responding party's motion record and factum, with proof of service, within 25 days after service of the moving party's motion record and factum; and

(c) a party who intends to refer to a transcript of evidence at the hearing shall ensure that it is included in the motion record.

Review of Registrar's Order

(5) A person affected by an order or decision of the Registrar may make a motion to a judge of the appellate court to set it aside or vary it by a notice of motion that is served forthwith after the order or decision comes to the person's attention and names the first available hearing date that is at least three days after service of the notice of motion.

Review of Single Judge's Order

(6) A person who moves to set aside or vary the order of a judge of an appellate court under subsection 7(5) or 21(5) of the *Courts of Justice Act* shall do so by a notice of motion that is served within four days after the order is made and states that the motion will be heard on a date to be fixed by the Registrar.

Registrar to Dismiss for Delay

(7) If the moving party has not served and filed the motion record and other documents in accordance with subrule (4),

(a) the responding party may make a motion to the Registrar, on 10 days notice to the moving party, to have the motion dismissed for delay;

(b) the Registrar may serve notice on the moving party that the motion will be dismissed for delay unless the motion record and other documents are served and filed within 10 days after service of the notice.

(8) The Registrar shall make an order in Form 61J.1 dismissing the motion for delay, with costs fixed at $750, despite rule 58.13, if the moving party,

(a) in the case of a motion under clause (7)(a), does not serve and file the motion record and other documents before the hearing of that motion, or within such longer period as a judge of the appellate court allows;

(b) in the case of a notice under clause (7)(b), does not serve and file the motion record and other documents within 10 days after the notice is served, or within such longer period as a judge of the appellate court allows.

PARTICULAR PROCEEDINGS

RULE 76   SIMPLIFIED PROCEDURE

APPLICATION OF RULE

76.01(1) The simplified procedure set out in this Rule does not apply to,

(a) actions under the *Class Proceedings Act, 1992*;

(b) actions under the *Construction Lien Act*, except trust claims;

(c) Rule 77.

Application of Other Rules

(2) The rules that apply to an action apply to an action that is proceeding under this Rule, unless this Rule provides otherwise.

AVAILABILITY OF SIMPLIFIED PROCEDURE

When Mandatory

76.02(1) The procedure set out in this Rule shall be used in an action if the following conditions are satisfied:

1. The plaintiff's claim is exclusively for one or more of the following:

i. Money.

ii. Real property.

iii. Personal property.

2. The total of the following amounts is $100,000 or less exclusive of interest and costs:

i. The amount of money claimed, if any.

ii. The fair market value of any real property and of any personal property, as at the date the action is commenced.

(2) If there are two or more plaintiffs, the procedure set out in this Rule shall be used if each plaintiff's claim, considered separately, meets the requirements of subrule (1).

(2.1) If there are two or more defendants, the procedure set out in this Rule shall be used if the plaintiff's claim against each defendant, considered separately, meets the requirements of subrule (1).

When Optional

(3) The procedure set out in this Rule may be used in any other action at the option of the plaintiff, subject to subrules (4) to (9).

Originating Process

(4) The statement of claim (Form 14A, 14B or 14D) or notice of action (Form 14C) shall indicate that the action is being brought under this Rule.

Action Continues to Proceed Under Rule

(5) An action commenced under this Rule continues to proceed under this Rule unless,

(a) the defendant objects in the statement of defence to the action proceeding under this Rule because the plaintiff's claim does not comply with subrule (1), and the plaintiff does not abandon in the reply the claims or parts of claims that do not comply;

(b) a defendant by counterclaim, crossclaim or third party claim objects in the statement of defence to the counterclaim, crossclaim or third party claim proceeding under this Rule because the counterclaim, crossclaim or third party claim does not comply with subrule (1), and the defendant does not abandon in the reply to the counterclaim, crossclaim or third party claim the claims or parts of claims that do not comply; or

(c) the defendant makes a counterclaim, crossclaim or third party claim that does not comply with subrule (1) and states in the defendant's pleading that the counterclaim, crossclaim or third party claim is to proceed under the ordinary procedure.

Continuance Under Ordinary Procedure — Where Notice Required

(6) If an action commenced under this Rule may no longer proceed under this Rule because of an amendment to the pleadings under Rule 26 or as a result of the operation of subrule (5),

(a) the action is continued under the ordinary procedure; and

(b) the plaintiff shall deliver, after all the pleadings have been delivered or at the time of amending the pleadings, as the case may be, a notice (Form 76A) stating that the action and any related proceedings are continued as an ordinary action.

Continuance Under Simplified Procedure — Where Notice Required

(7) An action that was not commenced under this Rule, or that was commenced under this Rule but continued under the ordinary procedure, is continued under this Rule if,

(a) the consent of all the parties is filed; or

(b) no consent is filed but,

(i) the plaintiff's pleading is amended under Rule 26 to comply with subrule (1), and

(ii) all other claims, counterclaims, crossclaims and third party claims comply with this Rule.

(8) The plaintiff shall deliver a notice (Form 76A) stating that the action and any related proceedings are continued under this Rule.

Effect of Abandonment

(9) A party who abandons a claim or part of a claim or amends a pleading so that the claim, counterclaim, crossclaim or third party claim complies with subrule (1) may not bring the claim or part in any other proceeding.

AFFIDAVIT OF DOCUMENTS
Copies of Documents

76.03(1) A party to an action under this Rule shall, within 10 days after the close of pleadings and at the party's own expense, serve on every other party,

(a) an affidavit of documents (Form 30A or 30B) disclosing to the full extent of the party's knowledge, information and belief all documents relevant to any matter in issue in the action that are or have been in the party's possession, control or power; and

(b) copies of the documents referred to in Schedule A of the affidavit of documents.

List of Potential Witnesses

(2) The affidavit of documents shall include a list of the names and addresses of persons who might reasonably be expected to have knowledge of matters in issue in the action, unless the court orders otherwise.

Effect of Failure to Disclose

(3) At the trial of the action, a party may not call as a witness a person whose name has not been disclosed in the party's affidavit of documents or any supplementary affidavit of documents, unless the court orders otherwise.

Lawyer's Certificate

(4) The lawyer's certificate under subrule 30.03(4) (full disclosure in affidavit) shall include a statement that the lawyer has explained to the deponent the necessity of complying with subrules (1) and (2).

NO WRITTEN DISCOVERY, CROSS-EXAMINATION ON AN AFFIDAVIT OR EXAMINATION OF A WITNESS

76.04(1) The following are not permitted in an action under this Rule:
1. Examination for discovery by written questions and answers under Rule 35.
2. Cross-examination of a deponent on an affidavit under rule 39.02.
3. Examination of a witness on a motion under rule 39.03.

Limitation on Oral Discovery

(2) Despite rule 31.05.1 (time limit on discovery), no party shall, in conducting oral examinations for discovery in relation to an action proceeding under this Rule, exceed a total of two hours of examination, regardless of the number of parties or other persons to be examined.

MOTIONS

Motion Form

76.05(1) The moving party shall serve a motion form (Form 76B) in accordance with rule 37.07 and shall submit it to the court before the motion is brought and heard.

Place of Hearing

(2) Unless the parties agree otherwise or the court orders otherwise, the motion shall be heard in the county where the proceeding was commenced or to which it has been transferred under rule 13.1.02.

Procedure

(3) Depending on the practical requirements of the situation, the motion may be made,
    (a) with or without supporting material or a motion record;
    (b) by attendance, in writing, by fax or under rule 1.08 (telephone and video conferences).

Motions Dealt With by Registrar

(4) When a motion described in subrule (5) meets one of the following conditions, the registrar shall make an order granting the relief sought:
    1. The motion is for an order on consent, the consent of all parties is filed and the consent states that no party affected by the order is under disability.
    2. No responding material is filed and the notice of motion or the motion form states that no party affected by the order is under disability.
(5) Subrule (4) applies to a motion for,
    (a) amendment of a pleading or notice of motion;
    (b) addition, deletion or substitution of a party whose consent is filed;
    (c) removal of a lawyer as lawyer of record;
    (d) setting aside the noting of a party in default;
    (e) setting aside a default judgment;
    (f) discharge of a certificate of pending litigation;
    (g) security for costs in a specified amount; or
    (h) dismissal of a proceeding with or without costs.

Disposition

(6) The court or registrar shall record the disposition of the motion on the motion form.

(7) No formal order is required unless,

(a) the court or registrar orders otherwise;

(b) an appeal is made to a judge; or

(c) an appeal or motion for leave to appeal is made to an appellate court.

76.06, 76.07 Revoked.

SETTLEMENT DISCUSSION AND DOCUMENTARY DISCLOSURE

76.08 Within 60 days after the filing of the first statement of defence or notice of intent to defend, the parties shall, in a meeting or telephone call, consider whether,

(a) all documents relevant to any matter in issue have been disclosed; and

(b) settlement of any or all issues is possible.

HOW DEFENDED ACTION IS SET DOWN FOR TRIAL OR SUMMARY TRIAL

Notice of Readiness for Pre-Trial Conference

76.09(1) Despite rule 48.02 (how action set down for trial), the plaintiff shall, within 180 days after the first statement of defence or notice of intent to defend is filed, set the action down for trial by serving a notice of readiness for pre-trial conference (Form 76C) on every party to the action and any counterclaim, crossclaim or third party claim and forthwith filing the notice with proof of service.

(2) If the plaintiff does not act under subrule (1), any other party may do so.

Certificate

(3) The party who sets the action down for trial shall certify in the notice of readiness for pre-trial conference that there was a settlement discussion.

PRE-TRIAL CONFERENCE

Notice

76.10(1) The registrar shall serve notice of a pre-trial conference at least 45 days before the scheduled date.

(2), (3) Revoked.

Documents

(4) Despite rule 50.04 (materials to be filed before pre-trial conference), at least five days before the pre-trial conference, each party shall,

(a) file,

(i) a copy of the party's affidavit of documents and copies of the documents relied on for the party's claim or defence,

(ii) a copy of any expert report, and

(iii) any other material necessary for the conference; and

(b) deliver,

(i) a two-page statement setting out the issues and the party's position with respect to them, and

(ii) a trial management checklist (Form 76D).

Trial Date

(5) The pre-trial conference judge or case management master shall fix a date for trial, subject to the direction of the regional senior judge.

Mode of Trial

(6) The parties may agree that the trial shall be an ordinary trial or a summary trial under rule 76.12; if they do not agree, the pre-trial conference judge or case management master shall determine the mode of trial that is appropriate in all the circumstances.

(7) If the trial is to be a summary trial under rule 76.12, the pre-trial conference judge or case management master,

    (a) shall fix a date for the delivery of all the parties' affidavits; and

    (b) may vary the order and time of presentation.

PLACING DEFENDED ACTION ON TRIAL LIST

Registrar

76.11(1) The registrar shall place a defended action on the appropriate trial list immediately after the pre-trial conference.

Trial Record

(2) At least 10 days before the date fixed for trial, the party who set the action down for trial shall serve a trial record on every party to the action and any counterclaim, crossclaim or third party claim, and file the record with proof of service.

(3) In the case of an ordinary trial, the trial record shall be prepared in accordance with rule 48.03.

(4) In the case of a summary trial under rule 76.12, the trial record shall contain, in consecutively numbered pages arranged in the following order,

    (a) a table of contents describing each document, including each exhibit, by its nature and date and, in the case of an exhibit, by exhibit number or letter;

    (b) a copy of the pleadings, including those relating to any counterclaim, crossclaim or third party claim;

    (c) a copy of any demand or order for particulars of a pleading and the particulars delivered in response;

    (d) a copy of any order respecting the trial;

    (e) a copy of all the affidavits served by all the parties for use on the summary trial; and

    (f) a certificate signed by the lawyer of the party filing the trial record, stating that it contains the documents described in clauses (a) to (e).

SUMMARY TRIAL

Procedure

76.12(1) At a summary trial, the evidence and argument shall be presented as follows, subject to any direction under subrule 76.10(7):

    1. The plaintiff shall adduce evidence by affidavit.

    1.1 The plaintiff may examine the deponent of any affidavit served by the plaintiff for not more than 10 minutes.

    2. A party who is adverse in interest may cross-examine the deponent of any affidavit served by the plaintiff.

    3. The plaintiff may re-examine any deponent who is cross-examined under this subrule for not more than 10 minutes.

    4. When any cross-examinations and re-examinations of the plaintiff's deponents are concluded, the defendant shall adduce evidence by affidavit.

    4.1 The defendant may examine the deponent of any affidavit served by the defendant for not more than 10 minutes.

    5. A party who is adverse in interest may cross-examine the deponent of any affidavit served by a defendant.

    6. A party shall complete all of the party's cross-examinations within 50 minutes.

    7. A defendant may re-examine any deponent who is cross-examined under this subrule for not more than 10 minutes.

8. When any cross-examinations and re-examinations of the defendant's deponents are concluded, the plaintiff may, with leave of the trial judge, adduce any proper reply evidence.

9. After the presentation of evidence, each party may make oral argument for not more than 45 minutes.

(2) The trial judge may extend a time provided in subrule (1).

(3) A party who intends to examine or cross-examine the deponent of an affidavit at the summary trial shall, at least 10 days before the date fixed for trial, give notice of that intention to the party who filed the affidavit, who shall arrange for the deponent's attendance at the trial.

Judgment After Summary Trial

(4) The judge shall grant judgment after the conclusion of the summary trial.

COSTS CONSEQUENCES

Opting In

76.13(1) Regardless of the outcome of the action, if this Rule applies as the result of amendment of the pleadings under subrule 76.02(7), the party whose pleadings are amended shall pay, on a substantial indemnity basis, the costs incurred by the opposing party up to the date of the amendment that would not have been incurred had the claim originally complied with subrule 76.02(1), (2) or (2.1), unless the court orders otherwise.

Plaintiff Denied Costs

(2) Subrules (3) to (10) apply to a plaintiff who obtains a judgment that satisfies the following conditions:

1. The judgment awards exclusively one or more of the following:
    i. Money.
    ii. Real property.
    iii. Personal property.
2. The total of the following amounts is $100,000 or less, exclusive of interest and costs:
    i. The amount of money awarded, if any.
    ii. The fair market value of any real property and of any personal property awarded, as at the date the action is commenced.

(3) The plaintiff shall not recover any costs unless,
    (a) the action was proceeding under this Rule at the commencement of the trial; or
    (b) the court is satisfied that it was reasonable for the plaintiff,
        (i) to have commenced and continued the action under the ordinary procedure, or
        (ii) to have allowed the action to be continued under the ordinary procedure by not abandoning claims or parts of claims that do not comply with subrule 76.02(1), (2) or (2.1).

(4) Subrule (3) applies despite subrule 49.10(1) (plaintiff's offer to settle).

(5) Subrule (3) does not apply if this Rule was unavailable because of the counterclaim, crossclaim or third party claim of another party.

Plaintiff May Be Ordered to Pay Defendant's Costs

(6) The plaintiff may, in the trial judge's discretion, be ordered to pay all or part of the defendant's costs, including substantial indemnity costs, in addition to any costs the plaintiff is required to pay under subrule 49.10(2) (defendant's offer to settle).

Defendant Objecting to Simplified Procedure

(7) In an action that includes a claim for real or personal property, if the defendant objected to proceeding under this Rule on the ground that the property's fair market

value exceeded $100,000 at the date the action was commenced and the court finds the value did not exceed that amount at that date, the defendant shall pay, on a substantial indemnity basis, the costs incurred by the plaintiff that would not have been incurred had the claim originally complied with subrule 76.02(1), (2) or (2.1), unless the court orders otherwise.

Burden of Proof

(8) The burden of proving that the fair market value of the real or personal property at the date of commencement of the action was $100,000 or less is on the plaintiff.

Counterclaims, Crossclaims and Third Party Claims

(9) Subrules (1) to (8) apply, with necessary modifications, to counterclaims, crossclaims and third party claims.

Transition

(10) In the case of an action that was commenced before January 1, 2002, subrules (2), (7) and (8) apply as if "$50,000" read "$25,000".

(11) In the case of an action that was commenced on or after January 1, 2002 and before January 1, 2010, subrules (2), (7) and (8) apply as if "$100,000" read "$50,000".

APPENDIX B
Rules of the Small Claims Court

RULE 1 GENERAL

CITATION

1.01 These rules may be cited as the Small Claims Court Rules.

DEFINITIONS

1.02(1) In these rules,

"court" means the Small Claims Court;

"disability", where used in respect of a person or party, means that the person or party is,

 (a) a minor,

 (b) mentally incapable within the meaning of section 6 or 45 of the *Substitute Decisions Act, 1992* in respect of an issue in the proceeding, whether the person or party has a guardian or not, or

 (c) an absentee within the meaning of the *Absentees Act*;

"document" includes data and information in electronic form;

"electronic" includes created, recorded, transmitted or stored in digital form or in other intangible form by electronic, magnetic or optical means or by any other means that has capabilities for creation, recording, transmission or storage similar to those means, and "electronically" has a corresponding meaning;

"holiday" means,

 (a) any Saturday or Sunday,

 (b) New Year's Day,

 (b.1) Family Day,

 (c) Good Friday,

 (d) Easter Monday,

 (e) Victoria Day,

 (f) Canada Day,

 (g) Civic Holiday,

 (h) Labour Day,

 (i) Thanksgiving Day,

 (j) Remembrance Day,

 (k) Christmas Day,

 (l) Boxing Day, and

 (m) any special holiday proclaimed by the Governor General or the Lieutenant Governor,

and if New Year's Day, Canada Day or Remembrance Day falls on a Saturday or Sunday, the following Monday is a holiday, and if Christmas Day falls on a Saturday or Sunday, the following Monday and Tuesday are holidays, and if Christmas Day falls on a Friday, the following Monday is a holiday;

"order" includes a judgment;

"self-represented", when used in reference to a person, means that the person is not represented by a lawyer, student-at-law or agent;

"territorial division" means,

(a) a county, a district or a regional municipality, and

(b) each of the following, as they existed on December 31, 2002:

    (i) The combined area of County of Brant and City of Brantford.

    (ii) Municipality of Chatham-Kent.

    (iii) Haldimand County.

    (iv) City of Hamilton.

    (v) City of Kawartha Lakes.

    (vi) Norfolk County.

    (vii) City of Ottawa.

    (viii) County of Prince Edward.

    (ix) City of Toronto.

(2) Revoked.

GENERAL PRINCIPLE

1.03(1) These rules shall be liberally construed to secure the just, most expeditious and least expensive determination of every proceeding on its merits in accordance with section 25 of the *Courts of Justice Act*.

MATTERS NOT COVERED IN RULES

(2) If these rules do not cover a matter adequately, the court may give directions and make any order that is just, and the practice shall be decided by analogy to these rules, by reference to the *Courts of Justice Act* and the Act governing the action and, if the court considers it appropriate, by reference to the *Rules of Civil Procedure*.

ORDERS ON TERMS

1.04 When making an order under these rules, the court may impose such terms and give such directions as are just.

STANDARDS FOR DOCUMENTS

1.05 A document in a proceeding shall be printed, typewritten, written or reproduced legibly.

FORMS

1.06(1) The forms prescribed by these rules shall be used where applicable and with such variations as the circumstances require.

TABLE OF FORMS

(2) In these rules, when a form is referred to by number, the reference is to the form with that number that is described in the Table of Forms at the end of these rules and is available on the Internet through www.ontariocourtforms.on.ca.

ADDITIONAL PARTIES

(3) If a form does not have sufficient space to list all of the parties to the action on the first page, the remaining parties shall be listed in Form 1A, which shall be appended to the form immediately following the first page.

ADDITIONAL DEBTORS

(4) If any of the following forms do not have sufficient space to list all of the debtors in respect of which the form applies, the remaining debtors shall be listed in Form 1A.1, which shall be appended to the form:

1. Certificate of judgment (Form 20A).
2. Writ of seizure and sale of personal property (Form 20C).
3. Writ of seizure and sale of land (Form 20D).
4. Direction to enforce writ of seizure and sale of personal property (Form 20O).

AFFIDAVIT

(5) If these rules permit or require the use of an affidavit, Form 15B may be used for the purpose unless another form is specified.

TELEPHONE AND VIDEO CONFERENCES — WHERE AVAILABLE

1.07(1) If facilities for a telephone or video conference are available at the court, all or part of any of the following may be heard or conducted by telephone or video conference as permitted by subrules (2) and (3):

1. A settlement conference.
2. A motion.

(1.1) If facilities for a video conference are available at the court, all or part of an examination of a debtor or other person under rule 20.10 may be conducted by video conference as permitted by subrules (2) and (3).

REQUEST TO BE MADE

(2) A settlement conference or motion may be heard or conducted by telephone or video conference or all or part of an examination under rule 20.10 may be conducted by video conference if a party files a request for the conference (Form 1B), indicating the reasons for the request, and the court grants the request.

BALANCE OF CONVENIENCE

(3) In deciding whether to direct a telephone or video conference, the judge shall consider,

(a) the balance of convenience between the party that wants the telephone or video conference and any party that opposes it; and

(b) any other relevant matter.

ARRANGEMENTS FOR CONFERENCE

(4) If an order directing a telephone or video conference is made, the court shall make the necessary arrangements for the conference and notify the parties of them.

SETTING ASIDE OR VARYING ORDER

(5) A judge presiding at a proceeding or step in a proceeding may set aside or vary an order directing a telephone or video conference.

RULE 2   NON-COMPLIANCE WITH THE RULES

EFFECT OF NON-COMPLIANCE

2.01 A failure to comply with these rules is an irregularity and does not render a proceeding or a step, document or order in a proceeding a nullity, and the court may grant all necessary amendments or other relief, on such terms as are just, to secure the just determination of the real matters in dispute.

COURT MAY DISPENSE WITH COMPLIANCE

2.02 If necessary in the interest of justice, the court may dispense with compliance with any rule at any time.

RULE 3 TIME

COMPUTATION

3.01 If these rules or an order of the court prescribe a period of time for the taking of a step in a proceeding, the time shall be counted by excluding the first day and including the last day of the period; if the last day of the period of time falls on a holiday, the period ends on the next day that is not a holiday.

POWERS OF COURT

3.02(1) The court may lengthen or shorten any time prescribed by these rules or an order, on such terms as are just.

CONSENT

(2) A time prescribed by these rules for serving or filing a document may be lengthened or shortened by filing the consent of the parties.

RULE 4 PARTIES UNDER DISABILITY

PLAINTIFF'S LITIGATION GUARDIAN

4.01(1) An action by a person under disability shall be commenced or continued by a litigation guardian, subject to subrule (2).

EXCEPTION

(2) A minor may sue for any sum not exceeding $500 as if he or she were of full age.

CONSENT

(3) A plaintiff's litigation guardian shall, at the time of filing a claim or as soon as possible afterwards, file with the clerk a consent (Form 4A) in which the litigation guardian,

    (a) states the nature of the disability;

    (b) in the case of a minor, states the minor's birth date;

    (c) sets out his or her relationship, if any, to the person under disability;

    (d) states that he or she has no interest in the proceeding contrary to that of the person under disability;

    (e) acknowledges that he or she is aware of his or her liability to pay personally any costs awarded against him or her or against the person under disability; and

    (f) states whether he or she is represented by a lawyer or agent and, if so, gives that person's name and confirms that the person has written authority to act in the proceeding.

DEFENDANT'S LITIGATION GUARDIAN

4.02(1) An action against a person under disability shall be defended by a litigation guardian.

(2) A defendant's litigation guardian shall file with the defence a consent (Form 4A) in which the litigation guardian,

    (a) states the nature of the disability;

    (b) in the case of a minor, states the minor's birth date;

    (c) sets out his or her relationship, if any, to the person under disability;

    (d) states that he or she has no interest in the proceeding contrary to that of the person under disability; and

(e) states whether he or she is represented by a lawyer or agent and, if so, gives that person's name and confirms that the person has written authority to act in the proceeding.

(3) If it appears to the court that a defendant is a person under disability and the defendant does not have a litigation guardian the court may, after notice to the proposed litigation guardian, appoint as litigation guardian for the defendant any person who has no interest in the action contrary to that of the defendant.

WHO MAY BE LITIGATION GUARDIAN

4.03(1) Any person who is not under disability may be a plaintiff's or defendant's litigation guardian, subject to subrule (2).

(2) If the plaintiff or defendant,

(a) is a minor, in a proceeding to which subrule 4.01(2) does not apply,

(i) the parent or person with lawful custody or another suitable person shall be the litigation guardian, or

(ii) if no such person is available and able to act, the Children's Lawyer shall be the litigation guardian;

(b) is mentally incapable and has a guardian with authority to act as litigation guardian in the proceeding, the guardian shall be the litigation guardian;

(c) is mentally incapable and does not have a guardian with authority to act as litigation guardian in the proceeding, but has an attorney under a power of attorney with that authority, the attorney shall be the litigation guardian;

(d) is mentally incapable and has neither a guardian with authority to act as litigation guardian in the proceeding nor an attorney under a power of attorney with that power,

(i) a suitable person who has no interest contrary to that of the incapable person may be the litigation guardian, or

(ii) if no such person is available and able to act, the Public Guardian and Trustee shall be the litigation guardian;

(e) is an absentee,

(i) the committee of his or her estate appointed under the *Absentees Act* shall be the litigation guardian,

(ii) if there is no such committee, a suitable person who has no interest contrary to that of the absentee may be the litigation guardian, or

(iii) if no such person is available and able to act, the Public Guardian and Trustee shall be the litigation guardian;

(f) is a person in respect of whom an order was made under subsection 72(1) or (2) of the *Mental Health Act* as it read before April 3, 1995, the Public Guardian and Trustee shall be the litigation guardian.

DUTIES OF LITIGATION GUARDIAN

4.04(1) A litigation guardian shall diligently attend to the interests of the person under disability and take all steps reasonably necessary for the protection of those interests, including the commencement and conduct of a defendant's claim.

PUBLIC GUARDIAN AND TRUSTEE, CHILDREN'S LAWYER

(2) The Public Guardian and Trustee or the Children's Lawyer may act as litigation guardian without filing the consent required by subrule 4.01(3) or 4.02(2).

POWER OF COURT

4.05 The court may remove or replace a litigation guardian at any time.

SETTING ASIDE JUDGMENT, ETC.

4.06 If an action has been brought against a person under disability and the action has not been defended by a litigation guardian, the court may set aside the noting of default or any judgment against the person under disability on such terms as are just, and may set aside any step that has been taken to enforce the judgment.

SETTLEMENT REQUIRES COURT'S APPROVAL

4.07 No settlement of a claim made by or against a person under disability is binding on the person without the approval of the court.

MONEY TO BE PAID INTO COURT

4.08(1) Any money payable to a person under disability under an order or a settlement shall be paid into court, unless the court orders otherwise, and shall afterwards be paid out or otherwise disposed of as ordered by the court.

(2) If money is payable to a person under disability under an order or settlement, the court may order that the money shall be paid directly to the person, and payment made under the order discharges the obligation to the extent of the amount paid.

RULE 5   PARTNERSHIPS AND SOLE PROPRIETORSHIPS

PARTNERSHIPS

5.01 A proceeding by or against two or more persons as partners may be commenced using the firm name of the partnership.

DEFENCE

5.02 If a proceeding is commenced against a partnership using the firm name, the partnership's defence shall be delivered in the firm name and no person who admits being a partner at any material time may defend the proceeding separately, except with leave of the court.

NOTICE TO ALLEGED PARTNER

5.03(1) In a proceeding against a partnership using the firm name, a plaintiff who seeks an order that would be enforceable personally against a person as a partner may serve the person with the claim, together with a notice to alleged partner (Form 5A).

(2) A person served as provided in subrule (1) is deemed to have been a partner at the material time, unless the person defends the proceeding separately denying having been a partner at the material time.

DISCLOSURE OF PARTNERS

5.04(1) If a proceeding is commenced by or against a partnership using the firm name, any other party may serve a notice requiring the partnership to disclose immediately in writing the names and addresses of all partners constituting the partnership at a time specified in the notice; if a partner's present address is unknown, the partnership shall disclose the last known address.

(1.1), (1.1.1) Revoked.

PARTNERSHIP'S FAILURE TO COMPLY

(2) If a partnership fails to comply with a notice under subrule (1), its claim may be dismissed or the proceeding stayed or its defence may be struck out.

ENFORCEMENT OF ORDER

5.05(1) An order against a partnership using the firm name may be enforced against the partnership's property.

(2) An order against a partnership using the firm name may also be enforced, if the order or a subsequent order so provides, against any person who was served as provided in rule 5.03 and who,

(a) under that rule, is deemed to have been a partner at the material time;

(b) has admitted being a partner at that time; or

(c) has been adjudged to have been a partner at that time.

AGAINST PERSON NOT SERVED AS ALLEGED PARTNER

(3) If, after an order has been made against a partnership using the firm name, the party obtaining it claims to be entitled to enforce it against any person alleged to be a partner other than a person who was served as provided in rule 5.03, the party may make a motion for leave to do so; the judge may grant leave if the person's liability as a partner is not disputed or, if disputed, after the liability has been determined in such manner as the judge directs.

SOLE PROPRIETORSHIPS

5.06(1) If a person carries on business in a business name other than his or her own name, a proceeding may be commenced by or against the person using the business name.

(2) Rules 5.01 to 5.05 apply, with necessary modifications, to a proceeding by or against a sole proprietor using a business name, as though the sole proprietor were a partner and the business name were the firm name of a partnership.

RULE 6 FORUM AND JURISDICTION

PLACE OF COMMENCEMENT AND TRIAL

6.01(1) An action shall be commenced,

(a) in the territorial division,

(i) in which the cause of action arose, or

(ii) in which the defendant or, if there are several defendants, in which any one of them resides or carries on business; or

(b) at the court's place of sitting that is nearest to the place where the defendant or, if there are several defendants, where any one of them resides or carries on business.

(2) An action shall be tried in the place where it is commenced, but if the court is satisfied that the balance of convenience substantially favours holding the trial at another place than those described in subrule (1), the court may order that the action be tried at that other place.

(3) If, when an action is called for trial or settlement conference, the judge finds that the place where the action was commenced is not the proper place of trial, the court may order that the action be tried in any other place where it could have been commenced under this rule.

6.02 A cause of action shall not be divided into two or more actions for the purpose of bringing it within the court's jurisdiction.

6.03 Revoked.

RULE 7 COMMENCEMENT OF PROCEEDINGS

PLAINTIFF'S CLAIM

7.01(1) An action shall be commenced by filing a plaintiff's claim (Form 7A) with the clerk, together with a copy of the claim for each defendant.

CONTENTS OF CLAIM, ATTACHMENTS

(2) The following requirements apply to the claim:

1. It shall contain the following information, in concise and non-technical language:

i. The full names of the parties to the proceeding and, if relevant, the capacity in which they sue or are sued.

ii. The nature of the claim, with reasonable certainty and detail, including the date, place and nature of the occurrences on which the claim is based.

iii. The amount of the claim and the relief requested.

iv. The name, address, telephone number, fax number if any, and Law Society of Upper Canada registration number if any, of the lawyer or agent representing the plaintiff or, if the plaintiff is self-represented, the plaintiff's address, telephone number and fax number if any.

v. The address where the plaintiff believes the defendant may be served.

2. If the plaintiff's claim is based in whole or in part on a document, a copy of the document shall be attached to each copy of the claim, unless it is unavailable, in which case the claim shall state the reason why the document is not attached.

(3) Revoked.

7.02 Revoked.

ISSUING CLAIM

7.03(1) On receiving the plaintiff's claim, the clerk shall immediately issue it by dating, signing and sealing it and assigning it a court file number.

(2) The original of the claim shall remain in the court file and the copies shall be given to the plaintiff for service on the defendant.

RULE 8   SERVICE

SERVICE OF PARTICULAR DOCUMENTS PLAINTIFF'S OR DEFENDANT'S CLAIM

8.01(1) A plaintiff's claim or defendant's claim (Form 7A or 10A) shall be served personally as provided in rule 8.02 or by an alternative to personal service as provided in rule 8.03.

TIME FOR SERVICE OF CLAIM

(2) A claim shall be served within six months after the date it is issued, but the court may extend the time for service, before or after the six months has elapsed.

DEFENCE

(3) A defence shall be served by the clerk, by mail or by fax.

(3.1) Revoked.

DEFAULT JUDGMENT

(4) A default judgment (Form 11B) shall be served by the clerk, by mail or by fax, on all parties named in the claim.

(4.1), (4.1.1) Revoked.

ASSESSMENT ORDER

(5) An order made on a motion in writing for an assessment of damages under subrule 11.03(2) shall be served by the clerk to the moving party if the party provides a stamped, self-addressed envelope with the notice of motion and supporting affidavit.

SETTLEMENT CONFERENCE ORDER

(6) An order made at a settlement conference shall be served by the clerk by mail or by fax, on all parties that did not attend the settlement conference.

SUMMONS TO WITNESS

(7) A summons to witness (Form 18A) shall be served personally by the party who requires the presence of the witness, or by the party's lawyer or agent, at least 10 days before the trial date; at the time of service, attendance money calculated in accordance with the regulations made under the *Administration of Justice Act* shall be paid or tendered to the witness.

NOTICE OF GARNISHMENT

(8) A notice of garnishment (Form 20E) shall be served by the creditor,

(a) together with a sworn affidavit for enforcement request (Form 20P), on the debtor, by mail, by courier, personally as provided in rule 8.02 or by an alternative to personal service as provided in rule 8.03; and

(b) together with a garnishee's statement (Form 20F), on the garnishee, by mail, by courier, personally as provided in rule 8.02 or by an alternative to personal service as provided in rule 8.03.

NOTICE OF GARNISHMENT HEARING

(9) A notice of garnishment hearing (Form 20Q) shall be served by the person requesting the hearing on the creditor, debtor, garnishee and co-owner of the debt, if any, and any other interested persons by mail, by courier, personally as provided in rule 8.02 or by an alternative to personal services as provided in rule 8.03.

NOTICE OF EXAMINATION

(10) A notice of examination (Form 20H) shall be served by the creditor on the debtor or person to be examined personally as provided in rule 8.02 or by an alternative to personal service as provided in rule 8.03.

FINANCIAL STATEMENT

(11) If the person to be examined is the debtor and the debtor is an individual, the creditor shall serve the notice of examination on the debtor together with a blank financial information form (Form 20I).

(12) The notice of examination,

(a) shall be served, together with the financial information form if applicable, at least 30 days before the date fixed for the examination; and

(b) shall be filed, with proof of service, at least three days before the date fixed for the examination.

NOTICE OF CONTEMPT HEARING

(13) A notice of a contempt hearing shall be served by the creditor on the debtor or person to be examined personally as provided in rule 8.02.

OTHER DOCUMENTS

(14) A document not referred to in subrules (1) to (13) may be served by mail, by courier, by fax, personally as provided in rule 8.02 or by an alternative to personal service as provided in rule 8.03, unless the court orders otherwise.

PERSONAL SERVICE

8.02 If a document is to be served personally, service shall be made,

Individual

(a) on an individual, other than a person under disability, by leaving a copy of the document with him or her;

Municipality

(b) on a municipal corporation, by leaving a copy of the document with the chair, mayor, warden or reeve of the municipality, with the clerk or deputy clerk of the municipality or with a lawyer for the municipality;

Corporation

(c) on any other corporation, by leaving a copy of the document with an officer, director or agent of the corporation, or with a person at any place of business of the corporation who appears to be in control or management of the place of business;

Board or Commission

(d) on a board or commission, by leaving a copy of the document with a member or officer of the board or commission;

Person Outside Ontario Carrying on Business in Ontario

(e) on a person outside Ontario who carries on business in Ontario, by leaving a copy of the document with anyone carrying on business in Ontario for the person;

Crown in Right of Canada

(f) on Her Majesty the Queen in right of Canada, in accordance with subsection 23(2) of the *Crown Liability and Proceedings Act* (Canada);

Crown in Right of Ontario

(g) on Her Majesty the Queen in right of Ontario, in accordance with section 10 of the *Proceedings Against the Crown Act*;

Absentee

(h) on an absentee, by leaving a copy of the document with the absentee's committee, if one has been appointed or, if not, with the Public Guardian and Trustee;

Minor

(i) on a minor, by leaving a copy of the document with the minor and, if the minor resides with a parent or other person having his or her care or lawful custody, by leaving another copy of the document with the parent or other person;

Mentally Incapable Person

(j) on a mentally incapable person,

(i) if there is a guardian or an attorney acting under a validated power of attorney for personal care with authority to act in the proceeding, by leaving a copy of the document with the guardian or attorney,

(ii) if there is no guardian or attorney acting under a validated power of attorney for personal care with authority to act in the proceeding but there is an attorney under a power of attorney with authority to act in the proceeding, by leaving a copy of the document with the attorney and leaving an additional copy with the person,

(iii) if there is neither a guardian nor an attorney with authority to act in the proceeding, by leaving a copy of the document bearing the person's name and address with the Public Guardian and Trustee and leaving an additional copy with the person;

Partnership

(k) on a partnership, by leaving a copy of the document with any one or more of the partners or with a person at the principal place of business of the partnership who appears to be in control or management of the place of business; and

Sole Proprietorship

(l) on a sole proprietorship, by leaving a copy of the document with the sole proprietor or with a person at the principal place of business of the sole proprietorship who appears to be in control or management of the place of business.

ALTERNATIVES TO PERSONAL SERVICE

8.03(1) If a document is to be served by an alternative to personal service, service shall be made in accordance with subrule (2), (3) or (5); in the case of a plaintiff's claim or defendant's claim served on an individual, service may also be made in accordance with subrule (7).

AT PLACE OF RESIDENCE

(2) If an attempt is made to effect personal service at an individual's place of residence and for any reason personal service cannot be effected, the document may be served by,

(a) leaving a copy in a sealed envelope addressed to the individual at the place of residence with anyone who appears to be an adult member of the same household; and

(b) on the same day or the following day, mailing or sending by courier another copy of the document to the individual at the place of residence.

CORPORATION

(3) If the head office or principal place of business of a corporation or, in the case of an extra-provincial corporation, the attorney for service in Ontario cannot be found at the last address recorded with the Ministry of Government Services, service may be made on the corporation,

(a) by mailing or sending by courier a copy of the document to the corporation or to the attorney for service in Ontario, as the case may be, at that address; and

(b) by mailing or sending by courier a copy of the document to each director of the corporation as recorded with the Ministry of Government Services, at the director's address as recorded with that Ministry.

WHEN EFFECTIVE

(4) Service made under subrule (2) or (3) is effective on the fifth day after the document is mailed or verified by courier that it was delivered.

ACCEPTANCE OF SERVICE BY LAWYER

(5) Service on a party who is represented by a lawyer may be made by leaving a copy of the document with the lawyer or an employee in the lawyer's office, but service under this subrule is effective only if the lawyer or employee endorses on the document or a copy of it an acceptance of service and the date of the acceptance.

(6) By accepting service the lawyer is deemed to represent to the court that he or she has the client's authority to accept service.

SERVICE OF CLAIM

(7) Service of a plaintiff's claim or defendant's claim on an individual against whom the claim is made may be made by sending a copy of the claim by registered mail or by courier to the individual's place of residence, if the signature of the individual or any person who appears to be a member of the same household, verifying receipt of the copy, is obtained.

(8) Service under subrule (7) is effective on the date on which receipt of the copy of the claim is verified by signature, as shown in a delivery confirmation provided by or obtained from Canada Post or the commercial courier, as the case may be.

(9) Revoked.

SUBSTITUTED SERVICE

8.04 If it is shown that it is impractical to effect prompt service of a claim personally or by an alternative to personal service, the court may allow substituted service.

SERVICE OUTSIDE ONTARIO

8.05 If the defendant is outside Ontario, the court may award as costs of the action the costs reasonably incurred in effecting service of the claim on the defendant there.

PROOF OF SERVICE

8.06 An affidavit of service (Form 8A) made by the person effecting the service constitutes proof of service of a document.

SERVICE BY MAIL

8.07(1) If a document is to be served by mail under these rules, it shall be sent, by regular lettermail or registered mail, to the last address of the person or of the person's lawyer or agent that is,

    (a) on file with the court, if the document is to be served by the clerk;

    (b) known to the sender, if the document is to be served by any other person.

WHEN EFFECTIVE

(2) Service of a document by mail is deemed to be effective on the fifth day following the date of mailing.

EXCEPTION

(3) This rule does not apply when a claim is served by registered mail under subrule 8.03(7).

SERVICE BY COURIER

8.07.1(1) If a document is to be served by courier under these rules, it shall be sent by means of a commercial courier to the last address of the person or of the person's lawyer or agent that is on file with the court or known to the sender.

WHEN EFFECTIVE

(2) Service of a document sent by courier is deemed to be effective on the fifth day following the date on which the courier verifies to the sender that the document was delivered.

EXCEPTION

(3) This rule does not apply when a claim is served by courier under subrule 8.03(7).

SERVICE BY FAX

8.08(1) Service of a document by fax is deemed to be effective,

(a) on the day of transmission, if transmission takes place before 5 p.m. on a day that is not a holiday;

(b) on the next day that is not a holiday, in any other case.

(2) A document containing 16 or more pages, including the cover page, may be served by fax only between 5 p.m. and 8 a.m. the following day, unless the party to be served consents in advance.

NOTICE OF CHANGE OF ADDRESS

8.09(1) A party whose address for service changes shall serve notice of the change on the court and other parties within seven days after the change takes place.

(2) Service of the notice may be proved by affidavit if the court orders that proof of service is required.

FAILURE TO RECEIVE DOCUMENT

8.10 A person who has been served or who is deemed to have been served with a document in accordance with these rules is nevertheless entitled to show, on a motion to set aside the consequences of default, on a motion for an extension of time or in support of a request for an adjournment, that the document,

(a) did not come to the person's notice; or

(b) came to the person's notice only at some time later than when it was served or is deemed to have been served.

RULE 9   DEFENCE

DEFENCE

9.01(1) A defendant who wishes to dispute a plaintiff's claim shall file a defence (Form 9A), together with a copy for each of the other parties with the clerk within 20 days of being served with the claim.

SERVICE OF COPY BY CLERK

(2) On receiving the defence, the clerk shall retain the original in the court file and shall serve a copy in accordance with subrule 8.01(3) on each of the other parties.

(3) Revoked.

CONTENTS OF DEFENCE, ATTACHMENTS

9.02(1) The following requirements apply to the defence:

1. It shall contain the following information:

i. The reasons why the defendant disputes the plaintiff's claim, expressed in concise non-technical language with a reasonable amount of detail.

ii. If the defendant is self-represented, the defendant's name, address and telephone number, and fax number if any.

iii. If the defendant is represented by a lawyer or agent, that person's name, address and telephone number, and fax number if any.

2. If the defence is based in whole or in part on a document, a copy of the document shall be attached to each copy of the defence, unless it is unavailable, in which case the defence shall state the reason why the document is not attached.

(2) Revoked.

ADMISSION OF LIABILITY AND PROPOSAL OF TERMS OF PAYMENT

9.03(1) A defendant who admits liability for all or part of the plaintiff's claim but wishes to arrange terms of payment may in the defence admit liability and propose terms of payment.

WHERE NO DISPUTE

(2) If the plaintiff does not dispute the proposal within the 20-day period referred to in subrule (3),

(a) the defendant shall make payment in accordance with the proposal as if it were a court order;

(b) the plaintiff may serve a notice of default of payment (Form 20L) on the defendant if the defendant fails to make payment in accordance with the proposal; and

(c) the clerk shall sign judgment for the unpaid balance of the undisputed amount on the filing of an affidavit of default of payment (Form 20M) by the plaintiff swearing,

(i) that the defendant failed to make payment in accordance with the proposal,

(ii) to the amount paid by the defendant and the unpaid balance, and

(iii) that 15 days have passed since the defendant was served with a notice of default of payment.

DISPUTE

(3) The plaintiff may dispute the proposal within 20 days after service of the defence by filing with the clerk and serving on the defendant a request to clerk (Form 9B) for a terms of payment hearing before a referee or other person appointed by the court.

(4) The clerk shall fix a time for the hearing, allowing for a reasonable notice period after the date the request is served, and serve a notice of hearing on the parties.

MANNER OF SERVICE

(4.1) The notice of hearing shall be served by mail or fax.

FINANCIAL INFORMATION FORM, DEFENDANT AN INDIVIDUAL

(4.2) The clerk shall serve a financial information form (Form 20I) on the defendant, together with the notice of hearing, if the defendant is an individual.

(4.3) Where a defendant receives a financial information form under subrule (4.2), he or she shall complete it and serve it on the creditor before the hearing, but shall not file it with the court.

ORDER

(5) On the hearing, the referee or other person may make an order as to terms of payment by the defendant.

FAILURE TO APPEAR, DEFAULT JUDGMENT

(6) If the defendant does not appear at the hearing, the clerk may sign default judgment against the defendant for the part of the claim that has been admitted and shall serve a default judgment (Form 11B) on the defendant in accordance with subrule 8.01(4).

(6.1) Revoked.

FAILURE TO MAKE PAYMENTS

(7) Unless the referee or other person specifies otherwise in the order as to terms of payment, if the defendant fails to make payment in accordance with the order, the clerk shall sign judgment for the unpaid balance on the filing of an affidavit by the plaintiff swearing to the default and stating the amount paid and the unpaid balance.

RULE 10   DEFENDANT'S CLAIM

DEFENDANT'S CLAIM

10.01(1) A defendant may make a claim,

(a) against the plaintiff;

(b) against any other person,

(i) arising out of the transaction or occurrence relied upon by the plaintiff, or

(ii) related to the plaintiff's claim; or

(c) against the plaintiff and against another person in accordance with clause (b).

(2) The defendant's claim shall be in Form 10A and may be issued,

(a) within 20 days after the day on which the defence is filed; or

(b) after the time described in clause (a) but before trial or default judgment, with leave of the court.

COPIES

(3) The defendant shall provide a copy of the defendant's claim to the court.

CONTENTS OF DEFENDANT'S CLAIM, ATTACHMENTS

(4) The following requirements apply to the defendant's claim:

1. It shall contain the following information:

i. The full names of the parties to the defendant's claim and, if relevant, the capacity in which they sue or are sued.

ii. The nature of the claim, expressed in concise non-technical language with a reasonable amount of detail, including the date, place and nature of the occurrences on which the claim is based.

iii. The amount of the claim and the relief requested.

iv. If the defendant is self-represented, the defendant's name, address and telephone number, and fax number if any.

v. If the defendant is represented by a lawyer or agent, that person's name, address and telephone number, and fax number if any.

vi. The address where the defendant believes each person against whom the claim is made may be served.

vii. The court file number assigned to the plaintiff's claim.

2. If the defendant's claim is based in whole or in part on a document, a copy of the document shall be attached to each copy of the claim, unless it is unavailable, in which case the claim shall state the reason why the document is not attached.

(5) Revoked.

ISSUANCE

(6) On receiving the defendant's claim, the clerk shall immediately issue it by dating, signing and sealing it, shall assign it the same court file number as the plaintiff's claim and shall place the original in the court file.

(7), (8) Revoked.

SERVICE

10.02 A defendant's claim shall be served by the defendant on every person against whom it is made, in accordance with subrules 8.01(1) and (2).

DEFENCE

10.03(1) A party who wishes to dispute the defendant's claim or a third party who wishes to dispute the plaintiff's claim may, within 20 days after service of the defendant's claim, file a defence (Form 9A) with the clerk, together with a copy for each of the other parties or persons against whom the defendant's or plaintiff's claim is made.

SERVICE OF COPY BY CLERK

(2) On receiving a defence under subrule (1), the clerk shall retain the original in the court file and shall serve a copy on each party in accordance with subrule 8.01(3).

DEFENDANT'S CLAIM TO BE TRIED WITH MAIN ACTION

10.04(1) A defendant's claim shall be tried and disposed of at the trial of the action, unless the court orders otherwise.

EXCEPTION

(2) If it appears that a defendant's claim may unduly complicate or delay the trial of the action or cause undue prejudice to a party, the court may order separate trials or direct that the defendant's claim proceed as a separate action.

RIGHTS OF THIRD PARTY

(3) If the defendant alleges, in a defendant's claim, that a third party is liable to the defendant for all or part of the plaintiff's claim in the action, the third party may at the trial contest the defendant's liability to the plaintiff, but only if the third party has filed a defence in accordance with subrule 10.03(1).

APPLICATION OF RULES TO DEFENDANT'S CLAIM

10.05(1) These rules apply, with necessary modifications, to a defendant's claim as if it were a plaintiff's claim, and to a defence to a defendant's claim as if it were a defence to a plaintiff's claim.

EXCEPTION

(2) However, when a person against whom a defendant's claim is made is noted in default, judgment against that person may be obtained only in accordance with rule 11.04.

RULE 11   DEFAULT PROCEEDINGS

NOTING DEFENDANT IN DEFAULT

11.01(1) If a defendant to a plaintiff's claim or a defendant's claim fails to file a defence to all or part of the claim with the clerk within the prescribed time, the clerk may, when proof is filed that the claim was served within the territorial division, note the defendant in default.

LEAVE REQUIRED FOR PERSON UNDER DISABILITY

(2) A person under disability may not be noted in default under subrule (1), except with leave of the court.

SERVICE OUTSIDE TERRITORIAL DIVISION

(3) If all the defendants have been served outside the court's territorial division, the clerk shall not note any defendant in default until it is proved by an affidavit for jurisdiction (Form 11A) submitted to the clerk, or by evidence presented before a judge, that the action was properly brought in that territorial division.

DEFAULT JUDGMENT, PLAINTIFF'S CLAIM, DEBT OR LIQUIDATED DEMAND

11.02(1) If a defendant has been noted in default, the clerk may sign default judgment (Form 11B) in respect of the claim or any part of the claim to which the default applies that is for a debt or liquidated demand in money, including interest if claimed.

(2) The fact that default judgment has been signed under subrule (1) does not affect the plaintiff's right to proceed on the remainder of the claim or against any other defendant for all or part of the claim.

MANNER OF SERVICE OF DEFAULT JUDGMENT

(3) A default judgment (Form 11B) shall be served in accordance with subrule 8.01(4).

DEFAULT JUDGMENT, PLAINTIFF'S CLAIM, UNLIQUIDATED DEMAND

11.03(1) If all defendants have been noted in default, the plaintiff may obtain judgment against a defendant noted in default with respect to any part of the claim to which rule 11.02 does not apply.

(2) To obtain judgment, the plaintiff may,

(a) file a notice of motion and supporting affidavit (Form 15A) requesting a motion in writing for an assessment of damages, setting out the reasons why the motion should be granted and attaching any relevant documents; or

(b) file a request to clerk (Form 9B) requesting that an assessment hearing be arranged.

INADEQUATE SUPPORTING AFFIDAVIT

(3) On a motion in writing for an assessment of damages under clause (2)(a), a judge who finds the plaintiff's affidavit inadequate or unsatisfactory may order that,

(a) a further affidavit be provided; or

(b) an assessment hearing be held.

ASSESSMENT HEARING

(4) If an assessment hearing is to be held under clause (2)(b) or (3)(b), the clerk shall fix a date for the hearing and send a notice of hearing to the plaintiff, and the assessment hearing shall proceed as a trial in accordance with rule 17.

MATTERS TO BE PROVED

(5) On a motion in writing for an assessment of damages or at an assessment hearing, the plaintiff is not required to prove liability against a defendant noted in default, but is required to prove the amount of the claim.

SERVICE OF ORDER

(6) An order made on a motion in writing for an assessment of damages shall be served by the clerk in accordance with subrule 8.01(5).

NO ASSESSMENT WHERE DEFENCE FILED

(7) If one or more defendants have filed a defence, a plaintiff requiring an assessment of damages against a defendant noted in default shall proceed to a settlement conference under rule 13 and, if necessary, a trial in accordance with rule 17.

DEFAULT JUDGMENT, DEFENDANT'S CLAIM

11.04 If a party against whom a defendant's claim is made has been noted in default, judgment may be obtained against the party only at trial or on motion.

CONSEQUENCES OF NOTING IN DEFAULT

11.05(1) A defendant who has been noted in default shall not file a defence or take any other step in the proceeding, except making a motion under rule 11.06, without leave of the court or the plaintiff's consent.

(2) Any step in the proceeding may be taken without the consent of a defendant who has been noted in default.

(3) A defendant who has been noted in default is not entitled to notice of any step in the proceeding and need not be served with any other document, except the following:

1. Subrule 11.02(3) (service of default judgment).
2. Rule 12.01 (amendment of claim or defence).
3. Subrule 15.01(6) (motion after judgment).
4. Postjudgment proceedings against a debtor under rule 20.

SETTING ASIDE NOTING OF DEFAULT BY COURT ON MOTION

11.06 The court may set aside the noting in default or default judgment against a party and any step that has been taken to enforce the judgment, on such terms as are just, if the party makes a motion to set aside and the court is satisfied that,

(a) the party has a meritorious defence and a reasonable explanation for the default; and

(b) the motion is made as soon as is reasonably possible in all the circumstances.

RULE 11.1   DISMISSAL BY CLERK

DISMISSAL — UNDEFENDED ACTIONS

11.1.01(1) The clerk shall make an order dismissing an action as abandoned if the following conditions are satisfied, unless the court orders otherwise:

1. More than 180 days have passed since the date the claim was issued or an order was made extending the time for service of the claim under subrule 8.01(2).

2. No defence has been filed.

3. The action has not been disposed of by order and has not been set down for trial.

4. The clerk has given 45 days notice to the plaintiff that the action will be dismissed as abandoned.

DISMISSAL — DEFENDED ACTIONS

(2) The clerk shall make an order dismissing an action as abandoned if the following conditions are satisfied, unless the court orders otherwise:

1. More than 150 days have passed since the date the first defence was filed.

2. Revoked.

3. The action has not been disposed of by order and has not been set down for trial.

4. The clerk has given 45 days notice to all parties to the action that the action will be dismissed as abandoned.

TRANSITION

(3) If an action was started before July 1, 2006, the following applies:

1. The action or a step in the action shall be carried on under these rules on or after July 1, 2006.

2. Despite paragraph 1, if a step in the action is taken on or after July 1, 2006, the timetable set out in subrules (1) and (2) shall apply as if the action started on the date on which the step was taken.

SAME

(4) If an action was commenced before July 1, 2006 and no step is taken in the action on or after that date, the clerk may make an order dismissing it as abandoned if,

(a) where an action is undefended, more than two years have passed since the date the claim was issued and the conditions set out in paragraphs 2, 3 and 4 of subrule (1) are satisfied; or

(b) more than two years have passed since the date the first defence was filed and the conditions set out in paragraphs 3 and 4 of subrule (2) are satisfied.

EXCEPTION WHERE TERMS OF SETTLEMENT SIGNED

(5) Subrules (1), (2) and (4) do not apply if terms of settlement (Form 14D) signed by all parties have been filed.

EXCEPTION WHERE ADMISSION OF LIABILITY

(6) Subrule (2) and clause (4)(b) do not apply if the defence contains an admission of liability for the plaintiff's claim and a proposal of terms of payment under subrule 9.03(1).

SERVICE OF ORDERS

(7) The clerk shall serve a copy of an order made under subrule (1) or clause (4)(a) on the plaintiff and a copy of an order made under subrule (2) or clause (4)(b) on all parties to the action.

RULE 11.2   REQUEST FOR CLERK'S ORDER ON CONSENT

CONSENT ORDER

11.2.01(1) The clerk shall, on the filing of a request for clerk's order on consent (Form 11.2A), make an order granting the relief sought, including costs, if the following conditions are satisfied:

1. The relief sought is,

i. amending a claim or defence less than 30 days before the originally scheduled trial date,

ii. adding, deleting or substituting a party less than 30 days before the originally scheduled trial date,

iii. setting aside the noting in default or default judgment against a party and any specified step to enforce the judgment that has not yet been completed,

iv. restoring a matter that was dismissed under rule 11.1 to the list,

v. noting that payment has been made in full satisfaction of a judgment or terms of settlement, or

vi. dismissing an action.

2. The request is signed by all parties (including any party to be added, deleted or substituted) and states,

i. that each party has received a copy of the request, and

ii. that no party that would be affected by the order is under disability.

3., 4. Revoked.

SERVICE OF ORDER

(2) The clerk shall serve a copy of an order made under subrule (1) in accordance with subrule 8.01(14) on a party that requests it and provides a stamped, self-addressed envelope.

SAME, REFUSAL TO MAKE ORDER

(3) Where the clerk refuses to make an order, the clerk shall serve a copy of the request for clerk's order on consent (Form 11.2A), with reasons for the refusal, on all the parties.

NOTICE OF SETTING ASIDE OF ENFORCEMENT STEP

(4) Where an order is made setting aside a specified step to enforce a judgment under subparagraph 1 iii of subrule (1), a party shall file a copy of the order at each court location where the enforcement step has been requested.

RULE 11.3   DISCONTINUANCE

DISCONTINUANCE BY PLAINTIFF IN UNDEFENDED ACTION

11.3.01(1) A plaintiff may discontinue his or her claim against a defendant who fails to file a defence to all or part of the claim with the clerk within the prescribed time by,

(a) serving a notice of discontinued claim (Form 11.3A) on all defendants who were served with the claim; and

(b) filing the notice with proof of service.

(2) A claim may not be discontinued by or against a person under disability, except with leave of the court.

EFFECT OF DISCONTINUANCE ON SUBSEQUENT ACTION

11.3.02 The discontinuance of a claim is not a defence to a subsequent action on the matter, unless an order granting leave to discontinue provides otherwise.

RULE 12   AMENDMENT

RIGHT TO AMEND

12.01(1) A plaintiff's or defendant's claim and a defence to a plaintiff's or defendant's claim may be amended by filing with the clerk a copy that is marked "Amended", in which any additions are underlined and any other changes are identified.

SERVICE

(2) The amended document shall be served by the party making the amendment on all parties, including any parties in default, in accordance with subrule 8.01(14).

TIME

(3) Filing and service of the amended document shall take place at least 30 days before the originally scheduled trial date, unless,

(a) the court, on motion, allows a shorter notice period; or

(b) a clerk's order permitting the amendment is obtained under subrule 11.2.01(1).

SERVICE ON ADDED PARTY

(4) A person added as a party shall be served with the claim as amended, except that if the person is added as a party at trial, the court may dispense with service of the claim.

NO AMENDMENT REQUIRED IN RESPONSE

(5) A party who is served with an amended document is not required to amend the party's defence or claim.

MOTION TO STRIKE OUT OR AMEND A DOCUMENT

12.02(1) The court may, on motion, strike out or amend all or part of any document that,

(a) discloses no reasonable cause of action or defence;

(b) may delay or make it difficult to have a fair trial; or

(c) is inflammatory, a waste of time, a nuisance or an abuse of the court's process.

(2) In connection with an order striking out or amending a document under subrule (1), the court may do one or more of the following:

1. In the case of a claim, order that the action be stayed or dismissed.

2. In the case of a defence, strike out the defence and grant judgment.

3. Impose such terms as are just.

RULE 13   SETTLEMENT CONFERENCES

SETTLEMENT CONFERENCE REQUIRED IN DEFENDED ACTION

13.01(1) A settlement conference shall be held in every defended action.

DUTY OF CLERK

(2) The clerk shall fix a time, date and place for the settlement conference and serve a notice of settlement conference, together with a list of proposed witnesses (Form 13A), on the parties.

TIMING

(3) The settlement conference shall be held within 90 days after the first defence is filed.

EXCEPTION

(4) Subrules (1) to (3) do not apply if the defence contains an admission of liability for all of the plaintiff's claim and a proposal of terms of payment under subrule 9.03(1).

ATTENDANCE

13.02(1) A party and the party's lawyer or agent, if any, shall, unless the court orders otherwise, participate in the settlement conference,

    (a) by personal attendance; or

    (b) by telephone or video conference in accordance with rule 1.07.

AUTHORITY TO SETTLE

(2) A party who requires another person's approval before agreeing to a settlement shall, before the settlement conference, arrange to have ready telephone access to the other person throughout the conference, whether it takes place during or after regular business hours.

ADDITIONAL SETTLEMENT CONFERENCES

(3) The court may order the parties to attend an additional settlement conference.

(4) The clerk shall fix a time and place for any additional settlement conference and serve a notice of settlement conference, together with a list of proposed witnesses (Form 13A) on the parties.

FAILURE TO ATTEND

(5) If a party who has received a notice of settlement conference fails to attend the conference, the court may,

    (a) impose appropriate sanctions, by way of costs or otherwise; and

    (b) order that an additional settlement conference be held, if necessary.

(6) If a defendant fails to attend a first settlement conference, receives notice of an additional settlement conference and fails to attend the additional settlement conference, the court may,

    (a) strike out the defence and dismiss the defendant's claim, if any, and allow the plaintiff to prove the plaintiff's claim; or

    (b) make such other order as is just.

INADEQUATE PREPARATION, FAILURE TO FILE MATERIAL

(7) The court may award costs against a person who attends a settlement conference if,

    (a) in the opinion of the court, the person is so inadequately prepared as to frustrate the purposes of the conference;

    (b) the person fails to file the material required by subrule 13.03(2).

PURPOSES OF SETTLEMENT CONFERENCE

13.03(1) The purposes of a settlement conference are,

    (a) to resolve or narrow the issues in the action;

    (b) to expedite the disposition of the action;

    (c) to encourage settlement of the action;

    (d) to assist the parties in effective preparation for trial; and

    (e) to provide full disclosure between the parties of the relevant facts and evidence.

DISCLOSURE

(2) At least 14 days before the date of the settlement conference, each party shall serve on every other party and file with the court,

    (a) a copy of any document to be relied on at the trial, including an expert report, not attached to the party's claim or defence; and

    (b) a list of proposed witnesses (Form 13A) and of other persons with knowledge of the matters in dispute in the action.

(3) At the settlement conference, the parties or their representatives shall openly and frankly discuss the issues involved in the action.

FURTHER DISCLOSURE RESTRICTED

(4) Except as otherwise provided or with the consent of the parties (Form 13B), the matters discussed at the settlement conference shall not be disclosed to others until after the action has been disposed of.

RECOMMENDATIONS TO PARTIES

13.04 The court may make recommendations to the parties on any matter relating to the conduct of the action, in order to fulfil the purposes of a settlement conference, including recommendations as to,

    (a) the clarification and simplification of issues in the action;

    (b) the elimination of claims or defences that appear to be unsupported; and

    (c) the admission of facts or documents without further proof.

ORDERS AT SETTLEMENT CONFERENCE

13.05(1) A judge conducting a settlement conference may make any order relating to the conduct of the action that the court could make.

(2) Without limiting the generality of subrule (1), the judge may,

    (a) make an order,

        (i) adding or deleting parties,

        (ii) consolidating actions,

        (iii) staying the action,

        (iv) amending or striking out a claim or defence under rule 12.02,

        (v) staying or dismissing a claim,

        (vi) directing production of documents,

        (vii) changing the place of trial under rule 6.01,

        (viii) directing an additional settlement conference under subrule 13.02(3), and

        (ix) ordering costs; and

    (b) at an additional settlement conference, order judgment under subrule 13.02(6).

RECOMMENDATIONS TO JUDGE

(3) If the settlement conference is conducted by a referee, a judge may, on the referee's recommendation, make any order that may be made under subrules (1) and (2).

CONSENT TO FINAL JUDGMENT

(4) A judge may order final judgment at a settlement conference where the matter in dispute is for an amount under the appealable limit and a party files a consent (Form 13B) signed by all parties before the settlement conference indicating that they wish to obtain final determination of the matter at the settlement conference if a mediated settlement is not reached.

SERVICE OF ORDER

(5) Within 10 days after the judge signs an order made at a settlement conference, the clerk shall serve the order on the parties that were not present at the settlement conference in accordance with subrule 8.01(6).

MEMORANDUM

13.06(1) At the end of the settlement conference, the court shall prepare a memorandum summarizing,

    (a) recommendations made under rule 13.04;

    (b) the issues remaining in dispute;

    (c) the matters agreed on by the parties;

    (d) any evidentiary matters that are considered relevant; and

    (e) information relating to the scheduling of the remaining steps in the proceeding.

(2) The memorandum shall be filed with the clerk, who shall give a copy to the trial judge.

NOTICE OF TRIAL

13.07 At or after the settlement conference, the clerk shall provide the parties with a notice stating that one of the parties must request a trial date if the action is not disposed of within 30 days after the settlement conference, and pay the fee required for setting the action down for trial.

JUDGE NOT TO PRESIDE AT TRIAL

13.08 A judge who conducts a settlement conference in an action shall not preside at the trial of the action.

WITHDRAWAL OF CLAIM

13.09 After a settlement conference has been held, a claim against a party who is not in default shall not be withdrawn or discontinued by the party who brought the claim without,

    (a) the written consent of the party against whom the claim is brought; or

    (b) leave of the court.

COSTS

13.10 The costs of a settlement conference, exclusive of disbursements, shall not exceed $100 unless the court orders otherwise because there are special circumstances.

RULE 14   OFFER TO SETTLE

14.01 A party may serve on any other party an offer to settle a claim on the terms specified in the offer.

WRITTEN DOCUMENTS

14.01.1(1) An offer to settle, an acceptance of an offer to settle and a notice of withdrawal of an offer to settle shall be in writing.

USE OF FORMS

(2) An offer to settle may be in Form 14A, an acceptance of an offer to settle may be in Form 14B and a notice of withdrawal of an offer to settle may be in Form 14C.

TERMS OF SETTLEMENT

(3) The terms of an accepted offer to settle may be set out in terms of settlement (Form 14D).

TIME FOR MAKING OFFER

14.02(1) An offer to settle may be made at any time.

COSTS CONSEQUENCES

(2) The costs consequences referred to in rule 14.07 apply only if the offer to settle is served on the party to whom it is made at least seven days before the trial commences.

WITHDRAWAL

14.03(1) An offer to settle may be withdrawn at any time before it is accepted, by serving a notice of withdrawal of an offer to settle on the party to whom it was made.

DEEMED WITHDRAWAL

(2) If an offer to settle specifies a date after which it is no longer available for acceptance, and has not been accepted on or before that date, the offer shall be deemed to have been withdrawn on the day after that date.

EXPIRY WHEN COURT DISPOSES OF CLAIM

(3) An offer may not be accepted after the court disposes of the claim in respect of which the offer is made.

NO DISCLOSURE TO TRIAL JUDGE

14.04 If an offer to settle is not accepted, no communication about it or any related negotiations shall be made to the trial judge until all questions of liability and the relief to be granted, other than costs, have been determined.

ACCEPTANCE OF AN OFFER TO SETTLE

14.05(1) An offer to settle may be accepted by serving an acceptance of an offer to settle on the party who made it, at any time before it is withdrawn or before the court disposes of the claim in respect of which it is made.

PAYMENT INTO COURT AS CONDITION

(2) An offer by a plaintiff to settle a claim in return for the payment of money by a defendant may include a term that the defendant pay the money into court; in that case, the defendant may accept the offer only by paying the money into court and notifying the plaintiff of the payment.

(3) If a defendant offers to pay money to a plaintiff in settlement of a claim, the plaintiff may accept the offer with the condition that the defendant pay the money into court; if the offer is so accepted and the defendant fails to pay the money into court, the plaintiff may proceed as provided in rule 14.06.

COSTS

(4) If an accepted offer to settle does not deal with costs, the plaintiff is entitled,

(a) in the case of an offer made by the defendant, to the plaintiff's disbursements assessed to the date the plaintiff was served with the offer;

(b) in the case of an offer made by the plaintiff, to the plaintiff's disbursements assessed to the date that the notice of acceptance was served.

FAILURE TO COMPLY WITH ACCEPTED OFFER

14.06 If a party to an accepted offer to settle fails to comply with the terms of the offer, the other party may,

(a) make a motion to the court for judgment in the terms of the accepted offer; or

(b) continue the proceeding as if there had been no offer to settle.

COSTS CONSEQUENCES OF FAILURE TO ACCEPT

14.07(1) When a plaintiff makes an offer to settle that is not accepted by the defendant, the court may award the plaintiff an amount not exceeding twice the costs of the action, if the following conditions are met:

1. The plaintiff obtains a judgment as favourable as or more favourable than the terms of the offer.

2. The offer was made at least seven days before the trial.

3. The offer was not withdrawn and did not expire before the trial.

(2) When a defendant makes an offer to settle that is not accepted by the plaintiff, the court may award the defendant an amount not exceeding twice the costs awardable to a successful party, from the date the offer was served, if the following conditions are met:

1. The plaintiff obtains a judgment as favourable as or less favourable than the terms of the offer.

2. The offer was made at least seven days before the trial.

3. The offer was not withdrawn and did not expire before the trial.

(3) If an amount is awarded under subrule (1) or (2) to a self-represented party, the court may also award the party an amount not exceeding $500 as compensation for inconvenience and expense.

RULE 15   MOTIONS

NOTICE OF MOTION AND SUPPORTING AFFIDAVIT

15.01(1) A motion shall be made by a notice of motion and supporting affidavit (Form 15A).

(2) The moving party shall obtain a hearing date from the clerk before serving the notice of motion and supporting affidavit under subrule (3).

(3) The notice of motion and supporting affidavit,

(a) shall be served on every party who has filed a claim and any defendant who has not been noted in default, at least seven days before the hearing date; and

(b) shall be filed, with proof of service, at least three days before the hearing date.

SUPPORTING AFFIDAVIT IN RESPONSE

(4) A party who prepares an affidavit (Form 15B) in response to the moving party's notice of motion and supporting affidavit shall serve it on every party who has filed a claim or defence and file it, with proof of service, at least two days before the hearing date.

SUPPLEMENTARY AFFIDAVIT

(5) The moving party may serve a supplementary affidavit on every party who has filed a claim or defence and file it, with proof of service, at least two days before the hearing date.

MOTION AFTER JUDGMENT SIGNED

(6) A motion that is made after judgment has been signed shall be served on all parties, including those who have been noted in default.

METHOD OF HEARING

15.02(1) A motion may be heard,

(a) in person;

(b) by telephone or video conference in accordance with paragraph 2 of subrule 1.07(1);

(c) by a judge in writing under clause 11.03(2)(a);

(d) by any other method that the judge determines is fair and reasonable.

(2) The attendance of the parties is not required if the motion is in writing under clause (1)(c).

MOTION WITHOUT NOTICE

15.03(1) Despite rule 15.01, a motion may be made without notice if the nature or circumstances of the motion make notice unnecessary or not reasonably possible.

SERVICE OF ORDER

(2) A party who obtains an order on motion without notice shall serve it on every affected party, together with a copy of the notice of motion and supporting affidavit used on the motion, within five days after the order is signed.

MOTION TO SET ASIDE OR VARY MOTION MADE WITHOUT NOTICE

(3) A party who is affected by an order obtained on motion without notice may make a motion to set aside or vary the order, within 30 days after being served with the order.

NO FURTHER MOTIONS WITHOUT LEAVE

15.04 If the court is satisfied that a party has tried to delay the action, add to its costs or otherwise abuse the court's process by making numerous motions without merit, the court may, on motion, make an order prohibiting the party from making any further motions in the action without leave of the court.

ADJOURNMENT OF MOTION

15.05 A motion shall not be adjourned at a party's request before the hearing date unless the written consent of all parties is filed when the request is made, unless the court orders otherwise.

WITHDRAWAL OF MOTION

15.06 A motion shall not be withdrawn without,

(a) the written consent of all the parties; or

(b) leave of the court.

COSTS

15.07 The costs of a motion, exclusive of disbursements, shall not exceed $100 unless the court orders otherwise because there are special circumstances.

RULE 16   NOTICE OF TRIAL

CLERK FIXES DATE AND SERVES NOTICE

16.01(1) The clerk shall fix a date for trial and serve a notice of trial on each party who has filed a claim or defence if,

(a) a settlement conference has been held; and

(b) a party has requested that the clerk fix a date for trial and has paid the required fee.

MANNER OF SERVICE

(2) The notice of trial shall be served by mail or fax.

RULE 17 TRIAL

FAILURE TO ATTEND

17.01(1) If an action is called for trial and all the parties fail to attend, the trial judge may strike the action off the trial list.

(2) If an action is called for trial and a party fails to attend, the trial judge may,

(a) proceed with the trial in the party's absence;

(b) if the plaintiff attends and the defendant fails to do so, strike out the defence and dismiss the defendant's claim, if any, and allow the plaintiff to prove the plaintiff's claim, subject to subrule (3);

(c) if the defendant attends and the plaintiff fails to do so, dismiss the action and allow the defendant to prove the defendant's claim, if any; or

(d) make such other order as is just.

(2.1) In the case described in clause (2)(b) or (c), the person with the claim is not required to prove liability against the party who has failed to attend but is required to prove the amount of the claim.

(3) In the case described in clause (2)(b), if an issue as to the proper place of trial under subrule 6.01(1) is raised in the defence, the trial judge shall consider it and make a finding.

SETTING ASIDE OR VARIATION OF JUDGMENT

(4) The court may set aside or vary, on such terms as are just, a judgment obtained against a party who failed to attend at the trial.

CONDITIONS TO MAKING OF ORDER UNDER SUBRULE (4)

(5) The court may make an order under subrule (4) only if,

(a) the party who failed to attend makes a motion for the order within 30 days after becoming aware of the judgment; or

(b) the party who failed to attend makes a motion for an extension of the 30-day period mentioned in clause (a) and the court is satisfied that there are special circumstances that justify the extension.

ADJOURNMENT

17.02(1) The court may postpone or adjourn a trial on such terms as are just, including the payment by one party to another of an amount as compensation for inconvenience and expense.

(2) If the trial of an action has been adjourned two or more times, any further adjournment may be made only on motion with notice to all the parties who were served with the notice of trial, unless the court orders otherwise.

INSPECTION

17.03 The trial judge may, in the presence of the parties or their representatives, inspect any real or personal property concerning which a question arises in the action.

MOTION FOR NEW TRIAL

17.04(1) A party may make a motion for a new trial within 30 days after a final order is made.

TRANSCRIPT

(2) In addition to serving and filing the notice of motion and supporting affidavit (Form 15A) required under rule 15.01, the moving party shall serve and file proof that a request has been made for a transcript of,

(a) the reasons for judgment; and

(b) any other portion of the proceeding that is relevant.

SERVICE AND FILING OF TRANSCRIPT

(3) If available, a copy of the transcript shall, at least three days before the hearing date,

(a) be served on all parties who were served with the original notice of trial; and

(b) be filed, with proof of service.

POWERS OF COURT ON MOTION

(4) On the hearing of the motion, the court may,

(a) if the party demonstrates that a condition referred to in subrule (5) is satisfied,

(i) grant a new trial, or

(ii) pronounce the judgment that ought to have been given at trial and order judgment accordingly; or

(b) dismiss the motion.

CONDITIONS

(5) The conditions referred to in clause (4)(a) are:

1. There was a purely arithmetical error in the determination of the amount of damages awarded.

2. There is relevant evidence that was not available to the party at the time of the original trial and could not reasonably have been expected to be available at that time.

RULE 18   EVIDENCE AT TRIAL

AFFIDAVIT

18.01 At the trial of an undefended action, the plaintiff's case may be proved by affidavit, unless the trial judge orders otherwise.

WRITTEN STATEMENTS, DOCUMENTS AND RECORDS

18.02(1) A document or written statement or an audio or visual record that has been served, at least 30 days before the trial date, on all parties who were served with the notice of trial, shall be received in evidence, unless the trial judge orders otherwise.

(2) Subrule (1) applies to the following written statements and documents:

1. The signed written statement of any witness, including the written report of an expert, to the extent that the statement relates to facts and opinions to which the witness would be permitted to testify in person.

2. Any other document, including but not limited to a hospital record or medical report made in the course of care and treatment, a financial record, a receipt, a bill, documentary evidence of loss of income or property damage, and a repair estimate.

DETAILS ABOUT WITNESS OR AUTHOR

(3) A party who serves on another party a written statement or document described in subrule (2) shall append to or include in the statement or document,

(a) the name, telephone number and address for service of the witness or author; and

(b) if the witness or author is to give expert evidence, a summary of his or her qualifications.

(4) A party who has been served with a written statement or document described in subrule (2) and wishes to cross-examine the witness or author may summon him or her as a witness under subrule 18.03(1).

WHERE WITNESS OR AUTHOR IS SUMMONED

(5) A party who serves a summons to witness on a witness or author referred to in subrule (3) shall, at the time the summons is served, serve a copy of the summons on every other party.

(6) Service of a summons and the payment or tender of attendance money under this rule may be proved by affidavit (Form 8A).

ADJOURNMENT

(7) A party who is not served with a copy of the summons in accordance with subrule (5) may request an adjournment of the trial, with costs.

SUMMONS TO WITNESS

18.03(1) A party who requires the attendance of a person in Ontario as a witness at a trial may serve the person with a summons to witness (Form 18A) requiring him or her to attend the trial at the time and place stated in the summons.

(2) The summons may also require the witness to produce at the trial the documents or other things in his or her possession, control or power relating to the matters in question in the action that are specified in the summons.

(3) A summons to witness (Form 18A) shall be served in accordance with subrule 8.01(7).

(4) Service of a summons and the payment or tender of attendance money may be proved by affidavit (Form 8A).

(5) A summons to witness continues to have effect until the attendance of the witness is no longer required.

INTERPRETER

(5.1) If a party serves a summons on a witness who requires an interpreter, the party shall arrange for a qualified interpreter to attend at the trial unless the interpretation is from English to French or French to English and an interpreter is provided by the Ministry of the Attorney General.

(5.2) If a party does not comply with subrule (5.1), every other party is entitled to request an adjournment of the trial, with costs.

FAILURE TO ATTEND OR REMAIN IN ATTENDANCE

(6) If a witness whose evidence is material to the conduct of an action fails to attend at the trial or to remain in attendance in accordance with the requirements of a summons to witness served on him or her, the trial judge may, by warrant (Form 18B) directed to all police officers in Ontario, cause the witness to be apprehended anywhere within Ontario and promptly brought before the court.

IDENTIFICATION FORM

(6.1) The party who served the summons on the witness may file with the clerk an identification form (Form 20K) to assist the police in apprehending the witness.

(7) On being apprehended, the witness may be detained in custody until his or her presence is no longer required or released on such terms as are just, and may be ordered to pay the costs arising out of the failure to attend or remain in attendance.

ABUSE OF POWER TO SUMMON WITNESS

(8) If satisfied that a party has abused the power to summon a witness under this rule, the court may order that the party pay directly to the witness an amount as compensation for inconvenience and expense.

RULE 19   COSTS

DISBURSEMENTS

19.01(1) A successful party is entitled to have the party's reasonable disbursements, including any costs of effecting service or preparing a plaintiff's or defendant's claim or a defence and expenses for travel, accommodation, photocopying and experts' reports, paid by the unsuccessful party, unless the court orders otherwise.

(2) The clerk shall assess the disbursements in accordance with the regulations made under the *Administration of Justice Act* and in accordance with subrules (3) and (4); the assessment is subject to review by the court.

(3) The amount of disbursements assessed for effecting service shall not exceed $60 for each person served unless the court is of the opinion that there are special circumstances that justify assessing a greater amount.

(4) The amount of disbursements assessed for preparing a plaintiff's or defendant's claim or a defence shall not exceed $100.

LIMIT

19.02 Any power under this rule to award costs is subject to section 29 of the *Courts of Justice Act*, which limits the amount of costs that may be awarded.

19.03 Revoked.

REPRESENTATION FEE

19.04 If a successful party is represented by a lawyer, student-at-law or agent, the court may award the party a reasonable representation fee at trial or at an assessment hearing.

COMPENSATION FOR INCONVENIENCE AND EXPENSE

19.05 The court may order an unsuccessful party to pay to a successful party who is self-represented an amount not exceeding $500 as compensation for inconvenience and expense.

PENALTY

19.06 If the court is satisfied that a party has unduly complicated or prolonged an action or has otherwise acted unreasonably, the court may order the party to pay an amount as compensation to another party.

RULE 20   ENFORCEMENT OF ORDERS

DEFINITIONS

20.01 In rules 20.02 to 20.12,
"creditor" means a person who is entitled to enforce an order for the payment or recovery of money;
"debtor" means a person against whom an order for the payment or recovery of money may be enforced.

POWER OF COURT

20.02(1) The court may,
    (a) stay the enforcement of an order of the court, for such time and on such terms as are just; and

(b) vary the times and proportions in which money payable under an order of the court shall be paid, if it is satisfied that the debtor's circumstances have changed.

ENFORCEMENT LIMITED WHILE PERIODIC PAYMENT ORDER IN FORCE

(2) While an order for periodic payment is in force, no step to enforce the judgment may be taken or continued against the debtor by a creditor named in the order, except issuing a writ of seizure and sale of land and filing it with the sheriff.

SERVICE OF NOTICE OF DEFAULT OF PAYMENT

(3) The creditor may serve the debtor with a notice of default of payment (Form 20L) in accordance with subrule 8.01(14) and file a copy of it, together with an affidavit of default of payment (Form 20M), if the debtor fails to make payments under an order for periodic payment.

TERMINATION ON DEFAULT

(4) An order for periodic payment terminates on the day that is 15 days after the creditor serves the debtor with the notice of default of payment, unless a consent (Form 13B) in which the creditor waives the default is filed within the 15-day period.

GENERAL

20.03 In addition to any other method of enforcement provided by law,
   (a) an order for the payment or recovery of money may be enforced by,
      (i) a writ of seizure and sale of personal property (Form 20C) under rule 20.06,
      (ii) a writ of seizure and sale of land (Form 20D) under rule 20.07, and
      (iii) garnishment under rule 20.08; and
   (b) a further order as to payment may be made under subrule 20.10(7).

CERTIFICATE OF JUDGMENT

20.04(1) If there is default under an order for the payment or recovery of money, the clerk shall, at the creditor's request, supported by an affidavit for enforcement request (Form 20P) stating the amount still owing, issue a certificate of judgment (Form 20A) to the clerk at the court location specified by the creditor.

(2) The certificate of judgment shall state,
   (a) the date of the order and the amount awarded;
   (b) the rate of postjudgment interest payable; and
   (c) the amount owing, including postjudgment interest.

DELIVERY OF PERSONAL PROPERTY

20.05(1) An order for the delivery of personal property may be enforced by a writ of delivery (Form 20B) issued by the clerk to a bailiff, on the request of the person in whose favour the order was made, supported by an affidavit of that person or the person's agent stating that the property has not been delivered.

SEIZURE OF OTHER PERSONAL PROPERTY

(2) If the property referred to in a writ of delivery cannot be found or taken by the bailiff, the person in whose favour the order was made may make a motion to the court for an order directing the bailiff to seize any other personal property of the person against whom the order was made.

(3) Unless the court orders otherwise, the bailiff shall keep personal property seized under subrule (2) until the court makes a further order for its disposition.

STORAGE COSTS

(4) The person in whose favour the order is made shall pay the bailiff's storage costs, in advance and from time to time; if the person fails to do so, the seizure shall be deemed to be abandoned.

WRIT OF SEIZURE AND SALE OF PERSONAL PROPERTY

20.06(1) If there is default under an order for the payment or recovery of money, the clerk shall, at the creditor's request, supported by an affidavit for enforcement request (Form 20P) stating the amount still owing, issue to a bailiff a writ of seizure and sale of personal property (Form 20C), and the bailiff shall enforce the writ for the amount owing, postjudgment interest and the bailiff's fees and expenses.

(1.1) If more than six years have passed since the order was made, a writ of seizure and sale of personal property may be issued only with leave of the court.

(1.2) If a writ of seizure and sale of personal property is not issued within one year after the date on which an order granting leave to issue it is made,

(a) the order granting leave ceases to have effect; and

(b) a writ of seizure and sale of personal property may be issued only with leave of the court on a subsequent motion.

(1.3) A writ of seizure and sale of personal property shall show the creditor's name, address and telephone number and the name, address and telephone number of the creditor's lawyer or agent, if any.

DURATION OF WRIT

(2) A writ of seizure and sale of personal property remains in force for six years after the date of its issue and for a further six years after each renewal.

RENEWAL OF WRIT

(3) A writ of seizure and sale of personal property may be renewed before its expiration by filing a request to renew a writ of seizure and sale (Form 20N) with the bailiff.

DIRECTION TO ENFORCE

(4) The creditor may request enforcement of a writ of seizure and sale of personal property by filing a direction to enforce writ of seizure and sale of personal property (Form 20O) with the bailiff.

INVENTORY OF PROPERTY SEIZED

(5) Within a reasonable time after a request is made by the debtor or the debtor's agent, the bailiff shall deliver an inventory of personal property seized under a writ of seizure and sale of personal property.

SALE OF PERSONAL PROPERTY

(6) Personal property seized under a writ of seizure and sale of personal property shall not be sold by the bailiff unless notice of the time and place of sale has been,

(a) mailed, at least 10 days before the sale,

(i) to the creditor at the address shown on the writ, or to the creditor's lawyer or agent, and

(ii) to the debtor at the debtor's last known address; and

(b) advertised in a manner that is likely to bring it to the attention of the public.

WRIT OF SEIZURE AND SALE OF LAND

20.07(1) If an order for the payment or recovery of money is unsatisfied, the clerk shall at the creditor's request, supported by an affidavit for enforcement request (Form 20P) stating the amount still owing, issue to the sheriff specified by the creditor a writ of seizure and sale of land (Form 20D).

(1.1) If more than six years have passed since the order was made, a writ of seizure and sale of land may be issued only with leave of the court.

(1.2) If a writ of seizure and sale of land is not issued within one year after the date on which an order granting leave to issue it is made,

(a) the order granting leave ceases to have effect; and

(b) a writ of seizure and sale of land may be issued only with leave of the court on a subsequent motion.

(2) A writ of seizure and sale of land issued under subrule (1) has the same force and effect and may be renewed or withdrawn in the same manner as a writ of seizure and sale issued under rule 60 of the Rules of Civil Procedure.

DURATION OF WRIT

(3) A writ of seizure and sale of land remains in force for six years after the date of its issue and for a further six years after each renewal.

RENEWAL OF WRIT

(4) A writ of seizure and sale of land may be renewed before its expiration by filing a request to renew a writ of seizure and sale (Form 20N) with the sheriff.

GARNISHMENT

20.08(1) A creditor may enforce an order for the payment or recovery of money by garnishment of debts payable to the debtor by other persons.

JOINT DEBTS GARNISHABLE

(2) If a debt is payable to the debtor and to one or more co-owners, one-half of the indebtedness or a greater or lesser amount specified in an order made under subrule (15) may be garnished.

WHERE LEAVE REQUIRED

(2.1) If more than six years have passed since the order was made, or if its enforcement is subject to a condition, a notice of garnishment may be issued only with leave of the court.

(2.2) If a notice of garnishment is not issued within one year after the date on which an order granting leave to issue it is made,

(a) the order granting leave ceases to have effect; and

(b) a notice of garnishment may be issued only with leave of the court on a subsequent motion.

(2.3) A notice of renewal of garnishment may be issued under subrule (5.3) without leave of the court before the original notice of garnishment or any subsequent notice of renewal of garnishment expires.

OBTAINING NOTICE OF GARNISHMENT

(3) A creditor who seeks to enforce an order by garnishment shall file with the clerk of a court in the territorial division in which the debtor resides or carries on business,

(a) an affidavit for enforcement request (Form 20P) naming one debtor and one garnishee and stating,

(i) the date of the order and the amount awarded,

(ii) the territorial division in which the order was made,

(iii) the rate of postjudgment interest payable,

(iv) the total amount of any payments received since the order was granted,

(v) the amount owing, including postjudgment interest,

(vi) the name and address of the named garnishee to whom a notice of garnishment is to be directed,

(vii) the creditor's belief that the named garnishee is or will become indebted to the debtor, and the grounds for the belief, and

(viii) any particulars of the debts that are known to the creditor; and

(b) a certificate of judgment (Form 20A), if the order was made in another territorial division.

(4) On the filing of the documents required by subrule (3), the clerk shall issue a notice of garnishment (Form 20E) naming as garnishee the person named in the affidavit.

(5) A notice of garnishment issued under subrule (4) shall name only one debtor and only one garnishee.

DURATION AND RENEWAL

(5.1) A notice of garnishment remains in force for six years from the date of its issue and for a further six years from each renewal.

(5.2) A notice of garnishment may be renewed before its expiration by filing with the clerk of the court in which the notice of garnishment was issued a notice of renewal of garnishment (Form 20E.1), together with an affidavit for enforcement request (Form 20P).

(5.3) On the filing of the notice and affidavit required by subrule (5.2), the clerk shall issue the notice of renewal of garnishment (Form 20E.1) naming as garnishee the person named in the affidavit.

(5.4) The provisions of these rules that apply with respect to notices of garnishment also apply with respect to notices of renewal of garnishment.

SERVICE OF NOTICE OF GARNISHMENT

(6) The notice of garnishment (Form 20E) shall be served by the creditor in accordance with subrule 8.01(8).

(6.1) The creditor shall serve the notice of garnishment on the debtor within five days of serving it on the garnishee.

FINANCIAL INSTITUTION

(6.2) If the garnishee is a financial institution, the notice of garnishment and all further notices required to be served under this rule shall be served at the branch at which the debt is payable.

PROOF OF SERVICE

(6.3) Service of the notice of garnishment may be proved by affidavit.

GARNISHEE LIABLE FROM TIME OF SERVICE

(7) The garnishee is liable to pay to the clerk any debt of the garnishee to the debtor, up to the amount shown in the notice of garnishment, within 10 days after service of the notice on the garnishee or 10 days after the debt becomes payable, whichever is later.

(8) For the purpose of subrule (7), a debt of the garnishee to the debtor includes,

(a) a debt payable at the time the notice of garnishment is served; and

(b) a debt payable (whether absolutely or on the fulfilment of a condition) after the notice is served and within six years after it is issued.

PAYMENT BY GARNISHEE

(9) A garnishee who admits owing a debt to the debtor shall pay it to the clerk in the manner prescribed by the notice of garnishment, and the amounts paid into court shall

not exceed the portion of the debtor's wages that are subject to seizure or garnishment under section 7 of the *Wages Act*.

EQUAL DISTRIBUTION AMONG CREDITORS

(10) If the clerk has issued notices of garnishment in respect of a debtor at the request of more than one creditor and receives payment under any of the notices of garnishment, he or she shall distribute the payment equally among the creditors who have filed a request for garnishment and have not been paid in full.

DISPUTING GARNISHMENT

(11) A garnishee referred to in subrule (12) shall, within 10 days after service of the notice of garnishment, file with the court a statement (Form 20F) setting out the particulars.

(12) Subrule (11) applies to a garnishee who,

(a) wishes to dispute the garnishment for any reason; or

(b) pays to the clerk less than the amount set out in the notice of garnishment as owing by the garnishee to the debtor, because the debt is owed to the debtor and to one or more co-owners of the debt or for any other reason.

SERVICE ON CREDITOR AND DEBTOR

(13) The garnishee shall serve a copy of the garnishee's statement on the creditor and the debtor.

NOTICE TO CO-OWNER OF DEBT

(14) A creditor who is served with a garnishee's statement under subrule (13) shall forthwith send to any co-owners of the debt, in accordance with subrule 8.01(14), a notice to co-owner of debt (Form 20G) and a copy of the garnishee's statement.

GARNISHMENT HEARING

(15) At the request of a creditor, debtor, garnishee, co-owner of the debt or any other interested person, the clerk shall fix a time and place for a garnishment hearing.

SERVICE OF NOTICE OF GARNISHMENT HEARING

(15.1) After having obtained a hearing date from the clerk, the party requesting the garnishment hearing shall serve the notice of garnishment hearing (Form 20Q) in accordance with subrule 8.01(9).

POWERS OF COURT AT HEARING

(15.2) At the garnishment hearing, the court may,

(a) if it is alleged that the garnishee's debt to the debtor has been assigned or encumbered, order the assignee or encumbrancer to appear and state the nature and particulars of the claim;

(b) determine the rights and liabilities of the garnishee, any co-owner of the debt, the debtor and any assignee or encumbrancer;

(c) vary or suspend periodic payments under a notice of garnishment; or

(d) determine any other matter in relation to a notice of garnishment.

TIME TO REQUEST HEARING

(16) A person who has been served with a notice to co-owner of debt is not entitled to dispute the enforcement of the creditor's order for the payment or recovery of money or a payment made by the clerk unless the person requests a garnishment hearing within 30 days after the notice is sent.

ENFORCEMENT AGAINST GARNISHEE

(17) If the garnishee does not pay to the clerk the amount set out in the notice of garnishment and does not send a garnishee's statement, the creditor is entitled to an order against the garnishee for payment of the amount set out in the notice, unless the court orders otherwise.

PAYMENT TO PERSON OTHER THAN CLERK

(18) If, after service of a notice of garnishment, the garnishee pays a debt attached by the notice to a person other than the clerk, the garnishee remains liable to pay the debt in accordance with notice.

EFFECT OF PAYMENT TO CLERK

(19) Payment of a debt by a garnishee in accordance with a notice of garnishment is a valid discharge of the debt as between the garnishee and the debtor and any co-owner of the debt, to the extent of the payment.

DISTRIBUTION OF PAYMENTS

(20) When proof is filed that the notice of garnishment was served on the debtor, the clerk shall distribute a payment received under a notice of garnishment to a creditor in accordance with subrule (20.1), unless,

(a) a hearing has been requested under subrule (15);

(b) a notice of motion and supporting affidavit (Form 15A) has been filed under rule 8.10, 11.06 or 17.04; or

(c) a request for clerk's order on consent (Form 11.2A) has been filed seeking the relief described in subparagraph 1 iii of subrule 11.2.01(1).

(20.1) The clerk shall distribute the payment,

(a) in the case of the first payment under the notice of garnishment, 30 days after the date it is received; and

(b) in the case of every subsequent payment under the notice of garnishment, as they are received.

NOTICE ONCE ORDER SATISFIED

(20.2) Once the amount owing under an order that is enforced by garnishment is paid, the creditor shall immediately serve a notice of termination of garnishment (Form 20R) on the garnishee and on the clerk.

PAYMENT IF DEBT JOINTLY OWNED

(21) If a payment of a debt owed to the debtor and one or more co-owners has been made to the clerk, no request for a garnishment hearing is made and the time for doing so under subrule (16) has expired, the creditor may file with the clerk, within 30 days after that expiry,

(a) proof of service of the notice to co-owner; and

(b) an affidavit stating that the creditor believes that no co-owner of the debt is a person under disability, and the grounds for the belief.

(22) The affidavit required by subrule (21) may contain statements of the deponent's information and belief, if the source of the information and the fact of the belief are specified in the affidavit.

(23) If the creditor does not file the material referred to in subrule (21), the clerk shall return the money to the garnishee.

CONSOLIDATION ORDER

20.09(1) A debtor against whom there are two or more unsatisfied orders for the payment of money may make a motion to the court for a consolidation order.

(2) The debtor's notice of motion and supporting affidavit (Form 15A) shall set out, in the affidavit portion,

(a) the names and addresses of the creditors who have obtained an order for the payment of money against the debtor;

(b) the amount owed to each creditor;

(c) the amount of the debtor's income from all sources, identifying them; and

(d) the debtor's current financial obligations and any other relevant facts.

NOTICE OF MOTION

(3) For the purposes of clause 15.01(3)(a), the notice of motion and supporting affidavit shall be served on each of the creditors mentioned in it at least seven days before the hearing date.

CONTENTS OF CONSOLIDATION ORDER

(4) At the hearing of the motion, the court may make a consolidation order setting out,

(a) a list of unsatisfied orders for the payment of money against the debtor, indicating in each case the date, court and amount and the amount unpaid;

(b) the amounts to be paid into court by the debtor under the consolidation order; and

(c) the times of the payments.

(5) The total of the amounts to be paid into court by the debtor under a consolidation order shall not exceed the portion of the debtor's wages that are subject to seizure or garnishment under section 7 of the *Wages Act*.

CREDITOR MAY MAKE SUBMISSIONS

(6) At the hearing of the motion, a creditor may make submissions as to the amount and times of payment.

FURTHER ORDERS OBTAINED AFTER CONSOLIDATION ORDER

(7) If an order for the payment of money is obtained against the debtor after the date of the consolidation order for a debt incurred before the date of the consolidation order, the creditor may file with the clerk a certified copy of the new order; the creditor shall be added to the consolidation order and shall share in the distribution under it from that time.

(8) A consolidation order terminates immediately if an order for the payment of money is obtained against the debtor for a debt incurred after the date of the consolidation order.

ENFORCEMENT LIMITED WHILE CONSOLIDATION ORDER IN FORCE

(9) While the consolidation order is in force, no step to enforce the judgment may be taken or continued against the debtor by a creditor named in the order, except issuing a writ of seizure and sale of land and filing it with the sheriff.

TERMINATION ON DEFAULT

(10) A consolidation order terminates immediately if the debtor is in default under it for 21 days.

EFFECT OF TERMINATION

(11) If a consolidation order terminates under subrule (8) or (10), the clerk shall notify the creditors named in the consolidation order, and no further consolidation order shall be made in respect of the debtor for one year after the date of termination.

MANNER OF SENDING NOTICE

(11.1) The notice that the consolidation order is terminated shall be served by mail or fax.

(11.2), (11.3) Revoked.

EQUAL DISTRIBUTION AMONG CREDITORS

(12) All payments into a consolidation account belong to the creditors named in the consolidation order, who shall share equally in the distribution of the money.

(13) The clerk shall distribute the money paid into the consolidation account at least once every six months.

EXAMINATION OF DEBTOR OR OTHER PERSON

20.10(1) If there is default under an order for the payment or recovery of money, the clerk of a court in the territorial division in which the debtor or other person to be examined resides or carries on business shall, at the creditor's request, issue a notice of examination (Form 20H) directed to the debtor or other person.

(2) The creditor's request shall be accompanied by,

    (a) an affidavit for enforcement request (Form 20P) setting out,

        (i) the date of the order and the amount awarded,

        (ii) the territorial division in which the order was made,

        (iii) the rate of postjudgment interest payable,

        (iv) the total amount of any payments received since the order was granted, and

        (v) the amount owing, including postjudgment interest; and

    (b) a certificate of judgment (Form 20A), if the order was made in another territorial jurisdiction.

SERVICE OF NOTICE OF EXAMINATION

(3) The notice of examination shall be served in accordance with subrules 8.01(10), (11) and (12).

(4) The debtor, any other persons to be examined and any witnesses whose evidence the court considers necessary may be examined in relation to,

    (a) the reason for nonpayment;

    (b) the debtor's income and property;

    (c) the debts owed to and by the debtor;

    (d) the disposal the debtor has made of any property either before or after the order was made;

    (e) the debtor's present, past and future means to satisfy the order;

    (f) whether the debtor intends to obey the order or has any reason for not doing so; and

    (g) any other matter pertinent to the enforcement of the order.

DUTIES OF PERSON TO BE EXAMINED

(4.1) A person who is served with a notice of examination shall,

    (a) inform himself or herself about the matters mentioned in subrule (4) and be prepared to answer questions about them; and

    (b) in the case of an examination of a debtor who is an individual, complete a financial information form (Form 20I) and,

        (i) serve it on the creditor requesting the examination, but not file it with the court, and

        (ii) provide a copy of it to the judge presiding at the examination hearing.

(4.2) A debtor required under clause (4.1)(b) to complete a financial information form (Form 20I) shall bring such documents to the examination hearing as are necessary to support the information that he or she provides in the financial information form.

WHO MAY BE EXAMINED

(5) An officer or director of a corporate debtor, or, in the case of a debtor that is a partnership or sole proprietorship, the sole proprietor or any partner, may be examined on the debtor's behalf in relation to the matters set out in subrule (4).

ATTENDANCE

(5.1) A person required to attend an examination may attend,
  (a) in person; or
  (b) by video conference in accordance with rule 1.07.

EXAMINATIONS PRIVATE, UNDER OATH AND RECORDED

(6) The examination shall be,
  (a) held in the absence of the public, unless the court orders otherwise;
  (b) conducted under oath; and
  (c) recorded.

ORDER AS TO PAYMENT

(7) After the examination or if the debtor's consent is filed, the court may make an order as to payment.

ENFORCEMENT LIMITED WHILE ORDER AS TO PAYMENT IN FORCE

(8) While an order as to payment is in force, no step to enforce the judgment may be taken or continued against the debtor by a creditor named in the order, except issuing a writ of seizure and sale of land and filing it with the sheriff.
  (9)-(15) Revoked.

CONTEMPT HEARING

20.11(1) If a person on whom a notice of examination has been served under rule 20.10 attends the examination but refuses to answer questions or to produce records or documents, the court may order the person to attend before it for a contempt hearing.

SAME

(2) If a person on whom a notice of examination has been served under rule 20.10 fails to attend the examination, the court may order the person to attend before it for a contempt hearing under subsection 30(1) of the *Courts of Justice Act*.

NOTICE OF CONTEMPT HEARING

(3) If the court makes an order for a contempt hearing,
  (a) the clerk shall provide the creditor with a notice of contempt hearing setting out the time, date and place of the hearing; and
  (b) the creditor shall serve the notice of contempt hearing on the debtor or other person in accordance with subrule 8.01(13) and file the affidavit of service at least seven days before the hearing.

SETTING ASIDE ORDER FOR CONTEMPT HEARING

(4) A person who has been ordered to attend a contempt hearing under subsection 30(1) of the *Courts of Justice Act* may make a motion to set aside the order, before or after receiving the notice of contempt hearing but before the date of the hearing and, on the motion, the court may set aside the order and order that the person attend another examination under rule 20.10.

FINDING OF CONTEMPT OF COURT

(5) At a contempt hearing held under subrule (1), the court may find the person to be in contempt of court if the person fails to show cause why the person should not be held in contempt for refusing to answer questions or produce records or documents.

SAME

(6) The finding of contempt at a hearing held under subsection 30(1) of the *Courts of Justice Act* is subject to subsection 30(2) of that Act.

OTHER POWERS OF COURT AT CONTEMPT HEARING

(7) At a contempt hearing, the court may order that the person,

(a) attend an examination under rule 20.10;

(b) be jailed for a period of not more than five days;

(c) attend an additional contempt hearing under subrule (1) or subsection 30(1) of the *Courts of Justice Act*, as the case may be; or

(d) comply with any other order that the judge considers necessary or just.

WARRANT OF COMMITTAL

(8) If a committal is ordered under clause (7)(b),

(a) the creditor may complete and file with the clerk an identification form (Form 20K) to assist the police in apprehending the person named in the warrant of committal; and

(b) the clerk shall issue a warrant of committal (Form 20J), accompanied by the identification form, if any, directed to all police officers in Ontario to apprehend the person named in the warrant anywhere in Ontario and promptly bring the person to the nearest correctional institution.

DISCHARGE

(9) A person in custody under a warrant issued under this rule shall be discharged from custody on the order of the court or when the time prescribed in the warrant expires, whichever is earlier.

DURATION AND RENEWAL

(10) A warrant issued under this rule remains in force for 12 months after the date of issue and may be renewed by order of the court on a motion made by the creditor for 12 months at each renewal, unless the court orders otherwise.

(11) Revoked.

SATISFACTION OF ORDER

20.12 If payment is made in full satisfaction of an order,

(a) where all parties consent, a party may file a request for clerk's order on consent (Form 11.2A) indicating that payment has been made in full satisfaction of the order or terms of settlement; or

(b) the debtor may make a motion for an order confirming that payment has been made in full satisfaction of the order or terms of settlement.

RULE 21   REFEREE

21.01(1) A person assigned the powers and duties of a referee under subsection 73(2) of the *Courts of Justice Act* may, if directed by the regional senior justice or his or her designate,

(a) hear disputes of proposals of terms of payment under rule 9.03;

(b) conduct settlement conferences under rule 13;

(c) hear motions for consolidation orders under rule 20.09; and

(d) assess receipted disbursements for fees paid to the court, a court reporter or a sheriff under the regulations made under the *Administration of Justice Act.*

(2) Except under subrule 9.03(5) (order as to terms of payment), a referee shall not make a final decision in any matter referred to him or her but shall report his or her findings and recommendations to the court.

22. Omitted (revokes other Regulations).

23. Omitted (provides for coming into force of provisions of this Regulation).

Glossary of Key Terms

acceleration clause   provides that if the debtor misses a payment, the entire debt is accelerated and becomes immediately due and payable

affiant   a person who swears to the truth of statements set out in her affidavit

affidavit   a sworn statement of facts that can be used as evidence in court proceedings in lieu of oral evidence

affidavit of documents   an affidavit in which a party identifies those documents that are relevant to the issues in the proceeding and that he has in his possession, power, and control and can produce; he must also identify those documents that he once had in his possession, power, and control but no longer has and those that he objects to producing; privileged documents, such as solicitor–client correspondence, will fall in the latter category; the documents being produced and relied on are contained in a document brief that is filed as evidence in the proceeding and may be referred to in court

assignment in bankruptcy   some debtors find that there is insufficient income to pay debts as they come due and they can retain a trustee in bankruptcy and assign most of their assets to the trustee for distribution to creditors, after which debtors may emerge from bankruptcy with most of their debts wiped out; an assignment in bankruptcy, sometimes called voluntary bankruptcy, is distinguished from a petition in bankruptcy, which is involuntary and where a creditor forces the debtor into bankruptcy by filing a petition in bankruptcy

Bankruptcy Court   in Ontario, several judges of the Superior Court with expertise in bankruptcy law have been assigned to sit in what is called Bankruptcy Court, which is not a formal statutory part of the Superior Court; its judges sit in Toronto, Ottawa, and London

certificate of appointment of estate trustee with a will   when someone dies with a will, he has usually named an executor (known as an estate trustee) to administer the estate in accordance with the will; an executor's authority is derived from the will itself; the certificate of appointment granted by the court merely indicates that the will is the last valid will and confirms the executor as estate trustee; an executor will often be named to act not only as estate trustee, but also as a trustee for the administration of any testamentary trusts contained in the will—such trusts are often established for beneficiaries who are under a disability, including minors and mentally incapacitated persons; these trusts may require the executor and trustee to administer them over a long period of time

certificate of appointment of estate trustee without a will   when someone dies without a will, it is necessary for someone, usually a relative, to apply to the court for a certificate of appointment of estate trustee without a will; until the appointment is made, no one has authority to do anything with the deceased's assets; once an appointment is made, the estate trustee may deal with the estate, settling its debts and distributing remaining assets to relatives in accordance with a statutory formula that determines the shares family members get

chattel   an item of tangible personal property (tangible means it is a thing, like a car); intangible personal property refers to a right to something of value—for example, a cheque, which is a right to payment

Children's Lawyer   a public official whose legal staff looks after the financial and other interests of children who are involved in or have an interest in civil proceedings

condition precedent   a situation where one must do A before one is allowed to do B—A is the condition precedent to the performance of the condition B

conditional sale contract   with this kind of contract, the vendor finances the debtor's purchase, taking security in the item sold; also called a purchase money security agreement or a hire-purchase agreement; a slang term for this kind of contract is "buying on the never-never," meaning that you never seem to stop paying in order to get title to (own) the chattel

consumer proposal   a plan put forth by a debtor to her creditors, through a trustee in bankruptcy, wherein a reduction of debt, interest, and/or a longer period to pay debts is suggested

contempt   a contemptuous act demonstrates disrespect or defiance of the court and the administration of justice

counterclaim   arises when A sues B and B defends A's claim and makes her own claim against A

Crown in right of Ontario   the legal title used to refer to the government of Ontario and how the government is usually named when it is a party to a legal proceeding

declaratory judgment   a judgment where the court declares the rights of the parties on some issue before it; also referred to as a declaration

default judgment   a plaintiff obtains a default judgment when the defendant takes no action and files no defence when he is sued—in that case, the defendant is deemed to have admitted the debt and the plaintiff may then present necessary documents to the court clerk, who will then, on behalf of the court, sign a judgment for the amount owing; no hearing is required, no oral submissions are made, and no judge is required to sign a default judgment

disbursements   amounts paid out by the law office on its own account to third parties on behalf of a client

discovery   a process where each party is asked questions under oath about the fact allegations in their pleadings and where the strength of the evidence with respect to the facts alleged can be tested; as well, credibility of the parties can be assessed and settlement options explored

estate trustee   the deceased's legal representative for estate administration purposes; the estate trustee may be named in the will or approved by the court

estate trustee during litigation   a grant made under a court order appointing someone to act for the estate when there is a dispute about the validity of the will or about who should administer the estate; during litigation the estate trustee has control of estate assets but has no authority to make payouts until the court has dealt with the validity of the will or decided who should administer the estate, as the case may be

***ex facie* contempt**   is contempt that occurs outside the courtroom

examination for discovery   a pretrial process where lawyers get to ask the opposite party (plaintiff or defendant) questions about the allegations in the statement of claim or statement of defence

execution   an act of the sheriff in enforcing a writ of seizure and sale (commonly referred to as a writ of execution), writ of delivery, or writ of sequestration; the word "execution" is also used to describe individual writs of execution on file; when a lawyer "searches executions" she is examining the sheriff's records to see if any writs of seizure and sale are filed with the sheriff

execution creditor   a creditor who has obtained a judgment and is in the process of executing or enforcing a judgment for debt

execution debtor   a debtor who is the subject of enforcement proceedings at the hands of an execution creditor

exigible   a word used to describe assets that the sheriff may seize when executing a writ of seizure and sale; if an asset is exempt from seizure it is referred to as a non-exigible asset

exigible assets   assets that are available to be legally seized under a writ of seizure and sale; non-exigible assets are those that are exempt from seizure under the *Execution Act* or under the provisions of another statute

full legal age and capacity   to sue or be sued, an individual usually has to have reached the age of majority and be mentally capable of taking part in a lawsuit; a person who is capable of participating and who is over 18 years of age is referred to as being of full age and capacity

gazetteer   a directory in which the entries are arranged by geographical location— various geographical places in the province are listed with corresponding small claims courts to use listed across from the geographical entry

guarantor   one who is obliged to pay a creditor when the principal debtor defaults

***in facie* contempt**   is contempt that occurs in the courtroom, in the face of the court

information   a sworn written statement made before a justice of the peace that can initiate criminal proceedings against a person

intestate, intestacy   when a person dies without having made a will, he is said to have died intestate; dying without a will is said to create an intestacy—that is, a situation where the estate will have to be administered without a will

issued and entered   a judgment or order is issued when it is signed by a judge or registrar and the court's seal is affixed to it; it is then entered—that is, recorded—by the registrar, using a system for referencing and recording an issued judgment; an entered judgment or order will usually have a stamp on it, indicating the microfilm or disk it was recorded on, or will be otherwise referenced so that it can be found in court files

judgment creditor   a creditor who has obtained a judgment for debt against a debtor

judgment debtor   a debtor against whom a judgment has been obtained

judgment proof   term used to describe a debtor against whom a judgment may be obtained, where the judgment will be unenforceable because the debtor has no assets to pay the judgment or the debtor has hidden or encumbered assets so that they cannot be easily seized; a judgment in these circumstances is sometimes described as a "paper judgment"—that is, it is worth no more than the paper it is printed on because it cannot be enforced in any practical way

lien   a claim to a right to sell or seize property, either real or personal, on the fulfillment of certain conditions

liquidated amount   a specific sum of money that can be easily and objectively calculated; if a debtor borrows $1,000 for a one-year period at 10 percent interest per year, the amount owing—$1,100—would be a liquidated amount because it is precise and specific and the total is easily calculated using an objective standard or formula

litigation guardian   an individual who conducts a lawsuit and instructs counsel on behalf of a party who is under a disability or who is not of full age and capacity

Mareva injunction   permits a creditor to obtain an injunction to secure the debtor's assets in a case where it is likely that the debtor will dispose of or remove all assets from the jurisdiction, before judgment, leaving no assets to satisfy the judgment debt

master   a judicial officer of the Superior Court who decides procedural issues on pretrial matters and performs some other judicial functions

motion   an application to the court within the main proceeding to settle a legal issue that has arisen in the main proceeding—for example, a plaintiff might bring a motion to court asking that the defendant provide more detail in the statement of defence; a motion is brought by a notice of motion, which states what remedy is sought and the reasons for it; the facts in support of the motion are usually presented in an affidavit

notice of motion   a document that states what remedy is sought and the reasons for it

Official Receiver   a government official in the Office of the Superintendent of Bankruptcy who receives proposals, examines bankrupts under oath, and chairs meetings of creditors

owner's equity   refers to how much of a property's value is actually that of the owner's—for example, if a house is worth $100,000 and is mortgaged for $50,000, the mortgagee is entitled to $50,000 to cover what is owing by the owner on the mortgage loan; the remaining $50,000 is free and clear of the mortgage claim and is the owner's equity in the house

partial indemnity   usual order for costs, based on a cost grid that establishes hourly rates for tariff items listed in the grid; provides less than full recovery of legal fees for the client

per annum   Latin for "per year"

personal property   consists of tangibles such as consumer goods, other goods, inventory and equipment, and intangibles including investments and securities

pleadings noted closed   the act of noting pleadings closed means that no party may file any further claims, defences, motions, or other court documents; this act brings the pretrial stage to a close—in a defended proceeding, the matter is then listed for trial; in a default proceeding, the defendant is barred from filing a statement of defence and the plaintiff is free to sign judgment

practice direction   a procedural directive issued by the chief justice of Ontario for the Superior Court or by a regional chief judge for a particular judicial region; a practice direction may clarify or supplement the procedural requirements of the *Rules of Civil Procedure*—at one time, there was some question about the authoritativeness of practice directions, but they are now clearly authorized by the *Rules of Civil Procedure*

privity of contract   a rule that only parties to a contract can enforce contract rights

Public Guardian and Trustee   a government office whose staff are responsible for looking after the interests of mentally incapable persons (formerly called mentally incompetent) where no attorney under a power of attorney, guardian of the person, or guardian of property has been appointed

purchaser in good faith   sometimes given in Latin as *bona fide* purchaser, this phrase describes an individual who has bought something in circumstances where there is nothing to tell her that the seller is trying to unload the asset quickly, get cash, and get away with the cash before creditors manage to seize the asset or its proceeds; where a bad-faith sale has occurred, there are usually signs that tip off a reasonable and prudent buyer—for example, a price below fair market value, secrecy in the transaction, undue haste, insistence on payment in cash, among other things—so that a purchaser would be presumed to be on notice that the seller's title is flawed or questionable and the purchaser is deemed to acquire ownership subject to the claims of creditors

receivable   refers to money that is owing to a creditor (also called an account receivable); because it describes a right to future payment or income, a creditor can sell or assign its receivables as a way of paying others—a creditor who has done this gives the purchaser or assignee of the receivable the right to be paid the amount of the receivable by the debtor

reference   a judicial proceeding used where it is necessary to inquire into an issue in an action in great detail; rather than tie up the court's time in a formal proceeding, a judge may order a reference to be held before a judge or other judicial official, such as a master, with expertise or time or both to delve into the matter using a less formal process than the process used in a formal trial

relief from forfeiture   a remedy granted to a debtor whose property has been seized by a creditor who has acted in an oppressive or capricious manner

retainer   a document that records the contractual relationship between legal service provider and client, usually stating that the legal service provider acts for the client and stipulating generally what the legal service provider has been retained to do; also used to describe an amount of money that the client pays the legal service provider as a down payment for services to be rendered—in this case, the legal service provider is required to account for how this money is used on the client's behalf; also used to describe a situation where a client does not hire a legal service provider for anything specific, but simply wants the legal service provider to be available to her to perform legal work for a specified period—in this case, the legal service provider does not have to account for the money and may use it for his own purposes; he is deemed to be entitled to the money for making himself available to the client, although he may charge for any services actually performed during the period of the retainer

reverse search   a reverse search allows you to submit an address, telephone number, or email address to obtain the name of a resident or subscriber

secured credit transaction   a transaction where the debtor has put up some asset of value as collateral that the creditor may use as security for the unpaid debt—if the debtor defaults, the creditor can recover what is owing by seizing the collateral; the debt is said to be secured by the creditor's rights in the collateral

specific performance   in an action for specific performance, the plaintiff claims that she cannot be properly compensated for breach of contract by payment of money damages; instead, she argues that the only just remedy is one where the defendant is compelled by the court to do what he was required to do under the contract—for example, if she has contracted to buy a house with a spectacular view, mere money cannot compensate for the loss of the view; the vendor will be compelled to perform the contract by completing the sale

stayed   a legal proceeding may be stopped from proceeding further, or stayed by a judge, until one of the parties does something they are obliged to do; for example, a plaintiff who is suing using an unregistered business name will have the proceeding stayed until he proves that he has registered the name as he is legally required to do

substantial indemnity   costs scale usually used as a punitive costs award that results in near indemnity for the winner on a dollar-for-dollar basis

superintendent of bankruptcy   a government official in Ottawa who supervises and oversees the administration of the *Bankruptcy and Insolvency Act*

taking of accounts   a court may order that there be a taking of accounts where an issue involving complex financial transactions needs to be examined in some detail in a less formal process than a trial; accounts may be taken before a judge or other judicial officers, usually masters of the Superior Court; the process is similar to that used in a reference

testamentary trust   a trust set up by the testator in a will to preserve and administer assets for specific purposes after the rest of the estate has been wound up—for example, for a child beneficiary; here, capital is set aside for investment by a trustee (often the estate executor and trustee), with the income to be used for the child's benefit until the child reaches an age set by the trust, at which time the capital may be paid out; if an individual sets up a trust during his or her lifetime, the trust is called an *inter vivos* trust; once a trust is set up, the person who establishes it, called a settlor, no longer owns or controls the trust property; the trustee is then the legal owner; however, the trustee's ownership rights are controlled by the trust terms, which require the trustee to use the property for the benefit of the beneficiary (sometimes called a *cestui que* trust)

testator   one who makes a will to dispose of his estate on death

title   the legal ownership of something; often refers to a document that indicates ownership or an ownership interest—to say someone has title to a car usually means that the car is registered with the province in the name of that person

to purge contempt   when an order has been made by the court finding someone in contempt, the person may avoid punishment for contempt by doing what was required of him; this is referred to as purging his contempt—for example, a person who refuses to answer questions on an examination may purge his contempt by re-attending and answering the questions

trial record   a record that consists of the pleadings, pretrial orders, a solicitor's certificate that the record is complete, and, depending on the nature of the case, other documents as well; once a record has been served and filed, the registrar will put the matter on the trial list 60 days later

trustee in bankruptcy   an individual, usually an accountant, who is licensed to act as a trustee under the *Bankruptcy and Insolvency Act*—such individuals advertise their services in the *Yellow Pages*; an individual or corporation that wishes to make a proposal or an assignment in bankruptcy begins by consulting a trustee; the trustee, once retained, is paid out of the debtor's/bankrupt's estate and becomes trustee over the estate for the benefit of the creditors to whom he is ultimately responsible for the administration and liquidation of the estate

unsecured credit   a loan or extension of credit to a debtor where the debtor has not given the creditor a right to seize property belonging to the debtor to satisfy the debt when the debt remains unpaid

white prints   large maps of subdivisions that are kept in a file of subdivisions and that show all of the lots in the subdivision; the white print will usually show an existing street or other identifiable landmark at the edge of the subdivision that will allow one to identify and locate a particular property, identified as a lot on the plan

with prejudice   a phrase used in connection with attempts to settle; when it is used (usually at the start of a letter), it signifies that the writer intends to make an offer that he is prepared to disclose to the court during the trial; such disclosure indicates that the party does not fear that disclosure will prejudice his case; rather the idea is that it will enhance his case by showing him to be reasonable, and otherwise presenting him in a favourable light

without prejudice   a phrase used in connection with attempts to settle; unlike "with prejudice" letters, this phrase means that statements will be made in the letter that are made solely in the context of an offer and the letter may not be disclosed to the court, even if it contains damaging statements or admissions; the making of an offer on a without-prejudice basis allows for a free and frank discussion of settlement, without the loss of the ability to present a case to the court, where the court is not prejudiced by admissions made in the course of settlement

writ of seizure and sale   also called a writ of execution; allows the sheriff to seize and sell goods or land belonging to the judgment debtor and apply the proceeds to the judgment creditor's claim